The Northwest
GARDENERS'
RESOURCE DIRECTORY

NINTH EDITION

Created by Stephanie Feeney

Debra Prinzing, Editor

SASQUATCH BOOKS
SEATTLE

A bouquet of thanks to Emery Rhodes, Marlis Korber, and the staff of Emery's Garden in Lynnwood, Washington. You have generously shared with me your passion for plants and gardens and supported my own career in countless ways. This book is also dedicated to my garden muses— Karen Page and Jean Zaputil, two longtime friends whose horticultural wisdom and design talent have greatly influenced me.

—D. P.

Printed in the United States of America
Published by Sasquatch Books
Distributed by Publishers Group West
Ninth Edition
08 07 06 05 04 03 02   6 5 4 3 2 1

The first eight editions of *The Northwest Gardeners' Resource Directory* were published by Cedarcroft Press, of Bellingham, Washington.

Guest essays appearing herein copyright by their respective authors.

Cover design: Kate Basart
Interior design:. Jenny Wilkson
Copy editor: Sigrid Asmus

Library of Congress Cataloging in Publication Data
ISBN 1-57061-303-6

If you would like to be considered for inclusion in the next edition of *The Northwest Gardeners' Resource Directory*, or if you are currently listed but wish to notify us of any changes, please send the appropriate information to nwgardener@sasquatchbooks.com. Be sure to include the name, address, phone number, email address, and website of your business or organization, as well as the name of a contact person.

Sasquatch Books
615 Second Avenue
Seattle, Washington 98104
(206) 467-4300
www.SasquatchBooks.com
books@SasquatchBooks.com

CONTENTS

FOREWORD

Having lived in other parts of the country, I know that the Pacific Northwest is one of the most dynamic gardening communities in the United States. As the president of the Northwest Horticultural Society, I have the opportunity to meet many colleagues from around the globe, and their enthusiasm for the region while they are visiting here never ceases to amaze me. When I took the director position at the Elisabeth C. Miller Botanical Garden in 1996, I fully expected to hold it for only a couple of years and then return to the Northeast. Six years later, I cannot imagine calling anyplace else home. I love the garden that is entrusted to me, the climate, and the dynamic scenery, not to mention the endless variety of plants available to me.

Gardening can be overwhelming to those who strive to practice both the art and science of growing plants and making gardens. There is so much to learn and see and do. When Stephanie Feeney dreamed up and published the first *Northwest Gardeners' Resource Directory* in the late 1980s, she let a genie out of the bottle. She showed us the richness of our gardening community, but more importantly, she showed us how to navigate through it successfully.

Compiling *The Northwest Gardeners' Resource Directory* is a monumental task. Debra Prinzing, like Stephanie, is thorough and single-minded in her pursuit to bring the reader the most current and accurate information. The most exciting new addition to the directory is the myriad websites and email addresses for the technologically advanced gardener. I am grudgingly coming into the twenty-first century, but do appreciate this access to websites for capturing the most current information, directions, and offerings of garden businesses and nonprofit organizations. Using the Internet saves time and energy. The comprehensive addition of websites makes this very valuable book essential.

Here at the Miller Botanical Garden, we are always looking for new plants, so I confess I use the list of nurseries herewith most often. Forever a plant junky, I found *The Northwest Gardeners' Resource Directory* an invaluable resource that helped to orient me upon my arrival in Seattle. It's now introducing me to new sources. Chapter 9, "Products, Materials & Professional Services," is my second favorite section. The Quest Yellow Pages don't tell you where to find manure sources, soil amendments, and someone to spread them for you (if you are not inclined to tackle it yourself), but this Directory will.

Aside from finding plants, products, and services, it's the "learning more about gardening better" that is an important endeavor for all of us. Classes, symposia, or even courses at the university and community college levels are listed here at your fingertips (especially in Chapter 3). Do you need to find a plant or horticultural society to meet cohorts (perhaps because your spouse is tired of hearing about your obsession)? The chapter on gardening societies (Chapter 2) will direct you to your particular gardening fetish. If you need places to spend your leisure time while traveling throughout the region, you can find great gardens to visit (Chapter 13). Or, find a plant festival or flower and garden show to attend (Chapter 12).

I lecture and write about gardening regularly, and any time I speak or pontificate on paper, I try to give each person hearing or reading me at least one practical piece of information. Stephanie, and now Debra Prinzing, have shared much more than one practical bit of information as they open up for us a gardening universe in a logical and accessible way, helping the Northwest gardener find what he or she is looking for. I refer to my dog-eared copy nearly daily.

The Northwest Gardeners' Resource Directory is the roadmap to gardening in the Pacific Northwest. It is an essential tool to getting the most out of gardening in our region.

—Richard Hartlage

Known for his charming Southern personality and witty observations on life and gardening, Richard Hartlage is director of the Elisabeth C. Miller Botanical Gardens in Seattle. He is the force behind the Miller Gardens' 2001 launch of "Great Plant Picks," promoting the best-adapted and performing plants for the Pacific Northwest. A native of Louisville, Kentucky, and a graduate in ornamental horticulture from North Carolina State University, Richard began his career working in nurseries, public arboretums, and private gardens in the Southeast and Northeast. He is the author of *Bold Visions for the Garden* (Fulcrum Press, 2001) and photographer for *Plant Life: Growing a Garden in the Pacific Northwest*, by Valerie Easton (Sasquatch Books, 2002)

INTRODUCTION

Gardening, in its essence, is about renewal, rebirth, and anticipation. And whether it's in joy or in sadness, we somehow continue returning to the garden to experience the excitement and comfort that comes with the seasonal patterns of new growth.

Ever since the spring of 2000, when Stephanie Feeney first approached me about the possibility of continuing the publication of her beloved creation, *The Northwest Gardeners' Resource Directory*, I have been caught up in her passion and enthusiasm for this project.

Stephanie and Larry Feeney ultimately passed the publishing torch to Sasquatch Books. And as horticultural luck would have it (kind of like the notion, "right plant, right place"), Sasquatch gave me the assignment of revising and updating Stephanie's work, the most recent edition of which was published in 1999.

I am deeply grateful to both Stephanie and Larry, two generous and engaging people who've enriched the lives of so many gardeners around the globe. We honor Stephanie's life and influence on the Northwest gardening community with this new book you're holding in your hands. Working on this project has shown me much about Stephanie's amazing talent for converting anyone she met into an instant new friend. As we worked on this book, countless gardeners throughout the United States and Canada (as well as many in Europe) shared their fond memories of Stephanie—and many had met her only via telephone or email conversations. I am also appreciative that Stephanie's dear friend and fellow writer Sarah Eppenbach has shared her memories of this remarkable woman in an essay from a celebration held in Stephanie's honor. If you didn't know her, I think Sarah's words will give you a peek into Stephanie Feeney's heart and spirit.

The Northwest Gardeners' Resource Directory has been given a full and exhaustive review and update for this Ninth Edition, a twelve-month endeavor that frequently prompted me to look at the smiling photo of Stephanie that's sitting on my desk and wonder, "How did you do it?" The giving spirit and goodwill of Stephanie continually nudged me on to finish this project—that and the encouragement, support, and extreme patience of Sasquatch editorial director Gary Luke and managing editor Joan Gregory. Thank you all.

This Ninth Edition builds on a solid foundation that's rooted in every aspect of gardening, garden touring, horticulture, and landscape design resources in our region. As we sit here with hundreds of excellent nurseries and garden centers under our noses, it's easy to take the Northwest gardening scene for granted. However, as I talked with each of the establishments featured here, reviewed their websites, and read their plant lists, one thing became certain: Everything you want or need in order to create the landscape of your dreams, grow the latest unique plant that's seduced you, or improve your knowledge as a gardener is right here in our corner of the world.

It's also here in this Directory, redesigned in an easy-to-read format. In these pages you'll meet several new public and nonprofit gardens to visit in British Columbia, Oregon, and Washington. I've unearthed new organizations to join, new sources for materials and supplies, and many great ways for you to get involved with a community of fellow gardeners. And when you contact an organization or company listed here, be sure to tell them how you found them—they'll appreciate hearing.

Remarkably, as a few established nurseries and emporiums in our backyard have closed their doors, an equal number has emerged to replace them. Fully 95 percent of the listings here contain new information that will simplify your search for the rare plant, right tool, important material, or frivolous piece of ornamentation. Look for the websites—they're everywhere.

To each of you, I share this wish: Great soil, few pests, equal parts sun and rain, and supportive fellow gardeners. Now that I've finally completed this project, I'm going outside to get my beds ready for spring.

Thanks for reading *The Northwest Gardeners' Resource Directory*.

—Debra Prinzing
www.debraprinzing.com

ACKNOWLEDGMENTS

I wish a basket of tulips to my loyal friend Charmel Bowden. She was the first one who took me seriously when I said, "I'm sick of being a business writer. I'd rather write about gardening." Being the networker that she is, Charmel picked up the phone and helped me make my first important contact in the gardening world.

I am grateful to two very talented Sasquatch interns, University of Washington English majors who spent hours tracking down resources, gathering data, and cheerfully participating in this project. Elizabeth Shen and Angela Overhoff will have great futures as writers and editors—hire them!

Two of my colleagues in the publishing world lent their support, as well. I am especially thankful for the help of Jessica Campbell, assistant editor at *Seattle Homes & Lifestyles* magazine, and Sharon Wootton, a fellow freelance garden writer (who's also responsible for my position as a contributor to *The Herald* newspaper's Home & Garden section). Jessica's and Sharon's willingness to take on the research for select chapters gave me hope that I would indeed—someday—finish this book! Thank you both, dear friends.

I also want to thank Brian Thompson and Marty Wingate for allowing me to continue Stephanie's practice of including great essays in the Resource Directory. Marty's wonderful piece on horticultural Latin makes me laugh out loud, but it also helps to demystify the botanical language I once feared. Thank you, Marty. And Brian has graciously written a helpful new essay that reveals how horticultural information has changed at Internet speed.

A special thanks to WSU Extension Agents Mary Robson and Holly Kennell for helping me update the information on Hardiness Zones—maybe they helped because I'm a Master Gardener, but more than likely, it's because these two are generous and smart women.

Richard Hartlage, who has shared his observations in the Foreword to this book, has been a dear friend and mentor. I am so thankful for your professional support, Richard.

Finally, I have to thank my fabulous family. My husband, Bruce Brooks, has been exceedingly patient and loyal, especially as the time I spent on this manuscript far outpaced the time I told him it would take (I am an eternal optimist). He is a cool guy, especially for someone who doesn't have a piece of gardening DNA in his genetic makeup. My sons, Benjamin and Alexander, have spent the past year in discussions about "what will we do when Mom is done with the book?" They are super boys who have never beheaded a bloom or trampled a flower in the countless gardens and nurseries to which they've been dragged. I love you all!

—D. P.

Stephanie Jo Scowcroft Feeney
August 16, 1948–December 5, 2000

IN REMEMBRANCE

Stephanie did not want eulogies or speeches. She did hope that those she knew from various activities and walks of life might come together and, through chatting and remembering, come to see and appreciate her life as a whole. And she loved bringing people of mutual interests together. So it seemed appropriate for those who loved and admired her to gather in the garden on an afternoon in May, a month Stephanie loved, when the vine tendrils reach exuberantly upward and the young shoots of the perennials SWOOSH, as Stephanie would say, into growth. Let us stroll these paths without program or agenda, inhale the perfume of blossoms and herbs, pause, perhaps, within the sheltering embrace of the kiwi arbor, chat with dear friends and newfound acquaintances, nibble and imbibe, and exult in the glory of this season of promise and renewal.

Those who knew Stephanie in the context of her Bellingham years—as a horticultural author, speaker, garden enthusiast—would not realize perhaps the many other roles she played in earlier years. Born in Billings of strong explorer's stock (her ancestors settled in Massachusetts four years after the founding of the Massachusetts Bay Colony, crossed the plains to the Oregon Territory by covered wagon, and built the first sternwheeler up the Frazer River to the Canadian gold fields), she left behind the open skies of Montana to learn design, communications, and architecture at Western Washington University and the University of Oregon, study low-income housing in Nairobi, and work at a crab cannery in the Aleutian Islands. But anyone knowing Stephanie during her Alaska years (when she truly knew not the difference between an annual and a perennial) identifies her with Drawing Conclusions, the graphic design firm she established in Juneau. She dedicated herself to her clients with her usual phenomenal energy, often rising at 4 a.m., even in the snowiest of Juneau's notoriously snowy winters, to walk down the hill to her office in the Valentine Building to resume work on a project.

Stephanie loved string quartet music—especially Haydn and Boccherini; the Mamas and the Papas; and Carlos Gardel. Like her mother, Myra, she insisted upon a fire in the fireplace except on the warmest of summer days (and then a fire in the evening would not necessarily be amiss . . .). She liked to drive! An adventurous but selective cook, she prepared Indian samosas, Mexican tamales, French bouillabaisse, Italian ravioli. She adored picnics and sleeping outdoors; her idea of camp cooking, say on a kayak run down the Yukon, ran to Chinese dumplings and pasta with smoked trout and caviar. She once served eggs benedict to guests she invited to a picnic brunch on a Juneau beach. She loved fine paper and publications, England, ferris wheels, and public radio. She believed in celebrating life's small victories, and greatly valued tradition. A true but exacting friend, she admired those who kept their word, lived up to their potential, and tried their hardest. She could not tell a joke (and did not pretend otherwise), but she could laugh at herself in the most charming manner.

No one who counted Stephanie as a friend or companion failed to be amazed at her enormous energy and enthusiasm. Truly she moved through each day at a pace few others could match. Perhaps we may suppose that, always impatient, ever impetuous, she simply SWOOSHED through life more quickly than those she left behind.

—Sarah Eppenbach
May 2001

chapter

1

ORGANIZATIONS THAT HELP GARDENERS

The business of gardening is one that can easily consume us, mostly because it's so rewarding. Who doesn't love to get lost in the garden for hours on end, creating our own private Eden of sorts? Yet gardeners of any level of experience or skill do get stumped from time to time. Where to turn? Fortunately, after you've exhausted the expertise of that knowledgeable friend or of the neighbor who seems to have a green thumb, you can turn to gardening problem-solvers at large. Here you'll find a generous world of resources ready at hand, thanks to volunteer organizations, public agencies, and nonprofit groups whose mission is to educate, inform, and inspire those who till the soil and nurture the plants that grow in that soil. This chapter will provide some reassurance that the gardening world is filled with folks who want to help you find solutions, answer your questions, and, most of all, build your skills . . . all to ensure you have success as a gardener. First-timers and veterans alike will find something useful here, so get out the yellow highlighter and mark the resources in your area. What's more, most of this help comes free for the asking! Some of the advice will require your time and effort; some of it will take only the smallest effort on your part. Don't be shy about making a phone call, visiting a drop-in Master Gardener clinic, or checking a website. These services and organizations are staffed by gardeners who began just like you, but have specialized or been at it a bit longer, and who have the benefit of their own mistakes and successes to pass along. The best part of getting free advice is that it will inspire you to share it with a beginner who you'll inspire to grow!

MASTER GARDENER PROGRAMS

Get in touch with a wealth of information through the Master Gardener programs in your area, either in person at a MG Clinic, or in the form of over 500 pamphlets available free or for a small fee. Cooperative Extension agents and the staff of the United States Department of Agriculture (USDA) are generally charged with helping *commercial* enterprises. So these days it's likely to be a Master Gardener volunteer working in the office to whom you can turn with that rust-covered rose branch or a baggie holding some mystery bugs that are chomping on your favorite perennial.

Master Gardeners at **Oregon State University (OSU) Cooperative Extension** and at **Washington State University (WSU) Cooperative Extension** are available throughout both states to answer (*noncommercial*) questions about any and all gardening issues. While you may telephone with a question—such as a pruning query—you may need to actually visit the office or a clinic, bringing specimens of the damaged or diseased plant or insects you want identified. If the answer is not immediately apparent, mail or phone follow-up is possible. Also, there are 4-H programs for young gardeners. Some Extension offices also offer the **Master Preserver, Master Wetlands,** and **Master Composter/Recycler** programs.

Master Gardeners can answer many of your questions, but how much more fulfilling to become a Master Gardener yourself! These trained volunteers offer free advice to residential gardeners with horticultural questions. Essentially, they offer help to gardeners with phone-in and in-person gardening questions; they also hold diagnostic clinics in a wide variety of venues, such as nurseries, plant sales, fairs, and public gardens. Master Gardeners work hard to create educational displays and demonstration gardens, and increasingly their ambitious and knowledgeable members are branching out to bring the benefits of gardening into children's classrooms and other institutions, including hospitals, nursing homes, prisons, and correctional facilities.

Western Oregon Master Gardener Programs

OREGON MASTER GARDENERS

http://osu.orst.edu/extension/mg/

This site will link you to the OSU online plant-disease control and pest management guidelines sites, as well as to program contacts in more than 25 Oregon counties.

BAKER COUNTY

Janice Cowan, Extension Agent; 2610 Grove Street, Baker City, OR 97814 | **Phone:** (541) 523-6418 | **Web:** http://osu.orst.edu/extension/baker

BENTON COUNTY

Barbara Fick, Extension Agent; 1849 NW 9th Street, Suite 8, Corvallis, OR 97330 | **Phone:** (541) 757-6750 | **Email:** barb.fick@orst.edu | **Web:** http://osu.orst.edu/extension/benton/mg.htm

CENTRAL OREGON (SERVING COOK, JEFFERSON, DESCHUTES, AND WARM SPRINGS COUNTIES)

Amy Jo Waldo, Extension Agent; 1421 S Highway 97, Redmond, OR 97756 | **Phone:** (541) 548-6088 | **Web:** http://osu.orst.edu/extension/deschutes/horticulture/hort

CLATSOP COUNTY

Justin Williams, Extension Agent; 2001 Marine Drive, Room 210, Astoria, OR 97103 | **Phone:** (503) 325-8573 | **Email:** clatsopmg1@hotmail.com | **Web:** www.clatsopmg.org

COLUMBIA COUNTY

Chip Bubl, Extension Agent; Courthouse, St. Helens, OR 97051 | **Phone:** (503) 397-3462 | **Email:** Chip.Bubl@orst.edu | **Web:** http://osu.orst.edu/extension/columbia/

COOS COUNTY

Amy Herron, Extension Agent; 290 N Central, Coquille, OR 97423 | **Phone:** (541) 396-3121 | **Email:** shirley.bower@orst.edu | **Web:** http://osu.orst.edu/extension/coos/

CURRY COUNTY

Doug Hart, Extension Agent; PO Box 488, Gold Beach, OR 97444 | **Phone:** (541) 247-6672 or (800) 356-3986 | **Email:** currymg@orst.edu | **Web:** http://osu.orst.edu/extension/curry/mg.html

DOUGLAS COUNTY

Stephen Renquist, Extension Agent; PO Box 1165, Roseburg, OR 97470 | **Phone:** (541) 672-4461 | **Email:** douglasmg@orst.edu | **Web:** http://osu.orst.edu.extension/douglas/

HOOD RIVER COUNTY

Steve Castagnoli, Extension Agent; or Elizabeth Daniel, Program Assistant; 2990 Experiment Station Drive, Hood River, OR 97031 | **Phone:** (541) 386-3343 | **Web:** http://osu.orst.edu/extension/hoodriver/

JACKSON COUNTY

George Tiger, Extension Agent; 569 Hanley Road, Central Point, OR 97502-1251 | **Phone:** (541) 776-7371 | **Web:** http://osu.orst.edu/extension/sorec/mastergarden.html

JOSEPHINE COUNTY

George Tiger, Extension Agent; 215 Ringuette Street, Grants Pass, OR 97527 | **Phone:** (541) 476-6613 | **Web:** http://osu.orst.edu/extension/sorec/mastergarden.html

KLAMATH COUNTY

Kerry Locke, Extension Agent; 3328 Vandenberg Road, Klamath Falls, OR 97603-3796 | **Phone:** (541) 883-7131 | **Email:** klamathmg@orst.edu | **Web:** http://osu.orst.edu/extension/klamath/

LANE COUNTY

Ross Penhallegon, Extension Agent; 950 West 13th Avenue, Eugene, OR 97402-3999 | **Phone:** (541) 682-4243 | **MG Hotline:** (541) 682-4247 or (800) 872-8980 | **Email:** lanemg@orst.edu | **Web:** http://osu.orst.edu/extension/lane/MG/

LINCOLN COUNTY

William Rogers, Extension Agent; 29 SE 2nd Street, Newport, OR 97365-4496 | **Phone:** (541) 265-4107 | **Web:** http://osu.orst.edu/extension/lincoln/

LINN COUNTY

Barbara Fick, Extension Agent; PO Box 765, Albany, OR 97321 | **Phone:** (541) 967-3871 or (888) 883-0522 | **Web:** http://osu.orst.edu/extension/linn/homehort.html

MARION COUNTY

Neil Bell, Extension Agent; 3180 Center Street NE, Room 1361, Salem, OR 97301 | **Phone:** (503) 588-5301 | **Web:** http://osu.orst.edu/extension/marion/

METRO TRI-COUNTY (SERVING MULTNOMAH, CLACKAMAS, AND WASHINGTON COUNTIES)

Jan McNeilan, Extension Agent; Jordis Yost, Program Assistant; 211 SE 80th Avenue, Portland, OR 97215 | **Phone:** (503) 725-2000 or (503) 725-2044 | **Master Gardener Program information:** (503) 725-2032 | **Web:** http://osu.orst.edu/extension/multnomah/

POLK COUNTY

Neil Bell, Extension Agent; Gail Miles, Program Assistant; PO Box 640, Dallas, OR 97338 | **Phone:** (503) 623-8395 | **Web:** http://extension.orst.edu/polk

TILLAMOOK COUNTY

Joy Jones, Extension Agent; 2204 Fourth Street, Tillamook, OR 97141-2491 | **Phone:** (541) 842-3433 | **Web:** http://osu.orst.edu/extension/tillamook.mg.html

UNION AND WALLOWA COUNTIES

Rich Topilec, Extension Agent; 668 NW First Street, Enterprise, OR 97828 | **Phone:** (541) 426-3143 | **Email:** rich.topilec@orst.edu | **Web:** http://osu.orst.edu/extension/union/masterg/mgarden.html

WASCO, SHERMAN, AND GILLIAM COUNTIES

Lynn Long, Extension Agent; 207 Courthouse Annex A, 400 East 5th Street, Room 222, The Dalles, OR 97058 | **Phone:** (541) 296-5494 | **Web:** http://osu.orst.edu/extension/wasco/mastergardeners/mghomepage.html

WASHINGTON COUNTY

18640 NW Walker Road, No. 1400, Beaverton, OR 97006-8927 | **Phone:** (503) 725-2300 | **Web:** http://osu.orst.edu/extension/washington

YAMHILL COUNTY

Linda McMahon, Extension Agent; 2050 Lafayette Avenue, McMinnville, OR 97128 | **Phone:** (503) 434-7517 | **Web:** http://osu.orst.edu/extension/yamhill/

Western Washington Master Gardener Programs

WSU MASTER GARDENER WEBSITE

http://gardening.wsu.edu

This is a very comprehensive WSU Cooperative Extension site with lots of information you'll want to download for your files. It's also a good place to keep abreast of the individual Master Gardener office activities, found under "Local Opportunities." There is even a searchable Specialty Nursery database for Western Washington that is really terrific! WSU/Cooperative Extension publications can be ordered from: Bulletins Office, WSU, PO Box 645912, Pullman, WA 99164-5912; (800) 723-1763; or order online from: http://pubs.wsu.edu/scripts/ PubOrders/webcat.asp/

CLALLAM COUNTY

Courthouse, 223 East 4th Street, Port Angeles, WA 98362 | **Phone:** (360) 417-2279 | **Master Gardener Helpline:** (360) 417-2279 | **Email:** lkennedy@co.clallam.wa.us | **Web:** http://gardening.wsu.edu/text/clallam.htm

CLARK COUNTY

Cileste Lindsay, Extension Agent; 11104 NE 149th Street, Building C, Room 100, Brush Prairie, WA 98606 | **Phone:** (360) 254-8436 | **Email:** ce6606@coopext.cahe.wsu.edu | **Web:** http://gardening.wsu.edu/text/clark/htm

COWLITZ COUNTY

Sheila Gray, Master Gardener Program Coordinator; 207 4th Avenue N, Kelso, WA 98626 | **Phone:** (360) 577-3014 | **Email:** sgray@wsu.edu | **Web:** http://gardening.wsu.edu/text/cowlitz/htm

GRAYS HARBOR

PO Box "R" 32 Elma-McCleary Road, Elma, WA 98541 | **Phone:** (360) 482-2934 | **Email:** linder@coopext.cahe.wsu.edu | **Web:** http://graysharbor.wsu.edu

ISLAND COUNTY

101 NE 6th (PO Box 5000), Coupeville, WA 98239 | **Phone:** (360) 679-7327 | **Email:** wsumg@co.island.wa.us | **Web:** http://gardening.wsu.edu/text/island.htm

JEFFERSON COUNTY

201 W Patison Street, Port Hadlock, WA 98339 | **Phone:** (360) 379-5610 | **Email:** deardorf@coopext.cahe.wsu.edu | **Web:** http://jefferson.wsu.edu/garden

KING COUNTY

Mary Robson, Extension Agent; Joan Helbacka, Master Gardener Program Coordinator; 919 S Grady Way, Suite 120, Renton, WA 98055 | **Phone:** (206) 205-3100 or (800) 325-6165, ext. 5-3100 | **Hotline:** (206) 296-3440, 10 a.m.-4 p.m., Monday-Friday | **Email:** joan.helbacka@metrokc.gov | **Web:** http://www.metrokc.gov/wsu-ce

The county Master Gardener program offers many programs, facilities, and contacts for information.

❀ Year-Round Clinics: Note: The MG Clinic at the Center for Urban Horticulture has been closed due to the May 2001 arson fire. A temporary clinic site is located at Ravenna Gardens in the University Village Shopping Center on Mondays, 4-8 p.m. Other year-round clinics include:

Fairwood Library, 17009 140th Avenue SE, Renton, WA; Saturdays, 10 a.m.- 2 p.m.;

Snoqualmie Valley / North Bend Library, 115 E 4th Street, North Bend, WA Second Wednesday of month (except December), 5:30-7:30 p.m.

Washington Park Arboretum, Graham Visitor Center, Sundays, noon-4 p.m. (Closed all UW holidays.)

❀ Neighborhood Clinics: April through October. For information, call Dial Extension, (206) 296-3425 or (800) 325-6165, ext. 63425, Tape #112, or see the website at http://www.metrokc.gov/DCHS/CSD/WSU-CE/Gardening/GardenResources/MGClinics.htm, or call (206) 205-3100 (King County Master Gardener line) or (206) 296-3440 (King County Master Gardener Hotline).

❀ Demonstration Garden: SE 16th Street and 156th Avenue SE, Bellevue (find driving directions in Chapter 13, "Gardens to Visit"). Open daily during Bellevue Community Gardens Park hours. MGs available March through October, Wednesday and Saturday, 9 a.m.-1 p.m. Demonstrations: Annuals, perennials, herbs, small fruits, tree fruits, vegetables, landscape trees / shrubs, composting, dried flowers, artichokes, and melons. Trials and experiments: Fruit and vegetables. Big opening day celebration in spring; free demonstrations on subjects such as drip irrigation, and organic pest and disease management.

❀ Dial Extension: (206) 296-3425 or (800) 325-6165, ext. 63425.

❀ Fact Sheets (FS): A series of very helpful fliers to help answer your gardening questions.

❀ Plant Sale: King County MG Fair & Plant Sale, April; at Center for Urban Horticulture, Seattle.

❀ Speakers: Master Gardeners are available as speakers. Request the official list (Bulletin FS-57).

❀ Workshops: Lots of them, free, at the Bellevue Demonstration Garden site; for groups, teachers, beginners, and veterans alike, call (206) 205-6386 to find out about demonstrations and classes; teaching materials (fact sheets, newsletters, articles for reprint, youth project ideas), and help in finding garden space or supplies.

❀ Training: Applications due in September for training the following January-March.

KITSAP COUNTY

Patt Kasa, Master Gardener Coordinator, Courthouse Annex, 614 Division Street, MS-16, Port Orchard, WA 98366 | **Phone:** (360) 876-7157 (MG Helpline) | **Email:** pkasa@wsu.edu | **Web:** http://kitsap.wsu.edu/hort/MG.htm

Training: Sign up on waiting list for training mid-January to mid-March.

LEWIS COUNTY

Debbie Burris, Master Gardener Coordinator, 345 W Main Street, Chehalis, WA 98532 | **Mailing address:** 360 NW North Street, MS:AES01, Chehalis, WA 98532-1900 | **Phone:** (360) 740-1212 |

Email: burrisd@coopext.cahe.wsu.edu | **Web:** http://gardening.wsu.edu/text/lewis.htm

MASON COUNTY

Debbie Burris, Master Gardener Coordinator, N 11840 Highway 101, Shelton, WA 98584 | **Phone:** (360) 427-9670, ext. 396 | **Email:** burrisd@coopext.cahe.wsu.edu | **Web:** http://graysharbor.wsu.edu

PACIFIC COUNTY

1216 Robert Bush Drive, PO Box 88, South Bend, WA 98586 | **Phone:** (360) 875-9331 | **Email:** ce6625@coopext.cahe.wsu.edu | **Web:** http://gardening.wsu.edu/text/pacific.htm

PIERCE COUNTY

Janet Sears, MG Volunteer Coordinator; 3049 S 36th Street, Suite 300, Tacoma, WA 98409 | **MG Hotline:** (253) 798-7170 or (800) 992-2456, ext. 7170 | **Email:** jsears@coopext.cahe.wsu.edu | **Web:** www.pierce.wsu.edu/

❀ Clinics: Year-round at the office, weekdays 9 a.m.-3 p.m.; more than 20 others during the season.

❀ Demonstration Garden: WSU Research/Extension Center, 7711 Pioneer Way E, Puyallup, WA. Open and staffed by a Master Gardener April-August, Tuesday and Saturday 10 a.m.-1 p.m. Demonstrating: Urban and environmentally sensitive gardening, annuals, perennials, herbs, small fruits, tree fruits, vegetables, landscape trees and shrubs, and composting. Trials and experiments: Fruit and vegetables.

❀ Plant Sale: Annually at the Demonstration Garden, call for details.

❀ Training: Deadline for application is November 15 for training the following January-March.

SAN JUAN COUNTY

221 Weber Way, Suite LL (office: 850 Spring Street), Friday Harbor, WA 98250 | **Phone:** (360) 378-4414 | **Email:** sjc@wsu.edu | **Web:** http://gardening.wsu.edu/text/sanjuan.htm

SKAGIT COUNTY

306 S 1st Street, Mt. Vernon, WA 98273 | **Phone:** (360) 428-4270 | **Email:** ce6429@coopext.cahe.wsu.edu | **Web:** http://skagit.wsu.edu

❀ Clinics: Phone-in clinic at the office, Wednesdays, 10 a.m.-2 p.m., April-October, and in Anacortes at Ace Hardware, Thursdays 9 a.m.-1 p.m., April-September.

❀ Demonstration Garden: Discovery Garden. (See Chapter 13, "Gardens to Visit.")

SNOHOMISH COUNTY

Holly Kennell, Extension agent; Jan Rainsberger, Master Gardener Coordinator; 600 128th Street SE, Everett, WA 98208 | **Phone:** (425) 338-2400 | **Email:** ce6431@coopext.cahe.wsu.edu or rainsber@wsu.edu (Jan Rainsberger) | **Web:** http://snohomish.wsu.edu

❀ Clinic: MG Hotline (425) 357-6010 | Phone-in clinic, Monday-Friday 10 a.m.-2 p.m. through April 11 and then 9 a.m.-4 p.m., April 14-September 26. Clinic schedule available from the office for 14 locations and many special events.

* Compost Demonstration Project: Call for details.

* Demonstration Garden: Jennings Park, 7027 51st Avenue NE, Marysville, open 8 a.m.-dusk. Master Gardeners available May 1-Sept. 30, Tuesday through Saturday, 10 a.m.-2 p.m.; call about special public tour dates, July, August, and September or call for your own guided group tour. Demonstrating: Annuals, perennials, herbs, small fruits, tree fruits, vegetables, containers/raised beds, lawn grasses, and wildflowers. Many new specialty gardens are planted each year, with the permanent planting of an English Cottage Garden and an orchard. An official All-American Display Garden.

THURSTON COUNTY

720 Sleater-Kinney Road SE, Lacey, WA 98503 | **Phone:** (360) 786-5445, ext. 7908 | **Email:** master@co.thurston.wa.us | **Web:** http://thurston.wsu.edu/Master%20Gardener/master_gardener.htm

* Demonstration Garden: Dirt Works/Yauger Park, Olympia, WA; Tuesday, June-September, from 9 a.m.-1 p.m., first and third Wednesdays, 6:30-8 p.m., second and fourth Saturdays, 9 a.m.-1 p.m., with special tours upon request. Demonstrating: Annuals, perennials, herbs, low-water-use plants, square foot gardening, butterfly gardens, ground covers, cover crops, turfgrass and its alternatives, IPM, and tree fruit. Trials: Fruit, vegetables, weed control, and solar soil sterilization.

* Closed Loop Park, Hawks Prairie Landfill, specializing in insect-tolerant, disease-resistant shrubs and perennials. Call (360) 923-9183 for details.

* Farmers Market, downtown Olympia; theme gardens on herbs, butterflies, shade; worm bin and composting demonstrations; landscaped stormwater drainage basin; MGs on-site weekends 10 a.m.-3 p.m. in season. Web: http://farmers-market.org/vendors/mg/mg.html

WAHKIAKUM COUNTY

Courthouse, PO Box 278 (office: 64 Main Street, Hanigan Building, Suite D), Cathlamet, WA 98612 | **Phone:** (360) 795-3278 | **Email:** ce6635@coopexe.cahe.wsu.edu | **Web:** http://gardening.wsu.edu/text/wahkiak.htm

WHATCOM COUNTY

Courthouse Annex, Suite 201, 1000 N Forest Street, Bellingham, WA 98225 | **Phone:** (360) 676-6736 | **Email:** whatcom@wsu.edu | **Web:** http://whatcom.wsu.edu/ag/homehort/mg/mgarden.htm

* Compost / Recycling Demonstration Projects at Hovander Homestead Park in Ferndale.

* Demonstration Garden: Hovander County Park, Ferndale; (360) 676-6736. Open daylight hours, May to mid-September. MGs available Wednesdays as they work, 9 a.m.-noon. The garden is a demonstration site for growing annuals, perennials, herbs, small fruits, tree

fruits, vegetables, landscape trees and shrubs, as well as how to use composting and drip irrigation techniques. A special feature is the large weed identification garden.

HOTLINES AND ONLINE HELP

Call-in Hotlines

While getting answers to some questions demands that you present an actual leaf, flower, or branch specimen for identification, the telephone can be an appropriate approach for types of questions like timing of pruning and fertilizing, winterizing, plant selection, and composting. Here are some information hotlines to call.

MASTER GARDENER OFFICES

Find the Master Gardener office nearest you; many provide quick answers for gardening questions. See the full listing of all western Oregon and Washington Master Gardener offices above, under "Master Gardener Programs."

ELISABETH C. MILLER HORTICULTURAL LIBRARY

Seattle, WA | **Phone:** UW PLANT (206-897-5268) (Monday-Friday, 9 a.m.-5 p.m.) | **Email:** hortlib@u.washington.edu

This quick-reference service for gardeners is provided by the Miller Library at the Center for Urban Horticulture. Wondering where to buy seeds for variegated ornamental corn, or what the experts say about flowering dogwoods? Call the Plant Answer Line for quick answers to your gardening questions. Modeled after the quick-reference service so popular in public libraries, the Plant Answer Line is tailored to fit the needs of Pacific Northwest gardeners.

OREGON INVASIVE SPECIES HOTLINE

Toll-free: (866) INVADER | **Web:** www.invasivespecies.org

WASHINGTON STATE UNIVERSITY (WSU), DIAL EXTENSION

King County Dial Extension Gardening: (206) 296-DIAL (3425) or (800) 325-6165, ext. 63425 | **Web:** www.metrokc.gov/dchs/csd/wsu-ce/DialExtension.htm (you can download a list of the tape numbers and topics for reference)

This tremendous resource for gardeners is available to you 24 hours a day, 7 days a week through King and Pierce Counties, WSU Cooperative Extension, and the USDA. (If you use the toll-free number you need to call weekdays during office hours.) With the **King County Dial Extension** (see phone numbers listed above), gardeners have access, through the convenience of the telephone, to over 250 informative recorded messages that run the whole horticultural gamut. When you call, have paper and pencil handy, because these 4- to-5-minute tapes are filled with substantive information. The **Pierce County Dial Extension** number is **(253) 596-6500** or **(800) 201-6500, code 3425;** it's sponsored by Pierce County Dial Extension and the *News Tribune* newspaper in Tacoma.

Internet Sources / Online Help

www.coopext.cahe.wsu.edu/~lenora

This Washington State University (WSU) site offers over 700 answer sheets to problems affecting vegetables, fruit trees, lawns, and ornamental trees and shrubs. For pest problems, both nonchemical and legal chemical management options are listed.

http://eesc.orst.edu

You'll find pages and pages of online gardening resources, articles, and ideas at this Gardening Information site managed by Oregon State University Extension & Experiment Station Communications. You can search the site, order publications or videos, link to related websites, and check gardening calendars.

http://gardening.wsu.edu/

This website answers hundreds of landscape and garden questions geared especially to the needs of Western Washington gardeners. Here you will find "Ask an Expert," where WSU Master Gardeners will personally answer your questions; the "Library" links you to publications written by the expert faculty and staff at WSU; "Local Opportunities" leads you to each Washington county's MG program offerings; "Timely Topics" provides a month-by-month list of gardening tips; "Stewardship Gardening" covers issues ranging from water-wise gardening, eco-lawns and composting to integrated pest management. Some library topics: Bamboo/invasive roots; ceanothus/root rot, winter damage; crabapple-scab and cider apple rust-resistant varieties; maples/aphids, scale, fungus on leaf and branches; skimmia/mites, and more.

www.icangarden.com

This is a great site for Canadian gardeners. Check the "Hints & Tips," and have a look at the Forum section that links gardeners by topic, including geographic region. There is also a good link to the Canadian Plant Hardiness Zone Map.

http://pep.wsu.edu/hortsense

Search the home gardener fact sheets for managing plant problems with Integrated Pest Management. Cultural controls and Washington-registered pesticides are included.

RADIO PROGRAMS AND NEWSPAPER COLUMNS

Radio Programs: Oregon

KEX 1190AM, Portland

Chris Totten, "Garden Doctor," Saturdays, 8-10 a.m.; call-in (800) 345-1190. Chris is a certified ecological hor-

ticulturist with a background in soils, fertility management, and pest control—plus a passion for plants.

KOTK 1080AM, Portland

Ed Hume, Saturdays, 10 a.m. to noon; call-in (503) 250-1080.

KUGN 590AM, Eugene

Rob Winters and **Steve Avery,** "Ask an Expert," Saturdays, 7-10 a.m.; (541) 485-0590 or (800) 590-5846. These two gardening experts host regular guests who join them in discussing plants and other gardening issues. They happily pass along plant sale, event, and club information, so consider taking them up on this generous publicity offer.

KXL 750AM, Portland

Mike Darcy, "In the Garden." Saturdays, 9-11 a.m. Talk show: (503) 417-7575 or (800) 827-0750. Mike interviews guests and is a very popular and knowledgeable expert.

Radio Programs: Washington

KIRO 710AM, Seattle

Ciscoe Morris, "Gardening with Ciscoe," Saturday and Sunday at 9 a.m.(some programs shortened during football season); (206) 421-KIRO or (877) 710-KIRO. Also visit www.ciscoe.com, where Ciscoe lists the names of his guests and how to get in touch with them.

KIXI 880AM, Seattle

Marianne Binetti, daily gardening tips at 9:30 a.m. and 4:30 p.m. Send your questions to www.binettigarden.com.

KOMO 1000AM, Seattle

Scott Conner, Saturday, 7-9 a.m. and Sunday, 7-10 a.m., call-in format (206) 421-1000 or (800) 874-8759. Scott is well known and respected for his breadth of gardening experience. He takes questions and hosts guests; also see Scott's website at: www.gardeninginthenw.com.

KUOW 94.9FM, Seattle

Carl Elliott, "The Radio Gardener," Wednesdays at 10:20 a.m., call-in Q&A (206) 543-5869 or (800) 289-5869. Be sure to check out the KUOW / Carl Elliott website at www.kuow.org/weekday_garden.asp, where Carl posts notes, tips, recommendations, and resources from the show.

KVI 570AM, Seattle

Ed Hume, Saturdays, 10 a.m., call-in format (206) 421-5757 or (888) 312-5757; also see Ed's website at: www.humeseeds.com.

Newspaper Columns: Oregon

Garden Showcase
PO Box 23669, Portland, OR 97281 | **Phone:** (800) 322-8541 | **Web:** www.gardenshowcase.com

Monthly, full-color, large-format magazine, covering Oregon and Washington topics. Local and regional horticultural experts submit regular columns: Ann Lovejoy, "Speaking Organically"; Lucy Hardiman, "Planting by Design"; Dan Hinkley, "The World of Gardening"; Mike Darcy, "Through the Grapevine"; Ray McNeilan, "Garden Q&A"; Jolly Butler, "Gardening 101"; and Ed Hume, "My Favorites."

The Oregonian

Each Thursday, *The Oregonian* publishes "Homes & Gardens of the Northwest," a section devoted to regional topics including plants, gardening, and landscape design. You can read archived articles and more on the Web: www.oregonlive.com/homeandgarden. Columnists include Dulcy Mahar, "Down to Earth"; Vern Nelson, the "Hungry Gardener"; and featured writer Kym Pokorny, who covers a variety of stories each week. You'll also want to see the plant feature "Bio: Flora," where illustrator Rene Eisenbart's renderings beautifully introduce gardeners to a seasonal perennial, bulb, vine, or other ornamental specimen.

The Register-Guard

"Home & Garden" is published monthly by the Eugene daily newspaper, typically on the second or third Thursday. You can read archived stories at www.registerguard.com. Regular columnists include Ellen Schlesinger, "Gardens in Season"; Liz Lair, "My Own Backyard"; Tracy Ilene Miller, "The Edible Garden"; and Stephen Anderson, "At the Wood's Edge."

Newspaper Columns: Washington

Northwest Garden News

A monthly tabloid published in Seattle, covering timely gardening topics, with book reviews, a calendar of events, and classifieds; it's available free at nurseries, garden shops, and many bookstores throughout western Washington.

Seattle Post-Intelligencer

"Northwest Gardens," Thursday edition, features columnists Ann Lovejoy, "From the Garden"; Marianne Binetti, "Ask Marianne"; and Marty Wingate, who writes about regional garden trends. Chris Smith writes "Good Enough to Eat," an edible gardening column. In early 2002, Ciscoe Morris joined the *P-I* line-up with a weekly to-do list for gardeners. The section also features book reviews, and there's a horticultural website and plant of the week. Read archived articles at www.seattlep-i.com or http://seattlep-i.nwsource/nwgardens/.

Seattle Times

Sunday Northwest Life section, "The Practical Gardener," by Mary Robson, Extension Agent. You can read archived columns at www.SeattleTimes.com and http:// gardening.wsu.edu/timely/index.htm. Sunday edition, *Pacific Northwest Magazine;* Valerie Easton writes a weekly column "Plant Life," and longer garden features monthly. You can read archived columns at http://seattletimes.nwsource.com/pacificnw/

Marianne Binetti

The well-known gardening author and syndicated garden columnist writes a weekly Gardening Column for about 20 area newspapers, including the *Seattle Post-Intelligencer* and the *Eastside Journal/South County Journal.* Read archived columns at www.binettigarden.com.

LIBRARIES

Many libraries have excellent selections of gardening magazines and may provide a collection of seed and plant catalogs too. Be sure to check their newspaper holdings for weekly columns, and don't overlook the video section (examples: *Square Foot Gardening, How to Grow Roses,* and *Water Gardening Tips*). Turn to libraries for patron access to the Internet. Today, libraries (such as Seattle's Miller Library) are also installing multimedia computer stations (where you can use CD-ROM programs) to keep in step with the rapid pace of software and technology development!

Elisabeth C. Miller Horticultural Library

Center for Urban Horticulture | **Street address:** 3501 NE 41st Street, Mail: CUH, UW Box 354115, Seattle 98195-4115 | **Phone:** (206) 543-0415 | **Web:** www.millerlibrary.org | **Open:** Monday, 9 a.m.-8 p.m.; Tuesday-Friday, 9 a.m.-5 p.m.; Saturdays (except July and August), 9 a.m.-3 p.m.

The library's Plant Answer Line provides a quick reference service for gardeners and is available Monday-Friday, 9 a.m.-5 p.m. by phone; (206) 897-5268 or (206) UW-PLANT, or anytime by email at hortlib@u.washington.edu.

With more than 10,000 volumes, including a top-notch collection of horticultural reference books, 400 journal and newsletter titles, extensive clipping and brochure files, and 1,000 current nursery and seed catalogs, this is indisputably the foremost horticultural library in the Northwest. And you're invited to visit! Old and rare, as well as new and select books cover a wide range of subjects, including gardening techniques, selecting and growing ornamental plants, vegetable and herb gardening, pests and diseases, garden design and history, gardens to visit, horticulture in urban environments, botany and plant ecology, environmental science, and native floras from around the world. The thorough and thoughtful librarians have created lists from their collection on specific topics to make it easier for you to hone in on the best resources. A multimedia computer station gives access to recommended websites, horticultural CD-ROMs, and online services such as the Anderson Horticultural Library's Plant Information Online. There is a small lending collection of books and videos for the public. (Brian Thompson, the Miller Library Systems and Technical Services librarian, has contributed an essay on new trends in gardening on the Internet, located on page 257 of this *Directory*.)

As a historical note, it's important to know that The Miller Library was destroyed on May 21, 2001, when Merrill Hall at the Center for Urban Horticulture was firebombed by terrorists. After a six-month closure, during which smoky, wet, and soot-stained books and files were treated and cleaned, the library reopened in December, using interim space in CUH's Isaacson Hall. All but about 15 percent of the collection was salvageable. The University of Washington has begun plans to rebuild Merrill Hall, where an enlarged and expanded library will be permanently housed, with completion slated for early 2004.

King County Hazardous Waste Library

130 Nickerson Street, Suite 100, Seattle, WA 98109 | **Phone:** (206) 263-3051 or (206) 263-3070 | **Email:** haz.waste@metrokc.gov | **Web:** www.metrokc.gov/hazwaste/hwl/ | **Open:** Monday-Friday, 8:30 a.m.-5 p.m.

Set up to help the residents of King County, this library offers you access to vast resources, from their extensive collection and through their online computer connections, such as DIALOG, the Chemical Information Service; Toxnet; MEDLINE; the EPA's online Library System, and the Hazardous Waste Collections database. Materials available include reference books, laws and regulations, policy and technical reports, video and audio tapes, and files of pamphlets, fliers, newspaper articles, and vendor brochures.

Kitsap Regional Library: Heronswood Nursery Project

1301 Sylvan Way, Bremerton, WA 98310 (see website for individual branches) | **Phone:** (360) 405-9100 | **Web:** www.krl.org/heronswood.htm

Donations from Heronswood Nursery in Kingston, Washington, have helped to fund the purchase of several hundred horticultural books and videos for this nine-library system. When you visit Heronswood, 50 cents from your admission supports this wonderful program. You can also view all the book and video titles at the website above.

Lawrence J. Pierce Library

Rhododendron Species Foundation, PO Box 3798, Federal Way, WA 98063-3798 | **Phone:** (253) 838-4646

On-site reference only, weekdays 9 a.m.-3 p.m. Call for access information to this small, but excellent resource of books on species rhododendrons and companion plants.

Leach Botanical Garden Library

6704 SE 122nd Avenue, Portland, OR 97236 | **Phone:** (503) 823-9503 | **Open:** Tues.-Sat., 9 a.m.-4 p.m.; Sun., 1-4 p.m. (Please call in advance as a courtesy.)

A wonderful resource for the Portland area, this library houses a large collection of horticultural and botanical books, periodicals, and textbooks. LBG members can check out books and anyone can use the material on-site.

Carroll O'Rourke Library

Lakewold Gardens, 12317 Gravelly Lake Drive SW, Lakewood, WA 98499 | **Phone:** (253) 584-4106 or (888) 858-4106

This small library is open to the public for reference use only. See the Lakewold listing in Chapter 13, "Gardens to Visit," for hours and driving directions.

Seattle Tilth

4649 Sunnyside Avenue N, Room 1, Seattle, WA 98103 | **Phone:** (206) 633-0451 | **Web:** www.seattletilth.org/reflib/reference library.html

Open hours vary by season, with summer office hours 9 a.m.-4 p.m. weekdays. The large reference library here covers urban and organic gardening, composting, homesteading, and small farming. Free pamphlets, too.

Washington Toxics Coalition

4649 Sunnyside Avenue N, Suite 540, Seattle, WA 98103 | **Phone:** (206) 632-1545, ext. 7, or (800) 844-SAFE | **Web:** www.watoxics.org

It is recommended that you call in advance to schedule a visit or receive help over the phone. The Toxics Coalition also has a wide variety of brochures, some free, some for purchase, that you can request by mail. Here you will find a terrific Information and Resource Library. Subject areas covered include toxicology, with health and environmental effects of specific chemicals; regulations at all levels, including model laws; pesticide use, covering agricultural and urban pesticides; alternatives, including methods of pest management and toxic waste reduction; professional referrals, including contact information for those in related scientific, medical, legal, and technical fields; and citizen organizing strategies for your environmentally sound community.

University of Washington Libraries

Seattle campus | **Web:** www.lib.washington.edu

The Natural Sciences Library (206-543-1243), located in the south Allen Library (next to Suzzallo, the main library) has an excellent botany collection. The Forest Resources Library (206-543-2758), in the basement of Bloedel Hall, is a good resource for information on trees and woody plants. The Architecture-Urban Planning Library (206-543-4067) in Gould Hall has a large collection on landscape architecture.

VanDusen Library

VanDusen Botanical Garden, 5251 Oak Street, Vancouver, B.C. V6M 4H1 | **Phone:** (604) 878-9274 (Main); (604) 257-8668 (Library) | **Email:** library@vandusen.org | **Web:** www.vandusengarden.org | **Open:** Tues.-Fri., 10 a.m.-3:30 p.m. (including Wed., 7-9 p.m.), Sun., 1-4 p.m.

The VanDusen Library collection complements the living resources of the Garden. It is the largest botanical and horticultural library with free public access in the province. Over 5,000 books, periodicals and other materials including seed catalogues are available for research and general information. Borrowing privileges extend to VanDusen members (two books for two weeks at a time from the circulating collection of 1300 books). If you are interested in helping out in the library, please contact the volunteer coordinator at (604) 257-8674.

WALKER HORTICULTURAL LIBRARY

Yakima Area Arboretum, Jewett Interpretive Center, 1401 Arboretum Drive, Yakima, WA 98901 | **Phone:** (509) 248-7337 | **Web:** www.ahtrees.org. | **Open:** Tues.-Fri., 9 a.m.-5 p.m.; Sat., 9 a.m.-4 p.m

The public is welcome to use this area's only horticultural library. Members are invited to check out all non-reference books. Enjoy more than 2,000 horticultural titles, including the lifetime collections of area botanists Ronald B. Tukey, Fred Carver, and Bill Luce. The library serves as a resource for technical materials but also houses children's books, popular gardening literature, nearly all Timber Press selections, and even has a section on light-hearted gardening mysteries.

COMMUNITY GARDENS / SMALL GARDEN PLOTS FOR RENT

For those who live where they cannot garden, these plots are a blessing. Be forewarned that they are very popular, so you should reserve yours well before spring (although some sites operate on a year-round basis). Water, a compost system, and some communal tools are usually provided, and often there's a forum for communicating with fellow site-mates. Camaraderie is one of the greatest benefits and something missed out on by those tending their home gardens. The national Association of Community Gardens has an excellent website where you can locate a garden near you through a searchable database: www. communitygarden.org/information/index.html.

PORTLAND COMMUNITY GARDEN SITES

Leslie Pohl-Kosbau, Portland Park Bureau, 6437 SE Division Street, Portland, OR 97206 | **Phone:** (503) 823-1612 | **Email:** pkleslie@ci.portland.or.us | **Web:** www.parks.ci.portland.us/Parks/CommunityGardens.htm

These garden sites are under the wing of Portland Parks and Recreation—and what a resource! The agency offers a Children's Gardening Program (in-school and after school); Earth and Gardening Group (a network for teachers and volunteers who garden with children); Native Habitats; a Display Garden and Compost Demonstration Site; a Demonstration Orchard (Gabriel Community Garden at SW 41st and Canby St in Gabriel Park); and Produce for the People (coordinates a program so excess produce from community gardens reaches local emergency food agencies).

You can rent space in 25 Community Garden Sites all

around Portland (request a brochure with map and addresses), 16 of which have *wheelchair-accessible plots*. Annual fees range from $12 for a 4 x 8-foot plot to $35 for a 20 x 20-foot plot (plus $10 deposit), $10 for an accessible, raised-bed plot. Even if you are well-situated with your own garden elsewhere, you can help this terrific program by volunteering your expertise or muscle power, or by attending events they sponsor—like "Seed the Earth" (a community seed and plant exchange and sale), usually held in April at the Fulton Park Community Garden, SW 2nd at Miles (just off Barbur Blvd above the Terwilliger curves); call or check the website for specific date and times.

OTHER OREGON COMMUNITY GARDENS

❀ Ashland: (541) 482-6001

❀ Beaverton: City of Beaverton, (503) 526-2487 or (503) 526-2434

❀ Bend: Hollinshead Community Garden, Betty Faller, (541) 389-8088

❀ Clackamas: Clackamas Community College, (503) 657-8400, ext. 211

❀ Corvallis: Lee Lawton, (541) 753-3115

❀ The Dalles: Chenowith Elementary School, (541) 296-9127

❀ Eugene: Parks and Recreation, (541) 682-5329; Food for Lane County, (541) 485-4355

❀ Gresham: Gresham Parks Department, (503) 618-2640

❀ Hillsboro: (503) 648-7202

❀ Lake Oswego: Tilth Garden at Lescher Farm / Lake Oswego Parks and Recreation, (503) 673-0351

❀ Medford: (541) 772-2780; West Medford Community Coalition, (541) 857-0653

❀ Milwaukie: Gladstone Community Garden: (503) 654-3535

❀ North Clackamas Park: (503) 653-8100

❀ Portland State University (for PSU students only): (503) 725-4392

❀ Salem: Community Sun Gardens, City of Salem Dept. of Community Services (503) 588-6336 or Dina Devoe, (503) 378-1847

❀ Tigard: (503) 228-3228

❀ Veronia: (503) 429-0301

SEATTLE COMMUNITY GARDENING; SEATTLE P-PATCH PROGRAM

700 Third Avenue, 4th Floor, Seattle, WA 98104 | **Phone:** (206) 684-0264 | **Email:** p-patch.don@ci.seattle.wa.us | **Web:** www.ci.seattle.wa.us/don/ppatch/

This program provides community garden space for residents of 44 Seattle neighborhoods. Over 1,900 (much-sought-after) plots serve over 4,600 urban gardeners. Some plots are handicapped-accessible with raised beds; all are organic. The program also provides special services for low-income, disabled, youth, and non-English-speaking gardeners. Get involved in supporting this great program and consider joining Friends of P-Patch, PO Box 19748, Seattle, WA 98109; (206) 684-0264.

OTHER WASHINGTON COMMUNITY GARDEN SITES

❀ Auburn: Auburn P-Patch Program, (253) 931-3043

❀ Bainbridge Island: Through the Park District, (206) 842-2306

❀ Bellevue: Parks and Community Services Department, (425) 452-7225 or (425) 452-6855. Bellevue operates two P-Patch gardens, offering approximately 105 400-square-foot plots. Apply in January. Plots are assigned to Bellevue residents and returning gardeners first.

❀ Bellingham Community Garden Sites (3 locations): Through the Bellingham Parks and Recreation Department, 3424 Meridian Street, Bellingham 98225, (360) 676-6985

❀ Bremerton: Through the Parks and Recreation Department, (360) 478-5305

❀ Edmonds: Good Shepherd Church in Lynnwood, (425) 774-1010

❀ Everett: City of Everett Office of Neighborhoods, (425) 257-8717

❀ Kent: North Green River Community Garden, (206) 296-4281

❀ Kirkland: Kirkland Community Garden, (425) 803-2845

❀ Lynnwood: Good Shepherd Community Garden, (425) 774-1010

❀ Mercer Island: Mercer Island Community Garden, (206) 236-3545

❀ Normandy Park: Normandy Park, (206) 248-7603

❀ Pacific: (253) 735-7334

❀ Redmond: Marymoor Park Community Garden, (206) 296-4281

❀ Renton: City of Renton, (425) 277-5530 or (425) 430-6700

❀ Tacoma: Community Garden Program, (253) 591-5330

❀ Tukwila: Parks and Recreation Department, (206) 768-2822

COMPOSTING, ORGANIC GARDENING, NATURAL LAWN CARE

Most communities have some type of home and yard waste recycling. Look in the phone book / yellow pages under "Recycling," "Public Utility," and/or "Solid Waste" to see what services may be available where you live. Master Gardeners generally have this information, too; see the listing of Master Gardener Programs above and find the one nearest you.

British Columbia Composting Programs

GREATER VANCOUVER REGIONAL DISTRICT
4330 Kingsway, Burnaby, B.C. V5H 4G8 Canada | **Compost Hotline:** (604) 736-2250 | **Web:** www.gvrd.bc.ca/services/garbage/compost

The GVRD is a partnership of 21 municipalities and one electoral area in southwestern British Columbia. There are several compost demonstration gardens available to gardeners living in the GVRD, which share great "water-wise" techniques. The website above will link you to specific demonstration garden locations, plus information on backyard composting, worm composting and lawn care.

Oregon Composting / Recycling

MASTER RECYCLER / COMPOSTER PROGRAM
OSU Extension Master Recycler Program, 211 SE 80th Avenue, Portland, 97215 | **Phone:** (503) 725-2035 | **Email:** megan.cogswell@orst.edu | **Web:** http://extension.orst.edu/ multnomah/recycling

Program concentrates on composting and alternatives to household hazardous wastes. This is where you turn for training, rather than have your compost questions answered on the spot (for that see below). This community education program provides 30 hours of training, offered in spring and again in fall (you reciprocate with 30 hours of volunteer educational help in the community). The program also provides speakers on a variety of topics, including home composting and vermicomposting.

METRO RECYCLING INFORMATION
600 NE Grand Avenue, Portland, OR 97232 | **Hotline:** (503) 234-3000 | **Email:** mri@metro.dst.or.us | **Web:** www.metro-region.org

Call with questions on composting, yard-waste recycling, hazardous products alternatives (including alternatives to pesticides), recycled products, and other local recycling resources. Ask when the next free workshops will be held, as there's an extensive offering. The hotline handles nearly 100,000 calls a year!

HOME COMPOSTING DEMONSTRATION SITES
Contact: John Foseid, Composting Expert, (503) 797-1674

Metro and Portland Parks and Recreation have built several sites, each featuring numerous active residential-scale composting systems, interpretive signs, and free composting literature. These centers are open to the public for self-guided tours from April through October. (These are *not* drop-off sites for yard debris. Call the Hotline number, (503) 234-3000, to find the drop-off site closest to you.) Workshops are offered at each location.

* Clackamas Community College: 19600 S Molalla Avenue, Oregon City

* Fulton Community Gardens: SW Barbur Blvd and SW Miles Street (Burlingame neighborhood)

* Kennedy Community Gardens, SW 103rd Street at Kennedy, Beaverton

* Leach Botanical Garden: 6704 SE 122nd Avenue, Portland

* Mount Hood Community College: 26000 SE Stark Street, Gresham

* Mary Woodward Elementary School, 12325 SW Catherine Street, Tigard

Washington Composting / Recycling

KING COUNTY BIOSOLIDS COMPOST

This product enhances landscapes and gardens, and can work as a soil amendment, mulch, or top-dressing to improve soil tilth. Marketed as "GroCo," the biosolid compost for residential landscapes is available throughout the greater Seattle area. Call GroCo at (206) 622-5141 for locations and prices. One yard of GroCo (you pick up) costs $13.95/yard. For more information, see http://dnr.metrokc.gov/WTD/biosolids/Compost.htm.

KING COUNTY RECYCLING / COMPOSTING INFORMATION LINE

(206) 296-4466 | **Web:** http://dnr.metrokc.gov/swd/resrecy/recycling/master.shtml

Residents of King County outside Seattle can call here for more information on waste reduction, recycling and composting programs, purchasing compost, or about discounts on compost bins. For information on becoming a Master Recycler Composter, contact Karen May at (206) 296-4353 or email karen.may@metrokc.gov. Training is held in the spring.

Organic Gardening

Master Gardeners are always helpful if you have questions in this area. See contact information listed earlier in this chapter.

OREGON TILTH

470 Lancaster Drive NE, Salem, OR 97301 | **Phone:** (503) 378-0690 | **Email:** organic@tilth.org | **Web:** www.tilth.org

Oregon Tilth is a member-based, nonprofit organization involved in research and education of organic growers, and is also an official organic certification agency. Tilth offers its members an excellent bimonthly newspaper, *In Good Tilth*, and has developed a Yard and Garden program that offers tips and how-to's on growing food organically. Membership is $25/year, and there are several chapters throughout Oregon.

SEATTLE TILTH

4649 Sunnyside Avenue N, Room 1, Seattle, WA 98103 | **Phone:** (206) 633-0451 | **Compost/Lawn & Garden Hotline:** (206) 633-0224 | **Green Gardening:** (206) 547-7561 | **Email:** tilth@seattletilth.org | **Web:** www.seattletilth.org

Office hours vary with the season, in summer they are Mon.-Fri., 9 a.m.-4 p.m. Join! Annual membership is $30 and includes a subscription to the monthly Seattle Tilth newsletter, discounts on classes, and a chance to network with like-minded gardeners interested in creating a healthy, sustainable future. Tilth has a large demonstration garden, an extensive offering of classes and workshops, a reference library covering urban and organic gardening, composting, homesteading and small farming, and free pamphlets.

WSU COOPERATIVE EXTENSION, KING COUNTY, URBAN FOOD GARDENERS

919 SW Grady Way, Suite 120, Renton, WA 98055-2980 | **Phone:** (206) 205-6386 | **Contact:** Sally Anne Sadler (email: sasadler@wsu.edu) | **Web:** www.metrokc.gov/DCHS/CSD/WSU-CE/Gardening/UrbanGardening/Index.htm

A great resource for both novice and experienced gardeners who want to find more information on composting, growing vegetables year-round, gardening with the fewest toxic chemicals, and how to improve the yield from your vegetable garden. The Urban Food Garden Program emphasizes intensive, organic, and water-wise vegetable and fruit gardening in urban settings. Take advantage of classes, demonstrations, fact sheets, articles and newsletters, and educational materials to help with classroom gardening projects. If you need help finding garden space to plant or the appropriate supplies, here is a good place to start.

WSU COOPERATIVE EXTENSION/MASTER GARDENERS

Washington State University (WSU), Dial Extension | **Phone:** (206) 296-DIAL (3425) or (800) 325-6165, ext. 63425 | **Web:** www.metrokc.gov/dchs/csd/wsu-ce/DialExtension.htm

The WSU Cooperative Extension and Master Gardener Programs have publications providing tips and guidelines for organic gardening methods. (See, for example, King County Dial Extension, (206) 296-DIAL, tape #1963, on Organic Vegetable Gardens.)

Natural Lawn Care & Natural Landscaping Programs

GREATER VANCOUVER REGIONAL DISTRICT

4330 Kingsway, Burnaby, B.C., V5H 4G8 Canada | **Phone:** (604) 432-6200 | **Email:** comm_ed@gvrd.bc.ca | **Web:** www.gvrd.bc.ca

The GVRD's Waterwise Gardening program educates residents of the 21 municipalities in Southwest British Columbia about "water-thrifty gardening" techniques. You can request a free copy of the 23-page "Waterwise Guide," which outlines water conservation, garden design, composting, lawn care and plant selection. There is a great list of drought tolerant plants suitable for Lower Mainland gardens. Use this link for a listing of publications, programs and resources (like local suppliers of worms and compost bins): www.gvrd.bc.ca/services/ garbage/compost/AddResources/resources.html.

Seattle Public Utilities

(206) 684-SAVE (7283) or (206) 633-0224 | **Web:** www.savingater.org or www.cityofseattle.net/util/rescons/ (This site also provides links to landscape professional organizations and related sites.)

Funded by a coalition of Puget Sound—area cities and water/sewer districts, these programs have produced a wonderful series of publications, available upon request via the phone or at the websites listed above. The series includes: *Natural Lawn Care, Growing Healthy Soil, Smart Watering, Choosing the Right Plants,* and *Natural Pest and Disease Control.* (See also the website spearheaded by Seattle Tilth, listed below.)

Seattle Tilth

(206) 633-0451 | **Natural Lawn & Garden Hotline:** (206) 633-0224 | **Web:** www.cityofseattle.net/util/rescons/

Answers questions about composting and organic gardening, particularly in an urban setting, for Seattle residents. Request information on how to obtain a compost bin, literature on composting, workshops, bin design plans, and more. (Seattle Tilth runs this program on contract through the city.)

Seattle Master Composter—Soil Builder Program / Seattle Tilth

Seattle Tilth, 4649 Sunnyside Avenue N, Room 1, Seattle, WA 98103 | **Phone:** (206) 633-0451 | **Compost Hotline:** (206) 633-0224

Seattle Tilth is an urban chapter of Washington Tilth, a regional network comprised of a diverse group of people interested in organic gardening, urban ecology, composting, recycling, and environmental issues. Tilth administers the Seattle Master Composter Program and maintains what is probably the most comprehensive demonstration site / resource library in the region, demonstrating many composting systems to choose from. When you visit, take the excellent self-guided tour. Find more good program information on Yard and Food Waste topics at www.ci. seattle.wa.us/util/composting/.

Help for Specific Problems

Noxious Weeds

In this case, the word "noxious weed" is a legal term, not just one used to designate an annoying plant. There are lists of plants, for in the entire United States and for each state, that designate which plants are illegal to grow, propagate, transport, or offer to buy or sell. Know what's legal and what's invasive by contacting the offices below.

Ivy O.U.T. (Ivy Off Urban Trees)

Washington Native Plant Society | 7400 Sand Point Way Northeast, Seattle, WA 98115 | **Phone:** (206) 527-3210 | **Email:** ivyout@wnps.org | **Web:** www.wnps.org/cps/ivyout.html

Ivy Off Urban Trees (Ivy O.U.T.) has been initiated by the Washington Native Plant Society with a grant from the Washington Department of Natural Resources and the U.S. Forest Service. The Central Puget Sound chapter of WNPS is working to remove the non-native, invasive English ivy from Seward Park in south Seattle. You can contact Ivy O.U.T. to learn about good native plant alternatives to English ivy.

King County Noxious Weed Line

(206) 296-0290 | **Web:** http://dnr.metrokc.gov/wlr/lands/weeds/

Watch out for those lovely exotic plants that are tough to control and crowd out plants beyond your backyard. If you need help identifying your weeds, or advice on removing them, call this resource or check the website, where you can download the current King County Noxious Weed List brochure and see images of these plants.

Oregon State Department of Agriculture, Plant Division Weed Control Program

635 Capitol Street NE, Salem, OR 97301-2532 | **Phone:** (503) 986-4636 (Plant Pest & Disease Programs), or (503) 986-4621 (Noxious Weed Control Program) | **Web:** http://www.oda.state. or.us/Plant/Plant_division_homepage.htm

Oregon Invasive Species Hotline

Toll-free: (866) INVADER | **Web:** www.invasivespecies.org

Washington State Department of Agriculture, Plant Services Division

PO Box 42560, Olympia, WA 98504-2560 | **Phone:** (360) 902-1922 | **Web:** www.wa.gov/agr/

The Plant Services Division certifies that plant material is free from infestation, and provides testing and inspection services to assure disease-free planting stock for various agricultural industries.

Washington State Noxious Weed Control Board

1111 Washington Street SE, Olympia, WA 98504 (PO Box 42560, Olympia, WA 98504-2560) | **Phone:** (360) 902-2053 | **Web:** www.wa.gov/agr/weedboard/index.html

The above website will also link you to all the County Weed Boards in the state, so you can contact a local resource. You can find a detailed list (and Photo Gallery) of Pacific Northwest noxious weeds at www.wa.gov/agr/ weedboard/weed_info/gallery.html. You may be very surprised to find plants you've been growing (and no doubt adore) or aspire to add to your garden!

WSU / Cooperative Extension

http://gardening.wsu.edu/text/nvproblm.htm

The website on native plants has good information on dealing with "Non-native Problem Plants."

Pesticides / Disposal

Leftover, unused, or unidentified pesticides can be very harmful when stored or disposed of improperly. Many people have such horrors lurking in the basement or piled along the back wall of the garage. Along comes a fit of spring cleaning and the guilt of what to do with the blasted things hangs heavily on one's shoulders. Whatever you do, DON'T flush them down the toilet or dump them down a storm drain or into a nearby creek! Help is at hand!

Pesticides / Disposal: National Sources

ENVIRONMENTAL PROTECTION AGENCY

(800) 858-7378

Call for toxicological information on pesticides seven days a week, 6:30 a.m.-4:30 p.m. PST.

PESTICIDE INFORMATION

U.S. Poison Control Center | (800) 858-7378

NATIONAL PESTICIDE TELECOMMUNICATIONS NETWORK

(800) 858-7378 | **Web:** http://ace.orst.edu/info/nptn/

Pesticides / Disposal: Oregon

METRO RECYCLING INFORMATION

Hotline: (503) 234-3000

Answers a range of questions, including all **recycling** (including lawn debris) queries and **pesticide disposal** questions. A full lineup of informative workshops, called "Learn About Common-Sense Gardening," is offered by Metro and the City of Portland Bureau of Environmental Services on alternatives to pesticides. Call this number to register.

NORTHWEST COALITION FOR ALTERNATIVES TO PESTICIDES

PO Box 1393, Eugene, OR 97440 | **Phone:** (541) 344-5044 | **Email:** info@pesticide.org | **Web:** www.pesticide.org

The NCAP is a five-state, grassroots membership organization that promotes sustainable resource management, prevention of pest problems, use of alternatives to pesticides, and the right to be free from pesticide exposure. NCAP strives to substantially reduce or eliminate the use of pesticides as a preferred method of pest control in the Northwest and elsewhere. The organization provides **alternatives fact sheets** like "Aphids: Least Toxic Aphid Management," "Encouraging Ladybugs," and "Rose Diseases: Least Toxic Management of Roses." Inquire about brochures (some are available free from the website; others can be ordered for $2 per publication by mail). NCAP also publishes **brochures**, such as *Gardens Without Pesticides*, *Children and Pesticides*, and *Growing Food Without Pesticides*. They offer **pesticide fact sheets**, too, so if you want to read up on the likes of Roundup, Finale, or Di-

azinon you can order copies or download them from the website.

OREGON POISON CONTROL CENTER

Pesticide Exposure 24-hour phone: (800) 222-1222

Pesticides / Disposal: Washington

KING COUNTY HAZARDOUS WASTE LIBRARY

130 Nickerson Street, Suite 100, Seattle, WA 98109 | **Phone:** (206) 263-3051 or (206) 263-3070 | **Email:** haz.waste@metrokc.gov | **Web:** www.metrokc.gov/hazwaste/hwl | **Open:** Mon.-Fri., 8:30 a.m.-5 p.m.

Check the listing under "Libraries" (above) to see the many ways these folks can help you!

SEATTLE HOUSEHOLD HAZARDS LINE

(206) 296-4692 | **Web:** www.metrokc.gov/hazwaste/house

Reduce the risk to pets, children, family, and the environment from exposure to products marked "Danger," "Warning," or "Caution." The Local Hazardous Waste Management Program in King County is a multiagency effort to reduce and manage hazardous waste from households, small businesses (such as landscape companies), and government agencies. The program collects leftover pesticides and provides education and information on alternatives to pesticides. Ask about the wide range of educational materials available, including brochures, videos, and consumer guides. Call to locate places that accept discarded hazardous products, including pesticides.

WASHINGTON POISON CONTROL CENTER

(800) 732-6985 or (800) 222-1222

Call here if you should have an accident, or need answers to questions about pesticides, insecticides, or other chemicals.

WSU COOPERATIVE EXTENSION OFFICES, PESTICIDE SAFETY INFORMATION

See the website at http://picol.cahe.wsu.edu/. You should also check "Pesticides: Learning About Labels," at http://pep.wsu.edu/factsheet/applylearning.htm.

WASHINGTON TOXICS COALITION

4649 Sunnyside Avenue N, Suite 540 E, Seattle, WA 98103 | **Pesticide Information Center:** (206) 632-1545 | **Web:** www.watoxics.com (also general information for homeowners and gardeners)

WTC can answer questions relating to alternative products and techniques to reduce our reliance on toxic chemical responses to pest and disease problems, and garden maintenance practices. Whether it's tent caterpillars or aphids, this knowledgeable group can provide you with sensible and successful solutions, and—what's more important—can help you understand more about what's at the root of the problem, such as insect lifecycles, insect biology, and overall control philosophy. They identify and promote nontoxic and environmentally sound alternative products and techniques, and publish well-documented Fact Sheets for $1 each. Their booklet, *Buy Smart, Buy Safe* ($5), is a consumer guide to products that are the least toxic.

Plant Problem Diagnosis

MASTER GARDENER DROP-IN CLINICS

These clinics (see "Master Gardener" listings earlier in this chapter for location details) offer some of the very best ways to seek a positive identification, to track down a knowledgeable opinion about an unhealthy garden, or to learn more about gardening techniques. You can bring in pests or plants (or parts thereof) for identification, and you can often find out about upcoming workshops, demonstrations, lectures, seminars, training, and other good stuff.

HORTICULTURAL EVENTS

Events such as the **Seattle Tilth Autumn Harvest Fair,** the **King County Master Gardener Harvest Fair,** and the various Fruit Society Fall Fruit Fairs (Oregon and Washington) bring together experts who are gregarious types, animated by the festive mood of the event, and full of great advice, so take the opportunity to ask a few questions! (Have an unidentified apple or pear growing in your garden you'd like to put a name to? These guys *delight* in the challenge of "name that mystery variety"!) See "Seasonal Sources & Events" in Chapter 7, "Plant Sales," for more information.

GARDEN CLUBS

Clubs are another excellent source of on-the-spot problem solving. Very few of these organizations are formed for the purpose of getting together purely for the social benefits. It's been our experience that anyone who shows up with a problem specimen or insect will have no lack of advice, and probably find some of the best horticultural minds in the community working for a solution! (See Chapter 2, "Clubs, Societies & Volunteer Opportunities," for a list)

NURSERY AND GARDEN CENTER STAFF

These people are generally very knowledgeable and, if not caught at the height of a busy sales day, interested in helping you with questions. Be aware that these are for-profit businesses, so the bottom line (of what can be sold to you) may influence the advice given. *Be wary* if a nursery staff member actively pushes only chemical solutions (particularly general-purpose sprays and powders) without any discussion of organic or mechanical methods (like a strong spray of water for aphids). See Chapter 5, "Nurseries," for nursery locations.

OSU COOPERATIVE EXTENSION, DEPARTMENT OF BOTANY AND PLANT PATHOLOGY

Plant Clinic, 1089 Cordley Hall, OSU, Corvallis, OR, 97331-2904 | **Phone:** (541) 737-3472

The OSU Plant Clinic is dedicated to helping you solve your plant problems by correctly identifying the cause and helping you choose the most appropriate control methods. See the program's extensive searchable database of plant diseases at www.bcc.orst.edu/bpp/.

For an Online Guide to Plant Disease Control, see http://plant-disease.orst.edu/index.htm—you'll be able to scan A to Z the Pacific Northwest Plant Disease Management Handbook and much of the OSU Extension Plant Pathology slide collection and photographs. (Published version of the handbook can be ordered at puborder@orst.edu.)

WSU COOPERATIVE EXTENSION, PLANT AND INSECT DIAGNOSTIC LABORATORY

Western Washington: Jenny Glass, Diagnostic Plant Pathologist, WSU Puyallup, 7612 Pioneer Way East, Puyallup, WA 98371-4998 | **Phone:** (253) 445-4582 | **Email:** glass@puyallup.wsu.edu | **Web:** http://gardening.wsu.edu/plantclinic/index.htm

Both commercial and residential horticultural clients are benefited by the services offered here—plant problem assessment, disease diagnosis, and insect identification. You are first directed to take a problem specimen directly to your County Extension Agent (the website lists contacts throughout the state). The Puyallup site is equipped to deal with Northwest Insect and Spider identification only; you will need to submit Form CO495 (available from your local WSU Cooperative Extension office), plus a $15 identification fee with your specimen.

HORTSENSE

http://pep.wsu.edu/hortsense/

See these useful home-gardener fact sheets for managing plant problems with Integrated Pest Management practices. Both cultural controls and Washington-registered pesticides are covered at their website.

Plant Selection

It's wonderful to cruise the aisles or paths of your favorite specialty nursery in search of a great plant you've never grown before. Seeing how a mature specimen settles into its permanent home—by observing it in a display border at a garden or nursery—is even more inspiring. You might be one of those gardeners who believes in shopping "in season," when you can buy what's in bloom (since that's when retail plant-sellers usually stock ornamental trees, shrubs, vines, perennials, and annuals for the landscape). But now you can take advantage of a new world of ideas, with these organized plant selection programs. Here's a list of some programs to get you started.

APPROPRIATE PLANTS FOR KITSAP COUNTY

Kitsap County Public Works | **Phone:** (360) 337-5777 | **Web:** solidwaste@co.kitsap.wa.us

Kitsap County Public Works, the WSU/Kitsap Cooperative Extension Service, and Kitsap Conservation District have published a useful guide for gardeners in this area. Learn which native plants, fruit trees, roses, rhododendrons, and other recommended landscape plants are suitable for this region. The publication also lists "plants to avoid." Call the above number and request *Appropriate Plants for Kitsap County*, KCPWFORM #3508, or order online.

GREAT PLANT PICKS

The Elisabeth C. Miller Botanical Garden, PO Box 77377, Seattle, WA 98177 | **Phone:** (206) 363-4803 | **Email:** lindap@miller garden.org | **Web:** www.greatplantpicks.org

Launched in 2001, Great Plant Picks is a regional-plant awards program designed to help the home gardener identify unbeatable plants for the Pacific Northwest garden. The program inspires gardeners in the maritime areas west of the Cascade Mountains, from Eugene, Oregon, in the south to Vancouver, BC, in the north. Great Plant Picks, an educational program administered by the Elisabeth C. Miller Botanical Garden (www.millergarden.org), a private, nonprofit garden located in North Seattle, was set up with the goal of creating a comprehensive list of superb plants for gardeners in the region. Look for each year's new introductions (selected by the top plant experts in the Northwest) at the Northwest Flower and Garden Show each February.

When you visit the GPP website, you can view vibrant photographs of the select plants (15 were chosen in 2001), download fact sheets, and read the judges' evaluations of the plants. You can also link to retail specialty nurseries that carry the varieties identified as "best choices" in the following categories: trees/conifers, shrubs/vines, and perennials.

TROUBLE-FREE PLANTS FOR THE PACIFIC NORTHWEST

Local Hazardous Waste Management Program in King County, 130 Nickerson Street, Suite 100, Seattle, WA 98109 | **Phone:** (206) 263-3051 | **Email:** haz.waste@metrokc.gov | **Web:** www.metrokc.gov/hazwaste/house/plantlist.html

The hazardous waste management program in King County recommends a good selection of plants that resist diseases and pests naturally (thereby reducing your need to use pesticides and other damaging chemicals). The selection features evergreen and deciduous shrubs, evergreen and deciduous trees, roses, rhododendrons, fruit trees, vegetables, and culinary herbs. This useful list also highlights a plant's mature size, flowering season, habitat, and beneficial features. You can link to other online lists for "good garden bugs" and other pesticide-free practices from this site, too.

PLANT INTRODUCTION SCHEME OF THE BOTANICAL GARDEN OF THE UNIVERSITY OF BRITISH COLUMBIA (PISBG)

http://www.ubcbotanicalgarden.org/research/indsutry/pisbg.php

Since 1985, this program has introduced and recommended plants for the gardening public, fostering links with the local nursery industry to ensure that good sources of interesting and reliable landscape plants are available. Through a separate program tied to the British Columbia Landscape and Nursery Association, the Botanical Garden is able to realize some royalties and license fees for the plants it develops and introduces. The program includes several wild-collected British Columbia natives, such as *Rosa woodsii* 'Kimberley', and *Penstemon fruticosus* 'Purple Haze'. The collection also includes plants derived from UBC's Asian collections, such as *Clematis chiisanensis* 'Lemon Bells'.

Soil Testing

* Call your local Master Gardeners office. (See listing of county phone numbers earlier in this chapter.)

* Contact the WSU Cooperative Extension in King County, (206) 205-3100 or (800) 325-6165, ext. 5-3100, and request a free packet of information on soil testing, including recommended sources. (WSU and OSU do not provide soil testing.)

* See "Soil, Amendments, and Rock" in Chapter 9, "Products, Materials & Professional Services," for private soil-testing company listings.

Tree Questions

CERTIFIED ARBORISTS

Are you looking for a trained professional to answer questions about a tree problem? Consider consulting a certified arborist. They have at least three years' experience and have passed a certification exam that tests a variety of tree-care knowledge. Examples of the kinds of work CAs are trained for include tree preservation and conservation; hazard tree evaluations (including steep slope and root problems) and removals; tree-loss evaluation; tree valuation; reforestation; tree planting; tree and shrub pruning and moving; and tree witness testimony. (See Chapter 9, "Products, Materials & Professional Services" for further more information on caring for trees and shrubs.)

MASTER GARDENERS

Master Gardeners provide diagnostic help at their clinics (see the list of offices under "Master Gardeners" earlier in this chapter). In Washington, you can call the Dial Extension number at (206) 296-DIAL to hear detailed taped messages on tree problems. Examples of tapes include #1615, "Aphids on Spruce"; #1647, "Problems with Madronas"; and #1642, "Dangerous Trees."

FRIENDS OF TREES

3117 NE Martin Luther King Boulevard, Portland, OR 97212 | **Phone:** (503) 282-8846 | **Hotline:** (503) 284-8733 | **Email:** fot@friendsoftrees.org | **Web:** www.friendsoftrees.org

Friends of Trees brings neighbors together for tree planting and tree-care projects along city streets, in urban natural areas, and on school grounds. The organization also distributes information on how to protect urban trees. Educational outreach efforts aimed at children and adults are helping to improve appreciation for Portland's great shade trees. The website has a wonderful array of resources, including information on "Branching Out," a program that makes the planting of trees in yards affordable.

INTERNATIONAL SOCIETY OF ARBORICULTURE, PACIFIC NORTHWEST CHAPTER

PO Box 811, Silverton, OR 97381 | **Phone:** (503) 874-8263 | **Email:** info@pnwisa.org | **Web:** www.pnwisa.org

Excellent materials, including *How to Hire an Arborist* and *Tree Care Information*, are available from this organization. The website discusses tree myths, the truth about topping, and how to save trees, and includes a guide to pruning techniques. You can also request a list of Portland/Vancouver/Oregon Certified Arborists, Puget Sound/Greater Seattle Area Certified Arborists, and professional arborists in British Columbia. A complete listing of all certified arborists is available from the ISA website at www.isa-arbor.com.

PLANTAMNESTY/SEATTLE

PO Box 15377, Seattle, WA 98115-0377 | **Phone:** (206) 783-9813 | **Email:** plantamnesty@plantamnesty.org | **Web:** www.plantamnesty.org

This passionate organization offers a valuable referral service that provides names of certified arborists who have passed the ISA exam as well as a rigorous PlantAmnesty exam. To learn more about PlantAmnesty's lively history and excellent workshops, see the related entry in Chapter 2, "Clubs, Societies & Volunteer Opportunities."

SEATTLE CITY ARBORIST

Seattle Municipal Building, 600 Fourth Avenue, Room 708, Seattle, WA, 98104 | **Phone:** (206) 684-7649 | **Web:** http://www.cityofseattle.net/td/arborist.asp

You'll get help with choosing just the right streetside tree on this website. Find out about becoming a Tree Steward, a program of volunteers that work with city staff "to protect and enhance Seattle's urban forest." Want a tree identified? Take a leaf to the City Arborist (call ahead). For other city arborists in other cities, call your local public utilities district or park department.

TREEMENDOUS SEATTLE

7400 Sand Point Way NE, Seattle, WA 98115 | **Phone:** (206) 985-6867 | **Email:** chris@seattletrees.org | **Web:** www.seattletrees.org

This public-private partnership was formed to unite and coordinate efforts of volunteers, communities, businesses, nonprofit organizations, and government agencies in order to plant, preserve, and maintain a healthy urban forest in the Puget Sound region. You can join this organization and learn more about planting more trees in your community. TREEmendous Seattle also operates an Urban Ecology Education Program that provides curriculum for science classes at area schools. See the great glossary on the website.

URBAN AND COMMUNITY FORESTRY PROGRAM

Washington State Department of Natural Resources, PO Box 47037, Olympia, WA 98504-7037 | **Phone:** (360) 902-1704 or (800) 523-TREE (8733) | **Email:** urban_forestry@wadnr.gov | **Web:** www.wa.gov/dnr/htdocs/rp/urban/urban.htm

Among other things, this program educates citizen groups and volunteers in planting and sustaining healthy trees and vegetation wherever people live and work in Washington State. Request a free copy of *TreeLink News*, a bulletin of programs for tree-lovers. The website offers great resources, such as USDA Forest Service bulletins on pruning, handling hazardous trees, and more.

WSU/PIERCE COUNTY MASTER GARDENERS AND THE (TACOMA) *News Tribune*

Call (253) 596-6500 or (800) 201-6500, code 3425, for tapes covering over 250 topics. Examples of their offerings include #5292, "Dogwood Diseases"; #5287, "Fertilizing Trees and Shrubs"; and #5461, "Tree Root Problems."

Utilities

British Columbia: According to the B.C. Utilities Commission, there is no provincial or national requirement to "call before you dig." However, as a matter of common sense, we recommend BC gardeners contact their local municipality planning office for advice on any major digging project. If you think you have electrical or gas lines in your landscape, you should call the appropriate utility company. BC Hydro operates an extensive educational program to help gardeners plant trees appropriately. Request a free copy of "Planting Near Power Lines" at (800) BCHYDRO or visit www.bchydro.com.

Oregon and Washington: Gardeners just *love* to dig. But beware of what lurks forgotten below! If you are digging any deeper than 12 inches, Oregon and Washington state laws require that you notify the Utilities Underground Location Center, a national clearinghouse. Call anytime, 7 days a week, 24 hours a day for this free service: Utilities Underground Location Center, (800) 424-5555; www.callbeforeyoudig.org.

chapter

2

Clubs, Societies & Volunteer Opportunities

The old adage goes something like this: You get out of something what you put into it. It's still great advice for anyone who wants to reap a rewarding harvest of knowledge, information, friends, and new garden-ing ideas. Gardening organizations, plant societies, and special-interest clubs are ideal "points of entry" for both beginning and veteran horti-cultural enthusiasts. This chapter offers you a great list to begin with, as we've endeavored to feature a wide array of groups large and small, from those with a broad, generalist focus right through to the narrow, genus-specific clubs.

Note that the contact persons listed served the organization at the time this publication was assembled and researched. Over time, these individuals, nearly always volunteers, may relinquish their duties to an-other member, so be forewarned that contact people frequently change, especially for nonprofit, all-volunteer groups.

Many clubs meet on a regular basis, usually once a month, to share information, plants, companionship, and a love of gardening. Some stage plant sales open to the public, sponsor community gardening projects, offer field trips, or host lectures. Plant societies abound, and may offer field trips, major tours, newsletters, conventions, libraries, and more, in addition to monthly meetings.

If you have a special interest not represented here, check the ultimate sourcebook for gardeners, Barbara Barton's *Gardening by Mail,* where you will find over 200 horticultural societies—international, national, and regional (anyone interested in the Aloe, Cactus & Succulent Society of Zimbabwe?). But why join or contact a foreign horticultural society? Because many can arrange private garden visits should you be traveling in their area, and they sponsor ongoing plant and extensive seed exchanges that can provide access to rare and unusual treasures, publish excellent periodicals, and provide many other valuable privileges. This is your window to the world of gardening—get involved!

Also check Chapter 7, "Plant Sales," and the "Major Regional Flower Shows" section in Chapter 12 for more details on club and plant society activities.

Editor's Note:

Collecting the information for this section is just about the hardest detective work we've undertaken for this *Directory.* The entries here represent just a small portion of the pages and pages of organizations in existence! If we've listed a contact for an organization and it turns out to be someone who has "retired" from the group, ask for another phone number and apologize for us! Another contact-finding strategy is to go to the website for a plant or horticultural group's national headquarters and work your way backwards to the British Columbia, Oregon, or Washington chapters. This step usually yields a local contact and phone number.

Because space here is limited, trying to decide who to include and who to leave out is most difficult. We've tried to provide information on a broad range of horticultural interest groups. If you feel there's an area that's been poorly covered, please contact us with that information for the next edition.

About International Organizations: You will note that some international plant and horticultural societies, most of which are based in the U.K., do not wish to receive your dues in U.S. or Canadian dollars. Because of the fluctuations in exchange rates, we have not listed the North American equivalent of international dues. We recommend you check the organization's website (most groups do publish their current due schedule on the Web) and if you are concerned about efficiency, use a major credit card when paying your dues.

The Role of the Internet

There is a *phenomenal* amount of information put up on the Internet by garden clubs, societies, and foundations. Just try a search for "Roses" or "Rhododendrons" and prepare yourself for major informational overload. Many of these sites are just plain gorgeous, others are purely informational, and some have a lovely balance of the two. If you've got the time and interest, follow the links you'll find on a favorite organization's site . . . they're likely to lead you through a labyrinth of fascinating connections around the globe.

HEY! I CAN DO THAT! VOLUNTEERING IN THE NORTHWEST

There's no question about it: Successful gardeners are a hardworking and energetic species. They're also a particularly generous and enthusiastic group that loves to share techniques, knowledge—heck, even cuttings and divisions from their own backyards! It's this passion for doing what we love most that must account for many gardeners' ability to juggle the demands of their landscape, their family, and in many cases a demanding work life... and then, miraculously, to also have time to share their knowledge, energy, and skills about horticultural matters with others. If you have the urge and the time, consider joining one of these groups, for the pleasure of sharing, and also to enjoy the personal growth that a lifetime pursuit of one's gardening education requires.

A good way to find out more about volunteering with a horticultural organization or public / private garden is to talk with its current volunteers who work at major events like the Northwest Flower and Garden Show and the Van Dusen Flower and Garden Show. Find out what they're up to and ask about other available opportunities. At a public garden, a horticultural library, or a study weekend, you'll undoubtedly see many people filling important jobs—and yes, more likely than not they're volunteers. They'd be glad to tell you how to get involved, too!

CENTER FOR URBAN HORTICULTURE

3501 NE 41st Street, Seattle, WA | **Mailing address:** PO Box 354115, University of Washington, Seattle, WA 98195-4415 | **Phone:** (206) 543-8616 | **Web:** www.urbanhort.org

Opportunities are available indoors and out: reception, propagation, data entry, processing books, technology, wetland/prairie restoration project, class monitors.

ELISABETH C. MILLER HORTICULTURAL LIBRARY

At the Center for Urban Horticulture (see address above) | **Phone:** (206) 543-0415 | **Email:** hortlib@u.washington.edu | **Web:** www.hortlib.org

Surround yourself with gardening books, periodicals, and fabulous obscure resources! Many library-related tasks allow you to assist the small, talented staff.

FRIENDS OF THE P-PATCH PROGRAM

This not-for-profit corporation exists in association with the Seattle Department of Neighborhoods; phone (206) 684-0264 to find out how to help support and nurture community organic gardening and the Seattle P-Patch Program. Your financial or volunteer support will help this worthy community organization assist low-income gardeners, youth, and local food banks. Membership is $5 on up; call for a brochure. A volunteer skill bank helps build new community gardens. There is a special need for sign makers, landscape designers, grant writers, construction help, haulers with big trucks, donors of building materials, and garden skill teachers for children and adults. Master Gardeners play a big role here as well. (See Chapter 1, "Organizations That Help Gardeners," for P-Patch and other community garden locations.)

MASTER RECYCLER/COMPOSTER PROGRAM

Similar to the Master Gardener Program, with a mix of classroom sessions, field trips, and work at demonstration sites. Fewer hours of training and "pay-back" are required for those involved here than for the Master Gardener Program and the classroom sessions may take place evenings or weekends. Call your County Extension office for information on local programs.

MASTER GARDENERS

Volunteerism and gardening are synonymous with Master Gardeners, the quintessential community service program that nurtures citizen-gardeners. This program is discussed at length in Chapter 1 "Organizations That Help Gardeners." There are Master Gardener Programs throughout Oregon (through OSU / Cooperative Extension) and Washington (through WSU/Cooperative Extension). In the major cities, though, it can be difficult to join the training, with waiting lists and lotteries the norm. Apply early!

METROPOLITAN PARK DISTRICT OF TACOMA

The Park District Horticultural Division maintains four greenhouses, four cold frames, six shade-houses, and three open nurseries. Volunteers are integral to the success of the work in these facilities and the gardens, which include the **W. W. Seymour Botanical Conservatory** (253/591-5330) or any of the individual gardens at **Point Defiance Park** (253/591-5328). There's also an **Adopt-a-Park** program (or garden, or project; 253/305-1062).

PLANT SALES

Plant Sales always need volunteers. Many of the big ones will accept help from non-members. (These sales sometimes need as many as 400 people to help out in lots of different ways.) Have you ever considered the advantage of being a part of the team that stages these feeding frenzies? Benefits include having a first glance at what will be offered for sale and where growers display it. (No fair hiding the best stuff, though!) There are often pre-sales to members and workers, held anywhere from a day in advance to an hour before the ravenous gardening public descends on the plant-laden tables. We know one Seattle couple who joined the Portland-based Hardy Plant Society in part because of its fabulous plant sales (they travel early to the sales and always volunteer for it, driving home with a car full of great new plants). Other plant hounds have figured out that an offer to help with post-sale cleanup is occasionally rewarded with a choice of leftover plants that didn't sell (not always slim pickings, by any means!).

Here are some suggested plant sales to contact:

❋**Arboretum Foundation.** Spring plant and fall bulb sales. Phone: (206) 325-4510; Web: www.arboretum-foundation.org

❋**Bellevue Botanical Garden Society.** Spring plant sale. Phone: (425) 451-3755; Web: www.bellevuebotanical.org

❋**Hardy Fern Foundation.** Spring fern festival. Phone: (206) 870-5363; Web: www.hardyferns.org

❋**Hardy Plant Society of Oregon.** Spring and fall sales. Phone: (503) 224-5718; Web: www.hardyplantsociety.org

❋**Northwest Horticultural Society.** Fall plant sale. Phone: (206) 527-1794; Web: www.northwesthort.org

❋**Rhododendron Species Foundation.** Spring and fall plant sales. Phone: (253) 838-4646 (Seattle), (253) 927-6960 (Tacoma); Web: www.rhodygarden.org

ARBORETUM OF THE CASCADES (FORMERLY THE PRESTON ARBORETUM)

29700 SE Highpoint Way, Preston, WA 98050 | **Mailing address:** PO Box 512, Preston, WA 98050 | **Phone:** (425) 888-3162 | **Email:** sbond@nwlink.com

If you are interested in being in on the ground floor of an exciting new arboretum, contact the Arboretum of the Cascades, formerly the Preston Arboretum and Botanical Gardens. The Arboretum of the Cascades currently operates an Environment Learning Center (by appointment only) and is embarking on a major expansion under the auspices of King County Parks Department. Susan Bond, executive director, is enlisting volunteers for this ambitious project, including helping implement the Master Plan for this 300-acre effort.

SEATTLE YOUTH GARDEN WORKS

4759 15th Avenue NE, Seattle, WA 98105-4404 | **Phone:** (206) 525-1213 | **Contact:** Nancy Neal, MA, Director | **Email:** info@sygw.org | **Web:** www.sygw.org

This unique employment and education program is directed at converting troubled teens (ages 14–22) from street life to trained teens growing seedlings into productive gardens. The youths earn an hourly wage as they learn about gardening, develop business savvy, and gain skills for sustaining their own lives. Volunteers must be at least 24 years old, have prior experience working with youth, and be available to make a six-month commitment (a minimum of one day a week for three to four hours). For positions in project administration, public relations, and fund-raising, no minimum age or prior experience is required. Volunteer orientation and training is provided.

TREE STEWARDS

City of Seattle, Central Building, 810 Third Avenue, Room 754, Seattle, WA 98104 | **Contact:** Liz Ellis | **Phone:** (206) 684-5008, TTY (206) 684-4009 | **Web:** www.ci.seattle.wa.us/td/treestew.asp

The City of Seattle has openings for its Tree Steward Program. Volunteers must have 30 hours' training by local forestry / gardening experts and then offer 60 hours of volunteer work. Training is offered twice a year, spring and fall. This is an excellent means of gaining skills in tree selection, maintenance, care of tree problems, and is a great way to learn where the resources are for getting things done! It also offers an opportunity for members of the community to make a big difference in their immediate neighborhoods. Help maintain and enhance Seattle's urban forest!

WOODLAND PARK ZOO

Volunteer Services, WPZS, 5500 Phinney Avenue N, Seattle, WA 98103-5897 | **Phone:** (206) 684-4845 | **Email:** kim.haas@zoo.org | **Web:** www.zoo.org (click to Volunteer section and complete the online application)

Volunteers at the zoo enjoy the flora and fauna of an enriching environment. Horticulture volunteers assist zoo horticultural staff in planting and maintenance of the gardens (on-the-job-training is provided), docents provide public education, volunteers also assist visitors with basic information. As the Zoo manages the wonderful 2.5-acre Rose Gardens at Woodland Park, you can also sign up to work with expert Rosarians. Docents take a 12-week training course and commit to two years and 30 volunteer hours each year.

SPECIALIST PLANT GROUPS

Abbreviations used in this section:
CUH = Center for Urban Horticulture, Seattle
GVC = Graham Visitor Center, Arboretum, Seattle
PGC = Portland Garden Club, 1132 SW Vista Avenue, Portland
VDBG = VanDusen Botanical Garden, Vancouver, BC
IMO = International Money Order

African Violets / Gesneriads

AFRICAN VIOLET SOCIETY OF AMERICA

2375 North Street, Beaumont, TX 77702 | **Phone:** (409) 839-4725 or (800) 770-2872 | **Web:** www.avsa.org

AVSA gives members continuous information on the latest developments in the African violet world, with ongoing conventions, events, and plant introductions. Membership includes an annual subscription to the *African Violet Magazine,* a bimonthly publication. Dues $20 annually.

AMERICAN GLOXINIA AND GESNERIAD SOCIETY

Web: www.aggs.org

An international organization, with members in many countries around the world and several officers located here in the Northwest. Membership brings *The Gloxinian,* a quarterly magazine; Round Robin letters; access to the library of books and slides; and the opportunity to buy plants and rare seeds of hybrid and species gesneriads not available from any other source. New members receive a copy of *How to Know and Grow Gesneriads,* and a packet of seeds. Dues $20 annually.

MT. HOOD GESNERIAD AND AFRICAN VIOLET SOCIETY

Vivian Scheans, 4660 SW Dogwood Drive, Lake Oswego, OR 97035 | **Phone:** (503) 620-4426 | **Email:** vscheans@teleport.com

A chapter of the AGGS. Monthly meetings where guests are welcome. The group also features an active plant and seed exchange.

PORTLAND AFRICAN VIOLET SOCIETY

A chapter of the AVSA, this group meets at 12:30 p.m. the last Saturday of each month (September–June) at Tabor Heights Methodist Church, 6161 SE Stark, Portland, OR. Meetings feature demonstrations, programs, and workshops, plus plants for sale and cuttings to trade. Visitors are welcome.

PORTLANDIA VIOLET CLUB

Blanche Bunker, 18005 SE Mill Court, Portland, OR 97233 | **Phone:** (503) 761-7861; Meetings at 10 a.m., third Saturday of each month (except July, August, and December).

PUGET SOUND GESNERIAD SOCIETY

Doreen Hovermale, 3814 N Frace Street, Tacoma, WA 98407 | **Email:** apirone@pirone.org

An AGGS chapter that meets monthly. These serious students of the Gesneriaceae family have 225 genera to keep them occupied (of which African Violets are but one). Members share information on growing, propagating, and showing *Gesneriads,* and some from this chapter have joined the collecting trips to the Southern Hemisphere organized through the national/international organization. Monthly newsletter and a seed fund (exchange).

SAINTPAULIA SOCIETY OF TACOMA

Nellie Sleeth, 2913 N Monroe Street, Tacoma, WA 98407 | **Phone:** (253) 752-4706

Study sessions on propagating, growing, design, and pest identification/control for members of the Gesneriad family. Monthly meetings. Shows are variable; yearly sale at Poole's Garden Center, 6th and Union, Tacoma, the first Saturday in October. Dues $5 annually.

SEATTLE AFRICAN VIOLET SOCIETY

Chris Hansen, 4825 Olympic Drive, Ferndale, WA 98248-9544

Founded in 1952, this group holds monthly meetings at 7:30 p.m. the third Tuesday of each month, September–

June, at Beacon Hill Presbyterian Church, 1625 S Columbian Way, Seattle.

VANCOUVER (BC) AFRICAN VIOLET AND GESNERIAD SOCIETY

Bill Price, 2909 Mathers Avenue, West Vancouver, BC V7V 2J7 Canada | **Email:** billpri@attbi.com

Meetings held 2 p.m. the third Sunday of the month, September–June, at VanDusen Botanical Garden, 37th and Oak Streets, Vancouver, BC.

Alpine / Rock Gardens

ALPINE GARDEN CLUB OF BRITISH COLUMBIA

Joy Curran, Membership Secretary, RR1 B38, Bowen Island, BC V0N 1G0 Canada | **Phone:** (604) 947-0457 | **Web:** www.icangarden.com

One of Canada's largest and most active plant organizations, the club is noted for offering an extensive free seed exchange (over 1,500 offerings), but please note: It's for *members only*. There's a big show in April, a spring sale in West Vancouver, and a fall sale (usually at VanDusen Garden). There are five bulletins annually, field trips, and Open Gardens during April and May. Meetings are at VDBG, monthly, September–June, visitors welcome. Dues $25 (Canada), $20 (U.S.) annually.

ALPINE GARDEN SOCIETY OF GREAT BRITAIN

AGS Centre, Avon Bank, Pershore, Worcestershire WR10 3JP England | **Phone:** (UK) 44 1386 554790 | **Fax:** (UK) 44 1386 554801 | **Email:** ags@alpinegardensociety.org | **Web:** www.alpinegardensociety.org

This group boasts more than 14,000 members and is one of the largest specialty plant societies in the world. By joining, you receive a substantial quarterly journal, newsletters, a seed list (and if you find yourself in the UK you might plan to take in AGS shows and events). If you are looking for travel options, consider joining an AGS expedition to such far-off places as Central Asia or East Africa.

NORTH AMERICAN ROCK GARDEN SOCIETY

PO Box 67, Millwood, NY 10546 | **Phone:** (914) 762-2948 | **Email:** nargs@advinc.com | **Web:** www.nargs.org

NARGS was founded in 1934 and has 34 chapters and 4,500 members around the world. There is a phenomenal seed exchange with over 5,000 offerings! The society publishes a journal and stages "study weekends" for members on the West Coast and East Coast. The $25 annual dues (one or two people at the same address, billed annually in the quarter you join) provide national benefits plus local chapter membership (nominal additional fee) and a Chapter Yearbook.

NORTH AMERICAN ROCK GARDEN SOCIETY, OFFICIAL REGIONAL CHAPTERS

The objective of NARGS chapters, some listed below, is "to encourage and educate members in the appreciation, propagation, culture, and conservation of alpine plants."

* **Emerald Chapter** (Eugene / Corvallis). Contact: Kristy Swanson, 99 River Loop 1, Eugene, OR 97404; Web: www.peak.org/~parsont/emerald/. Share garden visits, seminars, demonstrations, wildflower hikes, plant sales, seed swaps, newsletter, library, and more. For a free issue of the chapter newsletter or any other questions, email Louise Parsons at parsontnospam@peak.org.

* **Mt. Tahoma Chapter.** Contact: Bob Fincham, 4412 354th Street SE, Eatonville, WA 98328; Email: bobfincham@mashell.com; Web: www.nargs.org/meet/chap_mntaho.html. Monthly meetings (except July, August, December) in the Pierce County Administrative Center, 3005 112th Street E, Tacoma, WA. The chapter also sponsors field trips and garden tours, plant sales, auctions, and exchanges. Members help manage a 1-acre alpine garden at the Rhododendron Species Botanical Garden in Federal Way. Dues $7.50 per person ($10 couple) annually; monthly newsletter included.

* **Northwestern Chapter.** Contact: Fred Graff, Treasurer, 2630 West Viewmont Way, Seattle, WA 98199-3019; Phone: (206) 282-5512; Email: fgraff@galaxy-7.net; Web: www.nargs.org/meet/chap_nw/membership.htm. Meets monthly (except summer), guests welcome, quarterly bulletin. Local members pay an additional $10 to receive chapter newsletter and field trips.

* **Siskiyou Chapter.** Contact: Maki and Bernie Hartman; Email: hartman@medford.net; Web: www.nargs.org/meet/chap_sisk.html. The chapter meets at 7 p.m. the second Tuesday of each month (September–May) at Horton Plaza, 1122 Spring Street, Medford, OR.

SCOTTISH ROCK GARDEN CLUB

Hazel Smith, Harrylayock, Solgirth, Dollar, Fife FK14 7NE Scotland | **Email:** membership@srgc.org.uk | **Web:** www.srgc.org.uk

Founded in 1933 by enthusiasts interested in promoting the cultivation of alpine and rock garden plants, this is Scotland's largest horticultural society, with 4,500 members in 38 countries. By joining, you receive *The Rock Garden* (a biannual journal), a book list, and an excellent seed exchange list (more than 4,000 selections).

Aroids

INTERNATIONAL AROID SOCIETY

PO Box 43-1853, South Miami, FL 33143 | **Fax:** (954) 680-0305 | **Email:** Hyndman@aroid.org | **Web:** www.aroid.org

Membership ranges the globe from Brazil to the Netherlands, the south of France to Bellingham, Washington, offering lively online discussions on taxonomy and much information on propagation. There is a quarterly newsletter (view a sample issue online) and a scholarly annual publications, the *Aroideana* journal. Dues: $25 individual, $30 international.

Bamboo

AMERICAN BAMBOO SOCIETY

Michael Bartholomew, 750 Krumkill Road, Albany, NY 12203-5976 | **Email:** mab29@cornell.edu | **Web:** www.bamboo.org

The purpose of the national organization is to publish educational information and to introduce new species of bamboo to enthusiasts around the country. ABS produces a journal, hosts conventions, manages a reference library, and offers seeds, plants, trips. Dues $35 annually; includes one chapter affiliation.

* **Oregon Bamboo Association.** Contact: Mike James Long, PO Box 41086, Eugene, OR 97404; Phone: (541) 688-6635; Email: maj@efn.org. Promoting the utility and beauty of bamboo, this chapter of the ABS stages the Portland Bamboo Festival each July, with lectures, demonstrations, and plant sale. Dues $12.50, or $35 with joint membership in ABS.

* **Pacific Northwest Chapter.** Contact: Erika Harris, 12260 First Avenue S, Seattle, WA 98168-2014; Phone: (206) 242-8848; Email: clintonbamboo@sprynet.com. Welcoming all bamboo lovers, this chapter of the ABS provides information on the identification, propagation, use, culture, and appreciation of bamboo—for experienced growers or aspiring enthusiasts. With members from southern Oregon to Vancouver, BC, the chapter offers work parties, demonstrations, seminars, and lectures. The chapter also stages a summer festival at the Center for Urban Horticulture in Seattle, and fall and spring plant sales. Dues $15, or $35 with joint membership in ABS.

Bonsai

AMERICAN BONSAI SOCIETY

Jim Hagan, ABS Executive Secretary, PO Box 351604, Toledo, OH 43635-1604 | **Email:** rcase@swcp.com | **Web:** www.absbonsai.org

Membership includes a subscription to *Bonsai: A Journal of the American Bonsai Society*, online bonsai discussion groups, and invitation to a national offering of demonstrations, workshops, and sales by vendors. Dues $24 individual, $30 family.

BRITISH COLUMBIA CHAPTERS OF ABS

British Columbia Bonsai Clubs Federation; Contact: Roger Low, 3230 E 15th Avenue, Vancouver, BC V5M 2L4 Canada; Phone: (604) 435-5737.

OREGON CHAPTERS OF THE ABS

* **Bay Area Bonsai Society.** Contact: George and Eva Ahuna, 1434 N Tenth Court, Coos Bay, OR 97420; Phone: (503) 269-9696; or Kenneth Windred; Phone: (503) 888-3634.

* **Bonsai Society of Portland.** PO Box 10615, Portland, OR 97225; Phone: (503) 972-7799; Email: info@portlandbonsai.org; Web: www.portlandbonsai.org. Meets monthly (except June, July, Aug.) at the PGC. Visitors welcome. Newsletter, bonsai basics classes, guest artists, demonstrations and workshops. Annual shows and sales.

* **Cascade Bonsai Society.** Contact: Mark Tapley, 97 Randy Street, Ashland, OR 97520; Phone: (541) 482-2920; Email: stillite@jeffnet.org.

* **Corvallis Bonsai Society.** Contacts: Ruth Musil; Phone: (503) 757-8261. Bob Newton; Phone: (503) 753-6028; Email: boblnewton@aol.com.

* **Eugene Bonsai Society.** Contact: Mary Corrington; Phone: (503) 683-2882.

* **Far West Bonsai Society.** Contact: DeBoyd and Eileen Smith, 95650 Sixes River Road, Sixes, OR 97476; Phone: (503) 332-7633.

WASHINGTON CHAPTERS OF THE ABS

* **Dungeness Bonsai Society.** Contact: Bernice Newland, PO Box 1441, Sequim, WA 98382; (360) 683-3682; Email: ljrt@tenforward.com. Meets seven times a year, with workshops and demonstrations for members.

* **Puget Sound Bonsai Association.** Contact: Carolyn Higgins, PO Box 15437, Seattle, WA 98115-0437; Email: cjhiggs1@juno.com; Web: http://psba.8m.com/. First organized in 1973, now with over 350 members. PSBA meets six times each year and stages an Annual Show in the spring featuring members' trees. Initial dues are $25 individual, $30 couple; renewal memberships $15 individual, $20 couple.

* **Yakima Valley Bonsai Society.** PO Box 669, Yakima, WA 98907; Phone: (509) 248-7337 or (509) 965-0869; Email: zingmom@aol.com. Meetings held each month at the Yakima Area Arboretum, 1401 Arboretum Drive, Yakima. Organized to help others learn the art of bonsai and to sponsor workshops, films, field trips, collecting trips. Dues $15 individual, $25 couple.

OTHER NORTHWEST (NON-ABS AFFILIATED) BONSAI CLUBS

* **Vancouver Island Bonsai Club.** Contact: Randy Kowalchuk, PO Box 8674, Victoria, BC V8W 3S2 Canada; Phone: (250) 370-7562; Email: webmaster@ victoriabonsai.bc.ca; Web: www.victoriabonsai.bc.ca.

* **Portland Bonsai Society.** Contact: Bob Laws, 8808 NW 24th Avenue, Vancouver, WA 98665; Phone: (360) 574-0166; Email: rlaws@pacifier.com.

BONSAI CLUBS INTERNATIONAL

PO Box 8445, Metairie, LA 70011-8445 | **Phone:** (504) 832-8071 | **Email:** bcibizness@aol.com | **Web:** www.bonsai-bci.com

Members receive six issues of *Bonsai Magazine* per year, enjoy access to an extensive audio/video lending library, invitations to the annual convention, and more. Dues $36 annually.

Boxwood

AMERICAN BOXWOOD SOCIETY

Treasurer, ABS, PO Box 85, Boyce, VA 22620-0085 | **Phone:** (540) 667-4942 | **Email:** info@boxwoodsociety.org | **Web:** www.boxwood society.org

ABS membership brings a quarterly bulletin (available to non-members, $25/year). The ABS compiles a source-book, the *Boxwood Handbook* that lists nurseries nation-wide; (order at address above for $17, includes tax and shipping); funds research on *Buxus;* sponsors a Memorial Display Garden with some 85 *Buxus* species; and acts as the International Registration authority for cultivated *Buxus.* Formed 1961, presently 900 members, predominantly on the East Coast. Dues $25.

Bromeliads

THE BROMELIAD SOCIETY, INTERNATIONAL

PO Box 12981, Gainesville, FL 32604 | **Phone:** (352) 372-6589 | **Email:** WBC@bsi.org | **Web:** www.bsi.org

A trip to the Volunteer Park Conservatory in Seattle or the W. W. Seymour Conservatory in Tacoma may spark your interest in bromeliads—or if you venture anywhere in Florida, you'll see these amazing, textured flowers with their spiked foliage growing everywhere in residential gardens. Here is an organization that provides a great deal of information on these fascinating plants. Seed exchange, bimonthly journal. Dues $30/individual or $35/dual.

Bulbs

INTERNATIONAL BULB SOCIETY

PO Box 92136, Pasadena, CA 91109-2136 | **Phone:** (949) 369-8588 | **Email:** membership@bulbsociety.org | **Web:** www.bulbsociety.com

The IBS is dedicated to disseminating knowledge regarding the botany and horticulture of geophytic plants. Originated in Orlando, Florida, in 1933 as the American Amaryllis Society, IBS now publishes an international journal, *Herbertia;* a quarterly *Bulbs* newsletter, and sponsors the world's largest bulbous plant seed exchange. Dues $40 year.

Butterfly Gardening

NORTH AMERICAN BUTTERFLY ASSOCIATION

4 Delaware Road, Morristown, NJ 07960 | **Phone:** (973) 285-0907 | **Email:** naba@naba.org | **Web:** www.naba.org

This organization's focus is on public education about conservation and non-consumptive recreational "butter-flying." Membership brings the quarterly magazine *American Butterflies, Butterfly Garden News* (also a quarterly), biannual meetings, and local chapter seed exchanges.

NABA's Program for Butterfly Gardens and Habitats has produced a series of butterfly gardening brochures. Each one focuses on a particular region of North America and includes such information as top butterfly nectar flowers, nectar flowers that *don't* work in a region, top caterpillar food plants, common butterflies for your garden and yard, local and unusual butterflies for your garden and yard, and general comments about gardening in this region. Brochures for Western Washington (1998) and Southwest Oregon (1997) are available at $3 each, with PDF files available online. Dues $30.

* **Oregon Chapter,** NABA-Eugene/Springfield. Contact: Eric Wold, 2055 Shiloh Street, Eugene, OR 97401; Email: canoe@epud.net

* **Washington Chapter,** NABA-Washington State. Contact: Idie Ulsh, PO Box 31317, Seattle, WA 98103; Email: wabutterflyassoc@earthlink.net

NORTHWEST LEPIDOPTERISTS ASSOCIATION

Dr. Andy Brower, Department of Entomology, Oregon State University, Corvallis, OR 97331 | **Phone:** (541) 737-5531 | **Email:** browera@bcc.orst.edu

This informal group, with members ranging in age from 10 to over 80, is comprised of area members of the Lepidopterists Society. There's no membership fee but $5 brings the newsy biannual newsletter. There is an annual meeting, plus Fourth of July butterfly counts. If you have an interest in butterflies (and gardening for them) you'll find an opportunity for excellent contacts here.

XERCES SOCIETY

4828 SE Hawthorne Boulevard, Portland, OR 97215 | **Phone:** (503) 232-6639 | **Email:** xerces@teleport.com | **Web:** www.xerces.org

This is the only conservation organization solely devoted to the protection of invertebrates and their habitats. The name derives from the Xerces Blue butterfly (*Glaucopsyche xerces*), the first butterfly in America known to become extinct as a result of human interference. Members receive the quality, full-color, biannual magazine *Wings: Essays on Invertebrate Conservation.* The organization co-authored *Butterfly Gardening: Creating Summer Magic in Your Garden* (a beautiful book on practical information and inspiration for creating imaginative gardens to attract butterflies). Dues $25.

Cactus, Succulents, and Exotics

THE CACTUS AND SUCCULENT SOCIETY OF AMERICA

Mindy Fusaro, Treasurer, PO Box 2615, Pahrump, NV 89041-2615 | **Email:** cssa@wizard.com | **Web:** www.cactus-mall.com/cssa

Benefits include a members' seed list and the cactus and succulent journal *Haseltonia,* the oldest continuously published periodical on this subject. Also, the CSSA sponsors the publication of *To The Point,* a newsletter. Dues $35 individual, $40 international.

CASCADE CACTUS AND SUCCULENT SOCIETY

CCSS, 4318 First Avenue NE, Seattle, WA 98105 | **Phone:** (206) 633-5570 | **Email:** dblackmer@worldnet.att.com | **Web:** www.cascadecss.org

This group features lots of experienced growers willing to help newcomers and one another, plus an extensive library for members' use. Each meeting displays plants and a "cactus and succulent of the month." Annual Odd Plant Show and Sale, field trips, greenhouse tours, monthly newsletter *The Point*. Meets monthly (except August). Dues $20 ($40, benefactor level).

DESERT PLANT SOCIETY OF VANCOUVER (BC)

Moira Greaven, 6408 Marine Drive, West Vancouver, BC V7W 2S6 Canada | **Phone:** (604) 947-9240 | **Email:** paula@vividgreetings.com | **Web:** www.cactus-mall.com/dpsv

Members share an interest in studying, collecting, and growing, as well as the conservation of cacti and succulents. Dues $15.

OREGON CACTUS AND SUCCULENT SOCIETY

Michael Graves, 1314 SE 74th Avenue, Hillsboro, OR 97123 | **Phone:** (503) 649-4747 | **Email:** greensup@aol.com

PACIFIC NORTHWEST PALM AND EXOTIC PLANT SOCIETY

Frank Hunaus, 10310 Hollybank Drive, Richmond, BC V7E 4S5 Canada | **Phone:** (604) 271-9524 or (604) 987-1075 | **Email:** jayakerley@hotmail.com | **Web:** www.palms.org/pacific/

The Northwest's regional chapter for the International Palm Society. Members are dedicated to furthering the knowledge and distribution of palms in this region (BC, Oregon, Washington). Membership brings *Hardy Palm International*, a quarterly journal; chapter meetings with speakers; library; participation in the development of public palm gardens and garden tours of private gardens in this area; and an annual plant sale featuring rare and exotic palms and other plants. Dues $25 U.S., $30 Canadian.

VICTORIA CACTUS AND SUCCULENT SOCIETY

Glen Downey, 4131 Hawkes Avenue, Victoria, BC V8Z 3R9 Canada | **Phone:** (250) 479-5306

Carnivorous Plants

INTERNATIONAL CARNIVOROUS PLANT SOCIETY (ICPS)

PMB (Postal Mail Box) 330, 3310 E Yorba Linda Boulevard, Fullerton, CA 92831-1709 | **Email:** info@carnivorousplants.org | **Web:** www.carnivorousplants.org

Members receive the color publication *Carnivorous Plant Newsletter*, discounts at several carnivorous plant nurseries, and access to the society's seed bank. Dues $25.

PACIFIC NORTHWEST CARNIVOROUS PLANT CLUB

Tom Kahl, 8219 S 130th Street, Seattle, WA 98178 | **Phone:** (425) 226-3958 | **Web:** http://nurserysite.com/clubs/pnwcarnivorous/

This organization of enthusiasts (with members ranging from Oregon to British Columbia) is responsible for the hardy carnivorous plantings at the Rhododendron Species Botanical Garden, Federal Way. Send Tom a SASE for information. Dues $1 plus membership in ICPS (above).

Chrysanthemums

COLUMBIA RIVER CHRYSANTHEMUM SOCIETY (PORTLAND)

Shirlee Peters | **Phone:** (503) 246-6770 | **Email:** weehawktoo@qwest.net

Group meets at 7 p.m., third Wednesday of the month (February-October) at the Brentwood/Darlington Center, 7211 SE 62nd Street, Room C, Portland. October Show.

EVERGREEN CHRYSANTHEMUM ASSOCIATION

Curtis Jacobs, 22606 2nd Drive SE, Bothell, WA 98021-8356 | **Phone:** (425) 481-4763 | **Email:** cejacobs@Email.msn.com

Meets monthly (members live from Olympia to Bellingham). Originally a men's group organized in 1947 but now open to women, this group has a mission to encourage the cultivation of late-blooming English chrysanthemums. Only cultivars registered in England and a small list of exceptions may be entered in the show held the last weekend in October, which has the reputation as the largest display of large, late-blooming exhibition mums in North America. These plants are rarely found in nurseries or garden stores in Washington, so you'll learn about them via a couple of public plant sales (or members-only sales and a garden tour should you join). New members receive 10 exhibition cultivars free. Dues $15 individual, $20 couple.

NATIONAL CHRYSANTHEMUM SOCIETY

Web: www.mums.org

TACOMA CHRYSANTHEMUM SOCIETY

Florence Andreasen | **Phone:** (253) 537-4197 | **Email:** Flo-And@webtv.net

September show at Point Defiance Park, Tacoma, Washington.

Clematis

AMERICAN CLEMATIS SOCIETY

Edith Malek, PO Box 17085, Irvine, CA 92623 | **Phone:** (949) 224-9885 | **Email:** edith@clematis.org | **Web:** www.clematis.org

America's first clematis society. Originally organized as the Southern California CS, they have now gone national with the mission of encouraging and promoting the development and improvement of clematis. Membership includes a bimonthly ACS newsletter, access to special tours and trips, plant and product discounts, and clematis growing resources. Beautiful website! Dues $20.

BRITISH CLEMATIS SOCIETY

Russ Goodwyn, Membership Secretary, 2 Gatley Avenue, West Ewell, Surrey KT19 9NG, United Kingdom | **Phone:** 01276 476387

| **Email:** postmaster@britishclematis.org.uk | **Web:** www.british clematis.org.uk

Founded in 1991, the BCS has an international membership focusing on "the queen of the climbers." The society aims not only to impart knowledge to enthusiasts but to put gardeners in touch with expert growers and scientists. Member benefits include a subscription to *The Clematis*, regular newsletters, visits to gardens of interest for clematis lovers, an active seed exchange, exhibits, workshops, an extensive slide library, plus cultural advice on growing clematis.

Cottage Gardens

THE COTTAGE GARDEN SOCIETY

Clive Lane, at Brandon, Ravenshall, Betley, Cheshire CW3 9BH, United Kingdom | **Phone:** 44 1270 250776 or 44 1270 820258 (evenings) | **Web:** www.thecgs.org.uk/

This is a good source of information and camaraderie about old-fashioned plants and the friendly, informal traditions of the cottage gardening style. Founded in 1982 by a group of amateur gardeners in North Wales, its membership has grown to more than 9,000 (many from the United States). Members receive a quarterly newsletter (read sample articles on the website), an annual seed exchange, and can join summer garden visits. Novices as well as experienced enthusiasts are welcome. Annual subscription $15 U.S., payable in cash (download membership form from website).

NORTH AMERICAN COTTAGE GARDEN SOCIETY-NORTH AMERICAN DIANTHUS SOCIETY

Ms. Denis Garrett, NACGS-NADS Membership Secretary, PO Box 188, Pegram, TN 37143-0188 | **Email:** randbear@nets.com | **Web:** www.geocities.com/WestHollywood/2903/NACGS.html

The NACGS-NADS, originally two sister societies founded by cottage garden enthusiast Rand Lee, have merged. The organization continues to explore the informal mixed-ornamentals-and-edibles English cottage gardening styles (including cultivating dianthus) for North American climates, conditions, and cultivars. The society publishes *Small Honesties*, a 24-page quarterly journal containing articles on cottage gardening, with four pages devoted solely to the genus *Dianthus*. The group also offers an active seed exchange and Round Robin correspondence clubs. Dues $18 U.S., $20 Canada. Write the address above to request a sample issue of the quarterly journal, $4.50 per copy postpaid.

Daffodils

AMERICAN DAFFODIL SOCIETY

4126 Winfield Road, Columbus, OH 43220-4606 | **Phone:** (614) 451-4747 | **Email:** nliggett@compuserve.com | **Web:** www.daffodilusa.org

Members receive a subscription to a quarterly journal (good color photos) and other publications, as well as a listing of daffodil specialists and garden bulb dealers nationwide and overseas. Rare bulb/seed exchange. Dues $20.

CENTRAL WASHINGTON DAFFODIL GROUP

Sonja Razey, 1681 Cleman Drive, Naches, WA 98937 | **Phone:** (509) 653-2970 | **Email:** laurabee@wolfenet.com

OREGON DAFFODIL SOCIETY

Leonard Forster, 31875 Fayetteville Road, Shedd, OR 97377 | **Email:** dad@cafetoday.net

Dahlias

AMERICAN DAHLIA SOCIETY

1 Rock Falls Court, Rockville, MD 20854 | **Phone:** (301) 424-6641 | **Email:** AFisherADS@hotmail.com | **Web:** www.dahlia.org

The national organization publishes a quarterly bulletin and an annual *Classification Book* (mandatory reading for dahlia judges and serious dahlia growers!). New members receive a complimentary copy of the society's 64-page *Guide to Growing and Caring for Dahlias*. In the Northwest, be sure to visit the society's trial gardens at Point Defiance Park, Tacoma. Dues $20.

EVERGREEN STATE DAHLIA SOCIETY

Kathy Mackey, PO Box 4354, Tumwater, WA 98501 | **Phone:** (360) 956-1614

PORTLAND DAHLIA SOCIETY

Larry Sawyer, 11015 SW Berkshire Street, Portland, OR 97225 | **Phone:** (503) 646-8782 | **Email:** etoedtli@pacifier.com | **Web:** www.hevanet.com/pds/

This group has traced its roots to the Columbia Valley Dahlia Society, which started in 1928, with members from Oregon, Washington, and San Francisco! Today PDS offers members monthly meetings, a regular publication, and a major Labor Day weekend show at the Clackamas County Fairgrounds in Canby. Dues $7 individual, $10 couple.

PUGET SOUND DAHLIA ASSOCIATION

Ted C. Hastings, 22041 Peter Grubb Road, SE, Renton, WA 98058-0416; Hotline: (425) 836-4487 | **Web:** www.pugetsounddahlias.org

As the largest local Dahlia Club in America, this group provides members with monthly meetings and a newsletter (*PSDA Bulletin*), member sales of plants and tubers, a huge Spring Tuber and Plant Sale (open to the public), and a large annual show at Factoria Mall in Bellevue, held the weekend before Labor Day. Their annual publication, *Dahlias of Today*, includes cultural information on how to grow dahlias—written by the experts!—for $6 postpaid. PSDA plants and maintains demonstration gardens in Seattle's Volunteer Park and Bellevue's Botanical Garden. Dues $15.

SEATTLE DAHLIA SOCIETY

Bess Owens, 8204 21st Avenue NE, Seattle, WA 98115 | **Phone:** (206) 523-7867 | **Email:** tntball@worldnet.att.net

SKAGIT VALLEY DAHLIA SOCIETY

Carol Fiske, PO Box 434, Burlington, WA 98233 | **Phone:** (360) 757-2972 | **Email:** fiske@fidalgo.net

The group meets monthly, publishes a monthly newsletter, stages two tuber sales, and holds an annual August Dahlia Show at the Cascade Mall, Burlington.

SNOHOMISH DAHLIA SOCIETY

Danielle Parshall, 20212 65th Avenue SE, Snohomish, WA 98296 | **Phone:** (360) 486-6163 | **Email:** dparshal@scdahlias.org | **Web:** www.scdahlias.org

Founded in 1909, this is the oldest continuously meeting dahlia group in the United States, with an enthusiastic and helpful membership. SDS meets monthly, publishes a newsletter; sponsors a huge tuber sale in April at Everett's Legion Park Hall, and an annual Dahlia Show at Everett's Forest Park Floral Hall in mid-August. See images of members' gardens on the society's colorful website. Dues $10.

VANCOUVER (BC) DAHLIA SOCIETY

Rosa Beer, 14263 Grosvenor Road, Surrey, BC V3R 5H3 Canada | **Phone:** (604) 584-5124 | **Email:** themcnabbs@telus.net

VICTORIA (BC) DAHLIA SOCIETY

Joan Marsh, 11274 Chalet Road, Sidney, BC V8L 5M1 Canada | **Phone:** (250) 656-2072 | **Email:** barneym@telus.net

WASHINGTON STATE DAHLIA SOCIETY

Vivian Connell, 6807 154th Place SE, Snohomish, WA 98296 | **Phone:** (425) 338-7904 | **Email:** beaucon@gte.net | **Web:** http://home.attbi.com/~bekababe2/

This group's roots reach back to 1911; it became the Washington State Dahlia Society in 1934! With 80 members, the society sponsors monthly lectures from seasoned growers, competitions and shows, dahlia garden tours, and more. The annual show is held in September at South Hill Mall in Puyallup. Dues $10 individual, $15 family.

WHATCOM COUNTY DAHLIA SOCIETY

Cheryl Brandt, 8360 Valley View Road, Custer, WA 98240 | **Phone:** (360) 366-3285 | **Email:** dick@dkporter.net

Monthly meetings, newsletter, and spring tuber sale; show held mid-September at Bloedel Donovan Park, Bellingham.

Daylilies

AMERICAN HEMEROCALLIS SOCIETY

The national society's Region 8 encompasses members in British Columbia, Oregon, and Washington. Membership form available on the website; mail dues to Pat Mercer, AHS Executive Secretary, Dept. WWW, PO Box 10, Dexter, GA 31019; Phone: (912) 875-4110; Email: gmercer@nlamerica.com; Web: www.daylilies.org

Region 8 contact: AHS Regional Representative Luke Senior, 7423 Phillips Lane SW, Tacoma, WA 98498; Phone (253) 589-0305.

By joining the American Hemerocallis Society, you become a part of the Region 8 group. Members receive *The Daylily Journal* (a beautiful color publication) and an excellent regional newsletter (with very good black-and-white photos, cultural tips, and discussions of what members feel are the best hybrids). Other benefits include a by-mail plant auction, an annual sale and show, and regional meetings. Dues $18 individual, $22 family.

ALDERGROVE (BC) DAYLILY CLUB

Pam Erikson, 24642 51st Avenue, Aldergrove, BC V0X 1A0 Canada | **Phone:** (604) 856-5758 | **Email:** pamela1@istar.ca

COLUMBIA RIVER DAYLILY CLUB

Betts Daume, 21834 NE 147th Street, Brush Prairie, WA 98606 | **Phone:** (360) 256-9103 | **Email:** BettsPNW@aol.com

Members receive a newsletter; six meetings per year, with program alternating between Portland, Oregon, and Vancouver, Washington; plant sales; and garden tours for members.

PUGET SOUND DAYLILY CLUB

Dick Tripp, 11012 239th Place SW, Edmonds, WA 98020 | **Phone:** (206) 546-2724 | **Email:** rtripp@u.washington.edu

Organized in 1993, the club now has over 150 members areawide, including Oregon. It meets four times a year, offers a quarterly newsletter, *The Puget Daylily*, and holds garden tours, plant trades, and auctions for members. Dues $7.50; send to Jay Golub, 19512 SE 21st Street, Sammamish, WA 98075; Email: jgsgarden@foxinternet.net.

WILLAMETTE VALLEY DAYLILY CLUB

Frank Foster, 7647 Stayton Road, Turner, OR 97392 | **Phone:** (503) 769-1424 | **Email:** fosterfj@aol.com

Delphiniums

THE DELPHINIUM SOCIETY

Shirley E. Bassett, membership secretary, Summerfield, Church Road, Biddestone, Chippenham, Wiltshire SN14 7DP United Kingdom | **Email:** david.bassett@care4free.net | **Web:** www.delphinium.demon.co.uk

Established in 1928, this London-based group is a wonderful resource for the famed English delphiniums (which are indeed sturdier, and with more richly colored, more profuse florets than the Pacific Giants we are accustomed to seeing here). With membership come free seeds and a really valuable *Yearbook* (color photos, lots and lots of cultural and other information), and a fall bulletin. Dues $10 (they request U.S. cash as foreign checks are prohibitively expensive to process). Send an additional $5 for the Society's excellent *Handbook*.

Ferns

HARDY FERN FOUNDATION

PO Box 166, Medina, WA 98039-0166 | **Phone:** (206) 870-5363 | **Email:** hff@hardyferns.org | **Web:** www.hardyferns.org

This group is dedicated to establishing a comprehensive collection of the world's hardy ferns for display, testing, evaluation, public education, and distribution. The Rhododendron Species Botanical Garden in Federal Way houses HFF's primary display and test garden (with over 100 different species and cultivars); Lakewold Gardens, Tacoma, also houses a display garden. Members participate in a spore exchange, receive a quarterly newsletter, and have first access to new fern varieties. New members receive a *Directory of Fern Gardens and Nurseries*, a brochure on fern propagation, and a brochure on fern pests and diseases (along with remedies), the most recent newsletter, a spore list, a membership list, and a source list. The foundation sponsors an annual Fern Festival in June at the CUH, Seattle. Dues $10 student, $20 active, $25 family.

Fruit

CALIFORNIA RARE FRUIT GROWERS

The Fullerton Arboretum, California State University, PO Box 6850, Fullerton, CA 92634-6850 | **Phone:** (714) 638-1796 | **Email:** info@crfg.org | **Web:** www.crfg.org

Founded in 1968, the CRFG is the largest amateur fruit-growing organization in the world, with over 3,000 members representing every state and 30 foreign countries. The membership includes many nationally recognized botanical gardens, rare fruit enthusiasts, commercial fruit growers, and recognized fruit researchers. The group has a general interest in all aspects of fruit growing, with a primary focus on semitropical fruits and uncommon fruits and vegetables. There are seed, plant, and scion wood exchanges; garden tour opportunities; plant sales; and classes on pruning and grafting; also a bimonthly journal, *The Fruit Gardener*. The website has a Question and Answer page—ask the experts! Dues $25, $35 foreign.

FRIENDS OF FRUIT

Charles Bergeron, WWFRF Membership, 7920 88th Street Court SW, Tacoma, WA 98498-5906 | **Phone:** (253) 584-5216 | **Email:** cbmsb@juno.com | **Web:** www.wwfrf.org

This organization is also known as Western Washington Tree Fruit Research Foundation (WWFRF). Backyard fruit growers unite! This is a way you can actively participate in continuing the invaluable fruit-testing program at the Mt. Vernon Research and Extension Unit, affiliated with Washington State University. This group has been responsible for testing and introducing scab-resistant apples, curl-resistant peaches, apricot trees that bear and ripen delicious fruit in our climate, and novel new fruits such as Asian pears. The work makes it possible for us to be able to grow a wide variety of fruits without having to use pesticides and fungicides. After drastic budget cuts at WSU, WWFRF (which includes home orchard growers, nurseries, landscapers, and Master Gardeners) was formed in 1991 to help sustain the research effort. You'll receive an informative newsletter, free admission to seasonal field days, free admission once a month during harvest season to tour the unit and bring home boxes of complimentary fruit, as available ($15 admission charged to nonmembers), and a wealth of backyard orchard advice for the asking. Dues $25 individual, $40 family. For more info, see Chapter 13, "Gardens to Visit," and learn about Discovery Garden (in Mt. Vernon) for the newly emerging display garden supported by WWFRF.

HOME ORCHARD SOCIETY

PO Box 230192, Tigard, OR 97281-0192 | **Phone:** (503) 835-5040 | **Email:** lmills@europa.com | **Web:** www.wvi.com/~dough/HOS/HOS1.html

HOS chapters can be found at Clackamas Community College in Oregon City (Contact: Jim Cox, 503/234-3559) and Luelling Memorial in Yamhill County (Contact: Jeff Lukehart, 503/472-8730). Membership includes the quarterly *POME News*, a spring scion exchange, and a fall fruit show. Members are invited to visit and volunteer at the 1.6-acre Arboretum at Clackamas Community College, 19600 S Molalla Avenue, Oregon City, where there are sections devoted to various types of fruit, including heirlooms. The Arboretum is an experimental orchard where visitors can observe various fruit varieties, growth of different rootstocks, training methods, watering techniques, plant combinations, ground covers, pest-control methods, harvest timing, and more. Dues $15.

NORTH AMERICAN FRUIT EXPLORERS

1716 Apples Road, Chapin, IL 62628 | **Email:** vorbeck@csj.net | **Web:** www.nafex.org

NAFEX is a worldwide network of individuals devoted to developing, discovering, cultivating, improving, evaluating, and generally *appreciating* superior varieties of fruits and nuts. NAFEX holds an annual conference in summer at a facility involved in horticultural research. There is a large mail-lending library of horticultural books and publications for members. *Pomona* is the quarterly publication, the primary means of communication among members. For those particularly interested in one or more species of fruit or nut, 28 interest groups have been formed. Dues $10 year or $19 two years; Canadian members $15 year or $28 two years.

WESTERN CASCADE TREE FRUIT SOCIETY

WCFS Treasurer, 2625 13th Avenue W, Unit 306, Seattle, WA 98119-2054 | **Web:** www.wcsf.org

A nonprofit educational organization for aspiring hobby orchardists and backyard fruit growers. All events are open to non-members: Annual spring meeting with workshops, scionwood/rootstock and fruiting plant sale, slide shows and lectures, fall fruit show. Quarterly newsletter, *The Bee Line*. Dues: $15 for WCFS and a chapter membership (except Seattle Tree Fruit chapter: $23).

❀ **WCTFS / North Olympic Fruit Club,** Port Angeles– Port Townsend area. Contact: Robert Chisick; Phone: (360) 683-6684; Email: chisick@juno.com

❀ **WCTFS / The Peninsula (Kitsap) Chapter.** Contact: Scott Thompson; Phone: (360) 689-6706; Email: thompsonfarms@earthlink.net

❀ **WCTFS / The Piper Orchard Chapter** (Northwest Seattle). Contact: Ron Schaevitz; Phone: (206) 362-1227

❀ **WCTFS / Seattle Tree Fruit Society.** Contact: Marlene Falkenbury; Phone: (206) 522-2273

❀ **WCTFS / Tahoma Chapter.** Contact: Tim Shouse; Phone: (253) 840-9026; Email: ttrshouse@aol.com

Fuchsias

BC FUCHSIA AND BEGONIA SOCIETY

3242 E 47th Avenue, Vancouver, BC V5C 1C9 Canada | **Contact:** Lorna Herchenson, International Corresponding Secretary | **Phone:** (604) 929-5382 | **Email:** Lherchenson@telus.net or info@bcfuchsiasociety.com | **Web:** www.bcfuchsiasociety.com

This society is 40 years old and is known for its colorful annual show and competition each July at VanDusen Botanical Garden in Vancouver. Members receive a monthly newsletter and free fuchsia gardening information, as well as member discounts at area gardening shops. Dues $17 individual; $22 family.

NORTHWEST FUCHSIA SOCIETY

PO Box 33071, Seattle, WA 98133-0071

This is an umbrella organization made up of representatives from a number of local societies throughout Washington and Oregon. Their mission is to promote a love of fuchsias throughout the Northwest. Membership in one of the local clubs automatically makes you a member of the NWFS. They maintain an extensive library of fuchsia books and publish *The Fuchsia Flash* ten times a year, with articles of worldwide interest by fuchsia experts, with cultivation tips and lots of advice on problem solving (subscribe for $12 year; Contact: Donna Fellows, 610 Fifth Street, Steilacoom, WA 98388).

OREGON FUCHSIA SOCIETY

Contact: Sue Randall, 11689 SW Lancaster Road, Portland, OR 97219; (503) 246-7920 | **Contact:** Mallory Jarboe, 16851 S Bradley Road, Oregon City, OR 97045; (503) 631-3617; email: maljarboe@aol.com | **Web:** www.oregonfuchsia.com

This lively chapter holds monthly meetings with guest speakers, an annual plant auction, a cutting exchange, judged fuchsia show, field trips to growers, and other events. Membership includes a monthly bulletin, *Northwest Fuchsia Facts.* OFS operates a test garden with over 100 plants and 90 varieties at Leach Botanical Garden in Portland.

WASHINGTON AREA FUCHSIA SOCIETIES

❀ **Eastside Fuchsia Society.** Contact: Sonneva Wood; Phone: (425) 746-2406. Maintains a beautiful display garden at Bellevue Botanical Garden.

❀ **Fuchsia Fanciers.** Contact: Rod Steiger; Phone: (360) 245-3783. Display garden at Borst Park, Centralia.

❀ **Greater Seattle Fuchsia Society.** Contact: Frances Underwood; Phone: (206) 522-4312. Display garden at the Locks in Seattle (Ballard neighborhood); annual spring plant sale and show.

❀ **Lake Bay Fuchsia Society.** Contact: Ginnie Aardal; Phone: (253) 884-9744

❀ **North Cascades Fuchsia Society.** Contact: Phil Goertz; Phone: (360) 428-8739. Display garden at Church Creek Park, Stanwood.

❀ **North Olympic Fuchsia Society.** Contact: Donna Martin; Phone: (360) 681-7595

❀ **Peninsula Fuchsia Society.** Contact: Jay Siegel; Phone: (360) 779-3020. Show in August

❀ **Pilchuck Fuchsia Society.** Contact: Doug Symonds; Phone: (360) 569-8953. Display garden at Jennings Park, Marysville.

❀ **Puget Sound Fuchsia Society.** Contact: Irene Bergum; Phone: (425) 742-2606

❀ **Puyallup Valley Fuchsia Society.** Contact: Sally Wipf; Phone: (253) 922-6000. Display garden at Puyallup Library, and an annual show in August.

❀ **Sno-King Fuchsia Society.** Contact: Salcha Earley; Phone: (425) 290-9232. Display garden at Country Village, Bothell; and an annual show in August.

❀ **Tahoma Fuchsia Society.** Contact: Jackie Crossman; Phone: (253) 584-8973. Display and test garden at Point Defiance Park, Tacoma; annual show.

Heather

NORTH AMERICAN HEATHER SOCIETY

Susan White, 23920 Wax Orchard Road SW, Vashon Island, WA 98070 | **Email:** swvashon@aol.com | **Web:** http://home.earthlink. net/~diank0457/heathers/

The NAHS, founded in 1977 as the Pacific Northwest Heather Society, supports the advancement of knowledge about the many heather species, as well as our native mountain heathers. Members receive a quarterly newsletter, *Heather News,* a brochure that lists 14 heather display and trial gardens around the United States (6 in the Pacific Northwest) and may attend an annual conference. There's also an extensive heather slide and book lending library for members and chapters. Dues $15 year.

❋**Cascade Heather Society.** Contact: Alice Knight, 1199 Monte Elma Road, Elma, WA 98541; Phone: (360) 482-3258; Email: clknight@techline.com. One of five regional NAHS chapters. This chapter maintains the heather display beds at the Rhododendron Species Foundation in Federal Way, Washington. Dues $5 year, includes newsletter.

❋**Vancouver Island Heather-Plus.** Contact: Joyce Prothero, 281 Cudmore Road, Salt Spring Island, BC V8K 2J7 Canada; Email: jprothero@saltspring.com. Another NAHS chapter in the Northwest.

Herbs

THE CANADIAN HERB SOCIETY

VanDusen Botanical Garden, 5251 Oak Street, Vancouver, BC V6M 4H1 Canada | **Email:** info@herbsociety.ca | **Web:** www.herbsociety.ca

This national organization of herb enthusiasts promotes the cultivation, use, and enjoyment of herbs.

FRIENDS OF THE MEDICINAL HERB GARDEN

Botany Department, University of Washington, Box 355325, Seattle, WA 98195 | **Phone:** (206) 543-1126 | **Email:** kpossee@ u.washington.edu | **Web:** http://nnlm.gov/pnr/uwmhg/index.html

A dedicated group of volunteers is responsible for the maintenance of the 80-year-old Medicinal Herb Garden, managed through the Botany Department of the University of Washington, and funded solely by donations. Members collect seed for exchanges with other educational groups, publish a newsletter, have a terrific website on the Internet, and give tours and lectures about the garden and medicinal plants. Membership is $25.

Volunteer! Weeders of all skill levels needed. Work parties meet once a month, spring through fall, call for details.

HERB SOCIETY OF AMERICA

9019 Kirtland Chardon Road, Kirtland, OH 44094 | **Phone:** (440) 256-0514 | **Email:** herbs@herbsociety.org | **Web:** www.herbsociety.org

Founded in 1933, the society is concerned with the cultivation of herbs and the study of their history and uses. Membership includes a subscription to *The Herbarist*, quarterly newsletter, discounts on books and Society-sponsored symposia, and participation in members' seed exchange program. The national headquarters is located adjacent to the Holden Arboretum, at a house built in 1841 and listed on the National Registry of Historical Places. The society has awarded over $75,000 toward the advancement of promising research on herb topics such as archaeology, history, taxonomy, and genetics. It also supports The National Herb Garden, located on 2.5 acres at The National Arboretum in Washington, D.C. The website's "Garden Gallery" offers books and herb-related gifts. Dues $50.

Holly

HOLLY SOCIETY OF AMERICA

4738 Hale Haven Drive, Ellicott City, MD 21043-6669 | **Email:** secretary@hollysocam.org | **Web:** www.hollysocam.org

If you love the genus *Ilex*, this is the group for you. The Holly Society has helped to stimulate interest, promote research, and collect and share information on all types of holly. Membership includes four journals per year, and a cutting exchange at the annual meeting. Dues $25.

Hostas

AMERICAN HOSTA SOCIETY

Lu Treadway, AHS Membership Secretary, 246 Etheridge Road, Auburn, GA 30011 | **Email:** Hostanut@BellSouth.net | **Web:** www.hosta.org

Your membership dues bring a generous return, including two *hefty*, information-packed color journals per year, an annual convention that draws members from across the country and abroad, a garden visiting program as private gardens are opened to members, a list of hosta resources, regional activities, access to a slide program, and an *Annual Yearbook*. Dues $25 individual, $29 family.

❋**Northwest Region 6 / AHS.** Contact: Alan Tower, 3412 E 64th Court, Spokane, WA 99223; Phone: (509) 448-5837; Email: tower@ior.com

Hydrangeas

AMERICAN HYDRANGEA SOCIETY

Penny McHenry, PO Box 11645, Atlanta, GA 30355 | **Phone:** (404) 636-7886 | **Web:** http://dir.gardenweb.com/directory/ahs2/

Members meet three times annually at the Atlanta Botanical Garden with a lecture and information sharing and receive a quarterly newsletter; there's also a garden tour in June. Dues $15.

Iris

AMERICAN IRIS SOCIETY

Anner M. Whitehead, AIS Membership Secretary, PO Box 14750, Dept. E, Richmond, VA 23221-4750 | **Phone:** (804) 358-6202 | **Email:** aismemsec@aol.com | **Web:** www.irises.org

While many specialists and gardening experts belong to this organization, it is primarily for the amateur gardener who enjoys growing irises. New members receive an informative booklet and a quarterly *Bulletin* averaging over 100 pages. There are regional/chapter activities, judges training, book sales, technical assistance, a Youth Program, and additional specialist memberships (for Siberians, medians, spuria, Japanese, species, and other irises). Dues $20 individual, $25 family.

❋**Region 13 of the AIS** (Washington, Oregon, Alaska). Regional Vice President: John Ludi, 35071 SE Highway 211, Boring, OR 97009-9584; Phone: (503) 668-9230; Email: kludi@juno.com

❀**Columbia Basin Iris Society.** Contact: Beverly Petrak, President, 11209 Road Q NW, Quincy, WA 98848-9689

❀**Greater Portland Iris Society.** Contact: Barbara Aitken, 608 NW 119th Street, Vancouver, WA 98685-3802

❀**King County Iris Society.** Contact: Dwayne Booth, PO Box 95538, Seattle, WA 98145-2538; Phone: (206) 932-8903; Email: dwaynebooth@netscape.net, Web: www.leo9enterprises.com/kcis/kcisindex.html. This society holds monthly meetings (except late spring and summer) and stages annual plant sales for the public, plus garden tours, a summer picnic, and auction. Includes membership in Region 13 of the American Iris Society. Dues $8 individual.

❀**Median Iris Society.** Contact: Jim Craig, 16325 SW 113th Avenue, Tigard, OR 97224-3418; Email: craig iris@ipns.com

❀**Oregon Trails Iris Society.** Contact: Thomas Johnson, PO Box 18278, Salem, OR 97305-8278

❀**Pierce County Iris Society.** Contact: Charleen Duggan, 10015 257th Street Court E, Graham, WA 98338-7043. This group maintains an Iris Display Garden at Point Defiance Park in Tacoma, and holds a show in May and iris rhizome sale in August.

❀**Walla Walla Iris Society.** Contact: Richard W. Johnson, President, 638 Ash Street, Walla Walla, WA 99362-1502

❀**Yakima Valley Iris Society.** Contact: Kenneth Kennedy, 208 S 96th Avenue, Yakima, WA 98908-9771

Society for Japanese Irises

Terry Aitken, 608 NW 119th Street, Vancouver, WA 98685 | **Email:** aitken@e-z.net

Species Iris Group of North America (SIGNA)

Carla Lankow, 11118 169th Avenue SE, Renton, WA 98059 | **Email:** lankow@bigfoot.com

Ivy

American Ivy Society

PO Box 2123, Naples, FL 34106-2123 | **Email:** info@ivy.org | **Web:** www.ivy.org

Enthusiasts of the genus *Hedera* receive an annual *Ivy Journal*, three issues a year of *Between the Vines* newsletter, and assistance with identification. Dues $20.

Koi

These clubs are generally composed of people who are interested in keeping koi, in maintaining plants in and around their ponds, and who wish to provide a healthy and attractive environment for both fish and ponds. A number of the members in most koi clubs are also avid keepers of water gardens, so look to them for tips on successful pond-scaping.

Pacific Northwest Koi Clubs Association

Annual conference for all the clubs in the Pacific Northwest, including Alberta, BC, Idaho, Oregon, and Washington; see Web: www.pnkca.org for details.

Olympic Koi Club

Jerry Hames | **Phone:** (360) 876-2804 | **Email:** jerryhames@attbi.com | **Web:** http://community.silverlink.net/OKC/

This Kitsap County club was established in 1987 to promote and enlarge the hobby of keeping, breeding, and appreciating koi. Dues $20.

Northwest Koi and Goldfish Club

Virginia Hokkanen, 10907 NE Morris Street, Portland, OR 97220 | **Email:** showa@aracnet.com | **Web:** http://members.tripod.com/~nwkg/

NKGC's mission is the hobby of keeping, breeding, and exhibiting koi and goldfish. Members receive a monthly newsletter, enjoy tours of private ponds in Oregon and Washington, and meet monthly for lectures, fish auctions, and other events. The club library includes books and videos (see list on website) available for members' use, or you can email questions to club librarians. In June, there's a great Show and Competition, now in its 22nd year. Dues $20 U.S., $30 Canadian.

Oregon Koi and Watergarden Society

Nancy Mason, PO Box 1352, Roseburg, OR 97470 | **Email:** rkbrock@wizzards.net | **Web:** www.geocities.com/oregonkoiandwatergardensociety

Founded in 1988 in the Roseburg area, the club focuses on caring for water plants, koi health, competition, and pond techniques. Dues $24 year.

Puget Sound Koi Club

1936 SW 351st Street, Federal Way, WA 98023 | **Phone:** (253) 884-9684 | **Email:** koiaid@gte.net | **Web:** www.pugetsoundkoiclub.homestead.com

Meet the members of this active club for help on selection, care, and feeding of koi, and learn about Japanese gardening techniques, pond-building, and more. Dues $20; send to JoAnn Tyler, 17202 33rd Street, Court KPN, Lakebay, WA 98349.

Washington Koi and Water Garden Society

2121 168th Avenue NE, Bellevue, WA 98008 | **Email:** president@washingtonkoi.org | **Web:** http://washingtonkoi.org

Club meetings often feature experts in the field of plants, fish, and pond-building and maintenance. Fellow members are a valuable source of information and ideas. Pond tours are scheduled in summer, followed by a huge September koi show. Dues $25.

Lilies

NORTH AMERICAN LILY SOCIETY

PO Box 272, Owatonna, MN 55060 | **Email:** nals@ll.net | **Web:** www.lilies.org

Membership offers you a hardbound yearbook, a subscription to the quarterly bulletin, access to a seed exchange, slide collection, and circulating library, and annual shows and meetings in the United States and Canada. For *Let's Grow Lilies*, a 48-page official publication on hybrid lily culture with everything you need to know, send $3.50 to Dept. D of the NALS address above. Dues $20.

Affiliated regional societies:

❋**B.C. Lily Society.** Contact: John Taylor, 14751 109A Avenue, Surry, BC V3R 1Y7 Canada; Phone: (604) 589-0623

❋**Northwest Lily Society.** Contact: Donna Hathaway, 7811 SE Lincoln Street, Portland, OR 97215; (503) 777-0608. Monthly meetings, a biannual newsletter, library, bulb sale (to members only, March and October), and trips; also an Annual Lily Show. Dues $8.

❋**Victoria Lily Society.** Contact: Gordon Wallis, 4720 Spring Road, RR3, Victoria, BC V8X 3X1 Canada; Phone: (250) 479-6581

SPECIES LILY PRESERVATION SOCIETY

Maureen Barber, 336 Sandlewood Road, Oakville, Ontario, L6L 3R8 Canada | **Phone:** (503) 668-6443 | **Email:** ibarber@sympatico.ca | **Web:** www.lilies.org/slpg/ or Lily Net at www.camosun.bc.ca/~jbritton/lilynet.htm

Members of this NALS subsection collect and grow as many species as possible, especially rare lilies and those in danger of extinction. Members receive spring and fall bulletins, and participate in species lily bulb sales in the fall. Dues $7.

Mushrooms

KITSAP PENINSULA MYCOLOGICAL SOCIETY

1230 Fifth Street, Bremerton, WA 98337-1214 | **Web:** www.namyco.org/clubs/kpms

Annual wild mushroom show in Bremerton, newsletter, fieldtrip, and workshops. Dues $15.

NORTHWEST MUSHROOMERS ASSOCIATION

4320 Dumas Avenue, Bellingham, WA 98226

OLYMPIC PENINSULA MYCOLOGICAL SOCIETY

PO Box 33, Chimacum, WA 98325 | **Email:** mmuller@olympus.net

OREGON MYCOLOGICAL SOCIETY

1943 SE Locust Avenue, Portland, OR 97214 | **Phone:** (503) 659-1668 | **Email:** rogersmm@aol.com | **Web:** www.wildmushrooms.org

This group meets monthly, with a speaker and program, display table, books for sale and access to the extensive library, and an educational class. Field trips and special interest groups are offered too (Truffle Group, Culinary Group, Conservation) and there's a fall show. Dues: Initial joining fee (including first year's dues) $23 individual, $28 couple or family. Subsequent dues: $15 individual, $20 couple or family, $12 for seniors, students; send to Gerti and Hermann Opgenorth, 13716 SE Oatfield Road, Milwaukie, OR 97222.

PUGET SOUND MYCOLOGICAL SOCIETY

CUH, Box 354115, Seattle, WA 98195-4115 | **Phone:** (206) 522-6031 | **Web:** www.psms.org

This nonprofit educational society was founded in 1964 and has grown to be one of the largest such groups in the county. Its purpose is to foster the understanding of mycology as a science and a hobby. Members receive a newsletter, classes for beginners and advanced enthusiasts, and attend foray weekends during mushroom fruiting season. Discounts (generally 10 percent) are offered on field guides, cookbooks, and other materials sold at the meetings. Members may check out an assortment of books from a collection of over 100 volumes for personal study or research, plus videos of many of the lectures during the last several years. The Annual Wild Mushroom Exhibit, which draws thousands of visitors, is held each fall. Dues $20 individual or family, $10 students; send to Bernice Velategui, 2929 76th Avenue SE, #504, Mercer Island, WA 98040.

SNOHOMISH COUNTY MYCOLOGICAL SOCIETY

PO Box 2822, Everett, WA 98203; Hotline: (425) 317-9411 | **Web:** www.snonet.org/scms

Meeting since 1971, this nonprofit organization welcomes both novices and the more experienced. Monthly meetings (except during Jan., July, August) at the Everett Housing Authority Building. They have a comprehensive lending library and have built an extensive slide library; seasonal field trips scheduled. Annual Fall Mushroom Show in October. Dues $10.

SOUTH SOUND MUSHROOM CLUB

6439 32nd Avenue NW, Olympia, WA 98502-9519

VANCOUVER MYCOLOGICAL SOCIETY

Box 181, #101 - 1001 West Broadway, Vancouver, BC V6H 4E4 Canada V6H 4E4 | **Phone:** (604) 878-9878 | **Email:** Vancouver_myco@yahoo.com | **Web:** www.geocities.com/RainForest/Andes/8896

The first Vancouver area mushroom fair was held at VanDusen Botanical Garden in 1975 and the event quickly turned into an annual tradition. In 1978, the society was formed, bringing together mushroom farmers, professional mycologists, gourmet cooks, and "a variety of eccentric characters," according to the society's website. Dues $15.

Natives and Wildflowers

(See Chapter 4, "Northwest Native Plants," for lots more detailed information.)

ABUNDANT LIFE SEED FOUNDATION

PO Box 772, Port Townsend, WA 98368 | **Phone:** (360) 385-5660 | **Email:** abundant@olypen.com | **Web:** www.abundantlifeseed.org

Members support this incredible organization's conservation efforts to collect and conserve heirloom seed, Pacific Northwest native seed, and rare grain, vegetable, and flower seeds. Members receive a discount on purchases, a collection of heirloom seeds, and an excellent monthly newsletter. Educational programs, seed growers' conference, and more. Dues $30.

NATIVE PLANT SOCIETY OF BRITISH COLUMBIA

2012 William Street, Vancouver, BC V5L 2X6 Canada | **Phone:** (604) 255-5719 | **Email:** npsbc@hotmail.com

NATIVE PLANT SOCIETY OF OREGON

Jan Dobak, Membership, 2584 NW Savier Street, Portland, OR 97210-2412; General business address: PO Box 902, Eugene, OR 97440 | **Phone:** (503) 248-9242 | **Email:** membership@npsoregon.org | **Web:** www.npsoregon.org

NPSO members are dedicated to the enjoyment, conservation, and study of Oregon's native vegetation (13 chapters, 1,000 members). There's a monthly *Bulletin,* field trips, and an occasional journal, *Kalmiopsis.* The website is packed with terrific information and links. Dues $12 student, $18 regular, $24 family.

NATIVE PLANT SOCIETY OF OREGON CHAPTERS:

❁**Blue Mountain (Pendleton).** Contact: Jerry Baker; Phone: (541) 566-3381; Email: bm_president@npsoregon.org

❁**Cheahmille (McMinnville).** Contact: Dave Hanson; Phone: (503) 843-4338; Email: ch_president@npsoregon.org

❁**Corvallis.** Contact: Gaylee Goodrich and Esther MacEvoy; Phone: (541) 753-9227; Email: co_president@npsoregon.org

❁**Emerald (Eugene).** Contact: Nick Otting; Phone: (541) 344-4499; Email: em_president@npsoregon.org

❁**High Desert (Bend).** Contact: Stu Garrett, 1501 NE Medical Center Drive, Bend, OR 97701; Phone: (541) 389-6981; Email: hd_president@npsoregon.org

❁**Mid-Columbia.** Contact: Jerry Igo, PO Box 603, Mosier, OR 97040

❁**North Coast (Tillamook).** Contact: Vivian Starbuck; Phone: (503) 377-4141; Email: nc_president@npsoregon.org

❁**Portland.** Contact: Dee White; Phone: (541) 775-2909; Email: po_president@npsoregon.org

❁**Siskiyou (Ashland).** Contact: Molly Sullivan; Phone: (541) 552-9908; Email: si_president@npsoregon.org

❁**Umpqua Valley (Roseburg).** Contact: Richard Sommer; Phone: (541) 673-3709

❁**Willamette Valley (Salem).** Contact: Karl Anderson; Phone: (503) 315-7329; Email: wv_president@npsoregon.org

❁**Wm. Cusick (La Grande).** Contact: Frazier Nichol; Phone: (541) 775-2909

WASHINGTON NATIVE PLANT SOCIETY

7400 Sand Point Way NE, Seattle, WA 98115-6302 | **Phone:** (206) 527-3210 or (888) 288-8022 | **Email:** wnps@wnps.org | **Web:** www.wnps.org

Dedicated to the preservation, conservation, and study of the native plants of Washington, this public-education-oriented organization offers regular program meetings, special projects, field trips, workshops, and a quarterly journal, *Douglasia.* The Annual Study Weekend draws members from around the state to one of 13 active regional chapters in the state. Membership $25.

WASHINGTON NATIVE PLANT SOCIETY CHAPTERS:

❁**Central Puget Sound.** Contact: Michelle Connor, 3514 NE 57th Street, Seattle, WA 98105; Phone: (206) 522-5531; Email: mcconnor@u.washington.edu

❁**Central Washington.** Contact: Phelps Freeborn, 3409 Taylor Way, Yakima, WA 98908; Phone: (509) 454-0871

❁**Columbia Basin.** Contact: Dr. Steven Link, Biological Sciences, WSU-Tri Cities, 100 Sprout Road, Richland, WA; Phone: (509) 372-1526; Email: slink@tricity.wsu.edu; Web: www.wnps.org/cbasin/index.html

❁**Koma Kulshan (Bellingham).** Contact: Vikki Jackson, 2636 Franklin Street, Bellingham, WA 98225; Phone: (360) 734-9484; Field trip chair: Barry Wendling; Phone: (360) 671-8403; Email: ledum1@attbi.com

❁**Northeast Washington.** Contact: Suzanne Schwab, South 22508 Carman Road, Cheney, WA 99004; Phone: (509) 236-2210; Email: sschwab@ewu.edu

❁**Okanogan.** Contact: Caryl Campbell, PO Box 892, Winthrop, WA 98862; Phone: (509) 996-3458; Email: bearfight@methow.com

❁**Olympic Peninsula.** Contact: Wendy McClure, PO Box 395, Poulsbo, WA 98380; Phone: (360) 779-3820; Web: www.olympus.net/personal/dllewell/

❁**Salal.** Contact: Dr. Thomas Corrigan, PO Box 494, La Conner, WA 98257; Phone: (360) 466-3215; Web: www.wnps.org/salal/index.html

❁**San Juan Islands.** Contact: Bill Engle, PO Box 3327, Friday Harbor, WA 98250-3327; Phone: (360) 378-1840

❋ **South Sound.** Contact: Perry Lund, 2416 Lakeview Court SW, Olympia, WA 98512-9027; Phone: (360) 357-8590; Email: perrynkin@attbi.com

❋ **Wenatchee Valley.** Contact: Lauri Malmquist, 3352 Hansel Lane, Peshastin, WA 98847-9419; Phone: (509) 548-6458; Email: lam@televar.com; Web: www.geocities.com/RainForest/2745/

Orchids

AMERICAN ORCHID SOCIETY

Web: www.theaos.org

By joining the American Orchid Society (the largest special-interest horticultural organization in the world), you will become part of a close-knit association of breeders, growers and fanciers—amateurs and professionals—whose interest has been captivated by these fascinating flowers. Nearly 30,000 members worldwide utilize the vast array of Society educational resources—including the Society's respected magazines: *Orchids, Awards Quarterly,* and *Lindleyana*—to learn more about these fascinating plants.

OREGON ORCHID SOCIETIES:

❋ **Central Coast Orchid Society.** Contact: Elsie Flower; Phone: (541) 265-6674; Email: dflower@orednet.org

❋ **Cherry City Orchid Society.** Contact: Bergen Todd; Phone: (503) 378-7003; Email: toddwac@open.org

❋ **Mary's Peak Orchid Society (Corvallis).** Contact: Paula Hansen; Phone: (541) 753-7776

❋ **Oregon Orchid Society (Portland).** Contact: Rick Burian; Phone: (503) 245 7994; Web: www.ipns.com/calypso. Each meeting features a lecture/educational program and a display of blooming plants. Visitors welcome! Membership is open to anyone interested in orchids and includes a subscription to the *Calypso* newsletter. Two major shows annually.

❋ **Pacific Orchid Society (Coos Bay).** Contact: Carol Baughman; Phone: (541) 267-0147

❋ **Rogue Valley Orchid Society.** Contact: George Brown; Phone: (541) 608-0133; Email: yorgob909@cs.com

❋ **Sunset Empire Orchid Society (Astoria).** Contact: Dr. John Banholzer; Phone: (503) 325-3804; Web: http://home.pacifier.com/~snook/

❋ **Umpqua Orchid Society.** Contact: Gloria Webber; Phone: (541) 677-0520

❋ **Willamette Orchid Society.** Contact: Laurel Findlay; Phone: (541) 689-5389

WASHINGTON ORCHID SOCIETIES:

❋ **Federal Way Orchid Society.** Contact: Geraldine Flaten; Phone: (206) 244-5209

❋ **Fraser Valley Orchid Society (Canada).** Contact: Diana Burritt; Phone: (604) 581-9801

❋ **Grays Harbor Orchid Society.** Contact: Beryl Evey; Phone: (360) 289-9620; Email: berylevey@oly.com

❋ **Mt. Baker Orchid Society.** Box 1286, Blaine, WA 98230; Email: mt-baker@yahoo.com; Web: www.geocities.com/RainForest/canopy/2387. The group meets monthly at Charley's Greenhouse in Mt. Vernon; MBOS also helps organize the Orchid Show at the Northwest Flower and Garden Show.

❋ **Northwest Orchid Society.** PO Box 51021, Seattle, WA 98115-1021; Hotline: (206) 781-5805; Email: nwos@geocities.com; Web: www.geocities.com/RainForest/Canopy/2386. This group of 300 orchid enthusiasts meets monthly. Members include beginners, serious hobbyists, and commercial growers. Activities include a monthly bulletin, lectures, sales privileges at NWOS events, a circulating library, an annual orchid auction and show, and more. Visit the Seattle Public Library, downtown location, for a very large selection of orchid books and publications donated by this organization. Annual Show held each year in conjunction with the Northwest Flower and Garden Show. Dues $20.

❋ **Olympia Orchid Society.** Contact: Charles Stevenson; Phone: (360) 352-5468

❋ **Puget Sound Orchid Society.** Contact: Barbara Inman; Phone: (253) 848-4446; Email: valleyorchids@qwest.net

❋ **Tacoma Orchid Society.** Contact: Danielle Sessler; Phone: (253) 927-5801; Email: orchids_tac@yahoo.com; Web: www.geocities.com/orchids_tac. This group welcomes beginners curious about orchid culture and keen to learn. Plenty of help is available from serious hobbyist and commercial grower members, and the Society sponsors "Beginner's Programs." Members meet monthly with a silent auction table and lecture; monthly newsletter. The spring show and sale offers a "gigantic sales area!" Dues $12 year.

❋ **Verkist Orchid Study Group (Bellingham).** Contact: Marcia Manthey; Phone: (360) 384-0522

VANCOUVER ORCHID SOCIETY

Mark Elliott, President; PO Box 23932, APO, Richmond, BC V7B 1Y1 Canada | **Phone:** (604) 943-6479 | **Email:** melliott@mrl.ubc.ca | **Web:** http://members-http-7.rwc1.sfba.home.net/gsinger/vosweb/

Established in 1946, the VOS meets monthly except July and August at VDBG. The society hosts the Vancouver Orchid Show and Sale each May. Dues $20.

Passifloras

PASSIFLORA SOCIETY INTERNATIONAL

Butterfly World, 3600 Sample Road, Coconut Creek, FL 33073 | **Phone:** (954) 977-4434 | **Email:** info@passiflora.org | **Web:** www.passiflora.org

PSI was formed in 1990 to establish a central location for *Passiflora* enthusiasts to exchange information, obtain help with plant identification, and to locate seeds and plants. PSI publishes a wonderful quarterly newsletter for the serious amateur. Dues $30.

Penstemon

The American Penstemon Society

Ann Bartlett, 1569 S Holland Court, Lakewood, CO 80232 | **Email:** abart111@aol.com | **Web:** www.biosci.ohio-state.edu/~awolfe/penstemon/Penstemon.html

The APS, formed in 1946 as a coalition of gardeners from across the country, is dedicated to the advancement of knowledge about penstemons, their introduction into cultivation, and the development of new and improved cultivars. The genus *Penstemon* is one of the largest genera of wildflowers in the world, with about 250 species, all native to North America. Joining this group will bring a journal twice a year, a seed exchange of 50¢ packets (with up to 10 free seed packets to overseas members), a *Beginner's Manual* and tours. Dues $10.

Peonies

Pacific Northwest Peony Society

Cyndi Turnbow, 10944 Mill Creek Road SE, Aumsville, OR 97325 | **Phone:** (503) 749-1397

The PNW Peony Society was formed in 1996 to promote the enjoyment and knowledge of the peony. Membership includes two newsletters annually, an annual meeting, and garden tours. The annual meeting rotates between various western Washington and western Oregon cities. Dues $5.

Perennials

Northwest Perennial Alliance

Sue Troutner, 23110 SE 249th Court, Maple Valley, WA 98038 | **Phone:** (425) 413-1410 | **Email:** NPA@northwestperennialalliance.org | **Web:** www.northwestperennialalliance.org

NPA is a group of ardent gardeners (professionals and amateurs) with a passionate devotion to herbaceous plants and a commitment to furthering perennial gardening in the Northwest. This is a great place for beginning gardeners to learn new skills, be encouraged, and get hands-on experience. NPA's annual study weekend is fabulous (look under "Study Weekends" in Chapter 3). Members receive the quarterly Perennial Post newsletter, enjoy seed exchanges, plant sales, and great lectures. Two more benefits of membership include the extensive program of Open Garden tours of members' gardens and the April plant sale. Dues $25.

Volunteer! As a member of NPA, you have a special opportunity to join work crews under the guidance of first-class plant professionals and experts in the groups's

famed perennial border at the Bellevue Botanical Garden (2nd and 4th Sundays, 3rd Tuesday, and 1st Thursday of each month). As an incentive for hours worked, NPA offers educational classes with registration as a benefit of volunteer labor at the BBG border.

Perennial Plant Association

3383 Schirtzinger Road, Hilliard, OH 43026 | **Phone:** (614) 771-8431 | **Email:** ppa@perennialplant.org | **Web:** www.perennialplant.org

This is actually a national trade organization for commercial growers, but you are invited to check the website for information on new perennial plant introductions (and links to nurseries that carry them), plus connect with the PPA Speakers' Bureau if you should be seeking a guest speaker for your local garden club. This is the organization that names the much-anticipated Perennial Plant of the Year, usually launching an unsuspecting perennial into global notoriety as we all scramble to plant it in our gardens. Interested amateur gardeners and horticultural students are offered a discounted membership rate (see website).

Primulas

American Primrose Society

Julia Haldorson, PO Box 210-913, Auke Bay, AK 99821 | **Email:** Julia-haldorson@ak.net | **Web:** www.americanprimrosesoc.org

The society offers a quarterly magazine, slide programs, convention, seed exchange (species and hybrid, some available from no other source), plants, a Round Robin with enthusiastic *Primula* growers around the world, and annual plant shows and sales. Membership will also bring a chart containing information about the cultural preferences and natural habitats for many *Primula* species. Dues $25, U.S. and Canada.

❊ **Eastside APS Chapter (Washington).** Contact: Thea Oakley, 3304 228th Avenue NE, Redmond, WA 98053; Phone: (425) 880-6177; Email: othea@halcyon.com

❊ **Tacoma APS Chapter (Washington).** Contact: Candy Strickland, 6911 104th Street E, Puyallup, WA 98373; Phone: (253) 841-4192; or Cy Happy III, 11617 Gravelly Lake Drive, Tacoma, WA 98499; Phone: (253) 588-2585.

❊ **Valley Hi APS Chapter (Oregon).** Contact: Addaline Robinson, 41809 SW Burgarsky Road, Gaston, OR 97119-9047; Phone: (503) 985-1048

BC Primula Group

Dennis Oakley, 10060 Dennis Place, Richmond, BC V7A 3G8 Canada | **Phone:** (604) 274-0551

Rhododendrons

American Rhododendron Society

11 Pinecrest Drive, Fortuna, CA 95540 | **Phone:** (707) 725-3043 | **Email:** oars@arsoffice.org | **Web:** www.rhododendron.org

Membership includes chapter affiliation, education programs, a quality quarterly *Journal* (excellent color photos, well-written articles), a seed exchange, pollen bank, regional and national conferences, plant sales, truss shows, and book discounts. The ARS website is a fabulous resource on plant data and plant care. Dues $28 individual, $33 family.

ARS *Rhododendron and Azalea News*: Subscribe to this free, online newsletter by sending a request to betty spadey@aol.com.

BRITISH COLUMBIA ARS CHAPTERS

* **Vancouver Rhododendron Society.** Contact: Joe and Joanne Ronsley, 250 Oceanview Road, Box 422, Lions Bay, BC V0N 2E0 Canada; Phone: (604) 921-9444; Email: fearing@triumf.ca. Dues are $44 and include ARS membership.

* **Victoria Rhododendron Society.** Email: pfuller@vicsurf.com; Web: http://victoria.tc.ca/Recreation/RhodoSoc/. Meetings are held the first Thursday of the month, 7:30 p.m., at Garth Homer Centre, 811 Darwin Street, Victoria.

OREGON ARS CHAPTERS

* **District #4 Director:** Michael Robert, 1152 Fir Acres Drive, Eugene, OR 97401

* **Eugene Chapter.** Contact: Michael Robert (see above); Web: www.ars-eugene.org

* **Portland Chapter.** Contact: Steve Hopkins; Email: stevehopkins@prodigy.net; Web: www.arsportland.org. Group meets monthly at the PGC and hosts an annual Plant Sale at the Crystal Springs Garden.

* **Siuslaw Chapter.** Contact: Mike Bones, 90379 Oregon Coast Highway, Florence, OR 97439

* **Willamette Chapter.** Contact: Helen Maltby, 9430 54th Avenue NE, Salem, OR 97305; Email: spadherb@aol.com; Web: http://members.aol.com/WillChaptr/Willchap.html. Dues $28.

WASHINGTON ARS CHAPTERS

* **District #3 Director:** Fred Minch; Phone: (253) 845-8043; Email: fjminch@eskimo.com

* **Cascade Chapter.** 3030 E Beaver Lake Drive SE, Sammamish, WA 98075; Phone: (206) 391-2366; Email: rhodywater@aol.com; Web: www.arscascade.org

* **Komo Kulshan Chapter.** Contact: Alan Yoder, 8281 Bob Hall Road, Lynden, WA 98264; Phone: (360) 354-3817; Email: alan.yoder@worldnet.att.net

* **Pilchuck Chapter.** Contact: Jerry Rock, 13314 34th Avenue NW, Marysville, WA 98271; Phone: (360) 652-8908. Meets at 7 p.m. first Thursday of the month (except July and August) at Marysville Junior High School*f* Library, 1605 7th Street, Marysville.

* **Seattle Rhododendron Society.** Contact: Diane Thompson, 23209 - 53rd Avenue SE, Bothell, WA 98021; Phone: (425) 481-9075; Email: paulanddiane@earthlink.net Web: www.seattlerhododendronsociety.org. Group meets first Wednesday of the month, 7:30 p.m., at the GVC, Seattle (except July and August). Anyone in this area interested in rhododendrons has no doubt heard about the famous Meerkerk Rhododendron Gardens on Whidbey Island. It was to this group that Ann Meerkerk left her beloved estate, home to 3,000 rhododendrons. The gardens are maintained by a manager and Puget Sound area volunteers. The Hybridizers Study Group directs the Hybrid Test Garden there. Members of the society receive a monthly newsletter and attend monthly meetings with speakers and slide presentations; pollen, seed, cutting, and plant exchanges are available, also plant sales and lotteries, Meerkerk Garden activities, and a discount on book purchases. The chapter sponsors three truss shows each spring. There are also photography and Rhododendron Species study groups within the SRS membership. Dues: $28 (you will receive a free, one-gallon rhododendron plant when you attend your first SRS chapter as a new member).

* **Whidbey Island Chapter.** Contact: Frank Fujioka; Phone: (360) 331-4178; Email: frank@whidbey.com

* **Grays Harbor Chapter.** Contact: Audrey Holmeide, 507 Carl Way, Aberdeen, WA 98520; Phone: (360) 532-0726

* **Juan de Fuca Chapter.** Contact: Kathe Pryzgoda, 235 Wildwood Lanes, Sequim, WA 98362; Phone: (360) 582-0469

* **Kitsap Chapter.** Contact: Hank Heim, 10674 NE Manor Lane, Bainbridge, WA 98110; Phone: (206) 842-5464; Email: hrhelm@msn.com

* **Lewis County Chapter.** Contact: Mike Hedge, 919 Scammon Creek Road, Centralia, WA 98531

* **Olympia Chapter.** Contact: Connie Klein, 3627 South Bay Road NE, Olympia, WA 98506; (360) 456-1073; Email: rogersandklein@thurston.com

* **Olympic Peninsula Chapter.** Contact: Peggy Middleton, 161 Belvedere Drive, Port Townsend, WA 98036; Phone: (360) 379-9872; Email: middleton@waypt.com

* **Peninsula Chapter.** Contact: Gary Becker, 8806 Ray Nash Court NW, Gig Harbor, WA 98335; Phone: (253) 265-2796

* **Shelton Chapter.** Contact: Sue and Rick Penney, SE 112 Bay East Drive, Shelton, WA 98584

* **Tacoma Chapter.** Contact: Bill Brackman, 14610 114th Avenue Court E., Puyallup, WA 98374; Phone: (253) 848-2675; Email: myrnaandbill@aol.com

RHODODENDRON SPECIES FOUNDATION

Weyerhaeuser Corporate Campus, 2525 S 336th Street, Federal Way | **Mailing address:** PO Box 3798, Federal Way, WA 98063 | **Phone:** (253) 838-4646 | **Email:** rsf@rhodygarden.org | **Web:** www.rhodygarden.org

The RSF was created in 1964 for the preservation, distribution, and display of species rhododendrons. As a private, nonprofit organization, the RSF is internationally recognized as a leader in rhododendron conservation. Its staff and countless volunteers support programs in plant collection, plant and pollen distribution, education, and study. Benefits vary slightly with each membership level, but generally include free admission to the Rhododendron Species Botanical Garden, discounts in the Garden Shop and on classes, members-only plant and pollen programs, and the quarterly newsletter. Memberships: $15 student, $35 individual, $50 family, and up.

Volunteer! Opportunities abound in photography (the staff always needs good 35mm slides to add to their collection for classes, including species in the wild or landscape); in the garden shop; with mailings and mail-order plant distribution; and at the flower and garden shows. Want to be more involved with the garden? Be a docent, bloom recorder, research assistant, or help with garden maintenance. You don't need to be a member of the Foundation to volunteer.

Roses

Looking for roses? For an exhaustive linked listing of rose societies, look to this website: www.country-lane. com/yr/links.htm.

AMERICAN ROSE SOCIETY

PO Box 30000, Shreveport, LA 71130-0300 | **Phone:** (318) 938-5402 or (800) 637-6534 | **Email:** ars@ars-hq.org | **Web:** www.ars.org

Members receive a wide array of benefits, including the monthly *American Rose* magazine, a rose handbook and annual guide to rose culture, contacts with ARS Consulting Rosarians in every community, free admission to the Gardens of the American Rose Center, and participation in American Horticultural Society's reciprocal garden admission program to 100 select gardens and horticultural events in the U.S. The society also provides members with a great lending library and slide/video programs. Dues: $37 U.S., $42 Canadian, $34 seniors 65 and over.

ARS/PACIFIC NORTHWEST DISTRICT

This group consists of 31 rose societies in Alaska, BC, Idaho, Montana, Oregon, and Washington. Within its membership are 170 Consulting Rosarians, as well as other rose experts to advise rose growers, speak to garden clubs, and share their great knowledge. Should one of the regional society contacts listed below be incorrect, this is the group to which you should turn for updated information and contacts. You can reach the officers of the PNW district via the website: www.olyrose.org/pnwdistrict.htm.

BRITISH COLUMBIA CHAPTERS OF THE ARS

❈**Fraser Pacific Rose Society (Coquitlam).** Contact: Danielle Scott; Phone: (604) 820-2434; Email: keyrose@telus.net

❈**Peninsular Rose Society (Victoria).** Contact: Anne Williams; Phone: (250) 592-3055; Email: peninsular@nurserysite.com

❈**Vancouver Rose Society.** 6633 MacDonald St., Vancouver, BC V6N 4G6 Canada. Contact: Brenda Viney; Phone: (604) 936-1514; or Elizabeth Sheppard; Phone: (604) 856-5279; Email: esds@uniserve.com Web: www. vancouverrosesociety.org

OREGON CHAPTERS OF THE ARS

❈**Albany Rose Society.** Contact: Shirley Pierce; Phone: (541) 928-3888; Email: otisandshirley@proaxis.com

❈**Corvallis Rose Society.** Contact: Nancy Mandel; Phone: (541) 752-3769

❈**Eugene Rose Society.** Contact: Mark Whiddel; Phone: (541) 998-2052

❈**French Prairie Rose and Garden Club (Mount Angel).** Contact: Maureen Ernst; Phone: (503) 845-6208

❈**Medford Rose Society.** Contact: Ruth Tiffany; Phone: (541) 773-2289

❈**Portland Rose Society.** PO Box 525, Portland, OR 97207; Phone: (503) 777-4311; Email: generalinfo@portlandrosesociety.org; Web: www.portlandrosesociety. org. The group is very involved annually with the activities of the June Portland Rose Festival.

❈**Rogue Valley Rose Society (Grants Pass).** Contact: Barbara Edwards; Phone: (541) 474-5070

❈**Salem Rose Society.** Contact: Shirley Kay; Phone: (503) 246-3087

❈**Southwestern Oregon Rose Society.** Contact: Mary Ann Kreutzer; Phone: (541) 572-3426

❈**Tualatin Valley Rose Society.** Contact: John Lauer, 13670 SW 22nd Street, Beaverton, OR 97008; Phone: (503) 644-9356

WASHINGTON CHAPTERS OF THE ARS

❈**Fort Vancouver Rose Society.** Contact: Frank Hecker; Phone: (360) 695-2015

❈**Grays Harbor Rose Society.** Contact: Gail Lake; Phone: (360) 268-6128

❈**Kitsap County Rose Society** (formerly Olympic Peninsula Rose Society). Contact: Jamie Schnirch; Phone: (360) 895-3414

* **Lewis-Clark Rose Society.** Contact: Jerry Hendrickson; Phone: (509) 243-4404

* **Olympia Rose Society.** Contact: Helen Pressley; Phone: (360) 754-3971; Email: hpre461@aol.com; Web: www.olyrose.org

* **Puyallup Rose Society.** Contact: Mike Peterson; Phone: (425) 226-8388

* **Rainy Rose Society.** Contact: Colin Hammington; Phone: (253) 639-7656

* **Seattle Rose Society.** Contact: Judy Phillips; Phone: (206) 232-8637. Don Julien, editor of SRS's newsletter, maintains a great website for the society, filled with archived articles from *Rose Petals*, the monthly newsletter, a photo gallery, and membership information at www.bmi.net/roseguy.

* **Skagit Valley Rose Society.** Contact: Peggy Van Allen; Phone: (360) 766-6483

* **Tacoma Rose Society.** Contact: Patricia Kurz; Phone: (253) 756-1791; Email: rosewoman@earthlink.net; Web: http://home.earthlink.net/~rosewoman/

* **Tri-City Rose Society (Richland, Pasco, Kennewick).** Contact: Helen Newman; Phone: (509) 627-0880; Email: hnewman@owt.com; Web: www.owt.com/rose society/

* **Tri-Valley Rose Society (Marysville).** Contact: Dwayne Berg; Phone: (360) 659-8306

* **Walla Walla Rose Society.** Contact: Nancy Rose; Phone: (509) 525-4564

HERITAGE ROSE GROUP

916 Union Street, No. 302, Alameda, CA 94501 | **Phone:** (925) 335-9156 | **Email:** maggie94553@earthlink.net | **Web:** www.thefragrantgarden.com/hrg.html

There are 16 chapters of the HRG, a national organization of gardeners who love species and old roses, founded in 1975. Quarterly newsletter *The Heritage Rose Letter,* plus local meetings throughout the year. Dues $6.

PACIFIC NORTHWEST ROSE HYBRIDIZERS GROUP

John and Mitchie Moe, 830 S 373rd Street, Federal Way, WA 98003 | **Phone:** (253) 815-1072 | **Web:** www.olyrose.org/hybridizing.htm

This specialty organization, founded in 1993, fosters activity and interest in rose hybridizing and breeding. Meeting topics include all aspects of rose hybridizing: germination, best pollen parents, and seed propagation. Members exchange pollen and seeds. Meetings five times a year; visitors are always welcome! Newsletter published five times a year. Website features selected articles on rose hybridizing. Dues $5.

ROSE HYBRIDIZERS ASSOCIATION

Larry Peterson, 21 S Wheaton Road, Horseheads, NY 14845-1077 | **Email:** lpeterso@stny.rr.com | **Web:** www.rosehybridizers.org

Membership includes a seed exchange, newsletter, and hybridizing demonstrations. Dues $10 year.

WORLD FEDERATION OF ROSE SOCIETIES

Mrs. Jill Bennell, 46 Alexandra Road, St. Albans, Hertfordshire AL1 3AZ England | **Email:** mail@rnrs.org.uk | **Web:** www.worldrose.org

Sweet Peas

NATIONAL SWEET PEA SOCIETY

Mrs. M. E. McDonald, St. Annes, The Hollow, Broughton, Stockbridge, Hants, SO20 8BB United Kingdom | **Web:** www.sweetpeas.org.uk

Just as it's hard to resist the fragrance and charm of the sweet pea, it's hard to resist the attraction of this British organization (founded in 1900!). Membership includes the handbook *How to Grow Sweet Peas,* twice-yearly bulletins, an annual, and the chance to enter your novelty sweet peas in the trials at the Royal Horticultural Society's Wisley garden!

Trees / Arboretums / Parks

AMERICAN CONIFER SOCIETY

John Martin, PO Box 3422, Crofton, MD 21114-0422 | **Phone:** (410) 721-6611 | **Email:** conifersociety@aol.com | **Web:** www.conifersociety.org

Receive the quarterly bulletin packed with information devoted to the care and cultivation of conifers and their companion plants. Annual meeting, regional groups. For a complimentary copy of *A Brief Look at Garden Conifers,* write to the address above. Dues $25, $32 (outside the United States).

ARBORETUM FOUNDATION

2300 Arboretum Drive E, Seattle, WA 98112-2300 | **Phone:** (206) 325-4510 | **Email:** gvc@arboretumfoundation.org | **Web:** www.arboretumfoundation.org

Offices are at the Graham Visitor Center. The Arboretum foundation supports Seattle's 230-acre Washington Park Arboretum through membership, volunteer services, and fund-raising. Foundation events include plant sales and the Preview Party for the Northwest Flower and Garden Show. Members participate in special gardening classes and lectures at the Arboretum, receive discounts at the Foundation's gift and book shop, and subscriptions to the full-color *Washington Park Arboretum Bulletin,* and enjoy early entry to many foundation events, including plant sales. Members may also join special plant study groups or neighborhood-based Foundation Units, to further enhance gardening knowledge and camaraderie with other gardening enthusiasts. Dues $25 individual, $35 families (additional benefits provided for other member categories—see the website).

Volunteer! Opportunities include helping produce fund-raising events, hands-on Arboretum maintenance projects, propagating, potting, and selling plants in the greenhouse or plant donation areas, serving as an Arboretum tour guide, greeting visitors in the Graham Visitor Center lobby and gift shop, and helping teach kids about horticulture and ecology through the Arboretum's education programs.

FRIENDS OF THE TREES

PO Box 4469, Bellingham, WA 98227 | **Phone:** (360) 676-7704 | **Growing season address:** PO Box 253, Twisp, WA 98856 (March-May) | **Growing season phone:** (509) 997-9200 (March-May) | **Fax:** (509) 997-4812 | **Email:** friendsofthetrees@yahoo.com | **Web:** www.friendsofthetrees.net

Organized in 1978, this small, grassroots nonprofit corporation is dedicated to world reforestation and is active in Washington and beyond. Founder and chief tree advocate Michael Pilarski has developed a mailing list of 12,000, with 3,000 individuals outside the United States. While this organization operates on a shoestring, depending on donations from supporters to pay for sporadic newsletter mailings, much of its energy is devoted to workshops and educational activities. FTS also sells trees, seeds, and books. The newly launched website will introduce you to several of Pilarski's books available for purchase, including *Reforestation Forestry: An International Guide to Sustainable Forestry Practices* (1994) and *Subtropical & Tropical Medicinal Plant Checklist* (2001).

Volunteer! Friends of the Trees' internship program is staged at Sunny Pine Farm in the Methow Valley, where the organization operates a small, intentional community cultivating 25 acres of alfalfa, organic vegetables and herbs for essential oil distillation. Interns receive room, board and some financial compensation. Call (509) 997-4811 if you are interested. FOT also needs volunteers in the Bellingham area for administrative and Website assistance.

FRIENDS OF TREES

3117 NE Martin Luther King Boulevard, Portland, OR 97212 | **Phone:** (503) 282-8846; Hotline: (503) 284-8733 | **Email:** fot@friendsoftrees.org | **Web:** www.friendsoftrees.org

Friends of Trees is a nonprofit organization that promotes community partnerships to plant, care for, and preserve urban trees in order to strengthen neighborhoods, create an ecologically healthy environment, and enhance the quality of urban life. Membership includes a newsletter and notice of upcoming events. Dues $35 and up.

Volunteer! FOT offers a variety of opportunities in the field, in the community, at special events, and in the office. The excellent website lists many specific, current opportunities, including such projects as planting trees and seedlings in scores of neighborhoods, business districts, on school grounds, in natural areas, in parks, and along stream banks.

PLANTAMNESTY

PO Box 15377, Seattle, WA 98115 | **Phone:** (206) 783-9813 | **Email:** plantamnesty@plantamnesty.org | **Web:** www.plantamnesty.org

Founded in 1987 by Cass Turnbull, a passionate and witty landscaper whose mission is to "end the senseless torture and mutilation of trees and shrubs caused by malpruning," PlantAmnesty lives up to its mission of educating the public and landscaping professionals by providing them with the information they need to properly plan, install, and maintain their landscapes properly. PlantAmnesty members also help to shape public policy in order to promote the health and beauty of plants. Members receive a great quarterly newsletter, access to a "good gardener" (landscaper and arborist) referral service, pruning classes, workshops, resources such as a slide show and educational pruning video (starring Cass Turnbull), a cool adopt-a-plant program ("You call, you dig, you haul, that's all"), lots of How To (and How Not To) materials, and special events. Ask about the Heritage Tree Program in Seattle. PA also throws a dandy Gardener's Plant Sale and Fall Festival (includes donated nursery "seconds"), typically in September. Memberships: $30, $60, $120 on up.

Volunteer! PlantAmnesty needs you! Committee opportunities include Events, Tree Programs, Finance/Fund-raising, Board Development, Education, and Advocacy. Also: volunteer yard renovations for needy and deserving yards, hospitality for tours and events (that gets you in free!), and staffing educational booths at the Northwest Flower and Garden Show.

SEATTLE-ADOPT-A-PARK PROGRAM

Seattle Parks and Recreation | **Web:** www.cityofseattle.net/parks/Volunteers/index.htm

Created in 1982, this terrific program enables citizens of Seattle to assist in the care and maintenance of area parks. From corporate and business sponsorship to service league involvement, and from elementary school classes to individuals, there is a sense of shared responsibility as various groups provide help and enhance our community's "outdoor laboratories."

* North Division Contact: Theresa McEwan; Phone: (206) 615-0691; Email: Theresa.mcewen@cityofseattle.net

* Central Division Contact: Terri Arnold; Phone: (206) 386-1419; Email: terri.Arnold@cityofseattle.net

* South Division; Phone: (206) 684-4557

* Work parties: Contact Adam Cole, volunteer programs coordinator, at (206) 386-1419 or Email: adam.cole@ci.seattle.wa.us if your group wishes to schedule a work party. Team up with your neighbors, community group, or co-workers, and Seattle Parks and Recreation will design a volunteer project your team will enjoy.

SOUTH KING COUNTY ARBORETUM FOUNDATION

PO Box 72, Maple Valley, WA 98038 | **Phone:** (206) 366-2125 or (425) 413-2572 | **Email:** arboretum@skcaf.org | **Web:** www.skcaf.org

The Arboretum was established in 1965 to develop a native-plant-focused arboretum on 40 acres of the northerly portion of Lake Wilderness Park in partnership with the King County Park System. The grounds are managed and maintained purely by volunteers, and offer many opportunities for SKCAF members to show their support with time, talent, and money. Members attend general meetings, special events and programs. They also receive a newsletter, enjoy spring and fall plant sales, and more. Membership: $10 individual, $15 family.

TREEmendous Seattle

7400 Sand Point Way NE, Seattle, WA 98115 | **Phone:** (206) 985-6867 | **Email:** chris@seattletrees.org | **Web:** www.seattletrees.org

This worthy organization was established in 1992 to plant, maintain, and preserve trees in the City of Seattle. Through volunteers and community support, TREEmendous Seattle is involved in the actual work of planting and maintaining trees in the urban area, as well as creating a network of tree experts, volunteers, and funding sources. The group leads 200 active young urban foresters who are working with Seattle Parks and Recreation to restore green space. It also works with Seattle Public Utilities to organize street-tree planting projects and plant trees, with Seattle Public Schools to involve students and arborists in restoration at schools, and with the Seattle Transportation Department to expand the Tree Stewards training course and care for trees throughout the city. As part of the Seattle Millennium Project, TREEmendous in 2000 helped to unite neighborhoods, environmental groups, city departments, and other volunteers in planting 20,000 trees throughout the city. *The Gift of Life . . .* dedicate a tree to a friend or loved one (anniversary, birthday, graduation, any life passage or achievement), is another great program offered by TREEmendous Seattle ($50 and up). Membership: $25 individual.

Wildflowers / Naturescaping

North American Native Plant Society (formerly Canadian Wildflower Society)

PO Box 84, Postal Station D, Etobicoke, ON M9A 4X1 Canada | **Phone:** (416) 680-6280 | **Email:** nanps@nanps.org | **Web:** www.nanps.org

NANPS was founded in 1984 by a group of dedicated conservationists as the Canadian Wildflower Society, and has grown to hundreds of members throughout North America. The group's magazine *Wildflower* has gone independent; see www.wildflowermag.com.

NANPS serves as a communication link among native plant societies, botanical gardens, and plant-research centers across North America. An extensive seed exchange is available to members. Dues $10 per year Canadian within Canada, or $10 U.S. per year within the U.S.

Wild Ones – Natural Landscapers, Ltd.

PO Box 1274, Appleton, WI 54912 | **Phone:** (920) 730-3986 or Toll-free: (877) FYI-WILD | **Email:** woresource@aol.com | **Web:** www.for-wild.org

This national nonprofit organization is leading the way in natural landscape gardening, working to restore habitat, reduce lawns, and exploring the many other issues that surround this philosophy. The principles behind the movement are universal, so while the current chapters are clustered in the Midwest, membership will nevertheless bring a Northwest gardener a great deal of value (including *Wild Ones Journal,* an informative bimonthly newsletter). Dues $30.

General Interest

American Horticultural Society

7931 East Boulevard Drive, Alexandria, VA 22308-1300 | **Phone:** (703) 768-5700 or Toll-free: (800) 777-7931 | **Email:** membership@ahs.org | **Web:** www.ahs.org

It's fitting that the AHS is housed on the grounds of George Washington's River Farm, just outside the nation's capital. One of the oldest national gardening organizations in the country, AHS was formed in 1922, providing horticultural and gardening education and information. Get connected to great gardens around the world, and find education for every level of skill and a community of gardeners anywhere you travel. Members receive the bimonthly *The American Gardener* magazine, access to the Gardeners Information Service, a free seed-exchange program, free admission to public gardens and flower shows, and discounts from "the foremost gardening book service in the nation." Dues $35.

The BC Council of Garden Clubs

Lorna Herchenson, (604) 929-5382 | **Email:** lherchenson@telus.net

Founded in 1943, this organization represents a wide array of gardening clubs and groups across the province, with the goal of promoting horticulture with one voice. Conservation and civic beautification are two of the BC Council's objectives, bringing together nearly 100 local and regional groups. If you're looking for a group of special-interest or avid gardeners in your community the BC Council will point you in the right direction.

Hardy Plant Society of Oregon

1930 NW Lovejoy Street, Portland, OR 97209 | **Phone:** (503) 224-5718 | **Email:** admin@hardyplantsociety.org | **Web:** www.hardyplant society.org

Throughout the region, this highly respected group (over 2,000 members) is justly famous for the two *fabulous* plant sales (drawing over 70 participating growers in the spring and fall) and its programs for members and the plant-crazed public. HPSO is a nonprofit volunteer organization for beginning, experienced, amateur, and professional gardeners. Founded in 1985 and dedicated to the promotion of hardy herbaceous perennials, the society now has members throughout the Pacific Northwest and beyond. There are interest groups (organized geographically), a members-only seed sale, tours to noteworthy gardens, a very fine lecture and seminar program (speakers of national and international prominence), a monthly newsletter; and a biannual literary *Bulletin*. A favorite member benefit is the annual Gardens Open Today program, accompanied by a fat booklet of members' gardens open throughout the Northwest. It's just like a similar program in England, which is both admirable and an inspiration to other groups that are following HPSO's lead. The organization participates in the hardy plant study weekend rotation between Victoria, Seattle, and Portland. Dues $20.

HOBBY GREENHOUSE ASSOCIATION

8 Glen Terrace, Bedford, MA 01730-2048 | **Phone:** (781) 275-0377 | **Email:** kay@in-motion.net | **Web:** www.orbitworld.net/hga

Whether you own a backyard greenhouse or just garden on the windowsill, HGA is a great resource for plant information, gardening techniques, and ideas. Membership brings a quarterly magazine (sample copy $3.50) and a quarterly newsletter, the generous advice of experts, Round Robin letters from other members, seed exchange, and access to HGA's video resources, library, and books at a discount. Dues $22 U.S., $24 Canadian.

NATIONAL COUNCIL OF STATE GARDEN CLUBS

4401 Magnolia Avenue, St. Louis, MO 63110 | **Web:** www.garden club.org

The National Council serves as a link, resource, and clearinghouse of ideas for horticulture, floral and landscape design, flower shows, conservation, and environmental projects around the country. It is composed of 50 state garden clubs (plus D.C.), nearly 9,000 member clubs, and 235,000 members, and has 200 international affiliates. The organization publishes *The National Gardener,* a bimonthly magazine for garden club enthusiasts and members. If you are unable to find a garden club in your area, you can use a "garden club information request form" on the National Council's website to request a contact near you.

NORTHWEST HORTICULTURAL SOCIETY

Karin Kravitz, CUH, Box 354115, University of Washington, Seattle, WA 98195-4115 | **Phone:** (206) 527-1794 | **Web:** www.northwesthort.org

NHS provides a forum for gardeners and plant lovers in the Pacific Northwest to share their interests and learn about horticulture. Lectures, symposiums, workshops, and classes throughout the year benefit not only members but the general public, drawing top speakers in horticulture from across the country and abroad. NHS stages a fabulous plant sale at the CUH in September. Members can also participate in a seed exchange, join tours of notable gardens, and receive the NHS quarterly newsletter *Garden Notes*. The NHS has established a $100,000 Horticultural Education Fund, annually grants scholarships to students in horticulture at the University of Washington, and supports other projects that benefit horticulture in the Northwest.

The Society is a major financial supporter of the Elisabeth C. Miller Library (which needs the garden community's support now, more than ever), hosting one of best garden parties of the year—a posh auction of garden-related goods and services, generally in May. Dues $55 (with quarterly subscription to *Pacific Horticulture*), or $35 without subscription.

Volunteer! NHS needs enthusiastic volunteers to help with garden tours, lectures, the plant sale, and fundraising events. The Lecture Program brings many topnotch horticultural speakers, so this would be an excellent way to meet them.

THE OREGON STATE FEDERATION OF GARDEN CLUBS

Membership Chairman, PO Box 3252, Newberg, OR 97132

SALEM HARDY PLANT SOCIETY

PO Box 2027, Salem, OR 97308 | **Phone:** (503) 623-8937 | **Email:** shps@open.org | **Web:** www.open.org/~shps

SHPS is a nonprofit organization promoting the use of hardy perennial plants. It seeks to collect and disseminate source information about hardy plants and their availability. Educational programs include lectures, open gardens, nursery tours, plant exchanges, and a fall plant sale. Members participate in monthly meetings and receive a monthly newsletter. Dues $15.

SEATTLE TILTH ASSOCIATION

4649 Sunnyside Avenue N, Room 1, Seattle, WA 98103 | **Phone:** (206) 633-0451 | **Email:** tilth@seattletilth.org | **Web:** www.seattletilth.org

Seattle Tilth is a vibrant, nationally recognized nonprofit organization that promotes the art of organic gardening in an urban setting. It began in 1978 when neighbors sharing a vision for an urban agriculture and living environment joined together to remove a bleak expanse of asphalt and to breathe new life into the hidden soil beneath. Today, still operating on the grounds of the Good Shepherd Center where the organization began, Tilth members work to enhance local environments and community through education about organic gardening. Tilth runs a compost hotline, the Master Composter program, demonstration gardens, and a wonderful Children's Garden. Members receive a discount on all Tilth classes, an informative monthly newsletter, get in touch with gardening and other gardeners, have access to the Tilth library, and more. Dues $30.

Volunteer! Tilth offers training for those interested in the Children's Garden Program. If you are more interested in working in the Tilth produce/demonstration garden a few hours a week in exchange for skill-building workshops, call about the CORE Volunteer Program.

Help is very welcome for the Spring Edible Plant Sale and the Fall Harvest Fair, two major public events sponsored by Seattle Tilth.

THE WASHINGTON STATE FEDERATION OF GARDEN CLUBS

Wendy Larson, 16237 NE 29th Street, Bellevue, WA 98008 | **Email:** info@washingtongardenclubs.org | **Web:** www.washingtongarden clubs.org

Washington's 15 Districts have about 5,400 members in 230 clubs. The Washington State Federation of Garden Clubs is actively involved in sponsoring environmental workshops, civic beautification, and educational programs for all ages and levels of expertise. The group sponsors Flower Show Schools and Symposiums to train members to be nationally accredited Flower Show judges. There is also an extensive juried competition of members' horticulture, floral design, and garden crafts creations, held at the Northwest Flower and Garden Show. Members in Washington may subscribe to *Smoke Signals*, the state's quarterly publication; *WACONIAH*, a publication of the National Federation of Garden Club Pacific Region, and *The National Gardener*, the bimonthly national publication. Contact the state membership chairman by email (listed above) to find a Garden Club in your community.

WHATCOM HORTICULTURAL SOCIETY

PO Box 4443, Bellingham, WA 98227 | **Phone:** (360) 738-6833 | **Web:** http://home.earthlink.net/~cedarcroft/WhatcomHS/

Organized in 1989, the Whatcom Horticultural Society (originally called Whatcom in Bloom Garden Society), sponsors programs, lectures, tours, and publications for Whatcom area gardeners. WHS held a special place in the heart of this book's founder, Stephanie Feeney, for whose members she originally began typing up and photocopying lists of "great nurseries and gardens to visit" more than a decade ago. Thank you, Whatcom Horticultural Society members, for helping to launch this *Directory*! Novice and veteran gardeners alike are welcome to join WHS and all members benefit from the spring and fall lecture series, which attracts national and international gardening luminaries. WHS also supports various worthy horticultural causes (see the website for details). Dues $15.

Volunteer! This group exists solely through the efforts of volunteers, who help with the garden tours, lecture series, quarterly journal, membership, mailings, and more.

WILLAMETTE VALLEY HARDY PLANT GROUP

3093 Solomon Loop, Eugene, OR 96405 | **Web:** www.thehardy plantgroup.org

Organized in 1987 by a group of avid gardeners, the organization now numbers nearly 300. Members meet monthly (except summer), welcoming gardeners of all levels of experience. Benefits include a monthly newsletter; large plant sale annually (the Saturday before Mother's Day), gardening lecture series, the Open Gardens program, and field trips to area nurseries and gardens. The WVHPG supports a wonderful mixed border at the entrance to Alston Baker Park in Eugene. Dues $15.

BOTANICAL / PUBLIC GARDENS / ARBORETA

BELLEVUE BOTANICAL GARDEN SOCIETY

PO Box 40536, Bellevue, WA 98015 | **Phone:** (425) 451-3755 | **Email:** bbgsoffice@bellevuebotanical.org | **Web:** www.bellevue botanical.org

This nonprofit organization of amateur and professional gardeners assists the Bellevue Parks Department in establishing and maintaining the 36-acre garden, which opened in 1992. A great deal is happening here as the garden grows and the society sponsors many activities. Members receive a bimonthly newsletter, a 10 percent discount in the BBGS Gift Shop and at the Bellevue Smith & Hawken store, plus invitations to "members only" events. Many classes and lectures are "no fee" or "reduced fee" to BBGS members, and there is a rewarding members-only shopping time designated at the annual plant sale. Dues $25.

Volunteer! Opportunities abound! Lend a hand in marketing, community relations, fund-raising, at plant sales, as a garden greeter, in the gift shop, and beyond, including active outdoor "openings" in garden maintenance. Consider becoming a docent, as it is a terrific way to learn more about the garden and expand your horticultural knowledge. (See also the Northwest Perennial Alliance, in this chapter, for details on becoming involved in the NPA Border at the BBG).

THE BERRY BOTANIC GARDEN

Janice Dodd, 11505 SW Summerville Avenue, Portland, OR 97219 | **Phone:** (503) 636-4112 | **Email:** bbg@rdrop.com | **Web:** www.berrybot.org

This nonprofit organization was formed to preserve and enhance the gardens created by Rae Selling Berry, and is now in its 25th year. Beyond the personal gratification one gets in supporting the garden, members receive discounts on classes, plants, books, and other Berry-sponsored events and activities. You'll receive the newsletter, library privileges, and notices of all events. You can visit the garden without admission fees and bring along friends free of charge, too. When you join the Berry, you also support plant conservation in our region and around the world. Dues $35.

Volunteer! For self-enrichment and personal satisfaction, consider volunteering your time in the garden's horticultural, educational, or research activities. You could become involved as a guide or working in the garden itself, in propagation or the seed exchange, or help in the library or at plant sales. Help make a difference with an organization that relies heavily on volunteers to preserve this special garden. To volunteer, call Carolyn, (503) 636-4112, ext. 26.

THE BLOEDEL RESERVE

7571 NE Dolphin Drive, Bainbridge Island, WA 98110-1097 | **Phone:** (206) 842-7631 | **Web:** www.bloedelreserve.org.

The Reserve provides people in our region (and countless visitors from around the globe) an opportunity to enjoy nature through quiet walks in the garden and woodlands. The remarkable gardens and grounds will keep you coming back in every season, easily "paying for" the nominal cost of an annual membership. Members receive periodic newsletters, a 10 percent discount on purchase of Reserve book or videos, free admission for one year for groups of up to four adults (member must be present in group), and invitations to special events (concerts, lectures, programs) usually not offered to the public. Dues $35.

Volunteer! The Reserve maintains a volunteer staff of about 50 people who lead virtually all of the guided tours here, staff the visitor center, assist at the Gate House during the busy season, work with the garden crew throughout the gardens, and host all of the special events during the year. Contact the volunteer coordinator at the number above for more information.

BROOKLYN BOTANIC GARDEN

1000 Washington Avenue, Brooklyn, NY 11225 | **Phone:** (718) 623-7210 | **Email:** membership@bbg.org | **Web:** www.bbg.org

While not a Northwest garden, the Brooklyn Botanic Garden is deserving of your support, even from a distance. You may not be dropping by the lovely gardens on a regular basis, but you can admire the BBG from a distance through the "Subscribing Member" category for literary friends and supporters (and visit via the terrific website). Membership in BBG supports an important cultural resource and a leading center of horticulture, plant science, and education. Subscriber members receive quarterly issues of both the *21st Century Gardening Series Handbooks* annually (a $40 value!) and a terrific quarterly, *Plants & Gardens News*, plus reciprocal privileges at gardens around the country. Dues $35.

CONNIE HANSEN GARDEN CONSERVANCY

1931 NW 33rd Street, Lincoln City, OR 97367 | **Phone:** (541) 994-6338 | **Email:** conniehansengarden@hotmail.com | **Web:** www.conniehansengarden.com

A group of dedicated friends and admirers of the late Connie Hansen organized the conservancy in 1994 to help fund the preservation and maintenance of her garden for the joy of the public. The group is self-supporting, operating on dues, contributions, and an occasional grant. The CHGC's goal is to support and provide a local focus on garden-related activities, including horticultural classes, garden painting and art displays, tours, lectures, a library, plant sales, and meeting space. Dues: $25.

Volunteer! As the CHGC continues to develop its ambitious plans for the garden interpretive center, horticultural library, and educational classroom, perhaps you could offer a bit of your own expertise and good will.

DR. SUN YAT-SEN GARDEN SOCIETY

578 Carrall Street, Vancouver, BC V6B 2J8 Canada | **Phone:** (604) 662-3207 | **Email:** sunyatsen@telus.net | **Web:** www.discovervancouver.com/sun

This independent, nonprofit association bridges the two cultures of China and Canada. Membership brings unlimited garden visits, two free passes, subscription to the quarterly newsletter, advance notice and discount for all garden programs, an invitation to Mid-Autumn Moon Festival Party, and a 10 percent discount on purchases in the Garden Gift Shop. Dues $20.

FRIENDS OF THE CONSERVATORY

1402 E Galer Street, Seattle, WA 98112 | **Phone:** (206) 322-4112

Members receive a newsletter and announcements of special events, horticultural programs, and happenings at the Volunteer Park Conservatory. The Friends sponsor two annual fund-raising plant sales in May and September. Dues: $35.

Volunteer! There are opportunities at the Volunteer Park Conservatory for those who would like to work in the greenhouse propagating from the collection, in planning and working at plant sales, helping with the newsletter, or as docents in the Conservatory.

THE HOYT ARBORETUM FRIENDS FOUNDATION

4000 SW Fairview Boulevard, Portland, OR 97221 | **Phone:** (503) 228-8733 | **Email:** haffdir@ci.portland.or.us | **Web:** www.hoytarboretum.org

Enjoy Portland's Urban Forest of 175 spectacular acres of hiking trails and woody plants by becoming a supporter of the HAFF. Membership ensures that you will receive regular mailings and notices of special events and classes. Dues $25.

Volunteer! You can train to be a tour guide, greet the public at the Visitor Center, or serve on a work party for plant collection and trails. Call Tiffany Schuster at (503) 823-1649 for more details.

THE GARDEN CONSERVANCY

PO Box 219, Cold Spring, NY 10516 | **Phone:** (845) 265-2029 | **Email:** info@gardenconservancy.org | **Web:** www.gardenconservancy.org

While it's a well-established concept in Europe, the practice of preserving and managing exceptional gardens when their makers are no longer able to maintain them is relatively new to North America. The Garden Conservancy promotes such preservation efforts, offering technical advice and assistance, support, and advocacy nationwide on projects involving historic or otherwise horticulturally significant properties. Since 1989 TGC has undertaken several substantial projects, which now include the Abkhazi Garden in Victoria, British Columbia; the Chase Garden in Orting, Washington; and the

Mukai Farm and Garden in Vashon, Washington (see Chapter 13, "Gardens to Visit"). Members receive a subscription to TGC's newsletter, invitations to TGC-sponsored special events, discounts on purchases of the *Open Days Directory*, and discounts on purchases of Open Days garden admission coupon booklets. Dues $35.

JAPANESE GARDEN SOCIETY

Treasurer, 2300 Arboretum Drive E, Seattle, WA, 98122 | **Phone:** (206) 684-4725 or (425) 861-9109 | **Email:** volunteer.one@ verizon.net | **Web:** www.seattlejapanesegarden.org

The society is a nonprofit organization created to support the Seattle Parks Department in the preservation and maintenance of the Japanese Garden in the Washington Park Arboretum. Members meet quarterly with programs concerning the culture, plants, and design of Japanese gardens. Members also receive a quarterly newsletter and invitations to the society's special events, such as visits to regional Japanese gardens and Moon Viewing Ceremonies. Dues $10.

Volunteer! The Seattle Japanese Garden at the Washington Park Arboretum is such an esteemed treasure. Member volunteers may work as guides after completing a short training course. For those with more of a horticultural proclivity, consider offering your help through work parties that groom and maintain the garden.

JAPANESE GARDEN SOCIETY OF OREGON

PO Box 3847, Portland, OR 97208 | **Phone:** (503) 223-1321 | **Email:** japanesegarden@japanesegarden.com | **Web:** www.japanese garden.com

Membership benefits include early-morning access before the garden opens to the public, unlimited visits, invitations to special events and programs, a monthly newsletter, and a 10 percent discount at the Garden Gift Store. Dues $35.

KUBOTA GARDEN FOUNDATION

PO Box 78338, Seattle, WA 98178-9998 | **Phone:** (206) 725-5060 | **Web:** www.kubota.org

The foundation was established in 1989 as a nonprofit organization to provide a forum for those who love the Kubota Garden and want to help it prosper. The foundation hosts an annual meeting, publishes a seasonal newsletter, sponsors public guided tours and workshops, and holds spring and fall plant sales. Dues $25.

LAKEWOLD GARDENS

PO Box 98092, Lakewood, WA 98498 | **Phone:** (253) 584-4106 or (888) 858-4106 | **Email:** info@lakewold.org | **Web:** www.lakewold.org

Enjoy membership in this beautiful and well-kept estate garden here in our own Pacific Northwest. Membership includes a newsletter, free admission to the gardens, invitations to members-only events, and discounts to events such as the Picnic & Pops summer concert in August. Dues $10.

Volunteer! Be a tour guide, work in the plant refer-

ence library, help host social functions, or work under the Garden Manager on general gardening tasks or in special interest areas (water garden, parterres). Call for information on the next training.

LEACH GARDEN FRIENDS

6704 SE 122nd Avenue, Portland, OR 97236 | **Phone:** (503) 823-9504 | **Web:** www.parks.ci.portland.or.us/Parks/Leach/ Botanical Gar.htm

This nonprofit organization's mission is to educate and involve the community in the conservation and preservation of the botanical legacy of John and Lilla Leach. Members receive a newsletter; discounts on gift shop purchases, plants, and classes; checkout privileges at the library; and volunteer opportunities. There are spring and fall plant sales and other events. Membership is $20.

Volunteer! A variety of opportunities are available for tour guides, gardeners (outdoors or in the greenhouse), reception, fund-raising events, office help, and the education committee and gift shop.

PORTLAND CHINESE GARDEN SOCIETY

PO Box 3706, Portland, OR 97208 | **Phone:** (503) 228-8131 | **Email:** membership@portlandchinesegarden.org | **Web:** www.portlandchinesegarden.org

Members of this wonderful new project in the heart of downtown Portland receive free daytime admission to the Chinese Garden, a newsletter subscription, a 10 percent discount at the Gift Shop and Tea House, and invitations to special members-only events. Dues $35.

Volunteer! Help the "garden of awakening orchids" with a wide array of projects (see the website for specifics), including major events like the Chinese New Year Celebration, and ongoing duties such as greeting visitors, membership sales, and helping with children's events and guest services. For a volunteer application, email lwatson@portlandchinesegarden.org.

SEATTLE CHINESE GARDEN SOCIETY

2040 Westlake Avenue N, Suite 306, Seattle, WA 98109 | **Phone:** (206) 282-8040 | **Email:** info@seattle-chinese-garden.org | **Web:** www.seattle-chinese-garden.org

This nonprofit group is dedicated to the creation of a classical Chinese garden in the Puget Sound area. Sited on a peaceful 6-acre site in West Seattle with spectacular views of the city, harbor, and mountains beyond, the Seattle Chinese Garden Xi Hua Yuan will feature plant species from Sichuan and neighboring provinces. The garden's first showpiece, the Song Mei Pavilion, was installed and dedicated in 1999. Fund-raising has continued ever since, with approximately $5.4 million raised (including $1.5 million from The Boeing Company) by early 2002. Groundbreaking for Phase I is set for 2003. Members receive a quarterly newsletter and invitations to special exhibits, garden tours, and programs. Dues $20.

Volunteer! The society offers many ways to become

involved, through horticultural and educational programs, or training to be a docent.

YAKIMA AREA ARBORETUM

1401 Arboretum Drive, Yakima, WA 98901 | **Phone:** (509) 248-7337 | **Email:** arboretum@nwinfo.com | **Web:** www.ahtrees.org

The arboretum is a "living museum of botanical specimens," and it cultivates a greater knowledge and appreciation of trees and plants from around the world. Display gardens include a Japanese garden, trees of Washington, and the wetland trail, encompassing over 2,000 plant species spread across 46 acres. Members receive a newsletter, a discount in the Tree House Museum gift shop, library privileges, and an opportunity to buy at the plant pre-sale. Membership is $25.

OVERSEAS SOCIETIES

ALPINE GARDEN SOCIETY OF GREAT BRITAIN

See entry under "Alpine / Rock Gardens," above.

THE BRITISH CLEMATIS SOCIETY

See entry under "Clematis" above.

THE COTTAGE GARDEN SOCIETY

See entry under "Cottage Gardens" above.

HARDY PLANT SOCIETY OF GREAT BRITAIN

Mrs. Pam Adams, Administrator, Little Orchard, Great Comberton, Pershore, Worcs. WR10 3DP England | **Phone:** 44 (0) 1386 710317 | **Email:** admin@hardy-plant.org.uk | **Web:** www.hardy-plant.org/uk

About 40 years ago a group of gardeners and nurserymen got together to conserve older, rarer, and unusual plants and to make them more available to gardeners. Today, 12,000 members around the globe enjoy a wide range of activities for the enthusiastic "hardy planter." Members receive two issues of the full-color, substantive, and collectible journal, *The Hardy Plant*, three newsletters, a seed list and book list, workshops, and tours. This gives North American members access to *many, many* specialty study groups, for which the payment of an additional fee provides a newsletter/bulletin and often a very good seed exchange. Examples include the Correspondents Group (for far-flung gardeners), Hardy Geranium Group, Peony Group, Pulmonaria Group, Half Hardy Group, Variegated Plant Group, and more.

ROYAL HORTICULTURAL SOCIETY

Membership Department, 80 Vincent Square, London SW1P 2PE England | **Email:** info@rhs.org.uk | **Web:** www.rhs.org.uk

As a member of this venerable society, you can enjoy many benefits. The RHS was founded in 1804 and has grown to be the world's leading horticultural organization, with 300,000 members. Benefits of membership include free gardening advice from the RHS experts, free entry for you and a guest to the magnificent RHS gardens (there are four, including Wisley in Surrey and Harlow Carr in North Yorkshire), and free entry to 80 beautiful gardens across Britain and 20 in Belgium and France. Members also receive a monthly copy of *The Garden* magazine and privileged access and discounted tickets to the RHS Flower Shows, including Chelsea, Hampton Court Palace, and at Tatton Park in Cheshire. You can also take advantage of the RHS Seed List, where you can order from the thousands of different species and varieties collected annually.

SCOTTISH ROCK GARDEN CLUB

See entry under "Alpine / Rock Gardens" above

WORLD FEDERATION OF ROSE SOCIETIES

See entry under "Roses" above.

MARTY WINGATE:

"YOU SAY COTTON-EASTER, I SAY co-TON-E-ASTER"

As if we were about to get a tooth pulled without novocaine, most of us are led kicking and screaming into the world of botanical Latin. Give us flowers, give us trees, just don't give us *Metasequoia glyptostroboides*. Botanical names are difficult to learn, hard to pronounce, and taxonomists keep changing them anyway, so why should we learn them? Here's a reason—in fact, here are several: cherry laurel, spurge laurel, mountain laurel, Portuguese laurel, and California laurel; crape myrtle, wax myrtle, ground myrtle, and box-leaf myrtle. Are any of these laurels? Are any myrtles? Not a one.

Botanical Latin is a universal language. Gardeners can go anywhere in the world—even someplace like New York—and converse in plants without trying to figure out that kiss-me-at-the-gate is a regional name for the *herb saponaria*. And I don't even want to know why some people call *Campsis radicans* "cow itch."

The words in plant names can describe a quality ("mollis" means soft, like the leaves of *Alchemilla mollis*), or they can be clues to what the plant looks like—such as the heart-shaped leaves of *Tilia cordata*. They can be named for a person (the genus *Fuchsia* is named after Leonhart Fuchs), or after a place (*Oxalis oregana* is native to Oregon). But don't assume too much. I once thought *Cornus florida* meant that the Eastern dogwood came from that very state. In fact, "florida" means profusely flowering.

When we talk about plants, we use their family, genus, species, and cultivar names. The family name ends with "aceae." For example, Asteraceae is the name of the composite (daisy) family. The inevitable exception to this rule is that some taxonomists refuse to go along with the standardized ending, and continue to use the old names of families. That's why you may see Asteraceae written as Compositae.

The two-word plant name—genus and specific epithet—is referred to as a "binomial." In the binomial *Cornus kousa*, *Cornus* is the genus, and *kousa* is the specific epithet. *Prunus* (plums, cherries) and *Crataegus* (hawthorns) are two genera (plural) in the rose family (Rosaceae). Occasionally, a family will have only one genus: *Ginkgo biloba* is the only member of Ginkgoaceae.

The genus of a family of plants is divided into smaller groups called species. The genus *Rosa* is made up of many species—for example, our native Nootka rose (*R. nutkana*), and *R. mulliganii*, named for Brian O. Mulligan, former director of the Washington Park Arboretum.

When groups of a species are different, but not enough to make them into entirely new species, they are split into varieties or subspecies. The shore pine, *Pinus contorta* var. *contorta* and the lodgepole pine, *P. contorta* var. *latifolia*, are two extremely different-looking examples of this species.

A hybrid is a cross between two species. Some hybrids occur naturally (*Arctostaphylos* x *media* is a cross between *A. uva-ursi*, or kinnikinnik, and *A. columbiana*). Some crosses are done on purpose to get a better plant (bigger flowers, redder tomatoes). The "x" indicates the plant is a hybrid, although sometimes that clue is left off. Rarely, two genera will cross. The popular leyland cypress is a cross between *Cupressus macrocarpa* (the Monterrey cypress) and *Chamaecyparis nootkatensis* (the Alaskan cedar). In the name of the plant that results, the "x" is placed before the genus (showing there's been a combination of the two genera), as in x *Cupressocyparis leylandii*.

What about 'Peace', 'Stella d'Oro', and all those other names we really use? Those are names of cultivars—selected forms that occur naturally or from hybridization. Cultivar names are written in plain text with single quotes around the word.

There's no denying that the whole subject is ripe for parody. The Douglas fir (*Pseudotsuga menziesii*) has had a total of nineteen different names since it was collected by Archibald Menzies during Captain Vancouver's 1791–95 voyage. Recently, our dear garden mums were switched from *Chrysanthemum* to *Dendranthema* (a change that actually occurred more than thirty-five years ago). But after an outcry from gardeners, it was changed it back—so they are *Chrysanthemum* after all.

Certainly the most fun with botanical names must be found in Edward Lear's *The Complete Nonsense Book* (New York: Dodd, Mead & Co., 1912). Here is where we find drawings such as the one of a delicate, pendulous bloom of what looks like a bleeding heart—where, instead of pink hearts, there's a string of people with their feet tied

to the stem (ahh, it is, of course, *Manypeeplia upsidownia*), and another with the triangular porcine bloom of *Piggiwiggia pyramidalis*.

Look up a few plant names—plants you have in your garden—and practice saying them to anyone who will listen ("Here is my *Rosmarinus officinalis*—that means rosemary was used as a medicinal herb by the Romans, you know."). Practice saying them to the cat. Practice saying them to imaginary visitors. Start dropping the names in casual conversation ("I've so enjoyed my *Parthenocissus henryana* this year!"). It won't take long before you are hooked.

When she isn't trying to convince people that botanical nomenclature is fun and putting us all to shame, **Marty Wingate** writes for national and local publications, including the Thursday garden section of the *Seattle Post-Intelligencer*. She also writes for *Horticulture* and *Garden Showcase*. Marty has a master's degree in urban horticulture from the University of Washington *chapter* 3

EDUCATIONAL OPPORTUNITIES

Degree Programs

Study Weekends

Workshops & Classes

Lecture Series

I must have been four or five years old when I discovered my mother's garden. Past the tomatoes and behind the cucumbers was a tangle of snap pea plants. When I realized what they were, I plopped down in the dirt and popped as many peas as I could find into my mouth. When my mom found me covered with dirt and happily munching away, she decided it was time for my formal introduction to gardening. Out came the Fisher-Price spade and a little packet of seeds. I don't remember what we planted that first day, but I distinctly remember Mom showing me how to make rows in the soil and pat the seeds into place.

That was my first gardening class, kneeling in the dirt with Mom and my plastic shovel. Many amateur gardeners have had similar introductions to the world of horticulture and similarly informal continuing education. There's no substitute for getting your hands dirty when it comes to learning the ins and outs of the garden, but venturing out of the backyard and into a classroom every once in a while can be enormously enlightening.

When I first moved to the Northwest, much of what I learned in my mother's Midwestern garden went right out the window. Tricks for cultivating prairie grasses and heat-loving vegetables don't do much good in our mild, wet climate. Fortunately, educational opportunities abound here to fill in such gaps.

Whether you're a newcomer or a native Northwesterner, a beginner or an accomplished gardener, there's a class out there for you. Local parks and recreation departments offer one-day classes on composting. Nurseries hold seminars on native plants. Community colleges offer courses on design. The educational resources available to the Northwest gardener are numerous and are expanding to keep up with enthusiasm.

This chapter features classes and workshops that let you pick the brains of experts, familiarize yourself with new techniques, and get to know gardeners who share your interests. They can also serve as introductions to clubs and organizations or local botanical gardens. Most importantly, they can help you reach your gardening goals—whether you want to learn to design with color or just get that troublesome perennial to thrive. After a series of weekend classes, you might even decide to take advantage of one of the many degree programs offered in the area—a far cry from plastic spades and snap peas.

—Jessica Campbell

EDUCATIONAL OPPORTUNITIES

An immense variety of formalized educational opportunities can be found in the Pacific Northwest—for the novice, veteran, or specialty gardener; for students seeking professional degrees; and for those who simply want to expand their horizons.

Degree Programs in Oregon

CLACKAMAS COMMUNITY COLLEGE
19600 S Molalla Avenue, Oregon City, OR 97045 | **Phone:** (503) 657-6958, ext. 2770 | **TTY/TDD:** (503) 650-6649 | **Web:** www.clackamas.cc.or

Certificate and degree programs offered include a horticultural certificate, horticulture associate of applied science, and agriculture one-year transfer program.

OREGON STATE UNIVERSITY
Horticulture Department, 4017 Ag and Life Sciences Building, Oregon State University, Corvallis, OR 97331-7304 | **Phone:** (541) 737-3464 | **Web:** www.oregonstate.edu/dept/hort

The undergraduate program has two options: horticultural science (for careers directly or indirectly dealing with production, breeding, postharvest handling, marketing, and scientific study of horticultural crops), and turf and landscape management. The graduate program offers master of science, doctor of philosophy, and master of agriculture degrees.

PORTLAND COMMUNITY COLLEGE
17705 NW Springville Road, Portland, OR 97229 | **Phone:** (503) 614-7255 | **Web:** www.pcc.edu

A range of courses in horticulture and landscape technology are offered at both the downtown campus and the Rock Creek Campus.

UNIVERSITY OF OREGON
Department of Landscape Architecture, 5234 University of Oregon, Eugene, OR 97431-5234 | **Phone:** (541) 346-3634 | **Fax:** (541) 346-3626 | **Web:** darkwing.uoregon.edu/~landarch

The five-year program leads to a bachelor of landscape architecture degree, combining general preparation in the arts and sciences with a focus on environmental design studies. The goal is to produce a visually literate and environmentally responsible citizen capable of playing a professional role in the evolving landscape.

Degree Programs in Washington

UNIVERSITY OF WASHINGTON
College of Forest Resources, Box 354115, Seattle, WA 98195 | **Phone:** (206) 543-8616

Degrees offered include bachelor of science; master of science and master of forest resources; and doctor of philosophy in environmental horticulture, public horticulture, and urban forestry. Dr. Linda Chalker-Scott, academic advisor, can be reached at (206) 685-2595 or lindacs@u.washington.edu.

CLOVER PARK TECHNICAL COLLEGE
4500 Steilacoom Boulevard SW, Tacoma, WA 98499-4098 | **Phone:** (253) 589-5800 | **Web:** www.cptc.ctc.edu/cptc/

Certificate programs include retail floral marketing and greenhouse/nursery operation. An associate degree in applied technology in landscape management and golf course management is also offered.

EDMONDS COMMUNITY COLLEGE
20000 68th Avenue W, Lynnwood, WA 98036 | **Phone:** (425) 640-1739 | **Web:** www.edcc.edu

Edmonds Community College offers one-year certificates in general horticulture and horticultural therapy, as well as a grower's certificate. Also offered are two-year degrees in nursery specialization, landscape management, landscape installation, and landscape design, with day, evening, and summer courses offered. The horticultural therapy program offers students a one-year certificate. The school's goal is to offer students hands-on field experience while providing an excellent learning environment in the classroom. For example, Carrie Becker (of the highly-praised Bellevue Botanical Garden/Northwest Perennial Alliance design–installation–maintenance team) teaches a class using the BBG's extensive perennial borders as an on-site classroom.

LAKE WASHINGTON TECHNICAL COLLEGE
11605 132nd Avenue NE, Kirkland, WA 98034 | **Phone:** (425) 739-8356 | **Fax:** (425) 739-8298 | **Email:** Don.Marshall@lwtc.ctc.edu | **Web:** www.lwtc.ctc.edu/

Lake Washington Technical College offers both a certificate and an associate of applied science program, providing broad exposure in the field of horticulture. Coursework includes a combination of classroom instruction and hands-on experience. The emphasis encourages stewardship of the environment. The program networks with members of the horticultural industry to broaden students' experience and to provide exposure to varied opportunities. The program is self-sufficient through plant sales each spring prior to Mother's Day. (See Chapter 7, "Plant Sales," and Chapter 13, "Gardens to Visit.")

SOUTH PUGET SOUND COMMUNITY COLLEGE

2011 Mottman Road SW, Olympia, WA 98512 | **Phone:** (360) 754-7711, ext. 5219 or 5594 | **Web:** www.spscc.ctc.edu

The horticultural technology program at this two-year school provides a broad-based knowledge of horticulture principles, combined with hands-on experience. The college loans the students $4,000 in operating capital in a plant sales course. The students make the decisions on how to spend the money, what to grow, then manage the growing, and offer an annual plant sale, gaining valuable technical and promotional skills in this innovative program.

SOUTH SEATTLE COMMUNITY COLLEGE

6000 16th Avenue SW, Seattle, WA 98106-1499 | **Phone:** (206) 764-5336, ext. 219 | **Web:** www.sccd.ctc.edu/south/

The landscape horticulture program offers a one-year certificate, a two-year associate of applied science degree, and training toward industry certifications. Specializations include design/build, landscape management, and horticultural studies. The SSCC Arboretum is an important part of the landscape horticulture program. As part of their studies, students use the Arboretum as a laboratory for design and construction projects, plant identification, arboriculture, irrigation, and landscape management courses. The program facilities also include a retail garden center, a new greenhouse, and a large cold-frame structure, which are used by the students to propagate, grow, and market plants.

CLARK COLLEGE

Web: www.clark.edu

The Clark College website (Clark College is located in Vancouver, B.C.) features convenient links to other community colleges in Washington.

Scholarships

Many sources of financial aid are available, including internship programs. The best place to learn more about these is the school in which you are interested. It will surprise you how much funding is available! If you are in school, or are planning to attend a program, contact your department for more information on scholarships early in the application process. Many departments keep a notebook of funding sources. Some notable scholarships include:

* The Elisabeth C. Miller Memorial Scholarship, awarded by the Northwest Horticultural Society each spring to one or several deserving students in the field

of urban horticulture or landscape architecture; call (206) 547-1794.

* A scholarship sponsored by the Washington State Nursery and Landscape Association for students in horticulture; call (253) 863-4482, or email wsnla@nwrain.com.

* A scholarship sponsored by the Garden Writers Association of America for students interested in garden and horticultural writing; call (703) 257-1032 or email AssnCtr@idsonline.com. Also for students interested in garden and horticultural writing, there is a scholarship sponsored by the Garden Writers Foundation; call (703) 257-1032 or see www.gwaa.org/gwf/.

* The Washington Association of Landscape Professionals (WALP) awards a number of scholarships to students enrolled in community college landscape horticulture programs in Washington; call (800) 833-2186 or (425) 385-3333, or see www.walp.org.

* The Association for Women in Horticulture sponsors the Leah Moussaioff Memorial Scholarship for students working toward a certificate or degree in an area of horticulture, at a post high school program. Candidates must either be Washington residents or enrolled in a program at a Washington State institution. Application forms are distributed in April and due in June. For information, write: Scholarship Committee, AWH, P.O. Box 75093, Seattle, WA 98125-0093, or email: scholarship@awhort.org.

CLASSES AND WORKSHOPS

Many free or nearly free classes are offered throughout the region, in almost every community, large and small. Here are some ideas of places to watch for opportunities.

* Most community colleges offer community education and continuing education classes. One advantage is that they are usually evening or weekend offerings.

* Master Gardeners earn "pay-back" hours in various public-information forums, including clinics and classes, workshops, and seminars. Just pick up the phone, call your local office, and ask what is on the agenda for the season. (Early spring is the best time to call.) Find phone numbers in Chapter 1, "Organizations That Help Gardeners."

* Chapter 4, "Northwest Native Plants," lists classes, workshops, and seminars. Nurseries and garden centers offer workshops that relate to the season, including the big holidays. Request to have your name added to their mailing lists to receive the newsletter and watch your local newspaper for class announcements. Some will be more substantive than others. Let's face it— these free classes are often the incentive (although not always the only one) they offer to get you to come in to the nursery. See the entries in Chapter 5, "Nurseries," for those offering classes, workshops, and seminars.

* Many parks and recreation departments offer gardening or horticultural classes seasonally. Some are offered as evening talks or as weekend workshops. Call your local office for their schedule.

* Plant societies offer many workshops and lectures, and a few sponsor major lecture series. Some of the more substantive programs are listed in this chapter, but also have a look through the entries in Chapter 2, "Clubs, Societies & Volunteer Opportunities."

* Public gardens often sponsor specific classes or a series of them. Several are listed in this chapter.

Also, check your local newspaper gardening calendars for notice of educational events, including the following calendars:

* *Garden Showcase*, a monthly magazine with subscribers in Oregon and Washington, gives an extensive listing of classes, events, guided walks, and seminars. You can often find this publication at specialty nurseries; (800) 322-8541 or www.gardenshowcase.com.

* Miller Horticultural Library, Center for Urban Horticulture, Seattle, Bulletin Board and staff; (206) 543-0415 or www.millerlibrary.org.

* *Northwest Garden News*, a free monthly tabloid distributed in western Washington, provides a calendar of classes, events, and plant sales in Washington; (206) 725-2394 or norwesgard@earthlink.net.

* *The* (Portland) *Oregonian* gives gardening information in Thursday and weekend editions, and on its website, www.oregonlive.com.

* *Seattle Post-Intelligencer*; see the Thursday gardening section.

* *Seattle Homes & Lifestyles*; see "Garden Planner" or website at www.seattlehomesmag.com.

* *The Seattle Times*; see the Friday and weekend editions.

* *The Herald* (Everett, WA); see the Thursday Home & Garden section.

Classes and Workshops in Oregon

BARBARA BLOSSOM ASHMUN

Creative Garden Design, 8560 SW Fairway Drive, Portland, OR 97225 | **Phone:** (503) 297-1307 | **Email:** barbarablossom@earthlink.net

Contact knowledgeable, amicable garden designer, author, and lecturer Barbara Ashmun for her class schedule and open garden dates. Specialized workshops in the garden can be custom designed especially for your group.

BERRY BOTANIC GARDEN

11505 SW Summerville Avenue, Portland, OR 97219-8309 | **Phone:** (503) 636-4112 | **Email:** bbg@agora.rdrop.com | **Web:** www.berrybot.org

Berry Botanic Garden offers a variety of botanical and horticultural classes. Registration for classes and workshops is accepted by mail, in person, and by telephone (except tour registration). The garden's website has a comprehensive list and a printable registration form. Request a newsletter for classes and events. (See Chapter 12, "Flower and Garden Shows, Festivals & Events," and Chapter 13, "Gardens to Visit.")

CONNIE HANSEN GARDEN

1931 NW 33rd Street, Lincoln City, OR 97367-0776 | **Phone:** (541) 994-6338 | **Mailing address:** PO Box 776, Lincoln City, OR 97367-0776 | **Web:** www.conniehansengarden.com

Classes are free to garden members (except Japanese Flower Arranging); $5 for non-members.

HARDY PLANT SOCIETY OF OREGON

1930 NW Lovejoy Street | Portland, OR 97209 | (503) 224-5718 | **Email:** admin@hardyplantsociety.org | **Web:** www.hardyplantsociety.org

With a membership of more than 2,000 hardy souls, the Hardy Plant Society manages to sponsor quite an enviable lecture program, drawing speakers from near and far. Join the society, and you'll get the newsletter announcing lectures and symposiums. Some events are open to the public, while others are for members only.

HOYT ARBORETUM

4000 SW Fairview Boulevard, Portland, OR 97221 | **Phone:** (503) 228-8733 | **Web:** www.hoytarboretum.org

The visitors center is open from 9 a.m. to 3 p.m. most days. There is an automated voice mail system through which you can receive information on classes, workshops, and guided tours. You can also request a newsletter. The arboretum also offers many programs for children. Preregistration is required for most classes.

LEACH BOTANICAL GARDEN

6704 SE 122nd Avenue, Portland, OR 97214 | **Phone:** (503) 761-9503 | **Web:** www.portlandparks.org/Parks/LeachBotanicalGar.htm

Call the garden to request a listing of offerings. Preregistration is required, space in classes is limited. Members receive a discount on fees. Grade-specific outdoor classes are organized to introduce students to a variety of horticultural topics. The Johnson Creek Program is a knowledge-packed, hands-on classroom program for learning about plants, animals, birds, fish, and the challenges of water quality in Johnson Creek. Garden staff can bring a "suitcase" version of each of the programs to the classroom. These one-hour programs utilize slides, plants, and discussion to give students an experience similar to the one they would enjoy at the garden. Watch for the annual Nature Fair in August, where you will find many activities—from making leaf prints to learning about bugs in the garden.

LUCY HARDIMAN

Perennial Partners, 1234 SE 18th Avenue, Portland, OR 97214 | **Phone:** (503) 231-0025 | **Fax:** (503) 231-0326 | **Email:** Fredalu@aol.com

A well-known and highly respected garden designer and writer, who is often on the lecture circuit, Lucy Hardiman also offers a program of classes. Topics include gardening in containers (a subject she is justly famous for), color and fragrance in the winter garden, bodacious borders, small-garden design, vertical gardening, and designing with color. Request a copy of Lucy's class list for dates and times.

METRO BUREAU OF ENVIRONMENTAL SERVICES

Metro Regional Center, 600 NE Grand Avenue, Portland, OR 97232-2736 | **Phone:** (503) 234-3000 | **Email:** mri@metro.dst.or.us | **Web:** www.metro-region.org

Metro offers a variety of garden workshops, including several on composting. Call for a current schedule of topics.

MOUNT PISGAH ARBORETUM

33735 Seavy Loop Road, Eugene, OR 97405 | **Education office:** (541) 747-1504 | **Web:** www.efn.org/~mtpisgah/educate.htm

The arboretum's outdoor education program is the largest and longest-running outdoor science education program in the county. The arboretum's 200 acres of diverse ecological habitat provide a living classroom for schoolchildren and adults in pursuit of information on the topics of forest ecology, wetlands, and waterways. Spring nature walks introduce lichens and mosses, spring wildflowers, and plant identification. Weekend workshop topics include natural history, ethnobotany, nature photography, and papermaking with native plants. A three-day spring botany workshop covers biological terminology, scientific names, and plant family characteristics. Learn to key plants and learn about the relationship between floral elements and ecological requirements.

PORTLAND STATE UNIVERSITY

School of Extended Studies, Summer Session, Box 1491, Portland, OR 97207 | **Phone:** (503) 725-3276 | **Fax:** (503) 725-4840 | **Email:** register@ses.pdx.edu | **Web:** www.extended.pdx.edu

Portland State sponsors some gardening-related continuing education through their Haystack Program at Cannon Beach. Check for upcoming lectures listed on the website. Each fall, the program sponsors *Horticulture Magazine*'s gardening program, a daylong symposium with several speakers.

TUALATIN HILLS NATURE PARK

15655 SW Millikan Boulevard, Beaverton, OR 97006 | **Phone:** (503) 644-5595

This 200-plus acre lowland forest makes an ideal classroom for active and curious youngsters, and there are many opportunities for kids to take supervised educational walks in the company of knowledgeable staff trained to zero-in on the incredible diversity of life every-

where along the trails and waterways. The programs are organized by age groups.

Classes and Workshops in Washington

BELLEVUE BOTANICAL GARDEN

12001 Main Street, Bellevue, WA 98015-4536 | **Phone:** (425) 451-3755 | **Mailing address:** PO Box 40536 Bellevue, WA 98015 | **Web:** www.bellevuebotanical.org

Call for a schedule of offerings and visit this place with beautiful and educational perennial borders.

CENTER FOR URBAN HORTICULTURE

3501 NE 41st Street, Seattle, WA 98105 | **Phone:** (206) 685-8033 | **Mailing address:** PO Box 354115, Seattle, WA 98195-4115 | **Email:** access@u.washington.edu | **Web:** www.urbanhort.org

Of all the offerings of gardening and related educational opportunities in the Seattle area, this is the hot spot. Request a copy of the snazzy, jam-packed quarterly newsletter, *Urban Horticulture Presents*, which has all the CUH programs, gardening and horticulture classes, as well as those held at Washington Park Arboretum. The lecture schedules for the Northwest Horticultural Society and news from the Miller Library and the CUH are also included. You'll find a breathtaking array of lectures, classes, workshops, daylong symposiums, walks, field trips around the Northwest, and guided garden tours abroad. To request disability accommodation contact the office of the ADA coordinator at least ten days before the event: (206) 543-6450 (voice), (206) 543-6452 (TDD).

FUNGI PERFECTI

PO Box 7634, Olympia, WA 98507 | **Phone:** (360) 426-9292 | **Email:** mycomedia@aol.com | **Web:** www.fungi.com

The Stamets Seminars are in-depth workshops in mushroom cultivation, utilizing tissue culture, spawn generation techniques, substrate preparation, inoculation techniques, and strategies for maximizing yields. Each participant receives seven select mushroom strains for their unrestricted use.

GARDENING GETAWAYS

3626 41st Avenue W, Seattle, WA 98199 | **Phone:** (206) 285-1143 | **Fax:** (206) 282-0297 | **Web:** www.gardeninggetaways.com

Cindy Combs has put together a brilliant idea: gloves-on gardening escapes set at bed-and-breakfasts, working alongside a professional in the process of installing a garden on site. These are three-day, two-night workshops that typically include design basics, bed preparation, plant selection, planting, mulching, paths, ornamentation, and a discussion of ongoing maintenance.

HERONSWOOD NURSERY, LTD.

7530 NE 288th Street, Kingston, WA 98346-9502 | **Phone:** (360) 297-4172 | **Fax:** (360) 297-8321 | **Web:** www.heronswood.com

The Heronswood catalog carries the year's listing of classes and events and is usually distributed by early January. A

full list of classes is also available on the website. Also offered are private classes customized for your needs.

HIGHLINE COMMUNITY COLLEGE

S 240th and Pacific Highway S, Des Moines, WA 98198-9800 | **Phone:** (206) 878-3710 | **Mailing address:** PO Box 98000 Des Moines, WA 98198 | **Web:** www.highline.ctc.edu

Landscaping classes are offered through the Center for Extended Learning.

MASTER GARDENERS

See Chapter 1, "Organizations That Help Gardeners," for the Master Gardener groups that offer lectures, workshops, and related events.

NORTHWEST HORTICULTURAL SOCIETY

PO Box 354115, Seattle, WA 98195-4115 | **Phone:** (206) 527-1794 | **Web:** www.northwesthort.org

This venerable organization puts on a top-notch lecture series each year at the Center for Urban Horticulture and offers workshops throughout the year.

NORTH CASCADES INSTITUTE

2105 Highway 20, Sedro-Woolley, WA 98284 | **Phone:** (360) 856-5700, ext. 209 | **Email:** nci@ncascades.org | **Web:** www.ncascades.org

This nonprofit educational organization offers year-round field seminars that may be of interest to Northwest gardeners and naturalists. Request a catalog. Scholarships are available in the following categories: low-income, minority, teachers, pre-service teacher education, students, environmental educators in non-formal settings, and conservation professionals. Academic credit is available through Western Washington University.

PACIFIC RIM BONSAI COLLECTION

Weyerhaeuser Company, PO Box 9777, Federal Way, WA 98063-9777 | **Phone:** (253) 924-3153 | **Web:** www.weyerhaeuser.com

Guided tours are offered Sundays at noon; introductory bonsai lectures are offered alternate Sundays from May through September.

PLANTAMNESTY

PO Box 15377, Seattle, WA 98115-0377 | **Phone:** (206) 783-9813 | **Web:** www.plantamnesty.org

The organization most frequently turned to for information and education in tree pruning and care is Plant Amnesty. Classes are tailored for both professionals and the public, and founder Cass Turnbull maintains an active schedule teaching workshops all around the region. The newsletter and website list not only PlantAmnesty's own offerings but relevant classes sponsored by other organizations as well.

SEATTLE TILTH

4649 Sunnyside Avenue N, Room 1, Seattle, WA 98103-6900 | **Phone:** (206) 633-0451 | **Fax:** (206) 633-0450 | **Email:** tilth@seattletilth.org | **Web:** www.seattletilth.org

Lots of classes and workshops are offered for the urban organic gardener on a wide variety of topics taught in the spring and fall by many well-respected local gardeners. School field trips and summer classes for children complete Tilth's lineup. Preregistration is required. Most activities have a nominal fee; request a catalog.

THE TACOMA NATURE CENTER

1919 South Tyler Street, Tacoma, WA 98405 | **Phone:** (253) 591-6439 | **Email:** tnc@tacomaparks.com

This educational facility of the Metropolitan Park District of Tacoma offers a variety of environmental- and wildlife-related in-school programs, as well as field-trip opportunities. A number of videos adapted to use in the classroom are available, and the center offers teacher training workshops. While much of what the center concentrates on is more fauna than flora, teaching children about backyard and urban habitat, wetlands, watersheds, endangered species, and human impact on the environment will carry over to gardening-related applications.

WASHINGTON PARK ARBORETUM

PO Box 358010, Seattle, WA 98195 | **Phone:** (206) 543-8800 | **Fax:** (206) 325-8893 | **Web:** www.wparboretum.org

Educational Programs for kids or adults can be arranged with three weeks' advanced registration by calling the above number. Free tours of the arboretum depart from Graham Visitor Center Saturdays and Sundays at 1 p.m. There are no tours on holidays or Husky home-game Saturdays, and no tours in December. Call ahead to make sure the regularly scheduled tour will take place, or call to arrange a tour for your club, senior center, community center, or organization. The 60- to 90-minute guided walk is available daily from 10 a.m. to 3 p.m. The cost is $15 per group of 15 people or $10 per group of 15 for Arboretum Foundation members. The Arboretum Plant Study Program is a year-round series focused on varying sets of trees, shrubs, vines, and ground covers in the Washington Park Arboretum, including fieldwork in plant identification and discussions on plant selection, placement, and function within the urban environment. At least 20 plants each session will be studied over the year, Saturdays, from 9 a.m. to 12:30 p.m., with no repeats over the series, for a total of 240 plants! Instructors include the likes of Scott Conner, Randall Hitchin, and Eric Gay. The Arboretum Foundation Nature Crafts is a hands-on opportunity to create plant-related projects, under the direction of the Arboretum Foundation Nature Crafts Study Group and Education Committee. Preregistration is required. Call (206) 726-1954. A number of programs sponsored by the Arboretum Foundation teach youth and their families about nature.

The Youth Education Programs Guide is published twice a year and is free.

Explorer Packs (backpacks with field equipment, activity lists, and background information) are available to families and groups with children in kindergarten through eighth grade. The Arboretum has four Explorer Pack themes: Tree-tectives, Marsh Madness, Autumn Adventures, and Signs of Spring. Call to reserve a pack (two-hour check-out period). There are no longer any restrictions on when these packs can be checked out. Explorer Packs are $15 for a two-hour rental and suit groups of 15 to 30 kids. Family Packs are $5 for a two-hour rental and are suitable for groups of five or less. Family Packs have two themes: Family Tree, and Wetland Wonders. In addition to the Saplings Program, a series of pre-planned, grade-specific field trips, the arboretum offers planning assistance for self-guided field trips.

WOODLAND PARK ZOO

5500 Phinney Avenue N, Seattle, WA 98103-5897 | **Phone:** (206) 684-4800 | **TDD:** (206) 684-4026 | **Web:** www.zoo.org

See the zoo through the eyes of a horticulturist. Check the website, call, or email scott.shane@zoo.org.

chapter 4

NORTHWEST NATIVE PLANTS

Native plants continue to be prominent on the topic list when gardeners gather. Anyone with an interest in restoring property (or creating a new garden) with plants that feel at home in the region will now have a much easier time tracking down those plants in nursery catalogs, finding books specializing in the subject, or seeing native plants in the flesh at public gardens and nurseries.

Plants that have been seen only "in the wild" (whether that was an abandoned lot or along a hiking trail) are now spotlighted in shade gardens and backyard borders, while owners proudly talk about the advantages of their drought tolerance, easy care, and the tasteful way they blend with the natural environment.

No one in the Pacific Northwest introduces us to the rich palette of garden-worthy native plants more eloquently than Dr. Arthur Kruckeberg, through his scholarly yet affable book, *Gardening with Native Plants of the Pacific Northwest* (University of Washington Press, 1996). He has been a major influence and a strong advocate for the greater appreciation and use of our indigenous herbaceous and woody perennials, trees, and shrubs in cultivated settings.

But in deciding just how to accomplish this integration of native and not-so-native, one must weigh a number of important factors. For one thing, remember that within this region we are blessed with many microclimates that create widely divergent habitats. The nursery trade is often guilty of painting an entire collection of Northwest native plants with a single brushstroke, without designating the particular niche from which their offerings have come.

What's essential is to consider the natural conditions from which such plants are taken when deciding where and how to use them in a garden. The popular misconception that natives are inherently easier to care for must be dispelled, considering that once such plants are placed in a cultivated location they are already on "foreign soil." A garden is a garden, and by definition the gardener has intervened—henceforth the results flow from good judgment, skill, and luck.

Another thing to keep in mind is that before most plants are able to survive in the garden a period of nurturing is necessary to establish strong roots—and native plants are no exception. It is often thought that native plants are somehow "tougher" because of their ability to take care of themselves in nature under great restraints. But be prepared to find natives unwilling to make the transition into cushier quarters. This is another good reason to read Dr. K's book, because he relates conditions under which native plants will happily adapt, as well as noting which plants are best enjoyed in the wild.

—Sharon Wootton

ORGANIZATIONS, FOUNDATIONS, AND SOCIETIES

If you are interested in joining a club or society that specializes in a particular type of native plant, look in Chapter 2, "Clubs, Societies & Volunteer Opportunities," under the following headings for listings and descriptions:

❀ Alpines / Rock Gardens

❀ Butterfly Gardening

❀ Ferns

❀ Mushrooms

❀ Natives / Wildflowers

❀ Wildflowers / Naturescaping

NORTH AMERICAN ROCK GARDEN SOCIETY

PO Box 67, Millwood, NY 10546 | **Web:** www.nargs.org

A very extensive seed list (including wild-collected and garden-collected seeds) is available to members.

BACKYARD GARDENER WEBSITE

www.backyardgardener.com

Duncan McAlpine is the webfather here, and he offers extensive alpine and rock garden content and scads of excellent links to organizations worldwide. There's more than alpine meadows and rocks at Backyard Gardener,

which includes comments by columnists and sections on a variety of gardening challenges.

NATURESCAPING AND NATIVE PLANT STEWARDSHIP

Many established gardening programs teach the importance of enhancing, restoring, and preserving bird and wildlife habitat in harmony with the built and cultivated environment that surrounds our homes, businesses, and institutions. Whether your outdoor space is as restricted as a balcony or encompasses several acres, the decisions you make can benefit an amazing variety of birds and beasts, from butterflies and hummingbirds to bats and migratory songbirds.

BERRY BOTANIC GARDEN

11505 SW Summerville Avenue, Portland, OR 97219 | **Phone:** (503) 636-4112 | **Email:** bbg@rdrop.com | **Web:** www.berrybot.org

The garden maintains stored seeds of approximately 50 of the region's most rare and endangered taxa as part of the Center for Plant Conservation National Collection. They maintain samples of over two hundred more taxa, many of which are locally or regionally rare or endangered, but more common elsewhere. For the serious native plant student, the BBG participates in the Partners for Plants program. In conjunction with the Portland Garden Club, Gifford Pinchot National Forest, and Portland State University, for several years they have organized two intensive one-week sessions during which participants stay in the field and get hands-on experience in conducting a monitoring study or other projects of real conservation value. The program changes from year to year so check early in the year for current information.

CASCADE BIOMES, INC.

PO Box 22419, Seattle, WA 98122-0419 | **Phone:** (206) 322-0528 | **Email:** biomes@earthlink.net

This group educates home owners and landscape professionals about proper use of native plants in the urban landscape. (See "Literature" in Chapter 10 for the Native Plant Alliance book, *A Manual of Native Plant Communities for Urban Areas of the Pacific Northwest*, and Chapter 7, "Plant Sales.")

KING COUNTY SMALL HABITAT RESTORATION PROGRAM

King County Dept. of Natural Resources, Seattle, WA | **Phone:** (206) 296-8736 | **Web:** http://dnr.metrokc.gov/wtd/shrp/

The staff can help you design a native plant buffer, including advice on whether permits are required (say, if you are working near a stream). The program builds low-cost projects that enhance and restore streams and wetlands. Ask for the handy brochure, *Go Native! A Guide to Creating Your Own Native Plant Buffer.*

NATIONAL WILDLIFE FEDERATION

11100 Wildlife Center Drive, Reston, VA 20190 | **Phone:** (800) 822-9919 | **E-mail:** info@nwf.org | **Web:** www.nwf.org/habitats

Offers a backyard wildlife habitat protection program.

NATIONAL WILDLIFE FEDERATION NORTHWEST FIELD OFFICE

418 First Avenue W, Seattle, WA 98119 | **Phone:** (206) 285-8707 | **Email:** salmon@nwf.org

NATIVE PLANT SALVAGE PROGRAM, KING COUNTY DEPARTMENT OF NATURAL RESOURCES

(206) 296-1923, to volunteer to help salvage plants | **Web:** splash.metrokc.gov/wlr/pi/salvage.htm

Volunteers in King County are rescuing native plants from sites slated for development for use in revegetation projects (to restore stream banks, wetlands, and buffer areas near a variety of capital improvement and road projects). The website provides a very detailed blueprint for others wishing to follow this exemplary land stewardship program. If you have a site from which plants need a rescuing hand, call (206) 296-8065.

NATIVE PLANT SOCIETY OF OREGON

Contact: Jan Dobak, Membership Chair, 2584 NW Savier Street, Portland, OR 97210-2412 | **Web:** www.npsoregon.org

Statewide issue committees focus on rare and endangered species, conservation, legislation, education, and landscaping with natives. Issues include the use of native plants in government, commercial, and private landscaping and restoration projects, providing public education, and finding ways to meet the challenge of protecting wild populations against inappropriate exploitation.

THE NATURE CONSERVANCY

4245 N Fairfax Drive, Suite 100, Arlington VA 22203 | **Phone:** (800) 628-6860 | **Web:** www.tnc.org

This venerable international organization preserves plants, animals, and natural communities representing the diversity on Earth by protecting the lands and waters they need to survive. The Nature Conservancy operates the largest private system of nature sanctuaries in the world (more than 1,500 preserves in the United States alone). Some are postage-stamp size, others cover thousands of acres. All safeguard imperiled species. The Conservancy has protected more than 9 million acres of ecologically significant land, starting with a modest 60-acre land purchase in New York state in 1955. The Nature Conservancy emerged in 1951 from a professional association of ecologists seeking to turn their knowledge of nature into positive action for conservation. Your dues bring membership in the Washington chapter as well.

OREGON FLORA PROJECT

Contact: Scott Sundberg, Department of Botany and Plant Pathology, 2082 Cordley Hall, Oregon State University, Corvallis, OR 97331-2902 | **Phone:** (541) 737-4338 | **Email:** sundbers@bcc.orst.edu | **Web:** www.oregonflora.org

Coordinated by Scott Sundberg, the Oregon Flora Project is being directed from Oregon State University. To increase our scientific understanding of and public access to Oregon's native plants, the project produces a checklist, a comprehensive list of Oregon's native and naturalized plants, an Oregon Plant Atlas, distribution maps generated from an Internet-accessible database, *Flora of Oregon,* an illustrated identification manual for the plants of Oregon, and a newsletter.

WASHINGTON NATIVE PLANT SOCIETY

7400 Sand Point Way NE, Seattle, WA 98115-6302 | **Phone:** (206) 527-3210 or (888) 288-8022 | **Email:** wnps@wnps.org | **Web:** www.wnps.org

Membership brings many benefits, among which are opportunities to apply for funding of education and research projects, participation in native-plant salvage and restoration projects, and a chance to help protect threatened plants and habitats. They also run the Ivy Out program, with the goal of eradicating the invasive form of English ivy from Western Washington.

WASHINGTON NATIVE PLANT STEWARDSHIP PROGRAM

(See "Native Plant Stewardship" under "Classes and Workshops" below.)

WASHINGTON NATURAL HERITAGE PROGRAM

Washington State Department of Natural Resources, PO Box 47014, Olympia, WA 98504-7016 | **Phone:** (360) 902-1667 | **Email:** sandra.moody@wadnr.gov | **Web:** ww.wa.gov/dnr/htdocs/fr/nhp/wanhp.html

WNHP plays an important role in identifying, recording, monitoring, and safeguarding elements of natural diversity (plant communities, native species, etc.) that may lead to new medicines, disease resistance for crops, control of pests, and other benefits. As our concern for the loss of native species and their habitat grows, the need for solid scientific data and arguments for the protection of these elements is obvious. WNHP, within the Department of Natural Resources, has identified 2,330 vascular plant species in Washington, of which 451 are determined to be in imminent danger of extinction. The program publishes *Endangered, Threatened, and Sensitive Vascular Plants of Washington.* This resource serves as an excellent companion in identifying endangered, threatened, and sensitive plants.

WASHINGTON PARK ARBORETUM

University of Washington, PO Box 358010, Seattle, WA 98195-8010 | **Phone:** (206) 543-8800 | **Email:** wpa@u.washington.edu | **Web:** www.wparboretum.org

The Arboretum's 230 acres on Lake Washington hold an outstanding collection of trees and shrubs. Experienced volunteers lead 1- to 2-hour free tours every Saturday and Sunday at 1 p.m. (January-November except during Husky Saturday home games), featuring areas of seasonal interest. Meet at the Graham Visitor Center.

For organized groups, tours on various themes are available, with advance reservation and a small fee.

WASHINGTON RARE PLANT CARE AND CONSERVATION PROGRAM

At the Center for Urban Horticulture, 3501 NE 41st Street, Seattle, WA 98195 | **Phone:** Contact Sarah Reichard at (206) 543-8616, or program manager Laura Zybas at (206) 616-0780 | **Email:** reichard@u.washington.edu, or lzybas@u.washington.edu | **Web:** www.urbanhort.org or http://depts.washington.edu/rarecare/

Washington state has approximately 2,330 vascular plant species, of which about 450 are in danger. This innovative program concentrates on ex situ (off-site) conservation in the face of rapid environmental degradation and loss of habitat due to urbanization. The Center for Urban Horticulture is affiliated with the Center for Plant Conservation, based in St. Louis, Missouri. The program of native plant conservation involves propagating, growth, and then re-introduction of rare plant species back into their natural ecosystems. Call for information on becoming a volunteer.

WASHINGTON WILDLIFE BACKYARD SANCTUARY PROGRAM

Washington Department of Fish and Wildlife, 16018 Mill Creek Boulevard, Mill Creek, WA 98012 | **Phone:** (425) 775-1311. For those east of the Cascades, write N-8702 Division Street, Spokane, WA 99218 | **Web:** www.wa.gov/wdfw/wlm/byw_prog.htm

Write, please (limited staff, popular program) to request information about creating your own wildlife sanctuary garden. You will receive a packet of information about inventorying existing conditions on your property, then designing and implementing a plan ($5 check payable to WDFW if the packet is mailed, $3 if you pick it up at the office). You can subsequently apply for the Washington Department of Wildlife's Backyard Sanctuary certificate designating your property as wildlife habitat.

CLASSES AND WORKSHOPS

Below are descriptions of classes and workshops in Oregon and Washington that address Northwest native plants. For information about lecture series and additional class offerings, see Chapter 3, "Educational Opportunities."

Oregon

BERRY BOTANIC GARDEN

11505 SW Summerville Avenue, Portland, OR 97219 | **Phone:** (503) 636-4112 | **Email:** bbg@rdrop.com | **Web:** www.berrybot.org

Join the BBG and receive a discount on classes while you support their PNW plant conservation activities. There are many, many stimulating workshops, classes, tours, and other educational opportunities here, including workshops on native plants, propagation techniques, and where and how to acquire seeds and cuttings from wild and nursery-grown stock; also, take home loads of starts you can pot up from the Berry collections.

COLUMBINES AND WIZARDRY HERBS, INC.

Howie Brounstein, PO Box 50532, Eugene, OR 97405 | **Phone:** (541) 687-7114 | **Email:** howieb@teleport.com | **Web:** www.teleport.com/~howieb/howie.html

Check out this website, with its extensive list of links to wildcrafting, herbal plants, databases, and other native-plant-related sites, plus lots of information from Howie. The business offers apprenticeships (often for high school and college credit) and workshops.

HOYT ARBORETUM

4000 SW Fairview Boulevard, Portland, OR 97221 | **Phone:** (503) 228-8733 | **Web:** www.hoytarboretum.org

Explore a world of trees in the 175-acre Arboretum overlooking the Oregon Zoo. Hoyt offers more than 900 species of trees and shrubs, including one of the nation's largest conifer collections. Wander 10 miles of gentle trails. In the spring you can count on classes on wildflowers, mosses, and lichens; in the summer on native trees and shrubs, and in the fall several courses covering mushrooms. Join (get their newsletter), call for a schedule, and watch local gardening calendars.

JOHN INSKEEP ENVIRONMENTAL LEARNING CENTER

Clackamas Community College, 19600 S Molalla Avenue, Oregon City, OR 97045 | **Phone:** (503) 657-6958, ext. 2351 | **Email:** elc@clackamas.cc.or.us | **Web:** http://depts.clackamas.cc.or.us/elc/index.htm

The ELC was created within the premises of an abandoned jam cannery. The innovative environmental educational programs are aimed at teaching stewardship of the natural environment.

LEACH BOTANICAL GARDEN

6704 SE 122nd Avenue, Portland, OR 97236 | **Phone:** (503) 823-9503 | **Web:** www.parks.ci.portland.or.us; then click on Search A-Z, then "L" for Leach.

Leach Botanical Garden is committed to raising the public's understanding about and to the conservation of Pacific Northwest botany and horticulture. Many of the classes offered reflect this goal, such as "Winter Twig Identification," "Algae, Liverworts, and Mosses," and "Garden Trough Construction."

NATURESCAPING FOR CLEAN RIVERS

East Multnomah Soil and Water Conservation District, with the Portland Bureau of Environmental Services; contact Linda Robinson at (503) 797-1842 | **Email:** naturescaping@yahoo.com

Naturescaping holds free neighborhood workshops that promote native plants, natural landscaping, and water-friendly practices. Call to book a workshop that will teach you and your neighbors about integrated pest management, planting the right plant in the right place, how to deal with invasive plants, the importance of mulch and compost, the benefits of using native plants, and lots more!

Washington

BURKE MUSEUM OF NATURAL HISTORY AND CULTURE

PO Box 353010, University of Washington, Seattle, WA 98195-3010 | **Phone:** (206) 543-5590 | **Email:** recept@u.washington.edu | **Web:** burkemuseum.org/events.html.

Occasionally the Burke will hold classes and other activities related to native plants.

CENTER FOR URBAN HORTICULTURE

3501 NE 41st Street, Seattle, WA | **Phone:** (206) 543-8616 | **Web:** www.urbanhort.org | **Contact:** Sue Nicol, PO Box 354115, Seattle, WA 98195-4115

See a full listing of all the CUH/WPA events and activities in the handsome, fact-packed quarterly newsletter. Typical classes include "Native Seed Collection and Storage" and "Habitat Gardening with Native Plants." Also home to the Elisabeth C. Miller Horticultural Library.

HERONSWOOD NURSERY

7530 NE 288th Street, Kingston, WA 98346-9502 | **Phone:** (360) 297-4172 | **Email:** heronswood@silverlink.net | **Web:** www.heronswood.com

Seminars and tours are offered, some overseas, led by knowledgeable staff members ("Heronistas"), and occasionally by well-known plantsman Dan Hinkley.

NATIVE PLANT SALVAGE PROJECT

WSU Thurston County, 720 Sleater Kinney Road SE, Suite Y, Lacey WA 98503. Contact Erica Guttman for project information | **Phone:** (360) 704-7785 | **Email:** ericag@coopext.cahe.wsu

Under the auspices of the WSU Cooperative Extension, the salvage program here really has its act together. Ask for their newsletter and you'll find out about the many native plant and related classes and workshops. You'll keep up on the announcements of their plant salvage events and become inspired to join.

NATIVE PLANT STEWARDSHIP PROGRAM

Washington Native Plant Society, 7400 Sand Point Way NE, Seattle, WA 98115-6302 | **Phone:** (206) 527-3210 or (888) 288-8022 | **Email:** wnps@wnps.org | **Web:** www.wnps.org

This program provides approximately 100 hours of training emphasizing native plant ecology and conservation. Topics include native plant identification, ethnobotany, wetland plants, invasive species, landscaping with natives, and restoration. Like experts in the Master Gardener program do, Native Plant Stewards agree to provide a minimum of 100 hours of outreach, education, and work on native plant restoration projects in return for the training, which lasts 10 weeks, with meetings on Fridays from March to early May.

NATURAL CONNECTIONS

Contact: Jill Reifschneider, 14846 74th Place NE, Kenmore, Washington 98028 | **Phone:** (425) 481-4292 | **Email:** naturelinks@mindspring.com

Jill helps students plan, plant, and learn from school gardens that use Northwest native plants or provide wildlife habitat. She provides teacher training in "Project WILD," "Landscaping for Wildlife," and "Discovering Native Plant Stories" (which addresses specific Washington State Essential Academic Learning Requirements through an intimate study of plant structure and function). It's an integrated curriculum that engages students in the study of botany, ethnobotany, and the ecology of Northwest native plants.

NORTH AMERICAN ROCK GARDEN SOCIETY

Email: nargs@advinc.com | **Web:** www.nargs.org

The society, organized in 1934, is for gardening enthusiasts interested in alpine, saxatile, and low-growing perennials, and encourages the study and cultivation of wildflowers that grow well among rocks, whether such plants originate above tree line or at lower elevations. The Western Winter Study Weekends are held in late February.

NORTH CASCADES INSTITUTE

2105 State Route 20, Sedro-Woolley, WA 98284-9394 | **Phone:** (360) 856-5700, ext. 209 | **Email:** nci@ncascades.org | **Web:** www.ncascades.org

Your best bet is to ask for their catalog, which is heavy on natural history. The annual four-day Spring Naturalists Retreat is held in May, with top names in nature writing on hand. Classes range from birds to wildflowers to life in the treetops.

OLYMPIC PARK INSTITUTE

111 Barnes Point Road, Port Angeles, WA 98363 | **Phone:** (360) 928-3720 | **Email:** opi@yni.org | **Web:** www.yni.org/opi/

What an inspiring venue for students in search of the challenge of learning from knowledgeable instructors, as they address issues of the environment, flora, and fauna. Courses are fashioned for the Elderhostel program and for youth and families as well. Among topics of interest are forest ecology, natural history of the Olympic lowlands, mushrooms, alpine wildflowers, butterflies, plant families of the Olympics, and traditional plant uses. Ask for a catalog.

TACOMA NATURE CENTER

1919 S Tyler Street, Tacoma, WA 98405 | **Phone:** (253) 591-6439 | **Email:** tnc@tacomaparks.com | **Web:** www.tacomaparks.com/parks&gardens/tnc.htm

The center and its 54-acre wetland habitat offer a self-guiding booklet for the 2-mile path and plenty of opportunities to see native vegetation. Workshops are given during the annual native plant sale in October.

WASHINGTON NATIVE PLANT SOCIETY

7400 Sand Point Way NE, Seattle, WA 98115 | **Phone:** (206) 527-3210 or (888) 288-8022 | **Web:** www.wnps.org

The WNPS plays an important role in offering grant money for educational and research projects / programs related to improving our understanding of native plants. Past grants have funded *Celebrating Wildflowers*, a 220-page K-12 curriculum guide, a marvelous native plants of Washington video (see a review under "Literature" in this chapter), and teacher training workshops. Their generosity has provided for the development of native plant gardens on school grounds, teacher resource packets, and the *Watchable Wildflowers of the Columbia Basin* full-color guide (see "Literature" this chapter). Research grants are provided for the study of rare species and plant inventories. Grants have resulted in the discovery and study of native species formerly unknown in Washington. They also have a long tradition of giving to other environmental organizations whose work has a direct impact on the health and preservation of Washington's native flora. Call or check the website.

Annual **study weekends** are held for members; hikes are planned with experienced leaders who are familiar with the area and its flora.

The **Central Puget Sound Chapter** offers a valuable workshop preceding the monthly meeting on using Hitchcock's indispensable *Flora of the Pacific Northwest*. At each meeting a couple of plant species are featured. You'll learn about how to use a key in determining proper species identification. You can buy the book at the University Bookstore or at a discount at the meeting. Bring a hand lens and your enthusiasm. See the WNPS website for chapter meeting dates and location.

WASHINGTON PARK ARBORETUM

Contact: Sue Nicol, PO Box 354115, Seattle WA 98195-411 | **Phone:** (206) 543-8616 | **Web:** www.urbanhort.org or www.wparboretum.org

WPA offers many adult and youth programs through the Center for Urban Horticulture, often in the Arboretum. WPA walks are led by experienced volunteers, and begin at 1 p.m. on most Sundays. WPA also has Explorer packs—backpacks with field equipment, activity lists, and background information—for families and groups with children ages 5 to 12. Pre-registration and a small fee are required. The Saplings program introduces children to the wonderful world of plants. Other programs: Grades K-2, "Discover Plants!"; Grades 3-8, "Native Plants and People"; Grades K-8 "Wetland Ecology Walk." For registration information, call (206) 543-8801; email mravin@u.washington.edu.

NURSERIES AND PLANT / SEED SOURCES

Listed here are nurseries and seed sources that specialize in Northwest native plants. Look in "Nurseries" (Chapter 5) and "Seed Sources" (Chapter 6) for more specific details on these nurseries and about other sources that may carry natives in addition to non-native plants.

Further resources for finding native plants are:

❋ **Washington State University.** On the Web, go to http://gardening.wsu.edu/nwnative

❋ **King County Surface Water Management.** Web: http://splash.metrokc.gov/wlr/pi/npnursry.htm

❋ **Backyard Gardener.** Web: www.backyardgardener.com/nur.html. Includes links to nurseries with their own websites. (The Backyard list differs from the ones provided below because it includes lots of national and international sources.)

Oregon

BOSKEY DELL NATIVES

23311 SW Boskey Dell Lane, West Linn, OR 97068 | **Phone:** (503) 638-5945 | **Email:** boskydellnatives@aol.com

Lory Duralia specializes in native plants of Oregon; 300 different species are available seven days a week.

THE BOVEES NURSERY

1737 SW Coronado Street, Portland, OR 97219 | **Phone:** (503) 244-9341 or (800) 435-9250 | **Email:** bovees@teleport.com | **Web:** www.bovees.com

CALLAHAN SEEDS

PO Box 5531, Central Point, OR 97502 | **Street address:** 6045 Foley Lane | **Phone/Fax:** (541) 855-1164

The focal point of Callahan's is native tree and shrub seeds.

DOWN TO EARTH

532 Olive Street, Eugene, OR 97401 | **Phone:** (541) 342-6820 | **Web:** www.home2garden.com

This nursery is dedicated to environmental concerns, from its selection of native plants and drought tolerant varieties to its enormous selection of organic fertilizers, amendments, and remedies for the garden.

FORESTFARM

990 Tetherow Road, Williams, OR 97544-9599 | **Phone:** (541) 846-7269 | **Fax:** (541) 846-6963 | **Email:** forestfarm@rvi.net | **Web:** www.forestfarm.com (online ordering)

This grower is known for its enormous selection of over 6,000 kinds of native and non-native plants suitable for the Northwest, including trees, shrubs, vines, and perennials.

GOSSLER FARMS NURSERY

1200 Weaver Road, Springfield, OR 97478-9663 | **Phone:** (541) 746-3922

Be prepared to be wowed by what you see in Gossler's catalog or (if you're lucky to visit) in the series of great display gardens. Natives blend beautifully with ornamental trees and shrubs from other environs, and you'll discover interestingly named cultivars in the lineup.

GREER GARDENS

1280 Goodpasture Island Road, Eugene, OR 97401-1794 | **Phone:** (541) 686-8266 or (800) 548-0111 | **Web:** www.greergardens.com

The emphasis here is on rhododendrons, with more than 700 in the current catalog. Great display garden.

HANSEN NURSERY

PO Box 1228, North Bend, OR 97459 | **Phone:** (541) 756-1156 | **Email:** hansen.nursery@verizon.com

Plant list for $1; open by appointment. Hardy cyclamen specialist with some native bulbs.

WALLACE W. HANSEN, NURSERY & GARDENS

2158 Bower Court SE, Salem, OR 97301 | **Phone:** (503) 581-2638 | **Fax:** (503) 581-9957 | **Email:** plants@nwplants.com | **Web:** www.nwplants.com

A great selection and a 5-acre display garden filled with native plants.

OAKHILL FARMS NATIVE PLANT NURSERY

4314 Goodrich Highway, Oakland, OR 97462 | **Phone/Fax:** (541) 459-1361

Free catalog. This nursery offers 125-plus varieties of native trees, shrubs, ground covers, ferns, wildflowers, and wetland plants.

OREGON NATIVE PLANT NURSERY (FORMERLY PHEASANT VALLEY FARMS)

PO Box 886, Woodburn, OR 97071 | **Phone/Fax:** (503) 981-2353 | **Email:** dmalcolmchadwick@hotmail.com

Douglas M. Chadwick seed propagates native Oregon herbaceous perennials, representing all regions and most habitats in Oregon, including the Siskiyou and Cascade Mountains, the Columbia River Gorge, and the Willamette Valley. Free plant list.

RARE PLANT RESEARCH

13245 SE Harold Street, Portland, OR 97236 (by appointment) | **Fax:** (503) 762-0289 | **Email:** rareplant@aol.com

RUSSELL GRAHAM PURVEYOR OF PLANTS

4030 Eagle Crest Road NW, Salem, OR 97304 | **Phone:** (503) 362-1135 | **Email:** grahams@open.org | **Catalog:** $2

Gardens open by appointment. Rare and unusual Northwest and North American native plants.

SISKIYOU RARE PLANT NURSERY

2825 Cummings Road, Medford, OR 97501 | **Phone:** (541) 772-6846 | **Web:** www.siskiyourareplantnursery.com | **Catalog:** $3

A 2-acre display garden is open the first Saturday of each month. You'll be amazed at the selection of 1500 plants, including alpine natives.

SQUAW MOUNTAIN GARDENS

36212 SE Squaw Mountain Road, PO Box 946, Estacada, OR 97023 | **Phone:** (503) 630-5458 | **Fax:** (503) 630-5849 | **Email:** hennchicks@aol.com | **Web:** www.squawmountaingardens.com

Offers succulents for the rock garden.

TRILLIUM GARDENS

PO Box 803, Pleasant Hill, OR 97455 | **Phone:** (541) 937-3073 | **Email:** sales@trilliumgardens.com

Northwest natives and ornamental grasses. By appointment.

WILLOWELL NURSERY

10008 SW 60th Avenue, Portland, OR 97219 | **Phone:** (503) 245-3553 | **Email:** willowell@hevanet.com

Retail and wholesale, native plant rescue, and Naturescaping projects.

Washington

ABUNDANT LIFE SEED FOUNDATION

PO Box 772, Port Townsend, WA 98368 | **Phone:** (360) 385-5660 | **Fax:** (360) 385-7455 | **Email:** abundant@olypen.com | **Web:** www.abundantlifeseed.org

A nonprofit foundation promoting conservation and use of heirloom, Pacific Northwest native, and rare seeds. They distribute through a catalog and the World Seed Fund. Seeds are sold in retail amounts.

AUBE'S WOODLAND NURSERY

14111 Woodland Avenue, Puyallup, WA 98373 | **Phone:** (253) 841-3040

BARFOD'S HARDY FERNS

15606 Burn Road, Arlington, WA 98223-7190 | **Phone:** (360) 435-6009

BURNT RIDGE NURSERY & ORCHARDS

432 Burnt Ridge Road, Onalaska, WA 98570 | **Phone:** (360) 985-2873 | **Email:** burntridge@myhome.net

Northwest natives for the ornamental landscape.

CLOUD MOUNTAIN FARM

6906 Goodwin Road, Everson, WA 98247 | **Phone:** (360) 966-5859 | **Email:** info@cloudmountainfarm.com

Offers native plants, shrubs, ground covers, and perennials.

COLLECTOR'S NURSERY

16804 NE 102nd Avenue, Battle Ground, WA 98604 | **Phone:** (360) 574-3832 | **Email:** dianar@collectorsnursery.com | **Web:** www.collectorsnursery.com

COLVOS CREEK FARM

PO Box 1512, Vashon, WA 98070 | **Phone:** (206) 749-9508

Northwest and West Coast natives and drought-tolerant plants.

DEWILDE'S NURSERY

3410 Northwest Avenue, Bellingham, WA 98225 | **Phone:** (360) 733-8190

FANCY FRONDS

PO Box 1090, Gold Bar, WA 98251 | **Phone:** (360) 793-1472 | **Email:** judith@fancyfronds.com | **Web:** www.fancyfronds.com

Ferns, ferns, and more ferns.

FARMERS' MARKETS

Check your local farmers' markets; these events often attract native-plant growers who are not "open" for retail sales otherwise.

FOREST FLOOR RECOVERY NURSERY

Contact: Wanda Cucinotta, PO Box 89, Lummi Island, WA 98262 | **Phone:** (360) 758-2778 | **Email:** Forestflor@aol.com

The nursery contracts with the Department of Natural Resources to harvest (recover) and cultivate native and naturalized plants, shrubs, and mosses prior to logging of DNR Timber Sale land.

FROSTY HOLLOW ECOLOGICAL RESTORATION

PO Box 53, Langley, WA 98260 | **Phone:** (360) 579-2332 | **Email:** wean@whidbey.net

A native seed source with collections from southern Oregon north to central BC. For a stamped (57 cents), self-addressed, business-size envelope, they'll send a mail-order catalog.

FUNGI PERFECTI

PO Box 7634, Olympia, WA 98507 | **Phone:** (360) 426-9292 or (800) 780-9126 | **Fax:** (360) 426-9377 | **Email:** mycomedia@aol.com | **Web:** www.fungi.com

Certified organic mushroom spawn, growing kits, books, and classes.

HERONSWOOD NURSERY

7530 NE 288th Street, Kingston, WA 98346-9502 | **Phone:** (360) 297-4172 | **Fax:** (360) 297-8321 | **Email:** heronswood@silverlink.net | **Web:** www.heronswood.com

Dan Hinkley defines "native" as "grown on Earth," but you'll fall in love with his vast offerings.

INSIDE PASSAGE

PO Box 639, Port Townsend, WA 98368 | **Phone:** (360) 385-6114 or (800) 361-9657 | **Fax:** (360) 385-5760 | **Email:** inspass@whidbey.net | **Web:** www.insidepassageseeds.com

A Northwest natives–oriented enterprise. Contract growing; also, seeds for woody plants, wildflowers, and herbaceous plants.

MADRONA NURSERY

815 38th Avenue, Seattle, WA 98122 | **Phone/Fax:** (206) 323-8325 | **Web:** Bucherjohn@earthlink.net

Selection of native plants among stock.

MAXWELTON VALLEY GARDENS

3443 E French Road, Clinton, WA 98236 | **Phone:** (360) 579-1770 | **Email:** mvg@whidbey.com | **Web:** www.whidbey.net/mvg

Find 100 species of native plants in stock.

MEERKERK RHODODENDRON GARDENS

3531 S Meerkerk Lane, Greenbank, WA 98253 (on Whidbey Island) | **Phone:** (360) 678-1912 | **Web:** www.meerkerkgardens.org

New and rare rhododendron seed and pollen exchange. Annual sale of test plants.

MT. TAHOMA NURSERY

28111 112th Avenue E, Graham, WA 98338 | **Phone:** (253) 847-9827 | **Web:** www.backyardgardener.com/mttahoma

The nursery specializes in selecting, propagating, and selling rock garden, alpine house, and woodland plants, including Northwest species.

MOUNTAIN MEADOW NURSERY

7236 132nd Avenue NE, Kirkland, WA 98033 (by appointment only) | **Phone:** (425) 885-0785 or (425) 454-3766 | **Email:** nancyshort@aol.com

Woodland natives, with specialties along the lines of maidenhair ferns, native ground covers, shrubs, and trees, along with non-natives that snuggle in as happy companions.

MsK RARE PLANT NURSERY

20312 15th Avenue NW, Shoreline, WA 98117 | **Phone:** (206) 546-1281

Display Garden, open without appointment on Mother's Day weekend; many native plants among the trees, shrubs, perennials, ground covers, and hard-to-find plants.

NATIVES NORTHWEST

190 Aldrich Road, Mossyrock, WA 98564 | **Phone:** (360) 983-3138.

Trees and shrubs, about 80 percent native species.

NOTHING BUT NORTHWEST NATIVES

14386 NE 249th Street, Battle Ground, WA 98604 | **Phone/Fax:** (360) 666-3023 | **Web:** www.teleport.com/~nwplants/

Offers perennial, shrub, and tree species. Check out their grasses, vines, and perennials for woodland, meadow, or garden. They propagate virtually all their stock and try to offer plants not commonly available in other nurseries. Free plant list.

PLANTS OF THE WILD

PO Box 866, Tekoa, WA 99033 | **Phone:** (509) 284-2848 | **Fax:** (509) 284-6464 | **Email:** kathy@plantsofthewild.com | **Web:** www.plantsofthewild.com

Find a wide variety of container-grown native plants, wholesale and retail at this Eastern Washington site.

RAVEN NURSERY

22370 Indianola Road, Poulsbo, WA 98370 | **Phone:** (360) 598-3323 | **Fax:** (360) 598-6610 | **Email:** tworaven@ix.netcom.com

Native plants, daylilies, and maple species.

SHORE ROAD NURSERY

616 Shore Road, Port Angeles, WA 98362 | **Phone:** (360) 457-1536 | **Fax:** (360) 457-8482 | **Email:** plantman@olypen.com

Make sure to visit the great native display gardens.

SILVASEED COMPANY, INC.

PO Box 118 (317 James Street), Roy, WA 98580 | **Phone:** (253) 843-2246 | **Email:** silvaseed@qwest.net

Find seed for Northwest conifer species here; also custom seed collection and seed stratification; conifer seedlings in bulk.

SOUND NATIVE PLANT

PO Box 7505, Olympia, WA 98507-7505 | **Phone:** (360) 352-4122 | **Fax:** (360) 867-0007 | **Email:** sessnp@compuserve.com

Joslyn Trivett has a wide selection of container-grown trees and shrubs, ground covers, and wetland emergents of western Washington origin. The focus is on larger restoration projects and wetland mitigation.

WATERSHED GARDEN WORKS

2039 44th Avenue, Longview, WA 98632 | **Phone/Fax:** (360) 423-6456 | **Email:** info@watershedgardenworks.com | **Web:** http://watershedgardenworks.com/contactus.html

Wetland and riparian plants.

WETLAND PLANT COOPERATIVE / KING CONSERVATION DISTRICT

935 Powell Avenue SW, Renton, WA 98055 | **Phone:** (206) 764-3410, ext. 120 | **Email:** brandy.reed@kingcd.org | **Web:** http://www.kingcd.org/pro_wet_nur.htm

A native plant nursery administered by KCD, growing primarily native wetland plants grown from local seed, plus some shrubs and trees. Plants are available to citizens and community groups who can trade volunteer time at the nursery.

WEYERHAEUSER CO.

Rochester Regeneration Center, 7935 Highway 12 SW, Rochester, WA 98579 | **Phone:** (800) 732-4769

Seedling sales. For less than 5,000 seedlings, press 1 when you call.

WILDSIDE GROWERS

6360 Hannegan Road, Lynden, WA 98264 | **Phone:** (360) 398-7174 | **Fax:** (360) 733-2581 | **Email:** wildsidegrowers@home.com

Northwest native perennials and shrubs, with selections from prairie to alpine conditions.

WOODBROOK NURSERY

5919 78th Avenue NW, Gig Harbor, WA 98335 | **Phone:** (253) 265-6271 | **Fax:** (253) 265-6471 | **Email:** woodbrk@harbornet.com | **Web:** www.woodbrook.net

Many dozens of shrubs and trees native to the Northwest, from deciduous trees to conifer shrubs.

NORTHWEST NATIVE PLANT SALES AND EVENTS

Find an extensive list of sales in Chapter 7, "Plant Sales." Most events are annual and are generally held at the same time and place each year. Here are a few additional sales where native plants are available.

CASCADE BIOMES

PO Box 22419, Seattle, WA 98122-0419 | **Phone/Fax:** (206) 322-0528 | **Email:** biomes@earthlink.net

This company has an annual fall plant sale that aspires to make native plants more available to home owners and small-scale projects in western Washington. Request a catalog.

MOUNT BAKER–SNOQUALMIE NATIONAL FOREST

Contact: 21905 64th Avenue W, Mountlake Terrace, WA 98043 | **Phone:** (425) 775-9702

A sponsor of the annual Celebrating Wildflowers Festival. They offer a full calendar of free guided walks and children's activities throughout the spring and summer in the national forest. Find calendars at ranger stations, county visitor information centers, or REI.

OREGON ASSOCIATION OF CONSERVATION DISTRICTS

(503) 648-3174 (Salem) | **Email:** rgraves@netcnct.net | **Web:** www.netcnct.net/community/oacd/index.htm

Purchase plants through conservation district native plant sales. Plants are offered with the restriction that they be used for conservation: reforestation, bank stabilization, wildlife habitat, erosion control, or wetland restoration. Most counties have a plant list and many have a catalog. Place an order, then pick up the plants. The website has a comprehensive list of all the conservation district offices with contact information.

SOUTH KING COUNTY ARBORETUM

22520 SE 248th Street, PO Box 72, Maple Valley, WA 98038 | **Phone:** (425) 413-2572 | **Web:** http://www.skcaf.org/

Plant sales in May and September. Find 40 acres with trails through native forests, display gardens, and nursery.

TACOMA NATURE CENTER

1919 S Tyler Street, Tacoma, WA 98405 | **Phone:** (253) 591-6439

The annual "Festival of Natives" is held in the fall to take advantage of a better selection of plants at a time optimal for planting. Buy native plants, attend workshops, hear speakers, or take tours of the Nature Center and exhibits displayed by area native plant organizations.

WASHINGTON CONSERVATION COMMISSION

300 Desmond Drive, Olympia, WA 98504-7721 | **Phone:** (360) 407-6200 | **Email:** wscc@conserver.org | **Web:** www.conserver.org/wcc.html

Find the conservation district in your area and purchase plants through their native plant sales. Plants are offered with the restriction that they be used for conservation: reforestation, bank stabilization, wildlife habitat, erosion control, or wetland restoration. Most counties have a plant list and many have a catalog. Place an order, then pick up the plants.

WASHINGTON NATIVE PLANT SOCIETY

Contact to check for plant sale information: (206) 527-3210 or (888) 288-8022 | **Email:** wnps@wnps.org | **Web:** www.wnps.org/

LITERATURE ABOUT NORTHWEST NATIVE PLANTS

Two terrific resources for information on trees and woody plants are located on the Seattle campus of the University of Washington. The **Elisabeth C. Miller Library** at the Center for Urban Horticulture, 3501 NE 41st Street, subscribes to hundreds of plant-society publications and has them bound and shelved for easy access. They also print a detailed listing of books on Northwest native plants. Most are publications that are available on their shelves. Also, check the large collection at the **Allen Library** in the basement of Bloedel Hall for an extensive collection in the areas of botany, horticulture, and forest resources. Look under "Libraries" in Chapter 1, "Organizations That Help Gardeners" for details on contact information, location, and open times.

In Portland there are two excellent resources you can use for reference work (non-members) or to check books out (member benefit). The **Berry Botanic Garden Library** (11505 SW Summerville Avenue, Portland, OR 97219; (503) 636-4112) has an excellent collection that includes periodicals and plant society journals. The **Leach Botanical Garden Library** (6704 SE 122nd Avenue, Portland, OR 97236; (503) 823-9503) is a wonderful resource with a large collection of horticultural and botanical books, periodicals, and textbooks.

NORTH AMERICAN ROCK GARDEN SOCIETY

Email: nargs@advinc.com | **Web:** www.nargs.org

NARGS offers marvelous services to members through its online bookstore, which lists a wide selection of topical literature at 80 percent of the listed retail price (including any Timber Press book).

Books

Alpines: The Illustrated Dictionary
Clive Innes (Timber Press, 1995, 192 pp.)

Although not specific to the Northwest, this does provide information for those who grow alpine plants that may come from nurseries far away. It is well-documented, with cultural details and excellent color photos.

Butterfly Gardening: Creating Summer Magic in Your Garden
Created by the Xerces Society and The Smithsonian Institution (1998, revised and updated)

This is a rich and gloriously beautiful book on how to garden to attract butterflies and other invertebrates for their ecological value, for the biological diversity their presence in a garden fosters, and for the sheer delight of having them as companions as we work or relax in our gardens. It's composed of essays broadly and specifically covering the topic by writers, photographers, scientists, amateur lepidopterists, and gardeners. They are each and every one a fascinating good read and the photography is utterly riveting in its detail and incredible color. It will influence the selection of plants you make to include more that draw these important pollinators and gentle creatures.

Champion Trees of Washington State
Robert Van Pelt (University of Washington Press, 1996)

Bob Van Pelt is a man who truly loves trees, and the biggest ones throw this statuesque man into raptures of respect and awe, so much so that he dedicates a great deal of his life to seeking out the champions to see that they get credit for their achievements. Along with a small cadre of like-minded friends, he scours woodlands and urban parks, mountainous valleys and residential backyards, and, using internationally accepted standards, records their mythic measurements. This guide lists, describes, and pictures the largest native and introduced trees in Washington (there is a nomination form included if you have an arboreal candidate). Important and curious facts are included throughout, along with amazing drawings and lots of striking photos, often with a teeny-tiny human standing insignificantly nearby for scale. There are also lots of quick-reference sidebars, like the place name index of towns and cities with record trees.

Discovering Wild Plants: Alaska, Western Canada, The Northwest
Janice J. Schofield (Alaska Northwest Books, 1989, 355 pp.)

This is a well-written compendium that covers a broad swath of the Northwest, including Alaska and western Canada. Former home economist Janice Schofield is very attuned to the traditional medicinal, culinary, and practical uses of this area's trees, roots, wildflowers, herbs, seaweeds, and mushrooms. The thorough coverage of hundreds of plants includes each plant's name, other names it is known by, botanical name information, habitat and range, harvest calendar, and medicinal, cosmetic, and culinary uses.

Ethnobotany of Western Washington: The Knowledge and Use of Indigenous Plants by Native Americans
Erna Gunther (University of Washington Press, 1945; revised edition 1973, 7th printing 1995, 72 pp.)

This is the classic book on the relationship between a native people and their indigenous flora. Gunther, an ethnologist, recorded the information well before the people who could relate such information had died, and also before many of the plants themselves had disappeared. You'll love reading through the accounts of each plant's history, uses, and lore, and find plants you know and love taking on greater historical context. The book is supplemented with elegant line drawings; it even has its own garden, found at the entrance to the Burke Museum on the campus of the University of Washington in Seattle (corner of NE 45th Street and 15th Avenue NE).

Flora of the Pacific Northwest: An Illustrated Manual

C. Leo Hitchcock and Arthur Cronquist (University of Washington Press, 1981, 730 pp.)

An indisputable classic on the subject of identifying Northwest plants, it's especially valuable to gardeners for the wealth of personal experience reflected in the authors' observations.

Forest Giants of the Pacific Coast

Robert Van Pelt (University of Washington Press, 2001, 224 pp.)

Even after a century of intensive exploitation, the forests of the Pacific Coast remain unmatched in overall size, height, and age. This new guide to the largest 20 species of conifers in North America reaches from the southern Sierras to Vancouver Island, from the coast to northwestern Montana. Color maps, comparative drawings, color photographs of typical trees and cones, and individual profiles of 117 giant tree features are included. All are unique specimens that represent the extremes to which their species can grow.

Gardening with Native Plants of the Pacific Northwest

Dr. Arthur Kruckeberg (University of Washington Press, 2nd Edition, 1996, 382 pp.)

The professor emeritus of botany at the University of Washington and a champion of Northwest flora identifies 250 Northwest natives he would recommend for the garden. He gives practical information on propagation, plant lists for appropriate garden settings, and sources for plants and further information. Many clear line drawings and photographs help with identification. While scholarly, it is happily most approachable! His enthusiasm is infectious.

Grow Wild: Low Maintenance, Sure-Success, Distinctive Gardening with Native Plants

Lorraine Johnson (Fulcrum Publishing, 1998, 154 pp.)

As Lorraine Johnson, of the Canadian Wildflower Society, contemplated how to approach this topic, and how she could ever address the entire continent (both the United States and Canada), she whittled her challenge down by focusing on distinct regions. Luckily for us one of them happens to be the Pacific Northwest. The book is also broad in scope. The first chapter, "Healing the Land, The Promise and Possibilities of Native Plant Gardening," serves as an inspiring discourse on the values gardeners are putting in place as they turn to Mother Nature's beckoning hand. Then she turns to the specifics, with profiles of everyday gardeners and what trials, tribulations, and triumphs they have faced in creating their bit of paradise. Through her informed, opinionated yet easy-

going and affable style, Lorraine conveys much advice anyone contemplating how and why to approach naturalistic garden style and design can relate to and use.

Grow Your Own Native Landscape: A Guide to Identifying, Propagating, and Landscaping with Western Washington Native Plants

Michael Leigh (WSU Cooperative Extension/Thurston County, 1997, $5.50 plus s&h, 132 pp.)

It's easy to fall in love with this book! It starts out with "Which native plants should I use?" and begins with a terrific list for "Deep Shade and Moist Soils." This is followed by down-to-earth, easy-to-read advice on options for obtaining, propagating, and salvaging native plants—successfully. The guide profiles 90 plants in detail, including aquatics.

Landscaping for Wildlife in the Pacific Northwest

Russell Link (University of Washington Press, 1999)

The author has worked in landscape architecture for 10 years, and for several years has been a wildlife biologist for the Department of Fish and Wildlife. Link is highly respected in the area of wildlife habitat and its stewardship. His impressive book will no doubt become the "bible" on the topic, as he has meticulously covered the subject matter for home gardeners excited about understanding this approach to the flora, fauna, and land in the places where they garden. The book is prodigiously illustrated with informative line drawings; detailed examples that address the point being discussed; annotated plant, bird, and animal lists; detailed instructions on building the likes of nest boxes, naturalistic birdbaths, wildlife shelters, bird feeders, and ponds; and provides details about basic gardening skills like proper planting of bare-root trees and shrubs. "Insects and Their Relatives" provides a compelling argument for and discussion of attracting various buggy creatures to your garden, including pieces on mason and bumble bees, butterflies, and moths, and homes you can build for them. Finally, with his characteristic thoroughness, several appendices provide lots of Pacific Northwest–specific resource information (nurseries included).

Moss Gardening, Including Lichens, Liverworts, and Other Miniatures

George Schenk (Timber Press, 1997, 262 pp.)

Moss gardening is a sure-fire natural option. With the advent of specialist nurseries offering the botanical tools needed to delve more deeply into this realm, a whole new, dazzling world opens.

Mosses, Lichens and Ferns of Northwest North America

Dale Vitt, Janet Marsh, and Robin Bovey (Lone Pine Press, 1988, 296 pp.)

Among the most prominent feature of woodland and alpine areas are lichens, mosses, and ferns. Now that we've become more familiar with alpine gardening and native plants in the garden, it's time to seek out knowledgeable references to help key out specimens in the wild and better understand their habitat. This book offers clear color photographs of these often Lilliputian plants and keyed maps showing range and habitat.

Mountain Plants of the Pacific Northwest

Ronald J. Taylor and George W. Douglas (Mountain Press Publishing Company, 1995, 450 pp.)

These two professional botanists have given us an elegantly produced and utterly practical field guide to a broad range of plants, covering roughly the alpines down through those in the lowland hills. This book is very easy to use, well organized, and thoroughly researched, and also has photos that show the surrounding habitat as well as close-ups.

Native Plants in the Coastal Garden: A Guide for Gardeners in British Columbia and the Pacific Northwest

April Pettinger (Whitecap Books, 1996, 224 pp.)

April Pettinger has done a superb job researching her topic, and has written an engaging book for gardeners who are in search of inspiration and knowledge about native plants in our gardens and in their natural habitat. She identifies 250 species of fascinating, garden-worthy native plants and helps her readers imagine how they can be incorporated into their own gardens. She explains how to identify plant habitats, describes how to attract wildlife into the garden, and explores the history, geography, ecology, aesthetics, and environmental benefits of gardening with native plants.

Naturalistic Gardening: Reflecting the Planting Patterns of Nature

Ann Lovejoy, photographs by Allan Mandell (Sasquatch Books, 1998, 160 pp.)

While it's written for a wider audience too, this book favors Northwest gardeners, as local luminary Ann Lovejoy lives, writes, and gardens within the context of her topic at her home and gardening school on Bainbridge Island. Additionally, she identifies the plants, gardens, garden owners, and wild settings illustrated throughout the book in Allan Mandell's brilliant photos. She provides the clear voice and straightforward know-how needed to interpret those essences from nature that we want to recapture in our cultivated gardens, be they expansive or intimate, citified or countrified, realistic or impressionistic.

Nature Journaling: Learning to Observe and Connect with the World Around You

Clare Walker Leslie and Charles E. Roth (Storey Books, 1998, 182 pp.)

This book is a favorite for approaching the journaling process—from techniques of artistic expression to selecting the focus of one's journal, and from realistic sugges-tions on being a better observer to understanding what one wants to accomplish by keeping such a record.

Plants of the Pacific Northwest Coast of Washington, Oregon, British Columbia and Alaska

Jim Pojar and Andy MacKinnon (Lone Pine Publishing, Vancouver, BC, 1994, 526 pp.)

If you have even a whisper of a desire to improve your forays into the wilds of the Northwest's coastal areas, you really must bring this comprehensive field guide along. Without it, the journey can be very frustrating for a curious naturalist anxious to identify and learn more about the vast world of our rich and varied native flora. There just isn't any book as well researched and written, abundantly illustrated (1,100 color photographs, more than 1,000 line drawings, 794 range maps in color), and cleverly keyed, right down to their selection of "oddballs" (one-of-a-kind eccentrics that throw even the most avid naturalist sleuth into a tizzy).

Propagation of Northwest Native Plants

Robin Rose, Caryn E. C. Chachulski, and Diane L. Haase (Oregon State University Press, 1998, 256 pp.)

Anyone who has entered the fascinating world of plant propagation (whether by seed or vegetatively) will understand why having a detailed, reliable reference is essential to making your efforts productive. This book is a standard for novices and professionals alike as it profiles 135 species of Northwest native plants. Information is clearly presented, illustrated with line drawings, and includes extensive reference sources for each plant. An overview of propagation techniques addresses seed collection, cleaning and storage, pre-sowing seed treatments, seed sowing and covering, stem and root cutting, layering, division, grafting, micropropagation, and salvage.

Reflecting Nature: Garden Designs from Wild Landscapes

Jerome and Seth Malitz (Timber Press, 1998, 267 pp.)

This father and son duo have traveled and hiked together for over 20 years, and what they have brought back from those experiences for the rest of us are their thought-provoking interpretations of wild landscape vignettes for the cultivated garden. They are after the essences, the elements that speak to our hearts and imaginations, with a goal of recreating the spirit of the scene or plant grouping with their own plant design and detailing suggestions. While the examples they use come from woodlands across the country, there are common elements that makes this book appropriate for the Northwest gardener too. They favor a Japanese influence, both philosophically and in design considerations, that you'll find throughout the book.

Rock Garden Plants of North America: An Anthology from the Bulletin of the North American Rock Garden Society

Edited by Jane McGary (Timber Press, 1996, 460 pp.)

Rock-gardening enthusiasts will find this collection of articles gleaned from a 50-year accumulation of the NARGS *Bulletin* a special treasure. The coverage is organized by region, and the Far West is well represented through the writing of noted horticulturists and botanists like R. LeRoy Davidson and Sean Hogan.

Spirit of the Siskiyous: Journals of a Mountain Naturalist

Mary Paetzel (Oregon State University Press, 1998, 164 pp.)

The Siskiyous, part of the Klamath Range that runs from southwest Oregon into California, are a plant enthusiast's mecca. The journals of this so-called "amateur" naturalist provide a stunning and sensitive portrait of the place—but beyond that, she brings alive every creature and plant with remarkable detail. While she wrote this journal purely for herself, it is a marvelously good read. Her illustrations, many in color, are delights.

Vascular Plants of the Pacific Northwest

Leo J. Hitchcock, Arthur Cronquist, Marion Ownbey, and J. W. Thompson (University of Washington Press, five volumes, 1955)

A much-respected resource.

Wayside Wildflowers of the Pacific Northwest

Dr. Dee Strickler (The Flower Press, 1993, 272 pp.)

The extraordinary photographs here identify over 400 flower species, and are accompanied by notes on habitat range, plant features, and an outstanding glossary of botanical terms, making this an invaluable companion for outings into the Northwest.

Western Trees: A Field Guide

Martha Stuckey and George Palmer (Falcon Books, 1998, 143 pp.)

Easy to tuck in a pocket, easy to browse, this is an excellent companion to take along on a hike for those of us who may be tree identification impaired.

The Wildflower Gardeners' Guide

Henry W. Art (Garden Way Publishing, 1990, 180 pp.)

For gardeners who have faced the frustration of establishing wildflowers in a cultivated setting and for those who have yet to venture into this visually rich and rewarding area, professor Henry Art has compiled a series of books to guide your endeavors. One volume is specific to the Pacific Northwest, extending east to the Rocky Mountains and north up throughout British Columbia. The book addresses 33 of the most popular species, in a two-page spread format. For each plant, it gives historical and cultural profiles; thorough propagation information; native companion plants; a large, detailed line drawing; a map of the plant's range; and further plant requirements. There is a gallery of color photos, and a resource guide

that lists botanical display gardens, suppliers, and societies by state or province. This book is fun and easy to read, inspiring, and would make a valuable addition to your library (and a wonderful gift for a gardening friend).

Wildflowers Washington

C. P. Lyons (Lone Pine Publishing, 1997, 192 pp.)

This is one of the best field guides to take along for identifying wildflowers while you're out on a hike. It's a comfortable size to haul, yet jam-packed with easy-to-access information on over 500 flowers, each of them represented with beautiful (and useful) color photos. The front material provides a brief but interesting historical background on explorers Lewis and Clark, and plant seekers Archibald Menzies and David Douglas, and a discussion on ecosystems. A favorite feature is the inclusion of historical bits on the plants from the journals of Lewis and Clark and David Douglas.

Brochures / Guidebooks

Grow Your Own Native Landscape: A Guide to Identifying, Propagating and Landscaping with Western Washington Native Plants

King County Department of Natural Resources, 201 S Jackson Street, Suite 600, Seattle, WA 98104 | **Phone:** (206) 296-6519

You can purchase this useful reference in person for $5 at the above address or order by mail for $7.50.

Native Plant Alliance: A Manual of Native Plant Communities for Urban Areas of the Pacific Northwest

Charles M. Anderson ($7.50 plus tax, s&h), from Cascade Biomes, Inc., PO Box 22419, Seattle, WA 98122-0419 | **Phone:** (206) 322-0528

This manual describes and defines the region's plant, soil, and human communities (biomes). It addresses what is required to restore native plants to the many landscapes that have undergone extreme transformation through urban spread. This is a good place to get a handle on the importance of soil mycorrhiza, and procedures for reintroducing native plant communities in the succession typical of Northwest wilderness areas. If you are interested in the differences between methods used in establishing nursery-grown natives vs. salvaged plants, this easy-to-understand book covers the topic admirably. The second part of the book is filled with annotated plant lists for various situations ("Sunny Places," "Understory Layer," etc.), with botanical and common names and remarks about culture.

Watchable Wildflowers of the Columbia Basin

Bureau of Land Management, Wenatchee Resource Area, 915 Walla Walla Avenue, Wenatchee, WA 98801-1521 | **Phone:** (509) 665-2100

A mere $4 brings you this beautiful, 35-page, full-color booklet. If you visit the Columbia Basin area, this informative guide will help you understand the dynamics, geology, and natural history of its ecosystem and plant communities. Among the nicest features are the site-specific profiles to help you find wildflowers (example: each section covers an area, like "Douglas Creek–North" and includes driving directions, details of the locale's habitat and landscape, and then a specific plant list, including a "Unique Plant" feature). The booklet is also sold by some regional chapters of the Washington Native Plant Society. View a sample page at: http://www.geocities.com/RainForest/2745/watchab1.htm.

Winter in the Woods: A Winter Guide to Deciduous Native Plants in Western Washington, and Grow Your Own Landscapes

WSU Cooperative Extension / Thurston County, Native Plant Salvage Project | **To order:** (800) 723-1763

It's one thing to have leaves to help identify woodland trees and shrubs, but those who hike in winter will find this helpful and unusual guide indispensable!

Magazines / Journals

ALPINE ROCK GARDEN SOCIETY

The Society's quarterly *Bulletin* is a valuable membership benefit. These journals are scholarly in tone, beautifully illustrated with line drawings and color photographs, and are captivating good reads. You'll collect them.

NORTH AMERICAN ROCK GARDEN SOCIETY

The Society publishes a very fine quarterly, *Rock Garden*, with dozens of pages of substantive, well-written articles and stunning color photography for the aficionado. These are real keepers.

OREGON NATIVE PLANT SOCIETY

The Society produces a monthly *Bulletin* featuring notices of chapter meetings and activities, updates on conservation issues, and short informative articles. *Kalmiopsis*, published one or more times a year, features longer articles of interest to both lay and professional members of the Society.

WASHINGTON NATIVE PLANT SOCIETY

The quarterly journal, *Douglasia*, covers WNPS news and announcements, and always includes many content-rich articles on topics relating to native plants.

WASHINGTON PARK ARBORETUM

The *Bulletin of the Washington Park Arboretum* is published by the Arboretum Foundation. Volume 55, No. 3 (Fall 1992) is an issue dedicated to the subject of Northwest Natives with contributions by many knowledgeable local horticulturists. Also, see the article in Volume 57, No. 1 (Spring 1994) on "Attracting Birds with Northwest Native Shrubs," written by Kevin Burke.

Wildflower: North America's Magazine of Wild Flora

Subscriptions: Box 335, Station F, Toronto, ON M4Y 2L7 Canada | **Email:** subscribe@wildflowermag.com | **Web:** www.wildflowermag.com

This is a great publication that brings together the news of wildflower gardening, ecosystem restoration, plant rescue, pollination biology, conservation of rare and common native plants, book reviews, new book listings, original botanical art, native plant society addresses across the United States and Canada, wildflower photography, poetry, land acquisition strategies, botanizing travel accounts, and native plant and seed sales. Subscribe! It's a 52-page quarterly; $35 for 1 year, $70 for 2 years (checks or VISA accepted).

Posters

GOOD NATURE PUBLISHING

1904 Third Avenue, Suite 415, Seattle, WA 98101 | **Phone:** (206) 622-9522 or (800) 631-3086 | **Fax:** (206) 622-3066 | **Email:** tim@goodnaturepublishing.com | **Web:** www.goodnaturepublishing.com

This is the source for a visually stunning and educationally significant collection of natural history fine-art posters, featuring artists whose horticultural talents are expanded by their skill in rendering flora and fauna with accuracy and imagination. A portion of sales is generously contributed to the effort to reforest urban areas. Offerings include images of Western flora and fauna, garden herbs, and hummingbird gardens.

Videos

Native Plants of Washington

North Cascades Institute, 810 State Route 20, Sedro-Woolley, WA 98284-9394 | **Phone:** (360) 856-5700, ext. 209 | **Email:** nci@ncascades.org | **Web:** www.ncascades.org

This 70-minute video is beautifully photographed and presents its strong educational message through an emphasis on the eight ecosystems in Washington state and the native plants that have adapted to each area. This would be an especially good teaching tool to use with children. ($20 plus $2 s&h, plus tax)

Internet Resources

BERRY BOTANIC GARDEN

www.berrybot.org

This site has excellent informational pages on such topics as Plant Conservation at the Berry Botanic Garden, Saving Seeds for the Future, Seed Banking, Conserving the Forgotten Plants, and more.

CITY OF VANCOUVER

(604) 873-6011 | **Web:** www.city.vancouver.bc.ca

Find an extensive listing of native plant organizations and demonstration garden resource listings in British Columbia and Western Washington. Search for "native plants" at the website.

DUNCAN MCALPINE/ROCK AND ALPINE GARDENING

www.backyardgardener.com/index2.html

NATIVE PLANT SOCIETY OF OREGON

www.npsoregon.org

Here's a very good site with chapter information, state organization goings-on, an email discussion list, book reviews, other Web links of interest, and a page devoted to discovering Oregon's native plants—where to find them and when they are at their best.

OREGON ASSOCIATION OF CONSERVATION DISTRICTS

www.netcnct.net/community/oacd/index.htm

Find several useful fact sheets and tips here, including how to protect stream banks from erosion, and ideas for enhancing wildlife habitat.

TWO RAINY SIDE GARDENERS

www.rainyside.com

Rainyside is a Northwest site that has links (found at their "Maritime Northwest Native Plants" page) and a resource listing of nurseries (some are hot-linked, and several offer Northwest native plants or are seed sources).

WASHINGTON NATIVE PLANT SOCIETY

www.wnps.org

The WNPS has a well-organized site with chapter information, state organization news, a plant-collection ethics page, native plant bibliography, a page on "Gardening with Natives," and more.

WSU COOPERATIVE EXTENSION

http://gardening.wsu.edu

WSU's site has two "subsites" devoted to "Northwest Native Plants" and "Stewardship Gardening." Some of the topics covered include nurseries and other commercial sources, salvaging native plants, and the ethics of collecting native plants.

GARDENS AND ARBORETUMS TO VISIT

All these gardens include areas devoted to Northwest native plant collections. Remember to see the list of nurseries in this chapter that specialize in or offer a good selection of Northwest native plants, because they often have good display gardens. For gardens that appear here without a full description, you'll find detailed information in Chapter 13, "Gardens to Visit."

British Columbia

DAVIDSON ARBORETUM / RIVERVIEW HORTICULTURAL CENTRE

Riverview Hospital, 500 Lougheed Highway, Coquitlam, BC, V36 4J2 Canada | **Phone:** (604) 290-9910

GOVERNMENT HOUSE

1401 Rockland Avenue, Victoria, BC V8S 1V9 Canada | **Garden phone:** (250) 356-5139

The garden contains 20 acres and includes BC wildflowers.

PARK AND TILFORD GARDENS

440-333 Brooksbank Avenue, North Vancouver, BC V7J 3S8 Canada | **Phone:** (604) 984-8200.

QUEEN ELIZABETH PARK

South Vancouver between E 33rd Avenue (the entrance) and Cambie Boulevard (excellent map on website) | **Phone:** (604) 257-8400 | **Web:** www.city.vancouver.bc.ca/parks/parks&gardens/qepark.htm

ROYAL BRITISH COLUMBIA MUSEUM AND PROVINCIAL ARCHIVES NATIVE PLANT GARDEN

Downtown Victoria, at 675 Belleville Street at Government Street | **Phone:** (250) 356-7226

STANLEY PARK

Located just north and west of downtown Vancouver | **Phone:** (604) 257-6908 | **Email:** spes@vcn.bc.ca | **Web:** www.parks.vancouver.bc.ca

Check out the Stanley Park Ecology Society, located in the world-famous park. Volunteers offer programs, including Sunday Discovery Walks.

UNIVERSITY OF BRITISH COLUMBIA BOTANICAL GARDEN

6804 SW Marine Drive, Vancouver, BC V6M 4H1 Canada | **Phone:** (604) 822-9666

Features of interest to native-plant enthusiasts are the BC Native Garden that houses 8 acres of native woodlands and meadows, peat bogs, and ponds; the David C. Lam Asian Garden, a 30-acre woodland; and the E. H. Lohbrunner Alpine Garden, the largest of its kind in North America, a 2.5-acre volcanic rock and limestone hillside planted with more than 12,000 alpines representing various continents.

VANDUSEN BOTANICAL GARDENS

5251 Oak Street (at 37th), Vancouver, BC V6M 4H1 Canada | **Phone:** (604) 878-9274 | **Web:** www.vandusengarden.org

This 55-acre site in the heart of Vancouver has more than 7,500 plants from around the globe.

Oregon

BERRY BOTANIC GARDEN

11505 SW Summerville Avenue, Portland, OR 97219 | **Phone:** (503) 636-4112 | **Email:** bbg@rdrop.com | **Web:** www.berrybot.org

CECIL AND MOLLY SMITH RHODODENDRON GARDEN

5065 Ray Bell Road, St. Paul, OR 97137 | **Phone:** (503) 771-8386

Rhododendron hybridizer Cecil Smith created this spectacular rhododendron garden.

DARLINGTONIA BOTANICAL WAYSIDE

84505 US Highway 101, 5 miles north of Florence, OR | **Phone:** (800) 551-6949

A great outdoor site for carnivorous plants. See them from a convenient boardwalk.

HOYT ARBORETUM

4000 SW Fairview Boulevard, Portland, OR 97221 | **Phone:** (503) 228-8733

LEACH BOTANICAL GARDEN

6704 SE 122nd Avenue, Portland, OR 97236 | **Phone:** (503) 823-9503

MARTHA SPRINGER BOTANICAL GARDEN

Willamette University, 900 State Street, Salem, OR 97301 | **Phone:** (503) 370-6143 | **Web:** www.willamette.edu/dept/pplant/grounds/botanical.htm

Among the educationally oriented planting areas are several sections with Oregon native plants from various regions.

MOUNT PISGAH ARBORETUM

33735 Seavy Loop Road, Eugene, OR 97405 | **Phone:** (541) 747-3817 | **Email:** mtpisgah@efn.org | **Web:** www.efn.org/~mtpisgah/

The 208 acres here feature a mix of native and introduced trees, shrubs, wildflowers, and more. Check out the 2-acre wildflower garden.

OREGON GARDEN PROJECT

PO Box 155, Silverton, OR 97381-0155 | **Phone:** (503) 874-8100 or (877) 674-2733 | **Email:** jim@oregongarden.org | **Web:** www.oregongarden.org

This is a 220-acre, world-class botanical garden showcasing Oregon's horticultural diversity. Open houses are held regularly.

PAULING SCIENCE CENTER

19600 S Molalla Avenue, Clackamas Community College, Oregon City, OR 97045 | **Phone:** (503) 657-6958

The Center has 14 individual plant beds that showcase plants of the Northwest. Containing more than 100 native plant species, the garden provides both an outdoor laboratory for students, and a place for the community to come to enrich their understanding of native plants in a cultivated setting.

PEAVY ARBORETUM

McDonald Forest, 8692 Peavy Arboretum Road (Route 99W), Corvallis, OR 97330 | **Phone:** (541) 737-4452 | **Web:** www.oregonforests.org/guide/featured.htm

Displays here hold more than 200 native and exotic trees that can be viewed from five trails.

Washington

ARBORETUM OF THE CASCADES (FORMERLY THE PRESTON ARBORETUM)

29700 SE Highpoint Way, Preston, WA 98050 | **Mailing address:** PO Box 512, Preston, WA 98050 | **Phone:** (425) 888-3162 | **Email:** sbond@nwlink.com

This is a fledgling arboretum, now being built from scratch on a section of 260 acres north of I-90, near Preston. It will be devoted to native plants, including botanical "rooms" where combinations of natural species will be grown. They need volunteers!

BELLEVUE BOTANICAL GARDEN

12001 Main Street, Bellevue, WA 98005 | **Phone:** (425) 452-2750 | **Email:** TKuykendall@ci.bellevue.wa.us | **Web:** www.bellevuebotanical.org

See several individual gardens here, including alpine and waterwise plots, with demonstrations of the use of native plants and their cultivars in the urban landscape.

THE BLOEDEL RESERVE

7571 NE Dolphin Drive, Bainbridge Island, WA 98110-1097 | **Phone:** (206) 842-7631 | **Web:** www.bloedelreserve.org

The Reserve includes 150 acres; open by reservation.

BLUE HERON GARDEN

City of Lake Forest, Brookside Boulevard and NE 170th Street, Lake Forest, WA

This is a city demonstration garden featuring drought-tolerant native plants, gardening without pesticides and herbicides, and techniques for gardening and composting wisely near streams.

CENTER FOR URBAN HORTICULTURE

3501 NE 41st Street, Seattle, WA 98105 | **Phone:** (206) 543-8616

Among the Center's many offerings, find the 50-acre Union Bay Natural Area with wetlands and prairie restoration demonstrations and bird-watching. Visit Goodfellow Grove to see a display of native woody plants in a landscape setting.

THE CHASE GARDEN

Located in Orting, WA | **Mailing address:** Send a SASE to PO Box 98553, Des Moines, WA 98198 | **Phone:** (206) 242-4040 | **Web:** www.chasegarden.org

Group tours are available by appointment mid-April to mid-May to this 4.5-acre garden operated under the auspices of the Garden Conservancy. It includes fine example of Northwest gardening in the 1960s, with naturalistic woodland and understory of native shrubs and carpets of trillium, erythronium, and vanilla leaf.

DAYBREAK

Discovery Park (Magnolia neighborhood), Seattle | **Phone:** (206) 285-4425 | **Email:** info@unitedindians.com

A demonstration garden features Northwest native species useful to Pacific Northwest native peoples.

E. B. DUNN HISTORIC GARDEN TRUST

(206) 362-0933 | **Web:** www.dunngardens.org

Visit this Seattle garden by reservation only. Tours are scheduled April–September at 2 p.m. Thursdays, 10 a.m. and 2 p.m. Fridays, 10 a.m. Saturdays. Admission $5–7.

CARL S. ENGLISH, JR. BOTANICAL GARDENS

Adjacent to the Hiram M. Chittenden Locks (in Ballard), 3015 NW 54th Street, Seattle, WA 98107 | **Phone:** (206) 783-7059

The plantings include 1,500 varieties, with a few concentrations of natives.

EVERGREEN ARBORETUM AND GARDENS

At Legion Memorial Park, 144 Alverson Boulevard at 2nd Street, Everett, WA | **Phone:** (425) 257-8583 | **Web:** www.evergreenarboretum.com

A project of the Everett Parks Department in cooperation with the WSU Landscape Architecture Program and the Evergreen Arboretum Foundation, the Arboretum includes a water conservation garden and native plants, and now sponsors a garden tour.

ERNA GUNTHER ETHNOBOTANICAL GARDEN

Burke Museum, University of Washington (corner of NE 45th Street and 17th Avenue NE), Seattle, WA | **Contact:** Curator Susan Libonati-Barnes | **Phone:** (206) 543-5592

Established in 1984 and renovated in 1998.

HIGHLINE COMMUNITY COLLEGE – WASHINGTON NATIVE PLANT HABITAT GARDEN

2400 S 240th Street (located between Buildings 12 and 13), Des Moines, WA 98198 | **Phone:** (206) 878-3710, ext. 3522

The garden contains more than 100 native plant species representing distinct climatic areas: coastal, subalpine, and both sides of the Cascades. The plantings provide both an outdoor laboratory for students and a place for the community to come to enrich their understanding of native plants in a cultivated setting.

KITSAP COUNTY WATER-WISE GARDEN

Givens Community Center, 1026 Sidney Avenue, Port Orchard, WA

Tucked in behind the bus shelter in a courtyard setting, the Water-Wise Garden includes many small demonstration plantings for sunny and shady gardens, including native trees, shrubs, perennials, and ground covers.

LAKE HILLS GREENBELT

15416 SE 16th Street, Bellevue, WA 98007-5917 | **Phone:** (425) 452-6881

The 150-acre reserve here features a half-acre wildlife habitat demonstration garden, a pond, and a cedar haven with a 1-mile trail. Free one-hour nature walks are offered 10 a.m. Saturdays.

LAKEWOLD GARDENS

12317 Gravelly Lake Drive SW, Lakewood, WA 98499 | **Phone:** (888) 858-4106 | **Email:** info@lakewold.org | **Web:** www.lakewold.org

Formerly a private estate, Lakewold covers 10 acres on the west side of Gravelly Lake, 10 miles south of Tacoma. Each individual garden is a spectacular experience. Lakewold has one of the Northwest's best collections of rhododendrons and Japanese maples. Volunteer guides are available April through September by reservation.

DELBERT McBRIDE ETHNOBOTANICAL GARDEN

On the grounds of the Washington State Capital Museum | 211 West 21st Avenue, Olympia, WA 98501 | **Phone:** (360) 753-2580

More than 30 species here demonstrate the resourcefulness of the Native Americans of western Washington, who used the plants for food, medicine, and implements.

MEDICINAL HERB GARDEN

University of Washington, Seattle | **Phone:** (206) 543-1126

Located on Stevens Way across from the botany greenhouse, the plantings here include medicinal herbs native to this area.

MEERKERK RHODODENDRON GARDENS

3531 S Meerkerk Lane, Greenbank, WA 98253 (on Whidbey Island) | **Phone:** (360) 678-1912 | **Web:** www.meerkerkgardens.org

ELISABETH C. MILLER GARDEN

PO Box 77377, Seattle, WA 98177 | **Phone:** (206) 362-8612 | **Web:** www.millergarden.org

Open by appointment only March 1–Nov. 15. Tours 10 a.m. and 2 p.m. Wednesdays and Thursdays (call first).

OHME GARDENS

3327 Ohme Road, Wenatchee, WA 98801 | **Phone:** (509) 662-5785 | **Web:** www.ohmegardens.com

These hillside gardens are partly covered with native plants.

POINT DEFIANCE PARK NATIVE PLANT DISPLAY GARDEN

5400 N Pearl Street, Tacoma, WA 98407 (located near the park's entrance) | **Web:** www.tacomaparks.com

A 1.5-acre site demonstrates the range of Pacific Northwest biodiversity. The Tacoma Garden Club founded this site and continues to provide support and maintenance. The central ravine was transformed into a waterfall and pool, splitting the garden area in two and giving access to seven vegetation zones, including a bog area. Many rarely seen native plants can be found here, including Saskatoonberry, tanbark oak, chinquapin, Brewer spruce, and the native Douglas maple, *Acer glabrum* var. *douglasii*.

RHODODENDRON SPECIES BOTANICAL GARDEN

PO Box 3798, Federal Way, WA 98063 | **Phone:** (253) 838-4646 | **Fax:** (253) 838-4686 | **Email:** rsf@rhodygarden.org | **Web:** www.rhodygarden.org/

More than 10,000 rhododendrons grow on the 22 acres here, but there's also a 1-acre Alpine Rock Garden maintained in conjunction with the Mt. Tahoma Chapter of the North American Rock Garden Society.

RHODY RIDGE ARBORETUM PARK

17427 Clover Road, Bothell, WA 98012 | **Phone:** (425) 743-3945

SEATTLE CENTER

200 Second Avenue N (just northwest of the Pacific Science Center), Seattle | **Contact:** Customer Service at (206) 684-7200

Plantings here create a low-water-use garden.

SKAGIT DISPLAY GARDENS

At the Mount Vernon Research and Extension Center, 16650 State Route 536, Mt. Vernon, WA 98273-4768 | **Phone:** (360) 848-6120 | **Fax:** (360) 848-6159

This is a terrific collection of display gardens, including the Washington State University Master Gardener Discovery Garden, Skagit Valley Rose Society Demonstration Garden, and the Washington Native Plant Society Salal Chapter Garden. The Naturescaping Garden demonstrates ideas for creating a wildlife sanctuary in your yard or garden. Also look for the Skagit Vegetable Trials, under way here to identify the best available varieties and growing practices for the maritime climate, along with the All-America Selections Trials.

SOUNDSCAPE LAWN & GARDEN DEMONSTRATION GARDEN AT THE CENTER FOR URBAN HORTICULTURE

3501 NE 41st Street, Seattle, WA 98105

The demonstration garden features Northwest natives, located adjacent to the Center for Urban Horticulture grounds, just north of the campus. This is a self-guided tour with good signage.

SOUTH KING COUNTY ARBORETUM

22520 SE 248th Street, Maple Valley, WA | **Mailing address:** South King County Arboretum Foundation, PO Box 72, Maple Valley, WA 98038 | **Phone:** (425) 413-2572 or (206) 366-2125 | **Email:** arboretum@skcaf.org | **Web:** www.skcaf.org/index.html

The Arboretum encompasses 40 acres of the northerly portion of Lake Wilderness Park, in Maple Valley. Look for the Smith-Mossman Western Azalea Collection, which, when fully established, will be the largest selection of wild-collected Western azaleas.

SOUTH SEATTLE COMMUNITY COLLEGE ARBORETUM – NORTHWEST NATIVES GARDEN

6000 16th Avenue SW, Seattle, WA 98106 | **Phone:** (206) 764-5300

TACOMA NATURE CENTER

1919 S Tyler Street, Tacoma, WA 98405 | **Phone:** (253) 591-6439 | **Fax:** (253) 593-4152

The Native Plant Garden includes Hummingbird/Butterfly and Woodland Edge Gardens; native ground covers, shrubs, and trees, including many uncommon varieties.

VOLUNTEER PARK

11247 15th Avenue E, Seattle, WA | **Phone:** (206) 684-4743

Look for the water conservation demonstration garden, maintained by the Seattle Water Department and Seattle Parks and Recreation.

WASHINGTON PARK ARBORETUM

2300 Arboretum Drive E, Seattle, WA 98112 | **Phone:** (206) 325-4510

The north end of the area features representative native trees and shrubs. To observe wildlife habitat, visit the Foster Island and Waterfront Trail native plant communities, which attract many resident and migratory fowl, small mammals, frogs, fish, and water-loving insects.

WOODINVILLE WATER DISTRICT

17328 Woodinville-Duvall Road, Woodinville, WA 98072 | **Phone:** (425) 483-9104

A demonstration garden of low-water-use plants, including natives, will be rebuilt here after a construction phase is completed in summer 2002.

WOODLAND PARK ZOOLOGICAL GARDENS

5500 Phinney Avenue N, Seattle, WA 98103

The Park makes extensive use of Northwest native plants in its animal habitats (many feign foreign foliage but are hardy to our area). Take the self-guided tour of the Northwest Temperate Forest using the illustrated booklet *Tale of the Forest,* an especially useful tool when touring with kids.

chapter

5

NURSERIES

Virtually every nursery you find listed in this chapter has some unique feature that sets it apart, offering gardeners a reason to take the exit, find the back roads, or (increasingly) check the website. There is no single destination that can meet all your needs or satisfy your longings, and that's actually good news, because it means you can diversify your sources. As Stephanie liked to say, "there's no definitive Mecca, and the size of an establishment has nothing to do with the ultimate question of finding the rare bijou for that nagging hole in your herbaceous perennial border." Indeed, as much as an outing to the giant full-service nursery is a must, it's always a delight to visit the Northwest's many smaller nurseries, the ones that tend to specialize in "rare, unusual, or uncommon" plants, often lovingly grown from seed or cuttings passed along through the growers' own network of enthusiasts. In personal visits and in conversations and correspondence with every nursery listed here, we have met many, many hard-working and dedicated nursery owners (and super staff) anxious to provide sound advice and quality plants.

Who's Listed

Generally, nurseries throughout the Pacific Northwest are listed here. **No one pays to be in this directory!** We endeavor to ferret out businesses with substantive offerings worth your time to investigate. Not every place that puts plants out front for sale is listed, so you can appreciate the details and updates many of these nurseries have provided. For gardeners new to the Northwest, and for visitors, we also list several larger garden centers.

A word about **"wholesale growers"**: This *Directory* does not list nurseries that are exclusively wholesale, although some offer plants on both retail and wholesale terms. In the yellow pages, or perhaps on the sign out front, you will find an indication of whether, as a recreational plant fanatic, you will be welcome at this establishment. A "wholesale" designation generally indicates a nursery that caters "to the trade" (landscapers, retail outlets, professional gardeners, and the like). And generally they sell plants in large quantities at a discount to those who meet their qualifications. Many of these growers are madly working from sunup to sundown propagating and caring for their stock and do not have time to answer the questions of the hobbyist (even the knowledgeable one). Many have chosen this horticultural path because retail is not "in their blood." Whatever the reason, should you wish to approach a wholesaler about purchasing plants, call to see if there is a website, plant list, or catalog (or even contact the grower by mail) before you arrive on their doorstep.

General Notes on the Nurseries Chapter

Timing: Note that some of the nurseries listed below close their doors for the season about the time some slow-moving gardeners decide it's time to go out and buy what they've decided they need. There's no question that a well-prepared wish list toted around in spring will bag some of the best stuff. Then again, some things won't even arrive at the nursery until later. Don't hesitate to ask when you don't find what you want. You'll often find that the nursery has a schedule for receiving plants, or will take your name and call when plants come in. Many nurseries, large and small, are very service oriented and will seek something out for you that they don't normally have, or will offer discounts on quantity buys (a flat of thyme, for instance).

Email addresses and websites: The number of nurseries large and small that not only communicate by email but also share their goods and services virtually on the Web is exploding. You will often find photos of the nursery and/or display gardens, class offerings, promotional coupons, plant information, newsletters, and catalogs with secure online ordering capability. A word of warning, though! These sites and addresses come and go with remarkable speed. All of the addresses listed were updated just before going to press and we test-drove most of them.

@ Look for this symbol @ for some of the best nursery websites around. While this designation is somewhat subjective, we've highlighted retail nurseries that have well-organized sites, or sites that are particularly user-friendly. And we couldn't resist recognizing sites with beautiful plant images—a great way to virtually introduce gardeners to the real thing.

Hours of operation: This edition endeavors to streamline the constantly changing world of retail hours. Whenever possible, we have provided a broad entry, rather than minutiae, with these preferred times: Daily, Weekends, Weekdays, or by appointment only. If you suspect the nursery might close on Sundays in the dead of winter, or shorten its hours after daylight savings time begins, please call first.

Where a nursery is listed as **"Open: By appointment,"** please call before you drop in. These businesses are not unfriendly or exclusive—but they are usually run by a single person who may not be able to afford the luxury of attending to the nursery "front desk" on a daily basis should a customer unexpectedly drop by. (Sometimes it is also a matter of local zoning regulations.) Also, be aware that many specialty nurseries are located in a residential setting, often one not obvious from the street. Don't be shy, though! Often these sources are the brightest of gems, offering selection, quality, and an experience you'll cherish forever.

Catalogs: These are very time-consuming to compile, and expensive to print and mail. Consider sharing with a friend. Rarely does the nominal catalog fee cover printing and postage expenses. If you find a catalog you particularly enjoy, a quick postcard of recognition and thanks could go a long way to brighten the day of a harried nursery owner! Collecting a packet of interesting catalogs makes a thoughtful gift for a gardening friend.

Directions: We've endeavored to provide you with *generalized* driving directions to help you find nurseries and gardens to visit. You'll also need a good map for navigational purposes, or to get into the habit of calling or checking the nursery's website before you head out. Many smaller or more remote nurseries will send you a plant list and a map so you can be looking over their offerings before you arrive. With a few days pre-planning, your map study or call can make your trip much more enjoyable. We've visited many of the nurseries listed here; others have come with high recommendations from gardening friends.

Mail-order nurseries: These nurseries are intermingled through this largely Northwest listing. Increasingly, we're discovering that mail-order growers are loading much of their catalog on colorful and user-friendly websites for easy viewing. Note that nurseries east of the Mississippi have restrictions on sending plants other than specially washed and inspected ones to Oregon and Washington. This is to keep the dreaded Japanese beetle out of our area and gardens. Plants crossing the Canadian border are subject to the protocol of strict regulations (sometimes requiring permits), and always require inspection (see "Importing Plants" at the end of this chapter).

✉ Look for this symbol ✉ to find retail nurseries that offer plants, bulbs, seeds, and other products via mail order. Many will send you a catalog, plant list, or price sheet upon request (for a SASE or a nominal charge); others have converted their catalog to an online version, via their website. A few of the nurseries in this chapter are retail mail order only and are not equipped to handle in-person customers. Please take note of these limitations when ordering.

"Full service": This term means you can expect to find annuals, perennials, shrubs, trees (ornamental, fruit, etc.), roses, vines, ground covers, herbs, bulbs, seeds, pots, soil, tools, and all the other paraphernalia we gardeners like to collect.

❋ Gardens to visit: Look for this symbol ❋ to indicate retail nurseries that have designed and planted display gardens for customers to enjoy. You'll learn much more about the potential for success a specific tree, shrub, or perennial might have in your own garden when you see it planted in a nursery's display border, paired with companion plants. We've highlighted the displays worth visiting.

Someone missing? We contacted each nursery that appeared in the 8th edition of the *Northwest Gardeners' Resource Directory*, providing details about updating and revising the listings and information we had on file for them. If you wonder why a nursery is missing from this listing, it may be that after several unsuccessful attempts to get a response from the owners we instead have turned over the limited space to a business that we *know* is alive and anxious to get the word out to prospective customers. We often wonder how someone who cannot take a few minutes to respond to a brief query will treat you, as their customer. Listings are strictly at the author's discretion. Please let us know about nurseries you think should be added to the next edition.

A Selection of "Virtual" Nurseries

Although the retail websites are virtual, the plants, you can trust, are the real McCoy. Many nurseries have put catalogs online (you'll find dozens of them listed in this chapter), but there are some nurseries for which the Internet is actually home base. The few cyber-nurseries we list here are not to be confused with the tangible out-of-the-Northwest nurseries recommended at the end of this chapter.

Aesthetic Gardens

www.agardens.com | PO Box 1362, Boring, OR 97009 | **Fax:** (503) 663-6672; online orders are encouraged, but orders may also be faxed here. Aesthetic Gardens will email you with a toll-free contact phone number once you place an order.

This collective group of growers is motivated to offer "the most complete source of rare and unusual plant material in the Internet community." Their website offers everything from "A" (alpine plants) to "V" (vines), and much that's in-between. You'll find hundreds of conifers, rhododendrons, deciduous and evergreen broadleaf trees and shrubs, exquisite Japanese maples, perennials, bamboo, and small fruits and berries. At present, all the growers are located in Oregon and Washington. They'll select and ship plants directly from the field or greenhouse to you, and, in general, 1-gallon sizes are offered.

New Ornamentals Society

http://members.tripod.com/~hatch_L/nos.html | PO Box 12011, Raleigh, NC 27605 | **Email:** newplants@angelfire.com

This organization and its site are aimed at the professional, very serious enthusiast, and at the intensely plant-curious. As a society of horticulturists, taxonomists, and landscape designers interested in the best and newest ornamental landscape plants, NOS has developed a mind-boggling database and reference system for plants. The database documents plant descriptions, taxonomy, history, origins, and often nursery availability—information that comes from their membership. The most extensive and powerful access to the databases is offered on a subscription basis ($29/year). For those of you interested in what NOS offers the public gratis, log on, but do so when you won't be rushing off to dinner or a movie. For the horticulturally curious, this site is engrossing and can become addictive. Variegated-plant enthusiasts on the lookout for new, rare variegated taxa can search the vast listings using a simple search function. Check the "New Plant Page" to learn about great introductions and which nurseries carry them. One recently featured plant was *Hydrangea paniculata* 'Zwijenburg', also called the Limelight Hydrangea. The NOS site will link you directly to the nursery that has introduced this bright green flowering shrub from Holland.

WESTERN BRITISH COLUMBIA NURSERIES

Where to Find Listings of B.C. Nurseries

PLANTLOVERS.COM

www.plantlovers.com

Plantlovers is a North America-wide website for all things plants. Created in Vancouver and now reaching throughout Canada and the United States, this is the official host site for the VanDusen Flower & Garden Show in Vancouver. When you visit, click on the North American map to first reach western Canada; then click on British Columbia and you'll view a great listing of "secret sources" worth investigating. There is also a great listing of garden accessories retailers on this site.

DIRECT FARM MARKETING ASSOCIATION, SOUTHERN VANCOUVER ISLAND

www.islandfarmfresh.com

This site serves as a clearinghouse for dozens of farms, growers, nurseries, and agricultural locations on the south end of Vancouver Island, mostly outside Victoria. With detailed maps, schedules, links, and harvest dates, the website is a good place to start if you're planning a nursery-lover's visit to the island. Contact the association for a free map at produce@islandfarmfresh.com or call toll-free (877) 228-2289.

FARM FRESH GUIDE, LANGLEY AREA

Greater Langley Chamber of Commerce, #1, 5761 Glover Road, Langley, BC Canada | **Phone:** (604) 530-6656

Request a free copy of the "Farm Fresh Guide," which lists the Langley area's wonderful "country-style" farms, nurseries, and agricultural attractions.

Western British Columbia Nurseries

ART KNAPP PLANTLAND & FLORIST

1401 Hornby Street, Vancouver, BC Canada V6Z 1W8 | **Phone:** (604) 662-3303 | **Fax:** (604) 662-8268 | **Email:** artknapp@artknapp.com | **Web:** www.artknapp.com

With 16 stores across British Columbia, this enormous chain of full-service nurseries and garden centers will deliver high-quality plants material, garden tools and accessories, bulbs, seeds, koi and pond supplies, and unique gift items. The urban-focused Vancouver store serves lots of balcony and patio gardeners, so look for fabulous urns and containers, home and garden accessories, gifts, indoor plants, and more.

When you visit this and other Art Knapp outlets, be ready for well-organized departments, excellent selection, and a knowledgeable staff to assist you. Each store is designed to serve its local gardening community, with inventory that varies by the neighborhood. The Art Knapp Plantland website links to each store, providing a schedule for classes and special events, product information, and more. The site also hosts a gardening discussion group for customers.

BROOKSIDE ORCHID GARDENS

23711 – 32nd Avenue, RR #12, Langley, BC V2Y 2K5 Canada | **Phone:** (604) 533-8286 | **Fax:** (604) 533-0498 | **Email:** info@brooksideorchids.com | **Web:** www.brooksideorchids.com | **Directions:** From Vancouver, take the Trans Canada Hwy #1 east to Hwy 10, where you'll follow the "bypass" to 232nd Street (heading south). Cross the Fraser Hwy and continue to 32nd Avenue, turning left. | **Open:** Tuesday-Saturday

Brookside started production in its greenhouses in 1985, specializing in potted orchids and cyclamen. In recent years, extensive orchid trials and research have led Brookside to expand the varieties of orchids it breeds and produced—with 29 different genera in the current lineup. In 1997, Brookside added retail to its extensive greenhouse operations, opening an "on-farm" shop and publishing its first mail-order catalog. You'll see over 650 varieties of orchids in the annual catalog, and, of course, when you visit the Brookside shop (there's always complimentary tea and coffee to enjoy here, too). Popular orchids include brassia, cattleya, cymbidium, dendrobium, miltoniopsis, odontioda, oncidium, phalaenopsis, and more. See the website for Brookside's extensive festival and events calendar, Q&A page, and to subscribe to the free email newsletter. The nursery ships orchids throughout North America.

ELIZABETH'S COTTAGE PERENNIALS

24980 56th Avenue, Langley, BC V4W 1B1 Canada | **Phone:** (604) 856-5279 | **Email:** shepp@shaw.ca | **Web:** www.elizabethscottage.com | **Directions:** Head north on Interstate 5 to the U.S.-Canada border (which then becomes Hwy 99). Continue to the Fraser Hwy heading east. When you reach the town of Langley, turn north on 240th Street; continue to 56th Avenue and turn right. Elizabeth's Cottage is on the right. | **Open:** Seasonally, by appointment only. | **Plant list:** $2

Elizabeth and Donald Sheppard's motto is "perennial plants from a cottage garden," and at their small, English-style garden and nursery, you'll find old-fashioned and newer varieties of perennials. The display gardens here show how well perennials grow in and among 100 heritage and shrub roses (best enjoyed beginning in late May). The business got its start about five years ago when Elizabeth's passion for growing plants from seeds and cuttings led to "just too many plants, so a springtime weekend plant sale seemed like a good idea." Not looking back, she's turned growing and selling plants into a full-time endeavor.

ERICKSON'S DAYLILY GARDENS

24642 51st Avenue, Langley, BC V2Z 1H9 Canada | **Phone:** (604) 856-5758 | **Email:** pam_Erickson@mindlink.bc.ca | **Web:** http://pbmfaq.dvol.com/list/ericksondaylilies.html. Also see www.daylilygrowers.com, Pam Erickson's website, which serves as a clearinghouse for daylily clubs, events and information. | **Open:** By appointment only (directions provided when you schedule a visit). | **Catalog:** $2

Pam and Tom Erickson carry one of Canada's largest collections of award-winning daylilies. Active in the American Hemerocallis Society, Erickson's in 1995 was named the first official daylily display garden in Canada by AHS. The catalog features 1,100 daylily cultivars.

FOXGLOVE FARM AND GARDEN SUPPLY

104 Atkins Road, Salt Spring Island, BC V8K 1A3 Canada | **Phone:** (250) 537-5531 | **Fax:** (250) 537-5591 | **Email:** foxglove@saltspring.com | **Web:** www.gulfislands.com/foxglove | **Directions:** Foxglove Farm and Garden is on Atkins Road between the Fulford Harbour and Vesuvius Bay Ferry terminals on Salt Spring Island, close to the town of Ganges. | **Open:** Daily (closed Sundays August-March)

Foxglove has been the farming, gardening, and pet supply center on Salt Spring Island for 25 years, offering a wide array of landscaping and gardening products—and, of course, plants. You can find Westcoast, Mckenzie, Salt Spring, Pacific Northwest, and Ferry Morse seeds here. At the end of each March, there's an annual "lawn and garden open house" that officially kicks off spring gardening.

FRASER'S THIMBLE FARMS

175 Arbutus Road, Salt Spring Island, BC V8K 1A3 Canada | **Phone:** (250) 537-5788 | **Email:** thimble@saltspring.com | **Web:** www.thimblerarms.com | **Directions:** The nursery is located at Southey Point on the northernmost tip of the Island. | **Open:** Seasonal (Daily during summer months) | **Catalog:** $3 (spring and fall editions offered; plant list also on website)

Richard and Nancy Fraser's rare plant nursery is one of the oldest nurseries in the Gulf Islands with more than 400 species of native plants. Besides Fraser's many rare and unusual offerings, including heritage fruit trees, the nursery has a wide range of perennials, ornamental trees, shrubs, bulbs, and an amazing array of collector's plants. Among the specialties: asarum, dodecatheons, cyclamen, meconopsis, trilliums, erythroniums, ferns (100+ varieties!), fritillaria, violas, hardy geraniums, dicentra, and hardy ground orchids. They also carry Pacific Northwest native plant seeds and wildflower seeds, and sell "the usual fare" of gardening supplies, accessories, equipment, etc. Fraser's extensive plant list will tempt you to visit. If you can't, mail order is easily arranged, however, note the $50 minimum to U.S. addresses.

FREE SPIRIT NURSERY

20405 32nd Avenue, Langley, BC Canada V2Z 2C7 | **Phone:** (604) 533-7373 | **Fax:** (604) 530-3776 | **Web:** www.plantlovers.com | **Directions:** From Hwy 99, take Exit #8B (32nd Avenue/152nd Street) exit and head east at the first light onto 32nd Avenue. Continue east for 6.5 miles and look for Free Spirit's sign at the 204th Street intersection. Nursery is on the left. | **Open:** April-October, Thursday-Saturday (closed in July). Or by advance appointment. | **Plant list:** $1.50

Having studied and worked with the famed Dutch garden designer Piet Oudolf, Lambert Vrijmoed arrived in the Fraser Valley in the early 1990s. Along with his wife Marjanne Vrijmoed, he started Landmark Landscape Design, which was greatly inspired by Oudolf's philosophy. "But it was really hard to find the plants we wanted to use, so we began growing and propagating—intensively—on our two acres," Lambert explains. Free Spirit opened on a limited basis in 1994. Today, Lambert encourages U.S. customers heading north on holiday to stop by his nursery first. Then, while you're off playing in Vancouver, he'll arrange for inspection and the necessary phytosanitary forms; you can pick up plants and paperwork on your way back through the U.S.-Canadian Border. What plants would this be? Think ornamental grasses, epimediums, digitalis, woodland plants, shrubs, vines and "new wave" perennials. Free Spirit Nursery took a gold medal at the 2001 VanDusen Flower & Garden Show for its "Point of Passion" display, so you can be sure a visit to the nursery's lovely display gardens will inspire your own passion for plants, especially ones for which character, texture and form play a strong role.

GARDENWORKS

6250 Lougheed Hwy, Burnaby, BC V5B 2Z9 Canada | **Phone:** (604) 299-0621 | **Email:** inquiries@gardenworks.ca | **Web:** www.gardenworks.ca

GardenWorks' nine gardening centers in B.C. provide great plants, flowers, tools and supplies . . . along with helpful advice to make your gardening successful. The chain emphasizes four-season gardening, carrying the right plants that will star in your garden year 'round. Many of its staff members are trained horticulturists and have been certified by the Canadian Nursery Association. This is a full-service nursery that offers the broad inventory of conifers, deciduous trees and shrubs, vines, fruit trees, rhododendrons and azaleas, roses, tropicals, annuals, perennials, "basket stuffers" and seasonal specialties. The chain has developed the "GardenWorks" line of fertilizers and other amendments developed specially for just about any need B.C. landscapes require. You can get answers to your gardening questions in person, at garden clinics in the stores, through free information handouts, by phone or on the chain's website (check GardenLine answers to frequently-asked questions and "seasonal tips" for some good ideas each month of the year). The website also provides address and phone numbers for individual stores.

HANSI'S NURSERY

27810 112th Avenue, Maple Ridge, BC Canada | **Phone:** (604) 462-8799 | **Fax:** (604) 462-8042 | **Email:** hansinursery@telus.net | **Web:** www.g4graphics.net/hansis | **Directions:** From Vancouver, travel east on the Lougheed Hwy. Turn left on 272nd Street, then right on 112th Avenue. The nursery is on the right. | **Open:** March-October, by appointment only. | **Plant list:** Free

Find the rare and the collectible specialty trees, shrubs, perennials and alpine plants at this unusual nursery, operated by professional nurserywoman Hansi Pitzer. Hansi's is located on five acres of second-growth forest, on the north side of the Fraser Valley, east of Vancouver. "We supply our own water with two wells, there are no street lights or sidewalks here—we are country people and love the peace and tranquility," she says. The new catalog features perennials for moist, sunny or shady places, plus a wide selection of evergreen and deciduous shrubs, vines and trees. You'll also find this is a good source for willows, chamaecyparis, mahonia, yucca, taxus, and acacia—what a wide variety! Ask about scheduling a guided tour of the display gardens, too!

Hawaiian Botanicals and Water Gardens

6011 No. 7 Road, Richmond, BC Canada V6W 1E8 | **Phone:** (604) 270-7712 | **Fax:** (604) 270-7779 | **Email:** info@hawaiian botanicals.com | **Web:** www.hawaiianbotanicals.com | **Directions:** The nursery is located on the southeast corner of No. 7 Road and the Westminster Hwy. Travel north on Interstate 5 to the U.S.-Canadian border (the Interstate becomes Hwy 99 once you enter Canada). Head east on Westminster Hwy; turn right on No. 7 Road. | **Open:** Daily.

Jeanie and Jack Wooton operate Hawaiian Botanicals, which opened in 1991 to offer Canadian gardeners tropical and aquatic plants. They have a well-rounded selection of marginals, oxygenators, water lilies, and tropicals like bromeliads, gingers, and carnivorous plants at this Richland retail outlet. As a specialty aquatic nursery, Hawaiian Botanicals also carries fish, pond filtration systems, and accessories. Enjoy the impressive ponds, greenhouses, and plant displays when you visit.

Kelly's Country Garden

23930 16th Ave, South Langley, BC V2Z 1L1 Canada | **Phone:** (604) 534-3448 | **Fax:** (604) 533-7220 | **Email:** tccharles@sprint.ca | **Web:** www.kellyscountrygarden.com | **Directions:** Travel north on Interstate 5 and cross the U.S.-Canadian border (the Interstate becomes Hwy 99). Just past the border, go east on 16th Avenue. The nursery is located just beyond the intersection at 232nd Street on the right. | **Open:** Wednesday-Sunday

Special pleasures for any garden, Kelly's is a unique garden store and nursery, specializing in quality perennials, cedars, unusual planters, stylish accessories, antiques, and metal art. This small, family-run business combines individual garden spaces with old and new accessories. Antiques include an ever-changing selection of used and antique items such as boilers, washtubs, sap buckets, wheelbarrows, and chimney pots.

Jones Nurseries Garden Centre

16880 Westminster Hwy, Richmond, BC Canada V6V 1A8 | **Phone:** (604) 278-8671 | **Fax:** (604) 273-0650 | **Email:** inquiry@jones.com | **Web:** www.jonesnurseries.com. | **Directions:** Travel north on I-5 through the U.S.-Canadian border; this becomes Hwy 99 once you've entered Canada. Prior to reaching Vancouver, take the Westminster Hwy exit and travel east. Jones Nurseries is just beyond the No. 7 Road intersection on the right. | **Open:** Daily

Just a short drive outside Vancouver, Jones Nurseries is a family-owned plant grower and garden center. Here, you'll find a full range of products, from trees and tropicals to tools and gifts. Take advantage of the "Greenback Discount Program"—when you fill up the Greenback card with $300 worth of purchases, receive $30 toward your next purchase. Custom design services included.

Mandeville Garden Centre & Floral Design

4746 S.E. Marine Drive, Burnaby, BC Canada V5J 3G6 | **Phone:** (604) 434-4111 | **Fax:** (604) 434-0240. Mandeville also operates a seasonal store at 750 Marine Drive, West Vancouver, BC, (604) 913-1992. | **Email:** bhardy@summerwindsgc.com | **Web:** www.mandevillegardens.com | **Directions:** Located at the corner of S.E. Marine Dr. and Nelson Street. Enter the parking lot from Nelson, midway between S.E. Marine Dr. and Marine Way. The nursery is about a 5 minutes drive south from the Metrotown Shopping Centre, at Kingsway and Nelson in Burnaby. | **Open:** Daily, with extended seasonal hours

Founded in 1948, Mandeville was acquired by the SummerWinds Garden Centres of Canada in the late 1990s. Its newly renovated store, complete with spectacular display spaces, including a 500-square-foot European-style indoor garden that changes each season, will inspire your own efforts. This nursery and its staff go far beyond offering garden supplies and a good selection of plants—that goes without saying. In the Garden Store you'll find soils and amendments; grower and propagation supplies; pots, baskets, and containers; water supplies; and gifts for gardeners. Seed offerings include West Coast; Thompson & Morgan; Suttons, McKenzie, Cedar Creek, Seeds of Change, Nature's Garden (Native Canadian plants), Ferry Morse, Terra Viva Organics, and Market Land.

Take a break from choosing plants and enjoy a meal or snack at Willow's Café (be sure to sample the homemade butter and cream fudge). There's also The Mandeville Market, which offers seasonal produce, a floral design (fresh and silks) and gift department and a sizeable garden furniture department. Add to your garden knowledge by taking a class at The Gardener's School, with courses offered throughout the year. Learn useful, inspiring, hands-on techniques like how to divide perennials; garden design; creating a water garden; and orchid care, among so many other titles. Add your name to the mailing list for school updates and check the website to enroll in "The Ardent Gardener Program," which offers you exclusive savings, events and a points-earning program with purchases.

Meadowsweet Farms Garden Nursery

19656 Sixteenth Avenue, South Langley, BC Canada V2Z 1K1 | **Phone:** (604) 530-2611 | **Fax:** (604) 514-1768 | **Email:** meadowsweet@pacificgroup.net | **Web:** www.meadowsweet farms.com | **Directions:** From the U.S. traveling north on Interstate 5, cross the border at Blaine (Peace Arch) to Exit #2. Travel east on 16th Avenue | **Open:** Daily (closed November-March) with extended summer hours. | **Catalog:** $3

This is a really wonderful find for the discerning plant lover/gardener and highly recommended as a destination. You will find an intelligent and stimulating selection of well-grown plants herbaceous perennials, some lovely small trees and shrubs, nearly 300 varieties of hostas, ornamental grasses, aquatics, and marginals, ferns, vines, hardy fuchsias, and more. Proprietor Randal Atkinson is a fanatic about grasses and hostas, so you won't be disappointed in his selection. He also carries a number of the best gardening journals and magazines, such as *Gardens Illustrated, BBC Gardeners World, Practical Gardening, Garden Design, Pacific Horticulture, The Herb Companion*, and the like. Their catalog offers 60 pages of select new varieties from Europe, the United States, and Canada. The display borders that greet your arrival are luscious, with acres devoted to displaying the rare, unusual, and spectacular plant material sold here.

MINTER COUNTRY GARDENS

10015 Young Street North, Chilliwack BC V2P 4V4 Canada | **Phone:** (888) MINTERS or (604) 792-6612 | **Fax:** (604) 792-8893 | **Email:** minter@minter.org | **Web:** www.mintergardens.com | Second location: 45675 Knight Road, Sardis, BC, (604) 858-6162 | Show gardens: 52892 Bunker Road, Rosedale, BC, (888) MINTERS | **Directions:** Minter Country Gardens is near Harrison Hot Springs, about 75 miles east of Vancouver. You can reach the main store by traveling east of Vancouver on Trans Canada Hwy 1. Take exit #135 (see Harrison Hot Springs Resort signs). Minter Gardens is just across the overpass at the intersection for highways #1 and #9. | **Open:** Daily, April-October

Country Gardens has been an important part of the Chilliwack community for more than four decades, with Brian and Faye Minter as owners for more than three of them. The original Country Gardens store was relocated about five years ago to a beautiful 18-acre site on Young Street North. A second store, Country Garden World, operates in Sardis. A visit to Minter's is indeed a daylong event, as you'll want to save time to take in the many special events and sights. The Prins Dutch Venlo–style glass greenhouse, using the latest plant-growing technology (hot water in-floor heating, computer-monitored irrigation and fertilization, energy curtains, and vents), is amazing to see. You can enjoy the glorious display gardens, then shop for plants. Minter's is always on the lookout for new varieties; in fact Brian Minter is a regular at the Northwest Flower and Garden Show, where he usually lectures on new plant introductions for the residential garden. At the center of the Young Street North site, you'll enjoy a water park, many paths, and the botanical garden-style setting. Sunday afternoons, March through October (weather permitting), enjoy musical entertainment in the Minter Gardens' courtyard. Hungry? Before you leave, enjoy buffet dining in the Trillium Restaurant or grab a snack in the Bloomer's Garden Café. During warm weather, the nursery also operates The Garden Gazebo with ice cream, hot dogs, and popcorn.

OLD ROSE NURSERY

1020 Central Road, Hornby Island, BC V0R 1Z0 Canada | **Phone:** (250) 335-2603 | **Fax:** (250) 335-2602 | **Email:** oldrose@mars.ark.com | **Web:** www.oldrosenursery.com | **Directions:** The nursery is located on Hornby Island along Central Road (the main road), two miles from the ferry dock. To get to Hornby Island, which is in the Strait of Georgia, catch the ferry from Vancouver Island to Denman Island and then drive across Denman to the Hornby Island ferry. (See www.hornbyisland.net for recommended accommodations and activities.) | **Open:** Generally open afternoons from mid-June to mid-August; Spring and Fall weekends. All visits require an advanced appointment. | **Catalog:** Free, on website.

Tony and Carol Quin propagate and grow own-root roses for mail order throughout Canada, and for retail and wholesale buyers. The nursery began more than 12 years ago and has grown to surround their original Hornby Island home and cottage garden. Now, the roses have taken over the vegetable patch, too. The nursery's collection of more than 700 varieties of roses, including a wide range of climbing and rambling roses, Old Garden heritage roses, English, Rugosas, modern shrub roses and their hybrids, groundcover roses, and species or wild roses. Old Rose Nursery is a licensed propagator of David Austin's English Roses. Enjoy the Quin's display garden from mid-June through July. If you're planning a summer visit, contact the nursery to find out about the summer rose festival, usually in June.

PACIFIC RIM NATIVE PLANT NURSERY

44305 Old Orchard Road, Chilliwack, BC V2R 1A9 Canada | **Phone:** (888) 751-7427 or (604) 792-9279 | **Fax:** (604) 792-1891 | **Email:** plants@hillkeep.ca | **Web:** www.hillkeep.ca | **Directions:** Chilliwack Mountain is on the Fraser River, on the outskirts of the city of Chilliwack. By car, Pacific Rim nursery is about 3 hours northeast of Seattle and 1.5 hours east of Vancouver. From Hwy 99, head east onto Hwy 1 to Exit 109 (Yale Road West). From the exit ramp, turn left over the highway; turn right at the immediate fork and soon cross some railroad tracks to Industrial way. From Industrial, turn left on Old Orchard Road (there's a large white building with a red roof on the corner). Follow Old Orchard across water meadows and along the Fraser River, slowly climbing. Turn right on Shrewsbury Drive. At the end of pavement, you'll find the nursery's private dirt road, which snakes up the hill on a one-lane road (no room to pass so be sure to make that appointment!) | **Open:** April-October, by appointment. Mail-order sales year-round. U.S. customers take note: PRNP will help you acquire Phytosanitary Certificates (at cost, currently $12) should you wish to carry plants back across the border. | **Plant list:** extensive listing of plants and seeds on website.

Patricia Woodward (mother) and Paige (daughter) have made their home and nursery on a small, cultivated patch inside the Hillkeep Nature Reserve, an 80-acre private nature reserve at the top of Chilliwack Mountain. There they have a small display garden of native plants and a heart-stopping view of the Fraser Valley 100 feet below. In progress are a display rock garden of native alpine plants and a series of walks through special habitats on the rest of the reserve. Another daughter, Dorrie Woodward, is indispensable on seed-collecting expeditions and photographic documentations. The Woodwards grow more than 500 species native to the Pacific Northwest, nearly all from wild-collected seed. In their words,

"These plants are not only beautiful, they were born to thrive without cosseting. We have plants adapted to bog and streamside; steep slopes; meager soil; deep shade; pitiless sun; rainless summers; soggy winters; moving screes; rock gardens; and troughs. Did we mention blizzards?"

Their specialties include: bulbs, vines, alpine plants, grasses, ferns, trees and shrubs. The list is intoxicating: saxifrages; aquilegias; lewisias; penstemons (more than 30 kinds); Cypripediums (3 kinds, from seed); gentians; Pacific Coast Irises; dodecatheons; wild roses; a vast array of ground covers; lilies; Calochorti and other bulbs! Every plant comes with complete growing instructions. Wholesale and retail. If getting to Pacific Rim seems daunting, seek out the Woodwards at the various regional plant sales in B.C., including the Pacific Northwest Native Plant Sale, the VanDusen Botanical Garden spring plant sale and the Alpine Garden Club of BC sale (sale info usually listed on nursery website). If you want to really experience seed exploration, check into Paige's plant-study tours led in collaboration with botanists to places like China.

The Perennial Gardens

13139 224th Street, Maple Ridge, BC V4R 2P6 Canada | **Phone:** (604) 467-4218 | **Fax:** (604) 467-3181 | **Email:** info@perennial gardener.com | **Web:** http://perennialgardener.com | **Directions:** 45 minutes east of Vancouver; from Hwy #7 (Lougheed Hwy), take 224th Street north to the nursery from downtown Maple Ridge. From south of the Fraser River take the (free) car ferry just north of downtown Fort Langley. Factor the possibility of a wait here, depending on the Ferry gods. | **Open:** Seasonally, Wednesday-Saturday | **Catalog:** $5, for a 2-year subscription

Elke and Ken Knechtel propagate about 80 percent of the plants they sell and have their finger on the heartbeat of the serious gardener. It is obvious that they love plants, growing them and talking to others about their interest. They offer mail order to the U.S., and a visit to the website will provide all the incentive you'll need to buy from the 1,800-plus varieties offered. Perennial Gardens has many plants for shady sites, a nice selection of North American natives, hard-to-find herbaceous perennials, "bold" plants, sun-loving companions, ornamental grasses, and field-grown Japanese iris. Some of the larger collections include hardy geraniums, hostas, astilbes, ferns, and primula. Consider planning your visit around a workshop or talk, and come prepared to spend some very enjoyable and educational time wandering the many display gardens of mixed borders and invitingly planted creek and woodland shade gardens.

The Potting Shed Antiques & Garden Shop

1706 152nd Street, White Rock, BC V4A 4N4 Canada | **Phone:** (604) 541-6100 | **Fax:** (604) 541-9114 | **Web:** www.thepottingshed.ca | **Directions:** Take I-5 north to the U.S.-Canadian border, crossing through the Truck Crossing at Blaine, which brings you onto Pacific Hwy/176th Street. Continue north to 16th Street and turn left. Turn right on 152nd Street, go one block to 17th Street and the shop is on the corner. | **Open:** Daily (closed Mondays)

This charming urban garden shop, located just across the border into British Columbia, will transport you to the English country garden. You'll discover unique plant material selected by a staff horticulturist. The shop also designs custom containers and offers courtyard and garden design services. And of course, you'll love the salvaged garden antiques, vintage home décor, and furniture. We love the motto here: "Blurring the distinction between home and garden"

Ravenhill Herb Farm

1330 Mt. Newton Cross Road, Saanichton, BC V8M 1S1 Canada | **Phone:** (250) 652-4024 | **Email:** andnoel@pacificcoast.net | **Directions:** 25 minutes north of Victoria, 15 minutes from the Schwartz Bay ferry, 3 miles from Butchart Gardens. There is a detailed map at www.islandfarmfresh.com. | **Open:** April-July, Sundays only, Noon-5 p.m.

In 1979 Andrew Yeoman (the gardener) and Noel Richardson (the author) moved to what was to become Ravenhill Herb Farm, he a former geologist-school teacher-investment counselor and she a former librarian. Their years of developing a successful culinary following involves not only the building of a nursery (which sells culinary and landscape herbs) and shop (with Morris Holmes' fine garden benches and country-style cabinets plus Laura Victoria soap products made on the farm), but also the writing of several fine books on growing and cooking with herbs (see Chapter 10, "Literature & Periodicals"). There are stunning views of the wooded valley, the sparkling water of the inlet, and the pastoral countryside as backdrop to the lovely display beds of organic vegetables and herbs.

Rain Forest Nurseries

1470 227th Street, Langley, BC Canada | **Phone:** (604) 530-3499 | **Fax:** (604) 530-3480 | **Email:** sales@rainforestnurseries.com | **Web:** www.rainforestnurseries.com | **Directions:** To reach Rain Forest Nurseries from Vancouver or Seattle, take Hwy 99 to 8th Avenue East exit to Hwy 15. Turn right on 16th Avenue and proceed east to 227th Street. Turn right on 227th Street. | **Open:** Daily, February-November; by appointment during winter months. | **Catalog:** $5, 80 pages

Nestled among trees and ponds in a quiet country setting, Rain Forest offers a great selection of perennials, grasses, sedges and rushes, vines and creepers, ferns, sub-tropicals, tender perennials and annuals, trees and shrubs, roses and plants for bogs and water gardens. To compliment the plants, choose from cedar and terra cotta planters, quality garden furniture and trellises. Enjoy the innovative display gardens and uncommon plant selections or chat with Rain Forest's friendly staff. Informative workshops are also offered.

SHOP IN THE GARDEN & PLANT CENTRE

6804 SW Marine Drive, Vancouver, BC V6T 1Z4 Canada | **Phone:** (604) 822-4529 | **Fax:** (604) 822-1514 | **Web:** www.ubcbotanicalgarden.org. | **Open:** Daily

This small but well-stocked shop is at the entrance to the University of British Columbia Botanical Garden. Staffed mostly by enthusiastic volunteer "friends of the garden," the shop is a great place to buy the rare and unusual species featured throughout the many glorious displays. You'll enjoy the selection of perennials and small shrubs, plus a selection of seeds collected from more than 300 plants here.

SOUTHLANDS NURSERY

6550 Balaclava St., Vancouver, BC V6M 1L9 Canada | **Phone:** (604) 261-6411 | **Fax:** (604) 261-6429 | **Web:** www.southlandsnursery.com | **Directions:** Southlands is located at the corner of W. 49th and Balaclava Streets, 2 blocks south of SW Marine Drive on the way past UBC's Botanical Garden. From downtown Vancouver/Granville Street, it is safest to turn south across traffic at the traffic light just beyond Balaclava and double back to Balaclava. | **Open:** Daily, with extended summer hours

Thomas Hobbs, along with partner Brent Beattie, has brought style and creativity to this once-neglected neighborhood nursery. It's now an elegant nursery filled with fabulous plant material, inspiring displays, and creativity everywhere. Pick a drizzly day and lose yourself among the tree ferns, orchids, bromeliads, and bedding plants in season, and the new ancient greenhouse they have salvaged and worked their magic to restore. Wander amid imported terra cotta pots, irresistible statuary, and English wire benches all cleverly tucked about in the lovely old conservatory. Or any time of the year plan a serious snoop through the thorough range of trees, shrubs, vines (Passifloras to make you quiver!), perennials, roses, roses, roses,, and the less common annuals: You'll be delirious with indecision. You will find a selective offering of local rustic and imported furniture, a few essential gardening tools, supplies, seeds, and bulbs, and Whichford Pottery from England. Of course, you'll always find copies (even autographed ones) of Thomas Hobbs' popular book, *Shocking Beauty.*

TANGLEBANK FARMS NURSERY

29985 Downes Road, Abbotsford, BC V4X 1Z8 Canada | **Phone:** (604) 856-9339 | **Fax:** (604) 856-2688 | **Email:** tanglebank farms@uniserve.com | **Web:** www.plantlovers.com | **Open:** Monday-Saturday, March to June; Wednesday-Saturday, July to October | **Directions:** Take Hwy #1 to Mt. Lehman Exit (#83); travel north on Mt. Lehman Road, past Fraser Valley Auto Mall to Downes Road

Tanglebank Farms Nursery is a cottage-style, family-run nursery situated in rural west Abbotsford. Arnold and Brenda Falk specialize in growing a wide range of perennials, herbs, and ornamental grasses, from the old favorites to the widely sought after new varieties. In the gift shop, you'll find an assortment of terra cotta containers, gardening accessories, and beautiful, handcrafted herbal soaps, shampoos, and scents. When you visit, take a leisurely stroll through the gardens that surround the nursery and soak in "the country."

WRENHAVEN NURSERY

16651 – 20th Avenue, Surrey, BC V3S 9M9 Canada | **Phone:** (604) 536-7283 | **Directions:** Take I-5 north to the U.S.-Canada border. After entering Canada, continue on Hwy 99 to 8th Avenue East. Then take 168th Street to 20th Avenue. | **Open:** Daily (closed Tuesday) | **Plant list:** Free

Wrenhaven Nursery began in 1965 as C and T Azalea Nursery, and in recent years, it has passed into the second generation of gardeners. Hart Wellmeier, a well-known West Coast bonsai artist, and Tiina Turu operate this friendly nursery with an excellent reputation for its plant material. The nursery is set within a three-acre display garden where you'll find examples of every variety of plant grown and sold here in its mature form. The best viewing season is mid-April to mid-May when the gardens are spectacular. Wrenhaven is most noted for its extensive rhododendron, azalea, and bonsai stock, all field-grown on site, with an emphasis on hardiness and quality.

WESTERN OREGON NURSERIES

Publications and Other Sources of Information

❋ *Garden Showcase:* Subscribe to this full-color monthly publication for extensive coverage of western Oregon and western Washington nurseries and gardening-related businesses, at www.gardenshowcase.com. *Garden Showcase* offers a well-researched feature called "Hitting the Road," with maps, driving directions, and opening information to *many* area nurseries. From each issue's articles there is an indexed source-list of specific plants mentioned. (See Chapter 10, "Literature & Periodicals.")

❋ *A Gaga Gardener's Guide to Nearby Nurseries,* 3rd edition (2001). In the Eugene-Springfield area, look for Ellen Schlesinger's excellent *Gaga Gardener's Guide* that describes 45 of her favorite local growers and garden centers, complete with snappy insights and good maps. To order the latest edition, published in 2001, send $14 (plus $1.05 for shipping and handling), payable to: Waccabuc Books, PO Box 26009, Eugene, OR 97402, or call (541) 686-4646. For a visitor or newcomer, this is like having an insider's guided tour to all the best hort haunts. PS: One great feature is the listing of the best local plant sales and garden societies.

❋ When you're at the big plant sales, collect information on the vendors you'd like to visit at your own pace. And don't forget those fabulous **Farmer's, Saturday,** or **Weekend Markets** as plant sources and nursery resources.

ADELMAN PEONY GARDENS

5690 Brooklake Road NE, Brooks, OR 97305-9660 | **Phone:** (503) 393-6185 | **Fax:** (503) 393-3457 | **Email:** info@peonyparadise.com | **Web:** www.peonyparadise.com | **Directions:** From Portland, travel south on I-5 to the Brooks exit 263, just north of Salem, and then travel east 1.5 miles on Brooklake Road. | **Open:** Daily, May–June 15; fall shipping with September 15 deadline for orders; shipping September 15–October 15; wholesale and retail. | **Catalog:** Free

Carol and Jim Adelman offer an awesome selection of **herbaceous peonies**—more than 100 varieties—with 28,000 plants in the ground for the big spring show of blossoms. They have been open to the public since 1995 (the family's agricultural roots include apple-growing for 25 years), and you can come to their growing fields for a close-up inspection/selection of what to grow in your own garden. The Adelmans offer 1,500 container-planted peonies to satisfy those of us who prefer choosing these glorious plants by the bloom (and scent), and offer fresh-cut stems as well. If the weather is less than cooperative, you'll appreciate a sheltered display area. The nursery continues to feature "intersectionals," crosses between the tree peony and the herbaceous peony. (Plants like this are also called "Itoh" after the Japanese man who first made the cross.) This horticultural magic adds yellow and lavender to the color palette. The foliage is finely cut, the flowers are held close to the foliage, and the plant retains its herbaceous characteristic of dying to the ground in fall. Sign up for Adelmans' newsletters, which frequently feature cultural information, and (a very nice touch) directions to nearby nurseries. Check the website for a glimpse of the many peony fairies that grace this nursery (also known as Carol and Jim's growing supply of grandchildren).

AL'S GARDEN CENTER & GREENHOUSES

1220 N Pacific Hwy, Woodburn, OR 97071 | **Phone:** (503) 981-1245 | **Fax:** (503) 982-4608 | **Email:** gardening@als-gardencenter.com | **Web:** www.als-gardencenter.com | **Directions:** From I-5 traveling south from Portland, take the Woodburn exit 271, and head east to Hwy 99E; turn right (south) onto 99. Nursery is 3 blocks farther, on the left. | **Open:** Daily

Al's Garden Center & Greenhouse was founded by Alfred and Ann Bigej, who set up a roadside fruit stand here in 1948. Today, their son Jack guides this **full-service nursery,** which operates both retail and wholesale divisions. The third generation of Bigejs has joined the business, with Jack's oldest child, Darcy, serving as the CFO; son Mark, who has a degree in horticulture, is the store and operations manager. You'll truly get the sense that this family business loves plants and gardeners when you visit. Al's Garden Center features annuals, perennials, nursery stock, water gardening, outdoor living accessories, a complete garden and gift shop, and a seasonal Christmas shop. With their three growing facilities, Al's propagates 95 percent of the annuals and perennials here. The nursery has just started a tree-growing facility, which will enhance the selection offered to retail and wholesale customers alike. Seeds include Livingston, Lake Valley, Ed Hume, and Thompson & Morgan; there's a full line of tools, remedies, statuary, and garden accents—and furniture and soils, too. Take in the ongoing displays showcasing planting ideas; attend one or several seminars offered many Saturdays on topics including roses, fruit-tree pruning, hanging baskets, clematis, mole and gopher control, ponds, bonsai, and more. Learn about what's happening at Al's by requesting *Seeds of Thought,* the information-packed newsletter.

AMBER HILL NURSERY

11998 S Criteser Road, Oregon City, OR 97045 | **Phone:** (503) 657-9289 | **Fax:** (503) 657-1005 | **Email:** amberhillnursery@aol.com | **Directions:** Between Oregon City and Canby. From I-205, take the Park Place exit, then follow Hwy 213 toward Molalla. Take a right turn onto Leland Road (yellow flashing light), follow down to Criteser Road, and turn left; the nursery is about 0.7 mile farther. From Canby, travel 2 miles north on Hwy 99E, take the Haines and New Era exit, turn left onto New Era Road. At first cross street, turn left onto Central Pt Road to Criteser Road, and turn right. | **Open:** Seasonal, or by appointment. Look for Amber Hill at the Portland Farmer's Market and Beaverton Farmer's Market. | **Catalog:** $1, includes map; wholesale and retail.

Sherry Gardner and Terry Tosney specialize in the more **unusual varieties of perennials, shrubs, small trees, conifers, and ornamental grasses.** Many of the plants have interesting bark, blooms, autumn color, and winter interest. Come especially to tempt yourself with their rare and hard-to-locate Japanese maples (species as well as about 60 cultivars; glorious foliage and richly textured bark). You'll find plants ranging from 4-inch pots to specimen-sized trees. A visit to this nursery, situated amid pastureland with grazing horses and sheep, makes an excellent day of exploration.

ARBUTUS GARDEN ARTS

119 W Main Street, Carlton, OR 97111 | **Phone:** (503) 852-6530 | **Fax:** (503) 852-6570 | **Email:** jaczav@europa.com | **Web:** www.arbutusgarden.com | **Catalog:** Online; shipping year-round.

Located in the heart of Yamhill County's wine country, Arbutus Garden Arts offers local gardeners and wine enthusiasts a great destination for botanical and garden art, tools, books, and gardening supplies, PLUS noteworthy landscape plants of the xeriscape persuasion. Deb Zaveson and Norm Jacobs operate a small farm and nursery near Yamhill and opened Arbutus Garden Arts in a historic brick building in downtown Carlton two years ago. "We focus on plants that—once established—require little irrigation," Norm says. He invites customers to the couple's nearby display garden to see firsthand how well the hardy plants, shrubs, small trees, and perennials grow here. The nursery is acquiring land adjacent to the retail site, with plans to add a new shade house for more plants.

Depending on the time of year, intrepid plant hunters might find variegated dwarf conifers, over 30 varieties of *Acer palmatum,* yellow flowering Magnolia, colorful heuchera and pulmonaria, or brilliant fall coloring hamamelis, parrotia, and fothergilla.

Tools are chosen for function and durability, and range from stainless-steel border forks and shovels to a wide selection of pruning and arborist tools. (Ask about the "tool rehab" service for refurbishing or sharpening your own tools.) Heirloom and organic vegetable starts are offered each spring. Garden furniture and structures, including gliders, swings, benches, arches, and gates, will inspire your own garden planning. Visit the reading room where you can enjoy tea and cookies and always purchase books and magazines at 15 percent off publisher's list price. The adjacent art gallery features a wide array of fine garden art in metal, wood, ceramics, glass, and fiber.

BALTZER'S SPECIALIZED NURSERY

36011 Hwy 58, Pleasant Hill, OR 97455 | **Phone:** (541) 747-5604 | **Directions:** From I-5 take exit 188A (Klamath Falls-Oakridge) and go east on Hwy 58; the nursery is 4.5 miles on right. | **Open:** Friday–Monday

The "Specialized" in the nursery name refers to Robert and Nancy Baltzer's love of the Japanese maples they offer—over 100 varieties of them, from 1-gallon to mature specimen sizes. The couple started this nursery in 1980 and has been collecting and propagating unusual plants and accents for fine gardens ever since. The inventory includes **thousands of Japanese maples** to choose from, 95 percent of which are propagated here. Baltzer's also offers a wide variety of conifers: dwarf, weeping, and contorted, and pre-bonsai plants. Specimen trees— Japanese maples and conifers—are planted on the lovely 4-acre ridge site for you to enjoy. Find also non-plant ornaments for your Japanese garden: granite and hand-carved stone, lanterns, granite stepping-stones and slabs, imported black pebbles, and landscape stone.

BARN OWL NURSERY

22999 SW Newland Road, Wilsonville, OR 97070 | **Phone:** (503) 638-0387 | **Fax:** Same | **Email:** barnowlnursery@compaq.net | **Web:** www.barnowlnursery.citysearch.com | **Directions:** From I-5, take exit 288 to I-205. Travel east and take exit 3 (Stafford Road/Lake Oswego) south to Stafford Road. Turn right onto Stafford Road; go 1.5 miles to Newland Road, and turn left onto Newland to the nursery (driveway on right). | **Open:** Seasonal and by appointment | **Plant list:** Free

For over 19 years Christine and Ed Mulder have combined their respective skills and interests in herbs, education, cooking, garden building, and the nursery business to develop their extensive herb nursery, shop, and 18 different themed herb display gardens. They offer over **400 varieties of locally grown herb plants** (with a specialty in lavender and rosemary). You'll also discover herb-inspired skin-care products for gardeners and charming garden ornaments. The best time to take in this extravagant site is during the last two weeks in June, before the lavender harvest. Watch for the annual Herb Fest in

May; a Lavender Fest in June; and a Holiday Open House in November. Request a flyer on classes, workshops, events, and sales, too.

BIG TREES TODAY, INC.

4820 SW Hillsboro Hwy, Hillsboro, OR 97123 | **Phone:** (503) 640-3011 | **Fax:** (503) 640-2877 | **Email:** sales@bigtreestoday.com | **Web:** www.bigtreestoday.com | **Mailing address:** PO Box 1402, Hillsboro, OR 97123 | **Directions:** Two miles south of Hillsboro on Hwy 219 (Hillsboro Hwy). | **Open:** Daily (closed Sundays); we recommend you call first. | **Plant list:** Free; wholesale and retail.

Since 1979 BTT has been helping with the heavy-duty task of moving big trees in or out, in sizes from 10 to 40 feet, at roughly $300 to $2,500. If you are in need of privacy, shade, good garden "bones," feel the need for a mature arboreal addition to the landscape, or if you have a need to (sigh) remove a large tree for whatever reason, give Terry Hickman a call. He offers a wide selection of **"mature trees for exceptional landscapes,"** field-grown, high quality trees—and you'll love wandering the grounds as you select and tag your own special tree. The selection includes many Japanese maples, red maples, oaks, ash, zelkova, cedars, sequoias, and dogwoods. Watch for show specials at the Portland garden shows.

BLOOMER'S NURSERY, INC.

89719 Armitage Road, Eugene, OR 97408-9454 | **Phone:** (541) 687-5919 | **Web:** www.bloomersplantnursery.com | **Directions:** From I-5, take exit 195-A to the Gateway Mall. At the light at Game Farm Road, turn left (north) and go 0.7 mile to Armitage Road; turn right and go 0.5 mile to the (retail) nursery. | **Open:** Daily

This long-established and highly respected Eugene nursery and garden center propagates 80 to 90 percent of its stock at a separate location (wholesale to the trade). Bloomer's specializes in **trees and shrubs, natives, perennials, annuals,** and more. Garden statuary, hand-crafted Americana furniture, wire works, and birdbaths round out the hard goods department. Jim and Glenda Bloomer grow the trees and shrubs on their 27-acre farm north of Eugene. Make sure to order the plant list or stop by the nursery when you're heading through Eugene.

BLUE HERON HERBARY

27731 NW Reeder Road, Sauvie Island, OR 97231 | **Phone:** (503) 621-1457 | **Web:** www.blueheronherbary.com | **Directions:** From Portland, go north on Hwy 30 to the Sauvie Island Bridge; cross the bridge, turn left, and go under bridge to Reeder Road, then turn right onto Reeder Road. | **Open:** Seasonal | **Plant list:** Free with SASE

Mike, Penny, and Heather Hanselman began Blue Heron as a vinegar and wreath business. As they developed their wonderful Elizabethan display garden to demonstrate how herbs can be used in the landscape, the evolution to an herb nursery was only a short step away. The display garden features more than 300 varieties of culinary and medicinal herbs. Check out the "witches' garden" for an interesting use of herbs. You'll discover many **medicinal and Asian herb varieties** that may be less familiar, as well as a wide array of culinary and ornamental herbs. Come summer, inhale and enjoy 50-plus lavender varieties—wow!

BOSKEY DELL NATIVES

23311 SW Boskey Dell Lane, West Linn, OR 97068 | **Phone:** (503) 638-5945 | **Fax:** (503) 638-8047 | **Email:** boskydellnatives@ aol.com | **Directions:** From I-205, take the Stafford Road exit; go north on Stafford Road to Borland Road. Turn right, going east on Borland Road 2 miles to Boskey Dell Lane, and turn right. The nursery is located at the end of the lane on the right. | **Open:** Daily | **Plant list:** Free; wholesale and retail.

Lory Duralia offers a large selection of Northwest natives: penstemons, wildflowers, ferns, trilliums, trees, shrubs, ground covers, and wetland/riparian plants. Her motto: "Plant Oregon, Grow Native," which is great advice for anyone in the regional garden scene. Request a free brochure, which you'll find interesting (Boskey rescues about 25 percent of its plants from developing land and logging sites). The inventory here includes more than **300 varieties of Oregon native plants.** Home owners, garden groups, neighborhood associations, school classes, and others are encouraged to make a visit here as a field trip—ask questions and glean ideas from the native plant display gardens, including an **alpine pond** (especially beautiful in spring). Ask these pros about soil erosion problems, riparian restoration, and native meadow restoration. The nursery offers a number of free topical workshops and classes, including a trough-making workshop in spring.

THE BOVEES NURSERY

1737 SW Coronado Street, Portland, OR 97219 | **Phone:** (503) 244-9341 | **Email:** bovees@teleport.com | **Web:** www.bovees.com | **Directions:** Take I-5 south from Portland to the Terwilliger exit 297. Cross back over the freeway on SW Terwilliger to Boones Ferry Road (at Lewis & Clark Law School). Turn right onto Boones Ferry Road and travel to Arnold Road. Turn right on Arnold, go to 16th, then turn left onto SW Coronado. | **Open:** Wednesday–Sunday, and by appointment. | **Catalog:** $2; retail and mail order.

If you are a collector, you probably already know of the vast selection of species and hybrid rhododendrons offered by Lucie Sorensen-Smith, E. White Smith, and George Watson. Perhaps you have been lucky enough to visit their elegant garden, open to the public when the nursery is open, displaying their extensive collection of species and hybrid rhododendrons and azaleas amid the mature landscape of unusual trees and shrubs. Their catalog of **vireya (tropical and semi-tropical) rhododendrons** lists over 150 species alone. A separate catalog offers alpine and rock garden plants, ground covers, woodland shrubs, and a few special camellias, lilacs, dwarf conifers, and ferns.

BRIM'S FARM AND GARDEN

34963 Hwy 105, Astoria, OR 97103 | **Phone:** (503) 325-1562 | **Fax:** (503) 325-9231 | **Email:** briml@pacifier.com | **Web:** www.brimsonline.com | **Directions:** From Astoria, travel 1 mile south of the old Young's Bay Bridge. Look for the big blue building on the right (on business loop Hwy 101 Alternate). | **Open:** Daily (Sundays, seasonally)

Brim's (aka Mike and Linda Brim) began in this location in 1986 with a feed store; over the years they have grown into a full-fledged garden center. Some of the plants you'll find here—besides rhododendrons and azaleas—are magnolias, ginkgos, maples, kalmias, monkey puzzle trees, and hellebores. The nursery specializes in **plants for the Northwest maritime climate,** as well as plants (such as roses) known for disease-free characteristics. An abiding philosophy here is to turn first to the least toxic approach to pest and disease problems. Year-round, you can find a selection suitable for the region, including bare-root trees and shrubs in the winter. Soil amendments and fertilizers are offered in larger economy sizes. Bulk seeds hearken back to Brim's feed-store roots, and you'll want to try the **blended lawn seed tailored to specific needs.** Twice annual sales (spring and fall) are worth checking out. The website details ongoing classes on topics like coping with moles, lawn care, and container gardening. Brim's gives professional landscapers a 10 percent discount.

BROTHERS HERBS & PEONIES ✉ @

4100 Hwy 99W, Newberg, OR 97132 | **Mailing address:** PO Box 1370, Sherwood, OR 97140 | **Phone:** (503) 625-7548 | **Fax:** (503) 625-1667 | **Email:** rick@treony.com | **Web:** www.treony.com | **Directions:** Located 30 minutes south of Portland on Hwy 99W, in the heart of the Willamette Valley wine country. | **Open:** March–December, Monday–Saturday (closed Sundays), and by appointment | **Catalog:** $2, color; shipping season September–January; wholesale and retail.

Rick Rogers has moved his peony nursery to a new site, but little has changed, as he continues to sell **wonderful tree peonies;** he's even dubbed his website "treony," a nifty new name for these plants. Rick's love of peonies and genuine desire to share his skills and knowledge are contagious. When he was 16 his father offered him a "work opportunity" that involved digging some 25 old (as in 25–30 years old) tree peonies from the Walter Marx Garden (Marx once owned the largest mail-order perennial nursery in the United States, and was known for his peony breeding.) Rick remembers the magic scent of the roots as he was digging, and that experience inspired a love affair that has in turn given birth to this nursery. Some 20 years later, he has those very peonies as a solid foundation for the Brothers offerings, with herbs added to the menu. You'll find Japanese, Chinese, European, and American TPs, "the best collection this side of the Mississippi." Rick propagates own-root American peonies and imports Chinese varieties. Take in the Peony Bloom Fest during the last week of April through mid-June.

BROWN'S ROSE LODGE NURSERY

5211 Salmon River Hwy, Otis, OR 97368 | **Phone:** (541) 994-2953 | **Directions:** Located 8 miles east of Lincoln City on Hwy 18 (Salmon River Hwy) in the community of Rose Lodge. The nursery is visible from the highway—its driveway leads off Hwy 18 at about mile 5.2. It's easy to find. | **Open:** Daily (closed some "rainy Wednesdays" in the winter).

Wally and Karen Brown characterize their 25-year-old nursery as a mom-and-pop country garden center with a casual attitude and a surprising selection of **plants good for a coastal areas,** including some unusual varieties. They propagate fuchsias, orchid cactus, and several other varieties of unusual plants. You'll also find shrubs, trees, indoor plants, and seasonal annuals and perennials. This nursery always has the basics, from tools and seeds to books and bagged soil and amendments. Seeds sources include Lilly Miller and Ed Hume. This is exactly the kind of place you'll enjoy discovering on a foray into the country or a drive off the beaten path. You meet the nicest people and feel your discovery provides a little insight into the fabric of the place.

CAPRICE FARM NURSERY

10944 Mill Creek Road SE, Aumsville, OR 97325 | **Phone:** (503) 749-1397 | **Fax:** (503) 749-4097 | **Web:** www.capricefarm.com | **Directions:** From Portland on I-5, take Hwy 22 exit heading east toward Bend (Santiam Hwy) Take exit 12, heading south to Mill Creek Road and Caprice Farm is on the left. | **Open:** Seasonal and by appointment | **Catalog:** $2, refundable with order

If you fancy peonies, tree peonies, hostas, Japanese and Siberian irises, and daylilies, then contact Cindi and Charlie Turnbow. Cindi's parents Al and Dot Rogers, started the nursery in 1975 (Al Rogers is the author of a Timber Press book on peonies, considered one of the most indepth sources on these luscious plants) and sold it to daughter and son-in-law in 1996. The Turnbows have recently moved Caprice Farm to new farmland in the fertile Willamette Valley, with more than 11 acres for growing their crops. Order Caprice Farm's catalog or check the very nice website, which features color photos of their offerings.

CARTER'S GREENHOUSE AND NURSERY

5145 Waymire Road, Dallas, OR 97338 | **Phone:** (503) 787-3371 | **Fax:** (503) 787-1502 | **Directions:** From I-5 heading south take the Salem Parkway exit and follow this road through Salem to the Marion Street bridge. Cross over the bridge, going west on Hwy 22. Take Hwy 22 to Hwy 99W. Turn left onto Hwy 99W and travel south 6 miles to Monmouth. At the traffic signal in Monmouth turn right, heading west. After the stop sign, go 2 blocks to Whitman, turn left onto Whitman and follow signs to Falls City. Go about 10 miles to the intersection with Hwy 223 (Kings Valley Hwy), go straight across onto Bridgeport Road, then go 1 mile to a "T"; turn left (you'll still be on Bridgeport). Go past the school (on right), cross a bridge, and go 1.5 miles. Bridgeport becomes a gravel road and goes over a hill and into a little valley. The nursery is on Waymire Road, the first right-hand road off Bridgeport on this gravel stretch. The nursery is on the left. | **Open:** Tuesday–Saturday | **Plant list:** Free; wholesale and retail.

When Steve and Peggy Carter fax their plant list, the reference line across the top of the page reads: Carters' Cool Plants. There is indeed a pretty "cool" lineup of plants that make you say Ahah—I want one! The Carters grow and propagate **gunnera, meconopsis (blue poppy),**

hardy **English violas and primroses, hardy ginger, grasses, many natives, vines galore, and lots of hostas.** The list changes throughout the year, depending upon availability. *Aruncus aethusifolius* (dwarf goatsbeard), *Eryngium agavifolium* (sea holly), *Sedum* 'Matrona' (an upright sedum form), *Euphorbia amygdaloides* 'Rubra' (purple spurge) . . . these selections were among about 175 plants on an August list. Sound appealing? You betcha!

CASCADE BULB & SEED

PO Box 271, Scotts Mills, OR 97375 | **Phone:** (503) 873-2218 | **Email:** halinar@open.org | **Web:** www.homestead.com/cascade or www.open.org/halinar/cbs.htm | **Open:** By appointment only; directions provided when you call. | **Plant list:** Send a first-class stamp; list available via email. Shipping season is March–October (plants), November–May (seeds).

Joseph Halinar started Cascade Bulb & Seed in 1979 after receiving a PhD in plant breeding from the University of Wisconsin-Madison. His specialized list will be of interest to collectors and hybridizers, with mail-order offerings of lily (Asiatic, Martagon, Caucasian, Western American, trumpet), daylily, and allium seeds and plants. "My goal is to have the best lily seed list possible," he writes in a recent plant list. Joseph is especially excited about some of the *Lilium davidii* hybrids and crosses he's developing.

COOLEY'S GARDENS, INC.

11553 Silverton Road NE, Silverton, OR 97381 | **Phone:** (503) 873-5463 | **Fax:** (503) 873-5812 | **Email:** cooleyiris@aol.com | **Web:** www.cooleysgardens.com | **Mailing address:** PO Box 126, Silverton, OR 97381 | **Directions:** From Portland take I-5 south to the Woodburn exit to Silverton Hwy 214 through Mt. Angel and Silverton. Go west on Hwy 213 toward Salem. Cooley's is 12 miles east of Salem on Silverton Road. | **Open:** Daily (extended hours during bloom season, generally the last two weeks of May) | **Catalog:** $5, deductible from your order; shipping July–September; wholesale and retail.

Since 1928 three generations of the Cooley family have been breeding and propagating tall bearded iris in Oregon's Willamette Valley. Now one of the world's largest growers of bearded iris, the Cooley fields encompass over 200 acres. You are invited to stroll the 5 acres of wheelchair accessible display gardens and marvel at over a million iris in bloom in the fields. The best viewing time is generally mid-May until early June, when you'll also be treated to special flower arranging, wine-tasting, and musical events (check website and catalog for dates). If you haven't seen the fabulous catalog, the "Iris Fancier's Standard Reference Book," you are in for a real visual treat; there's a new edition each April. Your horticultural reference library will find no greater bargain, as over 300 varieties are photographed in nearly 4 x 4-inch close-up portraits, with good descriptions. They offer a 19-minute video on iris planting, care, hybridizing, flower arranging, and landscape use as a *free* service to garden clubs. They also offer a unique service on the plants you buy: for $2 you can purchase *nightmare insurance* on your order! If for

ANY reason you lose your plants ("the freeze of the century, a raid by the neighbor's pigs or kids, flood, tornado . . .") just write them by July the year following your order, and they'll get a replacement to you. No kidding.

CORNELL FARM

8212 SW Barnes Road, Portland, OR 97225 | **Phone:** (503) 292-9895 | **Fax:** (503) 292-1051 | **Email:** cornellfarm@hevanet.com | **Directions:** Located west of downtown Portland. Just off the interchange for US 26 and SR 217, get off on 217 and stay in the right lane, which puts you on East Barnes Road. Go 1 mile east toward Portland on SE Barnes Road (passing St. Vincent's Hospital). Watch for the nursery on the right and the gazebo near the road. | **Open:** Daily

Debby Barnhart and Ed Blatter are enthusiastic propagators, raising 95 percent of their offerings from seed, cuttings, divisions, bulbs, and roots. Their 5-acre nursery shares the landscape with a historic home in Portland's West Hills. Here you'll find a specialty in **flowers—over 1,200 varieties of perennials and annuals**—with a carefully selected collection of the best trees and shrubs for the Northwest. Cornell Farm is well known for its large, eclectic, and even fanciful potted gardens and containers, as well as its extensive selection of bulbs in the fall and potted bulbs in spring, and well worth a visit. The resurgence of house plants is respected here, with a lineup of common to unusual indoor plants of all sizes. Find, as well, seeds from Shepherd's and Unwins, and complete garden supplies, organic and biological garden controls/fertilizers, and a limited selection of tools. Delivery and garden consultations are also available. Holidays are celebrated at Cornell Farm, so visit in December when you'll find trees, wreaths, ornaments, and garden gifts. Call for dates on classes and the **October Pansy Festival.**

DANCING OAKS NURSERY

17900 Priem Road, Monmouth, OR 97361 | **Phone:** (503) 838-6058 | **Web:** www.dancing-oaks.com | **Directions:** Located west of Salem about 40 minutes. From I-5 south of Salem, take the Hwy 22 exit 253 west to Hwy 99W, and take it going south to Monmouth. Go through town and after 3 miles turn right onto Parker Road. At the intersection turn right onto Helmick Road, then very soon go left on Elkins Road. Stay on Elkins until it ends, then turn left onto Arlie Road and go 1.5 miles down Arlie; turn right on Maple Grove for about 0.75 mile and at the bend in the road go right on Priem Road. Hang in there. Proceed about 2 miles down this gravel road until it ends at the nursery. | **Open:** Seasonal and by appointment; ask for the brochure that includes a map (send SASE); wholesale and retail.

Fred Weisensee and Leonard Foltz have carved out a secluded setting for their nursery in the foothills of the Coast Range. They describe themselves as "hopeless collectors always seeking the new and unusual." You will have much to ponder here if your tastes run to **new, rare shrubs from China, hardy bananas, hellebores, hostas, heuchera, tiarellas, ornamental crabapples, ginkgos, enkianthus, named varieties of rugosa roses, and *Cardiocrinum giganteum.*** Wander the three-year-old spring woodland display garden, or the summer garden, and note the low garden wall made of terra-cotta tiles. Fred and Leonard have crafted the metal arches, arbors, and obelisks they have on display and for sale, and carry glazed Asian pots, too. Call ahead, then load up the car with adventuresome friends for a botanical expedition.

DARYLL'S NURSERY

15770 W Ellendale Road, Dallas, OR 97338 | **Phone:** (503) 623-0251 | **Fax:** Same | **Email:** daryllsnursery@msn.com | **Directions:** From Portland, take I-5 south to Salem Parkway. Follow signs to Dallas, and take the Dallas exit. Just past Hwy 99 from the left lane go 3.7 miles to a signal light. Stay in right lane, and go 2 more miles to the nursery. | **Open:** Tuesday–Saturday; wholesale and retail.

With combined experience of nearly 50 years in the business of growing and selling plants, Daryll Combs and Martine Rivera propagate close to 100 varieties of ornamental grasses, gunneras, *Romneya coulteri* (Matilija poppies), new and exciting perennials, vines, and shrubs, plus many hydrangeas and bamboo varieties. Daryll's started life in Santa Barbara, California, and moved to Oregon about ten years ago. The nursery is now building a new propagation house, which will, as Daryll says, greatly expand the plants "we are waiting to try, as there are always new goodies here." The couple is dedicated to customers, with such services as free delivery (so you can get that 15-gallon *Gunnera chilensis* hauled home for you). Daryll's selection ranges from a large number of **unusual trees** (birches, Camperdown elms, and redwoods, for example), to **pre-bonsai** plants and plants to attract hummingbirds and butterflies (buddleias, cistus). You'll find much here to peruse.

DELTA FARM AND NURSERY

3925 N Delta Hwy, Eugene, OR 97408 | **Phone:** (541) 485-2992 | **Fax:** (541) 485-1985 | **Email:** deltafarm@nu-world.com | **Web:** www.deltafarm.com | **Directions:** From I-5, take exit 195B and travel west on Beltline Road to the Delta Hwy N exit; then go north 1 mile to the nursery, on the right (across from River Ridge Golf Course). | **Open:** Seasonal and by appointment; at Lane County/Eugene Farmer's Market Saturdays from early April. | **Catalog:** Free (can also be downloaded from website); shipping in February–June.

Ron and Faye Spidell have been growing plants as a hobby for 40 years and commercially for 13, a business that grew out of feeding a large family from their own expansive home garden. Each year this tireless couple adds more growing space and more varieties for you to choose from (spread over 3 acres). **Fuchsias** have been a specialty from the very beginning of their life together—view 185 varieties on the bright new website; all **650 varieties** can be ordered via a secure shopping service. Now they offer you an enormous selection including hybrids from New Zealand, Holland, and England. Many of the hardiest are on display here, with the Spidells planting new ones all the time. "Our intent is to research to add to the list of frost-hardy fuchsias here in the Northwest," Faye says. Choose your fuchsia starts in early March, so you can extend your budget to try more varieties. Wait until you see what this couple has in store for you tomato and pepper fanatics! The list (including cultural tips) is positively mouthwatering. Find also many varieties of herbs, ferns, houseplants (tuberous begonias), veggie starts, and some geraniums.

DOWN TO EARTH

532 Olive Street, Eugene, OR 97401 | **Phone:** (541) 342-6820 | **Fax:** (541) 342-2261 | **New second location:** 2498 Willamette Street, Eugene, OR 97405; (541) 349-0556 | **Web:** www.home2garden.com | **Open:** Daily

Down to Earth does not fit the pattern of what you may expect in a garden center, though it provides the vast range of gardening what-nots that would let it fit that category. The "home, garden, and gift" store is a modern version of the old general store, but with so much more. Adjacent to the kitchen, furniture, and pet departments, Down to Earth's organic garden section reflects the dedication of Jack Bates and his staff to environmental concerns and an approach to horticulture that is thoughtful and imaginative. You'll find organically grown **vegetable starts,** and **Northwest native** and **drought-tolerant plants,** plus a wonderful selection of water garden plants, hard-to-find perennials, and **hardy exotics** to whet and satisfy your botanical appetite. The plant department has expanded from its previous quarters and remains packed with treasures that will hold a discerning plant lover's rapt attention.

Seeds include Territorial, Renee's, Seeds of Change, Thyme Garden, Shepherd's, and more; plus, organic garden remedies and fertilizers. During the holidays, you can buy live trees, plus fresh cut boughs and wreaths, not to mention garden-inspired gifts. Sign up to receive the newsletter for updates on local garden events.

DUCKWORTH'S NURSERY

84846 S Willamette Street, Eugene, OR 97405 | **Phone:** (541) 345-5408 | **Directions:** South of Eugene city limits 2.5 miles, at the junction of S Willamette and Fox Hollow Road. | **Open:** Daily

If you are on the hunt for a special **deciduous or evergreen tree or shrub** then definitely include a stop at Duckworth's as a part of your search process. Peggy and Paul Duckworth's service-oriented family business (they deliver and plant) has served the area's homeowners and gardeners for a quarter of a century, offering a particularly fine selection of over 3,000 large-scale woody plants, with less-mature and smaller individuals too. The nursery is set on 22 acres of woods.

EARTH'S RISING TREES

PO Box 334, Monroe, OR 97456 | **Phone:** (541) 847-5950 | **Fax:** Same | **Email:** earthsrising@juno.com | **Directions:** call for directions; expect 3 miles of gravel road. | **Open:** By appointment only; or find them at First Alternative Co-op, Corvallis, and the Eugene Farmers' Market. | **Catalog:** Free; shipping mid-December to May, then plants are discounted.

Delbert McCombs's fruit trees—apples: dwarf, minidwarf, semidwarf, crab, traditional, scab-resistant, classic dessert, new wave, and russet; peaches; pears; plums; and a Bing cherry—are among the very few Certified Organically grown you will find (usually with a great deal of effort) available commercially. The list focuses on **fruit-tree varieties for the maritime Northwest.** For 20 years McCombs has shared his life and ideals with the members of Earth's Rising Farm, a chartered cooperative on 60 acres nestled in the rolling hills near Corvallis. In reading about McCombs and his trees, you'll learn about the quality and care that have been invested into these plants. If you are interested in grafting fruit trees, consider an apprenticeship or call for workshop dates.

EDMUNDS' ROSES

6235 SW Kahle Road, Wilsonville, OR 97070 | **Phone:** (503) 682-1476 or (888) 481-7673 | **Fax:** (593) 682-1275 | **Email:** info@edmundsroses.com | **Web:** www.edmundsroses.com | **Directions:** From I-5 take exit 286 (18 miles south of Portland) and head east 1 mile. Turn right on SW 65th Avenue and right on SW Stafford Road, and travel a little more than 0.5 mile and then turn left onto Kahle Road. | **Open:** Daily | **Catalog:** Free, full color; shipping season is early December to mid-May.

This family-owned nursery has operated for 53 years with an emphasis on **modern roses of all types,** about a third of which the Edmunds propagate themselves. You will also find gloves, shears, soil-test kits, drip systems, and fertilizer for roses. Check out their website or stop by the nursery the third weekend of April for the big clearance sale.

EVANS FARM NURSERY

22289 S Molalla Hwy 213, Oregon City, OR 97045 | **Phone:** (503) 632-3475 | **Fax:** (503) 632-4967 | **Email:** evansfarmsgrdctr@ mymailstation.com | **Directions:** Take I-205 to exit 10 and head south on Hwy 213. The nursery is 6.2 miles farther down Hwy 213. | **Open:** Daily

Evans is a 144-year-old family farm and nursery that specializes in **conifers, broadleaf ornamentals, shrubs, and perennials (over 300 varieties).** While Evans is widely known for supplying other retail nurseries and landscapers, the good news is that you can buy direct from them at the on-site retail store. Evans has an extensive arboretum here where you can see trees and shrubs in their mature state. There are special events year-round, including ten workshops. You can learn about these and more in Evans' quarterly newsletter—call to add your name to the list.

FARMINGTON GARDENS

21815 SW Farmington Road, Beaverton, OR 97007 | **Phone:** (503) 649-4568 | **Fax:** (503) 649-4540 | **Email:** sales@farmingtongardens. com | **Web:** www.farmingtongardens.com | **Directions:** Take Hwy 26 west from Portland to 185th Street. Head south on 185th to Farmington Road, turn west and travel 2 miles to the nursery. | **Open:** Daily

Farmington carries a great variety of **perennials, grasses, and fresh nursery stock,** much of which is propagated here. Sign up for email announcements or add your name to the newsletter list to learn about special events, such as the yearly Green Thumb Sale, held in July.

FERGUSON'S FRAGRANT NURSERY

21763 French Prairie Road NE, St. Paul, OR 97137 | **Phone:** (503) 633-4585 | **Fax:** (503) 633-4586 | **Email:** info@fragrant nursery.com | **Web:** www.fragrantnursery.com | **Directions:** From I-5, take exit 278 (Donald-Aurora) and drive west 5 miles; turn right on French Prairie Road NE; the nursery is the first driveway on the left. | **Open:** Daily, March–October, or by appointment.

Danielle Ferguson opened her nursery in 1997 with an emphasis on gathering together **fragrant perennials and shrubs.** She especially loves to offer customers fragrant plants that also provide year-round color and texture. Ferguson's Fragrant Nursery also specializes in custom baskets. Visit (and smell) the display garden, especially beautiful and enjoyable from May through September. Information on workshops and events is frequently updated on the website.

FORESTFARM

990 Tetherow Road, Williams, OR 97544-9599 | **Phone:** (541) 846-7269 | **Fax:** (541) 846-6963 | **Email:** forestfarm@rvi.net | **Web:** www.forestfarm.com (on-line ordering) | **Directions:** Use a good map, but this will help: Location is 4-5 hours south of Portland. From I-5, take the first Grants Pass exit and go straight through town (exit runs into 6th Street through town, which runs straight into Hwy 238 at the south end of town, watch for Jacksonville Hwy, Murphy, Medford on sign). Follow Hwy 238 through Murphy (where it bends to the left). About 5 miles past Murphy the road takes a hard (90-degree) right turn and then a 90-degree left turn—here you go straight instead—onto Watergap Road (there is a sign to Williams as well). About 5 miles later, go right at the "T" intersection. Once in Williams, go right onto Tetherow Road (just before the General Store/Post Office). In approximately 0.75 mile you'll see a green mailbox (No. 990) on the right. When you pull in, open your car window and push the button to open the "deer gate." | **Open:** By appointment only (late in the week is best) | **Catalog:** $5 for 500-plus pages with thorough descriptions; year-round shipping.

This nursery is highly recommended for its enormous selection of **over 6,000 kinds of native and non-native plants suitable for the Northwest, trees/shrubs, vines, and perennials,** many of which are propagated here. Ray (armed with a master's in horticulture from UC Davis) and Peg Prag started Forestfarm more than 25 years ago with natives in mind. Then, that was virtually unheard of; now, Forestfarm's plant list is diverse and rich, encompassing (it seems) much of the plant kingdom. This small, family nursery has grown to 25 employees, including 3 to 6 international horticultural student/interns each year (the Prags have hosted interns from 14 countries over the years). Forestfarm's exceptional catalog offers a list of plants that make good wildlife habitat, ones for erosion control, for basketry, for uses as dyes, for attracting hummingbirds and butterflies, for cutting gardens, and plants with nitrogen-fixing abilities. A nice selection of species roses (most on their own roots) complements the list. The hefty tome is sprinkled throughout with words of wisdom, thought-provoking quotes, and horticultural puzzles. Your life will go on hold when this catalog comes, as you dream and make plans. Looking ahead, Forestfarm is involved with establishing a 500-plus-acre botanical garden, nature center, and educational facility called Pacifica (meaning "peaceful"). Check with the nursery for more details or call (541) 846-9230.

FRAGRANT GARDEN NURSERY

PO Box 4246, Brookings, OR 97415 | **Phone:** (541) 412-8840 | **Fax:** (541) 412-8841 | **Email:** pat@fragrantgarden.com | **Web:** www.fragrantgarden.com | **Catalog:** $.50; **sweet pea seed** list only, 75 varieties, Spencers and Old Fashioned; shipping year-round on seed.

The name says it all—Pat Sherman was in search of plants (primarily choice trees and shrubs) selected specifically for fragrance. In the past several years, she's refined the nursery's offerings to emphasize sweet peas from around the globe. The colorful and informative website will give you all you need (including seed-starting advice and sweet pea history) to get your own spring bouquets started. Pat has just relocated the nursery to Brookings, so please contact her about visiting the gardens.

FRESHOPS

36180 Kings Valley Hwy, Philomath, OR 97370 | **Phone:** (541) 929-2736 | **Fax:** (541) 929-2702 | **Email:** sales@freshops.com | **Web:** www.freshops.com | **Open:** By appointment only | **Plant list:** Free; shipping season March–May; wholesale and retail; hops rhizomes, ten brewing and ornamental varieties.

GARLAND NURSERY

5470 NE Hwy 20, Corvallis, OR 97330 | **Phone:** (541) 753-6601 | **Fax:** (541) 753-3143 | **Web:** www.garlandnursery.com | **Directions:** Located halfway between Albany and Corvallis on Hwy 20 "at the 5-mile mark." West of I-5; take exit 228 at Hwy 34 interchange, going west over the Willamette River, then north (right) on Hwy 20; or, at exit 233, the intersection of I-5 and Hwy 20, proceed west on Hwy 20. | **Open:** Daily

This highly respected, full-service nursery/garden center dates back to 1937, when William and Corlie Schmidt named their new enterprise for their daughter, Garland. In turn, Garland's only son, Donald (Powell), his wife Sandra, and their three children carry on the family tradition, having tirelessly worked to expand the business and its offerings to their loyal patrons. A great deal of thought and thoughtfulness has been invested in providing displays and in the informational signage. Plan a leisurely visit to meander the well-organized, 5-acre site, with its ample selection of **trees, shrubs, perennials, bonsai** (from Wee Trees), and water plants. The large gift and garden supplies shop is housed in the remodeled barn; find garden books and wild bird supplies, too. Call for dates to attend the Spring Open House in April and the Christmas Open House in November. Ask about the ongoing workshop series, offered spring and fall.

GOODWIN CREEK GARDENS @

PO Box 83, Williams, OR 97544 | **Phone:** (800) 846-7359 | **Fax:** (541) 846-7357 | **Email:** info@goodwincreekgardens.com | **Web:** www.goodwincreekgardens.com | **Open:** Year-round, by appointment and by mail order. | **Catalog:** Free; shipping year-round, weather permitting.

Jim and Dotti Becker operate their small family farm in the foothills of the Siskiyou Mountains of southwestern Oregon. They began as a cut-flower farm and have evolved into a plant and seed nursery that specializes in the **organic growing of herbs, perennials, everlasting flowers, and fragrant plants** (lavenders and scented geraniums included). Ninety percent of the seed is grown here. The selection also includes a large number of native American herbs and other plants, which, they stress, are nursery propagated, not dug in the wild. Goodwin Creek Gardens is well known for its selection of lavenders (over 50 cultivars in the current catalog). Look here for plants for dyeing or drying, along with detailed information on planting butterfly, hummingbird, and everlasting gardens. If your interests are in everlastings, the Beckers have passed along their hard-earned wisdom through two books on the subject, *An Everlasting Garden* and *Concise Guide to Growing Everlastings* (now out of print but may be available through used bookstores). Look for *Scented Geraniums* too, and consider inviting the Beckers to lecture for your own garden club. The nursery also offers herbal soaps, shampoos, and bath products. Order the free monthly email newsletter, *The Vole's Venue,* filled with lots of friendly advice about the plants and animals in your garden, garden crafts, recipes, and more (subscribe on the wonderful website).

GOSSLER FARMS NURSERY ☀ ✉

1200 Weaver Road, Springfield, OR 97478-9663 | **Phone:** (541) 746-3922 | **Fax:** (541) 744-7924 | **Directions:** Located 9 miles off I-5. Take exit 194A (to Springfield, McKenzie River) on I-105 then go left (east) on Main Street to 69th Street. Take a left, go to the end of 69th, and take a right on Thurston Road, then the next left on Weaver, and travel to the end. | **Open:** For orders/questions 8 a.m.–5 p.m.; visits by appointment only. | **Catalog:** $2; shipping season October–December and February–May.

Prepare for major temptation if you have a soft spot in your horticultural heart for rare shrubs (some found nowhere else in the country)! "Rarity isn't the only criterion: most important is that the plant is beautiful at least one season of the year." It is obvious that Marj Gossler (mom) and her talented sons Roger and Eric are true collectors at heart. This hobby turned regional nursery treasure started with a catalog in 1968. Now, it's grown to amazing proportions. Varieties from Gossler include 450–500 different magnolias, 150 rhododendrons, 40 varieties of hamamelis, as well as numerous other trees, shrubs, perennials, and bulbs. You'll find unusual ornamental trees and, where the species is quite common, you will often find interestingly named cultivars. There are some perennials and vines as well. But if it is **trees and shrubs of distinction** you are looking for, this is one of the finest sources in the country; stewartia, styrax, corylopsis, acers, aralia elata, berberis, cercidiphyllum, cornus, daphne, hydrangea, and hellebores pop off the list . . . among many more. The 3-acre (accessible) private display garden will wow you with some 5,000 different varieties of plants, beyond the ones shown in their catalog, and many mature specimens of those you may be considering from the nursery! The gardens are best to visit from February through October (bring camera and notebook as it's a fantastic reference source). Call to see if Gossler is hosting any "open gardens" to showcase special bloom times, such as hellebores or magnolias.

GRAY'S GARDEN CENTERS, INC.

737 W 6th Avenue, Eugene, OR 97402 | **Phone:** (541) 345-1569 | **Second location:** 4441 Main Street, Springfield, OR 97478 | **Phone:** (541) 345-1231 | **Email:** scott@graysgardens.com | **Web:** www.graysgardens.com | **Directions:** Eugene store: Take I-5 to I-105 west; take 6th Avenue exit (right) and nursery is located at the intersection of the off-ramp. | **Springfield store:** Located at 44th and Main Sts. | **Open:** Daily

Gray's, now a full-service garden center, first opened in Eugene in 1940 as a feed store, is the oldest and largest independent garden center in the Eugene-Springfield area (the Springfield location opened in 1950). This respected mainstay offers **trees, shrubs, and perennials**— old favorites along with less well-known varieties—and **more than 8,000 roses,** in season. The shop carries a broad selection of gardening supplies, including books; organic and nonorganic pest and disease controls, soils, fertilizers, and amendments; statuary, containers, pond supplies, tools, garden furniture, art, and gifts. Seeds include Ed Hume, Territorial, Lilly Miller, Ferry-Morse, Thompson & Morgan, Kew Botanical, and Renee's Garden. Both centers showcase design ideas such as water gardens/features, and perennial and annual beds. Check the website for a full schedule of weekend garden clinics.

GREER GARDENS ☀ ✉

1280 Goodpasture Island Road, Eugene, OR 97401-1794 | **Phone:** (541) 686-8266 or (800) 548-0111 | **Fax:** (541) 686-0910 | **Email:** orders@greergardens.com | **Web:** www.greergardens.com | **Directions:** From I-5, take exit 195B/Beltline Road and go west 2.5 miles. Take the Delta Hwy exit, and at the stop turn left onto Delta Hwy; travel 0.5 mile, then take Good Pasture Island Road exit. At the stoplight turn right and drive 0.3 mile to the nursery. | **Open:** Daily | **Catalog:** $3, with many gorgeous full-color photos and a large listing of books; includes fall catalog; shipping year-round all over the world.

Harold Greer and his family are second-generation rhododendron growers who are recognized authorities on rhododendrons. The nursery has an extensive selection (over 700 in the current catalog) of **rhododendrons** (including vireyas), and azaleas in many sizes. **Japanese maples** are also a famed specialty. Many (as in 4,500) **new, rare, and unusual trees, shrubs, and vines** fill the information-packed pages of their catalog, with a fair showing of such diverse interests as orchids, bamboo, rock garden plants, ornamental grasses, and bonsai (plants, tools, books) represented as well. The Greers' 3-acre display garden, in a natural woodland setting, features collections of unusual rhododendrons, Japanese maples, magnolias, and companion plants. It's best viewed April through June for a glorious rhododendron show.

HANSEN NURSERY ✉ @

PO Box 1228, North Bend, OR 97459 | **Phone:** (541) 756-1156 | **Fax:** Same; call first | **Email:** Hansen.nursery@verizon.net | **Open:** By appointment only; directions given at time of call. | **Plant list:** $1; shipping season fall through spring.

Robin Hansen specializes in **hardy cyclamen and North American natives** (no wild collection of plants assured). When Robin visited the late Edgar Kline, she was transfixed by seeing an entire bed of his glorious cyclamen. She has brought that love home, and now, 12 years later, she offers her progeny to others of like mind. She propagates 95 percent of her stock from seed, and offers as many as 15 cyclamen species available to ship. "Folks always ask which are the easiest to grow—I often think they should ask which are the most difficult to grow," she writes. The informative catalog does not show pictures of her plants, but relies on Robin's personal narrative, with warnings about invasive tendencies. And what you can't have, you want—which may be why some cultivars are limited to one per person or "withheld for increase." Those you can add to your wish list.

Robin is expanding her offerings to include more natives, such as brodiaeas and camassia. You can see this plantswoman's inventory up close and personal by shopping at numerous benefit plant sales, including Berry Botanic Garden, Leach Garden Sale, Tryon Creek Sale, Salem Hardy Plant Society Sale, Silver Falls State Park Mother's Day Sale, and others. Call or email for new dates each year.

WALLACE W. HANSEN, NURSERY & GARDENS ✉ @

2158 Bower Court SE, Salem, OR 97301 | **Phone:** (503) 581-2638 | **Fax:** (503) 581-9957 | **Email:** plants@nwplants.com | **Web:** www.nwplants.com/ | **Directions:** From I-5, take the Market Street exit. Drive east on Market Street, go 1 block to Lancaster Drive, and turn right (south) on Lancaster. Drive about 1.5 miles to State Street, turn left (east) onto State Street, and drive about 2.5 miles to 62nd Avenue. Turn right (south) onto 62nd and drive 1 mile to Macleay Road. Turn left (east) onto Macleay and drive 0.5 mile to Bower Ct. Turn right onto Bower Ct. to the nursery, just a fraction of a mile to the dead end; stay left, and you are at the nursery. | **Open:** Seasonal and by appointment | **Catalog:** $2, subsequently free for customers; flyers free; wholesale and retail.

Wallace Hansen, an engineer by training, makes it obvious that his heart is in growing **Northwest native plants,** and especially in helping others find, understand, and appreciate them for their gardens and landscapes. He also specializes in growing and selling trees, shrubs, ferns, and perennials—about 150 species. **Wetland plants,** mostly used for restoration work, are also offered. Plants

in Hansen's catalogs are organized by botanical name followed by the common name, with beefy descriptions of habit and habitat. You will find madrone, native rhododendrons and azaleas, native huckleberries, Pacific dogwood, silk tassel, hairy manzanita, rare native oaks and yews, trilliums, native lilies, red flowering currant, and many more. You are invited to walk through the 5 acres of wooded garden paths to see how the Hansens incorporate Northwest natives into their "wild" garden (best seen in late spring, early summer, and fall).

HARTS NURSERY

Jefferson-Scio Road, Jefferson, OR 97352 | **Phone:** (541) 327-1034 or (800) 356-9335 | **Fax:** (541) 327-1603 | **Email:** info@hartsnursery.com | **Web:** www.hartsnursery.com | **Mailing address:** PO Box 1070, Jefferson, OR 97352 | **Directions:** Located southeast of Salem. From I-5, take exit 238 and head east. After crossing the Santiam River, take the first right on Jefferson-Scio Road. Nursery is 1.9 miles on left side of road. | **Open:** Seasonal and by appointment

Harts grows a full complement of **annuals and classic perennials, grasses, herbs, and vegetables** in Oregon's Willamette Valley. Four generations of Harts have been innovators in the nursery business, growing this operation to be the largest annual and perennial operation in Oregon (800,000 square feet of covered greenhouses allow for state-of-the-art vegetative and tissue propagation). You'll see the Harts tag on countless plants in your local specialty retail nursery (check for dealers at the Harts website), but if you're in the market for bargains and selection, you can shop at Harts on-site garden center. Call ahead for seasonal hours.

HEDGEROWS NURSERY ✳

20165 SW Christensen Road, McMinnville, OR 97128 | **Phone:** (503) 843-7522 | **Fax:** Same | **Email:** hedgerows@onlinemac.com | **Directions:** Follow Hwy 18 west from McMinnville approximately 9 miles. At the junction of Hwy 18 and the Bellevue/Amity Hwy (and the site of the Lawrence Gallery), turn left and follow the blue signs 1.5 miles to Hedgerows. From the coast, travel on 18, turn right on Bellevue/Amity Hwy, and follow the blue signs. | **Open:** Seasonal or by appointment

In its eighth year, Hedgerows has begun to develop a big name among aficionados, and a visit to this deceptively small specialty nursery can yield a startlingly large cache to cart home. David Mason trained at the Royal Horticultural Society's Wisley Garden and during his career has been the garden supervisor at Wakehurst Place in Sussex and the manager of Longstock Park Nursery and Water Garden in Hampshire. He co-authored *The Complete Book of the Water Garden.* His wife and partner in the nursery, Susie Grimm, has gardened for 35 years. They travel annually to England to seek out the unusual for new introductions, as well as many **uncommon perennials, shrubs, and vines.** A taste of what you'll find here: euphorbias, penstemons, pulmonarias, cistus, hydrangeas, ceanothus, hellebores, diascias, campanulas, salvias, and rock garden plants, 98 percent of them propagated here.

The setting, in the wine country of Yamhill County, should induce most horticultural explorers to put a visit here on a "Must Do" list. The display beds at the nursery and around David and Susie's home are accessible and best seen in July, although there's something great to see spring through fall. Note: Their table at plant sales is always mobbed, so call ahead for local plant sale times and dates.

HEIRLOOM ROSES ✳ ✉ @

24062 NE Riverside Drive, St. Paul, OR 97137 | **Phone:** (503) 538-1576 | **Fax:** (503) 538-5902 | **Web:** www.heirloomroses.com | **Open:** Daily | **Catalog:** $5, with 200 color photos; shipping year-round.

The specialty here, as you might cleverly assume, is old garden roses. Just look at what the hefty catalog (listing about 700 varieties) has in store for rosarians: albas, bourbons, buck roses, centifolias, Chinas, damasks, David Austin's English roses, gallicas, ground-cover roses, hand-painted roses, American and Canadian winter-hardy roses, hybrid musks, hybrid perpetuals, moss roses, noisettes, patio roses, polyanthas, Portlands, ramblers, rugosas, shrub roses, single roses, species roses, tea roses, roses for hedges, roses for growing into trees, miniature roses, and unusual color roses. Golly! All of Heirloom's roses are grown on their own roots for hardiness and disease resistance. A visit to the amazing trio of display gardens at the height of the bloom, where **more than 1,500 varieties of roses** are featured, is sheer ambrosia (especially with this nursery's emphasis on fragrant roses). Owners John and Louise Clements suggest you come May through August. A Pruning Day event is scheduled each February; the Rose Fest is in August (also the month for an end-of-season sale, with 50 percent off many roses, call for dates). The Cottage shop carries a large selection of rose books, two videos, rose-related tools, gifts, and more.

HONEYHILL FARMS NURSERY ✳

Portland, OR | **Phone:** (503) 292-1817 | **Email:** honeyhill2@aol.com | **Open:** By appointment only; directions given when you call.

A decade ago, Jim and Audrey Metcalfe retired from the health-care industry and began selling their specialty: **hellebores and their companion plants** (*Cyclamen coum, Pulmonaria rubra, Primula denticulata, sarcococcas, Primula* x *juliana, Euphorbia* x *martinii, Omphalodes verna* and *O. cappadociea*) to retail and wholesale customers. They hybridize and propagate all their inventory, having begun this small nursery from the original seedlings in their own garden. "We quickly learned of the variety of species and colors . . . and we were hooked," Audrey says. Brighten your dreary winter with a visit in February or March (call or email them to make an appointment), to catch the impressive show, as the display gardens feature winter interest, with a focus on hellebores (good accessibility). Or call for details on Honeyhill Farms' participation in Portland area fall and spring plant sales. The couple can also

be booked to lecture on hellebores and other garden topics for garden clubs and groups.

HOUSE OF WHISPERING FIRS ✳

20080 SW Jaquith Road, Newberg, OR 97132 | **Phone:** (503) 628-3695 | **Fax:** (503) 628-3553 | **Email:** kkd@msn.com | **Web:** www.houseofwhisperingfirs.com | **Directions:** Take I-5 to Tigard and follow Hwy 99 through Tigard and Sherwood to Newberg. Go north on Hwy 219 (College Street) about 8 miles to Mountain Top Road (toward Scholls and Hillsboro). Go (left) west on Mountain Top Road and follow signs 0.4 mile to Jaquith Road, then turn right at 1.0 mile on Jaquith Road. | **Open:** Daily | **Catalog:** Free

Kathleen Thompson grows herbs and everlastings for her Victorian Gift Shop, which offers the botanical bounty of the garden and also herb plants for your own garden. She invites you to meander through her specialty display gardens that feature hostas, ferns, herbs, scented geraniums, mint, a knot garden, shade perennials, and a pond. Take time to marvel at—and walk through—the newly planted herbal conifer maze. Seating has been thoughtfully provided, and the paths are wheelchair accessible (with assistance). Call or write to request a class schedule.

HOYT ARBORETUM

4000 Fairview Boulevard, Portland, OR 97221 | **Phone:** (503) 228-8733 | **Fax:** (503) 823-4213 | **Email:** haffdir@ci.portland.or.us | **Web:** www.hoytarboretum.org | **Directions:** From Portland, take Hwy 26 west to the Washington Park-Zoo exit and follow signs, continuing past the zoo parking lot, the Forestry Center, and up Knight's Boulevard to Fairview Boulevard. Turn right and you will see the sign for the Arboretum Visitor Center parking. | **Open:** Daily

Every year the Hoyt Arboretum gears up for its big annual Dirt Cheap plant sale, staged one weekend during October. Here's where you can choose from **choice trees, shrubs, and some perennials.** (See Chapter 7, "Plant Sales.") If you're visiting throughout the year, though, stop by the Arboretum's Gift Shop, for a selection of perennials and seasonal annuals, many rare. There are always trees out back, so if you're in the market for something special, ask the staff about availability. The shop also offers a wide selection of garden-inspired books and gifts.

HUGHES WATER GARDENS ✳ @

25289 SW Stafford Road, Tualatin, OR 97062 | **Phone:** (503) 638-1709 | **For technical assistance:** (503) 638-2077; for orders (800) 858-1709. | **Fax:** (503) 638-9035 (also for ordering) | **Email:** water@teleport.com | **Web:** www.thewatergardenshop.com (online store/orders), or www.watergardens.com (information) | **Directions:** Located 20 miles south of Portland in Tualatin. Take I-5 to the I-205 interchange (Stafford Road/Lake Oswego exit) and follow to Stafford Road exit south (about 3 miles), or take I-5 to the Stafford Road/North Wilsonville exit and take Elligsen Road east to SW 65th, turn right to Stafford Road, and turn left to the nursery. | **Open:** March–October, Monday–Saturday, 9 a.m.–5 p.m., Sunday, 10 a.m.–5 p.m.; November–February, Monday–Friday, 9 a.m.–5 p.m.

Eamonn Hughes has designed and built water features in Europe and the Pacific Northwest for more than 20 years. His 10-acre nursery near Portland is now the largest supplier of water plants on the West Coast. Hughes Water Gardens propagates its own plants for both retail and wholesale clients. You can access the entire catalog online (hard copy no longer published). Retail customers are welcome at the nursery, set in the rolling hills of the Stafford agricultural area, near Wilsonville.

The staff at Hughes teaches free classes on the weekends during the season, with topics such as pond and waterfall construction and other water-gardening themes. You'll find many books here on water gardening, including Eamonn's own *Waterfalls, Fountains, Pools & Streams* (Sterling Press). The store carries pond liners, pumps, fountains, and all the other equipment necessary to build and maintain water features. There's a wonderful—and huge—selection of bog and aquatic plants, as well as water lilies and lotus. Hughes also carries quality imported koi and goldfish.

The display gardens feature waterfalls, streams, and ponds. See the fountain displays and a 20 by 50-foot formal reflecting pond built to showcase the water lily collection. Peak bloom for water lilies is June through September. The extensive natural ponds in the display gardens will delight you year-round. Note: Eamonn's pond-building video is no longer available.

JOHNSON BROTHERS GREENHOUSES

91444 Coburg Road, Eugene, OR 97408 | **Phone:** (541) 484-1649 | **Fax:** (541) 343-6810 | **Email:** jbgh@cyber-dyne.com | **Web:** www.jbgreenhouses.com | **Directions:** From I-5, take the Coburg exit and head west on Pearl Street to Willamette Street. Turn right, and stay on Coberg Road for about 1.5 miles. | **Open:** Daily

Vern Johnson started the nursery in 1986 as place for growing annuals and it's now a great year-round garden source in the Eugene area. While JBG grows and offers just about anything you might be interested in—from trees and shrubs to innovative hanging baskets and old-fashioned annuals to water plants and herbs, the stars of this nursery are its vast numbers and very interesting varieties of **perennials.** Garden enthusiasts have been known to wander this nursery remarking in wonder "Where on earth did they get this?" and "Haven't seen these offered *anywhere* in this area!" A new addition is the Crystal Palace, a 9,000+ square foot glass, steel, and poly perennial house. The nursery has also expanded its poinsettia offerings, with a wide selection of colors and sizes from "teacup" to 12-inch hanging baskets. Vern says his goal is to offer a wide variety of plants at reasonable prices and to provide knowledgeable and helpful staff to answer your garden needs and questions. Take note of the frequent seminars and garden center fare of tools, soil amendments, statuary, ponds, and more.

JOY CREEK NURSERY

20300 NW Watson Road, Scappoose, OR 97056 | **Phone:** (503) 543-7474 | **Fax:** (503) 543-6933 | **Email:** webmaster@joycreek.com | **Web:** www.joycreek.com | **Directions:** From Portland, travel north on Hwy 30 approximately 18 miles. Watch for Watson Road on the left just before entering the town of Scappoose. Turn left on Watson Road and continue on a short drive that wends up to the nursery. | **Open:** Seasonal, daily, and by appointment (with 24 hours' notice, please). | **Catalog:** $2, for "A Gardener's Catalogue," with a fall supplement; mail order nationwide and internationally (order before June 1 and save on many plants).

Mike Smith, Maurice Horn, and Scott Christy have worked together to create a nursery "that we always wanted to go to but could never find. Our goals are to help fellow gardeners have the gardens they have always dreamed of."

With ten years' experience running Joy Creek, this horticultural trio now offers **more than 2,000 perennials,** featuring penstemons, salvias, dianthus, hostas, hydrangeas, clematis, euphorbias, lavandula, lonicera, sedum, ornamental grasses, and rock garden plants, grown from seed, cuttings, and divisions. On-site nursery patrons receive a 10 percent discount.

You'll find a great selection of irresistible clematis varieties, many virtually unavailable elsewhere. You will also find **glorious display gardens.** All told, 2,500 varieties of plants are displayed in the 4 acres of gardens and stock fields. If you are looking for drought-tolerant plants, check out their dry border garden for ideas. Additional inspiration is provided through free classes every Sunday, April through early September, at 1 p.m. The classes are presented in an informal, hands-on format and last about 90 minutes to 2 hours; some recent topics are "The Party's Not Over" (on extending the blooming season), and "Divide and Conquer, Parts I and II." Order the catalog or check the lovely website for 2002 class and special event dates. We wish more nurseries would follow Joy Creek's lead and offer for sale the mulch and fertilizers they use in their own gardens.

LITTLE RED FARM NURSERY

1020 S 42nd Street, Springfield, OR 97478 | **Phone:** (541) 744-0372 | **Fax:** Same | **Email:** lrfnursery@yahoo.com | **Directions:** From I-5, turn onto I-105 (Springfield exit, also called SR 126) and travel east to 42nd Street. Turn onto 42nd Street and go south to the intersection with Jasper Road. You're there. | **Open:** Seasonal or by appointment

Bob and Gayle Kramer offer **more than 1,500 varieties of herbaceous perennials,** many of which are those hard-to-find discoveries you'll be glad to find here. The Kramers love to propagate many of these plants themselves. There's also a healthy selection of annuals and some small ornamental shrubs. In addition to plants, you'll find garden art, accessories, and ornaments, many of the objects crafted by artisans here in the Northwest and with some imported from England. Also, find some hand-picked antiques from England for the garden. Get your name added to the list for the annual Open House, usually the last weekend in April, which celebrates plants, food, and music.

LORANE HILLS FARM AND NURSERY

27634 Easy Acres Drive, Eugene, OR 97405-9726 | **Phone:** (541) 344-8943 | **Mailing address:** PO Box 5464, Eugene, OR 97405 | **Directions:** From Eugene, take Lorane Hwy to Territorial Road. Go right and drive 0.5 mile to Easy Acres Road, then turn right again on Easy Acres for 0.5 mile | **Open:** By appointment only

About ten years ago, architect David, and University of Oregon biology instructor, Evelyn (Hess) tentatively began their nursery business on a part-time basis. They have recently retired from their day jobs and can now concentrate more energy on their love of plants, from the newly emerging display gardens to the wide spectrum of **herbaceous perennials** and (their specialty) **beardless irises** (Japanese, Sino-Siberian, and beardless species), along with **native plants.** Evelyn reports that they continue to expand the herbaceous and woody native plant offerings, as this is a growing interest.

MAX & HILDY'S GARDEN STORE ✳

19350 NW Cornell Road, Hillsboro, OR 97124 | **Phone:** (503) 645-5486 | **Fax:** (503) 645-5680 | **Directions:** From Portland, head west on Hwy 26 to the NW 185th Avenue exit. Cross over the freeway, turning left at NW 185th and head south to NW Cornell Road, where you'll turn right; continue about 1/3 mile and the nursery is on the left. | **Open:** Daily

The true love shared between the sweet-natured rottweiler Hildy and the feisty Airedale Max lent their names to this wonderful, full-service nursery cum garden center. From the newsletter: "Although they are, alas, no longer with us, this unlikely couple will live on as a symbol of our passionate commitment to bringing you the finest of everything related to gardening."

This is a very nice, full-service nursery and garden store to visit, with knowledgeable staff and great discoveries. The seed selection continues to expand, offering Renee's Garden, Botanical Interests, Ed Hume, Thompson & Morgan, The Kew Collection, Livingston Seeds, Territorial, Mr. Fothergill's from England, and all the seed-starting supplies to get you underway. The Glasshouse is filled with orchids, tender and hothouse plants (like solanums, abutilons, and hardy bananas), plus pots and containers with finishes from classic to ornamental.

The inventory here includes "everything from the meat-and-potato plants to the sublime," according to recent reports. Look for **water garden plants** (and all the sundry adjunct equipment and supplies), **Japanese maples, elegant bonsai, and a great section of perennials, alpines, and natives.** The display bed features a small alpine planting that changes each season. Frequent class offerings feature popular Portland-area speakers like designer Lucy Hardiman, so call to add your name to the newsletter mailing list.

MITSCH NOVELTY DAFFODILS ✉@ ✳

6247 S Sconce Road, Hubbard, OR 97032 | **Phone:** (503) 651-2742 | **Fax:** (503) 651-2792 | **Email:** havensr@web-ster.com | **Web:** www.web-ster.com/havensr/mitsch | **Mailing address:** PO Box 218, Hubbard, OR 97032 | **Directions:** Going south on I-5 from Portland, take the Hubbard/Canby cutoff to 99E. Going south on 99E, turn left at the flashing light in Hubbard, then turn left onto Whiskey Hill Road. After about 3 miles, turn right at Meridian Road and go about 1 mile; then turn left onto Sconce Road. | **Open:** Display garden open daily; open during flowering season (mid-March to mid-April) for sales of fresh cut flowers. | **Catalog:** $3, deductible from order (color photos, map); shipping season September–October.

Elise and Dick Havens operate this wonderful destination for daffodil fanciers, begun by Elise's father, noted daffodil hybridizer Grant Mitsch. New introductions, specialty daffs, Jackson daffodils from Australia, popular cultivars with names like 'Zillion' and 'Relentless' fill the catalog and website. This is a **guide to all things daffodil,** and you'll learn a lot by visiting the display gardens (call first for specific hours) or perusing the identifying photographs and descriptions in Mitsch's catalog. Take note of cultivars with unusual color combinations (corals, lime green, and near-pink tones are especially appealing), daffodils recommended specifically for their scent and size, and cottage garden mixes.

NICHOLS GARDEN NURSERY ✉@ ✳

1190 Old Salem Road, Albany, OR 97321-4580 | **Phone:** (541) 928-9280 or (800) 422-3985 | **Fax:** (800) 231-5306 | **Email:** customersupport@nicholsgardennursery.com | **Web:** www.nicholsgardennursery.com | **Directions:** From I-5 southbound, take Millersburg exit 234; turn left and head south 0.7 mile to the nursery. | **Open:** Daily (closed Sundays) | **Catalog:** Free (catalogs sent outside the U.S. may require a nominal handling charge); access the full catalog online (and enjoy the great free recipes).

For over 50 years the Nichols family has offered **new and unusual herbs, vegetable seed varieties** to tempt, and interesting garden-related products. The nursery does not sell any seeds or plants that are genetically engineered, and all Nichols seeds are untreated and free of any chemicals. Their catalog provides a marvelous selection of herb plants, well described with botanical and common names, ultimate size, habit, culture, features, and more. Included are the standard favorites (sage, rosemary, and thyme) as well as the more obscure (epazote, Good King Henry, and safflower). Find garlic and shallot bulbs for fall planting, Egyptian onion sets, hop root cuttings, and saffron crocus bulbs. The nursery offers a selection of herbs both for growing indoors and for use in outdoor basket making. You'll also enjoy the many **herb-growing tips and recipes in the catalog.** Each May, Nichols invites customers to its Plant Day for refreshments, tours, special offers, and an expanded plant sale featuring selections not offered in the catalog. Call for the date! You'll be charmed by the herb display gardens, including a parterre bordered with miniature boxwood that surround varieties of lavender and germander. Come in midsummer for the best viewing, and bring a camera.

NORTHERN GROVES ✉ @

PO Box 1236, Philomath, OR 97370 | **Phone:** (541) 456-4364 or (541) 602-1315 | **Email:** bamboogrove@cmug.com | **Web:** www.teleport.com/~dbrooks/bamboo.html | **Open:** By appointment only | **Catalog:** $3, and also a mini-course in bamboo culture, or free on website.

Rick Valley grows and sells "useful bamboos and other plants," and has served as one of Oregon's most avid bamboo growers and spokesmen since 1981. What Rick likes best is leading the way with introductions that are new to the Northwest gardener; in fact, he's beginning to add native plants to his offerings.

While **hardy bamboo** is a favorite specialty, his passions also run to the edible landscape, as is reflected in his catalog. Rick is also active in permaculture education, ecological design, and consultation, centering on water, "landform," and horticultural systems.

NORTHWEST GARDEN NURSERY ✳

86813 Central Road, Eugene, OR 97402 | **Phone:** (541) 935-3915 | **Fax:** (541) 935-0863 | **Email:** nargsbs@efn.org | **Directions:** Central Road is about 10 miles west of Eugene and 6 miles west of Beltline Road on Hwy 126 (W 11th). From the north, take exit 195B onto Beltline Road. Turn left (south) onto Central Road at the end of the very long guardrail along Fern Ridge Reservoir, and travel 2.8 miles to the nursery (on the left at the sign and bamboo). | **Open:** Seasonal and by appointment; please leave pets at home and bring children only if you are prepared to supervise them closely.

Ernie and Marietta O'Byrne's specialty nursery, founded in 1992, is filled with wondrous plants and glorious gardens—a delight for plant-lovers. They specialize in out-of-the-ordinary herbaceous **perennials** for sun and shade and plants suitable for the rock garden. They offer a small but choice selection of **vines** and **shrubs** including clematis (species) and roses. "We are collectors of plants, therefore nursery plants reflect our personal tastes, especially what grows well in the garden, is unusual, and unusually beautiful," Marietta says. The O'Byrnes propagate about 80 percent of their own plants by seed, cuttings, and divisions. In spring, find an excellent collection of hellebores, meconopsis, woodland anemones, and various species primulas, pulmonarias, and saxifrage. In summer find Oriental poppies, epimediums, Pacific Coast hybrid irises, kniphofias, hardy geraniums, English hybrid delphiniums . . . and more. Nursery patrons are invited to visit the extensive **collector's garden,** about an acre plus of plants in the peace of the countryside. It features luxurious perennial borders in both sun and semishade, with woodlands underplanted with a tapestry of ground covers and hellebores, many ferns, primulas, meconopsis, and such, a rock garden with a collection of rare alpines, some troughs, a conifer, and also an ornamental grass garden mixed with heathers, kniphofias, and hot-colored plants. There is a pond with benches where you are invited to rest and contemplate. **Open Garden** days are offered; call for dates. The Helle-

bore Open Garden is typically the last two weekends in February. If you have a deep passion for wonderful plants and inspired plant combinations this must be a destination. For more on the garden, see *Fine Gardening* magazine, June 2000, and *Horticulture,* June 1999.

OAKHILL FARMS NATIVE PLANT NURSERY

4314 Goodrich Hwy, Oakland, OR 97462 | **Phone:** (541) 459-1361 | **Fax:** (541) 459-2095 | **Directions:** Located approximately 10 miles south of Roseburg. From I-5, take exit 142, and keep right onto Goodrich Hwy for 4 miles. From Eugene/Cottage Grove, take I-5 exit 148 and turn right at Pilot Truck Plaza onto Goodrich Hwy and travel 3 miles. | **Open:** By appointment only | **Catalog:** Free

Donna and Richard Rawson have owned Oakhill Farms since 1997, bringing customers a wide variety and astute selection of Pacific Northwest native plants for creating wildlife habitat, and developing drought-tolerant, hardier, and more trouble-free gardens, ponds, and woodlands. You'll find more than 125 varieties of native trees, shrubs, ground covers, ferns, wildflowers, and wetland plants, including many that are rare and unusual. Oakhill's plants are nursery grown and propagated from seed, divisions, or cuttings, usually available for sale in 2-inch to 15-gallon pots. Some varieties are offered bare-root. The nursery has expanded its selection of drought-resistant native shrubs with mountain mahogany (*Cercocarpus montanus*), buffaloberry (*Shepherdia canadensis*) and smooth sumac (*Rhus glabra*), among others. The Rawsons will gladly recycle your plastic pots. Check the back of their catalog for a membership application to join the Native Plant Society of Oregon.

ONE GREEN WORLD

28696 S Cramer Road, Molalla, OR 97038-8576 | **Phone:** (503) 651-3005 or (877) 353-4028 | **Fax:** (800) 418-9983 | **Email:** ogw@cybcon.com | **Web:** www.onegreenworld.com | **Directions:** Located 27 miles from Portland. From I-5, take the I-205 Oregon City exit, traveling east to Hwy 213 where you will head south. After you go through the town of Mulino, look for a sawmill on the right and turn right just after it onto Ebey Road. Continue to Cramer Road, turning right. One Green World is on the right. | **Open:** Seasonal or by appointment; orders taken weekdays. | **Catalog:** $3 (many color photos); informative, and also offers rootstock; books, some gardening supplies.

Jim Gilbert has long dedicated himself to the adventure of seeking out, growing, and offering an exemplary selection of unique **edible fruits and ornamentals from around the world.** In recent years he has made several trips to Russia, where he has found (and now offers) such delicious and nutritious fruits as Sea Berry and Honeyberry. From Hungary, find two new cherries, 'Danube' and 'Jubileum', and from the Nikita Botanic Garden in the Ukraine, two new persimmons.

Here you will find a source for such unusual plants as *Robinia pseudoacacia* 'Tortuosa', a couple of interesting Russian *Sorbus* hybrids, many hardy kiwis (including three Italian and two red-fruited varieties), ten varieties of cornelian cherry, two Japanese and two European varieties of plum, the natural sweetener plant stevia, and a very fragrant honeysuckle, *Lonicera etrusca* 'Donald Waterer'. Come March, One Green World hosts a day of free classes and demonstrations on growing home orchard fruit; with a separate day devoted to hands-on instruction in the arts of grafting and pruning. Check the website or call for dates (and to get on the mailing list).

OREGON NATIVE PLANT NURSERY (FORMERLY PHEASANT VALLEY FARMS)

P.O. Box 886, Woodburn, OR 97071-0886 | **Phone:** (503) 981-2353 | **Email:** dmalcolmchadwick@hotmail.com | **Directions:** Travel 30 miles south of Portland on I-5 to Woodburn (ext. 271). The nursery is located 2 miles west of the freeway interchange. When making an appointment, further directions are supplied. | **Open:** Daily by appointment, March-September | **Plant list:** Free

Douglas Chadwick seed propagates native Oregon herbaceous perennials. His plants represent all regions and most habitats in Oregon, including the Siskiyou and Cascade Mountains, the Columbia River Gorge, and the Willamette Valley. Specialties include native hollyhocks, shooting stars, choice native rhizomatous iris, and erythroniums (fawn lilies). Many choice alpine and rock garden subjects are available. Douglas encourages his customers to experiment with and establish low-maintenance and irrigation-free native gardens. April to June are the peak months to view display gardens.

OREGON TRAILS DAFFODILS

41905 SE Louden Road, Corbett, OR 97019 | **Phone:** (503) 695-5513 | **Fax:** (503) 695-5573 | **Email:** daffodil@europa.com | **Open:** By appointment only | **Catalog:** Free; shipping season September–October

OTD is a fourth-generation daffodil family business, with Bill and Diane Tribe carrying on the breeding work of Murray Evans (1912–1988) and also featuring cultivars bred by well-known hybridizer and exhibitor Bill Panill of Martinsville, Virginia. **The 400+ hybrid daffodil bulbs** they list are all grown on-site and offer a wide variety for show and garden pleasure. The catalog is very thorough and informative, especially for those of us who think there's not much more to know about daffodils— this will teach you a thing or two!

PONDERINGS PLUS

3360 N Pacific Hwy, Medford, OR 92501 | **Phone:** (541) 773-3297 | **Fax:** (541) 772-2169 | **Email:** gaylynn@internetcds.com | **Directions:** Take I-5 south from Portland to exit 35. The nursery is 5 miles on the left. Or take I-5 north to exit 31; turn left and then right at the next light. Continue west over I-5, turning right onto Hwy 99. The nursery is 2.5 miles on the right. | **Open:** Daily (closed Sundays in winter)

GayLynn and Larry Dunagan invite you to meander through their display perennial and water gardens, best seen from May through August. They run Ponderings Plus as the retail arm of a wholesale nursery called Mountain View Farms. Enjoy the same list of select perennials and **herbs** for shade, sunny, and dry locations

that they sell to the trade. The nursery also features **aquatic plants,** water gardening supplies, and statuary. There's usually a monthlong August sale, too, which is when the public can also tour the growing greenhouses.

PORTERHOWSE FARMS

41370 SE Thomas Road, Sandy, OR 97055 | **Phone:** (503) 668-5834 | **Fax:** Same | **Email:** phfarm@aol.com | **Web:** www.porterhowse.com | **Directions:** Take US 26 to Sandy. At Ten Eyek Road, turn left and follow direction signs to Roslyn Lake. Turn left at each intersection where a choice must be made. Then turn left onto Thomas Road (after the cemetery). The nursery is on the left, across from the park at Roslyn Lake. | **Open:** Daily, by appointment only | **Price list:** Free (check website for availability)

Don Howse is a passionate collector and prolific propagator (seed, cuttings, and grafting) of **dwarf and rare conifers, unusual broadleaf trees and shrubs,** rock garden perennials, plants for trough gardens, and plants for bonsai. You are invited to visit the nursery and gardens by appointment. Porterhowse Farms is now 20 years old, which explains why the 2.5-acre display garden is well-stocked with mature examples of plants listed in the catalog. Look for trough, alpine, and rock gardens, Bonsai display benches, and a newly developing arboretum (appearing on an additional 10 acres).

PORTLAND NURSERY

5050 SE Stark Street, Portland, OR 97215 | **Phone:** (503) 231-5050 | **Fax:** (503) 231-7123 | **Second location:** 9000 SE Division Street, Portland, OR 97266 | **Phone:** (503) 788-9000 | **Fax:** (503) 788-9002 | **Directions:** To reach the Stark Street location from I-84, take the 58th Avenue exit, and make an immediate right turn onto Glison Street. At NE 53rd, turn left to Stark Street, turn left and travel on Stark for 3 blocks. From I-205, take the Stark Street exit west and wend your way around Mt. Tabor (Stark turns into Thorburn and back into Stark). For the Division Street store, take the Division Street exit from I-205 and travel west. | **Open:** Daily, 9 a.m.–6 p.m. (closing hours vary by season)

As you might imagine, plants of all types—from lush indoor tropicals and **Northwest natives, specialty conifers, and rare and hard-to-find perennials, to time-honored annuals**—are all beautifully presented for your perusal and consideration. Come especially to enjoy the **roses,** and find just about the best selection you could dream of. There is an exemplary section of seeds, with varieties offered from all the best seed sources. Or visit anytime for the full range of gardening supplies and quality tools, and a well-stocked book nook. The nursery generously hosts a number of fundraising local flower shows and sales each year, sponsored by plant societies from the fuchsia fanciers to the hosta huggers. The Stark Street location now displays an imaginative parking strip—out with the grass, in with glorious color and bold texture!

RAINTREE GARDEN AND GIFT CENTER

84795 Hwy 101, Seaside, OR 97138 | **Phone:** (503) 738-6980 | **Fax:** (503) 738-4045 | **Directions:** Located on Hwy 101 halfway between Seaside and Cannon Beach. | **Open:** Daily

Dennis and Mary Lee Saulsbury are right where they've been for more than 25 years, even though the county has given them a new address. Raintree's nursery fare runs to **annuals, perennials, tropicals, and a broad range of evergreen and deciduous shrubs and trees.** The displays here change seasonally (if you are vacationing on the coast around Christmas, that's a particularly gorgeous time to stop by). The seed selection is excellent: Unwins, Lake Valley, and Ed Hume. The shop is always well-stocked with tools and supplies, books, bird supplies, interior and outdoor fountains, plant containers, and soil amendments.

RED'S RHODIES

15920 SW Oberst Lane, Sherwood, OR 97140 | **Phone:** (503) 625-6331 | **Fax:** (503) 625-8055 | **Email:** red@hardy-orchids.com | **Web:** www.hardy-orchids.com | **Directions:** From I-5, take the Tualatin/Sherwood exit, and go west, following signs for Sherwood on Sherwood-Tualatin Road. After about 3 miles watch for signs about "Old Town Sherwood" and "Antique Shops" and turn left onto Oregon Street. Go 2 miles to the end, turn left, and then immediately right (there is no other choice) onto Railroad Street. Go 2 blocks and turn left across the tracks onto S Sherwood Boulevard and go to a 4-way stop. At this stop sign go straight ahead. The road becomes Ladd Hill Road. Travel 1 mile to the second left onto Oberst Lane for 1 block, and turn right at Red's sign. | **Open:** By appointment only | **Plant list:** $1; shipping season December–March

"Red," aka Dick Cavender, and his wife, Karen, have operated this nursery based on highly-personal plant favorites for more than two decades. The plant list is a fascinating education in arisaemas (cobra lilies and Jack-in-the-pulpits), along with a large collection of **hardy terrestrial orchid species**—bletillas, calanthe, dactylorhiza—and roscoea. The Cavenders invite visitors into their collector's garden, sited on a hill with a panoramic view of the valley and four snow-capped mountains in the distance. You're able to tour over an acre of beds featuring 400 varieties of rhododendrons and azaleas, with many lovely Japanese maples, magnolias, and other flowering trees. The beds are heavily planted with all kinds of **rare and unusual herbaceous perennials and bulbs** including orchids, cyclamen, trilliums, and peonies. The pond contains several types of aquatic plants and a whole gaggle of goldfish. Press on to the three greenhouses to find collections of maddenii and vireya rhododendrons, other tender shrubs, and carnivorous plants. In April you'll be thrilled to see 150 flats of pleione orchids in bloom. Their growing fields of new and hybrid rhododendrons and azaleas (the emphasis is on *R. occidentale*, with some 30 selected forms and yellow hybrids). There is something in glorious bloom throughout the spring and early summer, with perennials and Japanese maples carrying color on into the fall. The Cavenders stock a number of great reference books about their favorite genus, including titles on pleione and wild orchids.

LON ROMBOUGH

PO Box 365, Aurora, OR 97002-0365 | **Phone:** (503) 678-1410 | **Email:** lonrom@hevanet.com | **Web:** www.bunchgrapes.com

While Lon's primary work lies in research, development, breeding, locating, consultation, and writing about **fruits, nuts, and other edible plants,** he also offers a fascinating list of **grape varieties,** some 130 strong. With a lifetime of professional work in horticulture, Lon is also known to thousands of us through his prolific contributions to most popular horticultural magazines: *Organic Gardening, Horticulture, Fine Gardening, National Gardening, The Growing Edge, Flower and Garden, Back Home, Indoor and Patio Gardening, HousePlant,* and publications of The Home Orchard Society, California Rare Fruit Growers, and others. He has written an extensive book on grape growing for all climates, scheduled for a February 2002 release from Chelsea Green Publishers (www.chelseagreen.com). Next up from Lon: a book on fruit growing in the Pacific Northwest.

THE ROSE GUARDIANS

PO Box 426, St. Paul, OR 97137 | **Phone:** (503) 393-1051 | **Fax:** Same | **Directions:** Provided when appointment is made. | **Open:** By appointment; request notification of Open Garden days (and sales). | **Catalog:** $5, plant list $1; fall and spring shipping dates.

Alice Stockfleth specializes in own-root roses, with a heavy emphasis on old-fashioned and David Austin roses grown in the Northwest. The catalog is without photos, but the descriptions are keyed to well-known references. There is an availability list specifying how many of each variety are currently offered (a welcome feature), and updates are sent out. The 2002 list features about **550 rose varieties.** Alice offers senior discounts, a wonderful perk, and sells her roses to nonprofit groups at wholesale prices for fund-raisers. If you are able to visit mid-May to mid-June, you'll view Alice's own roses in all their glory. If you have a specific list of roses in mind, call to receive a free "current availability" list.

RUSSELL GRAHAM PURVEYOR OF PLANTS

4030 Eagle Crest Road NW, Salem, OR 97304 | **Phone:** (503) 362-1135 | **Email:** grahams@open.org | **Directions:** From downtown Salem, take the Marion Street bridge across the river and turn right on Wallace Road. Head north (generally) on Wallace Road for about 2 miles then turn left onto Brush College Road, travel through the countryside 4 miles to Eagle Crest Road, and turn left. Go 1 mile on Eagle Crest Road until the pavement ends, and you're there. | **Open:** By appointment, and on Open Garden Weekends, March–June (call for dates). | **Catalog:** $2, mailed in summer (plants shipped in fall only; early orders are often rewarded with a free plant).

Russell and Yvonne are purveyors of fine plants and bulbs, including astrantias, primula, hardy cyclamen, species lilies, hardy ferns, and hellebores . . . RG has a loyal following of plant fanatics. The couple describe their specialties as "un-ordinary hardy perennials with many Northwest and North American natives. Mostly species." They do not go in for "weird, unusual, or rare plants" but rather try to offer **good, garden-worthy plants that are not readily available elsewhere.** Examples would be *Cardiocrinum giganteum*, species *Corydalis ochroleuca*, and *C. flexuosa*, and *Romneya coulteri*. Viola (American species and English bedding) selections are numerous, and you'll also find some outstanding hellebores and many named double primulas, including two blues.

For the Open Garden days be sure to dress for the weather—if you're sensibly shod you'll be able to take full advantage of what is on offer, and best see nearly 5 acres of perennials in nursery beds. You're invited to bring a picnic lunch as you relax enjoying the lovely view.

SCHREINER'S IRIS GARDENS

3625 Quinaby Road NE, Salem, OR 97303 | **Phone:** (503) 393-3232 or (800) 525-2367 | **Fax:** (503) 393-5590 | **Email:** info@schreinersgardens.com | **Web:** www.schreinersgardens.com (with online ordering) | **Directions:** From I-5 heading south from Portland, take exit 263 at Brooks. Travel west on Brooklake Road to Hwy 219 (River Road), turn left (south) on Hwy 219 to Quinaby Road, and turn left. | **Open:** Display gardens are open from Mother's Day in mid-May through the first week of June, 8 a.m.–dusk (verify best bloom time by calling the number above); office hours: Weekdays, year-round. | **Catalog:** $5, 72 pages of exquisite color, most irises shown at near full size.

The ideal growing conditions of the Willamette Valley drew the attention of this family of bearded-iris growers, who first became deeply involved in collecting and growing world-class irises back in the 1920s. That was in Minnesota, where harsh weather inspired the Schreiner family to scour the country for the very best site to establish their fledgling business. If you are serious about **bearded irises,** you already know this company, and the quality of its selections and the plants you receive. If you have even the slightest inclination to add these richly colored, textural plants to your garden you must order a copy of the catalog. As your garden unfolds, take the book out among your own plants and imagine where the addition of an accent of color or the elegant stately form of flower and foliage might be just the ticket for the perfect vignette. You're encouraged to visit (virtually, for an online tour or in person), where you can experience the beautiful iris blooms in person. The gardens here are lovely and feature great ideas for companion plants. The gift shop features a large array of gardening books, handcrafted artwork, and iris-inspired stained glass, pottery, sculpture, and potted flowers. Each spring, Schreiner's is filled with special events, including a Mother's Day event, a Memorial Day barbecue, and the Keizer Iris Festival. Call or check the website for a schedule. And doesn't this sound appealing—the Irises and Wine event staged with the nearby Amity Vineyards (the event frequently features a new release of an Amity wine).

SECRET GARDEN GROWERS

29100 S Needy Road, Canby, OR 97013 | **Phone:** (503) 651-2006 | **Email:** Secretgrwr@aol.com | **Web:** www.secretgardengrowers.com | **Directions:** From Salem, drive north on I-5 to the Woodburn exit.

Drive east through Woodburn, and stay on this road, which becomes Hwy 211 (no turns!) for about 7 miles. Then turn left onto S Needy Road, and look for the nursery sign. From Portland, take I-5 south to exit 282A (Canby/Hubbard), and go left on Arndt Road, turning right onto Barlow Road. Travel 4.5 miles and turn left on Zimmerman Road. Travel about 1 mile and turn right on S. Needy Road; look for the nursery sign on the left. | **Open:** Seasonal and by appointment

New in 1998, this country nursery is the dream-come-true of Pat Thompson, who for 20 years ran a successful landscape-design business (she still offers landscape design and consultation services and specialty garden maintenance). Pat grows all her stock, which includes a striking palette of perennials (many species salvias), ornamental grasses, shade-garden plants, some choice shrubs and trees, and shrub roses. The display gardens are evolving, and include the many garden habitats faced by Northwest gardeners: sunny borders, shady nooks, and pond/wetland areas. Put this new nursery on one of your "Days of Exploration" jaunts and take home some of Pat's horticultural treasures.

SISKIYOU RARE PLANT NURSERY

2825 Cummings Road, Medford, OR 97501 | **Phone:** (541) 772-6846 | **Fax:** (541) 772-4917 | **Email:** srpn@wave.net | **Web:** www.siskiyourareplantnursery.com | **Directions:** From I-5, take exit 33 (Central Point) and go east on Biddle Road, turning right (south) on Table Rock Road, then going left (east) on Midway Road to Cummings Road. Turn left to the nursery. | **Open:** Seasonal and by appointment; phone orders and inquiries Tuesday–Friday, 9 a.m.–5 p.m. PST. | **Catalog:** $3, with separate fall catalog (map to nursery); shipping year-round, weather permitting.

This is a very highly respected specialty nursery, known intimately by collectors and alpine plant aficionados across the country, and across the waters as well. Baldassare Mineo offers upwards of **1,500 plants** (from over 5,000 species under cultivation at the nursery), some *very* rare. He specializes in **alpines and other dwarf, hardy plants for the rock, alpine, and woodland garden,** with a new focus on larger, hardy, cottage-garden perennials. SRPN also has a good selection of dwarf shrubs, trees, conifers, and hardy ferns. Throughout the catalog are offers such as: Special Collections of . . . Easy to Grow Trough Garden Plants, . . . *Callunas*, . . . Campanulas, . . . dwarf conifers, . . . Hardy Ferns, and more. The catalog is illustrated with quality color photos of many of their plants and the descriptions are top-notch. The text emphasizes seasonal strengths such as outstanding foliage ("in Spring a specimen can look like a butter yellow cloud"), branching form ("can be enjoyed year-round even in winter when the bare branches make an elegant tracery"), and habit ("fine threads of foliage form a tight bun for the Lilliputian garden or trough"). If you are anywhere in the vicinity don't miss the opportunity to visit the nursery's beautiful **display garden,** which covers 2 acres. Be sure to peruse The Alpine House, where you'll find limited collector's stock and overstocked bargains. There is also a nice selection of books on alpine and rock garden plants. The fall catalog arrives in August, offering many new plants and over 100 **rare bulbs,** including the most extensive collection of anemones, erythroniums, and *Primula seiboldii* (Japanese primula) in the country. If you are lucky enough to live nearby, check into periodic classes.

SKIPPER & JORDAN NURSERY

29690 SE Orient Drive, Gresham, OR 97080 | **Phone:** (503) 663-1125 | **Fax:** (503) 663-4245 | **Mailing address:** 7800 SE Short Road, Gresham, OR 97080 | **Directions:** Located east of Gresham, 3 miles off Hwy 26 on Orient Drive at the corner of Orient Drive and Short Road. | **Open:** Daily | **Plant list:** Free upon request; wholesale and retail.

This family-owned and -operated nursery has grown quality evergreen trees and shrubs, ornamentals and shade/flowering **trees** for more than 30 years. Take advantage of this nursery's wholesale operation (good quantities and plants grown on-site) when you shop Skipper & Jordan's retail location.

SQUAW MOUNTAIN GARDENS ✉ @

PO Box 946, Estacada, OR 97023 | **Phone:** (503) 630-5458 | **Fax:** (503) 630-5849 | **Email:** hennchicks@aol.com | **Web:** www.squawmountaingardens.com | **Open:** By appointment only | **Catalog:** $3; shipping year-round.

With over 4,000 varieties (from around the world) of **sempervivum and sedums** to chose from, you will have a difficult time of it making your selections. For newcomers, there are sampler collections—satisfaction guaranteed—with a variety of color, texture, and growth habit. Janis and Arthur Noyes and Joyce Hoekstra run this family-owned, mostly mail-order nursery devoted to a love of **succulents** for the rock garden and perennial border (plus exotic specimens suitable for the summer garden). They also sell hardy ferns, a few broadleafs and evergreens, some perennials (a dozen dianthus), a large selection (over 100 varieties) of hardy hedera (ivies), and various ground covers and ornamental grasses. You'll find topical books, too, including one of the only available sources on sedums.

STANLEY & SONS NURSERY, INC.

11740 SE Orient Drive, Boring, OR 97009 | **Phone:** (503) 663-4391 | **Fax:** (503) 663-6672 | **Email:** conifer@teleport.com | **Web:** www.stanleyandsons.com | **Directions:** Located due east of Boring. Travel south on I-205 and take the Clackamas or Mt Hood exit (Hwy 212) east through the towns of Damascus and Boring. When you come out of Boring you will intersect Hwy 26. Continue over Hwy 26 and go 0.5 mile to the stop sign. Turn left and come down the hill. They are the third house on the right. | **Open:** By appointment to non-wholesale customers, $100 minimum order. | **Catalog:** Free; includes basic information on hardiness zones, sun/shade considerations, ultimate plant size, expected growth per year, and foliage.

Begun in 1976, Stanley & Sons has been a major wholesale supplier of rare and unusual Japanese maples and conifers in the region. The nursery has been keenly involved in selling actinidia (kiwi) and today devotes a quarter acre to fresh fruit production. Other specialties include aralia, more than **1,500 conifers, 40 species of sambucus, 65 varieties of heaths and heathers, 80 species of magnolia trees and shrubs,** and lovely sculpted pines. Stanley & Sons has an exemplary display collection of over 2,200 labeled plants on over an acre that would surely be of interest to any of us hungry to add these woody plants to our gardens and landscapes. Visit their website and also the virtual nursery they have helped found (see "Aesthetic Gardens" under "A Selection of 'Virtual' Nurseries" at the beginning of this chapter).

SWAN ISLAND DAHLIAS ✳ ✉

995 NW 22nd Avenue, Canby, OR 97013 | **Phone:** (503) 266-7711 | **Fax:** (503) 266-8768 | **Email:** info@dahlias.com | **Web:** www.dahlias.com | **Mailing address:** PO Box 700, Canby, OR 97013 | **Directions:** Located 20 miles south of Portland. From I-5, take exit 282A (Canby-Hubbard cutoff) to the traffic signal at Arnt Road, and turn left. Arnt turns into Knightsbridge Road. At Holly Street, turn left, go to NW 22nd, turn left again for 0.5 mile. | **Open:** Weekdays; shipping March–May. | **Catalog:** $4 (with map; spectacular quality color photography, excellent library dahlia reference); refundable; **Tuber list,** brochure free.

This quality grower has offered dahlia tubers for 75 years. The Gitts family (Nicholas and Ted) offer about 40 percent of their celebrated collection as introductions they hybridize themselves. Perhaps 'Optic Illusion' is their most famous flower. Their catalog offers knives like those they use in their dividing rooms, the "No Blot Indelible Pencil" they use to mark tubers, a "Dahlia Culture Guide," and dahlia seeds. Swan Island Dahlias sponsors a big indoor Festival featuring some 250 dahlia arrangements, on display the last weekend in August and Labor Day weekend. You can walk the 40 acres of dahlia fields daily (dawn to dusk) from August 1 through the first frost. Enjoy the fields in full, vivid bloom, as well as a smaller display garden that features more than 300 varieties.

TERRITORIAL SEED COMPANY

20 Palmer Avenue, Cottage Grove, OR 97424 | **Phone:** (541) 942-9547 | **Fax:** (888) 657-3131 | **Web:** www.territorial-seed.com | **Directions to store:** From I-5, take exit 174 in Cottage Grove; turn left at the stoplight and drive 0.2 mile to Palmer Avenue. | **Directions to trial grounds:** You are invited to investigate the trial grounds, open on Saturdays, 10 a.m.–2 p.m., August 21–September 18 (closed Labor Day). From I-5, take exit 170 south of Cottage Grove. Follow the signs to Cottage Grove Lake. Drive past the head of the lake and watch for the country school, about 3 miles. Turn right into Territorial's entrance road, about 300 feet *before* the school. | **Open:** Daily (closed Sundays during winter) | **Catalog:** Free (seeds, plants, gardening supplies, books).

Just about everyone knows about this highly respected seed company. Most vegetable enthusiasts have spent many long winter nights intimately curled up with Territorial's extensive catalog, or hours pondering their seed racks throughout the Pacific Northwest. But if you travel to Cottage Grove, you'll find a **great source for plants** too. There is a mouthwatering selection of vegetables, annuals and perennials, and fruits here, including tree fruits, caneberries, blueberries, strawberries, kiwis, figs, combination fruit trees, and more. If you are not from the area but are going to be traveling in that direction, maybe a visit to the nursery would add a new dimension to a company most of us only know through the medium of newsprint. There is a cozy little shop as well.

Territorial Select Transplants: As you are plotting your seed order, note that the catalog also offers collections of plants ready to pop into their season's home in your garden. Territorial maintains a mailing list to contact customers within the region, especially when spring and summer seminars are held. Make sure your name is on that list.

TRADEWINDS BAMBOO NURSERY ✉ @

28446 Hunter Creek Loop, Gold Beach, OR 97444 | **Phone:** (541) 247-0835 | **Fax:** Same | **Email:** glb@bamboodirect.com | **Web:** www.bamboodirect.com | **Directions:** Located just off Hwy 101 about 6 hours south of Portland. Hunter Creek Road is 1.3 miles south of Gold Beach on Hwy 101. Turn off onto "Hunter Creek Road/State Police" and go 100 feet; they are on the left. | **Open:** By appointment only | **Catalog:** $3, great color photos; plant list free with SASE, also lists books on bamboo; shipping February–November.

After a decade growing and selling bamboo, Gib and Diane Cooper have attracted a great following. They carry more than **200 species of bamboo,** specializing in clumping Sino-Himalayan varieties and bamboo from Central and South America. They propagate 90 percent of their bamboo, primarily by division, but also from seed. The catalog is very informative and obviously a great deal of thought has gone into organizing the information for the edification of their customers. You'll find books, tools, poles, and rhizome barrier material, plus fertilizer. Whether you're adding bamboo or removing it from the landscape, Tradewinds also provides bamboo consultation services. Visit the display garden here to see mature bamboo varieties.

TRANS-PACIFIC NURSERY

16065 Oldsville Road, McMinnville, OR 97128 | **Phone:** (503) 472-6215 | **Fax:** (503) 434-1505 | **Email:** gwroe@worldplants.com | **Web:** www.worldplants.com | **Directions:** Located 3 miles SW of McMinnville in sight of Hwy 18. | **Open:** By appointment only, or visit the annual open house, second weekend in October. | **Catalog:** $2; year-round shipping to West Coast customers.

If you relish the search for **the exotic, rare, and unusual,** your mouth will water and your garden gloves will twitch in anticipation as you peruse this collection of rarities. Jackson Muldoon and Gerry Roe got their start when Jack "followed the grafting season" to Australia and New Zealand. Gardeners here benefit from the partners' frequent collecting expeditions, recently including several to the Yunnan Province of China, Tibet, and Thailand. The nursery offers tender and hardy plants, from alpine to subtropical (98 percent of them propagated at the nursery). This is one of those catalogs you read with Phillips and Rix in one hand and a world atlas in the other. You

can also find Japanese maple seeds, harvested from one of the Northwest's premiere specimen nurseries. As much of Trans-Pacific's mail-order business has shifted to the Web, the catalog has been simplified for a seasonal emphasis. Be sure to refer to the website for the most up-to-date inventory, as well as color photos of many of the plants, and a free (online only) plant- and seed-finding service. Look for Jack and Gerry at the Hardy Plant Society of Oregon sales and at the Salem Farmers' Markets on Saturdays, April–October.

TRILLIUM GARDENS

PO Box 803, Pleasant Hill, OR 97455 | **Phone:** (541) 937-3073 | **Fax:** (541) 937-2261 | **Email:** sales@trilliumgardens.com | **Web:** www.trilliumgardens.com | **Directions:** Furnished when you schedule an appointment to visit. | **Open:** By appointment only | **Catalog:** Free availability list; wholesale catalog

Sheila Klest is a noted authority on Northwest native plants, the specialty of her nursery for more than 16 years. You'll also enjoy her selection of ornamental grasses. She has made presentations on the topic at Portland State University and at The Yard, Garden, and Patio Show. From the catalog, at the nursery, or at the Destination Imagination Plant Sale in late April or early May in Eugene, you will find native ground covers, perennials, shrubs, ornamental grasses, water plants, shade perennials, and ferns.

TUALATIN RIVER NURSERY & CAFÉ

65 S Dollar Street, West Linn, OR 97068 | **Phone:** (503) 650-8511 | **Fax:** (503) 638-9908 | **Web:** www.tualatinrivernursery.com | **Directions:** From I-5 south of Portland, take I-205 east. Take the West Linn/10th Street exit south and go under the freeway to Willamette Falls Drive. Turn right and proceed 4 blocks to Dollar Street (76 gas station on corner). Turn right and travel 1 mile to the nursery. | **Open:** Daily

John and Lori Blair specialize in **hardy perennials, ornamental grasses, bamboo, herbs, a tempting array of heirloom vegetables, a lovely selection of small trees including Japanese maples and dwarf conifers,** hebes, shrubs and plants for container gardens, and troughs. Territorial, Seeds of Change, Botanical Interests, and Renee's Garden Seeds are available. The original farmhouse is charmingly converted to a café and gift shop, the perfect place to repair after the engaging task of personally surveying the horticultural fare the nursery offers. The café has become very popular, and features homemade organic soups and a Sunday brunch (April–September). Special events include a Women's Faire in April, a Friday evening summer concert series, a September Tomato Tasting, and a holiday open house the second Saturday in November. The Grow Series is TRN's monthly free lecture program, so be sure to add your name to the nursery mailing list. Enjoy the display garden of perennials and shrubs before tucking into that pastry and latte back at the coffeehouse! (The five raised beds provide organically grown produce for the café.)

Valley View Nursery

1675 N Valley View Road, Ashland, OR 97520 | **Phone:** (541) 488-1595 | **Fax:** (541) 488-2454 | **Second location:** 1321 Center Drive, Medford, OR 97520 | **Phone:** (541) 773-7972 | **Fax:** (541) 722-8410 | **Email:** enbaron@home.com | **Web:** www.valleyview nursery.com | **Directions:** Ashland location, take exit 19 off I-5 and travel north 1.25 miles; Medford location, take exit 27—you can see the nursery from freeway. | **Open:** Daily

Eric Baron runs this full-service family company that started in 1978; today it is the Rogue Valley's largest plant grower (500,000 plants grown annually) and retailer. Shrubs, shade and flowering trees, conifers, large specimen trees, perennials, annuals, ornamental grasses, ground covers and seasonal baskets are just some of what you'll find here—all told, there are **1,200 varieties of plants, including 400 perennials.** The two locations also offer garden hard goods, organic remedies, pots and containers, fountains, patio furniture, and tools. Ask about the convenient planting and landscape design services. When you visit, enjoy the numerous display vignettes and large-scale plantings.

Whispering Springs Nursery

19425 Colby Lane, Hillsboro, OR 97123 | **Phone:** (503) 538-3942 | **Directions:** From Portland, travel west on Hwy 26 to Murray Road. Go south on Murray Road to Farmington Road; turn right onto Farmington and go about 12 miles to Hwy 219. Turn left and then turn right immediately, taking the Bald Peak exit. Drive on Bald Peak Road, continuing to the top of the mountain, past the State Park, about 6 miles. Turn left on Holly Hill Road 1 mile past the park. Proceed 0.7 mile to the greenhouse. | **Open:** Seasonal

Becky Snyder has "worshipped the Goddess Flora and sold plants for 20+ years." Besides inviting you to visit on Mother's Day for a glass of champagne punch, she welcomes you to her garden, where at an elevation of 1,100 feet she specializes in plants that are drought tolerant, low care, and good at covering banks, with lots of climbers and wildflowers. Easy access—and the garden is at its height in June. The nursery features the same kinds of plants Becky grows in her garden: tough perennials, unusual annuals, vines, wildflowers, and moss baskets. Becky propagates 99 percent of what she offers.

Whitman Farms

3995 Gibson Road NW, Salem, OR 97304 | **Phone:** (503) 585-8728 | **Fax:** (503) 363-5020 | **Email:** lucile@teleport.com | **Web:** www.whitmanfarms.com | **Directions:** Provided when you make appointment | **Open:** By appointment only | **Catalog:** $1, refundable (more of what is offered is shown on the website)

Lucile Whitman has put together a rather eclectic specialty farm that includes **currants** and **gooseberries, nuts,** and **oddments,** (species) **maples,** and **magnolias.** Along the lines of the *Ribes,* or fruiting currants on hand here, we find 41 varieties, simply described, and with unusually candid evaluation throughout! "Jostaberry: Bah! I only use this for understock for grafted gooseberries—see Red Josta below" or "*Ribes* 'Cherry': aphids love it." There are 31 gooseberries, and again this brutal honesty one doesn't find often—"*Ribes* 'Leveller': A huge sweet berry, but a challenge to grow."

Lucile propagates 99 percent of her stock and offers a wholesale list of "Edible and Ornamental Landscape Material," which includes nuts and a broader selection of ornamentals; it is available to anyone willing to meet the minimum quantities she sets. She offers larger-caliper (up to 2-inch) specialty trees, too. Also of interest, she has a large selection of dwarf apples perfect for patio trees or espaliering.

Wildwood Gardens

33326 S Dickey Prairie Road, Molalla, OR 97038 | **Phone:** (503) 829-3102 | **Fax:** Same | **Email:** gardens@molalla.net | **Mailing address:** PO Box 250, Molalla, OR 97038 | **Directions:** From I-5, take the exit onto Hwy 214 east (the road turns into Hwy 211, the Woodburn-Estacada Hwy) headed for Molalla. On the east side of Molalla, cross the bridge at Feyrer Park, then turn right onto Dickie Prairie Road and go 1 mile. You are there. | **Open:** By appointment, and on Memorial Day weekend | **Catalog:** $2, with many color photos of bearded iris (free to prior year's customers).

This is a **wonderful iris source, offering over 1,000 varieties, and all types.** Will Plotner has worked in the iris world for more than 25 years and is active in national and international iris organizations, so be sure to bring your questions. He specializes in bearded and water iris and also offers 100-plus varieties of Japanese iris and hundreds of hemerocallis (daylilies). The catalog also features garden wind-chimes, inexpensive but reliable plastic plant markers, and a great deal on Will's favorite gardening gloves ($2 with any plant order, $1 with orders over $50, and free with $100-plus orders).

Wildwood Nursery

8374 Old Hwy 99S, Winston, OR, 97496 | **Phone:** (541) 679-4006 | **Fax:** (541) 679-4881 | **Email:** ppddriggs@wmni.net | **Directions:** From I-5 take exit 119 west on Hwy 99S. Drive 3 miles to Winston, then Wildwood is the first nursery south of Winston, next to the South Umpqua River. | **Open:** Daily

Carl and Paula Riggs are restoring Wildwood Nursery to its 1920s glory; when it was one of Central Oregon's landscaping treasures. Originated in 1921 by Clarence Moyer, the nursery holds 18 acres of grand old trees, riverfront beauty, and spiritual peace. Moyer was a friend of Luther Burbank and a well-respected horticulturist in his own right; he lived almost half of his life on this land, dying in 1968 at the age of 98. Some of his contributions include Moyer's Red Nandina, the Moyer Prune, and numerous varieties of camellias and daffodils. He was also one of the first nurserymen to utilize the US Mail as a selling tool.

The nursery itself has been in continuous use since its founding and is included in the National Register of Historic Sites. The Moyer family's first cabin remains on the property, along with a later "catalog" home and a 600-gallon redwood water tank, one of only a few left in the state.

Wildwood is known locally for its wide variety of plant material, excellent service, and beautiful environment. In the spring, a waterfall of wisteria panicles cascades from the tops of towering myrtle trees near the old cabin. You can enjoy the cork oak planted by Luther Burbank in the early twenties as a gift for Mr. Moyer; the dawn redwood, once thought extinct; and a graceful stand of cedars of Lebanon; as well as many other unusual and spectacular trees remaining from the Moyer era.

WILLAMETTE FALLS NURSERY AND PONDS (TRUE VALUE HARDWARE)

1720 Willamette Falls Drive, West Linn, OR 97068 | **Phone:** (503) 656-7344 | **Fax:** (503) 650-9694 | **Email:** frank@willamettefalls.com | **Web:** www.willamettefalls.com | **Directions:** From I-5 south of Portland, take I-205 east. Take the West Linn/10th Street exit 6 south, and turn right at the stop sign. Proceed 2 blocks to Willamette Falls Drive, turn right, and proceed 3 long blocks to the Willamette Falls Nursery, on the right. | **Open:** Daily | **Plant list:** Available online, just after the first of the year

This hardware store opened in 1906 and was purchased and restored in 1990 by John and Gloria Lightowler. In 1994 the adjunct nursery opened. The building and the flavor of the business are right at home in this peaceful, historic Willamette neighborhood. An astute plant hunter will be drawn to this gem by a streetside, dry-climate planting featuring hardy subtropicals. When you meander out back, you'll find a **diverse selection of collector plants** (many from the O'Byrne's nearby Northwest Garden Nursery), as well as a large, luxuriously planted pond that provides great atmosphere as one circles its edge round and round, soaking in how many treasures are tucked in here and there.

The selection of aquatic plants is extensive, and manager Frank Patterson reports that you can take a free pond building and pond-care seminar throughout the year.

Willamette Falls propagates about 25 percent of what's sold here, including a large variety of abutilons, cannas, hellebores, heirloom and unusual annuals and annual vines, and some new-to-the-trade perennials, and difficult-to-find ones, too. "Our aim is to uncover more and more worthy plants that will be aesthetically and horticulturally satisfying to gardeners in the Pacific Northwest, to push the hardiness envelope to broaden the palette of plants available," Frank says. To that end, he's planning on an upcoming plant-buying excursion to California with Ernie and Marietta O'Byrne, so call ahead to learn when those nifty heat-loving plants arrive here.

Seeds on offer include Lilly Miller, Plantation, and Johnson's of England. In a homey neighborhood hardware store right on-site, you'll find the full range of tools, accessories (including pond paraphernalia), pest controls, and other necessities.

WINE COUNTRY NURSERY & AQUARIUM

4100 E Portland Road, Newberg, OR 97132 | **Phone:** (503) 538-1518 | **Fax:** (503) 537-9637 | **Email:** winecountryroger@aol.com | **Web:** www.winecountrynursery.com | **Directions:** Located about 22 miles from downtown Portland, opposite the "Entering Newberg" sign on Hwy 99W, and at the east entrance of Newberg. Reach the nursery by taking I-5 south to Hwy 99W. | **Open:** Daily

After an extensive career in marketing for Jantzen Inc., the famous swimwear firm in Portland, Roger Yost in 1995 opened Wine Country Nursery & Aquarium. He has raised his passion for plants to the scale of a full-service nursery, which fills about 6 acres of a 43-acre compound (the balance is devoted to organic farming, and growing arborvitaes and specimen trees; 2 acres are leased to Brothers Herbs & Peonies. The Wine Country Nursery specializes in **magnolias, dogwoods, and other flowering trees;** Japanese maples, perennials, ornamental grasses, "Stepables" (ground covers), vines and shrubs, and more than 300 varieties of roses. The Aquarium portion of this venture supplies preformed ponds, liners, pumps, filters and, of course, koi. You can gaze at more than 20 tanks of tropical fish and koi to select for your own home aquarium or pond. Wine Country also carries Territorial and Thompson & Morgan seeds, designer pots, hammocks, swings, arbors, benches, trellises, statuary, birdbaths, fountains, and metal sculpture for the garden.

WISTERIA HERBS & FLOWERS

5273 S Coast Hwy, South Beach, OR 97366 | **Phone:** (541) 867-3846 | **Directions:** Located 1 mile south of Newport on the east side of Hwy 101. Look for the tables full of plants. | **Open:** Seasonal

Linda Montgomery has just logged her 10th year in business (the 21st for a nursery at this site). Located on an old piece of property with wonderfully shaped evergreens, old rhododendrons, and "real good growing vibes," Wisteria Herbs & Flowers carries about **600 varieties of perennials and herbs**—cottage garden favorites. Linda propagates about 75 percent of her stock, with an emphasis on lavenders, campanulas, rosemary, scented geraniums, and old-favorites. She also sells fuchsia baskets and hardy fuchsias. The display garden here has 30 varieties of lavender, as well as displays featuring plants for shade, coastal wind, easy-to-grow perennials, and newer varieties. Put this nursery down as a "must visit" on your next trip to the coast.

WOODEN SHOE BULB COMPANY

33814 S Meridian Road, Woodburn, OR 97071 | **Phone:** (503) 634-2243 or (800) 711-2006 | **Fax:** (503) 634-2710 | **Email:** iverson@molalla.net | **Web:** www.woodenshoe.com | **Mailing address:** PO Box 127, Mt. Angel, OR 97362 | **Directions:** From I-5 south of Portland, take the Woodburn exit 271, and proceed east 6 miles to Meridian Road (flashing yellow light). Turn right onto S Meridian and drive about 2 miles. | **Open:** Daily (in bloom season); otherwise, call for gift shop and fall bulb pickup hours. | **Catalog:** Free; shipping season on fresh flowers February–April; bulb orders accepted until September 1.

Talk about a display garden—there are 90 acres here filled with tulips and daffodils. You are invited to visit throughout the spring to walk through the formal display beds that feature each of the 160 varieties of tulips available so you can compare color, height, and bloom time (then, of course, place an order for fall delivery). During mid-March to mid-April, there is a monthlong celebration that features a wide array of entertainment—hot-air balloon rides, seminars in the art of wooden-shoe making, magic acts, live music, vintage-car shows, and quantities more.

WOODLAND GARDENS NURSERY

86020 Lorane Hwy, Eugene, OR 97405 | **Phone:** (541) 344-6481 | **Directions:** Located in the SW Eugene area, 3 miles out the Lorane Hwy Go south on Chamber Street, and go over the hill to the stop at Lorane Hwy. Turn right and go 2.3 miles to the intersection of Lorane Hwy and McBeth Road. There's a Grange Hall on the left and the nursery sign on the right. Go up the (rather long) gravel driveway. | **Open:** Seasonal and by appointment

Linda Wills specializes in "well-behaved, garden-tested, easy-maintenance perennials," as well as hostas, and Siberian and Pacific Coast irises. She also offers an eclectic mix of perennials and shrubs. Her goal is to field-test what she offers in order to select out the **best perennial choices for Northwest gardens.** The display garden features hostas, trees, vines, and iris, most appreciated in the spring and summer months. There is an "open tea" in Linda's garden, usually the third Tuesday in June (check dates each year). Her son and daughter-in-law have joined the business, so now this is truly a family affair.

WESTERN WASHINGTON NURSERIES

Websites Featuring Listings of Washington Nurseries

SPECIALTY NURSERY ASSOCIATION

www.specialty-nurseries.com | 20055 235th Avenue SE | Maple Valley, WA 98038

This organization of Northwest Washington specialty nurseries publishes an annual *Specialty Nursery Guide*, available free at member nurseries and usually snatched up by thousands of gardening enthusiasts at the Northwest Flower and Garden Show each February.

Started in 1988, SNA was a joint effort of local nurseries and WSU Cooperative Extension. The 2001 edition, edited by Bill Sloan of B&J Nursery in Maple Valley, features 94 nurseries, from full-service outlets to small, specialized destinations. Here's where you can find helpful cross-referencing for categories like "Aquatics" or "Rock Garden Plants."

Online, you can search the database of Washington nurseries by county, by city, or by product. The visually stunning website is user-friendly, with listings of late-breaking tours, events, and shows. A "forum" for gardeners invites regional dialogue on horticultural topics and issues. Here's where you'll read various answers to questions like "How can I grow crocosmia from seed?" or "Where can I find information on an antique sprinkler?"

WESTERN WASHINGTON NURSERIES

A & D NURSERY

6808 180th SE, Snohomish, WA 98296 | **Phone:** (360) 668-9690 | **Fax:** (360) 668-6031 | **Email:** adpeonies@earthlink.net | **Web:** www.adpeonies.com | **Mailing address:** PO Box 2338, Snohomish, WA 98291 | **Directions:** 0.5 mile west off Hwy 9 on 180th SE, or from I-5 take 164th Street exit 183, head east 2.5 miles to Mill Creek Plaza. Turn right onto Bothell-Everett Hwy; at North Creek Shopping Center turn left onto 180th SE, drive about 3.5 miles to A & D (the sign, on the right, sneaks up on you, so watch for it). | **Open:** Seasonal and by appointment | **Catalog:** $2, refundable. Features peonies, tree peonies, daylilies, and hostas (that's not a full listing of what is available at the nursery, though), a map, and luscious color photos; shipping season is March–November.

This is a nursery with great country charm and it's a truly special place for lovers of **peonies, daylilies, and hostas.** Owners Don Smetana and Keith Abel acquired A & D in the mid 1980s, but the nursery dates back to the '70s with peonies from America's first major hybridizer. Today, they propagate nearly 85 percent of the nursery's stock, offering gardeners access to unique, rare, and hard-to-find plants.

A & D is the designated display garden of the American Hemerocallis Society and is the first and only such **daylily garden** in Puget Sound. The nursery's selection and collection of daylilies and extensive collection of peonies is probably the most comprehensive in the region. The Hosta Walk provides the opportunity to see hundreds of mature plants in a woodland setting among favored companions. You'll find thousands of varieties to choose from, including many of the latest introductions by hybridizers (on display in the gardens, with many available in pots).

In the delightfully rustic Potting Shed there are thousands of color slides of peonies and daylilies for customers to peruse. A & D Nursery Bloom Time Best Bets: single-type peonies, all through May; tree peonies, early-May through mid-May; double and Japanese peonies, late May through mid-June; daylilies, July through August; hostas, May and June for foliage, late summer for flowers. Please note that parking is limited and, especially at busy times, is reserved for customers picking up or purchasing plants.

A & R PROPAGATING (SEE THE RHODY RANCH NURSERY)

AITKEN'S SALMON CREEK GARDEN

608 NW 119th Street, Vancouver, WA 98685 | **Phone:** (360) 573-4472 | **Fax:** (360) 576-7012 | **Email:** aitken@flowerfantasy.net | **Web:** www.flowerfantasy.net | **Directions:** (6 miles north of Portland, 160 miles south of Seattle.) From I-5 take the 99th Street exit 5 west to Hazel Dell Avenue. At the signal turn right (north) on Hazel Dell to 114th Street, left on 114th Street to the stop sign at 7th Avenue NW. Turn right to the corner of NW 119th Street. | **Open: Iris:** April–October, daily 8:30 a.m. to dusk.

Orchids: by appointment only. | **Catalog:** $2; shipping mid-July through August. Check website for updates on availability.

Discussions with iris fanciers usually lead to a recommendation to contact Terry and Barbara Aitken, whose plant-breeding program began over 20 years ago. Aitken's evolved out of Terry's growing interest in hybridizing irises (and now orchids) and learning more about the wide variety of different irises that can be grown. **Dwarfs, medians, tall bearded, Siberians, Japanese, Louisianas, spurias, and Pacific Coast irises,** with over 1,000 varieties represented, illustrate how you can enjoy irises in bloom from early April through early July. Terry has won many medals from the American Iris Society for his introductions.

The nursery's **4-acre garden** displays quality blooms from the world's top hybridizers as well as their own introductions, with the best bloom showing April through June (the garden is accessible on level ground with wide paths). Their passion for orchids has now moved from an avocation to offering a wide collection of several thousand, available year-round. If you're looking for a deal, check with Aitken's in late August for year-end specials on discontinued or overstocked varieties.

ALL SEASON NURSERY, GARDEN & GIFTS

3829 Pleasant Hill Road, Kelso, WA 98626 | **Phone:** (360) 577-7955 | **Fax:** (360) 577-1169 | **Email:** allseason@tdn.com | **Web:** www.tdn.com/allseason | **Directions:** Traveling south on I-5 take exit 46, and stay to the right. At the "T," turn left onto Pleasant Hill Road, following the nursery sign, and go 2.5 miles. From the south, take exit 42 from I-5 and stay to the right as you exit. At the "T," turn left onto Pacific Avenue; the first left is Pleasant Hill Road, and the nursery entrance is 1 mile on your left. (Don't go past the little grocery.) | **Open:** Daily

Jim and Nancy Chennault have transformed their business from a landscaping concern to a year-round, **full-service nursery and gift shop.** Easily reached from I-5 (think "road trip"), All Season's mature display gardens are a signature element of this nursery. "You've got to see it to believe it," writes Nancy of the rose garden and ponds. Some portions of the garden date back to the 1950s; they've been refurbished as an ongoing priority for the past 17 years. The specimen trees and shrubs were retained and a number of new gardens now provide inspiration, including an **alpine garden with a three-pond series and a creek,** a demonstration vegetable garden, a perennial rock garden, and a seasonal cutting garden. (Note: The garden is not wheelchair accessible.)

To make so many of us really feel at home there is an "Orphan Garden," which they describe as "one-of-a-kind, rescued and collected plants and garden accents that nobody wanted." Doesn't that sound familiar? Check out the website for a class and event schedule and plan a little side stop on your next trip north or south along I-5.

A LOT OF FLOWERS

1212 11th Street, Bellingham, WA 98225 | **Phone:** (360) 647-0728 | **Fax:** (360) 647-9658 | **Directions:** In the historic Fairhaven District at the corner of 11th Street and Harris. Take exit 250 from I-5, head west on Old Fairhaven Parkway to the stop light on 12th, turn right onto 12th, then turn left (west) on Harris for 1 block. | **Open:** Daily (closed January)

This favorite "hort haunt" of Whatcom County folks offers select **annuals, perennials,** and **herbs,** plus a full line of Shepherd's Seeds. Special emphasis is put into the unique selection of **cut flowers,** garden art, accessories, and botanically themed **gifts,** as well as a terrific array of terra cotta (and other) pots and containers. This special spot combines display gardens and a cozy, welcoming shop on a tiny urban corner.

ALPINE HERB FARM / WONDERLAND TEA & SPICE

6375 Rutsatz Road, Deming, WA 98244 | **Phone:** (360) 592-5943 | Or call Wonderland Tea & Spice, 1305 Railroad, Bellingham, WA 98225 | **Phone:** (360) 733-0517 | **Directions:** From Mt. Baker Hwy (SR 542) take Hwy 9 south. Turn left on Rutsatz Road, just after the bridge. The farm is located 3 miles on the right. | **Farm Open:** Third Saturday in May, 9 a.m.–6 p.m. for annual Big Sale, display garden, and information sharing. | **Plant list:** $1 (note: dried herbs are shipped; not live plants)

Alpine Herb Farm's owner Linda Quintana is highly respected for her vast knowledge of the medicinal, culinary, and ornamental uses of herbs, quality plants, and products. With more than 20 years' experience growing organic herbs and spices, Linda offers **classes,** herbal products, **organically grown herbs** (including hard-to-find medicinals), old-fashioned flowers, annuals and perennials (offered at her Farm on the dates above and at the Bellingham shop in season), plants, and collected seeds. Also stunning wreaths, swags, and such from material she has dried from her extensive gardens. The future will bring us more **prairie** and **dryland plants** as Linda's purchased additional acreage that offers ideal growing conditions for her new venture.

ALPINE NURSERY, INC.

16023 SE 144th Street, Renton, WA 98059 | **Phone:** (425) 255-1598 | **Fax:** (425) 255-0709 | **Directions:** From Renton take NE 3rd Street (Cemetery Road) 3 miles east then turn right on 160th Avenue SE to the stop sign, and turn left. | **Open:** Daily

Hunting for quality grown **trees, shrubs, conifers, ground covers,** and **perennials**? For more than 30 years William Spiry's nursery, set in pleasant grounds on 4 acres, has offered well-grown trees, shrubs, and perennials, free gardening advice, and some more unusual offerings such as **topiaries** and **grafted dwarf conifers.** You'll find **garden center** fare including Botanical Interests seeds, water fountains, tools, gloves, and containers. Take note of the August and September plant sales.

ANTIQUE ROSE FARM

12220 Springhetti Road, Snohomish, WA 98296 | **Phone:** (360) 568-1919 | **Directions:** 2 miles south of Snohomish; or, from I-5 take Hwy 2 east. Take the Hwy 9 exit south 3 miles to Marsh Road traffic signal. Turn left then immediately right on Springhetti Road and proceed 1 mile. From I-405, take the Hwy 522 exit to Hwy 9. Take this exit and travel north to the traffic signal at Marsh Road. Turn right, then immediately right on Springhetti Road and proceed 1 mile. | **Open:** Seasonal. Annual Antiques, Crafts, & Rose Festival each June (usually the second two weekends). | **Rose list:** Free

Don and Jackie McElhose have transformed this old dairy farm into a charming country destination for lovers of **old garden roses** and **modern varieties** selected for the Northwest. There are over 200 varieties available, on their own roots, including albas, climbers, bourbons, Gallicas, mosses, hybrid musks, noisettes, damasks, David Austins, and floribundas. Whew! Some select perennial companions are available. There is a lovely **gift shop featuring antiques, folk art, birdhouses, ironwork, rose-related gifts, books,** and much more. Classes cover rose selection, care, and pruning; call for schedule.

Avalon Nursery

16720 Hwy 9 SE, Snohomish, WA 98296 | **Phone:** (360) 668-9696 | **Directions:** Located on the corner of 168th Street SE and Hwy 9 between Woodinville and Snohomish. From I-5, take the 164th Street exit 183 and travel east 2.5 miles to Mill Creek Plaza. Turn right onto Bothell–Everett Hwy. At North Creek Shopping Center, turn left onto 180th SE, and drive about 4 miles to Hwy 9. Turn left (north), and go 0.7 mile to the nursery. From I-405, take exit 23 onto Hwy 522. Past Woodinville, take the Hwy 9 exit north. | **Open:** Daily

Craig Tutt started Avalon in 1995 and specializes in water gardening and aquatics. Here you'll find pond supplies, liners, pumps, filters, koi (Japanese and domestic), pond kits, water lilies, and other companion plants for your water features. Craig is well known for his design work installing ponds and water features in the area, an added service the nursery offers. You can also pick up perennials, trees, annuals, and some shrubs from the small nursery stock. For inspiration, enjoy Craig's two koi ponds, bordered by mixed seasonal beds. There is also a 2,800-square-foot greenhouse in which Craig propagates many of his plants, plus a well-outfitted retail shop.

Bainbridge Gardens

9415 Miller Road NE, Bainbridge Island, WA 98110 | **Phone:** (206) 842-5888 | **Fax:** (206) 842-7645 | **Web:** www.bainbridge gardens.com | **Directions:** From Winslow on Bainbridge Island, take Hwy 305 north to NE High School Road, then turn left (west) to Miller Road NE. Turn right (north); the nursery will be on your left. | **Open:** Daily

Junkoh Harui, long a nurseryman on the Island, has returned to his father's garden/nursery to revive the family tradition of offering a peaceful destination to buy plants amid an inspiring setting. In this garden once abandoned when the family was forced to leave in the 1940s with thousands of other Japanese-Americans, Junkoh has been able to recapture the beauty, restore some original gardens, and nurture plants first grown by his father, including the aged Japanese red pine trees that the senior Mr. Harui started from seeds brought from Japan in the early 1900s.

The news at Bainbridge Gardens is that plantswoman and well-known author Ann Lovejoy (who lives just a hop, skip, and a jump from Bainbridge Gardens and has frequently taught classes at the nursery) has joined forces with Junkoh to become a partner in the business.

Ann's **organic gardening** practices have been widely adopted by the entire nursery, so the nontoxic treatments and enhancements offered in the garden store are now greatly expanding. Where else can you regularly buy freshly made "Soil Soup" aka compost tea several times a week (while supplies last)?

If you are looking for an amazing selection of **perennials, ground covers, roses, trees, ornamental shrubs, and grasses,** this nursery must be on your agenda. The most dazzling selection of **containers, large and small** and in great finishes, fills every corner of the property, often grouped in complementary colors to inspire your own designs.

Call to request a free color brochure, ask to be put on the *Bainbridge Gardener* newsletter mailing list, or visit the website. This is a definite day trip destination! Time your trip to take advantage of the excellent **New Rose Cafe** for lunch or a latte while relaxing in the garden terrace setting.

B & D Lilies

PO Box 2007, Port Townsend, WA 98368 | **Phone:** (360) 385-1738 | **Fax:** (360) 385-9996 | **Display Garden:** (360) 765-4074 | **Web:** www.bdlilies.com | **Directions:** To the Snow Creek display garden (located about two hours west of Seattle via ferry and the Hood Canal Bridge): After crossing the Hood Canal Bridge follow Hwy 104. At the intersection with Hwy 101 follow north (right) 1,000 feet to the propagation grounds/display garden. From Port Townsend travel south on Hwy 101 about 2 miles south of Discovery Bay, to 284566 Hwy 101. The garden features a true lily bulb display (tetraploid Orientals), best in late July. | **Open:** Primarily mail order, office open weekdays, 9 a.m.–5 p.m. but the display gardens/propagation fields and daylily sales at **Snow Creek** open mid-June to mid-August, Monday–Saturday, 9:30 a.m.–5 p.m. Remember an umbrella and sensible shoes if it's rainy. | **Catalog:** $3 each/$5 both, refundable with first order, Fall and Spring catalogs (extensive color, informative). Shipping mid-October through December with a few Oriental hybrids shipping in spring due to later harvest the preceding fall. Wholesale and retail.

B & D Lilies offers a broad selection of **hybrid and species lilies,** and offers rare and endangered species through seed propagation and tissue culture. Another catalog is available showcasing the large selection of **daylilies.** B & D has had popular booths at Flower and Garden Shows (Seattle, Portland, San Francisco, and Boise) February–March, with a vast selection of lily bulbs, and a knowledgeable staff answering queries and taking orders.

B & J Nursery

20055 235th Avenue SE, Maple Valley, WA 98038 | **Phone:** (425) 432-4724 | **Email:** bill_sloan@netzero.net | **Directions:** From

Renton, take Maple Valley Hwy to Hwy 18 and head northeast. Go north (left) on 236th Avenue SE for 0.7 mile (stay on main road). | **Open:** Seasonal and by appointment | **Plant list:** Free—there are actually two. One is organized alphabetically and includes pertinent information on each plant; the other is thoughtfully arranged by color and heights within each color. Wholesale and retail. Ask for a free landscape planning chart.

At this family business started 20 years ago, Bill and Barb Sloan sell over 150 varieties of their specialty: **rhododendrons** (mostly) and evergreen **azaleas** (some). They propagate about half of their stock and have three 100-foot huts sheltering their progeny. The species, yakushimanum and yak hybrids, are very popular. The display garden (rhododendrons are identified) is accessible, with the best bloom April/May. The Sloans generously invite any questions from visitors curious about rhododendron culture and are very helpful in suggesting the best varieties for any growing situation (sun, shade, moist, etc.).

BAKER & CHANTRY, INC. ORCHIDS

18611 132nd Avenue NE, Woodinville, WA 98072 | **Phone:** *(425)* 483-0345 | **Fax:** (425) 424-8795 | **Email:** bc_orchids@juno.com | **Web:** www.orchidmall.com | **Mailing address:** PO Box 554, Woodinville, WA 98072-8784 | **Directions:** From Hwy 522, traveling east, take the first Woodinville exit. At the stoplight at the top of the ramp, turn left (back over 522). You are on 132nd. B & C is 0.3 mile north on the left side directly opposite 186th Street. | **Open:** Daily

If you are an **orchid** enthusiast, whether a beginner or a more accomplished grower, do make the time to discover this unique place. You'll always find exquisite plants in flower and, if you're not yet hooked, may be tempted to give these rewarding treasures a try. B & C can send you home with plant(s), supplies, cultural information, encouragement, and information about the local orchid societies. Marlene Holl and Jim Greeno invite you to two open houses each year: one in spring (date varies), and the day after Thanksgiving and for the next nine days. Orchid growing supplies are, of course, available here, too.

BAKERVIEW NURSERY AND GARDEN CENTER

945 E Bakerview Road, Bellingham, WA 98226 | **Phone:** *(360)* 676-0400 or (360) 380-9097 | **Fax:** (360) 676-5418 | **Email:** bakerviewnursery@uswest.net | **Web:** www.bakerviewnursery.com | **Directions:** From I-5 take Meridian exit 256-A, turn right (north), past Bellis Fair Mall, go about 0.5 mile, and turn right onto E Bakerview Road. | **Open:** Daily

An area landmark in the nursery and garden center business, this **full-service nursery** on 5 acres provides a large selection of just about any type of plant material or ancillary need a gardener might have. This includes a large selection of indoor and outdoor plants, trees and shrubs, bulk soil and amendments, decorative pottery, and garden accessories. Enjoy a marvelous series of display vignettes and take note of Bakerview's large commitment to **water gardens,** to supply you with all you could possibly need for a new or existing pond. This is truly a place to find gifts for gardeners and non-gardeners alike. There is an informative newsletter, workshops through the seasons, and a reference library—and the coffee is always on with a cookie to help you through the day!

BAMBOO GARDENS OF WASHINGTON

5016 192nd Place NE, Redmond, WA 98074 | **Phone:** *(425)* 868-5166 | **Fax:** (425) 868-5360 | **Email:** bamboo@blarg.net | **Web:** www.BambooGardensWA.com | **Directions:** Take Hwy 520 to Redmond. At the intersection with the Redmond-Fall City Road (SR 202) travel south 2 miles to 196th Avenue NE. Turn right and follow to the nursery. | **Open:** Daily. Call for holiday hours and closures. | **Catalog:** With mail-order items (hard goods like bamboo poles, water pipes, supplies) only; no plants are shipped; wholesale and retail. | **Plant list:** Free

Bamboo Gardens of Washington is the **premier destination for bamboo** in the Pacific Northwest. For anyone terrified that bamboo will take over the landscape, this is the place to begin a bamboo conversion: Wander through the rustling groves and view several other-worldly display gardens. This excursion will refresh your soul and inspire your garden muse. A bend in the path opens up fantasies and mysterious escapes, all suggested by the alluring and widely varied bamboo foliage. As a specialty retail and wholesale nursery, Bamboo Gardens strives to provide the highest quality plants, stone garden ornaments, bamboo poles, and related products. Its knowledgeable staff will cheerfully help you select from 45-plus varieties of bamboo, 50 **ornamental grass** offerings, and an ever-expanding selection of **water-garden plants.** Sign up for a workshop or class, or hire an expert to tackle removal or control challenges in your own backyard (or install a new grove of nonspreading bamboo!). **Tools and barrier supplies** are available for the do-it-yourself crowd. Build a trellis or fence with bamboo—all the instructions and supplies are on hand to get you started.

BARFOD'S HARDY FERNS

15606 Burn Road, Arlington, WA 98223 | **Phone:** *(360)* 435-6009 | **Directions:** From I-5, take the Smokey Pt exit (Hwy 531 at 172nd Street NE). Head east on 172nd Street NE to Hwy 9; then turn left and go north to 204th Street NE. Turn right and head east on 204th Street, which will curve and become 209th before it intersects with Burn Road. Turn right on Burn Road and head south to 156th NE; turn right, and look for the barn and greenhouse on the right. | **Open:** By appointment only | **Plant list:** Free, upon request

Torben and Anna Barfod are well known in nursery circles, having for decades operated a retail nursery and large-scale growing facility in Bothell. Torben recently "retired," having sold the Bothell location to an organic landscaper (a fact that pleases him—and also helped to avoid the developer's wrecking ball). In Arlington, he grows a wide range of temperate-hardy ferns, selling to longtime wholesale customers. Some of his plants make their way to Fancy Fronds, the nursery operated by his longtime colleague Judith Jones. But if you're among those who want to talk with and learn from a master-grower, Torben welcomes your visits.

BASSETTI'S CROOKED ARBOR GARDENS

18512 NE 165th, Woodinville, WA 98072 | **Phone:** (425) 788-6767 | **Email:** leanettebassetti@aol.com | **Web:** www.bassettisgardens.com | **Directions:** From I-5 take Hwy 520 east to the end. At the signal (at the end of 520) go straight on Avondale Road for about 5 miles. Turn west (left) at the set of blinking lights onto NE 165th, turn right into gate; go to large barn. | From I-405, take exit 23/Hwy 522 (Monroe, Woodinville). Take the second exit in Woodinville at NE 195th, continuing to the Woodinville-Duvall Road. Turn right (south) on Avondale Road, then west (right) at the blinking lights on NE 165th. Proceed as above to barn. | **Open:** Seasonal or by appointment

Picnics under the arbor and weddings in the garden (July through September). Come to purchase **dwarf conifers, alpine plants** such as *Vaccinium,* rhododendrons, saxifragia, hebes, and lewisias, including plants in containers. Bassetti's is also famous for **garden sculpture,** garden accessories, and especially the very popular Annual Garden Sculpture Opening and Sale, usually in late June (call for dates and to add your name to mailing list for announcement) featuring many local artists (sculptors, blacksmiths, ceramicists, photographers, and other artists) and specialty nurseries scattered through the festive country setting. You are invited to meander Leanette and Bill's **famed display gardens,** which include an Alpine Garden, a perennial border with an arbor behind, Shade and Sculpture Gardens, Kitchen Garden, Italianate Garden, an Annual Flower Garden . . . plus, the 60-foot "crooked arbor." The pond and the container gardens are best viewed May through August.

About half the stock here is propagated by the talented Bassettis. The land here has longevity, as Leanette's parents bought this former dairy farm and peat bog in 1957. The nursery and gardens have been developed on land once used as pasture. Talk about great soil! Take note of **Garden Sculpture Show,** mid-June to August.

BAY HAY AND FEED

10355 Sunrise Drive, Bainbridge Island, WA 98110 | **Phone:** (206) 842-5274 | **Fax:** (206) 842-5100 | **Mailing address:** PO Box 4698, Rolling Bay, WA 98061 | **Directions:** From Hwy 305 on Bainbridge Island turn east on Day Road E, then turn right on Sunrise Drive NE. | **Open:** Daily

This is an old-fashioned farm and garden store, with chicks and ducklings in spring, wind-up toys in the gift shop, and a large, eye-catching selection of beautiful pots from around the world. It is easy to spend one's time poking around the many rooms and levels here, but most plant-lovers will very soon make their way out back to the nursery. While not huge, this charming spot offers an excellent range of well-chosen small trees (Japanese maples, conifers, deciduous trees), shrubs, perennials, annuals, herbs, and ground covers. Seeds include Territorial, Lilly Miller, Botanical Interests, Renee's Seeds, and Thompson & Morgan. Before you leave, check out

the large work-clothing department, with everything from sturdy Carharts to stylish gardening clogs. PS: There's a fantastic bakery and espresso bar next door!

BAYVIEW FARM AND GARDEN

2780 Marshview Avenue, Langley, WA 98260 | **Phone:** (360) 321-6789 | **Fax:** (360) 321-0959 | **Email:** bfg@whidbey.com | **Directions:** From the Clinton ferry dock drive 6.5 miles north to Bayview Road, then right 0.5 mile to Marshview Avenue, where you'll turn left. (From the north on Hwy 525, watch for Bayview Road after passing through Freeland, about 3 miles on left.) The nursery is adjacent to a big red barn. | **Open:** Daily

Maureen and Jim Rowley have grown plants for other nurseries throughout this region since 1988, and opened the retail operation in January 1993 with the goal of providing Whidbey gardeners a full-service specialty nursery and garden center. Maureen comes from a family business manufacturing an excellent line of greenhouses (her late father held patents on several greenhouse systems, so her horticultural knowledge is in the genes). The Rowleys propagate a small percentage of annuals and perennials. **Hanging baskets** are a specialty, although you can find a wide variety of "everything"—conifers, water plants, bamboo, specimen trees, fruit and nut trees, shade and flowering trees, roses, flowering shrubs, broadleaf evergreens, vines, ground covers, Japanese maples, rhododendrons, berries, lawn and turf, cover crops, and plants from China. Whew! It is especially gratifying to see the effort put into a **super selection of seeds** (Thompson & Morgan, Lake Valley, Unwins, Shepherd's, Renee's Garden, Seeds of Change, Territorial, Ed Hume), customer education/support, and lots of organic supplies—a strictly nontoxic approach to pest control! This year-round garden center has a good selection of **quality English gardening tools** and Wellies, extensive bulk soil amendments, books, and pots. Plus, if you're a gardener-farmer, Bayview's feed store stocks hay, grain, and sundries for all farm pets and livestock. You can buy Soil Soup/compost tea here on Thursdays and Saturdays, plus organic fertilizers, tools, supplies, gardening gifts, and more every day. The accessible display garden features a perennial border, laburnum arbor, wildlife/native plant display, and Farmer's Market community garden. Call for details on spring workshops, including the very popular Moss Hanging Baskets; a fall pruning workshop is also offered.

BEAR CREEK NURSERY

4999 Samish Way, Bellingham, WA 98226 | **Phone:** (360) 733-1171 | **Fax:** (360) 715-1436 | **Web:** Bear Creek is profiled at www.botanique.com and has space in the marketplace on the website at www.nwgardening.com. | **Directions:** From I-5 (northbound), take exit 246 and head east of the freeway. Turn left on Samish Way, watch for the handsome nursery sign on the right. From I-5 (southbound) take the Samish Way exit, turn left to cross back over the freeway, turn right on Samish Way for about 5 miles, past Lake Padden 1.5 miles, on the left. | **Open:** Seasonal and by appointment

Discover this peaceful, rural gem. Customers are warmly welcomed by a knowledgeable staff anxious to answer questions about the wide range of **rare and unusual plant varieties** available. They offer a dazzling assortment of choice bulbs, ornamental grasses, uncommon perennials, daylilies, peonies, and hardy geraniums. Also see the rock garden plants (many varieties of sempervivums and sedums) and those for the woodland (including a good selection of hardy ferns, hellebores, and trilliums). They have added a small but very special collection of vines, flowering shrubs, and trees. Two snazzy shade houses comfortably lodge their **shade-loving plants,** particularly a large selection of hostas. Jeanne Hager is a passionate plantswoman, very knowledgeable and eager to provide exciting selections for the intrepid gardener. Be sure to visit during April and May when the nursery's collection of **species rhododendrons** from China is at its peak. Allow time to roam the Hagers' ambitious garden to view mature beds of collector plants and clever combinations. Throughout the nursery you will find unique art and artifacts mingling with the plants. Tours and educational programs are available by prearrangement. (Note: Not wheelchair accessible.)

BEAUTY AND THE BAMBOO CO.

306 NW 84th Street, Seattle, WA 98117 | **Phone:** (206) 781-9790 | **Fax:** (206) 297-2810 | **Email:** bambu501@aol.com | **Open:** By appointment only; wholesale and retail | **Plant list:** Free

Stan Andreasen has over **200 varieties of bamboo** on view, just north of Ballard in Seattle's Greenwood neighborhood. A beautiful display garden helps bamboo seekers visually compare the varieties they may want—right in the landscape. He offers his bamboo potted in 1-, 5-, 10-, 15-, and 25-gallon sizes. All are cold hardy, ready to plant indoors or outdoors "anytime." Bamboo poles, pots, and plastic root barriers are sold at the nursery. Stan tells us that "no matter what bamboo need the customer is looking for, an honest education will be assured." Stan also gives free consultations, and frequently lectures for garden clubs and specialty nurseries.

BELLWETHER PERENNIALS

4662 Center Road, Lopez Island, WA 98261 | **Phone:** (360) 468-3531 | **Fax:** Same | **Email:** fruitandnut@rockisland.com | **Directions:** From the ferry, follow the road to Center Road (the second intersection from the ferry landing). Turn left onto Center and follow about 4 miles. Pass the school, then go about 0.2 mile beyond to a little yellow house with a red barn and a greenhouse. | **Open:** By appointment; usually open most Fridays and Saturdays in late spring–early summer. | **Plant list:** Free; please send a SASE with your request; wholesale and retail.

Jenny Harris grows and sells a laudable palette of unusual perennials and shrubs that are appropriate to her island environment (and thus to many of our own gardens), grown as organically as possible. This is how she puts it: "My specialty is growing **plants that need little care** (extra water, special soil, staking) yet are interesting and unusual." Hear, hear! She shares her display garden with a flock of old English bantams; the plants, at least, are unirrigated and many are pest- and disease-tolerant. Jenny propagates nearly 90 percent of her stock, many from seed. Look for plants in the Lamiaceae, Scrophulariaceae (salvias, penstemons, and her favorites, the verbascums), and Apiaceae families, along with hardy geraniums, grasses, heucheras, kniphofias, ceanothus, arctostaphylos, sedum, and euphorbias to name a few. Design services are offered, with an emphasis on perennial and shrub borders and native plants. Plans are in the works for a summer garden art festival . . . call for details.

BLACK LAKE ORGANIC NURSERY & GARDEN STORE

4711 Black Lake Boulevard SW, Olympia, WA 98512 | **Phone:** (360) 786-0537 | **Directions:** From I-5 at Olympia take Hwy 101 west (toward Aberdeen). Take the Black Lake exit, turn left and go 3 miles south. The garden is on the west shore of Black Lake, eight houses beyond the grocery store. | **Open:** Tuesday–Sunday, 9 a.m.–6 p.m., closed Mondays and major holidays

This **organic only** garden-supply store has been providing vegetable and herb starts (their own) along with fruit and nut trees since 1980. They are well regarded locally for their commitment to **native plants**: trees and shrubs, wildlife-attracting plants, a miscellany of ornamentals, and Territorial Seeds. Find organic fertilizers, amendments, pest controls, wildlife aids, garden tools, books, and lots of down-to-earth advice on lawn and landscape care without the need for pesticides and herbicides less friendly to the environment and wildlife. Annual newsletter.

BLUE HERON FARM

12179 State Route 530, Rockport, WA 98283 | **Phone:** (360) 853-8449 | **Fax:** Same | **Email:** als@fidalgo.net | **Directions:** 16 miles north of Darrington on SR 530 at corner of Rockport Cascade Road and E Sauk Road (milepost 66). Or on SR 20 at Rockport go 1 mile south on SR 530 to corner of Rockport Cascade Road and E Sauk Road. From I-5, take Arlington exit 208 and travel for 50 miles. | **Open:** By appointment only | **Plant list:** Free with SASE; wholesale and retail.

For 14 years this husband-and-wife team of Michael Brondi and Anne Schwartz have grown **hardy bamboo** as a specialty, along with native trees and shrubs chosen for their **permacultural value** (multiple functions in the landscape). Bamboo makes a lovely evergreen hedge and is available as a ground cover, all the way up to timber varieties. There are over 100 varieties of hardy bamboo grown here (25 to 30 varieties are available for sale) and what they don't grow, they will help you find. The nursery encourages visitors to wander through the beautiful groves of mature bamboo. Brondi and Schwartz are founding members of the Pacific Northwest Bamboo Society and active early members of Washington Tilth Producers, the organic farm organization.

Here's where you'll find advice on removing and controlling bamboo, plus the supplies, like lengths of **root barrier,** to tackle the job. Look for the many Pacific Northwest–friendly varieties, such as *Fargesia nitida,*

'Blue Fountain Bamboo', a shade- and cold-tolerant clumping type. Special free workshops and spring sales in April and May (call for dates). They also grow certified organic raspberries, blueberries, garlic, carrots, winter squash, and onions.

BONNIE'S GREENHOUSE

30135 Lyman-Hamilton Hwy, Sedro-Woolley, WA 98284 | **Phone:** (360) 826-3284 | **Directions:** From I-5 travel east on Hwy 20. Bonnie's Greenhouse is 6 miles east of Sedro-Wooley. Turn right on Lyman-Hamilton Hwy; nursery is on the left. | **Open:** Daily

Bonnie Gallagher inherited her love of plants from her mother. After working for a commercial greenhouse for eight years, she decided to launch her own venture in 1995. She specializes in **moss and custom hanging baskets,** but you will always find unusual annuals and perennials at Bonnie's. The nursery has a large selection of herbs, **sedums** (hens-and-chicks are a favorite of Bonnie's), vines like *Cobaea scandens* (cup and saucer vine), and rhodochiton. Looking for cutting and everlasting flowers? Bonnie has a wide selection of her favorites here, too. You are welcome to meander through her garden, which surrounds the house, adjacent to the nursery. So if you are making a trip along this route, be sure to add a diversion (and save room in your vehicle for plants!).

BONSAI NORTHWEST

5021 S 144th Street, Seattle 98168 | **Phone:** (206) 242-8244 | **Fax:** (206) 242-8242 | **Web:** www.bonsai_NW.com | **Directions:** Driving south of Seattle on I-5 take exit 154B, stay right. Take the first right onto 52nd. Turn right on 51st and drive to the corner of 144th. From I-5 driving north, take exit 153 and take Klickitat Road to the corner of 144th. | **Open:** Wednesday–Sunday | **Catalog:** $2, of bonsai tools; wholesale and retail.

Bonsai Northwest offers the largest selection in the Northwest of **bonsai** and pre-bonsai, as well as finished trees, specializing in azaleas. You'll also find a **wide selection of pots** (Japanese and Chinese), tools, wire, fertilizer, and soil—everything for the amateur or experienced bonsai enthusiast. A handy repotting and grooming service can give new life to your established plants. Take note of an **indoor display garden** and outdoor waterfall and pond. Many classes, workshops and lectures are offered throughout the year.

BOUQUET BANQUE (NURSERY) / FISHSTICKS (BASKETRY SCHOOL)

8220 State Avenue, Marysville, WA 98270 | **Phone:** (360) 659-4938 | **Email:** fishsticks@greatnorthern.net | **Web:** www.twigtwisters.com | **Mailing address:** PO Box 1417, Marysville, WA 98270 | **Directions:** From I-5 take the 88th Street exit 200 and travel east to State Street (Hwy 99). Across from the Co-op and NAPA (the second driveway on your right, to the west) cross the RR tracks, turn south through the gate at the nursery/shop sign, park in the field. | **Open (Nursery):** Tuesday, Friday, Saturday, and Sunday, 9 a.m.–5 p.m. or by appointment | **Open (Basketry School/Shop):** Open according to the catalog for classes and same as the nursery for supplies. | **Catalog:** Free, with

classes, nursery events; gardens at showiest May–October. mail-order supplies, not plants; wholesale and retail.

Judy Zugish describes her endeavor as "22 years of hands-on homestead gardening—one woman's obsession." On her 3 acres she tends a 20 x 60-foot greenhouse, exuberant English country-style gardens, herbs (basils are a specialty), perennials, and specific plants for weaving, and offers her experience as a floral designer. Garden art, from alder and hazelnut furniture and trellises to woven archways, appears throughout the wandering paths, with new projects always under construction.

Judy propagates collectible herbs, **native plants, weaving willows, and vines** and offers field-dug divisions from her garden. During midsummer, don't miss the Lily Fest with **7,000-plus Oriental lilies** in bud and bloom. Come fall, there's a dandy Plant Sale with terrific prices. Judy's interest in **fiber plants** inspired FishSticks Basketry School. Often materials are gathered from the garden and used fresh or dried. Here is where you can obtain a range of unusual materials for your own projects, should you be in search of western red cedar, Alaskan yellow cedar, Japanese pre-split bamboo, sweet grass, or skeined willow. Take a class and create your own willow fence, trellis, conical forms, furniture, or sculpture.

BOXHILL FARM

14175 Carnation-Duvall Road, Duvall, WA 98019 | **Phone:** (425) 788-6473 | **Fax:** (425) 588-9583 | **Email:** boxhill@mindspring.com | **Web:** www.boxhillfarm.com | **Directions:** Just south of Duvall on Hwy 203 at intersection of Big Rock Road (across from the new Safeway). | **Open:** Daily

Along with their stock of other plant genera, this delightful nursery specializes in **boxwood** (miniature, columnar, for topiaries, hedges, and knots). Boxhill is a revamped 200-acre former dairy farm with historic buildings and great views. Entering their fourth season, owners Bob and Marise Schader are striving to offer more and more of their own nursery stock.

A growing display garden blends nicely into the picturesque setting, and includes bamboos, grasses, trees, and perennials. The shop carries an assortment of custom handmade tools from Holland, organic gardening supplies, garden art, and natural granite boulder planters. Their nursery specializes in many buxus varieties, magnolias, bamboo (yellow, green, black, and striped), daylilies, and ornamental grasses. Their tasty fare also includes **flowering trees (crabapples), unusual trees,** perennials (some rare new varieties from England), Northwest natives, water plants, and a special Chinese collection (*Michelia* and friends).

BURNT RIDGE NURSERY & ORCHARDS

432 Burnt Ridge Road, Onalaska, WA 98570 | **Phone:** (360) 985-2873 | **Fax:** (360) 985-0882 | **Email:** Burntridge@myhome.net | **Web:** http://landru.myhome.net/burntridge/ | **Open:** By

appointment only; and at Olympia Farmer's Market Saturdays, April–November, 10 a.m.–3 p.m. | **Catalog:** Free with SASE

Burnt Ridge Nursery & Orchards is a family-owned farm, in business since 1980. The 20-acre farm is located in the foothills of the Cascade Mountains, with a beautiful view of Mount St. Helens. The mail-order nursery specializes in **disease-resistant bushes, trees, and vines that provide edible fruits and nuts.** They might be unusual, but that's why Michael and Carolyn Dolan seek out and grow almonds, aronia, Asian pear, and bald cypress, plus apples and apricots. Another specialty here are Northwest native plants for the ornamental landscape.

When you order from Burnt Ridge, expect nicely sized, healthy, well-rooted plant material that's done well in the owners' own orchards. Please call for directions, as this nursery is open by appointment only.

BURLINGAME GARDENS

1389 Ocean Beach Road, Hoquiam, WA 98550 | **Phone:** (360) 533-8463 | **Fax:** Same | **Email:** burlingamegdns@techline.com | **Web:** www.burlingamegardens.uswestdex.com | **Directions:** From I-5 at Olympia take exit 104, Hwy 8, "Ocean Beaches." Follow highway signs to Aberdeen/Hoquiam. You will be traveling on Hwy 101 north, which turns into Hwy 8 west, which turns into Hwy 12 west, then turns back into Hwy 101 heading north out of Hoquiam! The secret is to get on the freeway to the beaches and stay there until you get to Hoquiam and forget all that highway sign stuff! From Hoquiam follow 101 north for 3 miles to Ocean Beach Road. Turn left onto Ocean Beach Road to No. 1389, then follow the signs to the nursery. About 1-1/4 hours from Olympia. | **Open:** Seasonal weekends; open most holidays and by appointment | **Catalog:** $2.50

Gail and Mike Johannes operate this nursery off the beaten track, offering a specialty niche in plants for **winter interest:** hellebores, hamamelis, corylopsis, winter heaths and heathers, and dwarf conifers. While all specialties, these plants join **collector plants** in many other categories: hard-to-find perennials, with many heirloom varieties; hardy geraniums; seaside garden plants (phormiums, cistus, hebes); Mediterranean herbs; shade-tolerant perennials; ornamental grasses; and flowering and fragrant shrubs. Vine lovers will be thrilled with the 14 varieties of wisteria. Plan your trip to coincide with the spring bloom, mid-March to mid-June, to see many 50-year-old species and hybrid azaleas and rhododendrons, some of which tower to 25 feet. The gardens spread over an area of about 5 acres, and include perennial and mixed borders, rose gardens, and dwarf conifers.

BUSH'S

13419 208th Street NE, Arlington, WA 98223 | **Phone:** (360) 435-4987 | **Fax:** (360) 435-7009 | **Email:** ianbush@earthlink.net | **Directions:** From I-5 at Arlington take exit 208, proceed east on SR 530 to Arlington. Continue on through Arlington north on 530 toward Darrington. After the bridge immediately outside Arlington and just past the soccer fields on the left, turn left onto Arlington Heights Road (288th Street NE). Continue east on this road about 5 miles, past the fire station; turn right onto 123rd Street NE. From then on, any time you have a choice go left. You will come across a little wooden bridge on 208th. Bush's is the second driveway on the left after the bridge. | **Open:** By appointment only

Ian and Anne Bush have spent many years as "part-time" nursery owners, but recently Anne was able to make the move into a permanent place tending the love of their life, over 60 varieties of Pacific Northwest **hardy fuchsias.** When you go to the nursery you will be treated to Anne's garden as well, so if hardy fuchsias are your passion you will want to plan your visit to coincide with bloom (from the end of June until mid-October with the peak in late August). The nursery also offers fuchsia and ivy geranium **baskets,** fuchsia basket **starts,** and assorted **annuals** and **perennials.** In addition Ian grows a large number and variety of plants (in containers) native to the Northwest.

CASCADE NURSERY

8921 55th Avenue NE, Marysville, WA 98270 | **Phone:** (360) 659-2988 or (360) 653-6747 | **Directions:** Off I-5, take the 88th NE exit and travel east on 88th. At 55th Avenue turn left (north). | **Open:** Daily (closed Wednesdays in winter)

This 4-acre country garden, not far off I-5, is the domain of Fred and Betsy Huse, who have solid retail nursery backgrounds at Molbak's and Furney's. For 17 years, though, they have fashioned their niche away from the hustle and bustle, offering a **broad spectrum of plants** including unique, hard-to-find roses, perennials, and hydrangeas but also water plants, hostas, rhododendrons, conifers, and lots of trees and shrubs. Drop by in spring for colorful annuals and very special **Victorian hanging baskets.** September is a BIG sale all month—take note! The **gift shop** sparkles at holiday time, but keep them in mind throughout the year, because you'll find lots of gardening books, including a special selection for children.

CEDARBROOK HERB FARM & PETALS GARDEN CAFÉ

1345 Sequim Avenue S, Sequim, WA 98382 | **Phone:** (360) 683-7733 | **Fax:** (360) 681-3040 | **Email:** cedbrook@olypen.com | **Web:** www.lavenderfarms.com/cedarbrook | **Directions:** 2 miles west of Port Townsend (17 miles east of Port Angeles); take Sequim Avenue exit off bypass and head up the hill. | **Open:** Daily; best blooms, July and August

On what was originally the homestead of the pioneer Bell family, in 1967 Karman McReynolds started Washington's first herb farm here. Of the 12 acres, about 2 acres grow **herbs, everlastings,** and **garlic,** now tended by Terry and Toni Anderson. The current specialties are lavender plants and products, with more than 40 varieties of intoxicatingly fragrant and lovely lavender showcased in display gardens, not to mention 200 other herb varieties. The **Lavender Festival** is usually in mid-July; the 2001 weekend was set for July 21–22. Make a day of it and enjoy a culinary, herb-inspired meal at Petals Garden Café.

You will also find a large variety of culinary (fresh-cut basil by the bunch, June–September), landscaping, tea, fragrant, medicinal, and flowering herbs; herb seeds;

wonderful elephant and Italian garlic; and everlastings (plants, seeds, and dried).

Live plants and gift items can be shipped. Drop by Bell House, the **gift shop,** at Christmas for ornaments, noble fir wreaths and swags, everlasting and herb wreaths, and culinary gifts. Year-round, you'll find herbal body-care products, books, and herbal crafting materials. Custom orders are welcome.

CEDAR VALLEY NURSERY

3833 McElfresh Road SW, Centralia, WA 98531 | **Phone:** (360) 736-7490 | **Fax:** (360) 736-6600 | **Email:** boyd@myhome.net | **Open:** By appointment only; directions provided when you schedule a visit. | **Catalog:** Free upon request; wholesale and retail.

Cedar Valley Nursery was started in 1979 by Bob and Ann Kyte to provide disease-free strawberry plants to be released by the USDA. Through the magic of **tissue culture** their offerings have expanded to **raspberries** (11 varieties) and **blackberries** (22 varieties) specifically selected for success in Pacific Northwest growing conditions. The Kytes note: "Not everyone needs tissue-cultured plants. However, if quality cultivars, free of disease are important to you, we sincerely believe our plants are the best available." If you want to learn more about tissue culture, written for an interested lay person, the third edition of Ann's book, *Plants from Test Tubes: An Introduction to Micropropagation* is published by Timber Press (1996). Custom propagation by tissue culture is available. The nursery is now managed by Charlie Boyd, another expert berry grower.

CHANGING SEASONS

17637 Bennett Road, Mt. Vernon, WA 98273 | **Phone:** (360) 424-8417 | **Email:** tmiller@ncia.com | **Directions:** From I-5 take the Hwy 20 exit and go west approximately 0.5 mile to Pulver Road. Turn left onto Pulver and go 1 mile to Bennett Road, turn right and drive 0.3 mile to the blue house on the right. | **Open:** By appointment only

Many gardeners in this area know Heidi Zeretzke (or at least her plants) from the variety of plant sales she participates in annually. This talented woman not only offers consultation and landscape design services, she's also active in the local Master Gardener clinic. She propagates 75 percent of Changing Seasons' plant stock, good news for gardeners who want to know who grows the plants they buy.

Heidi's specialty of **hummingbird- and butterfly-attracting plants**—perennials, shrubs, and trees, with an ever-increasing selection of Northwest natives—has introduced these to and educated many who want to create their own backyard habitats. Her list also carries a number of uncommon (and well-loved) perennials, shrubs, and trees, too. Plants you are likely to find when you visit the nursery include verbascum, elsholtzia, ceanothus, Pacific Coast iris, cistus, variegated elderberry, clethra, hummingbird mint, Himalayan honeysuckle, Echinacea, *Penstemon pinifolius,* buddleia, corydalis, flowering white currant, Chinese foxglove, and weigela.

CHRISTIANSON'S NURSERY & GREENHOUSE

15806 Best Road, Mt. Vernon, WA 98273 | **Phone:** (360) 466-3821 or (800) 585-8200 | **Fax:** (360) 466-2940 | **Email:** chrisnsy@fidalgo.net | **Web:** www.christiansonsnursery.com | **Directions:** Southbound on I-5, exit at Hwy 20; go 5 miles to Best Road, turn left after 2 miles (be careful as you cross this busy highway!). Northbound on I-5, take exit 221, go west on Fir Island-Chilberg Road 5 miles, then north on Best Road 3.5 miles. | **Open:** Daily | **Rose list:** Free; wholesale and retail.

Serving the Northwest for over 50 years, Christianson's offers an **enticing selection of common and uncommon plants,** over 800 varieties of **old and new roses,** rare and unusual perennials, plus vines, shrubs, and trees. This charming nursery's frequent presence at the Northwest Flower and Garden Show can inspire anyone to bring the English cottage garden style to their landscape. The nursery frequently designs award-winning display gardens incorporating all sorts of salvaged farm and barn materials that serve as the authentic backdrop to complex designs.

John and Toni Christianson have invested enormous enthusiasm and energy to craft their destination nursery, located in the pastoral countryside of Skagit Valley. Among the historic glass greenhouses you'll find a rustic Garden Room, displaying garden tools, garden ornaments, apparel for gardeners, and on cool days a cozy fire. Firmly ensconced on the site you'll also find the old Lee Schoolhouse (circa 1888) relocated from across the valley to a loving home, where it houses classes and events and anchors the ambitious new perennial and rose garden. In the nursery you will find a continued commitment to roses (750 varieties, with over 90 varieties of English roses) along with more space for **perennials** and **unusual bedding plants** and always a terrific array of herbs (in a greatly expanded display area), ground covers, ornamentals, vines, and an extensive selection of fruit and flowering **trees and shrubs.** A tractor garage has been given new life as Primrose, Christianson's gift shop, which carries many one-of-a-kind items, along with English and French garden antiques. Count on a super selection of books, bulbs, seeds, and special gifts. The atmosphere throughout is cheery, with resident rabbits and exotic birds chattering in one of the refurbished greenhouses, not to mention the discerning llamas grazing nearby.

CHRISTIANSON'S STANWOOD NURSERY (FORMERLY STANWOOD NURSERY)

9816 271st Street NW, Stanwood, WA 98292 | **Phone:** (360) 652-7226 | **Web:** www.christiansonsnursery.com | **Directions:** From I-5 take the Stanwood/Camano Island exit and proceed west to Stanwood.

The Christiansons have taken on this respected established **full-service nursery** and have made it over in their inimitable style. It's a popular destination for neighboring gardeners and anyone on their way to Camano Island. Here you can find a fine (though smaller) selection of trees and shrubs, perennials, annuals, ornamental grasses, ground covers, and vines. The shop provides a large array of garden center fare—amendments, pest and disease controls, tools, and more. The gift shop carries a wide variety of the same interesting discoveries that you'd find in the Mt. Vernon store. Check out the expanded and informative website for classes and special events. Or call to add your name to the mailing list for the well-written newsletter, *Garden Gazette* (much of which may also be read online).

CINDY'S PLANT STAND

1199 Monte-Elma Road, Elma, WA 98541 | **Phone:** *(360)* 482-3258 | **Email:** clknight@techline.com | **Directions:** From Elma's downtown, 1.5 miles west. Take Hwy 12 exit at Schoweiller Road, go north 2 blocks, then right on Monte-Elma Road. | **Open:** Seasonal

Cindy Knight, "The Tomato Lady," grows as many as 75 varieties of **tomato plants** for sale, raising something close to 5,000 in a season for her vegetable, flower, and plant stand near Olympia that sells bedding plants, dahlia tubers, and some heather too.

Faithful tomato-plant patrons come annually from a great distance, relying on this "Tomatologist's" knowledge, quality, and unmatched selection, including many heirlooms. Come also, in summer, for the tomato test garden and in late summer/fall for the half-acre dahlia garden with approximately 300 varieties. Cindy reports that she has added an emphasis on **berries and succulents.** Farmer's Market fans will love her in-season offerings of fresh tomatoes, **fresh produce grown on the premises, and cut dahlias.** Holiday wreath-making classes and custom wreaths keep the nursery active after the first frost. Greenhouses and growing areas are easily accessible and Cindy offers tours on request (information, in the form of "Cindy's Tips," is gladly shared at any time).

CITY PEOPLE'S GARDEN STORE

2939 E Madison Street, Seattle, WA 98112 | **Phone:** *(206)* 324-0737 | **Fax:** (206) 328-6114 | **Web:** www.citypeoplesmercantile.com | **Directions:** From I-5 north or south, take exit 168 onto Hwy 520. Take the Montlake exit, and at the traffic signal continue straight, on Washington Park Boulevard. Wend your way through the Washington Park Arboretum. At the traffic signal at E Madison Street, turn right and go west 2 blocks. | **Open:** Daily

Anyone within shouting distance of the Washington Park Arboretum will soon hear about City People's, a charming garden center **ideal for urban gardeners.** One of the four owners is Steve Magley, the store manager and plantsman extraordinaire.

This is a fabulous destination to which a serious horticultural shopping expedition must be dedicated! While not large, this nursery packs in an impressive selection of fine plants, from unusual herbs to ornamental grasses,

from disease-resistant trees and shrubs suitable to urban settings to old rose varieties, plus vines, bulbs, and ground covers—and don't forget the water plants! There's also a full line of organic products and an excellent selection of bulk materials from winter cover-crop seeds to bone meal.

Seeds carried are Territorial, Seeds of Change, Thompson & Morgan, Botanical Interest, Renee's Garden, Shepherd's, and Ed Hume. Workshops and classes are offered regularly; ask for a schedule. Stop in year-round, and we bet you won't leave empty-handed! Vegetable starts (throughout the season) are a specialty, as is a large and varied selection of containers. Here is the spot to which you can escape on a cold winter's day (horticultural therapy) or on a sunny Saturday morning when you're itchin' to get dirt under your nails.

Note: This creative company also operates a sister store, located at 5440 Sand Point Way NE, Seattle, WA 98105; (206) 524-1200. The Sand Point store offers gardening supplies, tools, seeds, and a top-notch selection of herbs and vegetable starts through the entire growing season as well as a small but dependably well-chosen selection of perennials and annuals for urban gardens. Garden-inspired gifts and home décor make these stores a top choice for those in search of great design. These are terrific poking around kinds of stores, the kind of old-fashioned atmosphere you imagine from a bygone era.

CLINTON, INC.

12260 1st Avenue South, Seattle, WA 98168 | **Phone:** *(206)* 242-8848 | **Fax:** (206) 444-9428 | **Email:** clintonbamboo@sprynet.com | **Directions:** Located just north of Burien. Take Hwy 509 to the S 128th Street exit. Go west to 1st Avenue S and turn right. Look for their sign just past 124th Street. | **Open:** Seasonal and by appointment. (If time allows, Clinton Bamboo Growers will bring a select offering of its plants to the Northwest Horticultural Society plant sale in September. Otherwise, the nursery has shifted much of its attention to the retail nursery.) | **Plant list:** Free with SASE

A decade ago, a trio of friends turned a fascination for bamboo into a small urban nursery. Erika Harris, Vance Allen, and Lee Gartner had searched far and wide and were not able to find any bamboo species other than Black and Golden. They decided to grow and propagate many different **bamboos, as well as Northwest-hardy ornamental grasses.** In addition, they carry several tropical species of bamboo for interior uses.

The **display garden** (best time to view is late spring through summer) presently includes 30 of the 85 species of bamboo and their cultivars in the Clinton collection, ornamental grasses, herbs, and phormiums (easy access; minimal stairs). Perennials, water plants, and root barrier are also offered, and knowledgeable advice is readily at hand.

Accessibility note: You can avoid the four steps by taking a pathway around the side.

CLOUD MOUNTAIN FARM

6906 Goodwin Road, Everson, WA 98247 | **Phone:** (360) 966-5859 | **Fax:** (360) 966-0921 | **Email:** cloud-mt@pacificrim.net | **Web:** www.cloudmountainfarm.com | **Directions:** From the Mount. Baker Hwy, turn north at Nugent Corner on Hwy 9, right on Siper to Hopewell, then right to Goodwin Road, then left about 1 mile. From Everson, take the main street (South Pass Road) east to Goodwin Road; turn right, then watch for their sign. | **Open:** Weekends, seasonal; or by appointment. First weekend in October, **Fall Fruit Festival** (extravaganza!) | **Catalog:** $1 (map, informative); shipping season February–May.

Cloud Mountain Farm built its solid, region-wide reputation by offering a high-**quality fruit, nut,** and **ornamental tree and plant** selection—including **native plants,** shrubs, bamboo, vines, canes, ground covers and perennials. The inventory has expanded to include more dwarf conifers, unusual (hardy) fruits, rhododendrons, and Japanese maples. Cultivars have been very carefully selected (and most of them test-grown by the nursery itself before sale) to ensure local hardiness and adaptability. They also have **books, tools,** and **supplies** appropriate to the subject, including trellis supplies (non-stretch wire, posts, anchors, and wire tighteners, bamboo for Belgian fences).

This is also a working farm noted for its innovative approach to growing "new" apple varieties (less than 100 years old) in the espalier style of the Dutch apple farmers. Tom and Cheryl Thornton have been establishing their farm/nursery in this lovely rural setting on the western edge of the Cascade Mountain range in northwestern Washington. Enjoy a visit to more than 20 acres of nursery stock and apple orchards on the lower slopes of Sumas Mountain. Stroll through the display gardens designed to showcase mature specimens of nursery plants. If you're in the nearby vicinity, consult with Cloud Mountain's landscape design and installation service. Free workshops are listed in the catalog.

COASTAL GARDEN CENTER (FORMERLY WILD BIRD GARDEN AND NURSERY)

4986 State Route 105, Grayland, WA 98547 | **Phone:** (360) 268-0804 | **Fax:** Same | **Email:** wildbird@techline.com | **Directions:** 20 miles southwest from Aberdeen, on SR 105, milepost 29; 1 mile south of Westport-Grayland intersection. | **Open:** Daily, April–October

Cynthia Becker specializes in **seasonal ornamentals, coastal garden plants,** easy-to-grow plants, and plants with year-round color and interest. Despite the name change, she continues an emphasis on flora and fauna, with Grays Harbor's best selection of wild-bird feeders. Find Territorial Seeds, garden art, and other gifts here; garden design and landscape services round out the offerings.

COENOSIUM GARDENS

4412 354th Street E, Eatonville, WA 98328 | **Phone:** (360) 832-8655 | **Fax:** Same | **Email:** bobfincham@mashell.com | **Web:** www.coenosium.com | **Directions:** Given at time appointment is made (but the good news is that Coenosium is only 35 miles from Mt. Rainier). | **Open:** By appointment, weekends preferred |

Catalog: $3, refundable ($5, international customers); shipping is between mid-March to mid-June, and late September to Thanksgiving.

Robert and Dianne Fincham, who founded and run this primarily mail-order nursery "of rare plants for the discriminating person," have been propagating and selling their beloved plants for 20 years. (A hobby that "got out of control," they admit.) It's somehow fitting to learn that Coenosium is an old Greek word for "plant community."

The nursery began its life in Pennsylvania in 1979 and set down roots in Washington in 1996. For customers not familiar with the wide range of conifers offered, two videotapes are available (each is two hours long) to help you visualize the plants. A third video offers *Grafting Methods for Propagating Ornamentals.* Bob is considered an authority on **dwarf conifers,** which makes this THE place to begin if you are willing to learn. Reading the informative catalog and visiting the website is a great education—can you believe there are over 1,500 conifer cultivars at this nursery alone? The couple propagates all plant material from their own stock plants and supplies many other specialty nurseries.

The Finchams are continually adding new plants to a 2½-acre **display garden** that features some large and rare specimens (moderately accessible). In addition, should you decide to make a visit, the nursery has a nice assortment of conifers and deciduous items in 3-gallon and larger sizes.

COLDSPRINGS GARDEN NURSERY

18013 W Snoqualmie Valley Road NE, Duvall, WA 98019 | **Phone:** (425) 788-5262 | **Fax:** (425) 844-2492 | **Email:** wiinc@prodigy.net or csprings98029@yahoo.com | **Directions:** Located 1 mile north of the intersection at Woodinville-Duvall Road and West Snoqualmie Valley Road (or 1 mile west and north of Duvall). Look for sign at road, turn uphill, and park across from the garden shed. | **Open:** Seasonal

Ann and Mary Kenady began by selling extras from their large garden, and Coldsprings Garden Nursery has grown steadily for nearly eight years. Thanks to a talented builder in the family, this place is outfitted with great garden buildings and greenhouses. Enjoy the informal garden displays beginning with Coldsprings' April opening. The slope overlooking Snoqualmie Valley offers great views, several ponds, a waterfall, rock garden, perennial beds, trees, and trails, all covering several acres. It's not easy for those with mobility impairment, although some areas can be negotiated.

About half the stock is propagated in the greenhouses here, with an emphasis on **unusual, new perennials** hardy in zone 7, plus special tender perennials. Vines, shrubs, and small trees, as well as ornamental grasses and sedges are available. Perennials here include: allium, campanula, crocosmia, petasites, darmera, eryngium, euphorbia, many geraniums, helleborus, nepeta, persicaria, polemonium, pulmonaria, saxifraga, and more. Look for sales at the beginning (April) and end (September) of season.

Call to add your name to the mailing list. You'll score points with the Kenady family if you arrive with your own boxes or flats for any purchases. Shop here early in the season to find the best selection, as some plants are available in limited quantities.

COLLECTOR'S NURSERY

16804 NE 102nd Avenue, Battle Ground, WA 98604 | **Phone:** (360) 574-3832 | **Fax:** (360) 571-8540 | **Email:** dianar@collectors nursery.com | **Web:** www.collectorsnursery.com | **Directions:** From I-5 take the 179th Street exit east to 102nd Avenue, and turn right; nursery is on the right. | **Open:** Open House weekends (once a month). Check catalog or web for dates. Nursery is also open by appointment. | **Catalog:** $2

Bill Janssen and Diana Reeck blend art, science, and pure fun as they bring their fascination with the plant world to the gardening public. They are particularly fascinated with "**the rare, the bizarre, the beautiful.**" We are the beneficiaries of that passion that's on the lookout for elusive botanical treasures. Bill and Diana propagate 95 percent of their plants. An avid plant hunter, Diana has taken three collection expeditions to wild places like China's Yunnan Province. She and Bill tap into a network of like-minded enthusiasts for seeds and cuttings of elusive and uncommon plants they study to bring to customers and fellow gardeners. Last year alone, there were 150 new plant offerings in the catalog. If **hostas** are your fondness, ask Bill about his hybridizing program. Just a few examples of what you will find in the catalog: a very large selection of **choice** and **rare conifers,** species clematis, daphnes, Asian plants, tricyrtis, variegated plants, hellebores, and epimediums, which they are now hybridizing. Over 3,000 cultivars have settled nicely into the 2-acre display garden, including conifers, perennials, and shade plants. They also offer custom propagation services.

COLVOS CREEK NURSERY

Intersection of Point Robinson Road and SW 240th, Vashon Island, WA 98070 | **Phone:** (206) 749-9508 | **Fax:** (206) 463-3917 | **Email:** colvoscreek@juno.com. | **Mailing address:** PO Box 1512, Vashon Island, WA 98070 | **Directions:** From any ferry, follow Vashon Hwy to SW 204th. Turn left on 204th and continue east then south to Maury Island; past the KIRO towers, go left at the "Y" onto Pt Robinson Road and continue 1 mile up the hill to the nursery | **Open:** Fridays and Saturdays, 10 a.m.–4 p.m. and by appointment | **Catalog:** $3 (listing more than 1,400 plants); wholesale and retail.

Registered Landscape Architect Michael Lee has developed a small nursery specializing in **Northwest and West Coast natives, drought-tolerant** plants, and **genera popular among plant collectors,** including acers, ilex, sorbus, quercus, eucalyptus, betula, cistus, and arctostaphylos. This nursery exists to offer hard-to-find plants of all kinds. Mike emphasizes Northwest and West Coast natives and drought-hardy trees, shrubs, and perennials for landscapes here in the dry-summer parts of zones 7–9.

A **display garden** located "cross-island" features much of his stock, so you can view mature specimens as they're tested for hardiness. Unusual plants in the Colvos Creek lineup include *Acacia pravissima,* an odd large shrub, and *Agapanthus* Headbourne Hybrids, the hardiest strain of these classy perennials.

Get on the mailing list for notification of the September sale, which features plants from Colvos and several other Vashon nurseries.

CONNELL'S DAHLIAS

10616 Waller Road E, Tacoma, WA 98446 | **Phone:** (800) 673-5139 or (253) 531-0292 | **Fax:** (253) 536-7725 | **Email:** connells@ oz.com | **Web:** www.connells-dahlias.com | **Directions:** From I-5 take the Hwy 512 exit 127 and proceed east on Hwy 512. From Hwy 512 take the Portland Avenue exit north; turn right onto 104th Street, then right on Waller Road E. | **Open:** Daily; call ahead in June and July for appointment. | **Catalog:** $2 (color, comes out in January); shipping season is in April.

This 30-year family operation has passed to the Connell sons, who continue to grow dahlia tubers—and exciting new hybrids—for area gardeners. Connell's is known for its large selection of nearly 400 top dahlias and 30 gladiolus. Didn't plan ahead last spring? Select from Connell's inventory of dahlia plants (available only at the office on Waller Road). Attend the Open House August 23–September 2, 2002, at which time you are invited to tour the gardens for pleasure or determine a dahlia order. Demonstrations on digging, dividing, and storing dahlias will be given. Display gardens are best for viewing mid-August to early October, Monday–Saturday, 9 a.m.–5 p.m.

CORA'S NURSERY & GREENHOUSE

902 24th Street, Anacortes, WA 98221-2810 | **Phone:** (360) 293-5478 | **Directions:** On Commercial Avenue, the main street coming into Anacortes from Hwy 20, watch for the Les Schwab Tire Co. and turn right; go 1 block; the nursery is at 24th and Q Avenue; park on Q Avenue. | **Open:** Daily at her home/nursery (set up for self-service when Cora is not there)

For many years Cora Zoberst has grown plants from seed for her small urban garden (small but packed to the gills with interesting things she likes and grows well). Her backyard nursery hosts an interesting mix of plants, especially **herbaceous perennials.**

Gardeners from the San Juan Islands who know about this quiet little hidden spot pop in to see what's available, especially as Cora "tries to have at least one of everything I offer for sale planted somewhere in my own garden." Talk about dedication!

Check out her amazing selection of clematis (16 varieties this year). An annual Green Thumb Sale the first Saturday of May will get you started for the season. From December 1, she offers lovely evergreen wreaths and crosses.

COTTAGE CREEK GARDEN NURSERY

13300 Avondale Road NE, Woodinville, WA 98072 | **Phone:** (425) 883-8252 | **Fax:** (425) 702-9243 | **Directions:** From north or south, take I-5 or I-405 to SR 520 east. At the end of SR 520 in Redmond, continue east onto Avondale Road NE. Follow Avondale

Road NE to the north for 4.5 miles to approximately 133rd (and the nursery). | **Open:** Daily | **Rose list:** Free; nursery offers wholesale and retail

Around press time, Cottage Creek Garden Center changed hands: former owner Robert Nelson sold the established nursery to Robert Pope. You can still learn much about antique and shrub roses by visiting the display gardens here, and the nursery's spring listing of **500-plus rose varieties** is still a great way to learn about the best roses for Northwest growing conditions.

Cottage Creek also carries an extensive selection of perennials, and an exuberant lineup of **hostas, hardy geraniums, Himalayan blue poppies,** and other good things.

Vine lovers are given the opportunity to watch characteristics of plant growth and habit on the 48-foot arbor and 128 feet of continuous trellis. Look for Ed Hume seeds in the shop that also has lots of hand tools, fertilizers, soil amendments, trellises, and such. Robert Pope and manager Edward Chavez are expanding the plant selection, the garden gifts department and now offer landscape and maintenance services.

COUNTRY GARDENS

36735 SE David Powell Road, Fall City, WA 98024-9201 | **Phone:** (425) 222-5616 | **Fax:** (425) 222-4644 | **Email:** daduck@nwlink.com | **Web:** www.nwlink.com/~dafox/ | **Directions:** Take US 90 from Seattle east to exit 22. Follow the Preston-Fall City Road 4.9 miles north to David Powell Road. Turn right (east) and continue 2.6 miles to the end of the road (intersection of David Powell Road and SE 56th Street). Continue through the electronic gate and on up hill; use the first driveway on the right. | **Open:** By appointment only (generally available daily, especially Friday–Sunday); shipping season year-round. | **Catalog:** Free and on the Web

This small, Howe Family–run nursery offers in excess of **60 hydrangea species** and cultivars, 100-percent propagated on the premises. They are actively introducing new and uncommon hydrangeas that hail from Europe and South America. Needless to say, these offerings are not easily found at other nurseries. In the wings, for instance, they have an additional 140 species and cultivars they are propagating. They welcome group tours and make slide presentations to garden clubs and other interested organizations. The website is extremely informative for anyone fascinated with this lovely garden plant.

THE COUNTRY STORE AND GARDENS

20211 Vashon Hwy SW, Vashon Island, WA 98070 | **Phone:** (206) 463-3655 | **Email:** tcsag@centurytel.com | **Web:** www.vashoncountrystore.com | **Directions:** On the main road that runs from one end of the Island to the other, 7.5 miles from any ferry. | **Open:** Daily

If you live on the Island, you know. If you don't, why not plan a great day of exploration discovering this old-fashioned style **country garden center** on 10 acres of fields and flowers. Owner since 1970, Vy Biel not only propagates 90 percent of her selection of (largely field-grown) unusual perennials, herbs, vines, trees, and shrubs, but packages her own seed selections of perennials that are difficult to find elsewhere. Commercial seeds include Territorial, Thompson & Morgan, Botanical Interests, and Ferry-Morse. The gardens and nursery feature a wide array of **butterfly-friendly and deer-resistant plants** (how's that for two ends of nature's spectrum?), plus decorative pots and nifty tools.

You'll be enchanted by the 1900-style buildings and wide selection of must-haves typically and not-so-typically found in a country store, such as antiques, rain gear, rubber gardening footwear, and unusual regional foods. Vy has just taken over a new website at www.good jam.com, where you can order Vashon's own yummy fruit jams and locally made gourmet foods. She continues to develop the display beds, showing visitors great options for dry sun, wet shade, and dry shade conditions. (See Chapter 8, "Emporiums: Gardening Shops.")

COURTYARD NURSERY

6400 Capitol Boulevard SE, Tumwater, WA 98501 | **Phone:** (360) 943-4360 | **Fax:** Same | **Directions:** From I-5, traveling south, take the Airdustrial exit in Tumwater and drive east on Airdustrial to the traffic signal at Capitol Boulevard. Turn left (north) on Capitol and go about 4 blocks. The nursery is on the right. | **Open:** Tuesday–Sunday or by appointment; wholesale and retail.

This busy Tumwater nursery features **trees** (Japanese maples, alpine firs, magnolias, and holly); **shrubs** (berberis, hydrangea, rhododendron), and **perennials** (sedums, succulents, ferns, and grasses). The current owners, Bob and Melanie Lee, have operated Courtyard Nursery for five years, building on the base of a previous nursery operation dating back 20 years. This enables the family to showcase an established display garden illustrating mature plants. The display garden also shares the talent of sister business Olympic Landscaping, **specializing in large rock work.**

Courtyard carries garden art, wooden benches, and metal sculpture, but plants are indeed the emphasis here, with the inventory changing frequently.

CRICKLEWOOD NURSERY

11907 Nevers Road, Snohomish, WA 98290 | **Phone:** (360) 568-2829 | **Email:** cricklewod@aol.com (not a typo—only one "o") | **Directions:** From the north, take Hwy 2 (southbound, to Snohomish), turn right at 2nd and Lincoln Street (Old Snohomish-Monroe Road), go 2 miles; turn right on Treosti Road, go 0.1 mile, turn left on Shorts School Road and go 1.5 miles, then turn left on Nevers Road. From the south on Hwy 522, take the Monroe exit, turn left on the Old Snohomish-Monroe Road, go 4 miles to 127th SE, turn left, go 1 mile to 140th SE, turn right, go 0.2 mile to Nevers Road, and turn left. | **Open:** Friday–Saturday, 10 a.m.–4 p.m., late March to early May, other times, by appointment only. Look for Evie at Snohomish Farmer's Market on Thursday evenings beginning the second Thursday in May; and at the Woodinville Farmer's Market on Saturday, beginning the second Saturday in May; shipping is from March–October.

For 25 years, Cricklewood has been the very small and specialized nursery of Evie Douglas, a one-woman horticultural whiz (with occasional help from her husband).

Evie propagates 100 percent of her stock, including many hardy geraniums, penstemon, hellebores, **own root and old English roses,** and cottage border **perennials.** She loves gold and variegated-foliage plants, and while the stock changes from year to year oddball genera are always to be found here. The best part about shopping at Cricklewood, of course, is talking about plants with the woman who personally grows and propagates them!

Evie's small cottage garden is open to visitors, with the main lawn and borders easily accessible. Peak viewing is in May and June, but there is something of interest year-round.

CULTUS BAY NURSERY

7568 Cultus Bay Road, Clinton, WA 98236 | **Phone:** *(360) 579-2329* | **Fax:** (360) 341-5232 | **Email:** mfisher@whidbey.com | **Directions:** From the mainland, take Whidbey Island/Mukilteo exit off I-5. Take Washington State ferry to Mukilteo/Clinton and head north on Hwy 525 for 2.7 miles. At the Red Apple Shopping Center turn left onto Cultus Bay Road, go 4 miles south. The nursery is at the intersection of Cultus Bay Road and Bailey Road. You will see a sign for the nursery on your right, where you will enter a long driveway. **Open:** Weekends, with extended seasonal hours and by appointment. Novmber–December opens for a couple of *really special* weekend events featuring the **best winter plants** and holiday goodies.

This is just the kind of small specialty nursery experience that makes you want to plan a weekend on Whidbey. Off the beaten track, but definitely worth the drive, Cultus Bay began in 1986 with the desire to provide inspiration and practical education to gardeners. Mary and her staff only sell what they have personally grown in their own gardens. Picturesque, charming, and inviting, this nursery has been featured in *Sunset, Country Homes/Country Gardens, NW Best Places, The Seattle Times,* and Pamela Harper's book *Color Echoes* (1994).

When you first arrive, you'll find a long, narrow, tree-lined drive that leads to open fields, where a lovely **Victorian-style farmhouse** sits—the home of Mary Fisher, her gardens, and her nursery. The display beds have expanded and changed over the years: the front herbaceous border has transformed to include trees, shrubs, grasses, and euphorbia. Another hellebore growing bed was added last year to provide field-grown plants. Tom Fisher just added a **small pond** ("We'll see where that takes us," says Mary). Just added: **one-of-a-kind garden accessories from local artists,** birdbaths, feeders, trellis work, hand-painted containers, and other delights, plus garden sculpture by Mark Fessler.

Get on the mailing list to attend some of the special new Cultus Bay Nursery events, including an early June "high tea," auction, and garden gala to benefit South Whidbey Schools Foundation.

PS: This place is kid-friendly. Mary has been known to engage in subversive horticultural acts like giving pots of plants to five-year-olds who then get excited about gardening!

DAN'S DAHLIAS

994 S Bank Road, Oakville, WA 98568 | **Phone:** (360) 482-2406 | **Fax:** (360) 482-2407 | **Email:** info@dansdahlias.com | **Web:** www.dansdahlias.com (you can order on-line) | **Directions:** From I-5, coming from the north, take the Hwy 8 exit 104 west to Alma. At the junction with Hwy 12 turn onto Hwy 12 and travel south, and continue through Malone. At Porter, turn west, crossing the RR tracks and the Chehalis River on bridge. At South Bank Road turn left to Dan's. | **Open:** Display garden and production field open August till frost (mid-October), daylight hours. Peak bloom is in September. | **Catalog:** Free; shipping in April for May planting (orders taken year-round).

Dan started growing and selling fresh **dahlias and tubers** at the age of ten, continuing on through his high school years, when he was named the 1990 National Future Farmers of America Floriculture Proficiency winner. In May of 1995, he graduated from WSU with a degree in landscape architecture, and he currently works in that field. Luckily for us, he continues to sell cut flowers and take orders for tubers from the garden and at the Olympia Farmer's Market. His catalog lists over **500 varieties**! If you are web-connected, go to visit his website, where you will see a photo of his 3-acre growing fields—they're spectacular.

DAVE'S TASTE OF THE TROPICS

1618 NE 189th Street, Shoreline, WA 98155 | **Phone:** *(206) 364-4428* | **Fax:** (206) 366-0604 | **Directions:** From I-5, take the 175th Street exit and travel east approximately 1 mile to 15th Avenue NE. Turn left onto 15th and travel north to Perkins Way. Turn on Perkins Way, then right onto 16th and then left onto 189th. Look for the palms out front and listen for the ukulele (just kidding about the uke). | **Open:** By appointment only | **Plant list:** $1; shipping May–August; wholesale and retail

Dave Alvarez specializes in "tropicalismo"—**palms, bananas, tree ferns, passion flowers, and agaves**—and also offers cactus, cannas, and bamboo. A visit to this home/nursery provides you with an opportunity to see Dave's display plantings to tempt your tropical tastebuds.

DAYBREAK GARDENS

25321 NE 72nd Avenue, Battle Ground, WA 98604 | **Phone:** *(360)* 687-5641 | **Open:** By appointment only | **Product list:** Free (with map)

Dave and Donna Burnett concentrate on both **indoor and outdoor bonsai starters** and pre-bonsai plants; they've also styled **trees for small-space gardens.** All the materials and instruction their customers will need for the art of bonsai are on hand. Items available at the nursery in addition to plants (organic fertilizers, safe pesticides, topical books, bonsai tools and supplies—including distinctive hand-crafted ceramic pots, general pruning tools, unique watering systems, and greenhouses) reflect the Burnetts' concern for proven organic growing techniques and top-quality products. They have operating watering systems and working models of Sky Bright molding fiberglass greenhouses for your inspection.

Classes for bonsai, general pruning, and greenhouse growing are offered in season.

DeLanceys' Garden Center

1951 Main Street, Ferndale, WA 98248 | **Phone:** (360) 384-1043 | **Fax:** (360) 384-8105 | **Directions:** From I-5 take exit 262 and travel west into Ferndale. Just past the RR trestle you'll need to prepare for a left hand turn into the nursery parking area. | **Open:** Daily (closed November through mid–February, unless you call for an appointment)

Mike and Anita DeLancey purchased this **neighborhood nursery** in 1988. After enduring three large floods from the nearby Nooksack River, they've operated seasonally. But you can always call for an appointment during the winter and stop by if the ground is dry! The couple grows annuals, **fuchsia baskets, and zonal geraniums** for which they can be justly proud. Locals and regulars from as far away as Seattle know this is a terrific place to pick up the season's bedding plants, most of which are grown right at the nursery. Their shrub and perennial selection offers customers a wider range than they'd find in chain stores, and certainly the atmosphere is very personable at this full-service garden center. In the fall, the nursery has a dazzling array of colorful mums (according to Anita, "our 4-inch-size plants are as big as most grower's 6-inch pots!"). You'll also find tools, seeds (Lilly Miller, Ed Hume, and Thompson & Morgan, from England) and bulbs.

DeWilde's Nurseries Inc.

3410 Northwest Avenue, Bellingham, WA 98225 | **Phone:** (360) 733-8190 | **Fax:** (360) 734-9746 | **Directions:** From I-5, take exit 257, and go south on Northwest Avenue about 0.2 mile. | **Open:** Daily

DeWilde's has been in the nursery business in Whatcom County for 50 years. The nursery is in the capable hands of Larry and Margaret Rudy, the second generation in this family business. They are particularly noted for their locally grown nursery stock, **specializing in large trees** that are available for viewing by appointment (not located at the nursery site). At the nursery they offer a wide variety of trees, shrubs, ground covers, herbs, perennials, and annuals acclimatized for the Pacific Northwest. The shop carries gloves, Ed Hume seeds, tools, and more. This is a good source for bark, turf, topsoil, and amendments (including mushroom compost), delivered or U-pick-up style.

DIG Floral & Garden

19028 Vashon Hwy SW, Vashon Island, WA 98070 | **Phone:** (206) 463-5096 | **Fax:** (206) 463-4048 | **Mailing address:** 23731 147th SW, Vashon Island, WA 98070 | **Directions:** From the West Fauntleroy ferry, stay on the arterial, Vashon Hwy, for 5.7 miles; turn left at the first driveway (clearly marked with signs); from the Pt. Defiance ferry, turn left onto Vashon Hwy for 7.9 miles. After you pass Mom's Deli (BP Gas Station) turn right and watch for signs. | **Open:** Daily (November–December, weekends only, or call for appointment)

A day on Vashon Island isn't complete without a stop to visit DIG and its creative owner Sylvia Matlock. This energetic plant lover sources top-quality Island-grown plants (from the likes of Puget Garden Resources' Pete Ray). Sylvia always has a keen eye out for remarkable growers throughout the region, such as the very innovative Log House Plants, which now supplies DIG's old-fashioned annuals and herbs. Each year Sylvia introduces an expanded selection of **top-notch shrubs,** such as *Ceanothus* 'Maire Simone', *Choisya* 'Sundance', and several varieties of phormiums including 'Yellow Wave' and 'Sundowner'. If you're hunting down sources for the likes of *Angelica gigas, Acanthus aurea, Corydalis* 'China Blue', *Helleborus orientalis* 'Dark Strain', or that alluring and elusive little *Datura* 'La Fleur Lilac', come visit DIG. Most recently, Sylvia has discovered and added stock from Viva Plants: hardy *Fuchsia* 'Chung' and *Phygelius* 'Sensation', among other great offerings.

Along the entry drive is a **display bed** that will grab your attention—it's home to a dazzling selection of plants, imaginatively co-mingling annuals, specialty perennials, and shrubs. Sylvia is brilliant at pulling together **garden art, functional and ornamental, from an astonishing variety of artisans.** You'll also find a big commitment to container gardening, with super pots and Sylvia's glorious plant combinations. The nursery is arranged to encourage strolling, with wide, well-placed aisles and lots to discover. Check DIG's class schedule for some wonderful offerings, including ones on garden lighting, dry-stack stone walls, and paths.

Edgewood Flower Farm

2017 Meridian Avenue E, Edgewood, WA 98371 | **Phone:** (253) 927-0817 | **Fax:** (253) 952-9051 | **Email:** eff@nwrain.com. | **Web:** www.edgewoodflowerfarm.com. | **Directions:** Easy access from I-5 (at Federal Way, 3 miles south of Enchanted Village or 3 miles north of the Puyallup Fair) take exit 142B onto SR 161 and follow the signs for Puyallup. Edgewood's address is on Meridian (which is also Hwy 161). | **Open:** Daily

For more than 25 years, Bill and Donna O'Ravez have built a reputation for the quality selection, inviting atmosphere, and charming garden shop at their destination garden center. This is the place to head on a dreary winter day for uplifting "garden therapy." The gorgeous Victorian moss baskets, **fuchsia baskets,** and selection of "European Balcony Geraniums" in small pots and finished baskets draw loyal locals and convert newcomers to regulars. There is always a tremendous selection of spring and summer annuals and perennials, roses (including David Austins), plus **specimen trees and shrubs,** with the added pleasure of shopping in a well-organized and amply stocked nursery. There are display gardens throughout with an inspirational English Country Garden design influence. This carries over into the shop, a destination in its own right, where you find an appealing selection of gardening books, those very special finds for cheery home decor, personal care products, and so much more. Of course, they carry tools, clothing, and gadgets for avid gardeners, too. Ask to be on the mailing list and take some of Edgewood's great classes—moss-basket design and more! If you need a beverage break, just order a latte from the espresso stand.

EMERY'S GARDEN

2829 164th Street SW, Lynnwood, WA 98037 | **Phone:** (425) 743-4555 | **Fax:** (425) 743-0609 | **Web:** www.emerysgarden.com | **Directions:** From I-5 take the 164th Street exit 183 and travel west 1 mile to 164th Street SW and Alderwood Mall Parkway (about a half-mile north of Alderwood Mall). | **Open:** Daily

In its sixth year, Emery's Garden is the creation of naturalist and plantsman Emery Rhodes. He's created an urban oasis, showcasing superb and hard-to-find nursery stock, and has put together a growing display garden that illustrates plant combinations, water features, specimen trees, and garden artwork.

You'll find that this is one of the largest and most diverse tree and shrub nurseries in the region. The **Japanese maples** here are outstanding. The staff is intent on selecting trees that are most suitable to the maritime Northwest, ensuring a successful garden experience for both new and longtime customers. Emery's huge selection of **perennials** is sure to please the experienced gardener while also ensuring beginners successful gardens year after year. For color there is nothing better than visiting the trio of greenhouses, where you'll find annuals and hanging baskets in every season.

Emery's general manager Marlis Korber and all the staff have a genuine respect for the partnership of the environment and gardening. They strive to offer **organic and earth-friendly fertilizers, compost and amendments,** and teach sensible practices such as drought-tolerant garden design and landscaping with native plants.

In the hands of buyer Amy Tullis, the continually expanding Garden Store features **well-designed and nature-inspired gifts, and accessories for the home and garden** (indoors and out)—everything for the "gardening lifestyle." Emery's has a wide selection of local and imported pottery containers, plus a Fine Gardening department with top-of-the-line tools, gloves, and gardening accessories for those who want their supplies to last.

If you visit with your family, steer the children to the kids' sand pit (located conveniently in the center of the nursery and filled with pint-sized garden tools), or take them to the "secret" aviary, where Emery's own collection of endangered and exotic birds happily thrives. No less beautiful, but a bit more ordinary, the nursery hens, roosters, and baby chicks range freely over the grounds. (Any of you who came to Duane Kelly's talk about the Northwest Flower and Garden Show a few years back will remember how a fussy hen squawked and clucked from the rafters throughout his goodhearted presentation.) That's nature! The barn, in fact, can hold up to 100

students at Emery's University, the usually free gardening classes taught year-round. To stay on top of all the activity at Emery's, be sure to add your name to the "Weedy Reader" mailing list or visit the nursery's website.

ENCHANTED LILY GARDEN

12827 164th Avenue NE, Redmond, WA 98052 | **Phone:** (425) 883-7318 | **Fax:** Same | **Email:** sunlily@msn.com | **Directions:** From I-405 take Totem Lake exit (NE 124th Street); go east about 3 miles, crossing the Redmond-Woodinville Road, to 164th Avenue NE; go north to 12827 164th, and turn left down the lane through the woods. | **Open:** Wednesday to Sunday or by appointment; call first for hours. | **Plant list:** SASE required; available in spring

Founder and lily fanatic Ann Hawes and chief helper/spouse Alex Toft founded the Enchanted Lily Garden in the early 1990s as an effort to "reintroduce" lilies to area gardens. "For a long time, the general view among 'old time' gardeners was that lilies were difficult to grow," Ann explains. "We are out to prove them wrong."

This nursery takes pride in offering large, quality bulbs and makes every effort to create success for the beginning lily grower. You can find Ann and Alex's favorite blooms both potted up and sold as cut flowers (June to September). They're both happy to share cultural and historical information on **Oriental lilies (and also offer Asiatics, trumpets, species, and new hybrids).** In fact, daylilies, arisaema, and species lilies are propagated on site. Other specialties include hostas, selected Asian perennials, and hellebores.

Alex and Ann sell copper slug rings (an effective and organic system of protecting tender emerging shoots), bulb-protecting perforated pots, books, and ornamental slug-bait houses.

Visit the **display garden** (wood-chip pathways, but in early spring boots are recommended) and time your visit to coincide with the colorful Asiatics' bloom in May or the heavenly sweet-scented trumpets in July, followed by the elegant Orientals (if you're sensitive to heavy fragrances, avoid July and August). Call to arrange a garden tour or lecture for your group. Make note of the Spring Lily Sale, usually during the last two weeks of March. Ann is an avowed "lilyholic" and she hopes her enthusiasm is infectious. It is!

FAIRIE PERENNIAL AND HERB GARDENS NURSERY

6236 Elm Street SE, Tumwater, WA 98501 | **Phone:** (360) 754-9249 | **Fax:** (360) 943-7699 | **Email:** DaveHerbs@aol.com | **Web:** www.fairiegardens.net | **Directions:** From I-5 take the Trosper Road exit 102, going east. Turn right on Capitol Way to X Street, then turn left to Elm Street. | **Open:** Seasonal, or by appointment. At the Olympia Farmer's Market from April 1. | **Plant list:** Free with SASE, and on website

David Baird and Steve Taylor have worked since 1985 transforming their modest residential half-acre site into a thriving nursery with many lush display areas. This magical place is a tribute to the two mens' love of gardening and plants. They offer a list of **1,000 herbs, ornamental grasses, shrubs, and perennials,** and invite visitors to see them growing and labeled in a series of inviting display gardens. There are many plants, and forms of more familiar ones not readily found elsewhere—for instance, the five varieties of germander: caucasian, creeping, curly wood, variegated, and wall. Plus, we love that outrageous herbaceous perennial form of angelica, *A. gigas sinensis*. There is a fat selection of hardy geraniums, lots of sages (Garden, Berggarten, Clary, Golden, Holt's Mammoth, Jerusalem, Pineapple, Purple, Russian, Tricolor, Turkish, and Uliginosa), and a current flame, *Eupatorium* (var. 'Little Red'). The **mature display gardens** are packed with ideas for your Culinary Garden, Water Garden, Fragrance Garden, or Medieval Paradise Garden. The new Dry Garden, planted in 1999, is a step beyond the Celtic Rock Garden. Taking a walk down the meandering path of the Blue-Yellow Garden would reveal nepeta (catmint), perovskia (Russian sage), santolina, hops, mallow, *Galium verum* (lady's bedstraw), oenothera (evening primrose), lavendula, and Cecile Brunner roses happily communing. Visit the small garden shop—a source for useful herbal products, ointments, sleep pillows, bath/scrub bags, and unusual sundials and garden ornaments. Workshops from April through August.

FAIRLIGHT GARDENS

30904 164th Avenue SE, Auburn, WA 98092 | **Phone:** (888) 526-8612 or (253) 631-8932 | **Fax:** (253) 630-5630 | **Email:** bamboo1@foxinternet.net | **Web:** www.fairlightgardens.com | **Directions:** Just off the Kent-Black Diamond Road on the east hill of Kent. From Kent, go east on Smith Street up the hill to Kent-Kangley Road; go to the first stoplight past Lake Meridian (152nd SE). Turn right and go 1 mile (the road goes under Hwy 18 and turns into Kent-Black Diamond Road). Go for another mile and turn right on 165th Avenue SE, and follow signs to nursery. From Auburn, take Hwy 18 east to the Auburn-Black Diamond Road exit. Turn right and make sure you stay on the main road, going over the river and past the fish hatchery, for 3 miles. Turn left on 168th Way SE, and go to Kent-Black Diamond Road; turn left to 165th and follow signs to the nursery. | **Open:** Seasonal or by appointment | **Plant and class list:** Free with SASE

Operating for more than a decade, this small South King County nursery carries an extensive selection of culinary, medicinal, and fragrance **herbs** (over 350 types offered) and **bamboo** (over 50 types offered). Enjoy their woodsy setting on 12 acres of towering fir trees that surround the Japanese koi pond and display gardens. The gift shop is full of herb- and fragrance-inspired gifts, bulk herbs, herb-related magazines and books, tools and pots, a great selection of bamboo poles, and much more. During the holiday season Judy and Don Jensen share their evergreen wreath–making machine (this is a terrific opportunity for a small fee; call for details and appointment). Judy is a master herbalist and teaches classes about herbs and their various uses, and Don, the bamboo master, teaches classes to help gardeners in the fine art of using bamboo in the landscape. This pair also gives lectures for garden clubs and libraries.

FANCY FRONDS

40830 172nd Street SE, Gold Bar, WA 98251 | **Phone:** (360) 793-1472 | **Fax:** (360) 793-4243 | **Email:** Judith@fancyfronds.com | **Web:** www.francyfronds.com| **Mailing address:** PO Box 1090, Gold Bar, WA 98251-1090 | **Directions:** From I-5 go east on SR 2 heading toward Stevens Pass (15 miles to Gold Bar). From I-405 take 522 east to Monroe/SR 2 and then east to Gold Bar. At the east end of the town of Gold Bar, just past the Mountain View Diner on the right, watch for electronic Pass Condition sign. Just 20 feet beyond turn right onto Dorman Road, come across RR tracks, and follow Dorman when it turns abruptly to the left. Take the second private road on the right (between two fenced fields), marked 408th Avenue SE, to 172nd Street SE. Turn right on 408th, which becomes 172nd when it curves to the left. Follow along to the plain cedar fence (greenhouse just inside). Call button at the gate if it is closed. Parking outside on the grass by fence. Welcome to the Fronderosa! | **Open:** By appointment only; Open House second weekend in August featuring specialty nurseries and artists. | **Plant list:** $0.57 with a SASE to PO Box above; a very handy addition to your horticultural library.

Judith Jones, with the kids and cats, has settled into this peaceful country setting in Gold Bar, Washington. Judith was long associated with Barfods Nursery (formerly of Bothell; now in Arlington), known for its vast selection of ferns. Here, she continues to offer a **worldwide selection of temperate ferns,** specializing in Victorian cultivars, xeric ferns, and tree ferns. A glance through the introduction to her catalog is dizzying, revealing spore donors scattered to all corners of the earth, from the Czech Republic and Germany, Chile and other South American countries to Japan and England, not to mention Tasmania and San Francisco. All so Judith can "make fresh ferns daily," which is what you'll find her doing if you drop by most days. She has **new introductions every year** and is available to provide a slide lecture on this underappreciated subject. Her installations (working with other nurseries and artists) have won several gold medals at the Northwest Flower and Garden Show. You will also, as ever, find her at such plant sales as the Arboretum, King County Master Gardeners, Northwest Horticultural Society, Hardy Plant Society of Oregon, the Leach and Berry Botanical Garden sales, and more.

Kerry McQuire's fabulous original concrete garden sculptures (**Garden GOYLES**) are on view—and for sale as well.

FAYLEE GREENHOUSES

7388 Sportsman Club Road NE, Bainbridge Island, WA 98110 | **Phone:** (206) 842-4489 | **Email:** vroomhe@yahoo.com | **Directions:** From the Seattle-Bainbridge Island Ferry dock on Bainbridge, drive north (straight) on Hwy 305 to the second traffic light, then go west (left) on High School Road. At the first flashing yellow light, take a left on Sportsman Club Road; continue across Finch Road on the dirt extension of Sportsman Club Road. A hanging basket marks the top of the road. Greenhouses are on the right. From Poulsbo, head south on Hwy 305 to High School Road; then head west and continue same as above. | **Open:** Seasonal, by appointment, and at the Winslow Farmer's Market.

Elizabeth and Herman Vroom moved to Bainbridge from Holland (after meeting in Zambia where they were both teachers), with the dream of starting a nursery specializing in annual flowers for containers, window boxes, borders, and hanging baskets. They learned their floral-basket craft from Dutch master Bert Verhoog. Here, they named their nursery "Faylee," after their two daughters (Tessa Fay and Anika Lee). You can choose from **30 styles of hanging basket designs,** already planted, or commission your own floral mix. Each Faylee design has a theme, like "White Shadow," a lush, all-white basket designed for a bright location in full shade. The white comes from prolific-blooming trailing begonia, impatiens, variegated hedera, spotted lamium, and the delicate asparagus fern. Faylee draws from 200 plants in creating custom baskets. Many of us try to plant containers that evoke that **lush, English moss-basket feel** . . . but Faylee's technique is unparalleled—starting with 29 tiny plants and nurturing them to abundance. Even so, when you'd like to try your own hand at a basket, the nursery offers a full line of supplies—hardware, moss, soil, plants, and various brackets. This is an innovative venture worth supporting. "We care for the environment; we use beneficial insects, recycle plant pots, and grow organic and heirloom vegetables in organic soil," Elizabeth adds.

Call for dates to take the spring hanging-basket workshops, or sign up children (ages 4 and up) for the Mother's Day hanging-basket classes.

FLOWER WORLD, INC.

9322 196th Street SE, Snohomish, WA (near Maltby) | **Phone:** (425) 481-7565 or (360) 668-9575 | **Fax:** (360) 668-5602 | **Mailing address:** 19127 99th Avenue SE, Snohomish WA 98296 | **Directions:** In Maltby, near Snohomish, hidden back down country lanes, but there are many signs to guide you. From SR 522 take the Maltby exit and watch for FW signs, or take 188th SE off Hwy 9 and watch for FW signs. | **Open:** Daily

As you drive down the lane into Flower World you are greeted each year with more display beds scattered through the entry grounds. This **nursery is ENORMOUS** (wear sensible shoes); it's a fascinating place to explore even in nasty weather, as much is under cover, and parts of it feel like being in a conservatory. Don't expect to find the rare or unusual, but do take a good-sized vehicle so you can stock up on everything from perennials and annuals to herbs, trees (ornamental and fruit), shrubs, clematis, roses (14,000 a season are grown here), grapes, berries, an astounding selection of fuchsias, and a gazillion houseplants. You'll also be able to find water-gardening supplies, statuary, bird feeders, pots in all media, pavers, and retaining-wall systems. Then they offer spring and fall bulbs, poinsettias in November and December, and Ed Hume and Burpee seeds. The hot July event is a monthlong sale with all plant material 15 percent off.

FOLIAGE GARDENS

2003 128th Avenue SE, Bellevue, WA 98005 | **Phone:** (425) 747-2998 | **Fax:** Same | **Email:** foliageg@juno.com | **Web:** www.foliagegardens.com | **Open:** By appointment only; one Open House a year for customers. | **Catalog:** $2 (two issues a year); shipping spring and fall.

Sue and Harry Olsen grow hardy native and exotic ferns, including the common and the rare, natives and imports (especially Japanese evergreens). This is the oldest mail-order source for **spore-grown hardy ferns** in the United States, with its start in the late 1960s. That's when Sue became enamored with a planting of *Dryopteris erythrosora* (wood fern family). Unable to find any for sale, she decided to try growing a few from spores. Some 300 erythrosoras sprang to life, creating an addiction. "One fern led to another and the small basement propagating table soon was replaced with sets of shelves," she writes in the small but information-packed catalog. Today, with the nursery, garden, and Olsen home all sharing one-half acre of space, Foliage Gardens is still small, but special. All material is nursery propagated; none is collected.

A one-hour video is available, called *Short Course on Ferns* ($32.50, includes postage/insurance). Sue is available for speaking engagements; and her ferns are often available at area garden shows and plant sales, including the Hardy Fern Foundation sale and the Hardy Plant Society of Oregon sale. The nursery also sells dwarf and semidwarf Japanese maple cultivars. Don't you love this Foliage Gardens sentiment? "May all your ferns be shaded by maples."

FOREST FLOOR RECOVERY NURSERY

PO Box 89, Lummi Island, WA 98262 | **Phone:** (360) 758-2778 | **Email:** Forestflor@aol.com | **Directions:** Call ahead. Lummi Island is a 20-mile drive from Bellingham, and requires that you make a 15-minute ferry ride. The ferry leaves at 10 minutes past the hour from Gooseberry Pt and on the hour from Lummi Island. | **Open:** By appointment and for the Annual Nursery Plant Sale during the Memorial Day Weekend Tour of Studios on the Island. | **Plant list:** Free with SASE, and free via email; shipping season September–May; wholesale and retail.

Wanda Cucinotta has gardened for a quarter century and lived most of her adult life in rural Washington. Her deep appreciation for native species and her concern for the habitat destruction wrought on our forests through most logging practices led to the creation of an innovative and remarkable business. She contracts with the Department of Natural Resources to recover (harvest) and cultivate native and naturalized plants, shrubs, and mosses prior to logging of DNR Timber Sale land. She has a fascinating nursery and woodland "display garden" that will captivate and inspire any of you planning to introduce native species into a cultivated (garden or natural) area. Wanda is very knowledgeable about these **hardy and drought tolerant plants.** She works hard to make sure that they are well-adapted to a cultivated life before they leave the nursery and that she has answered any questions you have about successfully growing these forest refugees. Besides containerized plants, she also offers **Woodland Dish Gardens** (Lost Forest Gardens) and impressive hanging baskets (no, not the petunia and fuchsia baskets found elsewhere—these are softer and woodsier, with mosses, woodland flowering plants, licorice, and other ferns).

FOXGLOVE FARM

4126 Ginnett Road, Anacortes, WA 98221 | **Phone:** (360) 293-8817 | **Email:** Sheryl@cnw.com | **Directions:** From Whidbey Island on Hwy 20, just north of Deception Pass Bridge, turn west onto Rosario Road, then right on Sharpe Road to Ginnett Road. From Anacortes, travel south on Rosario Road, turn left on Sharpe Road to Ginnett Road. Look for signs. | **Open:** Wednesday–Sunday

Sheryl Jones's charming, small nursery 6 miles south of Anacortes specializes in **fragrant and medicinal herbs,** unusual and antique annuals, less-well-known perennials, and woodland and native plants. She propagates some favorites, including 'Perennial Larkspur', 'Black Viola', sweet William 'Sooty', and cerinthe, plus "whatever catches my interest," as she says. The setting is lovely, and plants for sale in the nursery are displayed in beds bordering a beautiful pond, home to many wild ducks in spring and summer. Fresh herbs and cut flowers are offered too, and you are invited to make use of one of the picnic tables or seating areas. This is one of those "surprise" nurseries tucked back down a country lane. Since Sheryl also landscapes in the area and may not be here when you come, she's set up a "drop box" so customers can pay for plant purchases on the honor system.

FREMONT GARDENS

4001 Leary Way NW, Seattle, WA 98107 | **Phone:** (206) 781-8283 | **Fax:** (206) 781-7675 | **Email:** fremonted@aol.com | **Directions:** From I-5 north or south take the Mercer Street exit. At the bottom of the exit ramp, turn right onto Fairview and continue through the light. Turn left onto Valley Street and stay to the right, merging onto Westlake Avenue. Continue on Westlake along the west perimeter of Lake Union all the way to the Fremont Bridge (about 2-3 miles). Cross the bridge and go to the second light at Fremont Avenue and 36th Street. Turn left and continue on 36th, which becomes Leary Way NW; the nursery is at the corner of 40th NW and Leary Way NW. Parking is available on the south side of the building. | **Open:** Daily

Lorene Edwards Forkner and her staff of like-minded plant enthusiasts have created a magical nursery packed into a tiny site that is filled to overflowing with very special, often very hard-to-find plants. Every nook and cranny here is home to a new discovery: choice perennials, garden-worthy cultivars from the owner's favorite growers, annuals, vines, woody plants, and a large selection of heirloom vegetables. "While we concentrate on hardy perennials, we are prone to lapse into tender beauties, as well," Lorene confesses.

This **hard-working** and **knowledgeable plantswoman** has used her horticultural skill to create an urban nursery on the kind of site that shares many challenges her customers face. There is good humor and trusty advice

should you come with problems to solve or queries to explore. Ask for the informative quarterly newsletter, "Horticultural Wisdom from the Center of the Universe," and enrich your gardening life with a creative class or events. Visit the retail store that offers **unique merchandise "for garden living."** You'll find vases, art-glass garden globes, clever jewelry, botanical cards, and quirky ornamentation for the garden. On a more pedestrian level, be assured Fremont Gardens carries a broad range of organic amendments in bulk and package as well as nontoxic pest and disease controls.

PS: This nursery loves seeds and offers a **comprehensive selection of antique and modern sweet pea seeds** each spring, with more seeds from Renee's Garden, Shepherd's, Unwins, Lake Valley, Seeds of Change, Territorial, Fragrant Garden, and a new line called "Fremont Gardens Select Seeds" offering 'Black Ball' bachelor button, 'Coffee & Cream' calendula, 'Bull's Blood' beet, and Ruby Orach. The display garden warms Fremont Gardens' south wall and shows off year-round ideas. Design services bring the same talent that won two gold medals at the Northwest Flower and Garden Show into your backyard.

F.W. BYLES NURSERY

PO Box 7705, Olympia, WA 98507-7705 | **Phone:** (360) 352-4725 | **Fax:** (360) 352-1921 | **Email:** Byles@juno.com | **Web:** www.mapletrees.net | **Open:** By appointment (plants can be seen at The Barn Nursery, details below) | **Plant list:** $2 for mail order

Known for their vast collection of **Japanese and related maples,** F.W. Byles carries more than 400 varieties. The catalog cover says it all: "Small Maples, Big Color." You'll find many rare and/or unusual ones for landscape, patio, and garden use. Most are propagated at the nursery by owners Frank and Gudrun "Judy" Byles. The expansive plant list provides great detail on each tree's habit, form, sun requirements, and growing tips for "best effects," not to mention helpful insight into the Japanese cultivar names. Did you know *Omurayama* means "Village on a Mountain," *Shojo* means "Red Faced Monkey," and *Kinran* means "Woven with Golden Strings"? The maples are arranged on the list by habit and leaf color—such as "Upright, Red Leaf," or "Weeping, Green Leaf." Another category is for "Bark Interest Trees," including species, with divine descriptions like "white striping on deep purple bark" and "develops deep coral to salmon color on bark in winter." Descriptions are brief but pack in a lot of information. F.W. Byles has also recently added the inventory of noted Japanese maple grower Thomas Howard Hughes (and Judy's father), owner and operator of Hughes Nursery in Montesano, who died in 2000.

The larger **retail collection** of Japanese and related maples is found at The Barn Nursery, 9440 Old Highway 99 SE, Olympia, WA 98501, which is open year-round, 10 a.m.–6 p.m. From I-5 take exit 101 and go east to the second traffic signal. Turn right onto Capitol

Boulevard/Hwy 99 SE and go 3 miles. You'll find three 20 by 90-foot greenhouses full of Japanese maples.

FURNEY'S NURSERY INC.

21215 Pacific Hwy S, Des Moines, WA 98198 | Phone: (206) 878-8761 | Fax: (206) 592-8656 | Mailing address: PO Box 13150, Des Moines, WA 98198 | Directions: From I-5 heading south from Tukwila, take exit 151 west to Hwy 99 (Pacific Hwy S), then turn left (south) 1 mile. | Open: Daily; wholesale and retail.

In the nursery business here since 1942, Furney's is a family-owned, full-service **garden center** and a large propagator and grower (they have 175 acres of growing fields in Oregon's Willamette Valley). While Furney's closed its established downtown Bellevue location in the late '90s, it hasn't disappeared from the retail nursery scene. This is a top-notch plant outlet with an extensive tree and shrub selection—container, b & b (ball-and-burlap), and bare root. Here you'll find a broad array of **virtually all types of plants,** and especially bedding plants, annuals, perennials, fruits and berries, along with a complete line of gardening supplies. On the less-common side you will find topiaries, tropicals, and bog plants. If you are decorating your garden and searching for statuary or fountains, or if you are on the hunt for gifts (especially to a gardener), here's a place to start. Furney's also offers garden design consults.

THE GARDENERS

3155 Point White Drive NE, Bainbridge Island, WA 98110 | Phone: (206) 842-3112 | Directions: On Bainbridge Island, from Hwy 305 turn west onto High School Road. At Fletcher Road turn left (south) and follow the road to Lynnwood Center. At Lynnwood Center turn right onto Pt White Road and follow for 1 mile, then turn right up a steep blacktop driveway. At the top of the hill take the dirt road to the right, and pass 3 houses to the last house on the driveway. You've arrived. | Open: Seasonal, and by appointment

The Bowdens operated a landscape maintenance business for 20 years, but about seven years ago Elizabeth just got tired of the ubiquitous annuals that were readily available and began poring over seed catalogs to find the less-common varieties that are best for container gardening, cutting, fragrance, and annual vines. Her specialty, then, is to focus on unusual annuals one is not likely to find offered, except perhaps as seed, so she offers convolvulus, daturas, two varieties of ricinus, cerinthe, three of midsummer-blooming chrysanthemums, and nine varieties of nicotianas. And as for vines, ipomoeas, rhodochiton, eccremocarpus, and *Tropaeolum peregrinum* are just a few examples.

THE GARDENS AT PADDEN CREEK

2014 Old Fairhaven Parkway, Bellingham, WA 98225 | Phone: (360) 671-0484 | Fax: Same | Directions: From I-5 at exit 250, take the Old Fairhaven Parkway and travel west. Look for the nursery on the left. From Chuckanut Drive, turn right (east) at the stoplight at the Old Fairhaven Parkway and go about a mile. | Open: Daily, March–September

Mary Cragin has just entered her eighth year running this charming nursery near Fairhaven. Display beds demonstrate the use of ferns, shade plants, and plants for sunny or wet spots, and a **tribute border to Gertrude Jekyll's color theories** joins the nice little garden shop in offering a broad range of well-selected plants, including structural plants to provide living architecture for your garden. The goldfish-filled pond is a great laboratory for testing winter hardiness and the invasive qualities of water plant varieties. This nursery has made a name for itself offering one-of-a-kind garden ornaments, handsome wrought iron trellises, obelisks, lantern hangers, sturdy statuary and winter-hardy pottery, and offers a small selection of quality, built-to-last tools, the basics and Renee's Seeds, too. You'll also find rocks of great character for the garden (delivery available in Whatcom and Skagit Counties). Their opening in spring is highlighted by a breathtaking selection of hellebores, including Mary's prize black doubles. "We're now growing *Helleborus orientalis* from seed," writes Mary. "The plants in our display beds turned out to be great parents!" Here is a nursery that delights in helping customers with all sorts of design challenges—on-site, on-the-fly, or at the client's home. You're encouraged to send in snapshots documenting how it all turned out.

GARDEN CITY HEIRLOOMS

426 Avenue H, Snohomish, WA 98290 | Phone: (360) 563-0314 | Email: kksgarden@aol.com | Catalog: Yes; shipping season April–May. | Open: Mother's Day weekend or by appointment

Karen and Rick DeYoung run this family-owned farm that grows and sells heirloom vegetable varieties from seed. Karen's interest in **heirloom gardening** began when she was working as a chef's apprentice in France in the early 1980s. This small nursery is committed to organic gardening practices in greenhouse and field, and sells a tasty selection of veggie starts and some organic produce grown on-site, including beans, peas, and carrots. Karen writes, "My interest in growing heirlooms, in addition to preservation of the species, is nostalgia, pure and simple."

If you visit, you'll quickly catch her enthusiasm for such rarities as DiCicco broccoli, introduced in 1890 in Italy; Viroflay Giant spinach—dating back to 1885; and White Portugal onion, a find from the 1780s. And don't forget, when you reintroduce heirloom plants to the garden you're also enjoying varieties that are likely more disease- and pest-resistant, with better flavor and texture. You can also find some wonderful antique vines, perennials, and annuals, with common names that suggest another time: "Love in a Puff" and "Kiss Me Over the Garden Gate" are two of many to enjoy in your own garden. Order the catalog—it's a mini history lesson on gardening practices over the ages.

THE GARDEN OF EDEN NURSERY

1903 Shaw Road East, Puyallup, WA 98372 | Phone: (253) 845-7027 | Email: Greenthumbbiz@aol.com | Web: www.gardenofedennursery.com | Directions: From I-5 north or south, take Hwy 512 east to the Pioneer Street exit. Head east approximately two miles to Shaw Road. Turn right and you'll see the nursery on the left. | **Open:** Daily (closed Monday)

In May 2001, John Richardson and Bruce Tilley bought The Garden of Eden from its creators Pete and Linda Ziemke Garden of Eden. Founded in 1975, this established nursery and landscape design firm is now it the hands of two enthusiastic guys who fell in love with the idea of running a nursery (even though they come from non-horticultural backgrounds). "We were always interested in this field, and we just said, 'let's go for it,'" John confesses. The pair has brought a newfound energy to the grounds, display gardens, and nursery here, endeavoring to be both a great gardener's destination and superior local resource. The nursery is in a park-like setting, known for its rare and unusual grafted plants, and an extensive collection of Japanese maples. There is a picturesque spring-fed koi pond and gazebo, and many paths to wander as you select trees, shrubs, perennials, ground covers, and more. This spot comes highly recommended by our friends in Pierce County Master Gardeners—who borrowed some fabulous trees from Bruce and John for the volunteer group's 2002 Northwest Flower & Garden Show display.

GardenScapes—The Herb and Perennial Farm

4556 Terrace Way SE, Port Orchard, WA 98366 | **Phone:** (360) 871-7245 | **Fax:** (360) 871-6571 | **Email:** gardenscapes@silverlink.net | **Web:** www.egardenscapes.com | **Directions:** From Hwy 16, south of Bremerton, exit to Hwy 160 (Sedgwick Road/Southworth Ferry). Go approximately 6 miles east on Sedgwick Road to Wilson Creek Road. Turn left onto Wilson Creek Road and then take the first left, onto Grandview, which turns into Terrace Way after the curve. Look for the nursery sign on the left. From the Southworth ferry dock, drive off the ferry onto Southworth Drive. Follow approximately 1 mile to Wilson Creek Road, then turn left onto Wilson Creek Road, go 1 block, turn right onto Cottonwood, and left onto Terrace Way. | **Open:** Seasonal or by appointment; wheelchair accessible.

Susan Dearth and Marilyn Hepner have created a bit of paradise here on the Olympic Peninsula, pursuing a dream of starting a **small nursery tucked into a peaceful rural setting.** Herbs are a specialty, but perennials, vines, hanging baskets, and some shrubs are offered as well. They have built a greenhouse and propagate around 70 percent of what they offer. Display gardens installed over seven years ago are now showing the maturity that now makes this a destination garden too. Along with **herbal theme gardens** (medicinal, tea, fragrance, everlasting, and culinary) and a traditional knot garden, there are perennial borders and a U-pick lavender bed. A water garden was completed in 2001. Summer and fall are the best seasons to view the gardens here.

Besides plants, you will find pots, books, garden art, and some gardening supplies. Ask to be on the quarterly newsletter list so you can plan on one of the many appealing classes, like the popular Victoria hanging-basket workshop (where you can create a replica of those luscious baskets that hang from the lampposts in downtown Victoria—check the website for great images). If you're in a hurry, just buy one already planted by Mary or Susan.

Garden Spot Nursery

900 Alabama Street, Bellingham, WA 98225 | **Phone:** (360) 676-5480 | **Fax:** (360) 738-4730 | **Email:** marcy@garden-spot.com | **Web:** www.garden-spot.com | **Directions:** From I-5 take exit 255. From the south, turn left to cross over the freeway, then take the first left at the stoplight onto James Street. From the north this exit becomes James Street. Travel south to Alabama Street, and turn left (east) 1 block. | **Open:** Daily; call for seasonal changes

An eye-catching seasonal flower bed (10 by 125 feet) along Alabama Street will surely draw you in to investigate. In the spring, it is ablaze with daffodils and tulips; more color emerges in summer perennials. By fall and winter, you'll find still more to interest you, with great plant material for Northwest gardens.

Marcy Plattner is famous for her uncanny ability to offer an exceptional selection of interesting, quality plants, varieties you won't find elsewhere, along with **unique and special garden accessories.** With John and Marcy's purchase and development of the 3 rural acres they lovingly refer to as "The Farm," more and more plants are being propagated and grown specifically for the nursery. The extra-sumptuous **hanging baskets** are from their own greenhouses as well. Also on offer are herbs, native species plants, perennials, ornamental grasses, vegetable starts grown from Territorial Seeds, drought-tolerant plants, annuals, wildflowers, and a marvelous bevy of unusual vines, especially clematis, together with a broad and well-chosen selection of old and new roses. Sedums, shrubs, and trees for the small garden and plants for winter interest are Marcy's latest specialties. An ever-expanding selection of **top-quality seed companies** are represented, including Territorial, Shepherd's, Lilly Miller, Renee's Garden, and from England, Mr. Fothergill, and Thompson & Morgan. The nursery is known for their knowledgeable staff and creative plant display areas, so you can lose yourself in stimulating conversation or thoughtful contemplation. Stop by year-round to shop for garden-related or inspired gifts, the practical or the whimsical, along with gardening hats, tools, supplies, books, and magazines. The popular spring and fall Garden Talks and Workshops generally fill fast, so sign up early! During the third week in June, come for the "Pot 'em for you day," when gardeners bring their planters and baskets and the Garden Spot crew designs and plants glorious containers. ("It's like a big party as everyone waits their turn," Marcy says.)

Garden Spot (The Wallingford)

Wallingford Center, 1815 N 45th Street, Seattle, WA 98103 | **Phone:** (206) 547-5137 | **Fax:** (206) 547-4409 | **Directions:** From I-5 take the N 45th Street exit 169 and travel west on 45th to the Wallingford Center (park free in the lot). | **Open:** Daily

This nursery, garden emporium, and flower shop is tucked away in and spills out onto the terrace level. New owners John and Marian Jarosz have been busy stocking the nursery with a top-notch array of fresh plants that cover the whole range from annuals and perennials to appropriate **small trees and noteworthy shrubs for the city garden.** Their intention is to be a great resource for the urban gardener! So not only are they dedicated to continue serving Wallingford locals, but also loyal customers from around Seattle, and adventuresome gardeners on the go from afar. Look here for seeds (Territorial, Botanical Interests, Seeds of Change, Thompson & Morgan), hand tools, organic fertilizers, soils, compost, and hay in the fall.

GARDEN TREASURES NURSERY

15011 35th Avenue SE, Snohomish, WA 98296 | **Phone:** (425) 338-0393 | **Directions:** From I-5 northbound, take exit 183 (164th Street SW) and head east; this becomes Mill Creek Road, then Seattle Hill Road. Continue on Seattle Hill Road until you come to 35th Avenue SE. Turn left and Garden Treasures will be on your right. From I-5 southbound, take exit 186 (128th Street SW) and head east; continue on 128th Street until you come to 35th Avenue SE, then turn right for 1.2 miles and Garden Treasures will be on your left. | **Open:** Daily

Lynda and Rick Condon purchased Garden Treasures in 2000, following Lynda's long career with Van Bloem Gardens (where she earned a great reputation as "the Bulb lady" at Northwest nurseries). Now, she's devoting her creative energy to updating and renovating a country nursery. Garden Treasures is carving out a niche as the place to discover **interesting garden art** crafted by local artisans. As you walk through the nursery and its gift shop, you'll notice fun and sophisticated garden art that you've probably not seen elsewhere. Lynda's idea is to help gardeners "accessorize" their outdoor living spaces. The Condons continue to add new lines of plants from local nurseries, along with recruiting new artists to showcase here. Each September, the nursery hosts a Garden Art AfFair" with dozens of artists, jazz, food, and children's activities.

GRAY BARN GARDEN CENTER & LANDSCAPE CO.

20871 Redmond-Fall City Road, Redmond, WA 98053 | **2nd location:** Bella Bottega Shopping Center, 8980 161st NE in downtown Redmond (Corner of 161st NE & NE 90th) | **Phone:** (425) 868-5757 or (425) 376-1116 | **Fax:** (425) 868-8595 | **Web:** www.graybarn.com | **Directions to main store:** From Seattle, travel to the Eastside via I-5 exit 168, crossing the Evergreen Point Bridge on Hwy 520. Follow north on Hwy 520 to Redmond. Take the exit to Redmond/Hwy 202 (Redmond Way/Redmond-Fall City Road); at the traffic signal, turn right onto the Redmond-Fall City Road and drive south about 2 miles. The nursery is at a traffic signal. Turn right onto Sahalee Way. | **Open:** Daily

The signature gray barn has housed a nursery for several years, but it was not until 1997 that new owners came along and renovated the facility. Long ago, this barn served the farm that occupied this site, and even today customers tell tales of playing in the hayloft, now a spacious home to garden art, home furnishings, and a gift gallery. The main floor is a garden center with tools, seeds, pots, soil amendments, pest controls and the like. In the nursery that surrounds the barn you will find the full range of plants, with a greenhouse up front for seasonal color plants. Perennials are displayed under a sheltered roof and there is a sales yard for trees and shrubs in sizes from 1 gallon to landscape specimens. The staff prides itself on seeking out varieties that are "hot new picks"—those that have been developed to be disease resistant or are bred for better or unusual color. If you are looking for something particularly special there is also a collector's corner of one-of-a-kind and uncommon plants they've discovered. Planting displays are based on such themes as a Japanese garden, a waterfall/water garden, a shade garden, a formal garden, and one featuring edibles.

GREEN ACRES GARDENS & PONDS

15011 Vail Road, Yelm, WA 98597 | **Phone:** (360) 894-2940 | **Web:** www.greenacresponds.com | **Directions:** From Tacoma at I-5 take exit 133 and follow signs for Hwy 7 through Spanaway. At the intersection with Hwy 507, take Hwy 507 continuing south. After you cross the Nisqually River turn left on Vail Road and drive about 5 miles to the nursery. | **Open:** Weekends or by appointment

Sue and Jack Markham came to the nursery business as so many other enthusiasts have. In 1989 they decided to install a pond in their wooded landscape but found it difficult to find expert advice, much less all the paraphernalia they needed to construct, plant, populate, and maintain this new water feature. They've come a long way since then! Their endeavor drew others with questions they had found answers to. One thing led to another and now they have ten ponds with streams, falls, and other water features. The nursery offers **an exceptionally full array of aquatics,** with an extensive selection that includes lotuses and both tropical and hardy water lilies. The plant lineup also includes bamboo, hostas, ferns, Japanese maples, own-root roses, and unusual perennials, most of which are propagated here. The hands-on nature of this family-run venture means customers enjoy mature plants at starter prices! And, yes, you will find everything you'll need to get started with a pond or water feature, including the fish, their food, and many kinds of garden- and pond-related ornaments.

THE GREENERY

14450 NE 16th Place, Bellevue, WA 98007 | **Phone:** (425) 641-1458 | **Email:** watts-greenery@msn.com | **Open:** By appointment only; directions provided when you call.

Lynn and Marilyn Watts started The Greenery as a hobby in 1960, propagating most of the plants they sell in this small, woodland nursery. They specialize in **species rhododendrons** for the collector, and a wonderful selection of newer dwarf hybrids. They also offer **Northwest natives:** ground covers, flowering plants, trilliums, ferns, and shrubs, especially showcasing plants that make good companions for rhododendrons, such as trillium, erythronium, and cypripedium. There is a display garden.

THE GREENHOUSE NURSERY

Hwy 101 at 81 S Bagley Creek Road, Port Angeles, WA 98362 | **Phone:** (360) 417-2664 | **Fax:** Same | **Email:** diana@olympus.net | **Directions:** On the Olympic Peninsula, the nursery is between Sequim and Port Angeles on Hwy 101, 0.2 mile east of the Port Angeles Wal Mart. | **Mailing address:** 81 S Bagley Creek Road & Hwy 101, Port Angeles, WA 98362 | **Open:** Seasonally, or by appointment; wheelchair accessible.

Diana started a decade ago by growing hanging baskets to sell at the Farmer's Market. She was very successful, yet unsatisfied with having to move plants to the customer. Then in 1997 the doors opened at her **small specialty nursery,** rumored to have the best plant selection in the north Olympic Peninsula. An ever-expanding display garden featuring available perennials and shrubs features some of the 1,000 varieties in stock at any given time. No trees are allowed, though, as the display gardens are built on top of the nursery's septic system. You can also find hobby greenhouses and Whitney Farms products here.

HAYES NURSERY

12504 Issaquah-Hobart Road SE, Issaquah, WA 98027 | **Phone:** (425) 391-4166 | **Fax:** (425) 391-9586 | **Mailing address:** 16610 246th Place SE, Issaquah, WA 98027 | **Directions:** Travel east on I-90 and take the Issaquah/Front Street exit 17 and go south on Front Street 3.6 miles; the nursery is on the left. From Hwy 18, take the Issaquah/Hobart exit and go north on Issaquah-Hobart Road about 3.5 miles. | **Open:** Daily

This is the type of garden center that carries a wide selection of trees and shrubs—the old favorites along with new and less-common varieties, many in specimen and dwarf sizes as well. There are bare-root fruit trees for those of us who get organized for an early start, a huge selection of annuals and perennials (the uncommon as well as old favorites), and a nice selection of top-quality roses. The retail store offers gardening supplies and remedies, as well as fun garden gifts.

There are **several display gardens:** a bird and butterfly attracting garden, slope/hillside garden, picnic garden, and a bird sanctuary, two water-feature gardens (including one that showcases koi), a grass garden, a rockery garden, an Asian-style garden, and a "relaxation" picnic garden. There is a shop featuring water-garden equipment, supplies, and plants, garden pest and disease controls, statuary, handmade pottery, tools, books, and gift items. Seeds carried include Seeds of Change, Botanical Interests, Luther Burbank, and Burpee. Spring classes are popular and geared to the home gardener.

HAZELWOOD GARDENS RHODODENDRON NURSERY

11230 SE 80th Street, Newcastle, WA 98056 | **Phone:** (425) 255-3318 | **Email:** rhodiesrus@msn.com | **Directions:** Located 5 miles south of Bellevue (5 miles north of Renton). From I-405, take exit 7, and head east (uphill) for 1 mile to the first stop sign at 116th; then head north for 0.5 mile to SE 80th Street, turn left (west), and follow the signs. | **Open:** Seasonal and by appointment

Bonnie Johnson writes, "This is a business that started from a hobby that got out of hand. Duane (Johnson) began taking cuttings in 1974 and had such success that soon he was giving rhododendrons to all his friends. When they wouldn't invite him over without the warning not to bring any more plants, he was forced to start selling them to the public! This has turned into a passion to find new and different varieties, and with this area being one of the richest for hybridizing, we spend much of the fall visiting local hybridizers to get their new and exciting hybrids. The selection changes each year with new local introductions as well as those coming from around the world."

The Johnsons have expanded their horticultural palette beyond the 165 varieties of **rhododendrons** they now offer to include **deciduous azaleas** and **Kalmia latifolia,** nearly all propagated on site with all the kalmia from tissue culture. They have added another acre, too, which helps protect this wooded setting from development. The 2-acre display garden shows mature plantings with companion plants. Trails crisscross through the garden, which is on a hillside, and this provides constantly changing vistas through the woodsy canopy (you're invited to help weed as you go along!). Deer are present most of the year, as are hundreds of birds. In rainy weather be sure to don appropriate footgear. The best color viewing is from April through mid-May, around Mother's Day, and in the fall from about October 10 through the end of the month. Bonnie and Duane are enthusiastic teachers and happily answer questions on the care and propagation of their plants.

HEATHS AND HEATHERS

502 E Haskell Hill Road, Shelton, WA 98584-8429 | **Phone:** (360) 427-5318 or (360) 432-9780 | **Orders:** (800) 294-3284 | **Fax:** (360) 432-9780 | **Fax for orders:** (800) 294-3284 | **Email:** handh@heathsandheathers.com | **Web:** www.heathsandheathers.com | **Open:** mail order only, weekday hours 8 a.m.–3 p.m. | **Catalog:** $1.50 or download free from website; shipping season September–June 15; wholesale and retail.

Karla Lortz, also Secretary of the North American Heather Society, has taken over the mail-order heath and heather business formerly owned by Bob, Alice, and Cindy Knight. With more than 750 varieties, this is possibly the **broadest selection of heathers** in the United States. Heaths and Heathers propagates 80 percent of its inventory, adding new varieties regularly, including importing new cultivars to the United States each year. The big news about heathers is discovering the varieties that extend a typical spring blooming season to just about every month, brightening up dark winter days. Most heathers are hardy and require little care once established.

This wonderful resource endeavors to raise plants that are as environmentally friendly as possible. Perched on the edge of Puget Sound, the nursery uses no chemical pesticides or fungicides. Beds of 4-inch plants are watered in "capillary sand beds," which allow plants to wick up the amount of water they need, thereby not wasting water. Plants are shipped in recycled and surplus boxes, so don't look for a fancy logo or nifty packaging.

Since Heaths and Heathers isn't open to the public, check the website for the nursery's frequent appearances at Northwest plant sales, and look for the booth at the Northwest Flower and Garden Show each February.

HERONSWOOD NURSERY, LTD.

7530 NE 288th Street, Kingston, WA 98346 | **Phone:** (360) 297-4172 | **Fax:** (360) 297-8321 | **Email:** heronswood@silverlink.net | **Web:** www.heronswood.com (catalog online) | **Directions:** Provided at the time your appointment is confirmed. | **Open:** By appointment (except for **Garden Open Days**). Nursery is mail order *only* February 1–May 15. | **Catalog:** $5, for a two-year subscription—keep ordering from it, though, and it will come. In it, **2,400 specific plant varieties** are all described within 240 pages (which for Dan Hinkley must have been quite a feat of self-restraint!). You'll refer to it often as a botanical reference book when you find yourself wondering "What the heck is *Decaisnea fargesii*?" or "How many forms of eupatorium do I have to choose from?" Shipping seasons are March to mid-May and mid-September to October. | **Garden Visits:** The extensive Heronswood Gardens are generally open only to nursery customers. You'll be treated to the large woodland area, perennial borders, and *apotager*, with some great Little & Lewis sculpture throughout. Schedule visits Monday to Friday, 9 a.m.–1 p.m., with some exceptions. You are provided access to the gardens at the time of a nursery visit. Groups of six and more are required to schedule a **Garden Tour** (actually a great option, as these are guided and a great opportunity for garden clubs, arboretum units, and small groups of individuals). The current fee (subject to increase) is $100 per hour, from which a donation of $50 will help support the Eastern Black Sea Forestry Research Institute in Turkey.

If you are lucky, passionate plantsman and head heron Dan Hinkley could be your guide, though he may be off and hard at work for voracious plant lovers on a collection trip to Japan, Taiwan, Nepal, China, Korea, or the United Kingdom, or on one of the lecture tours that take him worldwide. The 3-acre display garden is not wheelchair accessible. Parents are strongly encouraged to bring young children in backpacks, as the nursery is not stroller-friendly, and strollers are not allowed in the display gardens.

Open Garden Days: Check the website, catalog, or call for these special dates, scheduled on a Friday, Friday and Saturday, or a Saturday only. Each February, Heronswood hosts its annual **Hellebore Open,** which helps raise your winter garden spirits while raising funds for the Miller Horticultural Library; call for details. Other Open days in Spring (June), Summer (July), and Fall (September) give you the entire year to enjoy Heronswood's horticultural beauty. These are popular events, so arrive early. No reservation required. Heron helpers populate the garden to answer the million and one questions you will have; bring a sharp pencil, a big notebook,

and a portable reference (like their catalog). Stroll the gardens (with lust in your heart) then shop in the nursery to relieve your longing. Many plants are marked at special prices at these times and light refreshments are available.

And what about the nursery, you might ask? Well, avid plant collectors, hang onto your horticultural hats! Treat yourself to a delicious selection of under-used plants, most of which are propagated on the premises, many from seeds and cuttings from plants found far away in Great Britain, New Zealand, Tasmania, Nepal, Japan, Korea, Taiwan, China, Chile, and from across the United States. mail order is a primary business at Heronswood, though thousands of intrepid gardeners make the pilgrimage to this Kitsap Peninsula nursery each year via a planned tour or a reservation to shop, to pick up pre-ordered plants, to attend a class or special event, or on one of the Open Garden days. In any event, we strongly suggest you first peruse the hefty catalog, serving forth **shrubs, trees, conifers, perennials, temperennials** (as in tender not temporary, although if you leave them out over a cold winter then they are also temporary), **vines,** and **ornamental grasses** and **sedges** (you needn't have your Hortus on hand because the catalog provides quite a bit of cultural information, and it's far more inspirational, less expensive, and infinitely more amusing than Hortus, too). For those with the inclination, this is arisaema heaven.

HIGHFIELD GARDEN

4704 NE Cedar Creek Road, Woodland, WA 98674 | **Phone:** (360) 225-6525 | **Open:** mail order only | **Catalog:** $1

Irene Moss grows 95 percent of the plants she offers, having gotten her start along this path when a friend innocently (?) brought seed packets from her lovely border to share! We are all the beneficiaries, as Irene did so well that now she has her own specialty nursery with an extensive selection of hardy geraniums, sold in 4-inch pots and well-priced. She lists a **nice range of perennials** with lots of interesting varieties, like *Pulmonaria* 'Benediction', *Epimedium grandiflorum* 'Higoense', *Campanula trachelium*, and *Stacys* 'Countess Helen Von Stein' as just a few examples. You will find her faithfully tending her table at the Arboretum, Northwest Perennial Alliance, and Master Gardener sales in Seattle, and in Oregon the Hardy Plant Society of Oregon, Leach Garden, Berry Botanical Garden, Salem Arts Fair (July), and annual plant sales.

HUMMINGBIRD FARM & NURSERY

2319 Zylstra Road, Oak Harbor, WA 98277 | **Phone:** (360) 679-5044 | **Fax:** (360) 679-6926 | **Email:** humming@whidbey.net | **Web:** www.hummingbird-farm.com | **Directions:** On Hwy 20, Whidbey Island, there is a handy directional sign pointing the way to Hummingbird Farm, south of Oak Harbor, north of Coupeville on the big curve around Penn Cove. Find it, then you'll turn to the west and just keep driving until you get to Hummingbird Farm—

you'll know it when you see it by the periwinkle blue fence that borders the display garden. | **Open:** April–September; call for fall and winter hours.

The gardens at Hummingbird Farm & Nursery may attract more visitors than hummingbirds, having appeared on the cover of *Country Living Gardener,* in *Sunset* magazine, and on the Ed Hume *Gardening in America* television program. The display gardens are picturesque, so bring a camera! The front cottage garden is enclosed in a snazzy periwinkle blue fence and shows off lusty plant combinations that demonstrate luscious color combinations, architectural structure, and tantalizing texture. Lighthearted accents characterize the smaller garden, from the honeysuckle-draped obelisk to whimsically painted corner-post birdhouses. In this garden you'll find that separate beds **feature hummingbird and butterfly plants, fragrance, and, in the moon garden, white flowers.** On the north side of the nursery is a shade border featuring a bog garden and appropriate plantings. There is also a rugosa rose display underplanted with lavender. The nursery offers many of the plants that have won your heart in the displays. You'll find herbs (lots of lavenders), perennials (many salvias, both the hardy and the more tender varieties), and annuals. Easy-to-read descriptive profiles are your introduction to uncommon plant varieties. You'll be inspired by the collections, which include hardy fuchsias, verbascums, eryngiums (sea holly), aquilegias (columbines), hardy geraniums, and euphorbias.

Hummingbird has expanded its **evergreen and small flowering shrub department,** with a focus on varieties offering multiple seasons of interest. The nursery also features ornamental grasses, native plants, and vines. In the nursery shop (a picturesque remodeled barn) you'll find signature dried flowers, garden books, supplies (organic fertilizers, Felcos, Territorial and Shepherd's Seeds), accessories (locally crafted rustic furniture, garden art, gift items—and of course hummingbird feeders). Seeds, tools, organic fertilizers, and a special organic compost are also in stock. A well-stocked reference library is on hand, as are informational handouts. Hummingbird's website is worth a visit, too, for a virtual tour of the display gardens—and a peek at what's growing.

Hunter's Hardy Perennials

1425 N 36th Street, Renton, WA 98056 | **Phone:** (425) 255-6756 | **Email:** smatehunter@yahoo.com | **Web:** www.nwroses.com | **Directions:** From I-405 north, take exit 6 and head west (left) to the first stop. Turn left on Park Avenue N and continue 6 blocks to N 36th Street. Turn right and go uphill to the fifth driveway on the right. From I-405 south, take exit 7 and turn right onto Lake Washington Boulevard. Turn left on N 40th Street, right on Park Avenue to N 36th Street, then left on N 36th, and go uphill to the fifth driveway on the right. | **Open:** Seasonally, or by appointment

Casey Hunter began this garden with the help of his mother-in-law who suggested and supplied a few perennials she had left from garden club sales. He began experimenting with propagation techniques, searching for vibrant, easy-care, and unique perennials (many of which have been shared from other gardeners and are difficult to find in retail nurseries). The nursery now propagates 80 percent of its stock. Most recently, Hunter's has added roses (20 varieties of Weeks Roses, selected specifically for the Northwest), but making up the backbone of this nursery are the **225 varieties of perennials.** Casey strives to keep plant prices affordable and the selection distinctive; specialties include hardy, upright fuchsias, ground covers, hostas, rockery and basket stuffers, and hanging baskets.

Open during spring and summer, Hunter's showcases its best offerings in two large perennial gardens and two large rose gardens, allowing you to see how plants look when mature and with companions. Call to find out about the end-of-season sale, which sells plants at up to 50 percent off (the remainder are free to good homes, Casey promises).

Indoor Sun Shoppe

911 NE 45th Street, Seattle 98105 | **Phone:** (206) 634-3727 | **Email:** staff@indoorsun.com | **Web:** www.indoorsun.com | **Directions:** Take the I-5 exit for NE 45th and go a few blocks east (toward the University of Washington); the Shoppe is on the right (south side), with free parking behind the store, entered from 9th Avenue NE. | **Open:** Daily

Anyone who has traveled this popular route through the University District has surely been intrigued by the warm glow of plant lights and the exotic foliage peeking out from the front windows of this landmark plant shop. If you haven't taken the time to drop in to see what is behind the glowing facade, do. You'll be transported into a wonderful world that seems like a botanical conservatory, with hundreds of **tropical varieties** and houseplants, **carnivorous plants, orchids, cacti,** and the like. There is a real need for information on the pest and disease problems of indoor plants and here you can find beneficial insects, other controls, and free advice gleaned from over 25 years in business! A comfortable atmosphere invites you to linger over a latte, perhaps with a new book or magazine from their wide selection. (See also Chapter 8, "Emporiums: Gardening Shops.")

Jade Mountain Bamboo, Inc.

5020 116th Street E, Tacoma, WA 98446-5009 | **Phone:** (253) 588-0662 or (253) 537-3938 | **Fax:** (253) 582-1933 | **Directions:** From I-5 take exit 127 and travel east on Hwy 512. After about 7 miles take the Canyon Road exit and at the stop sign turn right. Cross through the first intersection (112th Street E) to the next intersection, then turn right onto 116th Street E; the nursery is on the left. | **Open:** By appointment only | **Catalog:** $2, shipping year-round; wholesale and retail.

Phil Davidson (formerly of Torii Station Bamboo), together with Dale and Joanna Chesnut, has opened a new specialty nursery, with **cold-hardy temperate bamboo** as the focus; they also offer some tropical bamboo suitable for indoor use.

JULIUS ROSSO NURSERY CO.

6404 Ellis Avenue S, Seattle, WA 98108 | **Phone:** *(206)* 763-1888 or (800) 832-1888 | **Fax:** (206) 762-2544 | **Email:** info@rossonursery.com | **Web:** www.rossonursery.com | **Mailing address:** PO Box 80345, Seattle, WA 98108 | **Directions:** From I-5 take the Albro exit 161 and drive west on Albro Pl S. The nursery is at the corner of Albro and Ellis. | **Open:** Daily

Julius Rosso Nursery was founded in 1958, a family business tucked into an unlikely urban 4-acre site in Georgetown, on the northern tip of Boeing Field. For many years a wholesale nursery, Rosso is now open to retail customers, many of whom like to think the offbeat location is their own best-kept secret. Rosso offers everything from ground covers to full-sized trees, with native plants and ornamental varieties, perennials, flowering and evergreen shrubs, fruit trees, evergreens, hedging plants, roses, herbs, seasonal vegetable starts, and grasses. And if you're in the market for a Monkey Puzzle tree, here's a good place to look. Ed Hume Seeds are on the shelves, as are seeds from Northern Italy, which are excellent varieties for the Northwest garden. There is also a wide selection of roses. Rosso is one of the area's first retail nurseries to embrace the use of compost tea, stocking the Soil Soup system and supplies. You can buy your own batch of Soil Soup here on Saturday mornings or by request during the week.

JUNGLE FEVER EXOTICS

5050 N Pearl Street, Tacoma, WA 98407 | **Phone:** *(253)* 759-1669 | **Fax:** (253) 759-0637 | **Directions:** From I-5 in Tacoma, take Hwy 16 west to the 6th Avenue exit, and stay in the center lane. Turn left at the intersection of N 51st and Pearl Street. From the Peninsula, take Hwy 16 east, then take the Pearl Street exit (the second one after the Narrows Bridge) and proceed as above. The gardens are 3 blocks south of the Pt Defiance Park entrance. | **Open:** Daily in summer; call ahead for winter hours.

One customer told owner Jerry Cearley, "This place has a vibe going." Another called it "the coolest place in Tacoma." Whether you're into crazy settings or not, this Tacoma nursery is the **horticultural destination for anyone in search of tropical plants.** Jungle Fever grows and sells garden exotics—palms, bananas, plants with oversized foliage, vines, and trailing fronds. Jerry is the horticulturist and his partner Darlene Allard is the artist, and the two have combined forces in one lush environment of plants and art. You can cure your own "jungle fever" with unique, locally crafted garden art (functional and decorative). Among the plants, you'll find **hardy exotics,** including bamboo, bigleaf perennials, ornamental grasses, water plants, ferns, herbs, drought-tolerant Mediterranean and California natives, cannas, hardy gingers, vines, and choice perennials. The front of the nursery is a traffic-stopping tropical border. Around the side, you'll find a xeriscape setting with Southwest and Mediterranean natives. A year ago, Jerry and Darlene bought the home behind their nursery, so that garden is

in progress, too. Don't be surprised if it transports you to the tropical Rain Forest!

KENT'S GARDEN & NURSERY

5428 Northwest Road, Bellingham, WA 98226 | **Phone:** *(360)* 384-4433 | **Fax:** (360) 380-6228 | **Directions:** From I-5 take the Northwest Road exit 257, and drive north (right from the freeway exit), about 10 minutes for about 4 miles. | **Open:** Daily; by appointment only December–February.

Ginny Crump and Nancy Henshaw have been in business here since 1979, offering their plants and trees to retail customers at very reasonable prices. They grow about 60 percent of the inventory, and an excellent selection of **good-sized trees, conifers, and vines** is available, with ground covers, hedging plants, a widening assortment of perennials, and a large assortment of broadleaf evergreen and deciduous shrubs . . . everything from the basics to the rare and unusual. The nursery maintains 30 acres for growing; the **retail nursery is housed on 3.5 acres with demonstration gardens, sitting areas, a garden shop, and garden gift store** filled with lovely items, and the staff is friendly and knowledgeable. An Asian display garden and a children's garden are in the making for 2002. Call for the new class schedule.

KILLDEER FARMS

21606 NW 51st Avenue, Ridgefield, WA 98642 | **Phone:** *(360)* 887-1790 | **Fax:** (360) 887-3009 | **Email:** geraniums@killdeerfarms.com | **Web:** www.killdeerfarms.com | **Directions:** Take exit 9 off I-5 and head west on 179th Street. Turn right at the first stop, onto NW 41st Avenue. Turn left on 209th Street and travel to NW 51st Avenue. Turn right, and the nursery is 0.5 mile on the left. | **Open:** Seasonal and by appointment; mail order year-round. | **Catalog:** Full-color, free online; printed list free upon request.

Killdeer Farms specializes in propagating and growing **geraniums, pelargoniums, fuchsias, impatiens, and ferns of all types.** If you want to be amazed at the wide array of geranium and pelargonium genera available to gardeners, visit the website for a colorful introduction. The nursery features one of the largest collections offered anywhere (wholesale and retail), with more than 600 varieties to choose from. While there isn't a display garden here, you are invited to tour the production greenhouses.

KINDER GARDENS NURSERY & LANDSCAPING

1137 S Hwy 17, Othello, WA 99344 | **Phone:** *(509)* 488-5017 | **Fax:** (509) 488-6513 | **Directions:** 30 miles south of Moses Lake on Hwy 17. | **Open:** Daily (closed Sunday and Monday during summer and winter months) | **Plant list:** Free; wholesale and retail.

While this *Directory* is aimed at gardeners on the wet west side of the Cascades, there are many who live in microclimates in which plants grown on Washington's dry eastern side are appropriate and sought after. Also, because many of you are adventurous travelers, it's great to know about Dennis and Claudia Kinder's 3-acre nursery for your next road trip eastward through the heart of the Columbia Basin. The specialty here is growing both evergreen and deciduous shrubs and trees (350 varieties), with lots of handsome and useful conifers, ground covers, and vines, so this is a great resource. **Ornamental and conservation plants** join **hedging and windbreak material.** Prices vary for bare-root and containerized plants. Special landscaping trees and shrubs listed in the 16-page catalog are too plentiful to list here, but include dogwoods, Japanese maples, rhododendron varieties, 'Trost's Dwarf' and purple weeping birch, purple weeping beech, golden chain tree, weeping hemlock, various hinoki cypress, columnar scotch pine, and Colorado blue spruce. Volume discounts are offered and there's a great "buy one, get one free" end-of-season sale each year; call for details. The Kinders invite visitors to wander their arboretum of labeled plants in theme gardens that include two large ponds with waterfalls, aquatic plantings, and fish.

LAKEWOLD GARDENS SHOP

12317 Gravelly Lake Drive SW, Tacoma, WA 98499 | **Phone:** (253) 584-4106 | **Fax:** (253) 584-3021 | **Email:** info@lakewold.org or gardenshopping@aol.com | **Web:** www.lakewold.org | **Directions:** In Tacoma, only a few minutes off I-5; take exit 124 and go west 1 mile, following the signs to Lakewold Gardens. | **Open:** Varies by season; call for hours.

This wonderful shop, located in the Lakewold estate's old carriage house (circa 1920), is known for its small but **choice and distinctive offering of plants**: perennials, vines, trees, and shrubs. Here you will find the elusive Himalayan blue poppy (*Meconopsis sheldonii, M. betonicifolia,* and *M. grandis*), the signature plant for which the gardens are famous. Seeds are also an important offering here, including the British Plants of Distinction, Chiltren's, and Renee's Garden Seeds. Also, the Down-to-Earth line of organic amendments from Eugene. (See also Chapter 8, "Emporiums: Gardening Shops," and Chapter 13, "Gardens to Visit.")

LAZY-S-NURSERY

37050 28th Avenue S, Federal Way, WA 98003 | **Phone:** (253) 838-8041 | **Fax:** (253) 927-2047 | **Directions:** Follow I-5 to Enchanted Village, located just south of Federal Way. Head east on S 360th Street, turn right on 28th Avenue S, and go to S 371st Street; the nursery is on the left. | **Open:** Daily, except Wednesdays

Rock garden enthusiasts and those on the hunt for rare tree species either already know Mark Sieloff's Lazy-S or will be drawn there soon. Mark's father, Jim Sieloff, started the nursery in 1972 on the old Duncan homestead, circa 1888 (on the Federal Way historic register). Mark has owned Lazy-S since 1988. He propagates and specializes in **hard-to-find dwarf, semi, and large conifers** (like miniature spruce, hemlock, and beech); flowering and less common trees, like dogwoods, satomi, the fragrant epaulette tree, magnolias (see Oyama, with a red center!), *Styrax japonica, Syrax obassia* (and others), Japanese kousa, and, among his offerings of Japanese

'Shindeshojo', and Butterfly. Enjoy Mark's all-season bonsai display when you visit, and choose from his unusual varieties of shrubs and bonsai material.

THE LILY GARDEN ✉ @

4902 NE 147th Avenue, Vancouver, WA 98682-6067 | **Phone:** (360) 253-6273 | **Fax:** (360) 253-2512 | **Email:** thelilygdn@aol.com | **Web:** www.thelilygarden.com | **Open:** Office, 8 a.m.–5 p.m. | **Catalog:** Free, 48-pages, full color. mail order only, best hours to reach office, Tuesday–Thursday, 1–4 p.m. PST

Judith Freeman specializes in lilies, including varieties unavailable elsewhere, such as her own Columbia-Platte hybrid introductions. Her original business is Columbia-Platte Lilies Inc., which was founded in 1979. The Lily Garden catalog was introduced in 1993, offering over 100 different kinds of Lilium—Asiatic, LA, Trumpet, Orienpet, and Oriental hybrids, as well as species. The nursery grows all its plants (many their own hybrids) and guarantees all bulbs, so customers can be sure that the bulbs they buy are healthy, of flowering size, and true to name. Notable lilies include: 'Silk Road', 'Scheherazade', 'Tinkerbell', 'Ariadne', 'Rosepoint Lace', 'White Butterfiles', 'Brushstroke', 'Peach Butterflies', 'Tiger Babies', 'Classic', 'Red Velvet', 'St. Patrick', *Lilium leucanthum*, 'White Henryi', 'Anastasia', 'Arabesque', 'Catherine the Great', 'Silk Screen', 'Leslie Woodriff', 'Black Beauty', 'Sorbonne', 'Muscadet', *Lilium auratum, Lilium speciosum* var. *rubrum,* 'Casa Blance', and 'Stargazer'.

THE LILY PAD

3403 Steamboat Island Road, #374, Olympia, WA 98502 | **Phone:** (360) 866-0291 | **Fax:** (360) 866-7128 | **Email:** info@lilypadbulbs.com | **Web:** www.lilypadbulbs.com | **Open:** Mail order and Olympia Farmer's Market | **Catalog:** $1, full color; shipping season is October–April; wholesale and retail.

Jan Detwiler specializes in lilies (Asiatic hybrids, Easter lily/longiflorum—Asiatic crosses, trumpets, and Oriental hybrids) and bare-root plants: hardy perennials, (aconitum, dicentra, and hellebores, for example), daylilies, and tree and herbaceous peonies, many of which she propagates herself. Everything The Lily Pad sells is "trialed" in its 9-acre fields and determined hardy for Northwest gardens. If you are on Jan's mailing list you'll receive coupons for great savings at her booth at Flower and Garden Shows and for special clearance event notices. Check out the annual "clearance sale" at the Olympia Farmer's Market, usually the last weekend in April and the first weekend in November.

MADRONA NURSERY

815 38th Avenue, Seattle, WA 98122 | **Phone:** (206) 323-8325 | **Fax:** Same | **Email:** bucherjohn@earthlink.com | **Web:** www.specialty-nurseries.com | **Directions:** From I-5 in Seattle, go east on James Street, left on 37th, right on Columbia, then left on 38th (or take Lake Washington Boulevard west to Fullerton, which becomes 38th). | **Open:** By appointment only | **Plant list:** Free with SASE

Ann Bucher's enthusiasm for plants grew from a hobby to a small nursery located at her home (actually, and in a rather uniquely urban way, onto the only available space of the flat rooftops above the garage and house). She tries to offer **perennials** not readily available elsewhere and can provide personal advice and suggestions for her customers. The perennials (she's adding more hardy geraniums, hellebores, and astrantias) are joined by a small but increasing selection of **native plants** (vancouveria and trillium) and a small selection of trees and shrubs (*Sarcococca confusa,* sweet winter box)—all grown from seed or divisions. She focuses on **woodland plants for shady situations.** When asked about her "display" garden she says, "Both garden and gardener are disheveled in early spring, but the flowers are worth seeing. June and July there is a pretty good show." There is no way to avoid the steps, which may limit accessibility. The shady back garden is glorious in early spring, with hellebores, trilliums, hepaticas, and erythroniums. The front, sun-loving perennial garden explodes come summer. Once you're on Ann's mailing list, you'll receive a notice of the annual Open House.

MAGNOLIA GARDEN CENTER

3213 W Smith Street, Seattle, WA 98199-3217 | **Phone:** (206) 284-1161 | **Fax:** (206) 284-0081 | **Email:** maggarcen@aol.com | **Web:** www.magnoliagarden.com | **Directions:** From I-5 in Seattle take the Stewart Street exit 166. At Denny Way (and from downtown Seattle), turn right and follow Denny Way west to Western Avenue, which turns right and becomes Elliott Avenue. On Elliott, drive north to the Magnolia Bridge (exits on right), take the bridge to Magnolia village, turning right onto 32nd Avenue, then onto Condon Way. The nursery is located 1 block north of McGraw at 32nd Avenue W and Smith Street. | **Open:** Daily

Margaret and Chuck Flaherty have poured a lot of energy into jazzing up the selection, providing ever-changing, **creative container plant displays,** and offering their customers a staff of plant lovers anxious to help solve problems or provide knowledgeable advice. They offer a full range of plants and are very savvy about hunting up uncommon varieties, thoughtfully selected for success in the Northwest garden. The store is stocked with a full line of supplies and tools for urban (including container) gardening. Classes and workshops are offered on Saturdays. Magnolia Bluff and this nursery make a delightful and rewarding day of exploration.

MALONE'S LANDSCAPE & NURSERY

24322 228th Avenue SE, Maple Valley, WA 98038 | **Phone:** (425) 413-0979 | **Fax:** (425) 413-0410 | **Web:** www.maloneslandscape.com | **Directions:** Traveling south on I-405, take exit 4 (Hwy 169) to Maple Valley and Enumclaw. Malone's is located on the corner of Hwy 169 and 228th Avenue SE, about 12 miles from I-405. | **Open:** Daily

A gardening destination point! Malone's Landscape & Nursery is **well stocked with quality trees, shrubs, and a full range of perennials, herbs, and ground covers.** Colorful hanging baskets, fuchsias, and annuals provide year-round color and interest in the nursery. The gift shop transforms for the seasons, offering you the latest in gardening gifts, décor for the home (indoors and out), and great garden supplies. If you need help with landscape design, ask for details on Malone's excellent landscaping services (a sister business).

MARY'S COUNTRY GARDEN

23329 172nd Avenue SE, Kent, WA 98042 | **Phone:** (253) 639-1243 | **Email:** mlfrey@aol.com | **Directions:** From Hwy 167 in Kent take the Central Avenue exit and drive south to James Street. Turn left (east) onto James, which becomes SE 240th Street. At Hwy 516, continue east on SE 240th to 172nd Avenue SE. Turn left onto 172nd and drive about 0.3 mile; the nursery sign is on your left. | **Open:** Seasonal and by appointment

Mary Frey answered our question about what she thinks makes her nursery special with a delightful quote: "My nursery began naturally because of my love of gardening and propagation. I call it 'a nursery for the liberated gardener' because my customers are open to new and unusual plants. Children are welcome, and often do not want to leave." Among Mary's specialties are **primroses, hardy fuchsias, and campanulas.** You're offered a lovely selection of perennials, herbs, vines, and small shrubs (she propagates about half her stock), as well as seed from plants in the garden. She is also willing to help you hunt up something she doesn't have! As a home-based nursery, the display garden is Mary's own, with perennial and herb gardens and a woodland of native plants. She gives slide shows to garden clubs and libraries.

MAXWELTON VALLEY GARDENS

3443 E French Road, Clinton, WA 98236 | **Phone:** (360) 579-1770 | **Fax:** (360) 579-1496 | **Email:** mvg@whidbey.com | **Web:** www.whidbey.net/mvg | **Directions:** From the Mukilteo ferry, depart from Clinton, going north on Hwy 525. Turn left on Cultus Bay Road and right on French Road (this works out to be about 5 miles from the ferry to the nursery). From the north going south on Hwy 525, turn right on Maxwelton Road, then left on French Road. | **Open:** Daily | **Plant lists:** Free at the nursery or by mail with SASE (one first-class stamp per list).

Ron Kerrigan and his partner Bill Halstead bought this 9-acre property on Whidbey Island in 1985 as their home (and now nursery), with a dream to reclaim the native habitat destroyed by years of cattle grazing. The plants they sought to reintroduce were not easily available, which led to their developing a horticultural specialty in the plants they most avidly sought themselves, including ones for **difficult conditions such as dry shade, wet soils, stream banks subject to drying sun and wind, and aggressive browsing of deer and rabbits.** (Sound familiar, anyone?)

With a horticultural degree from Edmonds Community College and experience in charge of the greenhouses at the Center for Urban Horticulture, Bill came armed with the expertise to direct the restoration plans. Maxwelton now offers **Northwest native plants;** fragrant rhododendrons; woodland shade plants; plants for dry shade; drought-tolerant plants; unusual perennials; Pacific Coast, Japanese, and Siberian irises; and flowering shrubs and trees. The property is gradually evolving to include access to the woodland, criss-crossed by two streams, and a **nature trail system liberally marked with informational signage** (wear appropriate footgear). There is excellent labeling on their plant stock, and detailed plant lists are organized by special conditions—"Plants to attract birds and butterflies," "Plants for seaside gardens," "Plants for general drought tolerance," to name a few. A good time to visit is April–June for woodland wildflower bloom or late November to see the salmon spawning. Dogs are welcome on these trails, as this pair passionately supports adopt-a-dog programs. Bill Halstead extends the nursery's reach on Whidbey Island and the mainland through his landscape design consulting.

McComb Road Nursery

751 McComb Road, Sequim, WA 98382 | **Phone:** (360) 681-2827 | **Fax:** (360) 681-7578 | **Email:** mccomb@olympus.net | **Directions:** On the Olympic Peninsula, travel west on Hwy 101. Take the first Sequim exit (Washington Street). In Sequim, turn right (north) on 5th Avenue to the Old Olympic Hwy. Turn left (west) onto the highway and travel west to McComb Road. The nursery sign is on the left; follow signs. | **Open:** Daily

New owners Neil Burkhardt and Jane Stewart have taken on this established nursery aiming to make it their own. Neil graduated from the respected Lake Washington Technical College Environmental Horticulture Program, and served a stint with garden designer Phil Wood. Now he's moved west to offer his expertise and enthusiasm to create a "new" nursery. The display gardens have a habitat and ecosystem focus, and plant selection is based on successful cultivation in the Pacific Northwest. The nursery offers **quality unique plants, ponds, garden supplies, garden gifts, and art.** In addition, there is a seminar series (call for schedule), and in August, "Music at McComb" performances to help you enjoy a bit of respite before fall garden chores begin.

Millennium Farms

1504 NW 299th Street, Ridgefield, WA 98642 | **Phone:** (360) 887-4485 | **Fax:** (360) 887-4486 | **Email:** michael@mfarms.com | **Directions:** From I-5 heading south from Woodland, take Pioneer Street exit 14. Go east to the "Y" intersection, and turn north on NW 11th Avenue 1.5 miles, then turn left onto NW 299th Street. | **Open:** Weekends or by appointment; also at Vancouver's Farmer's Market on Saturdays. | **Catalog:** $2; shipping season April to early June; wholesale and retail.

Missy and Michael Stucky begin each growing season offering organic, heirloom, and old-fashioned herbs (over 500 varieties) plus vegetable and flower starts for the home gardener. There are over 100 varieties of **heirloom tomatoes, peppers, melons, beans, squash, and potatoes.** Missy, a Master Gardener, has 30-plus years of experience growing these plants. Michael comes from a line of Mennonite farmers known for growing the best-tasting

vegetables and grains available, many from seed brought from their homelands in the 1880s. In early August you can come to the farm for eggs and fresh produce picked to order. Their product must be tops, as it is featured by a number of Portland's award-winning restaurants.

Minter's Earlington Greenhouses

13043 Renton Avenue S, Seattle, WA 98178 | **Phone:** (425) 255-7744 | **Fax:** (425) 271-9896 | **Email:** minternursery@compuserve.com | **Directions:** Located in the Skyway area, west of the Renton Airport; from I-5, take exit 154 east onto I-405, then take the Renton exit 2, turning left at the traffic signal after exiting I-405. Proceed north on Rainier Avenue for 1 mile. Turn left onto Renton Avenue S. As you follow Renton Avenue S, the nursery is less than 1 mile on the left. | **Open:** Daily

Ron Minter and Paul Farrington have turned a neighborhood nursery (established circa 1938), into the hippest garden place in South Seattle. The pair not only modernized the plant offerings of a beloved garden center, they kept this landmark from becoming another condominium project along the way. In addition to an **excellent array of herbs, perennials, ornamental grasses, 90 varieties of roses, and dozens of fuchsias** (including hardy cultivars), you will be thrilled by the attention given to collector plants and to varieties that have proven hardy, pest- and disease-resistant, and of excellent form. With 50,000 square feet under glass as well as extensive sales display areas tucked in throughout the 4-acre site, this is an excellent destination in every season. Minter's propagates and grows most of its own plants, with a very popular emphasis on specialty geraniums and sun-loving coleus varieties. The **greenhouse** is home to tropicals and luscious plants like tibouchina, brugmansias, abutilon, and lots of unique Asian vegetable starts—and at Christmas, poinsettias as far as the eye can see. Call for the class list, which encompasses moss basket, container design, and autumn centerpiece projects. In the early spring, you can take a useful rose pruning workshop. The seed department includes Burpee and Ed Hume. Coffee and tea are served anytime! The shop carries a great hard-goods selection, plus garden art and accessories.

Mitchell Bay Nursery ✳

6451 Mitchell Bay Road, Friday Harbor, WA 98250 | **Phone:** (360) 378-2309 | **Email:** mbfarm@rockisland.com | **Directions:** Mitchell Bay Road, 8 miles northwest of Friday Harbor on San Juan Island (near Snug Harbor Resort). | **Open:** Seasonal, or by appointment

Mitchell Bay Nursery is the San Juan Island nursery of Colleen Howe and Bruce Gregory, with a large cottage garden to inspire you. Inside the fence you'll find perennials, vines, and shrubs for sun and shade. The garden surrounds a nearly 100-year-old pink farmhouse, so bring a camera! Outside, and of special interest to any island or suburban gardener (and these days even many in the heart of a bustling town) is an amazing unfenced deer-proof planting where Mitchell Bay is testing and demonstrating the *Sunset* list of deer-resistant plants. The specialty here includes a limited tree selection, and many ornamental shrubs, unusual perennials, vines, and grasses. Colleen and Bruce propagate all the plants they offer, which is for them a way of testing also for local cold hardiness. For all of the 25-plus years they have lived on the island, Colleen and Bruce have always had a sideline farming enterprise of one kind or another. Currently they market their organically grown Asian pears and two varieties of kiwi, both locally and at food co-ops on the mainland. They also make and sell various soaps and gardeners' hand salve, so look for it in Seattle area co-ops and markets.

MOLBAK'S GREENHOUSE AND NURSERY

13625 NE 175th Street, Woodinville, WA 98072-8558 | **Phone:** (425) 483-5000 | **Fax:** (425) 398-5190 | **Web:** www.molbaks.com | **Directions:** From I-405 take the Woodinville exit onto SR 522, get into the right lane, and take the first exit. Turn right, and go to the stoplight on NE 175th; turn left and proceed to the nursery, which is on the right. | **Open:** Daily

This is a **BIG nursery and garden center,** best approached from its main entrance, where the stunning front borders (changing by the season) have helped to define downtown Woodinville's image. There's hardly a type of plant you could be looking for that you would not find here, **well-grown and beautifully displayed.** Under "one (extensive) roof" find also furnishings for indoor and outdoor rooms, an excellent gift shop, and more. A vast houseplant department is flanked by a very fine collection of baskets. If seeds are one of your soft spots, plan to spend a lot of time poring over the extravagant selection from all over the world. There is also an excellent section of seeds (and tools and gardening togs, too) specifically for children. Plants are well-marked, cultural information is prominently displayed, and an information center dispenses expert advice freely. For aqua gardeners there are water plants, pond liners, pumps, fountains, ornaments, and more. To revive your energy should you be overwhelmed by the extent of plants and paraphernalia, enjoy a beverage at the espresso bar as you sit amongst the tropical houseplants and next to the conservatory/aviary, and then browse the well-stocked adjacent book nook. In fact, consider making a selection there before repairing to your respite.

Beginning and veteran gardeners alike will love Molbak's expanded website, where you'll find an extensive calendar of events, weekly specials, a map of the nursery, and more than 200 downloadable plant-care sheets. During the peak spring planting season, you can call Molbak's and ask to be connected to the a member of its HIT-team (Horticultural Information Team) and talk with a *human* plant expert for troubleshooting and advice.

If you have never taken in Floral Fairyland, one of the many major theatrical productions staged each year for children (whether you have one in tow or not), GO! The

sets for these elaborate classics are stunning—a tremendous gift to the community. During the holidays, Molbak's is a major destination for poinsettia-lovers and folks in search of the lush, festive color offered by Molbak's greenhouses, always filled with several special new poinsettia offerings. Count on Molbak's to usher in spring with a dazzling array to get anyone's spirits juiced up. Be sure to visit in fall when your garden sags or in winter when the bare border looks oh-so-bedraggled.

MOONROSE PERENNIALS

114 N Second Street, La Conner, WA 98257 | **Phone:** (360) 466-0338 | **Mailing address:** PO Box 847, La Conner, WA 98257 | **Directions:** Take the La Conner exit off I-5; follow signs to La Conner. On Morris Street, you'll turn right to Second. MoonRose is on the corner of Second and Centre. | **Open:** Daily

Laura Campbell's MoonRose has relocated to charming La Conner, where this talented woman once again has transformed an ordinary yard into a work of art. Combining her **passions for antiques and garden design,** this turn-of-the-century home offers a splendid palette for her talents, both indoors and out. Within, and decorated with flair, each room is filled with antiques, primitive furniture, farm and garden artifacts, architectural salvage, wrought iron, period lighting, and lovely linens. Outside, a fence surrounds the work-in-progress yard and garden—displaying an array of **perennials, vintage roses, trees, shrubs, and whimsical container plantings,** all for sale! Among the cache, you'll find a small but creative selection of gardening books, tools, baskets, and gifts for the gardener. The only thing missing is the latte stand, but you'll find that around the corner. . . .

MOOREHAVEN WATER GARDENS ✳

3006 York Road, Everett, WA 98204 | **Phone:** (425) 743-6888 | **Fax:** (425) 514-5488 | **Email:** Cmoore1023@aol.com | **Web:** www.moorehaven.com | **Directions:** From Hwy 99, turn west on Hwy 525 (Mukilteo Speedway); turn right onto Beverly Park Road, then right on York Road; the nursery is about 1 block on the right. | **Open:** Daily

Tucked back in a peaceful, wooded neighborhood is one of this area's finest **water garden** nurseries. If this place seems familiar, it's probably because you've seen Chris and Val Moore's numerous water garden wonderlands at the Northwest Flower and Garden Show. Here, you can wander their 4 acres of raised "water beds" and ponds, the greenhouse "conservatory," the mature permanent gardens, and the **aviaries** (pining for a peacock or a partridge?). You'll love the wide selection of aquatic plants, as well as the amazing choice of domestic and imported **koi,** goldfish, and tadpoles. Moorehaven also offers statuary, ponds, liners, pumps, and pond equipment, books, and, of course, excellent advice. The new website offers downloadable information sheets—a free and handy resource.

MOUNTAIN MEADOW NURSERY

7236 132nd Avenue NE, Kirkland, WA 98033 | **Phone:** (425) 454-3766 or (425) 885-0785 | **Email:** nancyshort@aol.com | **Directions:** From I-405 going north, take NE 70th Street exit 17 and travel east on NE 70th Street about 1 mile to 132nd Avenue NE and turn left. The nursery is on the east side of the street. From I-5 going south, take the Redmond exit 18, which puts you on NE 85th Street. Travel east to 132nd Avenue NE at a traffic signal, and turn right onto 132nd NE; the nursery will be on your left. | **Open:** By appointment only | **Plant list:** Free upon request

This small backyard family nursery is the dream of Nancy Davidson Short, made real with the enthusiastic complicity of daughter and son-in-law—Mary Anne (the propagator par excellence) and George (resident man of all work) Le Doux. The real passion here is for **Northwest natives, especially ferns:** maidenhair, deer fern, oak fern, *Woodwardia fimbriata*, the Oregon Chain fern, sword ferns, and more. Also find native ground covers like *Cornus canadensis, Oxalis oregana,* and *Dicentra formosa,* and shrubs like *Ribes sanguineum, Philadelphus lewisii,* and *Mahonia aquifolium.* Mountain Meadow also offers plants that combine readily with naturalistic landscaping and that are compatible with Northwest natives, including Japanese maples, half a dozen different epimediums, tiarellas, and mahonias. This trio is always on the hunt for the more difficult yet very worthy native plants, especially ground covers and shrubs. The display garden is coming along; while plants are still young, they are spreading and show off well—enough to give you a good feeling about the plants you choose to bring home. Natives, of course, take center stage. These gardens feature the amazing range of that most glorious of Northwest colors, green, and are thus handsome through all the seasons.

MSK RARE PLANT NURSERY ✳

20312 15th Avenue NW, Shoreline, WA 98177 | **Phone:** (206) 546-1281 | **Open:** By appointment only

This is a **very special nursery** and well worth calling for an appointment. Mareen Kruckeberg specializes in plants native to temperate-climate countries. All stock is grown in the nursery. Original seeds and cuttings come from all over the world. Find perennials, rock garden plants, ground covers, evergreen oaks, ferns, unusual deciduous trees and conifers, and natives other nurseries do not carry, such as their miniature troughs and other imaginative containers, all beautifully planted. Annually the nursery hosts a **Mother's Day Sale,** Friday, Saturday, and Sunday, 9 a.m.–6 p.m. Thanks to a conservation easement, the 4-acre Kruckeberg site has now been preserved as a Botanic Garden.

MT. TAHOMA NURSERY ✳

28111 112th Avenue E, Graham, WA 98338 | **Phone:** (253) 847-9827 | **Email:** rlupp@aol.com | **Web:** www.backyardgardener.com/mttahoma | **Directions:** From I-5, take the Hwy 512 east exit, and travel east. From Hwy 512 (Valley Freeway), take the exit onto Hwy 161 (Meridian Avenue E), go south through Graham to 280th Street SE, and turn left, then go to 112th Avenue E, and turn left. | **Open:** By appointment only. | **Catalog:** $2, shipping year-round

Since 1986 specialist grower Rick Lupp has run a small nursery, offering a lovely selection of **choice rock garden and woodland plants** and Washington State **native alpines,** as well as plants from faraway places. Small shrubs and dwarf conifers are ideal for those gardening with space restrictions. All plants are on their own roots (not grafted) and have been grown in this moderate climate, with lowest temperatures around minus 5°F). Rick specializes in androsace, dwarf campanula, fall gentiana, primula, and dwarf shrubs. You will also find a wide selection of troughs for rock garden plantings. When you visit, tour the raised alpine beds, best seen March and June (although walking is a bit rough on the trail).

MUNRO'S NURSERY

7622 Simonds Road NE, Kenmore, WA 98028 | **Phone:** (425) 488-1141 | **Fax:** Same | **Email:** mmunro@wolfenet.com | **Directions:** Head northeast from Seattle on Lake City Way/Bothell Way. Turn right on 68th Avenue NE in Kenmore, then left on NE 170th, which becomes Simonds Road NE. The nursery is less than 1 mile up the hill on the left. Look closely: there is no sign out front except a simple "Plant Sale" sign. Look for the ever-changing plant display. | **Open:** Daily, appointment recommended | **Plant list:** Free, via email request; wholesale and retail.

You may have run across Munro's Nursery at the Northwest Flower and Garden Show (and area plant sales); now it's possible to buy direct from Jerry Munro year-round. The nursery is at the Munro homestead in Kenmore, and features some trees and shrubs Jerry began planting here in 1934, so this nursery has been in continuous operation for more than 50 years. Blooming and foliage displays begin in March and look fabulous through the fall. Munro's specializes in perennials, including **many woodland natives, with hardy new shrub and tree introductions from around the world.** Stock includes numerous trillium species, hostas, meconopsis, dicentra, and corydalis, many propagated on site. Munro's offers manglietia, michelia, and other rare Magnolia relatives, taiwania, styrax relatives, cunninghamia, and hamamelis relatives.

NAYLOR CREEK NURSERY ✳ ✉ @

2610 W Valley Road, Chimacum, WA 98325 | **Phone:** (360) 732-4983 | **Fax:** (360) 732-7171 | **Email:** naylorck@olypen.com | **Web:** www.naylorcreek.com (order online, see tempting photos of the nursery, find map, jump in car . . .) | **Directions:** From the Hood Canal Bridge take SR 104 approximately 5 miles to the Port Townsend exit. Turn right onto Beaver Valley Road and proceed to and through Chimacum. Don't blink until you see the school on the left, then turn left onto W Valley Road, then go 2.6 miles. From Port Townsend take SR 20 south to Four Corners, turn left to Chimacum, and at the school turn right onto W Valley Road. | **Open:** Seasonal and by appointment | **Catalog:** $2, some color; shipping season mid-March–October; wholesale and retail.

Jack Hirsch and Gary Lindheimer specialize in shade-tolerant perennials. **Hostas** lead the pack with over 800 varieties (by any reasonable standard this is major hosta-mania!). Over the past decade-plus these mad collectors have been assembling their hoard of rare species, new hybrid introductions, and old standards. But visitors also flock here for the very fine selection of **shade-loving companion plants**: astilbes, arisaemas, hellebores, pulmonarias (50 varieties), and epimediums, to name some stars from their impressive lineup. There's also a stunning new introduction of theirs called *Brunnera macrophylla* 'Silver Wings'—wow! To provide their customers with well-established plants the following season, the owners make divisions in fall, 75 percent of them from their own stock plants. Their raised-bed garden will provide much to ponder with "1,000s of plants on display." Access on foot is easy, in an idyllic country setting. If you think you struggle with a shady garden, liberate you imagination with a visit to Naylor Creek Nursery.

NELSON RHODODENDRONS AND AZALEAS

706 Sapp Road, Sedro-Woolley, WA 98284 | **Phone:** (360) 856-0138 | **Directions:** From I-5, take exit 232 east on Cook Road to Sedro-Woolley. Turn left at the first traffic light and left at the second traffic light. Go less than 1 mile and turn left on Sapp Road. The nursery is on the right. | **Open:** Seasonal, and by appointment

If you are a **rhododendron, azalea,** and **kalmia** aficionado and a believer in the quality of field-grown plants, you will undoubtedly appreciate the work of Bernard and Karol Nelson in providing so many hardy specimens for your perusal. Here you will find a mind-boggling selection, from dwarf to medium to tall growth habits, with both newer hybrids and old favorites. As you speak to the Nelsons, members of the American Rhododendron Society since 1965, you'll have the opportunity to consult with two highly respected growers who have propagated their own plants at this specialized nursery since 1971.

NORA'S NURSERY

5761 Cape George Road, Port Townsend, WA 98368 | **Phone:** (360) 379-3920 | **Fax:** Same | **Email:** orders@norasnursery.com | **Web:** www.norasnursery.com | **Directions:** Provided when you schedule an appointment. | **Open:** By appointment only | **Plant list:** Extensive list on website

Nora's is a specialty nursery growing **unusual, hard-to-find perennials, herbs, grasses, shrubs, and vines.** Many cultivars are selected for desirable qualities such as foliage, color, and growth habit. Historically interesting plants, originally grown for dye material, as well as medicinal and fragrance varieties—and/or bird and butterfly magnets—are also featured. Recently, Nora's absorbed the healthy and interesting plant inventory of the former Woodside Gardens in Chimacum, Washington, expanding Nora's offerings by more than 200 varieties. Nora's goes beyond plants, as it is a small farm raising sheep, goats, llamas, and rabbits for the spinnable fiber they produce (with wool, mohair, cashmere, angora, and llama fiber available for purchase). You can also find "homegrown" blankets and other items here.

NOTHING BUT NORTHWEST NATIVES

14836 NE 249th Street, Battle Ground, WA 98604 | **Phone:** (360) 666-3023 | **Fax:** Same | **Email:** nwplants@teleport.com | **Web:** www.teleport.com/~nwplants/ | **Directions:** From I-5, take the exit east for Battle Ground. From Battle Ground, take Hwy 503 north to 244th Street, and turn right. At the stop sign turn left onto 132nd Avenue, then turn right onto NE 249th Street. Continue east past the stop sign about 1 mile to the nursery. | **Open:** Seasonal, and by appointment. | **Plant list:** Free

Kali Robson, proprietor/botanist, and manager Tom Henn have started a new nursery (1998) that specializes, as the name so aptly suggests, in **nothing but Northwest natives.** A look at NBNN's plant list shows you it's a great primer for native choices: ferns, many wonderful perennials, including *Aruncus sylvester, Erigeron glaucus, Mimulus lewisii, Sedum oreganum,* and *Trillium ovatum;* shrubs: *Amelanchier alnifolia, Garrya elliptica,* and *Ribes sanguineum;* conifers: *Abies grandis, Pinus ponderosa,* and *Tsuga heterophylla.* Kali and Tom both come from very strong academic and career backgrounds in botany and natural resource management. Their plant progeny include a strong listing of perennial, shrub, and tree species, and they actively seek out species to add to their list of **plants that are difficult to find in nurseries.** When you visit, take in the rock garden and woodland and pond displays for inspiring ideas. They feature plants to attract birds and butterflies, plus those that help in erosion control and restoration. Check the website or call for special workshops (usually timed to coincide with Open House weekends at nearby Collector's Nursery and at the Clark County Home & Garden Idea Fair in April. NBNN also offers workshops at Interstate Rock Products. (See Chapter 9, "Products, Materials, & Professional Services.")

NO THYME PRODUCTIONS

8321 SE 61st Street, Mercer Island, WA 98040 | **Phone:** (206) 236-8885 | **Fax:** (206) 230-8685 | **Email:** info@nothyme.com | **Web:** www.nothyme.com | **Open:** By appointment only, directions provided (plus, "Mercer Island is small," Nancy says). | **Catalog:** Free; shipping for plants late March to late October; non-plant items, year-round.

Any catalog that declares boldly on the cover, "Plants lovingly grown to the music of Bach and Joni Mitchell, pesticide free" is enough to win your heart from the get-go. Said catalog is fun to peruse for its charming illustrations, too. What began as catalog art has inspired a new aspect to her business: "Books you shouldn't live without." You can order great herb-gardening books (like *Growing 101 Herbs that Heal*) and nonfiction writers like Beverley Nichols (an Englishman, writer, and a great garden enthusiast). Nancy sprinkles words of wisdom here and there that invoke little chuckles, "May this spring find you content with your garden. I hope you are able to spend many hours with your hands busy in the dirt as your mind is free to travel wherever it pleases."

Herbs, of which there are over 300 here, ranging

from the obscure to culinary standbys, are $3 each. As with most of us, Nancy falls head over heels for some snazzy plant, then goes gung-ho growing as many varieties as she can. Mints, scented geraniums, and sages are the stars of this catalog, as are herbal collections for those interested in starting their own kitchen gardens. Tender perennials include *Polygonum odoratum* (Vietnamese coriander), *Stevia rebaudiana*, and *Leonotus nepetifolia*. She offers a select offering of seeds, including Renee's Garden and Botanical Interests.

OASIS WATER GARDENS ☀ ✉

404 S Brandon Street, Seattle, WA 98108 | **Phone:** (206) 767-9776 | **Fax:** (206) 767-0906 | **Directions:** From I-5, take Corson-Michigan exit 161, go west on Michigan to 4th Avenue S, turn right (north) to S Brandon, then turn right. | **Open:** Weekdays (closed Monday) | **Plant list:** Free; shipping March–September

Whether you are populating a pond (**koi and goldfish**) or planting a bog or wetland with web-footed water lovers (over 100 varieties to choose from), looking for the sensory pleasure a fountain brings to a garden, or are gussying up a water feature with **exotic water lilies** (50 varieties to choose from, both hardy and tropical, not to mention lotus), here is an excellent place to start. Owners Dianne and Bob Torgerson will enthusiastically field your questions or leave you to ponder on your own. Look also to Oasis for your **pond and water feature supplies** and equipment and check with Dianne on class offerings. What's new? A large selection of rose granite lanterns, pagodas, and water basins and a large selection of ceramic urns and water basins. In the greenhouse you will surely be charmed by the large population of fire belly toads, barking tree frogs, Pacific Northwest tree frogs, a bronze frog, and one each of the southern and northern leopard frogs.

OLYMPIC COAST GARDEN

500 N. Sequim Avenue, Sequim, WA 98382 | **Phone:** (360) 683-6244 | **Fax:** (360) 683-0675 | **Email:** Olympic_coast@tenforward.com | **Directions:** From Hwy 101 in Sequim, take the main interchange onto Sequim Avenue traveling north (toward the water) to the corner of Sequim Avenue and Fir Street (across the street from the high school). | **Open:** Daily, closed Sunday in off-season

Roger Pierce, the very knowledgeable plantsman who originally founded Olympic Coast Garden as a mail-order nursery specializing in field-grown perennials, moved the business into its present location in 1998—creating an all-purpose retail nursery. He and his wife Susan combine their vast experience, creating and selling **hanging baskets** (for which they propagate many unusual trailing plants not available from other growers), 'Martha Washington' or 'Regal' geraniums (they grow a wide assortment of 600 each season), and fuchsias, bedding plants, vegetable seedlings, and perennials. The nursery offers Territorial, Renee's Garden, Ed Hume, and Lilly Miller seed collections, along with good general

nursery fare like bagged soil, a wide range of pots, organic fertilizers, pest- and disease-controlling products (stressing environmentally safe choices like their favorite, "Sun-Oil," a horticultural oil that does a good job of killing pests), plus weekly deliveries of new houseplants. "An important part of what we do is trying to help anyone who comes into the store with helpful advice or to diagnose problems on any garden question they might have," Roger says.

There are actually two display gardens to visit, with one at Olympic Coast's "holding nursery," at 219 S Sequim Avenue. It features climbing roses, with mixed perennials and ornamental grasses, and it's packed with color from mid-spring to mid-fall. If you're in search of sweet-smelling plants, this garden offers night-scented stocks, winter honeysuckle, and true valerian . . . all of which can be appreciated from the city sidewalk in front of the garden. At the main nursery there are other displays, varying with each season. If you are puttering around the Olympic Peninsula, stop by to check them out!

OLYMPIC NURSERY

16507 140th Place NE, Woodinville, WA 98072 | **Phone:** (425) 483-9254 or (800) 570-8883 | **Fax:** (425) 485-9451 | **Email:** sales@olympicnursery.com | **Web:** www.olympicnursery.com | **Directions:** From Hwy 522 east, take the Woodinville/Hwy 202 exit. Turn right after exiting. At the traffic signal on NE 175th Street, turn left onto NE 175th. At the traffic signal at 140th Pl NE, turn right. The nursery is on the right at about 0.2 mile. | **Open:** Daily

This is a good source to check when you are looking for **larger-caliper trees** (2-inch and up for deciduous trees) and tall evergreens (which run in the range of 6 to 18 feet—instant screening when you need it). Olympic redesigns its display garden each year, and so you can find lots of ideas for landscaping with large deciduous and evergreen trees, large shrubs, native and wetland plants, and privacy plantings. Delivery and installation are available, as is a special-order service. Certified arborists are on staff too. If you can wait until October, call for details on a "huge" fall clearance sale—great tree bargains. Live Christmas trees in season.

OUDEAN'S WILLOW CREEK NURSERY

7421 137th Avenue SE, Snohomish, WA 98290-9022 | **Phone:** (360) 568-6024 | **Fax:** (360) 568-4904 | **Email:** cambrp@premier1.net | **Web:** www.oudeanswillowcreeknursery.com | **Directions:** From downtown Snohomish, follow Second Street east over Hwy 2, then turn left onto 131st Avenue SE, then right onto 84th SE at the Dutch Hill Elementary School, left onto 139th Avenue SE, left onto 80th SE, right onto 137th Avenue SE, and follow the road past the end of the pavement 300 feet along the gravel road. | **Open:** Weekends, or by appointment | **Plant list:** Free with SASE, or on the website; wholesale and retail; year-round shipping with possible 1-2 week delay in bad weather conditions.

Oudean's has fine-tuned its specialty to all genera of **carnivorous plants** (hardy and tropical, indoor and outdoor varieties). They have added many species carnivorous plants, especially sarracenia, pitcher plants. (See a wonderful display in bloom at Oudean's greenhouse in April and outdoors during the summer and early fall.) Did you know you can buy seeds from Oudean's own sarracenia hybrids and species? The nursery propagates 80 percent of its own plants (20 percent of the stock comes from tissue culture grown on from 6 months to 2 years). You'll find an all-red Venus fly trap introduction from the Atlanta Botanical Garden, *Dionaea muscipula* 'Akai Ryu' ('Red Dragon'), and ten new species and hybrid nepenthes, plus Mexican butterworts, the pinguicula. Oudean's also has **bog display gardens, many creative container gardens** (make your own bog), and offers lots of free care sheets detailing carnivorous plant cultural information. Individual questions are happily answered by phone, in person, or via email.

PARIS GARDENS (SEE ROSEHIP FARM & GARDEN)

PAT CALVERT GREENHOUSE

2300 Arboretum Drive East, Seattle, WA 98112-2300 | **Phone:** (206) 325-4510 | **Fax:** (206) 325-8893 | **Email:** Gvc@arboretum foundation.org | **Directions:** See directions in Chapter 13, "Gardens to Visit" | **Open:** Year-round, Tuesday, 10 a.m.–noon; and the first Saturday of the month, April–September, 10 a.m.–2 p.m.

Located adjacent to the Graham Visitors Center at the Washington Park Arboretum, the propagation team here offers starter plants of rhododendrons, ground covers, perennials, bonsai, camellias, conifers and other trees, and shrubs. There are many **choice varieties selected from plants in the Arboretum.** Some examples are callicarpas, daphnes, eucryphias, euonymus, hydrangeas, ilex (hollies), magnolias, rose species, sorbus, stewartia, syringas (lilacs), and viburnums. There is a 6 x 100-foot perennial border by the Greenhouse specializing in drought-tolerant plants (maintained by the volunteers). This is an all-volunteer-run facility sponsored by the Arboretum Foundation and moneys earned go back to support Arboretum projects. You, as a Foundation member, have the enviable opportunity to spend time here learning and practicing propagation. Requests are accepted, as time and difficulty dictate, to propagate something for you from the Arboretum collection. The Greenhouse will be open for sales during the annual Arboretum Foundation Book Sale in March, at the FLORAbundance Plant Sale in April, and at the October Bulb Sale, at the Graham Visitor Center at the Arboretum.

PAUL SAYERS LANDSCAPING AND NURSERY ✽

24612 132nd Street SE, Monroe, WA 98272 | **Phone:** (360) 794-5777 | **Fax:** Same | **Directions:** From I-5 in Everett, take the Hwy 2 exit east to Monroe; follow Hwy 2 through downtown Monroe to the last stoplight in town and turn left at Old Owen/Main Street. Follow past Monroe Golf Course, and when the road reaches a "Y," veer left onto Florence Acres Road. Follow to dead-end; Paul Sayers is on the left side, almost to the end. From I-405, take the Woodinville/Monroe exit onto Hwy 522 heading east, and follow

to the last Monroe exit. At the light, turn left onto Hwy 2, heading east. Follow Hwy 2 to the last light in town, turn left at Old Owen/Main Street, and proceed as noted above. | **Open:** Saturdays only, March–June, or by appointment. | **Plant list:** Upon request; wholesale and retail.

This charming, small family business began in 1994 with landscaping as the main emphasis; the nursery evolved as Paul and Gwen Sayers sought to provide healthy plant stock for their landscaping clients. Gwen began expanding the nursery side of things by propagating a wide array of perennials to help fill the beds and display gardens Paul designed. Soon the number and variety of perennials grew to the point where she could sell extras to other gardeners. For the past several springs, Gwen has opened for business each Saturday, selling perennials she propagates to neighbors, garden clubs, and people who see her sandwich boards along the old highway and decide to follow them (what plant maniac wouldn't do that?). You can expect to find **delphiniums, poppies, lupines, ornamental artichokes, and euphorbias, along with starts for cutting gardens and a variety of water plants.** Ornamental trees, shrubs, rhododendrons, azaleas, flowering cherries, and plum trees are also available. The Sayers also sell a select lineup of supplies and garden equipment, trellises, obelisks, hanging baskets, benches, and birdbaths.

This nursery's best-kept secret is a magical display garden at the back of the property, where Paul shows off his many talents in water-garden design and landscaping. You are invited to wander along paths, over bridges, and around a sizeable pond—and to marvel at a beautiful waterfall display. A second display area with koi ponds and water plants is in the works. Most of these two displays are easily accessible. Enjoy the explosion of perennials in mid-May, but remember the gardens are beautiful here year-round.

PENINSULA GARDENS

5503 Wollochet Drive NW, Gig Harbor, WA 98335 | **Phone:** (253) 851-8115 | **Fax:** (253) 851-8104 | **Email:** pengard@ix.netcom.com | **Web:** www.peninsulagardens.com | **Directions:** Take I-5 to westbound Hwy 16, follow until you cross over the Narrows Bridge. Take the Gig Harbor City Center exit, then a left to go over the overpass. The gardens are on the left side of the road, approximately 1.5 miles. | **Open:** Daily

For 23 years Peninsula Gardens has been bringing its high-quality selection of plants, gardening supplies, and gifts to Gig Harbor customers. In addition to the emphasis on great plants, owners Marlin and Bette Cram put a priority on customer service, and have a knowledgeable staff that helps customers in any horticultural endeavor. **Water gardening supplies** (including fish) are a specialty here. Visit the newly remodeled garden gift center and try out the patio furniture department. The nursery website is packed with information and details on seasonal classes and events. This is a special find, whether you're living on the peninsula or just visiting there.

PEPPER'S GREENHOUSE & NURSERY

11973 Havekost Road, Anacortes, WA 98221 | **Phone:** (360) 293-2213 | **Email:** bacopa@pioneernet.net | **Directions:** Take Hwy 20 to Anacortes. Turn left at the first traffic light (onto 32nd) and left at the stop sign onto "D" Street, which becomes Havekost Road. Go 2.5 miles and turn left at the nursery sign, following the drive through the woods and keeping to the left. | **Open:** Seasonal and by appointment

This is a delightful spot, tucked back off the road in a cleared site surrounded by woods. For 27 years Judy Pepper has provided her faithful clientele at this family-run nursery with an *excellent* selection of annuals and custom **hanging baskets,** pots and potting soil, fertilizer, statuary, and stepping-stones. Come the holidays, you'll find living and fresh-cut trees and fresh wreaths. A small but lovely display garden here always catches your interest.

PERENNIAL GARDENS

4221 South Pass Road, Everson, WA 98247 | **Phone:** (360) 966-2330 | **Directions:** From Everson, take the main street east (becomes South Pass Road). Watch for the nursery on the right. | **Open:** Year-round, drop-ins welcome. To be sure someone is on-site, it's best to call ahead for an appointment. "I'm open any time I'm here—and that's most of the time," Donna says.

Enjoy a relaxing drive out into the country and drop in to pick up something for your garden from the large selection of healthy, field- and container-grown plants sold by Donna Jensen, a veteran gardener with 50-plus years of experience that she freely shares. While small in terms of personnel, this is one of those specialty nurseries where customers have the opportunity to "talk plants and gardening" with the grower, with no pressure to purchase. Primarily you will find **perennials** ("herbaceous and woody, easy care, drought-tolerant, and different") but Donna also offers a selection of **ground covers and some woody plants.** Specialties are non-bearded irises, daylilies, true geraniums, some grasses, and heathers. If you're not convinced that it's possible to have a beautiful organic garden, here's a place to see how it's done. Perennial Gardens practices the art of self-sustaining gardening: mulch well with compost in a well-prepared bed, and use as few chemicals and as little water as possible. Donna will recycle your extra pots and hanging baskets.

PETERSEN'S PERENNIALS

7802 67th Avenue SE, Snohomish, WA 98290 | **Phone:** (425) 334-3685 | **Directions:** From I-5, take exit 194 onto Hwy 2, then take a right turn from the trestle onto Homeacres Road. Go to 52nd Street SE, turn left (at the "T"), and continue up the hill, past the church, then turn right at the second stop sign. Turn right onto 78th Street SE. They're on the left, next corner. | **Open:** Seasonal and by appointment

Karen Petersen describes her nursery as evolving from "desk to dirt" as she gave up her office job of 15 years to offer a specialty in **"hard-to-find perennials."** You'll find over 70 varieties in gallon containers, and she has also selected shrubs that make compatible partnerships in perennial borders. Display beds bordering the entrance to the garden provide a chance to assess how plants available in the nursery do in a garden setting and settled in with their companions.

PIRIFORMIS

1031 N 35th Street, Seattle, WA 98103 | **Phone:** (206) 632-1760 | **Fax:** (206) 632-5682 | **Web:** www.piriformis.com | **Directions:** From I-5 take the 45th Street exit 196 and travel west on 45th. Drive through the Wallingford District to the traffic signal at Stone Way, and turn left (south) to N 35th. Turn right (west) a block or so to the nursery. | **Open:** Daily

This pint-sized nursery specializes in **low-maintenance (drought-tolerant and low-water-use) plants,** but its charming and talented owner Tory Galloway has also garnered a following among gardeners looking for innovative planting schemes, inspiration for winter garden designs, and a quirky selection of salvaged farm implements and antique "junk" (you know, the things that reincarnate as garden art). For 13 years a landscape contractor, Tory and her colleagues won a coveted gold medal at the 2001 Northwest Flower and Garden Show for designing a winter garden that looks like Seattle really does in the winter. Kudos, and here's to more wonderful flower show displays! You will also find unusual and tasteful stepping-stones, for instance, and handsome garden ornaments created by local crafts(wo)men. Tory also offers new and used tools, potting soil, compost, and fertilizers. There are many changing displays, but you'll always find inspiration for the garden in the parking strip along the nursery's border—it proves that drought-tolerant does NOT have to be dull. If you have a specific question on a tricky garden site, visit the Piriformis website for a neat "search" program. Type in "dry shade" and see what pops up.

PLANTASIA SPECIALTY NURSERY & DISPLAY GARDENS ❋ @

3938 88th Avenue SW, Olympia, WA 98512 | **Phone:** (360) 754-4321 | **Fax:** (360) 956-9228 | **Email:** plantasiagardens@home.com | **Web:** www.plantasiagardens.com | **Directions:** From I-5, take exit 101 south of Tumwater, then take Air-Industrial Way west. At the traffic signal turn left onto Littlerock Road and go 2 miles. At 88th Avenue SW turn right (west) and watch for nursery sign on the right. | **Open:** Saturdays; the display gardens are open April–July and September. | **Plant list:** $7 color catalog, or free online.

The specialized nursery stock available here includes pond plants, perennials, uncommon shrubs, rock garden plants and, for collectors, hardy geraniums, pulmonarias, ferns, hostas, and lavender. And to give their visitors a look at how they have used these plants, Evonne and Mark Peryea open their acre-plus garden each year to the public to inspire home gardeners with what they call "the do-able." You will find **15 specialty gardens** (plus 8 water features) here, including a moon garden; Celtic garden; herb, sedum, and rock displays; a hydrangea island, and more. Then there's a dwarf conifer garden, an arboretum, a perennial garden, and an annual cutting garden. Especially fun for children and for those with a sense of whimsy, the garden ornaments on hand range from an alligator, turtle, giant snail, fairies, and angels to gargoyles and a large Buddha. There is a garden gift shop here too, with home and garden décor, water fountains, and pond plants. A recently added website is a true "plantasia," with 8,000 items offered online (including Renee's and Select Seeds and others). Design, installation, and delivery services are offered. A 38,000-entry garden encyclopedia is a great reference tool you'll return to frequently. Best of all, you can visit this place of magic in person.

PLANTS OF THE WILD ✉ @

PO Box 866, Tekoa, WA 99033 | **Phone:** (509) 284-2848 | **Fax:** (509) 284-6464 | **Email:** Kathy@plantsofthewild.com | **Web:** www.plantsofthewild.com | **Open:** Weekdays, by appointment only | **Catalog:** Free; shipping year-round; wholesale and retail.

This nursery (in far eastern Washington) specializes in **native plants,** many of which are appropriate to westside gardens. You'll find the catalog is well organized and offers brief but useful plant descriptions. This would be an excellent source for plants for naturalistic gardening, erosion control, land reclamation, and wildlife shelter. Plants offered include vines, ground covers, wildflowers, bunchgrass, small and large shrubs, deciduous trees, and conifers. Prices are very reasonable. Fabulous and informative website.

PLETHORA OF PRIMULA

244 Westside Hwy, Vader, WA 98593 | **Phone:** (360) 295-3114 | **Catalog:** $2

While April Boettger has been on her own as POP for a few years now, she worked for several years with a highly respected primrose guru, the late Herb Dickson, at his Chehalis Rare Plant Nursery, where she learned a great deal about her beloved Primulaceae family, which includes the **auriculas** (her specialty). While most of us are accustomed to the pyrotechnics of the grocery-store variety of primroses, collectors and aficionados have loved these related botanical treasures achieved through the art of the master hybridizers, recently made more available from specialty growers. Novices would do well to send for April's catalog, which will provide a marvelous primer along with offering oodles of advice and enthusiasm. Find her also at the Olympia Farmer's Market Fridays and Saturdays in May and June and at plant sales in Washington and Oregon.

POLLOCK AND SON'S

7901 NE 179th Street, Battle Ground, WA 98604 | **Phone:** (360) 573-6370 | **Fax:** (360) 574-2862 | **Web:** www.specialtynursery.com | **Directions:** From I-5, take the 179th Street exit east (near Clark County Fairgrounds). Travel 3.25 miles on NE 179th Street; find the nursery at the corner of NE 72nd Avenue. | **Open:** Daily except Sunday (closed December–February, when you can call for appointment).

Collectors' quality Japanese maples and unique conifers are the stars of this Vancouver-area nursery, sit-

uated on 6 acres. Debbie and Bob Pollock and their sons display a beautiful collection of amazing plants, with over 125 varieties of Japanese maples—from 1 gallon to specimen size. Laceleafs, variegated, dwarf, and other varieties will wow you. Plus, you'll find rhododendrons, native plants, perennials and annuals, dogwoods, magnolias, and plants for wildlife, along with hanging baskets and containers. The nursery offers landscape design consulting and installation.

PORTLAND AVENUE NURSERY

1409 E 59th Street, Tacoma, WA 98404 | **Phone:** (253) 473-0194 | **Fax:** (253) 473-4178 | **Directions:** From I-5 southbound, take exit 135 to Portland Avenue; head south to E 59th. From I-5 northbound, take exit 134 and head south on Portland Avenue to E 59th. | **Open:** Daily

This 3-acre urban oasis in the heart of Tacoma specializes in **Japanese maples and unique and unusual conifers.** Here's where you'll find an excellent selection of trees, shrubs, roses, and perennials. A complete garden center also features cedar furniture and statuary. The year-round displays will inspire you.

PUGET SOUND KIWI COMPANY

1220 NE 90th Street, Seattle, WA 98115 | **Phone:** (206) 523-6403 | **Fax:** Same | **Email:** kiwibob@umailme.com | **Open:** By appointment only | **Catalog:** Free for a SASE; free informative brochures on growing kiwifruit and figs

Bob Glanzman is a noted **kiwifruit** (*Actinidia deliciosa*) enthusiast and offers the widest selection of actinidia species (*A. kolomikta, polygama, arguta,* and *melanandra*) scions around. Bob is the coordinator of the North American Fruit Explorers Kiwi Interest Group (www.nafex.org) and assistant editor of the *Kiwifruit Enthusiasts Journal,* an exhaustive tome on the topic. He offers kiwi plants, kiwi books, and now offers fig trees suited to the Puget Sound climate.

PURPLE HAZE LAVENDER

180 Bell Bottom Road, Sequim, WA 98382 | **Phone:** (360) 683-1714 or (888) 852-6560 | **Fax:** (360) 681-5427 | **Email:** info@purplehazelavender.com | **Web:** www.purplehaze lavender.com (you can almost inhale the mesmerizing fragrance of lavender when you visit this attractive site) | **Directions:** From Hwy 101 in Sequim, turn onto West Sequim Bay Road (west of Visitor Center), and drive about 1 mile to Bell Bottom Road. | **Open:** Daily | Product **Catalog:** No shipping on plants; wholesale and retail.

The Olympic Peninsula's reputation for all things lavender is well-known—just call it "Provence West." Among the many fragrant farms is Purple Haze, run by growers Mike and Jadyne Reichner. Their 5-acre certified organic farm located in the Dungeness Valley is in an ideal climate for growing the **40 varieties of lavender** here. Choose from angustifolias, lavandins, stoechas, and lantanas, among others. New is the "Purple Haze Collection" of hard-to-propagate lavenders: 'Lodden blue', 'Royal velvet', 'Hidcote giant', 'Sachet seal', and

'Melissa'. The nursery sells lavender plants, and you can come to pick your own bouquets from June into September. There are weekend classes with an amazing array of topics to teach and inspire you in the hundreds of uses to which you can put that bouquet of lavender! The shop features **lavender-inspired products,** from the culinary (Herbs de Provence) to relaxing sachets, lotions, and oils. If you have a group of willing friends, consider organizing a retreat or customized class, as the handsome new Drying Shed is a novel, cozy, and fragrant place to gather.

RAFT ISLAND ROSES, NURSERY AND GARDEN

7201 Rosedale Street NW, Gig Harbor, WA 98335 | **Phone:** (253) 265-3647 | **Directions:** From I-5 take the Hwy 16 exit 132 and travel west; drive over the Tacoma Narrows Bridge and proceed 3 miles to the Gig Harbor City Center exit. At the end of the exit ramp proceed directly across to Stinson Avenue. Follow Stinson for 0.5 mile. Near the bottom of the hill at a 4-way stop, turn left onto Rosedale Street and travel west on Rosedale for 2 miles. The nursery is on the right. | **Open:** Daily | **Plant list:** Rose list free with SASE

The nursery boasts **10,000 rose shrubs, with a specialty in miniatures,** and about one-third of the inventory is own-root roses. Here you will find hanging roses and other types of flowering baskets, old garden roses, hybrid teas, floribundas, polyanthas, climbers, and ground-cover roses, including a great number that are non-patented. Frank and Mike Gatto have experienced many years of rose growing and care and they display their love of roses throughout the garden in a number of vignettes (including climbing roses). This specialty nursery also carries 100 varieties of fuchsias, heathers, annuals, and perennials—great companions for roses. Call for details on the annual rose festival.

RAINSHADOW GARDENS

6298 S Double Bluff Road, Freeland, WA 98249 | **Phone:** (360) 321-8003 | **Directions:** On Whidbey Island; from the north, drive down the island's main thoroughfare, Hwy 20, which turns into Hwy 525. About 1 mile past Freeland turn right (west) on Double Bluff Road and go about 2 miles to the gardens' steep driveway uphill on your right. From the south (Seattle), take the Mukilteo ferry to Clinton and proceed north on Hwy 525 about 8 miles; turn left on Double Bluff Road to the RainShadow driveway on the right. | **Open:** Seasonal and by appointment

Rising from the richly enhanced soil of a former dairy farm, and with a spectacular view west from a bluff overlooking Useless Bay and the Cascade Mountains, this small nursery offers a warm welcome; the owners have a genuine desire to talk about interesting plants. Anne Davenport and partner John Holbron, Jr., specialize in the plants they love, primarily **unusual trees and shrubs,** with a smattering of uncommon perennials too. There are a number of display garden areas (including a large and impressive bonsai collection), and a nursery of worthy plants to consider making your own.

RAINSHADOW GREENHOUSE

205 W Washington Street, Sequim, WA 98382 | **Phone:** (360) 683-0919 | **Directions:** In the heart of Sequim at 2nd and Washington Streets. | **Open:** Daily (closed Sundays in winter)

This year-round garden shop and nursery is a unique and appealing destination in Port Townsend, so it draws locals and visitors alike. A great feature here is the selection of lifelike, full-sized **topiaries,** very beautifully crafted. If your visit is in the gardening season you'll find a full range of nursery fare, from roses to trees and shrubs as well as a good selection of perennials. In the more dreary months you'll cheer yourself with a fine collection of houseplants, poinsettias at the holidays, and the always visually clever displays. Horticulturist owner Lelani Wood describes her garden gift selection as "eclectic" (our favorite kind) and her shop's style as "Quite unique."

RAINTREE NURSERY

391 Butts Road, Morton, WA 98356 | **Phone:** (360) 496-6400 | **Fax:** (360) 496-6465, orders daily 10 a.m.–4:30 p.m. PST, toll free at (888) 770-8358. | **Email:** info@raintreenursery.com | **Web:** www.raintreenursery.com (online ordering encouraged) | **Directions:** 100 miles from Seattle or Portland, 57 miles south and east of Olympia; from I-5, take exit 71 onto Hwy 508 east, and travel 24 miles through beautiful countryside to Butts Road; turn left to the nursery (see the map in catalog and on website). | **Open:** Saturdays, year-round; open additional days December–May, and by appointment. | **Catalog:** Free and packed with great information. Shipping season is December–May; wholesale and retail.

Started in 1972 by Sam Benowitz, Raintree has supplied more than 1 million edible plants to Pacific Northwest gardeners since that time. By specializing in **organically grown, disease-resistant plants for gardens west of the Cascades,** Raintree has garnered a passionate following. The nursery offers a great, free catalog packed with wonderful information on growing the stock it carries—and more: tree fruits, vines, unusual fruits, subtropicals, nuts, bamboo, and landscaping plants (also rootstock, grafting tools and supplies, books on all aspects of home fruit production, fruit tree pots, amendments, and the like). Visit to see demonstration plantings of espaliers, tree pruning techniques (best viewed late winter through spring), and vines. Check the catalog for a great detailed discussion on hardiness zones from western Washington through western Oregon and the sub-zones they delineate for better variety selection. See the catalog or website for details about all-day classes each March and all-day Edible Landscaping seminars every spring. Summer visitors will see mature plantings in fruit and may be able to swing a taste testing! Annual season-end close-out sale, late April to early May (call for availability and prices).

RAVENNA GARDENS

2201 Queen Anne Avenue N, Seattle, WA 98119 | **Phone:** (206) 283-7091 | **Second location:** University Village, NE 45th at 25th

Avenue NE; (206) 729-7388 | **Web:** www.ravennagardens.com | **Open:** Daily

This wonderful plant and products outlet is dedicated to serving urban gardeners in Seattle and Portland. The creation of veteran retailer Gillian Mathews and her colleagues, Ravenna Gardens offers anyone a plant-buying treat. While plants are not at center stage, they are given a high priority when it comes to **careful selection and creative presentation,** thanks to Gillian's own active involvement in the Northwest horticultural scene—and thanks to her talented managers and buyers. In the spirit of a shop you'd see on the corner of some vibrant European city, Ravenna Gardens' plant racks, tables, and pots spill outdoors onto sidewalk space. Spring, summer, and early fall bring choice perennials and annuals; come harvest time, there will be gourmet, heirloom-style pumpkins and gourds. Holidays bring fresh, fragrant, and festive plants (freshly cut and living). At the University Village location you'll find a mini-nursery nestled under the oversized trellis and at each of the building's four entrances—you'll be surprised at the very diverse selection of plants in such a modest space. There are always **lovely ornamental trees and handsome shrubs,** burly wisteria and dwarf conifers intermingling with herbs, annuals, and a tasty array of perennials, all just right for an urban gardener with limited space as a selection consideration. **Containers filled with innovative plant combinations** give you ready-made garden choices, too. Ravenna Gardens carries Renee's and Thompson & Morgan seeds, plus a well-edited inventory of good-quality tools, garden ornamentation, and hard goods. On many Thursday evenings, you'll find local Master Gardeners on hand to answer questions or teach a class. Garden designer Mark Henry is a favorite of the folks at Ravenna Gardens, so be sure to take in one of his popular container design workshops when they're offered. The displays at both Seattle stores are thoughtfully and creatively executed and that's enough to make you want to visit—and succumb to a tempting plant or two!

RAVEN NURSERY

22370 Indianola Road, Poulsbo, WA 98370 | **Phone:** (360) 598-3323 | **Fax:** (360) 598-6610 | **Email:** tworaven@ix.netcom.com | **Open:** By appointment; directions provided at time an appointment is scheduled. | **Plant list:** For wholesale only (no list specifically for retail customers)

Beatrice Idris is a small grower of **maples** (*Acer* species—no cultivars of *A. palmatum*); **Abies species** (true fir), and a few other conifers; and some flowering trees, daylilies, and irises. She describes herself as by training a plant ecologist, and has planned her garden and nursery, on beautifully forested acreage in North Kitsap County, as a balanced, healthy ecosystem. Her garden features a fall display of maples; the extensive collection of daylilies bloom from June to August and the beardless iris collection shows best from April to June.

RHODODENDRON SPECIES BOTANICAL GARDEN

2525 S 336th Street, Federal Way, WA 98063 | **Phone:** (253) 838-4646 (Seattle callers) or (253) 927-6960 (Tacoma callers) | **Gift Shop/Plant Pavilion:** (253) 661-9377 | **Fax:** (253) 838-4686 | **Email:** rsf@rhodygarden.org | **Web:** www.rhodygarden.org | **Mailing address:** PO Box 3798, Federal Way, WA 98063-3798 | **Directions:** From I-5 from the north or south, take exit 143 going east to Weyerhaeuser Way S. Turn right, following the signs to the parking for the Botanical Garden; the garden's small entry lot offers a few handicapped parking spaces. | **Catalog:** $3.50 to nonmembers; a condensed fall catalog is free with SASE; shipping (or pickup) is available in the spring or fall. | **Open:** Seasonal; call for hours.

The plant-sales pavilion offers species rhododendrons propagated from the specimens in the **22-acre Botanical Garden,** which are joined by offerings of alpine plants, ferns, heathers, bamboo, roses, carnivorous plants, and bonsai starter plants. Because the plants sold here reflect the true fabric of the Botanical Garden, you have a splendid opportunity to view varieties in the context of a garden setting. Before disappearing into the garden, make a perusal of the quality selection of books and gifts offered in the gift shop. And if you didn't already know, ordering from the Rhododendron Species Foundation's fabulous **mail-order catalog of species rhododendrons** and companion plants is open to the public (with preference given to orders from RSF members). What an opportunity to obtain species rhododendrons not available or rarely found elsewhere. The handy listing includes "Species for Beginners," "Species with Fall Color," "Vireyas," "Fragrant Species," and "Species for Bonsai." The RSF also offers rhododendron species pollen.

THE RHODY RANCH NURSERY

3225 E Masters Road, Port Angeles, WA 98362 | **Phone:** (360) 457-9743 | **Email:** rhodyranch@tenforward.com | **Directions:** The nursery is 3 miles east of Port Angeles off Hwy 101. Turn north on Masters Road, just east of Kmart, and travel to the end. | **Open:** Daily except Sunday; closed in winter except by appointment. | **Catalog:** $2, refundable with purchase; well organized by color

Formerly known as A&R Propagating, this nursery on the north Olympic Peninsula features a 4.5-acre display garden developed by the late Dr. Francis J. Skerbeck and his son Andy Skerbeck. The **display garden** here features several hundred species and hybrid rhododendrons and azaleas, as well as heather, kalmia, birch, chamaecyparis, and a host of ornamental and native plants. The displays are especially noteworthy for giving you a glimpse of how young plants will look at maturity. The **nursery** offers nearly 300 varieties of rhododendrons and azaleas, plus ground covers, perennials, and companion plants. About 80 percent of Rhody Ranch's stock is propagated and/or grown at the nursery. When you visit, take in the views of Vancouver Island and the Olympics, and keep eyes and ears open for the nearly daily visits from a pair of bald eagles, not to mention numerous songbirds, quail, migratory birds, and black-tailed deer (the deer a bit unfortunately for the azalea collection, Andy reports).

ROADHOUSE NURSERY

12511 Central Valley Road NW, Poulsbo, WA 98370 | **Phone:** (360) 779-9589 | **Directions:** From Hwy 3 in Silverdale, take Hwy 303 toward Bremerton. Take the Central Valley exit and turn north 2 miles. | **Open:** Daily (closed Mondays); closed Thanksgiving–January 31.

Jan and George Bahr run a true mom-and-pop nursery, as they are the only employees at this well-regarded nursery. The couple live and work here in a 1904 home that began life as a dance hall (and who knows what else!? Jan asks)—thus the name Roadhouse. Water gardens, **aquatic plants, and all things pond-related** give Roadhouse a delightful focus. Says Jan, "My first water garden was an old clawfoot bathtub which I converted to a water garden as a 4-H project. That bathtub has been moved to the nursery and is still serving as one of our display water gardens."

Here you'll find 20 to 30 water lily varieties, 6 to 10 water iris choices, and many other plants for wet places, 60 percent of which are propagated here. The Bahrs also carry goldfish and koi, pool liners, pumps, fish food, some medications, nets, filters, aquatic plant fertilizers, and lots and lots of free, practical advice for pond builders or pond owners. Jan has installed a 3,400 gallon koi pond, a display garden, and a pond with stream and waterfall for your edification and entertainment. Along with the watery wares there is a small retail nursery, with annuals, perennials, shrubs, and trees.

The displays are best appreciated June through August. Although the property slopes, it is wheelchair accessible with assistance. There are many places to sit and relax—and to enjoy some great water garden ideas.

ROBYN'S NEST NURSERY ✉ @

7802 NE 63rd Street, Vancouver, WA 98662 | **Phone:** (360) 256-7399 | **Email:** robyn@robynsnestnursery.com | **Web:** www.robynsnestnursery.com | **Directions:** Provided for plant will-call only | **Catalog:** $2 (free online); shipping season mid-April–October

The nursery is primarily mail order, so send for Robyn's tempting catalog or check her website. **Shade plants** are a specialty, with **over 400 varieties of hostas,** some rare or hard to find. Robyn's trip to Japan with other fanatics to see hostas in private gardens and in native habitat yielded plants she is propagating from for the nursery. The catalog listings are brief but informative. In the special hosta section, for example, the names of the hybridizers are included, and the section is thoughtfully prefaced by giving credit to several area hybridizers whose work is represented. Other shade lovers—astilbes, ferns, and epimediums—are offered in abundance too.

ROCKYRIDGE NURSERY

2027 Bobb Court SE, Olympia, WA 98513 | **Phone:** (360) 459-3152 | **Directions:** From I-5, take Mounts Road/Nisqually exit 116 and

head east. Travel about 3 miles to Reservation Road, and turn left onto Reservation Road to 25th Avenue. Follow left on 25th Avenue, then turn left on Quiemuth Street SE to the end of the road. Turn right and then immediately left on Bobb Court and follow to the end of the cul-de-sac. | **Open:** Daily (call in advance for best directions), and at the Olympia Farmer's Market April and May (Friday–Sunday).

Dolores and Jim Krob describe their business as a "Ma and Pa" nursery **specializing in rhododendrons and azaleas,** old and new, field grown and in containers, large and small. It's nestled in a quiet wooded setting, a little off the beaten track perhaps, but worth exploring! Here you'll find field-grown rhododendrons that are 6 or 7 feet tall—great specimen sizes. The display gardens are best in spring to show off the rhodys, azaleas, and their companions.

ROCKY TOP GARDENS

53 Fourth Street, Olga, WA 98279 | **Phone:** (360) 376-2042 | **Mailing address:** PO Box 203, Olga, WA 98279 | **Directions:** Provided at time appointment is scheduled | **Open:** By appointment only | **Plant list:** Lists plants currently available

Nancy Bartholomew's vast horticultural experience, including an early stint at Dan Hinkley's Heronswood Nursery, has long inspired her one-woman show on Orcas Island. She focuses **on plants for cutting gardens, for feeding the bird, bee, butterfly and hummingbird population, and on bulbs.** Perennials and shrubs are primarily sold in 4-inch and 1-gallon sizes. Some of Nancy's special offerings include omphalodes, euphorbia, weigelas, buddleias, pulmonaria, hydrangea, aconitum, asters, campanulas, dianthus, hardy fuchsias, hardy geraniums, lonicera, penstemon, ribes, solidago, thalictrum, and veronica. Kind of like an A to Z of neat plants you've gotta have. Look for Rocky Top Gardens at several popular plant sales, including the Arboretum Sale, the King County and Snohomish County Master Gardeners Plant Sales, and the Jefferson Land Trust Festival of Trees in Port Townsend.

The venture has taken a slightly slower pace in recent years, but Nancy continues to be very involved with the plants she grows, and she offers a great selection, especially if you need a plant fix while vacationing or touring Orcas Island.

ROOZENGAARDE, A DIVISION OF WASHINGTON BULB CO., INC. ❀

15867 Beaver Marsh Road, Mt. Vernon, WA 98273 | **Phone:** (800) 732-3266 (store) or (800) 488-5477 (toll-free orders) | **Fax:** (360) 424-3113 | **Email:** info@tulips.com | **Web:** www.tulips.com (online ordering encouraged) | **Directions:** From I-5, take the Mt. Vernon exit 226 and go west (into town). At the first stoplight, turn right; at the next stoplight go straight (on Division Street) over the bridge. At the stoplight at Wall Street, turn left, then make a sharp right as Wall becomes McLean Road, and go about 3 miles. At Beaver Marsh Road turn left. | **Open:** Daily; closed Sunday, except for special events | **Catalog:** Free, full-color, with about 185 varieties of spring-flowering bulbs; fresh flowers shipped year-round.

Roozengaarde is set in a lavishly planted landscape, reminiscent of Holland in the height of spring, and you'll find the garden in bloom in season, and their cheery shop open year-round. Bulb orders are taken March through August for fall delivery. If you visit in person, the time to go is spring: from March to May, view the **dazzling display garden** (the best way to select bulbs for your own garden). Picnic tables, benches, restrooms, and plenty of parking are provided. The shop offers fresh flowers year-round (consider "tulip tidings from the Skagit Valley," shipped anywhere), home/garden décor, and bulb sales. Virtually all their bulbs are grown locally—talk about fresh! Take in the Holiday Festival each November (call for dates). Bulbs are sold in the store September through November, with occasional fall planting seminars at the store.

RoseHip Farm & Garden

338 S Fort Casey Road, Coupeville, WA 98239 | **Phone:** (360) 678-3577 | **Fax:** (360) 678-6620 | **Directions:** On Whidbey Island, coming from the south, take the Mukilteo ferry to Clinton and follow Hwy 525 (turns into Hwy 20) until you reach Coupeville (about 30 minutes). Turn left at the traffic light on Main Street and at the 4-way stop sign, turn left on Terry Road. Go straight, then turn right on Fort Casey Road and go about 0.7 mile. From the north take Hwy 20 onto Whidbey Island via the Deception Pass Bridge and follow Hwy 20 through Oak Harbor on to Coupeville. At the traffic light on Main Street turn right, then follow the directions given above. | **Open:** April–October, Wednesday–Sunday, 9 a.m.–5 p.m.

Linda Bartlett and Valerie Reuther have taken over the former Paris Gardens (founded in 1995 by Maryanne Gardener). "Our focus is in working to keep Maryanne's passion for **own-root roses and unusual perennials,** and add a commitment to organic methods, **drought-tolerant plants, and organic vegetables,**" Valerie explains. This energetic pair spent a season working with Maryanne and, since then, have launched a vibrant lineup of programs to entice locals and long-distance clients. In addition to the many roses (beautifully displayed in the demonstration gardens), RoseHip offers clematis, deer-resistant and drought-tolerant perennials, unusual annuals, grasses, shrubs, and fragrant perennials—about one-third of them propagated here. There is a commitment to buying from local, small wholesale growers who specialize in the hard-to-find choices, including plants from Maryanne Gardener herself.

Organic soil, compost, and amendments are on hand, as are tools, gardener's soaps and lotions, handmade pots, metalwork for the garden, and gifts.

When it comes to the displays, you'll enjoy trellises, arbors, and fences placed throughout the garden, all of which create lovely vertical elements to show off the roses. From the wonderful early show of the bulbs through the irises, roses, and lilies, to the grasses, asters, mums and fall foliage there is something of focal interest through all the seasons.

There is also a fun Mother's Day event in the garden, along with frequent class offerings. Check on dates for the mid-October "apple pie contest and garlic races."

Rosebriar Gardens & Design

416 Rainier Avenue S, Seattle, WA 98144 | (206) 723-3796 | **Mailing address:** 4610 S Thistle Street, Seattle, WA 98118 | **Email:** yesroses@earthlink.net | **Directions:** From I-90 west, take the Rainier Avenue S (northbound) exit; the nursery is on the right at King Street and Rainier Avenue S. From I-5, take the Dearborn Street exit and turn east; then turn left on Rainier Avenue S to King Street. | **Open:** Wednesday through Sunday | **Plant list:** Yes

Garden designer Rose Lee is an itinerant nurserywoman who first operated Rosebriar in the parking lot of a used-auto dealership (she was a huge improvement for the neighborhood). She has now relocated closer to Seattle's International and Central Districts, offering more **healthy and choice plants** than you'd imagine one could fit into a tiny urban lot. Rose specializes in **disease-resistant roses for Northwest gardens,** propagating many antique varieties and hard-to-find roses herself. You can also find Chinese tree peonies, an enormous selection of iris, daylilies, hydrangeas, perennials, field-grown specialty azaleas, fruits and berries. The nursery's annual Garden Party is usually held the first weekend after Memorial Day, so call to add your name to Rose's mailing list. In the spring, she always offers helpful rose pruning, selection, and care workshops. And if you're into bargains (and who isn't, when it comes to plants?) choose your roses and fruit trees early in the season, as they go for 20 percent off when still bare-root. If you're looking for design ideas, peruse the tricky rockery wall that's probably keeping most of a neighboring property from falling on Rosebriar. Rose has planted this terraced bank to show how you can garden in a vertical state!

The Rose Petaller

10209 SW 211th Place, Vashon Island, WA 98070 | **Phone:** (206) 463-6513 | **Fax:** (206) 463-2180 | **Email:** BBAllen@wolfenet.com | **Web:** www.bballen.com | **Mailing address:** PO Box 1229, Vashon Island, WA 98070 | **Directions:** Off Vashon Hwy, about mid-island. Turn west on SW 211th Pl and it's the property straight down the road. | **Open:** By appointment only | **Plant list:** Free with SASE

Sheryl Allen gardens "intensely" on 1 acre of Vashon Island land, and when you tour the gardens here you'll find a pond at the bottom of the hill and enjoy canine and feline companions. Sheryl grows own-root roses and perennials, and while the list varies by the year, she will entertain you with stories about each of them. Expect to find centifolia, China, polyantha, English, gallica, noisette, rugosa, hybrid musk, and moss roses among The Rose Petaller's offerings. Prices are very reasonable and this makes yet another excuse for a day trip to lovely Vashon Island!

RUSSELL WATERGARDENS, NURSERY, AND DESIGN CENTER

24808 Redmond-Fall City Road, Redmond, WA 98053 | **Phone:** (425) 488-2496 | **Fax:** (425) 481-9056 | **Email:** russell.services@ gte.net | **Web:** www.russellwatergardens.com | **Directions:** From I-5, take SR 520 eastbound and continue to the light at Redmond-Fall City Road, and turn right onto the road. | **Open:** Daily

Russell Watergardens, a recent addition to the list of nurseries specializing in water features, recently opened its doors with a series of large water-garden displays. Owners John and Pamela Russell invite you to stroll among cascading waterfalls of all sizes and the large ponds filled with koi. Enjoy all types of aquatic plants, meandering streams, babbling brooks, and small reflecting pools filled with goldfish. The nursery offers a large inventory of aquatic plants, plus Aquascape Design's Pro Pond Eco System kits, and Aquascape Design's professional product line, including BioFalls biological filters, CleanSweep skimmer filters, pumps, plumbing, liners, and underwater lighting. There's everything for the "do-it-yourself" water gardener here, including consultations with professional water-garden builders. Or if you like, imagine any one of the beautiful Russell Watergardens in your own backyard—you can discuss your idea with a pond designer and have the nursery crew professionally install it for you. The nursery is also stocked with plant, tree, and perennial material that is perfectly suited for landscaping around and near a water garden. Take in one of the nursery's Build-a-Pond days to learn the "tricks of the trade" that count in placing a beautiful water element.

SAKUMA BROTHERS FARMS

PO Box 427, Burlington, WA 98233 | **Phone:** (360) 757-6611 | **Fax:** (360) 757-3936 | **Email:** sakumab@sos.net | **Directions:** From I-5, take exit 232 (Cook Road) and travel 1 mile west; Sakuma Brothers Farms is the first driveway on the left after the stop sign. | **Open:** Daily | **Plant list:** Free; wholesale and retail

While primarily wholesale, Sakuma Brothers also sells to retail customers, offering many of their popular varieties in smaller minimum quantities (like 25 plants instead of 1,000). The farms are best known as growers of **fine fruit and berry plants**; many knowledgeable gardeners look here for their strawberries, both June bearing (30 varieties) and Everbearing/Day Neutral types (10 varieties) and raspberries, including July–August bearing (8 varieties) and Fall bearing (6 varieties). You can purchase tissue-cultured plants as well, including blackberries (20 varieties including boysenberry, marionberry, and loganberry); raspberries (8 varieties); and tayberries (a blackberry/raspberry hybrid).

SAVAGE PLANTS AND LANDSCAPE

6810 State Hwy 104, Kingston, WA 98340 | **Phone:** (360) 297-8711 | **Fax:** (360) 297-8717 | **Email:** savagenursery@earthlink.net | **Directions:** From the Kingston ferry terminal, travel west on Hwy 104 about 2 miles. | **Open:** Daily, spring to fall; call for winter hours

This is the family business of Jim and Joan Savage, now in its tenth year. The "savage stock" includes a wide range of plants, among them shrubs, specimen trees, ornamental grasses, perennials, and annuals, along with a newly expanded herb selection. **Specimen trees and unusual perennials** are the pride of this small group of plant lovers. As for artistic displays, look for ideas on using plants in garden designs (nicely paired with hardscape examples). Shop for classical cast iron and terra cotta pottery as you stop to think, "What a beautiful and clever idea." There is some very savvy plant buying here that will please the most discerning of plant enthusiasts. If you need more inspiration, peruse the local garden artwork and a small but beautiful collection of trellises, birdbaths, and outdoor furniture.

SAXE FLORAL & GREENHOUSES

2402 NE 65th, Seattle, WA 98115 | **Phone:** (206) 523-3646 | **Fax:** (206) 523-4415 | **Directions:** From I-5 take the 65th Street exit and travel east to 25th Avenue NE (nursery is located just north of University Village at 25th and 65th). | **Open:** Daily

An old, established urban neighborhood nursery, Saxe Floral & Greenhouses is great fun to mosey around. Owner Nancy L. Javete invites you to discover a labyrinth of greenhouses, covered and open air sales areas, and more. This **year-round garden center** has it all, from vegetable starts and annuals in spring to bonsai, trees, shrubs, perennials, herbs, and fresh flowers, and gifts in the gift shop.

SEA-TAC DAHLIA GARDENS

20020 Des Moines Memorial Drive, Seattle, WA 98198 | **Phone:** (206) 824-3846 | **Fax:** Same | **Email:** patheck@prodigy.net | **Directions:** Located south of Sea-Tac Airport; from I-5 take the S 200th Street exit 151 and head west about 2 miles to Des Moines Memorial Drive. Turn left (south) for 1 block (3 houses); the nursery/house is on the left. | **Open:** Daily; garden open during bloom season, August–October. | **Plant list:** Free

About ten years before retiring from his career of 32 years with the Boeing Company, Louis Eckhoff began to hybridize and grow dahlias that he could share with the gardening public and dahlia fanciers across the country. On 1 acre of land, he and his wife Patti now grow over 7,000 of their favorite flower! They offer over **350 different dahlia varieties,** specializing in cut-flower sizes, but offering all sizes of blossoms from 1 inch to the dinner plates measuring in at 14 inches. This couple has introduced about 40 dahlia varieties since 1979. They have a ready willingness to help anyone with a dahlia question—from propagation to cultivation and anything in between. In August and September, when the garden is open, come to evaluate the selection. Take a camera and notebook, too, to help keep your overstimulated memory straight! Garden club field trips are welcome. You can also purchase the Eckhoffs' own hand-picked dahlia seeds.

SHORE ROAD NURSERY

616 Shore Road, Port Angeles, WA 98362 | **Phone:** (360) 457-1536 | **Fax:** (360) 457-8482 | **Email:** plantman@olypen.com | **Directions:** Located between Sequim (7 miles) and Port Angeles (6 miles) on the Olympic Peninsula; take Shore Road north from Hwy 101. | **Open:** March–December, Tuesday–Saturday, 10 a.m.–5 p.m. (best to call ahead if you are coming from afar) | **Plant list:** $2

David Allen is a botanist and environmental consultant and restoration specialist, so it is easy to see why his nursery specializes in the **native plants** he knows so well. In a former 10-acre hay field, he has created a special place, including a series of display gardens that feature an inspiring use of natives. The display areas include a "fire ring" garden, herb garden, quail garden, retention pond garden, and more. You'll be charmed by the way plants and hardscape elements are combined: grape covered arbors, rock walls, and seating areas included. Each season includes seed collection and taking of cuttings to propagate Shore Road's eclectic inventory of ornamentals, an assorted selection of trees, shrubs and herbaceous perennials. Plants range from plugs to 20-foot trees that David will custom-grow for your project. He is also known for his consulting work, performing botanical surveys, revegetation, restoration, habitat and landscape design. This is a great place for your garden club to tour—or invite David to speak to your group.

SHORTY'S NURSERY INC.

10006 SE Mill Plain Boulevard, Vancouver, WA 98664 | **Phone:** (360) 882-0699 | **Fax:** (360) 882-4085 | **Directions:** About 8 blocks west from I-205 on SE Mill Plain Boulevard. | **Ridgefield location:** 705 NE 199th Street, Ridgefield, WA 98642; (360) 887-3936 | **Open:** Daily.

Shorty's got its start in 1965 in North Clark County, where it still operates its Ridgefield store. In 1996, Shorty's grew to add a new store in Vancouver. Both locations offer area gardeners 5 acres, each with a **broad selection of garden and landscaping plants.** And even though it's an independent specialty nursery, Shorty's recently tied with a big-box chain nursery as "the most recognized nursery in the county." Hurray for small nurseries! According to General Manager Angelo Branch, Shorty's has one of the largest inventories and selections of trees and shrubs in the Vancouver/Portland metropolitan area. Shorty's propagates many of its perennials and annuals, too. Gardening tools, soil, mulch, remedies, and supplies are also stocked here, and the seed selection includes Ed Hume, Lake Valley, and Lilly Miller. The full-service personality of Shorty's extends to handy rentals of lawn equipment.

SKAGIT HEIGHTS DAHLIA FARM

57542 Hobson Road, Bow, WA 98232 | **Phone:** (360) 766-6612 | **Directions:** From I-5 northbound, take exit 236 and head west on Bow Hill Road. Travel just 0.3 mile and turn right on Hobson Road; you'll see a large driveway sign for the farm. | **Open:** Seasonal; open August–September for viewing the dahlia fields in bloom. | **Catalog:** $1 for postage; shipping is in May.

Of course, as this is a dahlia farm, the time to visit is in late summer and early fall, when you will be greeted by a display of over 750 brilliant varieties to select from. Founder Genevee Schluemer says, "It all started 45 years ago as a hobby; the more varieties I acquired, the more ground we opened up for planting. It got big enough that my husband took an interest in it and thereby we became a 4-acre commercial dahlia farm." You can place your orders in the fall for the best selection, and then also in the early spring when sales and distribution take place.

SKAGIT VALLEY GARDENS

18923 Johnson Road, Mount Vernon, WA 98273 | **Phone:** (360) 424-6760 | **Fax:** (360) 424-5331 | **Directions:** From I-5 just south of Mt. Vernon, take exit 221 and then take the frontage road along the west side of the freeway about 2 miles to the big red barn that houses the nursery and shop. | **Open:** Daily

This is the nursery you see south of Mt. Vernon as you speed by on I-5—the big red barn with the colorful display garden adjacent. SVG is a **full-service nursery, garden center, gift shop, and deli.**

Specializing in unusual conifers and a large, diverse selection of **perennials,** SVG also carries a very fine range of annuals, many interesting and quality trees and shrubs, vines, top-quality bulbs, fruit and vegetable starts, glorious fuchsia baskets they create themselves, herbs, pond plants, and a full line of water-gardening supplies, equipment, and pond-building materials. We have been impressed with the efforts on the beautifully landscaped water features, both in the sales area outside and in the enormous new greenhouse/sales area, where you can sit peacefully enjoying a latte, soup, or a sweet. The last hanging basket is barely out the door when SVG begins to create a Christmas wonderland of theme decorated trees in all sizes and shapes. It's a must-see holiday destination spot. Check out the classes and special events and turn to this nursery for great gardening information, problem solving, and great customer service. Their seed department offers Territorial, Botanical Interests, and Ed Hume seeds.

SKY NURSERY

18528 Aurora Avenue N, Shoreline, WA 98133 | **Phone:** (206) 546-4851 | **Fax:** (206) 546-8010 | **Email:** sky@skynursery.com | **Web:** www.skynursery.com | **Directions:** Near the NE corner of 185th Street and Aurora Avenue N. From I-5, take exit 176 and head west 1.5 miles to Aurora/Hwy 99. Turn right and travel north 10 blocks. | **Open:** Daily

This **full-service nursery** offers a wide selection for gardeners, from seeds and plants to red worms for your compost; find **bonsai supplies** and plants, bulk materials (delivery available), organic and environment-friendly products, water gardens, plants and supplies, and always lots of free advice from a knowledgeable staff. If you share the fervor over fish these days, come to see the display garden set around a model koi pond (stocked with very friendly fish). This is really **a gardeners' garden** store, with such a broad range of quality plants and products—trees, shrubs, hedging plants, ground covers, fruit trees and canes, roses, annuals, perennials, water plants, bulbs, vegetable starts, herbs throughout the year—that they will have the seasonally appropriate plants in top shape ready for you to plant. **Seed** offerings include Territorial, Thompson & Morgan, Lilly Miller, Burpee, and Ed Hume. Enjoy the recently expanded houseplant section, too. Each September welcomes Sky's "Garden Party," with speakers, refreshments, and entertainment. Take in the "Odd Plant Show and Sale" (space provided courtesy of the nursery), where you'll find carnivorous plants, aroids, and other nifty unusual plants. Proceeds from the Garden Party are dedicated to the Landry Memorial Horticultural Scholarship at Edmonds Community College. There's even a free quarterly newsletter where you can read about Sky's excellent seminars and great planting tips.

SMITH CREEK NURSERY

14519 Westwick Road, Snohomish, WA 98290 | **Phone:** (360) 568-3471 | **Email:** smithcrk@juno.com | **Directions:** From I-5, take the Hwy 2 exit 194 and follow east 2 miles past Snohomish. Turn left onto Westwick Road (100th Street SE) at mile marker 10. The nursery is a quarter mile farther, on the left. | **Open:** April–August, Tuesday–Saturday, 10 a.m.–5 p.m.

Sheila Smith's secluded country nursery specializes in **herbs,** with 300 varieties on offer. You'll find herbs for culinary, medicinal, and ornamental uses, and among these many unusual varieties. She also offers the avid gardeners who are drawn to this pleasant nursery a good selection of annuals, perennials, vines, and flowers for drying. Sheila's display garden features herbs and scented geraniums. Her gift shop is filled with many handcrafted items from local artists, handwoven baskets, soaps, stained glass, garden furniture, and stepping-stones.

SMOKEY POINT PLANT FARM

16622 Twin Lakes Avenue, Arlington, WA 98223 | **Phone:** (360) 652-3351 | **Fax:** (360) 652-3655 | **Web:** www.theplantfarm.com | **Directions:** From I-5, take the Smokey Point exit 206 (north of Marysville 3 miles), turn west on 172nd Street NE for 1-1/2 blocks, turn south on 27th, and follow the road around the bend to the left, then to the right—the nursery is essentially on the frontage road along the west side of I-5. | **Open:** Daily

Co-owners Mary Archambault (manager) and Joel Hylback debuted this enormous nursery (not to be missed by any plant lover driving along I-5) in 1994 with a single greenhouse. They have expanded considerably, acquiring the Larson Farm in 1997 for growing stock. In 2000, the koi pond and shade porch were added; take a stroll on the "Bridge Over the River Koi," which features the friendly, colorful, large and small koi, surrounded by a beautiful display garden.

An energetic staff has filled this 6.5-acre nursery with **a full line of nursery stock,** including lots of uncommon varieties not found in other garden centers. Find also bulbs, water plants, statuary/fountains, pest and disease controls, and pots. SPPF offers one of the broadest selections of plant materials for outdoor use. Backed by **40 acres of growing fields,** this nursery raises strong, healthy plants and presents them in a pleasing and organized way. If you can't find what you're looking for, just ask. Someone will track it down! SPPF offers basic gardening supplies with an emphasis on organic controls, seeds from Lake Valley, Burpee, Territorial, Ferry-Morse, Seeds of Change, Thompson & Morgan, Unwins, and Ed Hume—plus some "cool" varieties from the Italian Seed Co. As for gardening supplies and accessories, there is a greenhouse filled with a huge assortment; find fertilizer, gloves, stakes, trellises, tomato cages, seed-starting supplies, containers, garden art, furniture, and more. When you visit, be sure to say hello to Chester, the cat-in-residence.

SOOS CREEK GARDENS

12602 SE Petrovitsky Road, Renton, WA 98058 | **Phone:** (425) 226-9308 | **Email:** sooscrk@w-link.net | **Web:** www.w-link.net/~sooscrk | **Directions:** From the north on I-5 take the I-405 exit traveling east, then take the Hwy 167 (Valley Freeway) exit south. Take the Valley General Hospital exit at 41st Street and proceed east by coming over the freeway overpass (or if you are coming from the south, in Kent, take the 43rd Street exit east). Go east 2 miles on 176th Street (Carr Road), which becomes Petrovitsky Road. The nursery is on the left. | **Open:** Seasonal and by appointment | **Plant list:** Free; shipping April–July; wholesale and retail.

If you are blessed with a pond or garden in a boggy or wet situation, then Helmut and Lourdes Brodka have a wide palette of plants to choose from. They started 21 years ago to develop their 5-acre "unkempt wilderness" property into a **woodland garden.** Plant-selling was an accidental outcome, but isn't that wonderful!? You are welcome to wander their ponds, creekside, woodland, and gardens (which supply their nursery plants) to glean ideas. If you are just creating or equipping a water feature, they will order your liners, pumps, and filters. Here you will also find **hardy bog and water plants** (including water lilies), 95 percent of which the Brodkas propagate themselves, bamboo, some natives, and some not-so-common trees and shrubs. You can also find seashells, woodcarvings, and dried flowers for sale at Soos Creek Gardens.

SOUND NATIVE PLANTS

PO Box 7505, Olympia, WA 98507-7505 | **Phone:** (360) 352-4122 | **Fax:** (360) 867-0007 | **Email:** sessnp@compuserve.com | **Open:** By appointment only | **Plant list:** Free with SASE; wholesale (and retail at wholesale prices, if you don't need "hands-on service"); $100 minimum order.

Sound Native Plants is the largest nursery in western Washington devoted exclusively to growing native plants. All of SNP's stock is of western Washington genetic origin and well-suited to environmental restoration. Founders Ben Alexander and Susan Buis got their start in growing native plants and managing environmental restoration projects while working for the Olympic and Yosemite National Parks. They offer a wide selection of container-grown plants—trees and shrubs, wetland emergents, and ground covers—and willow and other riparian species as live stakes and for use in fascines. They are deeply involved in restoration planning and planting projects for wetland mitigation, steep slope and marine bluff stabilization, and stream-side restoration and erosion control.

SOUTH SEATTLE COMMUNITY COLLEGE GARDEN CENTER

6000 16th Avenue SW, Seattle, WA 98106 | **Phone:** (206) 764-5323 | **Fax:** (206) 763-5156 | **Directions:** See Chapter 13, "Gardens to Visit" | **Open:** Seasonal, plus ongoing special sales and workshops

This garden center is operated by current and former students of SSCC's Landscape/Environmental Horticulture program. Here, under the talented guidance of manager Penny McCormick, you'll find a wide range of plants from perennials, deciduous, and broadleaf evergreen shrubs, some small trees and dwarf conifers, old-fashioned and rugosa roses, ground covers, native plants and interior plants. Some of this plant material has been propagated by the students. More than anything, you'll enjoy the enthusiasm of the staff—they're all here because of a love of horticulture. Mark your calendar for the annual fall sale in October, an annual spring sale in May, and a year-end closing sale at the end of June. The garden center also offers ongoing seminars and workshops, so call for a current schedule of classes—and sales.

SPOONER CREEK NURSERY

5100 Lincoln Road, Blaine, WA 98230 | **Phone:** (360) 371-5551 | **Fax:** (360) 371-0191 | **Email:** manana02@sprynet.com | **Directions:** From I-5 going north, take exit 270 for Semiahmoo Resort; watch for nursery on the left (near the resort). | **Open:** Daily

Carrillee and Bob Fischer have logged several years as the new owners of this established nursery, devoting their energies to an extensive one-acre demonstration garden that's under construction (a trio of ponds and several distinct theme areas are planned). While they stock the full line of plants virtually any gardener would come seeking, there is an especially nice selections of rhododendrons, deciduous azaleas, kalmias, and roses (old English and antique varieties). Pond plants, fruit trees, evergreens, perennials, and annuals are offered, and "we're suckers for fragrant plants," says Carrillee. The retail shop carries a full line of gardening supplies and tools, birdseed, bark, top soil, etc. and the nursery offers classes and demonstrations appropriate to the season. This nursery's main claim to fame is its customer service (thanks to a super-friendly staff).

SQUAK MOUNTAIN GREENHOUSES AND NURSERY

7600 Renton-Issaquah Road SE, Issaquah, WA 98027 | **Phone:** (425) 392-1025 | **Directions:** Only 1 mile east of I-90 in Issaquah. From I-5, take the exit for I-90 east and follow to Issaquah. Take the Renton-Issaquah Road (Hwy 900) exit 15 southbound 1 mile. You will see the nursery sign and a large yellow mailbox on the left. | **Open:** Daily; closed Sundays.

This is a destination-quality, **full-service garden center located in a beautiful natural setting.** When you leave the freeway and arrive at Squak Mountain, you feel as though you've left the bustle and stress far behind. The nursery showcases a magnificent **waterfall feature,** constructed with over 200 tons of rock and beautifully planted. Display beds throughout the 10-acre grounds showcase great landscaping ideas. The garden center features 1 acre of growing greenhouses, a newly completed Garden Shed, and a full complement of great plants. Annuals here come directly from Squak Mountain's growing benches, including primroses, geraniums, fuchsia baskets, bedding plants, vegetables, mums, pansies, and poinsettias. Don't miss the stunning moss baskets created by veteran staff designers. A step inside the lofty Garden Shed is another treat, where you'll find garden gifts, décor, and unique tools—plus great patio furniture. This structure is transformed into a wonderland with decorations and ornaments come the holidays. The nursery is staffed by friendly, knowledgeable garden lovers . . . people who are happy to help you in selecting from a generous selection of roses, shrubs, trees, perennials, herbs, vines, ground covers, and ornamental grasses. A plant lover's paradise! PS: Add your name to the mailing list for a charming quarterly newsletter.

STAR NURSERY & LANDSCAPING

13916 42nd Avenue S, Seattle, WA 98168 | **Phone:** (206) 241-2115 | **Fax:** (206) 241-2677 | **Directions:** 1 mile north of Sea-Tac airport and 1 block east of Pacific Hwy S at 140th Avenue S. | **Open:** Weekdays | **Plant list:** For wholesale customers only

Star Nursery, a family-owned business since 1965, is primarily a wholesale operation, but retail customers are welcome. There are 17 acres here, with an **enormous selection of landscaping plants,** mostly propagated on the premises and field-grown for hardiness. Specialties are **evergreen and deciduous azaleas, rhododendrons, dwarf conifers, and grafted trees.** One of the features here that has gained applause from landscape professionals is the nursery's dedication to root pruning stock annually to build up strong, fibrous root systems—for plants that can be moved happily at any time. Star also sells some ground covers, vines, perennials, and heathers/heaths.

STEAMBOAT ISLAND NURSERY

8424 Steamboat Island Road, Olympia, WA 98502 | **Phone:** (360) 866-2516 | **Email:** steamboat@olywa.net | **Web:** www.olywa.net/steamboat | **Directions:** From I-5, take exit 104 onto Hwy 101 and proceed to the Steamboat Island Road exit; follow Steamboat Island Road for 7 miles, and find the nursery on the right. | **Open:** Weekends, March–October, and by appointment. Wholesale and retail.

Laine McLaughlin started her horticulture career after graduating from UC Davis, working in wholesale and retail nurseries after coming to Seattle in 1977. After getting a master's in environmental studies from The Evergreen State College, she was inspired to grow native plants. Since 1994, Laine has operated Steamboat Island Nursery, where she grows "something of everything"—trees, shrubs, perennials, temperennials, vines, annuals, grasses, and ferns. Her display gardens are continually evolving, featuring some deer-resistant and drought tolerant plants (for shade and sun); plus a winter garden and container planting ideas. Laine's specialties are extensive and include *Brugmansia* x *versicolor* 'Charles Grimaldi', *Cerinthe major purpurascens*, *Eucalyptus* spp. (19 species—all hardy!), *Salix magnifica*, *Solanum laciniatum* (kangaroo apple), *Vancouveria planipetala* and plants with year-round interest, such as bark, fall color and winter flowers. It's so inspiring to hear her say "I'm a zonal denialist," as Laine is willing to try plants that others consider borderline for Northwest planting zones. She has a special interest in plants that can tolerate wet winters, as Olympia averages about 44 inches of rain annually (quite a lot more than Seattle, in fact). You'll also find frost-resistant pots from Europe and Asia. Add your name to the twice-yearly newsletter mailing list and look for this wonderful plantswoman at sales, including Rhododendron Species Foundation, Northwest Perennial Alliance, and Northwest Horticultural Society events.

STONE HOLLOW FARM

21302 SE 1st Street, Sammamish, WA 98074 | **Phone:** (425) 391-2218 | **Email:** elainstonehollow@aol.com | **Directions:** East of Lake Sammamish. From Redmond along E Lake Sammamish Parkway, take Thompson Road (about 3 miles from Redmond, on the left. Make a sharp left turn, uphill) to 212th SE. Turn left on SE 8th Street, left on 214th SE and left on SE 1st Street (a short, private, gravel cul-de-sac). From Issaquah, follow E Lake Sammamish Parkway to 212th Way, zigzag uphill to 212th SE, turn right on SE 8th, left on 214th SE, and left on SE 1st. | **Open:** Friday–Saturday and by appointment | **Plant list:** Free

Plant lover, propagator, and Master Gardener Elaine Keehn (an ex-biochemist) specializes in **drought-tolerant perennials, hardy hebes, penstemon, and geraniums**—and a few other favorite small shrubs. Elaine occasionally offers seeds from her garden. She also sells slug houses, decorative cement/tufa leaves for the garden, and hypertufas. Classes are occasionally offered, and Elaine always shares her expertise with customers. Make friends with a plantaholic who has taken her avocation seriously! You are welcome to browse through the mature plantings in her 1-acre display garden, designed to be drought-tolerant and that thrives pesticide-free.

SUMMERSUN GREENHOUSE CO.

4100 E College Way, Mt. Vernon, WA 98273 | **Phone:** (360) 424-1663 | **Fax:** (360) 424-7934 | **Email:** summerr@cnw.com | **Web:** www.summersun.com | **Directions:** From I-5, take the College Way exit and go east about 5 miles. The nursery is on the left. | **Open:** Daily

Summersun has done a very nice job of expanding the nursery, with an excellent selection of **good-sized trees and shrubs,** including many varieties one does not find readily. A beautiful new perennial display garden creates an inviting parklike setting to show them off. The nursery also carries a full selection of annuals, ground covers, grasses, trees, shrubs, and poinsettias. The large greenhouse/shop offers a huge choice of **bedding plants, herbs, houseplants,** pots, and baskets. There is a good line-up of classes at the nursery (check the website or call for details). The **Annual Poinsettia Festival** is held during the three days immediately following Thanksgiving, showing off 300,000 brilliant blooms—an event to put you properly in the holiday mood. In the holiday spirit, refreshments, a half-hour tour of their facility, and a gift poinsettia are provided.

SUNDQUIST NURSERY

3809 NE Sawdust Hill Road, Poulsbo, WA 98370 | **Phone:** (360) 779-6343 | **Fax:** (360) 697-6971 | **Mailing address:** PO Box 2451, Poulsbo, WA 98370 | **Directions:** (If you have an appointment or plan to visit on an Open Garden Day.) From the ferry terminal at Edmonds/Kingston, follow Hwy 104 directly off the ferry, travelling west. At about 4 miles, where Hwy 104 turns right to Hood Canal, stay straight on Hwy 307 (Bond Road) toward Poulsbo. At 2 miles turn left on Sawdust Hill Road. From Poulsbo, head toward Kingston on Hwy 307 (Bond Road). At milepost 3, turn right onto Sawdust Hill Road. This portion of Sawdust Hill Road is a dead-end dirt road. The first driveway on the right is a preschool where the garden walks begin and plant sales take place. Park on the road shoulder. Nils forewarns that "watchful neighbors will call the sheriff if the road might be blocked or they suspect something might be wrong." | **Open:** By appointment only, and on Open Garden Days (usually in June, July, and September)

Nils Sundquist is garnering a great reputation as the "grass guy," a plantsman truly fluent in **ornamental grasses,** plus "practical favorite and designer perennials," hardy ferns and select natives. He's frequently on hand with loads of wonderful plants at some of the area's top plant sales. Nils and his wife Kristen are first and foremost wholesale growers, which is why they limit Sundquist Nursery to appointments and Open Garden Days. It's an opportunity worth planning for. You'll enjoy the ambitious garden design that surrounds the family's 1928 farmhouse. While Nils complains that he bites off more than he should, each year the gardens continue to expand. Recently, drystack rock walls have utterly transformed the landscape, suggesting rural New England. Thousands of narcissus illuminate this pastoral setting each spring (check for dates to attend Sundquist's annual Daffodil Day in early April); later, sweeps of chocolate candelabra primroses brighten the damp ground beside a gunnera near Kristen's preschool. Nils's ornamental grass border is considered one of the largest and most representative in Puget Sound. Unusual trees and shrubs are integrated into the pastoral setting, and he maintains an extensive shrub rose planting. Nils, an avid plantsman, favors an ever-evolving palette that includes **old favorites plus rare and sought-after selections** to gratify the savvy plant enthusiast, and specializes, in his nursery, in perennials, ornamental grasses, ferns, hardy fuchsias, lavenders, and unique shrubs, including many hydrangeas. Even so, he likes to say his display gardens are "a good study in low-maintenance estate gardening on a proletarian budget."

SUNNYSIDE NURSERY

3915 Sunnyside Boulevard, Marysville, WA 98271 | **Phone:** (425) 334-2002 | **Fax:** (425) 335-3580 | **Email:** sunnysidenursery@msn.com | **Directions:** From I-5, take exit 199 and go east to State Street; turn right 1 block to 3rd, turn left, and follow for 2 miles (3rd becomes Sunnyside Boulevard). From Hwy 9, take the Soper Hill exit and drive west for 2 miles. | **Open:** Daily (closed in January)

Owners Steve and Pauline Smith have brought a great deal of enthusiasm and expertise to this old Snohomish County country nursery, established over 50 years ago. Tucked in a rural setting, the 2-acre nursery is easy to reach from I-5 or Hwy 9—a peaceful side trip just minutes off the freeway. Sunnyside is an inviting nursery to wander through, with several robust display gardens (including a lovely garden in the Smiths' own back yard, just next door). Steve, aka "The Whistling Gardener," is known for his obsession for **tropicals,** and each summer he shows off his expertise by creating a 100-foot border filled with cannas, banana plants, and other **heat-loving varieties.** There is an excellent selection of the full range of plants, with many less common varieties featured. If you love your fuchsia baskets, reserve a spot in the greenhouse, where Sunnyside will "baby-sit" them during the winter for a small fee. The garden center shop is fully stocked with supplies, books, and tools, classes are offered year-round, and there is a great play area for non-gardening kids! During the holidays, get a group of friends together and plan a wreath-making party at the nursery. Sunnyside will help you with instruction and supplies. Call to request their newsletter for spring and fall class schedules.

SWANSON'S NURSERY

9701 15th Avenue NW, Seattle, WA 98117 | **Phone:** (206) 782-2543 | **Fax:** (206) 782-8942 | **Email:** garden@swansonsnursery.com | **Web:** www.swansonsnursery.com | **Directions:** Just north of Ballard. From I-5, take exit 172 westbound; drive west 2 miles and turn right on 15th Avenue NW. Continue 2 blocks to yellow flashing light and make an angled left turn. Continue north on 15th Avenue NW for 4 blocks. Nursery is about 1 mile into a residential neighborhood (it was rural until progress snuck in over the years). | **Open:** Daily | **Mailing list:** Call or fax Tami Littell at the numbers above to add your name and receive Swanson's colorful promotional postcards bearing discount coupons for upcoming specials, as well as class information.

This large, **full-service nursery,** tucked into a north Seattle neighborhood since 1924, meanders over 5 acres—and so do you, in and out of greenhouses and shade pavilions, on a quest of discovery (don't forget your red wagon, provided because they know you'll want to keep many great finds along the way). You'll especially appreciate the expansive selection of trees, shrubs, vines, herbs, ornamental grasses, and perennials. Plant collectors will be impressed with a growing selection of unusual varieties. Wander the greenhouses for houseplants, cactus, and bedding plants. Swanson's carries Territorial, Fragrant Garden, Renee's Garden, Burpee, Thompson & Morgan, Seeds of Change and Shepherd's Seeds. The display garden provides great seasonal plant ideas you won't be able to resist trying. Along the lines of plant companions, find here sturdy and handsome Asian-inspired wood arbors, trellises, and screens, made-to-order planters, plus some books and other specialty items, and a great selection of hand tools and accessories for gardeners. Plan an expedition over lunch or tea time and rest your weary bones in the excellent **Festivities** bistro, then scout the adjacent sophisticated gift, tabletop, and accessories shop, Panache. Saturday morning seminars are usually at 10 a.m. and are offered nearly year-round. Call for a schedule or check the website.

SWANS TRAIL GARDENS

7021 61st Avenue SE, Snohomish, WA 98290 | **Phone:** (425) 334-4595 | **Email:** schroder@premier1.net | **Directions:** From I-5, take exit 194, SR 2, east toward Snohomish. Stay in the right lane and follow Homeacres Road through 2 stop signs (and a right-hand turn). Turn left onto Homeacres Road and follow for 3 miles. Turn left on 60th Street and follow for 1/2 mile to Walther's gas station. Turn right on 61st Avenue and follow for 1 mile, continuing on after the stop sign. At the dead-end, the nursery is the sixth driveway on the left. Look for a barn with a blue roof. | **Open:** Seasonal, or by appointment

Alice Schroder is a self-described "plant-addict" who started Swans Trail five years ago to "keep the 'fixes' coming." She only sells plants she's grown and experimented with personally, offering mainly **hardy herbaceous perennials** with a sprinkling of interesting annuals, shrubs, and vines. Alice says 90 percent of her "babies" are grown here from seeds, which she acquires through various organizations, weird seed nurseries in the United States and abroad, wild collecting, and other "secret" methods. She sounds like a seed sleuth you'll want to know. At Swans Trail, you'll find anywhere from 200 to 400 species of plants, including many campanulas, seven types of digitalis, geraniums, primulas, and more.

The nursery sits amidst a 2-acre display garden that features spring woodland plantings of rhododendrons, erythroniums, *Primula sieboldii,* and more. Varying color borders continue through summer, showing off a large pond with grasses and bold plantings. Not handicapped accessible.

SWEETWATER LAVENDER, LTD. ✳

58 Jacobs Road, Coupeville, WA 98239 | **Phone:** (360) 687-1790 | **Orders and catalog requests:** (800) 884-9287 | **Email:** lavender@whidbey.net | **Directions:** From Seattle, take I-5 north to the Mukilteo/Whidbey Island ferry. Once on the island, follow Hwy 20 for 26 miles. Sweetwater is located 1 mile east of Coupeville on SR 20 (near Rhododendron State Park) at Jacob's Road. | **Open:** Seasonal, April–October | **Catalog:** Free (gifts and books shipped, but no plants)

Gordon Edwards and Susan Morgan grew tired of the city and corporate world, but discovered lavender-farming as a way of life on trips to England and Jersey (an island off the coast of France), where the "lavender lure" took hold. They grow 95 varieties of lavender in display gardens, a kitchen garden (herbs), a knot garden, a sunflower house, a perennial flower garden, a pond, and a field filled with 25,000 lavender plants.

Come to see lavender at its peak the first two weeks of July (although plants begin to bud in June). It's Provence at your doorstep! Call for dates and times of the annual Lavender Harvest, wand-making classes, tours, and lectures.

THOMPSON'S GREENHOUSE

6412 State Route 9, Sedro-Woolley, WA 98284 | **Phone:** (360) 856-2147 | **Directions:** 3 miles north of Sedro-Woolley on SR 9 | **Open:** Seasonal.

Alongside State Route 9 in a peaceful setting north of Sedro-Woolley, Stephen and Brenda Thompson's cheery little nursery packs in lots of variety, both in the broad range of plants carried and in selection. The long row of greenhouses attest to the Thompsons' propagation program; the specialties here are **perennials, annuals, and vegetable starts.** But there are also lots of choices among the trees, shrubs, ground covers, berries, flowering trees, roses, herbs, sedums, and patio plants. There's also a growing selection of clay and cedar pots and garden art. Visit for the annual sale during the first week in June.

THORNTON CREEK NURSERY

12237 1st Avenue NE, Seattle, WA 98125 | **Phone:** (206) 363-3820 | **Fax:** (206) 366-8551 | **Email:** lplants@earthlink.net | **Directions:** From the north (Edmonds), exit I-5 to the right (heading west) onto N 145th Street. At the first traffic light, turn left (south) onto 1st Avenue NE. The nursery is on the right, after the 5-way stop. From the south (downtown Seattle), exit I-5 at N 130th Street and go left (west) to the first traffic light. Turn left (south) onto 1st Avenue NE. | **Open:** Open garden/sales in May and September, call for dates; and open by appointment.

This small, home-based urban nursery specializes in **perennials, unusual annuals,** a variety of clematis, and **ornamental grasses.** Linda Orantes strives to offer a wide variety of plants not readily available in larger nurseries, so she seeks out seed from English sources and from the Bellevue Botanical Garden NPA border. "I love to grow penstemon, salvia, geraniums, primulas, and so many more," she confesses. With propagation in her veins, Linda is also peddling her progeny at several ma-

jor plant sales and at the University District Farmer's Market (most Saturdays in June–July). Her display garden is a constantly expanding collection of plants as her eclectic interests evolve. A "flat city lot," the garden has good access on the periphery by sidewalks, but is tricky to navigate on the paths. Call for spring and fall sale dates at the nursery.

THORSETT LANDSCAPE NURSERY ✳

13501 SE 226th Place, Kent, WA 98042 | **Phone:** (253) 631-5838 | **Fax:** (253) 630-7244 | **Email:** info@thorsett.com | **Web:** www.thorsett.com | **Directions:** On the east hill of Kent. From Hwy 167, take the S 212th Street exit and travel east. Follow to 132nd SE and turn right to the nursery. | **Open:** Daily | **Plant list:** Free with SASE or on website; mail order on perennials in spring; wholesale and retail.

This family business, run by Allen and Elizabeth Thorsett for more than two decades, is located on a county homestead of 10 acres. It's a **full-service nursery,** so you'll find a broad range of plants, topsoil and amendments, garden furniture, planters, and much more. Thorsett's offers lots of **perennials,** with a dedication to unusual varieties and **trees,** field grown, from younger landscape to specimen sizes; they specialize in magnolias, dogwoods, and Japanese maples, but you'll find the likes of stewartia and parrotia as well. Shrubs, annuals, and a large selection of garden baskets fill the nursery. The fall harvest tradition draws excited schoolchildren here for field trips and a pumpkin-picking session in the field. It makes a charming memory from this friendly nursery. There are year-round, substantive classes for adults, too, including private classes for garden clubs, and a great newsletter. Visit the **English Tea Garden** and reserve your place for the summer tea parties, usually in June.

TILLINGHAST SEED CO.

623 E Morris Street, La Conner, WA 98257 | **Phone:** (360) 466-3329 | **Fax:** (360) 466-1401 | **Mailing address:** PO Box 738, La Conner, WA 98257 | **Directions:** From I-5, take exit 221 or 230 and follow signs to La Conner. Tillinghast Seed Co. is the first business on the right at the entrance to La Conner. | **Open:** Daily

The romantic old general store run by Arberta Lammers is genuine—not a fabricated marketing ploy. When A. G. "Gus" and Emma Tillinghast founded the company in 1885, they offered only high-quality seeds. Today, Tillinghast is a unique general store, which includes a flower shop, a kitchen and gourmet food shop, a garden center, a greenhouse, and an acre of nursery. This is the Northwest's oldest seed store, and seeds remain the heart of this business. On any spring morning, the store is filled with gardeners selecting seeds for their crops and swapping advice. Lining the walls are upward of 750 wooden bins filled with seed packets—more than 1,000 varieties of vegetables, herbs, and flowers. Come for conversation, information, and (always) hot coffee.

TOWER PERENNIAL GARDENS

4010 E Jamieson Road, Spokane, WA 99223 | **Phone:** (509) 448-6778 | **Fax:** (509) 448-1661 | **Email:** atower@mindspring.com | **Directions:** The retail nursery is located at the intersection of E Jamieson Road and the S Palouse Hwy. Take I-90 exit 283B (S Freya Street), turn left. Proceed south on S Freya Street to E Jamieson Road. | **Open:** Daily | **Catalog:** Free; shipping season April–October; wholesale and retail.

Alan and Susan Tower started their mail-order nursery business as part of a lifelong passion for gardening. By 1996, when Alan saw demand for Tower hostas "explode," he left his clinical psychology practice and took the plunge full-time into hostas. With his involvement with the American Hosta Society as Regional Director, it is not surprising to find the Towers' enthusiastically offering over **350 hosta varieties**, among them some introductions of rare species available (exclusively through the Towers) from George Schmid, author of *The Genus Hosta*, the definitive work on these plants. The catalog still focuses on hostas, with representative imports and expedition-collected varieties too. You'll also find a small selection of hardy perennials (ranging from the common to the rare), trees, shrubs, ornamental grasses, and daylilies. The nursery offers **an exceptional collection of plants**: hardy geraniums, arisaema and amorphophallus, alpines, herbs, woodland shade plants, plants for sunny borders, peonies, dwarf conifers—emphasizing the unique, unusual, and new. The nursery propagates more than 50 percent of its stock in seven greenhouses. If you are going to be in the Spokane area this season, make a point of dropping by to see how the extensive display gardens (herb, rock, sun, shade, and a new koi pond and water garden) are developing on this 8-acre pastoral site, with its 100-year-old rustic barn and farmhouse. Call for a special events schedule that includes live musicians playing in the garden, free refreshments (including the regionally famous Louise's Orange Pecan Cookies), plant specials, and classes. Events usually coincide with Mother's Day, Memorial Day, and include Hosta Heaven (June), Daylily Festival (July), and a Fall Celebration (September).

TSUGAWA NURSERY

410 Scott Avenue, Woodland, WA 98674 | **Phone:** (360) 225-8750 | **Fax:** (360) 225-5086 | **Email:** tsugawan@pacifier.com | **Web:** www.tsugawanursery.com | **Directions:** From I-5, take exit 21, and travel 0.5 mile north on the frontage road along the freeway to the nursery. | **Open:** Daily

This nursery is a family owned and operated business that has its roots in the Tsugawa berry farm, originally founded in 1947. In 1981, the family purchased a defunct nursery in Woodland, renaming it Tsugawa Nursery. In the next 20 years, their place has grown to become well-established as the **area's best spot to shop for garden and landscape plants and supplies.** As a full-service garden center, Tsugawa's is well known in southwest Washington because it has become a great source for supplies

and basics, as well as a destination for those in search of water garden supplies, equipment, and plants. There's a large bonsai department, a complete selection of quality imported tools, Japanese landscape materials, flower arranging supplies, and lots of plants—countless varieties of Japanese maples, bamboo, perennials, roses, shrubs, and trees. Plus, Tsugawa offers design and delivery services.

TWIN CREEKS PEONIES

41506 292nd Way SE, Enumclaw, WA 98022 | **Phone:** (360) 802-9740 | **Fax:** (360) 802-2046 | **Email:** peonygrow@aol.com | **Directions:** From Seattle, take I-5 south to the Auburn-Enumclaw exit; turn left onto Auburn Way (Hwy 18, then SR 164) and go through Muckleshoot area until you reach SE 416th Street. Turn left and go all the way to the end of 416th. Twin Creeks is at the end of the street. | **Open:** Friday and Saturday, 10 a.m.–5 p.m., or by appointment. | **Plant list:** Free; mail order in the fall only.

Two creeks (or "criks," as she refers to them) cross on Joyce Myers's scenic Enumclaw country estate, giving the garden its name. Here's where this industrious peony-lover has turned her passion into a business, growing **peonies** to sell both as plants and as **cut flowers in season.** Many varieties are on display in Twin Creeks' display gardens and borders around the home; it's not surprising that peonies also look at home in a Japanese-inspired garden. Peonies are available in spring in pots (and also as fresh-cut flowers). In September and October, the plants are sold as bare-root stock.

VALLEY NURSERY

20882 Bond Road NE, Poulsbo, WA 98370 | **Phone:** (800) 797-2819 or (360) 779-3806 | **Fax:** (360) 779-7426 | **Email:** valleynursery@silverlink.net | **Web:** www.valleynursery.com | **Directions:** From Poulsbo, take Hwy 305 north to Bond Road. Turn right to nursery. | **Open:** Daily | **Plant list:** Free; rose/fruit tree list also available. Mail order on bare-root roses only; shipping season late January to early March.

Gardeners who live in this area consider Valley Nursery prime stomping grounds. They have been in business here since 1973, operating on 6 acres in a country setting. A **full-service nursery and garden center,** the nursery's goal is to carry the best-adapted plants for Northwest gardens. They're noted for a great selection of fruit trees and berries, roses, perennials, ground covers, dwarf conifers, annuals, and hanging baskets—in short, a full selection of landscape and garden material. The garden shop is likewise fully stocked with everything from tools to lawn and garden seed and books. Take a class (available year-round, and most are free), attend special seasonal events, and sign up for the informative quarterly newsletter. This is an extremely pleasant nursery to peruse, with many, many tempting plants for discerning gardeners.

VAN LIEROP BULB FARM, INC.

13407 80th Street E, Puyallup, WA 98372-3608 | **Phone:** (253) 848-7272 or (800) 666-8377 | **Fax:** (253) 848-9142 | **Directions:** Located 2 miles east of downtown Puyallup off of Pioneer Avenue at 80th Street E. | **Open:** Seasonal, with spring and fall retail hours. | **Catalog/Brochure:** Free; shipping season is January–May and September–November; wholesale and retail.

Owned and operated by the Van Lierop family since 1934, the nursery puts on a spring show of over 300 varieties of crocus, daffodils, hyacinths, and tulips, as well as less well-known bulbs, in a lovely setting on the farm. There is a beautiful gift and garden shop (also open before Christmas for great gifts), and you can order bulbs and fresh-cut flowers from the attractive catalog.

Village Green Perennial Nursery

10223 26th Avenue SW, Seattle, WA 98146 | **Phone:** (206) 767-7735 | **Directions:** From the West Seattle Freeway, take the Delridge Way exit, go south about 3.5 miles, turn right (west) on Barton Pl (becomes Barton Street) to 26th Avenue SW, then turn left (south) and go 3 blocks. | **Open:** Seasonal

Teresa Romedo's very happy and lushly planted garden is a true testament to her lifetime love of gardening. If you have a pond and/or stream, as she has, come to see what her skillful design decisions have brought to life in these often difficult planting sites. You'll love wandering around with the feeling of being invited through a garden gate into a mad plantswoman's private domain, where seemingly thousands of plants go slightly wild (but with a spark of spirit and genius) in the overall landscape.

Teresa has an associate degree in landscaping from South Seattle Community College and propagates about 75 percent of the plants in her nursery. Her specialties are **old English roses** (on their own roots), lots of **perennials** (with an English cottage garden flower emphasis), and a good selection of hardy geraniums and unusual asters. The companionship of lilacs, hydrangeas, and irises with dwarf hinoki cypress and *Viburnum opulus* adds to a well-rounded selection. Teresa features a couple of English Teas in the garden each year, inviting the Daughters of the British Empire over to serve in proper style, and displaying artists' work in the garden. Several "twilight sales" are staged in the garden during spring and summer—you can shop until dark falls! Add your name to her mailing list to hear about sales and other events. Her shop features a good selection of large garden pots and planted containers, stepping-stones, herbal soaps, vinegars, jellies, and iron artwork from local artists. As Teresa says, "We have a very good time!"

Walker Mountain Meadows

82 Leadville Avenue, Quilcene, WA 98376 | **Phone:** (360) 765-4747 | **Email:** wmm@olypen.com | **Directions:** The nursery is 0.5 mile off Hwy 101 between Brinnon and Sequim. From Hwy 101 turn at the Whistling Oyster Tavern onto Linger Longer Road, go approximately 0.5 mile, over the bridge, and take the second right onto Leadville. The nursery is on the left. | **Open:** Seasonal and by appointment. | **Catalog:** $3, credited to your first order

This family-owned and operated nursery originated 12 years ago when Kristen and Don Kench (with the help of children Jared, Scott, Jamie, Kurtis, and Austin) turned a love of growing different and unusual plants into a reality—Walker Mountain Meadows Nursery.

Just a few examples of what you will find: **a large selection of trees** (Japanese maples from 12 inches to large specimen trees, *Nothofagus antarctica*, fernleaf beech, weeping white pines, weeping larch, katsuras); water and bog plants (several varieties of water and bog iris, including the stunning 'Black Gamecock'; eight varieties of papyrus, zebra rush, and corkscrew rush); and the Black Viola, the Fortnight Lily, and the Walking Iris. The seeds the Kenches have searched worldwide to find are repackaged in "Try Me Packs." You'll also discover a small, interesting selection of South African bulbs and calla lilies in several colors. If you can't make a trip to Quilcene, write or call to order the catalog, or seek out the Kench clan at garden shows in Seattle, Portland, Vancouver (WA) and San Francisco. Walker Mountain Meadows frequents the many regional plant sales, too.

Walsterway Iris Gardens

19923 Broadway, Snohomish, WA 98290 | **Phone:** (360) 668-4429 | **Directions:** From Hwy 522, turn west (left) at the traffic signal at Maltby. Take an immediate right at the stop sign, then continue to the "Y," veering left over railroad tracks. Continue 0.25 mile on Broadway; the gardens are on the right. | **Open:** Daily (closed Monday and Tuesday) | **Plant list:** $1; shipping July 15–August.

This is one of those country nurseries you'll want to discover in flower while lazing though the back roads. Ralph and Fran Walster specialize in **tall bearded iris** (500 varieties), **Japanese iris** (140 varieties), and **Siberian iris** (100 varieties)—all propagated here. Operated by this energetic couple for 15 years, Walsterway Iris Gardens began as a backyard hobby of Ralph's mother, Edith Walster. Peak bloom for bearded and Siberian irises is mid to late May, Japanese iris arrive in late June. The display garden will inspire you to tuck iris rhizomes into every available corner of your garden. When you visit, Fran and Ralph will dig the siberian and Japanese iris at the same time you choose them. They take orders for the bearded iris and ship after bloom season (see dates above). If you miss the show, they have captured their horticultural progeny in beautiful color photos filling several large albums. The nursery has added a gift shop featuring iris-inspired items like umbrellas, suncatchers, and other colorful fare. PS: This little gem is near Flower World Nursery, so it's easy to make a day of nursery hopping.

Watershed Garden Works

2039 44th Avenue, Longview, WA 98632 | **Phone:** (360) 423-6456 | **Fax:** Same | **Email:** watershedgardenworks@compuserve.com | **Directions:** Take the first Longview/Kelso exit off I-5, following signs for Ocean Beaches or Hwy 4. Travel west through Longview on Hwy 4 or Ocean Beach Hwy, until you reach 44th Avenue. Turn left and the nursery is located at the end of a 2-block dead-end street, at the last home on the right. | **Open:** By appointment; find the Edwards at the Saturday Farmer's Market in Longview/Kelso and the Sunday Farmer's Market in Astoria, Oregon. | **Plant list:** Free; shipping late fall to early spring; wholesale and retail.

Scott and Dixie Edwards worked on water quality for Kitsap County agencies for several years until the late 1980s, when they stepped into the gardening world. The reason? They couldn't find many of the plants they needed for projects, "so we decided this need was our way back to the farm," Dixie says. Watershed grows **Northwest natives** (including some Alaska natives, more found down through Oregon, and some Northern California plants). The Edwardses propagate 90 percent or more of their plants (growing 50 percent from seeds collected in the wild). They prefer seed-grown plants for the improved root structure, and this is evident in the health and vitality of their inventory: many kinds of native willows, Pacific wax myrtle, Pacific madrone, red osier dogwood, vine maples, bigleaf maples, Oregon ash, devil's club, cascara, red flowering currant, elderberry, cedar, Pacific yew, many forms of carex, scirpus, tiger lily, fragaria, and twinflower, among others. You can also purchase seeds directly from this innovative nursery.

WATSON'S GREENHOUSE & NURSERY

6211 Pioneer Way E, Puyallup, WA 98371 | **Phone:** *(253)* 845-7359 | **Fax:** (253) 845-8921 | **Directions:** This one is tricky to find, so it's best to call for directions. From I-5 northbound, take Puyallup exit 135; drive past the Bingo Hall and veer to the right on Pioneer Way at first stop light; continue past the Shell station on the right and Watson's will be on the left in 4 miles. From I-5 southbound, take the Puyallup-Bay Street exit and follow signs to Puyallup, turning left under the freeway. Then follow directions above, continuing past the Bingo Hall. | **Open:** Monday–Friday, 9 a.m.–6 p.m.; Saturday, 9 a.m.–5 p.m.; Sunday, 10 a.m.–5 p.m.

This family-owned nursery was started in 1984 by Dan and Fran Watson; daughters Maidee Gregory and Terri Elliott have now joined forces with their parents to operate Watson's as one of the area's full-service nurseries and garden centers. With 32,500 square feet of covered shopping area, the nursery is filled with annuals, herbs, perennials, houseplants, home décor, and gifts. Be sure to check out the expanding selection of garden art, too. Watson's growing facility allows the nursery to bring a wide variety of plants to the gardening public. Each year, the family grows no fewer than **60,000 geraniums,** fills thousands of mixed hanging baskets and planters, and also offers fuchsias and ivy geraniums. Come the holiday season, the charming, state-of-the-art glass greenhouse is filled with theme trees, poinsettias, holiday music, and the occasional visit from Santa.

WELLS NURSERY

1201 Blodgett Road, Mt. Vernon, WA 98274 | **Phone:** *(360)* 336-6544 or (800) 761-9355 | **Fax:** (360) 336-5606 | **Email:** wellsmv@aol.com | **Web:** www.wellsnurseries.com | **Directions:** Located directly adjacent to (east side of) I-5 at exit 226, the main Mt. Vernon exit; on Blodgett Road. | **Open:** Daily | **Catalog:** For wholesale customers only

This long, slender sliver of a nursery can be seen from I-5—it's the one in Mt. Vernon right alongside the freeway with those graceful, tall, rather eccentric dwarf and ornamental **conifers** and stunning **Japanese maples** along the fence. If you appreciate high-quality evergreens and dwarf conifers, ornamental trees, and flowering shrubs, then you will really enjoy a walk through this nursery. There is much to choose from among the **vines** here, including clematis, wisteria, and passifloras, and be sure to seek out the glorious resident climbing hydrangea. You'll also find a great selection of bamboo and hedging materials. There is an amazing selection of really choice stuff here, well worth a stop to investigate. What may escape your attention is that Wells Nursery has been in business over 60 years and has acres of growing fields nearby in the rich Skagit Valley soil. They're also well known for developing many of the trees and shrubs found in the nursery, and it's interesting to note that the majority of Wells's material wends its way to East Coast professional landscapers, garden centers, and nurseries.

If you've passed by for years, now is a good time to pop in for a look. You'll enjoy the display garden centered around a lovely pond. And for the serious gardener, there is a small arboretum at Wells's growing grounds (by appointment only). Many of the plants developed over the past six decades, now numbering 51, are on view in the garden. It is worth a visit to see what can be done with a small planting area. Also, Wells holds some pretty impressive 50-percent-off sales. Call to get on the mailing list for an invitation to the special events.

WELLS MEDINA NURSERY

8300 NE 24th Street, Medina, WA 98039 | **Phone:** *(425)* 454-1853 | **Directions:** From I-5, take Hwy 520 eastbound, then take exit 168 (Evergreen Point floating bridge) toward Bellevue. Take the first exit after crossing the bridge and turn right (south) onto 84th Avenue NE. At NE 24th Street, turn right 1 block. From Hwy 405, take the exit onto Hwy 520 westbound toward Seattle, and exit at 92nd Avenue NE. Go over the freeway heading south on 92nd Avenue NE to NE 24th Street. Turn right to the nursery 1 block. | **Open:** Daily

Wells Medina began life in 1971 as the inspiration of Ned Wells. It has grown over the years as a family business keen to have its patrons enthuse about the marvelous plant choices found there for every gardener, from quality, well-grown common plants to the great rarities. Ned has now handed over the reins to his two daughters, Wendy Wells and Lisa Wells Freed, who now energetically own and operate Wells Medina.

When horticultural luminaries are in town, this is where they are taken for a look-see. There is a Northwest orientation here, with **conifers, Japanese maples, Rhododendrons,** other flowering **trees and shrubs,** shade trees, an excellent selection of **vines,** ground covers, unusual and old favorite **annuals** and **perennials,** ornamental grasses, and herbs, all specialties. Many of the unusual plants or varieties you've been searching for they have found first, awaiting your arrival. There are also pots (indoor and out, large and small); a reference library for the convenience of their patrons; and seeds from Territorial, Thompson & Morgan, and Lilly Miller. In the fall you'll find an extensive selection of bulbs. And then there's that *stunning* display border designed by the highly respected Withey/Price duo that will knock your socks off! The sisters have added a new emphasis with fabulous display pots, showcased at the summer container design competition. In October, there's a wonderful "Celebrate the Reds" event that combines fall color with wine tastings, all to benefit the Washington Park Arboretum. Call for details. You can count on Wells Medina to be in top form year-round.

WEST SEATTLE NURSERY

5275 California Avenue SW, Seattle, WA 98136 | **Phone:** (206) 935-9276 | **Fax:** (206) 935-1494 | **Directions:** From I-5, take the West Seattle Freeway exit to Fauntleroy Way, make a right turn onto Alaska (unmarked, but watch for the Schucks/Hancock Fabric sign), and travel to California Avenue SW; turn left on California, for 4-5 long blocks, and the nursery is on the right, at SW Brandon. | **Open:** Daily, with extended holiday hours

This **full-service nursery/garden center** is very proud of its big selection of garden plants that range from unusual **perennials** to **trees** (over 100 varieties), **shrubs,** and seasonal annuals for the urban landscape, including a selection of roses you might not find elsewhere and a wide array of houseplants. Seeds include Territorial, Seeds of Change, Fragrant Gardens (devoted to sweet peas), Ed Hume, and Renee's Garden; garden necessities include a wide range of amendments, fertilizers, tools, gloves, terra cotta and decorative pots/containers, statuary, benches, books, and gifts for the garden and home. Throughout the nursery grounds there are attractive planting displays and pieces of Northwest garden art. The nursery sponsors two "Art in the Garden" shows annually, in early spring and early fall. WSN now offers several garden design and care services, including on-site garden consultations and garden design. If you are on West Seattle Nursery's mailing list you'll learn about the many classes and events. Stop by during the holidays to enjoy the dazzling Christmasy atmosphere, use the wreath-making machines, and choose from a great selection of living and fresh-cut Christmas trees.

WHITNEY GARDENS AND NURSERY

Olympic Peninsula on State Hwy 101 at Brinnon, WA 98320 | **Phone:** (360) 796-4411 or (800) 952-2404 | **Fax:** (360) 796-3556 | **Email:** info@whitneygardens.com | **Web:** www.whitneygardens.com | **Mailing address:** PO Box 170, Brinnon, WA 98320-0080 | **Directions:** On the Olympic Peninsula, along the Hood Canal on State Hwy 101 at Brinnon. | **Open:** Nursery open daily; garden open for a small fee | **Brochure:** Free, with best blooming time schedule and tour information | **Catalog:** $4, extensive color, a real bargain and makes an excellent reference on rhododendrons. Shipping as weather permits, September through May.

Ann and Ellie Sather are carrying on what began in 1970 as a hobby for George and Ann Sather. Set on 7 serene acres, this internationally respected garden/nursery (a true horticultural museum) specializes in **hybrid and species rhododendrons** with myriad companion plants: azaleas, maples, magnolias, kalmias, camellias, perennials, and conifers. The selection here is immense. The early blooming rhododendrons start showing color in February, with fragrant rhododendrons and azaleas at their best in late April and early May. Spring bloom peaks around Mother's Day and in fall there is spectacular autumn foliage color. The display gardens are beautiful in any season, from great fall foliage to blooms emerging in mid-March. Whitney Nursery also offers Burpee seeds, plus soils, bark, several types of organic manure, fertilizer, containers, and more.

WIGHT'S HOME AND GARDEN

5026 196th Street SW, Lynnwood, WA 98036 | **Phone:** (425) 775-3636 | **Fax:** (425) 672-1404 | **Directions:** From I-5 driving north from Seattle, take the Lynnwood-44th Avenue W exit 181A. Turn left onto 44th Avenue W and drive north to 196th, then turn left onto 196th and drive west to 50th Avenue W. From I-5 driving south from Everett, take the Lynnwood/196th Street exit 181, turn right (west) onto 196th Street SW and travel west to 50th Avenue W. | **Open:** Daily, with extended holiday hours.

It began as a small, rural roadside nursery in 1963, so the Wight's you see today has come a long way! Wight's has consistently been named as one of *Nursery Business Retailer* magazine's "Top 100 Garden Centers in America." This is the type of exemplary garden center that offers extra help for its customers, with Washington Certified Nursery Persons always on duty, and more assistance through popular free workshops and classes. The mature display gardens demonstrate several gardening styles and there are annual seasonal sales (roses in March, a Sidewalk Sale in July, a Red Tag Nursery sale in October, and an after-Christmas half-price sale). Wight's offers a full range of plants: **quality annuals and perennials, hundreds of varieties of roses and rhododendrons, unusual conifers, fine Japanese maples, and hard-to-find large-caliper trees.** With the explosive popularity of water gardening, you'll want to see the excellent selection here of pond supplies, equipment, fountains, and statuary, not to mention water-loving plants. Wight's seed department includes Lilly Miller, Northrop King Certified Organics, Thompson & Morgan, Ed Hume, Burpee, and Botanical Interests. There is a florist shop, as well as patio furniture, gifts, and a vast array of home and garden décor, all artfully displayed. Wight's is renowned for its Wonderland of Christmas, which begins November 1 and is a must-see event for adults and children alike.

WILD BIRD GARDEN AND NURSERY (SEE COASTAL GARDEN CENTER)

WILDSIDE GROWERS

6360 Hannegan Road, Lynden, WA 98264 | **Phone:** (360) 398-7158 | **Fax:** (360) 733-2581 | **Email:** wildsidegrowers@home.com | **Directions:** From I-5, take exit 255 and follow it east (Sunset Dr-Mt. Baker Hwy) to the traffic signal at Hannegan Road. Turn left and follow about 7 miles. The nursery is just north of Ten Mile Road (halfway between Bellingham and Lynden). | **Open:** By appointment only

Susan Taylor and Veronica Wisniewski specialize in Northwest native perennials and shrubs with selections to suit conditions from prairie to alpine. They also offer North American native plants, all propagated in-house, from seed collected in the wild and from their own growing stock. You'll find choice natives from about 150 species such as *Iris tenax* and *Lomatium nudicaule* to nine varieties of penstemon, *Rudbeckia occidentalis,* and some native bulbs. You'll also find Susan and Veronica at area plant sales, including the Fairhaven/Bellingham Neighbors Plant Sale in March and the Washington Park Arboretum's Spring Plant Sale.

WILEYWOOD NURSERY

17414 Bothell Way SE, Mill Creek, WA 98012 | **Phone:** (425) 481-9768 | **Fax:** (425) 483-9506 | **Email:** simpos@conceptsnet.com | **Directions:** From I-5, take the 164th Street exit 183, and travel east to Bothell Way, then turn right (south) and go 10 blocks. From I-405, take exit 26 and drive north 4 miles to the nursery, on the left. | **Open:** Daily

While it's pretty much a standard garden center with a wide selection, Wileywood has a few standouts, one of which would have to be their friendly reception to children, offering diversions to keep them happy while gardening parents concentrate on matters (momentarily) more important. There is also a large selection of rhododendrons, with over 150 hybrids, and the rose department boasts 100 varieties. Seed companies represented are Burpee, Ed Hume, and Lilly Miller. Services include a full-service florist and a U.S. post office outlet. You can recycle plastic pots here, too.

WINDMILL GARDENS

5823 160th Avenue E, Sumner, WA 98390 | **Phone:** (253) 863-5843 or (800) 628-6516 | **Fax:** (253) 263-8397 | **Email:** info@windmillgarden.com | **Web:** www.windmillgarden.com | **Directions:** From I-5 at Federal Way, take Hwy 18 to exit 182 east. Exit onto Hwy 167 south, then exit onto Hwy 410 traveling east. Take the third Sumner exit at 166th Avenue E, turn left (north) onto 166th Avenue E, turn left onto 60th Street E, then right onto 160th Avenue E. | **Open:** Daily. | **Plant list:** Free with SASE; wholesale and retail.

Windmill Gardens opened in 1968 as a wholesale grower offering forced bulbs for a cut-flower business, and has expanded greatly over the intervening years. From 1982, Windmill has incorporated **a retail nursery, full-service florist, a gift shop, and a 1.5-acre display garden.** You'll find a wide variety of unusual conifers and a broad range of roses, from antique to modern hybrids. Fuchsias (over 60 varieties) and fuchsia baskets are a specialty, and you'll appreciate the great selection of perennials. As it's a full-service nursery, though, you will also find a good selection of all types of plants in a lovely setting. There are constant programs to attract new customers and keep Windmill's regular fans returning. Look for Tea Thymes (an extensive workshop series featuring garden experts like Marianne Binetti and Ed Hume), Fuchsia Fantasia (end of March), Spring Garden Fest (April), Salsa Fest (May), a formal high tea accompanied by a string ensemble (various dates), a fall Harvest Festival, and Garden of Lights (holidays). If you're in the market for a special garden venue (wedding, anniversary, or other gathering), you can choose Windmill Gardens, as several facilities on the grounds are available for rent, including a gazebo and the signature windmill building. Check the website or call for a preview and rates. Look to Windmill Gardens for special seasonal events and classes year-round, and keep informed with their handsome and informative newsletter.

WIND POPPY FARM & NURSERY

3171 Unick Road, Ferndale, WA 98248 | **Phone:** (360) 384-6804 | **Fax:** Same | **Email:** grass@windpoppy.com | **Web:** www.windpoppy.com | **Directions:** From I-5, north of Bellingham take Slater Road exit 260. Drive west to Elder Road (Union 76 gas station/Jordans Store). Turn right onto Elder to Unick Road. The nursery is at the second house on the right. | **Open:** By appointment only | **Plant list:** Free with SASE; wholesale and retail.

Karen and Bruce Teper have opened a much-needed nursery featuring **ornamental grasses.** They also carry excellent perennials, including species poppies. If you have an ambition to add more ornamental grasses to your life, Wind Poppy is a terrific destination, with 150-plus varieties, 75 percent of which the Tepers propagate themselves. The knowledgeable, easygoing Tepers are ideal guides through the multitudes of plants you may not know yet. The family display garden (level and accessible) showcases perennials in the spring, fantastic ornamental grasses in the fall, and a new testing garden for large ornamental grasses. Seek out Wind Poppy at some of the larger plant sales in Seattle, including Northwest Horticultural Society, Northwest Perennial Alliance, and Arboretum Foundation events.

WINDY MEADOW NURSERY

7020 Dahlberg Road, Ferndale, WA 98248 | **Phone:** (360) 384-5348 | **Fax:** (360) 380-4954 | **Directions:** From I-5 north of Bellingham, take exit 266/Grandview Road. Travel 1.5 miles east and find the nursery, located on the right. | **Open:** Seasonally, by appointment only

Windy Meadow is primarily a wholesale nursery and countryside collector's garden with a glorious view of nearby Mount Baker. Dedicated to providing the world's finest flowers, Windy Meadow grows 400 varieties of unusual annuals and perennials, hanging baskets, and fall mums. The garden is tended by Jennifer Titus and includes **more than 2,000 species of trees, shrubs, annuals, perennials, bulbs, and vines** in borders and "layers" of color and texture. Come July, the nursery's disease-resistant Asiatic lilies (part of an aggressive breeding program) reward visitors with thousands of blooms. A **Delphinium elatum** breeding program has taken on a life of its own, with several hundred plants held out for evaluation each year. Make it a point to visit during Windy Meadow's open house, usually the first weekend in May, when you can learn more about this innovative plant source and buy plants direct from the growers.

WINTERGREEN TREE FARM & GARDEN SHOP

13606 S Machias Road, Snohomish, WA 98290 | **Phone:** (425) 337-8120 | **Fax:** (425) 337-9534 | **Directions:** From I-5, take the Hwy 2 exit 194 east. Then take the Hewitt Avenue exit and proceed east to Lake Stevens Road. Turn left to Machias Cutoff and follow east (becomes Machias Road); Wintergreen is on the right. From Snohomish at 2nd and Maple Avenue, go north (heading out of town). Maple Avenue becomes Snohomish-Machias Road. After 5 miles, there is a stop sign at Centennial Trail. Turn right onto S Machias Road and go 0.5 mile to the farm. | **Open:** Seasonal

If you have heard of the wholesale grower called Henry's Plant Farm, and were itching to get in to see Henry's amazing plants, here's a great deal. Wintergreen Tree Farm is the retail arm, and here you will find many, **many varieties of annuals and perennials for sun and shade.** There is a lovely selection of hostas, ferns, ligularias, and hebes. Plants from many of the area's specialty growers make their way here as well. In addition to a lineup of container plants, Wintergreen offers **large mixed hanging baskets and patio pots.** Two display gardens invite an easy-access walk, spring through fall, through an English country design with continuous color (in pinks and lavenders), and a classic country design with the hotter colors of bright annuals and perennials. Rain or shine you'll be drawn into the rustic barn full of botanically themed decoration for home and garden. You'll be charmed by this gathering of many unusual pieces. Call for current classes and events. Come the holidays, take a drive to the country for U-cut and precut Christmas trees.

WOODBROOK NURSERY

5919 78th Avenue NW, Gig Harbor, WA 98335 | **Phone:** (253) 265-6271 | **Fax:** Same | **Email:** woodbrk@harbornet.com | **Web:** www.woodbrook.net | **Mailing address:** 1620 59th Avenue NW, Gig Harbor, WA 98335 | **Directions:** From I-5 at Tacoma, go west on SR 16, then take the Gig Harbor/City Center exit, and turn left at the traffic light onto Wollochet Drive NW. Drive for 2.3 miles, turn right on Artondale Drive NW (becomes 78th Avenue NW) for 1.8 miles. Look for the small sign on the right. | **Open:** Seasonal and by appointment | **Plant list:** Free price list with plant descriptions; wholesale and retail.

Ingrid Wachtler has been interested in native plants for years. Since she has begun to grow them, she has been amazed at how many she was unfamiliar with that have significant ornamental merit. The list here is well chosen, consisting of deciduous and broadleaf evergreen trees, conifers, and deciduous shrubs, with a preponderance of **Northwest natives.** You'll also find ground covers, perennials, ferns, and vines for your landscape—a great selection. Ingrid offers quantity discounts and holds spring and fall sales.

WOODSIDE GARDENS (SEE NORA'S NURSERY)

FARMER'S MARKETS / PLANT SALES

About 60 public markets in Washington are active these days, and many of them provide an urban outlet for small and specialty growers and nurseries that are perhaps not set up to handle retail shoppers, or that are located in rural areas not accessible to the general buyer. If you frequent farmer's markets, you'll soon learn that what is brought for sale is often the best of what is growing in the nursery. Consider attending markets away from your own community—it's a good way to explore other areas to find variety in plants and produce. You can get lists of markets from:

❀ **Washington State Farmer's Market Association,** PO Box 30727, Seattle, WA 98103-0727; (206) 706-5198; www.wafarmersmarkets.com.

❀ The **Puget Sound Farm Direct Marketing Association** publishes a *Farm Fresh Guide* each spring to highlight everything from U-pick farms and farmer's markets to roadside plant and flower markets in King, Pierce, Skagit, and Snohomish Counties. The guides are available at most local libraries, some Chamber of Commerce offices, the growers' farms, or by sending a first-class stamp to Farm Fresh Guide, Attn.: Sue Larson-Kinzer, Editor, 1733 NE 20th Street, Renton, WA 98056. The *Farm Fresh Guide* is also available online at the Puget Sound Fresh website: www.pugetsoundfresh.org.

Many small and specialty growers, not otherwise accessible to the voracious plant-buying public, bring their plants to special plant sales like those sponsored by the **Arboretum Foundation,** the **Northwest Horticultural Society, Master Gardeners,** or the **Hardy Plant Society of Oregon,** and to big meetings of horticultural organizations like the **Northwest Perennial Alliance Study Weekend** or the **North American Rock Garden Society Study Weekend.** When a nursery owner or grower belongs to a garden club or similar organization, they may bring plants for sale too. (See Chapter 2, "Clubs, Societies & Volunteer Opportunities," and Chapter 7, "Plant Sales.")

SPECIALTY NURSERY ASSOCIATIONS

These groups and organizations have pulled together their collective acts (not without many volunteer hours of a few energetic souls) and put out very informative (and free) guides that provide a listing for member nurseries and related companies.

The **Kitsap Peninsula Visitor and Convention Bureau** has published *A Resource Guide for the Gardener and Lover of Gardens*, an informative free brochure. It profiles 24 nurseries, gardens to visit, and garden shops, several of which are new discoveries. You can also learn the locations of several WSU–Kitsap County Master Gardener demonstration sites. To request a free copy, call (360) 297-8200 or email info@visitkitsap.com.

The **Specialty Nursery Association / Specialty Nursery Guides** are available from the association at 20055 235th Avenue SE, Maple Valley, WA 98038, or online at www.specialtynurseries.org.

The **Specialty Nursery Association of Clark Co.** publishes a guide to its member nurseries each spring. You can write for a free copy at PO Box 326, La Center, WA 98629, email shaccmail@aol.com, or call (360) 263-8890.

The **Washington State Nursery and Landscape Association** (www.wsnla.org) annually publishes a "Retail Nursery Map," available free at many nurseries. You can request it by calling (800) 672-7711 or writing WSNLA, PO Box 670, Sumner, WA 98390.

MAIL-ORDER AND ONLINE NURSERIES OUTSIDE THE NORTHWEST

CANYON CREEK NURSERY

3527 Dry Creek Road, Oroville, CA 95965 | **Phone:** (530) 533-2166 | **Fax:** Same | **Email:** johnccn@sunset.net | **Web:** www.canyoncreeknursery.com | **Open:** By appointment only | **Catalog:** $1; shipping spring and fall.

Located in a rugged canyon in Northern California, this family-run, mail-order nursery has the **largest lineup of fragrant violets in the United States,** as well as **a fine selection of uncommon perennials.** John and Susan Whittlesey's collection is not vast, but it is well considered. You will not find trendy upstarts but rather their tried and true favorites, including excellent selections of salvias (nearly 50 listed), hardy geraniums, 13 euphorbias, a few cultivars of kniphofias, agastache, and more than 45 different violas and violets (including some from one of England's top hybridizers, Richard Cawthorne); many *V. odoratas*; doubles and semi-doubles; Parmas; species violets, and—hang on, dianthus fans—nearly 20 dianthus varieties, including many historic ones. The prices seem reasonable and the information-packed web-

site beautifully illustrates a partial inventory of the full array carried in the Canyon Creek Nursery catalog.

COMPLETELY CLEMATIS SPECIALTY NURSERY

217 Argilla Road, Ipswich, MA 01938-2617 | **Phone:** (978) 356-3197 | **Fax:** Same | **Email:** vines@clematisnursery.com | **Web:** www.clematisnursery.com | **Open:** Weekdays, 8 a.m.–3 p.m. EST | **Catalog:** $3

Completely Clematis is a small nursery specializing in all types of clematis, with a special interest in small-flowered species and hybrids that are easy and rewarding to grow. The catalog and website highlight over 200 varieties (with more clematis added frequently). For the most thorough reference, order the catalog. This nursery is most helpful in sharing its expertise on climate and zone questions, tailoring planting instructions to the United States, rather than the United Kingdom. "The life expectancy of a properly planted and cared for clematis is indefinite: there is a *C. Montana* at Hill of Tarvit in Fife, Scotland, that is over 80 years old and shows no signs of flagging," according to the website. So take heart! Success with clematis is easy if you choose the right variety for your situation, plant it properly, and continue to give it appropriate care.

CRYSTAL PALACE PERENNIALS

PO Box 154, St. John, IN 46373 | **Phone:** (219) 374-9419 | **Fax:** (219) 374-9052 | **Email:** info@crystalpalaceperennials.com | **Web:** www.crystalpalaceperennials.com | **Open:** Daily; wholesale and retail. | **Catalog:** $3, refundable with first order, thoughtfully organized with lots of helpful supplementary material

Founded by Greg and Sue Speichert in 1989, Crystal Palace Perennials is a small, family owned and operated nursery with a mission to help customers succeed with ponds and their plants. Here you will find one of the largest collections of **plants that grow in, around and near the pond** (naturally occurring or man-made), with roughly 200 species and cultivars, not counting 100 water lilies. The network Greg and Sue consult in search of rarities reaches around the world, and the benefit to you is a long list of uncommon hardy and tropical water plants and pond marginals. They are also active propagators involved in wetland mitigation to save rare and endangered natives. Should you find yourself in the area (about one hour outside Chicago), take the opportunity to experience their ever-expanding display garden (especially May through August, Monday–Saturday). The catalog doubles as a primer on pond gardening, offering lots of advice from the voice of experience. In that vein, the Speicherts offer a book, *Water Gardening in Containers,* and they co-publish *Water Gardening: The Magazine for Pondkeepers.* (See also Chapter 6, "Seed Sources," and Chapter 10, "Literature & Periodicals.")

KLEHM'S SONG SPARROW PERENNIAL FARM

13101 E Rye Road, Avalon, WI 53505 | **Phone:** (800) 553-3715 | **Fax:** (608) 883-2257 | **Email:** info@songsparrow.com | **Web:**

www.songsparrow.com or www.klehm.com | **Catalog:** $4 ($10 US outside the United States).

Long appreciated for its solid reputation as one of the country's top sources of **estate peonies and wonderful new hybrid peonies,** Klehm's Nursery has been renamed to better reflect the broader range of plants grown and sold here: peonies, tree peonies, hostas, daylilies, roses, bearded iris, lilies, clematis, grasses, vines, perennials, trees, shrubs and conifers. Klehm's Song Sparrow Perennial farm offers a wide range of top-quality plants that exhibit ornamental merit for North American gardens. The nursery offers proven favorites and the finest new introductions from breeders around the world.

LILYPONS WATER GARDENS

PO Box 10, Buckeystown, MD 21717-0010 | **Phone:** (301) 874-5133 or (800) 999-LILY | **Fax:** (800) 879-5459 | **Email:** info@lilypons.com | **Web:** www.lilypons.com | **Open:** Daily, March–November, 9 a.m.–5 p.m. | **Catalog:** $5, color

Before more local sources sprang up, many **water lily** enthusiasts turned to Lilypons. The catalog and website provide exceptional references for identification (and selection, too—beyond what you are likely to find in your area). This renowned water garden plant-nursery began in 1917; its name was "borrowed" from the opera diva Lily Pons in 1936. Lilypons propagates 90 to 95 percent of their stock of water lilies, lotus, and water-margin plants. The catalog also lists a full line of pond liners, pumps, filters, vacuums, fish food, plant tablets, containers, and more. Today, a fourth-generation Thomas, Margaret Thomas Koogle, presides over the family business, following in the footsteps (or should we say steppingstones?) of founder G. Leicester Thomas. If you can schedule a visit to the grounds, still operating at the original site in Maryland, you'll be treated to a tour of the display ponds.

LOGEE'S GREENHOUSES

141 North Street, Danielson, CT 06239 | **Phone:** (888) 330-8038 or (860) 774-8038 | **Fax:** (888) 774-9932 | **Email:** logee-info@logees.com | **Web:** www.logees.com (order online) | **Catalog:** $3

Since 1892, Logee's has offered **tropical and subtropical plants from around the globe.** The luscious color catalog is excuse enough to build that conservatory or greenhouse you've dreamed about! Consider this a MUST HAVE catalog for tender plants you can't get anywhere else—575 varieties and counting. The zonal range has been extended, too, encompassing choice perennials for more hardy climates.

OLD HOUSE GARDENS – HEIRLOOM BULBS

536 Third Street, Ann Arbor, MI 48103 | **Phone:** (734) 995-1486 | **Fax:** (734) 995-1687 | **Email:** OHGBulbs@aol.com | **Web:** www.oldhousegardens.com | **Catalog:** $2

Scott Kunst is fanatically dedicated to antique and heirloom bulbs (from the 1500s to the 1930s) and works hard to offer the most authentic varieties he can, so if you're trying to replicate a garden that would have been planted in an earlier era, he will have already searched high and low to ferret out those historic bulbs. Of course, antique bulbs can be a glory in any garden, often as graceful as wildflowers, richly fragrant, enduringly tough, and often intriguingly different. Scott's catalog is delightful, providing engaging reading and inspiration to spare. You will also want to look here for books (including reprinted Victorian bulb catalogs), forcing vases, tools, and supplies. A landscape historian by profession, Scott is available to provide a slide presentation and talk on preserving historic plants and landscapes. He has also partnered with Seed Savers Exchange to pioneer heirloom-bulb preservation. The collaborative effort has created a public awareness campaign among gardeners, naming the "endangered bulb of the year" and featuring some of Old House Gardens' rare bulbs in Seed Savers' catalog. (Find Seed Savers online at www.seedsavers.org.)

PLANT DELIGHTS NURSERY

9241 Sauls Road, Raleigh, NC 27603 | **Phone:** (919) 772-4794 | **Fax:** (919) 662-0370 | **Email:** office@plantdel.com | **Web:** www.plantdel.com | **Catalog:** "10 stamps or a box of chocolates" (interpret this as you will).

Among the Plant Delights here is an engagingly humorous catalog, its gentle joshing bordering occasionally on the sarcastic. Earlier issues have been subtitled along the lines of "Raiders of the Lost Park" and "It's not easy being variegated," as this nursery boldly announces its mission to sell unusual perennials. You'll find an online catalog of 1,000-plus offerings, including arisaema, asarum, cannas, crinum lilies, epimediums, ferns, hardy palms, hardy ginger lilies, hellebores, heuchera, hosta, lobelia, ornamental grasses, pulmonaria, Solomon's seal, tiarella, verbena . . . and more.

The website, in operation since 1997, has allowed Plant Delights to offer low-quantity plant orders. Here, you'll also find daily logs from plant expeditions, favorite plant articles, and great links. If you are visiting Raleigh, North Carolina, enjoy a visit, where you'll meet 6,000 different kinds of plants in the "Juniper Level Botanic Garden."

RICHTERS

357 Hwy 47, Goodwood, Ontario L0C 1A0 Canada | **Phone:** (905) 640-6677 | **Fax:** (905) 640-6641 | **Email:** orderdesk@richters.com | **Web:** www.richters.com (order online).

The Richters' selection of herbs (including plants, bulbs, rootstock, tubers, and seeds) is unsurpassed, offering medicinal, culinary and aromatic choices. The catalog is a delight to receive each winter as you begin to plot herbal adventures for the coming season. You'll find **over 900 varieties of favorite and hard-to-find herbs,** including new introductions like curry leaf, lemon mint marigold, and the stevia herb (whose leaves produce that all-natural sugar substitute). Richters has been a family-run business for more than 30 years, located about 40 minutes outside Toronto. If you're in the area, a visit is recommended: you'll find an herb "rockscape" that depicts the Niagara escarpment, plus garden sculptures, seasonally changing displays, and fragrant paths. Take in one or more of the ongoing, mostly herb-related classes and special activities. Richters offers its own line of culinary, medicinal, ornamental, and aromatic herb seeds, including non-GMO and "sow natural" certified organic lines. There are also organic specialty seed potatoes. All added up, its excellent descriptions and lots of color photos make this a "must have" catalog—or visit the great website, that provides loads of information.

THE ROSERAIE AT BAYFIELDS

PO Box R, Waldboro, ME 04572-0919 | **Phone:** *(207) 832-6330* | **Fax:** (800) 933-4508 | **Email:** zapus@roseraie.com | **Web:** www.roseraie.com

The Roseraie at Bayfields presents over 300 varieties of roses available for shipping bare root from February to May (and during November for fall planting in Zones 5B and warmer). With its reputation for seeking out and offering "practical roses for hard places," this is a useful and instructive resource. You'll find own-root and grafted roses, with a good selection of old roses, species, English, and special-use roses. If you can't make it to Maine, where you can walk through a lovely array of raised-bed rose displays, visit Roseraie's "second best site" online. You'll find color images and many additional resources on rose selection, planting, and care. The Roseraie Round Table is a lively online bulletin board that invites participation.

SEQUOIA NURSERY

2519 E Noble Avenue, Visalia, CA 93292 | **Phone:** *(559) 732-0309* | **Fax:** (559) 732-0192 | **Email:** sequoianursery@miniatureroses.com | **Web:** www.sequoianursery.com | **Catalog:** Free

Now in his nineties, Ralph Moore has operated this rose nursery since 1937. Moore is **one of the world's most respected rose hybridizers, specializing in miniatures** (he has been called the "Father of Modern Miniature Roses"), and the list of awards he and his roses have won is lengthy and shows no sign of letting up. In 1999, the first-ever American Rose Society all-miniature international show was staged in his honor. It is not surprising that the catalog and new website showcase Ralph's work in miniatures. But be sure to check the Supplemental List, where you will find hundreds of additional offerings, many of them difficult to locate elsewhere, and all at extremely reasonable prices. Rosarians-in-the-know trust Sequoia to provide healthy roses, true to description.

WE-DU NURSERIES

2055 Polly Spout Road, Marion, NC 28752-9338 | **Phone:** (828) 738-8300 | **Fax:** (828) 738-8131 | **Email:** wedu@wnclink.com | **Web:** www.we-du.com | **Open:** Weekdays | **Catalog:** $3

We-Du Nurseries specializes in **American, Japanese, Chinese, and Korean wildflowers, rock garden plants, unusual perennials,** species irises and daylilies, hardy bulbs, and native and woody ornamentals. Located in the foothills of the Blue Ridge Mountains, We-Du grows plants on about 30 acres with widely varying microclimates. (North Carolina is USDA zone 7B, but many of the plants grow near Boston in zone 6B, which will give you an idea of how they might do in your area.) They write: "We feel that our flora include many beautiful plants suitable for the perennial border, which have been entirely neglected by the gardening public."

WHITE FLOWER FARM

PO Box 50, Litchfield, CT 06759 | **Phone:** *(800) 503-9624* | **Fax:** (860) 496-1418 | **Email:** hort@whiteflowerfarm.com or custserv@whiteflowerfarm.com | **Web:** www.whiteflowerfarm.com | **Catalog:** $5 (four issues per year), includes $5 credit toward purchase; or, at present, you can order the catalog free online.

The farm offers a quintessential catalog for annuals, perennials, bulbs, ornamental shrubs, trees, roses, woody vines and climbers, floral gifts, containers, and cool tools. White Flower Farm definitely has a beautiful lineup of plants to choose from. The text is well written, which makes these catalogs keepers, especially in your perennial reference library. Online, you can see the inventory, plus obtain more information, more photographs, and more plant varieties. If you're in the Litchfield area, call for details on the summer Open House to tour the White Flower Farm display gardens (frequently pictured in the catalog). It's usually in July. Check the website for their White Sale and "only on the Web" special deals.

YUCCADO NURSERY

PO Box 907, Hempstead, TX 77445 | **Phone:** *(979) 826-4580* | **Email:** info@yuccado.com | **Web:** www.yuccado.com

YuccaDo is an organic nursery specializing in the fabulous **plants of Southwest Texas and Northern Mexico,** where you'll find plants and trees grown specifically for their drought- and heat-tolerant characteristics. The current fascination in our region for wonderful agaves, bromeliads, cycads, palms, and subtropicals has sent us searching for sources. Here's one great place to start—and you'll find they lend their expertise with a great sense of fun. You're encouraged to visit YuccaDo (located about 60 miles outside Houston) during one of the nursery's open garden days (usually one weekend each month, March to October). Visits benefit the adjacent Peckerwood Garden, through which YuccaDo fosters a lively seed preservation and seed exchange relationship. The garden is a valuable repository of rare and unusual native plants from Mexico and the Southwest United States.

HARDINESS ZONES

For obvious reasons, the "hardiness" of particular plants is of vital interest to the gardener. Yet many of us are quite baffled by the systems set up to designate zones indicating minimum average temperatures to guide us as we select plants for our gardens. For American gardeners, there are three separate (and "conflicting") rating systems: Arnold Arboretum, Sunset's *Western Garden Book*'s proprietary climate maps, and the USDA Zone Hardiness Map.

Hardiness based on cold has been traditionally chosen to indicate zones because low winter temperatures provide a level of stress that tests the limits of a plant's ability to survive. Both the Arnold Arboretum zone map and the more familiar USDA Zone map depend for their ratings on winter temperatures. But low temperatures are not the only factors that are important to consider for plant survival. Annual rainfall and heating units are also very important considerations. No one zonal map will answer all the specific questions about what causes a plant to thrive or expire in a particular garden location.

Local Northwest gardeners now realize that while the USDA and Arnold systems may be functional east of the Great Plains, they do not satisfactorily address the varying influences in the many Western regional climate areas. For a more in-depth understanding, gardeners here might consider using the 24 climate zone system developed by Sunset. Their climate zone system, uniquely used by the Menlo Park, California-based publisher, includes specific information on factors such as latitude, elevation, and water availability, supplemented by the results of testing "indicator" plants. The 2001 edition of the Sunset's *Western Garden Book* provides maps showing topographical information, clearer distinctions between the 24 zones, and insets detailing micro-climates. While most gardens themselves have a number of micro-climates affecting plant health, the Sunset system allows the gardener to begin studying local climate conditions with an excellent framework. The newest USDA Plant Hardiness Zone Map was released in 1991, its first update in twenty-five years. It's used nationally by nursery catalogs and plant suppliers to indicate winter hardiness. Gardeners in the Pacific Northwest, even when using the Sunset guide for specific information, will naturally refer to this because it helps in understanding plant information produced nationally. Some microclimate information is included, but without the detail in Sunset. The map shows the lowest temperatures likely in U.S. areas based on horticultural and meteorological data collected from 1974 to 1986. It's most valuable for comparisons of temperature conditions in various regions.

You can view the USDA Plant Hardiness Zone Map and learn more information at the United States National Arboretum website: http://www.usna.usda.gov/Hardzone/.

BRINGING PLANTS ACROSS THE BORDER

Bringing Plants from British Columbia to the United States

As of enforcement that became effective January 2002, the United States is requiring a Canadian Phytosanitary Certificate for all propagated plant material (including houseplants, orchids, bedding plants, and even cuttings) entering the United States.

A Phytosanitary Certificate (Phyto) is an official document issued by the plant protection organization of the exporting country to the plant protection organization of the importing country. It indicates that the plants and plant products covered by the certificate are free from quarantine pests, practically free from other injurious pests, and that they conform to the country's phytosanitary import requirements. A Phytosanitary Certificate is not a trade document.

The Canadian Food Inspection Agency (CFIA) has a website that outlines the regulations; see www.inspection.gc.ca/english/plaveg/internat/internate.shtml.

Prior to January 2002, policies allowed USDA inspectors at the border crossings to authorize some plant entry at their own discretion without a Phyto. "Now, if you don't have a Phyto, we don't have an option anymore," explained one USDA. inspector. "So some people are just abandoning their plants at the border."

We recommend U.S. visitors to Canada take the following steps to ensure they can successfully bring those wonderful plant discoveries home:

❋ Plan ahead. No more impulse buying! We recommend you contact the nurseries you plan on visiting in advance and ask about their policies for arranging for a Canadian plant inspector to check the plants and provide you with the necessary paperwork. The Phytosanitary Certificate costs $12.35 Canadian for up to $1,600 Canadian in plants intended for noncommercial (residential) use. (Some nurseries may charge a nominal fee for arranging the inspection, however.)

❋ Several nurseries have recommended U.S. customers begin their visit to British Columbia with a day of plant buying. "If you visit us first, then while you're touring Vancouver for a few days, we can arrange for the Phyto and have everything ready for you to pick up on your way back through the border," said one nurseryman in Tsawwssen.

❋ If you're lucky enough to be at a major plant sale or event, such as the VanDusen Flower & Garden Show, there may be a Canadian Food Inspection Agency plant inspector on site who can examine your plants and prepare your Phyto while you wait. If you're heading to a flower show or plant sale, it's a good idea to contact the producers in advance and inquire about this.

* If you wish to obtain your own Phyto, you must contact one of the CFIA offices 24 to 48 hours in advance to schedule a visit with your plants. Ask to speak with a Plant Inspector. These offices are open only Mondays through Fridays, 8 a.m. to 4 p.m. so you're out of luck on the weekends.

Here are the offices:

CFIA, 10362 Royal Avenue, New Westminster (located about halfway between Vancouver, B.C., and the Peace Arch border crossing); (604) 666-2891.

CFIA, Pacific Custom Broker Building, 17637 First Avenue, Room 207, Blaine (Pacific Hwy. truck crossing); Kara Soares, (604) 541-3366 or Remy McKenzie, (604) 541-3371.

CFIA Abbotsford (near the Sumas border crossing); (604) 854-8029.

Bringing Plants from the United States to British Columbia

While Canada still allows you to bring houseplants across the border without a Phyto, you must obtain the paperwork for any other propagated plant. For orchids, Canada also requires a CITES (Convention on International Trade in Endangered Species) form, which is supplied by the grower.

* We offer Canadian gardeners a similar caveat of "plan ahead" as you return home with plants from the United States. You will need to obtain a Phytosanitary Certificate issued by the United States Department of Agriculture (USDA) or a state department of agriculture agency.

* As we've recommended to U.S. plant-buyers, call the nursery or nurseries you're planning to visit in advance and ask if they can arrange for a Phyto. The Northwest Flower & Garden Show in Seattle also arranges to have USDA inspectors on hand to issue plant Phytos for international visitors. The USDA charges $50 for a single Phyto form, which covers 1 to 100 plants. To save money, several friends can group their plants together under one form.

* If you wish to make an appointment to obtain your own Phyto, contact offices of the USDA or the Washington Department of Agriculture (which is authorized to issue Phytos) 24 to 48 hours in advance. Ask to speak with a Plant Inspector. These offices are only open Mondays through Fridays, 7:30 a.m. to 4 p.m., so you're out of luck on the weekends. Here are the offices:

USDA office at Seattle-Tacoma International Airport; (206) 764-6547.

USDA Plant Protection and Quarantine office in Blaine; (360) 332-8891.

WSDA office in Puyallup; (253) 445-4516. This office can also direct you to inspectors around the state.

WSDA office in Bellingham; (360) 676-6739.

Good Luck!

chapter 6

SEED SOURCES

The pleasure of growing high-quality, unique vegetables, trees, flowers, and herbs from seed is one that, for many of us, ranks high in our gardening experiences. If you're among those dedicated to the practice, the following compendium will perhaps read like a list of your closest friends. If this is new to you, we hope you'll be among the many who will be inspired to write for catalogs to give this satisfying approach to gardening a whirl. In addition to these sources, have a look in the "Reference" section in the gardening books you consult (especially ones written about the Pacific Northwest), where you'll often find invaluable listings, compiled and endorsed by the author. And watch for seed exchanges, offered through specialty garden clubs and societies, for a wild selection rarely found commercially! Additionally, we highly recommend digging around on the Internet to find where seeds are available, often along with cultivation, propagation, and harvesting advice. We've reviewed some great sites in this chapter—but of course, the Internet is a vast frontier . . . following the links can sometimes yield rewarding discoveries. And when the seed catalogs start to roll in around mid-December, there's always a veritable "cyberimplosion," as the excited messages fly through the ether. It's awfully convenient to have an international grange at your fingertips!

U.S. SEED SOURCES

ABUNDANT LIFE SEED FOUNDATION

930 Lawrence Street (PO Box 772), Port Townsend, WA 98368 | **Phone:** (360) 385-5660 | **Fax:** (360) 385-7455 (office open 10 a.m.–4 p.m.) | **Email:** abundant@olypen.com | **Web:** www.abundantlifeseed.org | **Catalog:** $2 donation

Abundant Life is a nonprofit foundation dedicated to the preservation of genetic diversity, with an emphasis on **rare or endangered seeds.** They acquire, preserve, and distribute open-pollinated seeds, concentrating on rare heirloom vegetables, medicinal herbs, and Pacific Northwest natives. ALSF also provides education on cultivation and seed saving. All seeds are fungicide-free and many are certified organic. The 2001 catalog offered over 1,000 vegetables, grains, and edible seeds, herbs, flowers, wildflowers, and berries, plus broadleaf and coniferous trees and shrubs. They also list a large selection of books you might have a hard time finding elsewhere, on topics such as alternative agriculture, herbs, growing from and collecting seed, plant identification, references and resources, and health and nutrition aspects. Visitors are welcome to Abundant Life's seed test garden at 27th and Discovery Road in Port Townsend.

THE BANANA TREE

715 Northampton Street, Easton, PA 18042 | **Phone:** (610) 253-9589 | **Fax:** (610) 253-4864 | **Web:** www.banana-tree.com | **Catalog:** Online; plants and seeds

Many of our fellow gardeners here in the Northwest have developed a perverse interest in growing plants with **tropical and exotic foliage.** In order to extend the range of these plants and their growing season, many gardeners are installing glasshouses where the more tender exotics can live year-round or migrate in fall. Here is a terrific resource if your interest lies in tempting the hardiness gods and you are fortunate enough to have an appropriate home for the likes of the dwarf Jamaican Red Banana, or if you are an avid Asian vegetable grower (find seed for varieties from bok choi to joi choi to mei qing choi). A collector's Mecca.

BOUNTIFUL GARDENS

18001 Shafer Ranch Road, Willits, CA 95490 | **Phone:** (707) 459-6410 | **Fax:** (707) 459-1925 | **Email:** bountiful@sonic.net | **Web:** www.bountifulgardens.org/ | **Catalog:** Free

Bountiful Gardens is a project of Ecology Action, an environmental research and education organization formed in 1970 (BG has been around since 1982) headed up by John Jeavons. The group's research mini-farm is involved in **biointensive growing,** and offers open-pollinated, untreated seeds of vegetables and grains, compost crops, herbs, and flowers (mostly heirloom varieties, many organically grown). Note the listing of exclusive new seeds and books.

CALLAHAN SEEDS

PO Box 5531, Central Point, OR 97502 | **Phone:** (541) 855-1164 | **Open:** By appointment | **Catalog:** $1

An extensive list of woody plant seeds with an emphasis on hardiness (including about 600 species of Northwest native trees and shrubs). Seeds are available in small packets and bulk. Frank Callahan, a botanist and "Big Tree Hunter," has led numerous seed collecting expeditions into Mexico.

CASCADE BULB AND SEED

PO Box 271, Scotts Mills, OR 97375 | **Phone:** (503) 873-2218 | **Email:** halinar@open.org | **Web:** www.homestead.com/cascade | **Open:** By appointment | **Seed and plant list:** Online, or send first-class stamp

Offering Asiatic, martagon, trumpet, and aurelian lilies, daylilies, and many more.

THE COOK'S GARDEN

PO Box 535, Londonderry, VT 05148 | **Phone:** (800) 457-9703 | **Fax:** (800) 457-9705 | **Web:** www.cooksgarden.com | **Catalog:** Free

Visit Cook's display garden, right next to Gardener's Supply Company if you find yourself in the Burlington, Vermont, area. Ellen and Shep Ogden are hands-on gardeners and enthusiastic cooks who exude a value system that emphasizes environmental respect and an appreciation for quality. If this philosophy appeals to you, you will probably love reading their packed-to-bursting catalog. They search the world for the best varieties, looking to top breeders in Holland, England, Denmark, Germany, and Japan as well as the United States. In one year they may consider over 20,000 different individual plantings, bringing only the best home to grow in their test gardens and then introducing the top candidates in their catalog. Find an expanded range of space-saving mixtures for small gardens; and great collections (Fragrant Flowers, Cut Flowers, Vines, Sunflowers, Children's Flower Garden, Cottage Garden). The plant section is expanded too, and you'll still find lots of crop cover material, soil builders, small hand tools, seed-starting systems, and cookbooks (including their own).

DeGIORGI SEED COMPANY

6011 N Street, Omaha, NE 68117-1634 | **Phone:** (800) 858-2580 | **Fax:** (402) 731-8475 | **Email:** lisadechant@degiorgiseed.com | **Web:** www.degiorgiseed.com | **Catalog:** Free

Founded in 1905. With over 1,200 flower and vegetable varieties to select from, you'll need to assert your best decision-making skills! Not for the wishy-washy and non-committal.

FERRY-MORSE SEED CO.

PO Box 1620, Fulton, KY 42041-1620 | **Garden helpline:** (800) 283-3400 | **Fax:** (800) 283-2700 | **Email:** mail@ferry-morse.com | **Web:** www.ferry-morse.com | **Catalog:** Online

Unique to Ferry-Morse Seeds is the toll-free number they offer for your gardening questions. It's a nice gesture from one of **America's oldest and largest seed companies**—founded in 1856! Until the 1950s you could order seeds from their catalog, but after that their seed packets were available only in retail garden centers. Today, one can still find their seeds in retail stores, and the catalog is back—twenty-first–century style—in online form. This state-of-the-art online catalog is amazing, offering full-color packet pictures of most varieties, lots of garden design plans, growing and preserving tips, a "flower by color" feature (allowing one to search their seed archives by specific color), posters, garden products, books, and CDs. Check out the recently added organic seed line. Perhaps the nicest thing about Ferry-Morse is the "Guarantee to Grow," which should comfort those gardeners who want to become more ambitious!

FILAREE FARM

182 Conconully Highway, Okanogan, WA 98840 | **Phone:** (509) 422-6940 | **Email:** Filaree@northcascades.net | **Web:** www.filareefarm.com | **Catalog:** Online, or print version $2 (cost added to your first order)

Filaree Farm offers the **largest selection of organic seed garlic** in North America. They have collected unique strains from around the world and list more than 100 of them in an information-packed catalog. They also offer cover crop seeds.

FRAGRANT GARDEN NURSERY

PO Box 4246, Brookings, OR 97415 | **Phone:** (541) 412-8840 | **Fax:** (541) 412-8841 | **Email:** pat@fragrantgarden.com | **Web:** www.fragrantgarden.com | **Catalog:** Online

Pat Sherman has done her homework in testing, evaluating, and offering the best bets in **Sweet Peas** (120 varieties)—so well, in fact, that the Fragrant Garden boasts one of the most comprehensive sweet pea collections in the United States, with a huge number of Spencer varieties, Old Fashioned types, Winter Elegance types, and Cuthbertson types. Pat has spent many seasons growing sweet peas to get it just right and has gone to enormous effort to search out varieties from England. She has not only carefully studied the evaluations of the British National Sweet Pea Society and several growers in the UK, but has compared them to her own experience in Oregon. She passes along her sage advice to her customers. Her seed racks are available at several better garden centers in the Pacific Northwest (listed on the website).

FRANKLIN HILL GARDEN SEEDS

2430 N Rochester Road, Sewickley, PA 15143-8667 | **Phone:** (412) 367-6202 | **Email:** info@franklinhillseeds.com, or for catalogs: catalogues@franklinhillseeds.com | **Web:** www.franklinhillseeds.com | **Catalog:** Free; also online

Franklin Hill Garden Seeds, established in 1996, specializes in **heirloom and unusual annual and perennial flower seeds.** As a gardener working in the commercial flower-seed industry, owner David Quatchak began to realize that more and more of the flower seeds available to the home gardener are by-products of the commercial floriculture industry. It is his belief that many plants and varieties not suitable for mass production as transplants by commercial greenhouses are slowly being lost and that our gardens are the poorer for it. Many of the classic garden flowers, those plants that created the rich, varied, romantic, and often fragrant gardens once commonly found in America's backyards are gone, but Franklin Hill Seeds hopes to bring these back via their unique and invaluable seeds.

FROSTY HOLLOW ECOLOGICAL RESTORATION

PO Box 53, Langley, WA 98260 | **Phone:** (360) 579-2332 | **Fax:** (360) 579-4080 | **Email:** wean@whidbey.net | **Seed list:** Free with SASE (business size)

Steve Erickson and Marianne Edain have now put out their nineteenth seed list! Their small company began through meeting the needs of an esoteric hobby for a few botanically inclined gardeners and what they do is now finding widespread recognition in residential gardens and landscape restoration. You can order from Frosty Hollow's offering of habitat-collected seeds of Northwest native plants, trees and shrubs, wildflowers, perennials, grasses, and wetland plants, sold by the pound, quarter pound, ounce, and gram (pre-season orders are recommended, however, to ensure you get what you want). They also consult on ecological landscaping and restoration. The collection range is from southern Oregon to central British Columbia.

FUNGI PERFECTI

PO Box 7634, Olympia, WA 98507 | **Phone:** (360) 426-9292 or (800) 780-9126 | **Fax:** (360) 426-9377 | **Email:** mycomedia@ aol.com | **Web:** www.fungi.com | **Catalog:** $4.50; free brochure

Certified organic **mushroom spawn,** growing kits, supplies, and books—for the likes of shiitaki, maitake, reishi, oyster, button, enoki, *Corprinus comatus,* and *Stropharia rugoso-annulata.* Amateur and commercial inquiries welcome. Also, request information on beginners' and masters' seminars.

GOODWIN CREEK GARDENS

PO Box 83, Williams, OR 97544 | **Phone:** (800) 846-7359 | **Fax:** (541) 846-7357 | **Email:** info@goodwincreekgardens.com | **Web:** www.goodwincreekgardens.com | **Catalog:** $1

Jim and Dotti Becker's selection of seeds runs to herbs, ornamental perennials, and everlastings. A feature here and not common in other catalogs is a listing of the number of seeds to expect in a packet. They give the botanical and common names and a brief description.

THE GOURMET GARDENER

12287 117th Drive, Live Oak, FL 32060 | **Phone:** (800) 404-GROW (4769) | **Fax:** (407) 650-2691 | **Email:** information@gourmetgardender.com | **Web:** www.gourmetgardener.com | **Catalog:** Free

More than 150 **hard-to-find herb, vegetable, and edible flower seeds** from sources sought out worldwide. Specializing in European heirloom varieties, this company tests each one in their gardens (one in France and one in the United States) before offering them for sale, selecting varieties they feel are the most flavorful and robust.

HIGH ALTITUDE GARDENS (FORMERLY SEEDS TRUST)

PO Box 1048, Hailey, ID 83333-1048 | **Phone:** (208) 788-4363 (weekdays, 9 a.m.–5 p.m.) | **Fax:** (208) 788-3452 | **Email:** higarden@micron.net | **Web:** www.seedtrust.com | **Catalog:** Free

This catalog for "high altitude, short growing season gardens" (their varieties have proven successful west of the Cascades as well) offers open-pollinated, largely organically grown **unusual vegetable, herb, native grass, and wildflower seeds.** Of special interest to some of you will be the wide selection of tomato offerings grown from seed they brought back from the Siberian Institute of Horticulture in 1989. Siberians adore tomatoes, and fierce competition reigns from dacha to dacha to grow the earliest and tastiest. Saving seeds has taken place for generations. For $2 each HAG offers several instructional brochures borne of the hard lessons they've learned over 17 years and suggestions from valued customers and friends on growing vegetables, tomatoes, wildflowers, wildflower mixes, native grasses, and herbs (most of this is available online, too). They also offer a separate price list with fuller descriptive text ($1 plus SASE) on the seeds of "classics and heirlooms," and one on "elusive wildflowers."

HOBBS & HOPKINS, LTD.

1712 S Ankeny Street, Portland, OR 97214 | **Phone:** (503) 239-7518 or (800) 345-3295 | **Fax:** (503) 230-0391 | **Email:** info@protimelawnseed.com | **Web:** www.protimelawnseed.com | **Catalog:** Online

This **specialty lawn seed** company is getting our attention with the likes of their "Fleur de Lawn" flowering lawn seed mix containing dwarf grasses and tiny annual and perennial flowers such as English daisy and baby blue eyes. In the business since 1979, they have moved with changing sensibilities, offering site-specific mixes for reclamation, wetlands, bio-filters, low-growing plants, cover crops, and a fragrant herbal mix that has a delightful texture. H&H creates mixes specifically for the needs of different regions, and test their products for several years to assure that they perform as promoted. If you are struggling with a bad grass day and need help deciding what direction to take, visit their test site of native grasses, ecology lawns, lawn-seed mixes, and wildflower mixes. There are no fewer than 90 demonstration plots to see year-round.

HORIZON HERBS

PO Box 69, Williams, OR 97544 | **Phone:** (541) 846-6704 | **Fax:** (541) 846-6233 | **Email:** herbseed@chatlink.com | **Web:** www.chatlink.com/~herbseed | **Catalog:** $2

The Chech family are purveyors of Strictly Medicinal® "Seeds and Live Roots, Certified Organically Grown."

Their extensive catalog of over 700 varieties provides you with lots of cultural information.

J. L. HUDSON, SEEDSMAN

Star Route 2, Box 337, Redwood City, CA 94020 | **Email:** inquiry@ jlhudsonseeds.net | **Catalog:** Free; also online, or request by email to: catalog@jlhudsonseeds.net

J. L. Hudson's *Ethnobotanical Catalog of Seeds* is for the serious gardener in search of the interesting and unusual. This company was started in 1911 by Harry E. Saier with the goal of enriching the diversity of your garden by making **rare, unusual, and old-fashioned seeds** available, and to encourage the free circulation of seeds and information. Also offered: Gibberellic acid (GA-3) kits and supplies for use in germinating difficult seeds.

ED HUME SEEDS

PO Box 1450, Kent, WA 98035 | **Fax:** (253) 859-0694 | **Email:** humeseeds@aol.com | **Web:** www.humeseeds.com | **Price list:** Free | **Catalog:** Online

Since 1977, Ed Hume Seeds has operated as a local, family-owned business. Ed's seed line is specially selected for **short season and cool climate areas,** which makes his varieties perfect for high altitudes and early or late planting in warm climates. The company uses only current crop seeds and, as a result, inventory that is unused at the end of the year is donated to worldwide charities instead of being held over for resale the following year. Look for seed packet displays at grocery stores and garden centers. Order online from Ed's website, where you'll find lots of gardening information, a year-round gardening calendar, links to other gardening-related sites, and full-color photos of the seed packets. Ed offers his "Moonbook" garden almanac as shareware and "Successful Seed Gardening" as freeware on his website.

INSIDE PASSAGE

PO Box 639, Port Townsend, WA 98368 | **Phone and fax:** (360) 385-5760 | **Email:** inspass@whidbey.net | **Web:** www.insidepassage seeds.com | **List:** Free with SASE

Forest Shomer, of Abundant Life Seed Foundation fame, started this Northwest natives–oriented enterprise in 1992 to provide fresh seed for more than 160 species of "woody plants, native wildflowers and herbaceous plants, and adventitious flowers and herbaceous plants." He collects under the guidelines of the Washington Native Plant Society and stores his seeds without fungicides.

IRISH EYES – GARDEN CITY SEEDS

PO Box 307, Thorp, WA 98946 | **Phone:** (877) 733-3001 (orders) or (509) 964-7000 (customer service) | **Fax:** (800) 964-9210 | **Email:** potatocs@irish-eyes.com | **Web:** www.irish-eyes.com or www.gardencityseeds.com | **Catalog:** Free

This company is the result of a recent merger that brought together Irish Eyes (well known for outstanding **seed potatoes,** garlic, shallots, leeks, and onions), and Garden City Seeds (formerly of Hamilton, Montana, and specializing in **organically grown seeds,** soil enhancements, and safe pest-control). Newly located in the beautiful, fertile Kittitas Valley of central Washington, they offer high-quality organic, untreated, and high-germination seeds, proven by seed trials and with the focus on early harvest varieties—those varieties that will grow well in northern, maritime, and high-altitude zones. Customers of both companies will be pleased to find their old favorites in the new catalog. Also, they will find many "new" items, including new varieties of regular and organic potatoes, garlic, shallots and elephant garlic, and extended offerings of garden supplies, books, fertilizers, and ways to control pests safely.

JOHNNY'S SELECTED SEEDS

Foss Hill Road, Albion, ME 04910-9731 | **Phone:** (207) 437-4301 | **Fax:** (800) 437-4290 | **Email:** staff@johnnyseeds.com | **Web:** www.johnnyseeds.com | **Catalog:** Free

The Johnny behind the name is Rob Johnston, Jr. He began this company in Albion, Maine, in 1973, at age 22, when he saw the need for a specialty-seed grower serving the short season (pertinent to the Pacific Northwest) and ethnic vegetable grower. At that time he was a visionary. Now, as this book attests, his vision foretold the wave of the future. Early on he began a breeding program as well; it now includes pumpkins, squash, peppers, and lettuce. He approached his business in a then-unconventional way, believing plants nurtured on organic soil—and not exposed to herbicides and pesticides—produced superior and healthier seed. He is very conscious of how his seeds do "in the real world." The catalog offers over 900 garden-tested seed varieties for vegetables, herbs, and flowers. It's a very useful publication (with many color photos!), providing lots of cultural information not generally found even in gardening manuals.

MOLBAK'S GREENHOUSE AND NURSERY

13625 NE 175th Street, Woodinville, WA 98072 | **Phone:** (425) 483-5000 | **Web:** www.molbaks.com

An enormous selection of seed companies is represented here, including a very nice section with seeds just for kids. Many of the companies we just can't resist, like Seeds of Change, Shepherd's, and Territorial Seeds, are joined by dozens of others. And, of course, Molbak's carries everything you'll need to get those seeds planted and germinating, including an excellent selection of books on growing from seed, potting mix, grow lights, peat pots, and much more.

NICHOLS GARDEN NURSERY, HERBS AND RARE SEEDS

1190 Old Salem Road NE, Albany, OR 97321-4580 | **Phone:** (541) 928-9280 | **Fax:** (800) 231-5306 | **Email:** nichols@nicholsgarden nursery.com | **Web:** www.nicholsgardennursery.com | **Catalog:** Free; also online

For over 50 years purveyors of fine seeds and herb plants, Nichols—the family garden, nursery, and shop—is open year-round, Monday-Saturday. Find garden and everlasting seeds, culinary and ornamental herb plants

and seeds, gourmet vegetable seeds from around the world, ecology lawn seed, even true tea plants. Check out the fabulous recipe section on the website, as well as the "Thymely Tips."

PERENNIAL PLEASURES NURSERY

PO Box 147, East Hardwick, VT 05836 | **Phone:** (802) 472-5104 | **Fax:** (802) 472-6572 | **Email:** annex@antiqueplants.com | **Web:** www.antiqueplants.com | **Catalog:** $3

Since 1980, Rachel Kane has specialized in **heirloom flowers and herbs from the 17th to 19th centuries** (with some more modern treasures tucked in for good measure). For those of you with horticultural hearts that yearn to capture times past, you'll find soul mates at Perennial Pleasures. They have collected 1,000-plus plants, most of historical interest, including an extensive list of culinary and medicinal herbs. The catalog is a delight to read, well written and filled with historical and cultural tidbits. You'll also find an excellent selection of books, especially on garden history and garden restoration.

PETERS SEED & RESEARCH

PO Box 1472, Myrtle Creek, OR 97457 | **Phone:** (541) 874-2615 | **Fax:** (541) 874-3426 | **Email:** psr@pioneer-net.com | **Web:** www.pioneer-net.com/psr | **Catalog:** $1

Tim Peters has been in the plant breeding and agricultural research arena for a quarter of a century, but 1994 was the first year he offered a mail-order seed catalog from his considerable open-pollinated vegetables, fruit, and grain stock. Here you will find what they believe to be the only source in the world for **truly perennial grains.** A few years ago it was a lot easier to characterize a company as offering "rare and unusual" varieties; today, PSR is among the many excellent companies out there to choose from. If you're looking for a fascinating selection of genuinely unique plants of high quality, then send for this list. Shipping dates are in early April, mid-May, and late July. You can also become a supporting member of PSR's breeding program ($5 annually), which brings a newsletter and access to exclusive varieties not available elsewhere.

PINETREE GARDEN SEEDS

Box 300, New Gloucester, ME 04260 | **Phone:** (207) 926-3400 | **Fax:** (888) 527-3337 | **Email:** pinetree@superseeds.com | **Web:** www.superseeds.com | **Catalog:** Free; also online

Pinetree Garden Seeds was begun in 1979 to provide home gardeners with seeds in appropriately sized packages. It's a concept that distinguishes this company among those of us gardeners who don't really want to get (or pay for) more seed in a year than we can use. Today, their 168-page catalog includes bulbs, plants, tools, and a distinguished selection of gardening books. But for many, the real attraction of this company is their list of 800 varieties of vegetable, flower, vine, ornamental grass, wildflower, and herb seeds. Now if you have a potager or kitchen garden, you'll love the mouthwatering selection of vegetables: Continental, French, Italian, Oriental, Latin American, and Native American (as well as homey favorites from across the United States).

RAINIER SEEDS, INC.

PO Box 1064, Davenport, WA 99122 | **Phone:** (800) 828-8873 | **Fax:** (509) 725-7015 | **Email:** kmiller@rainierseeds.com | **Web:** www.rainierseeds.com | **Catalog:** Free

This eastern Washington company focuses on native grass seed, wildflower mixes, turf grass, and specialty seeds. They boast that they're the largest producers / conditioners of **native plant seed** in the western United States. Many of their varieties are suitable for backyard sanctuary programs, reclamation, and revegetation.

REDWOOD CITY SEED COMPANY

PO Box 361, Redwood City, CA 94064 | **Phone:** (650) 325-7333 | **Web:** www.ecoseeds.com | **Catalog:** Free; also online

An alternative seed company specializing (since 1971) in the preservation of open-pollinated vegetable varieties. "We are one of the 15 **open-pollinated seed** companies (out of 230 nationwide) who are preserving half of all the old-fashioned vegetable varieties in North America. You can see how important each of the 15 companies are, and that about a third of the items in our catalog were introduced by us to the gardeners of the United States and Canada. We hope to educate gardeners to the fact that when they buy our traditional varieties they will become the current link between the ancient past and the hopeful future of their existence."

There's a contagious passion about a wide variety of herbs and vegetables here, but none compare with Redwood City's Hot Peppers section, which carries on shamelessly for several pages of catalog and website. The superb catalog is available online or in print form, free of charge. Also, consider ordering the catalog supplements, which list seasonal, rare, or unusual seeds and those only available in small quantities, published twice a year for $2, or free on their website. Kids are invited to participate in their "Seeds for Kids" program that features varieties RCS themselves voted on for inclusion. Read more about the program on their website.

RENEE'S GARDEN

Phone: (831) 335-7228 (horticultural helpline) or (888) 880-7228 (business line) | **Web:** www.reneesgarden.com | **Catalog:** Free

When you visit Renee's website you will have the cyber-opportunity to shop Renee Shepherd's new seed company from the comfort of your home. Renee is the pioneer who founded Shepherd's Garden Seeds in 1983. Ultimately she sold her successful business to White Flower Farm (which kept the name), continuing to work for them for a few years. Then she left to try her wings elsewhere, but found she missed being in the seed business, so she has now started a new wholesale company. Home gardeners, though, can shop on her website, and a glorious place to shop it is! You will find her characteris-

tic attention to **beautiful botanical illustrations,** useful seed packets with growing directions, a quick-view planting chart, growing tips, harvesting info, companion plants, and even cooking ideas. Enjoy the added little gift of recipes on the packages, almost as good as reading Renee's popular cookbooks. Her seeds are sold in retail outlets, too.

ROCKY MOUNTAIN RARE PLANTS

1706 Deerpath Road, Franktown, CO 80116-9462 | **Fax:** (775) 281-2911 | **Email:** staff@rmrp.com | **Web:** www.rmrp.com | **Catalog:** $1, or free online

Rebecca Day-Skowron and Bob Skowron specialize in seeds of alpine and xeric plants from around the world. Their catalog is a delight to read—informational, beautifully illustrated with pen-and-ink drawings, and supplemented with seed germination data and growing hints. Search the fantastic website by plant name and you'll be rewarded with great color photographs of hundreds of alpine varieties.

SEEDHUNT

PO Box 96, Freedom, CA 95019-0096 | **Email:** seedhunt@aol.com | **Web:** www.seedhunt.com | **Seed list:** $1

Ginny Hunt has put together a brilliant seed list for those who seek plants for their **"Mediterranean" climate** gardens. She has many, many salvias, perennials, shrubby perennials (try *Abutilon palmeri*), annuals, ornamental grasses—seeds not available elsewhere. The list text is short, snappy, and informational. All seed packets are $2.75, plus $2 shipping and handling per order.

SEEDS OF CHANGE ORGANIC SEEDS

PO Box 15700, Santa Fe, NM 87506-5700 | **Phone:** (888) 762-7333 | **Email:** gardener@seedsofchange.com | **Web:** www.seedsofchange.com | **Catalog:** Free

Seeds of Change offers a fabulous range of **open-pollinated vegetable, culinary and medicinal herb, and flower seeds.** They have a terrific website, with lots of substantive content as well as excellent color photographs. The Main Seed List offers their top 200 most popular seed varieties, new introductions, customer favorites, and seed collections. All seed packets contain complete descriptions, plus planting, watering, and harvesting instructions. All purchases support seed donations to hundreds of community organizations annually.

Seeds of Change also produces the Deep Diversity Catalog, whose specific purpose is to help conserve a worldwide range of diverse and unusual plants. This catalog is the heart of their mission, commitment, and research. Seventy pages, it is available by mail only. Send a check or money order for $4 to Deep Diversity, c/o the address above. The catalog also offers quality tools (including sturdy, hand-forged Bulldog Tools, the epitome of the historic craft of British garden-tool making), gardening equipment, supplies, and culinary products.

SELECT SEEDS

180 Stickney Road, Union, CT 06076-4617 | **Phone:** (860) 684-9310 | **Fax:** (800) 653-3304 | **Email:** info@selectseeds.com | **Web:** www.selectseeds.com | **Catalog:** Free; also online

Marilyn Barlow discovered a forgotten garden and from its hardy survivors came the inspiration to specialize in **heirloom varieties** largely lost to commerce. Her selection is brilliant and includes many fragrant plants. This is where we go to find the best seeds for vines (such hard-to-find delights as rhodochiton and *Ipomoea tricolor* 'Flying Saucers', a glorious selection of sweet peas, and the variegated Japanese hop). Also, you'll finally find the figleaf hollyhock — one of the notable eye-catchers of the garden, but so hard to find! And how about the foxglove, *Digitalis parviflora* 'Terracotta'? And don't miss her collection of eight annuals chosen for their outstanding fragrance and luminous white evening flowers.

SHEPHERD'S GARDEN SEEDS

30 Irene Street, Torrington, CT 06790 | **Phone:** (860) 482-3638 | **Fax:** (860) 482-0532 | **Email:** custserv@shepherdseeds.com | **Web:** www.shepherdseeds.com | **Catalog:** Free

Shepherd's Garden Seeds has gathered together an offering of more than 500 seed varieties, largely from international sources — French, Finnish, Italian, British, Japanese, Chinese, and even American heirloom cultivars — for vegetables, herbs, and flowers. They have sought out seeds from those who cherish a long heritage of fine quality over mass production. Look forward to their charmingly illustrated catalog, then sharpen those pencils and get ordering!

R. H. SHUMWAY'S SEEDS

PO Box 1, Graniteville, SC 29829-0001 | **Phone:** (803) 663-9771 | **Fax:** (888) 437-2733 | **Web:** www.rhshumway.com | **Catalog:** Free; also online

For 129 years this "Pioneer American Seedsman" has brought customers a remarkable selection of choice **rare flower and vegetable seed.** You'll be drawn right into this old-time styled catalog by its offerings of plants we crave, such as unusual vines like momordica, *Lapageria rosea*, the rare heirloom blue nasturtium *Tropaeolum azureum*, plants like abutilon, unusual melons, and bizarre gourds. Also through this company, you can order the **Seymour's Selected Seeds** catalog featuring the best varieties from England (if using their website, click on "Links" to find Seymour's).

TERRITORIAL SEED COMPANY

PO Box 158, Cottage Grove, OR 97424-0061 | **Phone:** (541) 942-9547 | **Fax:** (888) 657-3131 | **Retail store:** 20 Palmer Avenue, Cottage Grove, OR 97424-0061 | **Phone:** (541) 942-0510 | **Email:** tertrl@territorial-seed.com | **Web:** www.territorial-seed.com | **Catalog:** Free; also online

Territorial defines its purpose clearly. They aim to improve people's self-sufficiency and independence by enabling gardeners to produce an abundance of good tasting, fresh-from-the-garden food 12 months a year. With 44 acres of trial grounds and an organic research farm, located in London Springs, Oregon, the folks at Territorial are devoted to providing varieties proven for gardens west of the Cascades and consider their farm representative of an ordinary-to-difficult garden site in the Northwest. Each year Territorial's research staff grows and evaluates thousands of varieties. Those that appear in their catalogs have passed stringent requirements. Seeds for over 800 **vegetable, herb, flower, and cover crop varieties** are offered, none of them genetically modified or engineered. Many are open-pollinated and treasured heirloom cultivars. Territorial also offers a large selection of garden transplants, garlic bulbs, onion plants, seed potatoes, and perennial fruit plants, which are available seasonally. They publish two catalogs yearly, one each for spring and winter gardening. Their catalogs include extensive cultural information and a list of gardening supplies to help gardeners achieve successful harvests throughout the entire year.

THOMAS JEFFERSON CENTER FOR HISTORIC PLANTS

Monticello, PO Box 316, Charlottesville, VA 22902 | **Phone:** (434) 984-9860 | **Fax:** (434) 984-0358 | **Email:** twinleaf@monticello.org | **Web:** www.monticello.org/shop/ | **Catalog:** $2, or free online

Send for "Twinleaf," the Center's charming and informative booklet. It arrives each January and you'll always enjoy reading the essays and perusing the listing of historically cultivated varieties of annuals, perennials, vines, and bulbs, many marked with a symbol indicating that the selection was grown by Jefferson, who was, of course, an accomplished gardener. The Center offers a small but inviting collection of seeds, plants, and bulbs along with a few select gift items. They are thrilled to finally be able to offer *Jeffersonia diphylla*, a rare woodland perennial. And here's an uncommon vine, *Vigna caracalla*, described by Jefferson as "the most beautiful bean in the world" — the fragrant purple and white blossoms spiral like snail's shells and hang in luscious clusters on 15–20-foot vines. (If you are able to visit Monticello, the selection of seeds and plants there is larger than offered via mail order.)

THOMPSON & MORGAN

PO Box 1308, Jackson, NJ 08527-0308 | **Phone:** (800) 274-7333 | **Fax:** (888) 466-4769 | **Web:** www.thompson-morgan.com | **Catalog:** Free; also online

An English company, established in 1855, T&M markets seeds with a catalog aimed at their loyal American customers. (The 2002 catalog will be their 147th.) The company carries an overwhelming selection of over 2,000 seed varieties, with 360 new ones in 2002 (just try to resist!). The full-color catalog is very useful in identifying flower color and foliage effects, and they continue to add helpful pictographs for cultural information. T&M is renowned for their traditional as well as unusual and rare plant selections — perennials, annuals, herbs, trees, and shrubs, and (of course) vegetables. Along with seeds they also offer an increasing number of seedling starts.

TILLINGHAST SEED CO.

623 E Morris Street, La Conner, WA 98257 | **Mailing address:** PO Box 738, La Conner, WA 98257 | **Phone:** (360) 466-3329 | **Fax:** (360) 466-1401

This company has been providing local gardeners with a large selection of seeds for 117 years (no catalog, alas). Entering their charming, old-fashioned store, with original wooden seed bins, is like stepping back in time. It's the genuine article, not a marketing ploy.

TRANS-PACIFIC NURSERY / WORLD PLANTS

16065 Oldsville Road, McMinnville, OR 97128 | **Phone:** (503) 472-6215 (message phone; in most instances, they are unable to return phone calls) | **Fax:** (503) 434-1505 | **Email:** groe@worldplants.com | **Web:** www.worldplants.com | **Catalog:** Free; order via email or by sending a SASE

World Plants has essentially changed its format and now offers mostly plants, although **Japanese maple seeds** are still available. Each autumn they harvest seed from one of the premier specimen Japanese maple nurseries in the Northwest; over 100 varieties of *Acer palmatum* of every description are collected. Last year, they offered a mixture of these seeds, and also a mixture of laceleaf varieties only. In some years that are exceptional for seed they are able to offer a choice of some individual varieties as well. They are also offering, for the first time, seed of the *Acer* species (not named cultivars). This is used mostly to grow rootstock for grafting named cultivars, although seedlings are often very nice trees in their own right. It's an inexpensive way to grow groves of maples, seedlings for bonsai, or grafting rootstock.

WILD GARDEN SEED – SHOULDER TO SHOULDER FARM

PO Box 1509, Philomouth, OR 97370 | **Phone:** (541) 929-4068 | **Catalog:** $5

Frank and Karen Morton are probably known across America for their work, more than their names, as they are among the originators of the "fresh-cut salad" industry, with restaurant sales from one shore of this country to the other. That all began back in 1983. Also about that time they began plant breeding on their farm for their own purposes and in 1993 began offering unusual seed varieties to Peace Seeds in Corvallis. For the past few years they have published a catalog of their offerings, from packets to pounds. Have a look here if the growing of **wild salad greens;** insectary plants that attract, feed and shelter beneficial insects; and native prairie species (collected wild on their property where they have integrated the cultured with the wild) interests you. Their catalog discusses their philosophy in greater detail.

SEED SOURCES OUTSIDE THE UNITED STATES

This is just a small and eclectic collection of seed sources from the global array, but we have sifted through many and are proud to introduce you to the ones we've listed here. They have impressive seed lists, from the esoteric to the all-inclusive, with many varieties you will not be able to find in much of North America. We encourage you to indulge in these companies . . . please don't shy away from them simply because they're on different soil! And for the proverbial record, we would like to remark that when we write for new or updated information to all the nurseries and seed sources in this *Directory*, the foreign sources always get back to us immediately with courteous replies and politely volunteer plenty of information. There really is something to be said for such pleasant business dealings. So if you are tempted by one of these vendors, go for it. Also (usually) when requesting a catalog, send U.S. bills instead of a check. We have never had a problem with this and we sympathize with the request—fees to cash foreign checks are astronomical!

ASHWOOD NURSERIES

Ashwood Lower Lane, Ashwood, Kingswinford, West Midlands, DY6 0AE, United Kingdom | **Phone:** 44 1384 401996 | **Fax:** 44 1384 401108 | **Email:** ashwoodnurs@hotmail.com | **Web:** www.ashwood-nurseries.co.uk/ | **Catalog:** $2 (U.S. bills only)

The Ashwood name is synonymous with **lewisias** and nearly 20 years of breeding work, with many RHS gold medals—and they hold the National Collection. The catalog shows a remarkable color range. Also find seed for hellebores (*Helleborus* spp.), *Primula auriculas,* and Cyclamen (*Cyclamen* spp.). Their color catalog represents these plants and their own particular strains with breathtaking clarity. One would be a hard-hearted soul to not feel at least a twinge of lust.

AURORA FARM

3492 Phillips Road, Creston, BC V0B 1G2 Canada | **Phone:** (250) 428-4404 | **Fax:** (250) 428-4404 | **Email:** aurora@kootenay.com | **Web:** www.kootenay.com/~aurora | **Catalog:** $3 (mail-order catalog for American customers: PO Box 697, Porthill, ID 83853)

Aurora Farm was the first biodynamic seed company in North America and, as far as they know, remains the only North American source for (nonhomeopathic) biodynamic herbal preparations. This family-run business offers open-pollinated, untreated, **biodynamic seeds,** herbal tea, and herbal alternative remedies. The list is short but most interesting. If you are unfamiliar with the principals and philosophy of biodynamics, their site offers an excellent introduction.

B & T WORLD SEEDS

Rue des Marchandes, Paguignan, 34210 Olonzac, France | **Phone:** 33 468 91 29 63 | **Fax:** 33 468 91 30 39 | **Email:** matt@b-and-t-world-seeds.com | **Web:** www.b-and-t-world-seeds.com/

The Sleighs have made the trek from Somerset in the west of England to a tiny village in the south of France and brought with them the family seed business—**probably the largest offering of collected seed in the world,** at over 30,000 species, just the organization of which boggles the mind. You'll enjoy searching through the 700 sub-lists on their wonderful website (in order by category, such as "Natives of U.S. Northwest," "Windy Condition Plant, Shrub and Tree List," "Chinese Natives and Introductions," etc.). But you're also offered a choice of a paper catalog ($23), the Master List on "Seedy Rom" ($30), or you can download the catalog. In any event, when one comes upon a particularly wonderful plant that one feels they must, must have, the chances are it can be found here ready to be grown from seed. Payment via credit card, IMO (International Money Order), or bank drafts made out in UK or French currency (no U.S. checks). Going to be in France? Check out their charming B & T Bed and Breakfast.

BARNHAVEN PRIMROSES

11 Rue du Pont Blanc, 22310 Plestin Les Graves, Brittany, France | **Phone:** 33 02 96 35 31 55 | **Email:** Barnhaven@wanadoo.fr | **Web:** www.barnhaven.com | **Catalog:** $3 (U.S. bills only)

This most famous of purveyors of **primrose seed** took its original beginning from five packets of Sutton's seeds, purchased by Florence Bellis in 1935 and sent to her in Oregon. All the polyanthus offered by Barnhaven are direct descendants of those seeds. Florence Bellis's primroses are now in the capable and dedicated hands of Angela Bradford at her nursery in Brittany. (You can request the catalog in French or English.) Their plants are grown to be hardy, spending their life outside under the protection of an open-ended tunnel, where they are carefully hand-pollinated. Be forewarned, though—the catalog provides luscious descriptions.

THE BUTCHART GARDENS

Box 4010, Victoria, BC V8X 3X4 Canada | **Phone:** (250) 652-4422 | **Fax:** (250) 652-1475 | **Email:** email@butchartgardens.bc.ca | **Web:** www.butchartgardens.com | **Catalog:** $1 Canadian, or $1 U.S. bill (credited to your first order)

Annuals, biennials, perennials, and rock garden seeds are available, with many old-fashioned favorites sold as collections ("Cottage Garden," "Window Box," "Children's Collection," etc.). Seed is packed at Butchart Gardens, and is also sold in their garden Gift Store.

CHADWELL HIMALAYAN PLANT SEED

81 Parlaunt Road, Slough, Berks SL3 8BE United Kingdom | **Phone:** 44 1753 542823 | **Catalog:** $3 (U.S. bills only)

Chris Chadwell is a modern-day plant explorer specializing in the **Himalaya,** with seed gathered from his many horticultural expeditions. Chadwell offers a selection of unusual but high-quality alpine, perennial, shrub, and tree seeds from the Himalaya, Japan, New Zealand, and North America. Some of the seeds are available on a per-packet basis by ordering from the catalog; the rest can only be obtained by subscribing to his annual plant-hunting expeditions.

CHILTERN SEEDS

Bortree Stile, Ulverston, Cumbria LA12 7PB United Kingdom | **Phone:** 44 1229 581137 (24-hour phone for orders and queries. Message: "During usual working hours you will normally hear a friendly female living voice, inevitably at other times an inanimate machine will greet you. But don't be afraid!" Nice touch!) | **Fax:** 44 1229 584549 | **Email:** info@chilternseeds.co.uk | **Web:** www.chilternseeds.co.uk | **Catalog:** $5 (U.S. bills only)

A privately owned family concern, Chiltern Seeds was established 26 years ago by Douglas and Bridget Bowden, who, with their modern approach to the development of Chiltern Seeds, are justifiably proud of the "old-fashioned" personal service they extend to all their many customers. The aim of the company is to introduce into general cultivation **unusual, rare, and even endangered species,** and to introduce gardeners to the fascination of growing from seed. Virtually every plant commonly grown from seed is represented here. Exporting to over 90 countries, they also import rare seeds from all over the world—indeed, much time is spent in seeking new collectors and suppliers to provide even more items to add to the 4,600 already in their catalog, making it the largest of its kind in the world. One of the highlights of our winter is the time we spend overindulging in an (overly) ambitious seed order, with something like Penelope Hobhouse's *Flower Gardens* in one hand and this sinfully tempting catalog in the other. A how-to-germinate leaflet comes with the seeds.

COMPASS SEEDS

The Coach House, Carnwath, Lanark ML11 8LF United Kingdom | **Phone:** 44 1555 841450 | **Fax:** 44 1555 841480 | **Email:** seeds@btinternet.com | **Web:** www.compass-seeds.com | **Catalog:** $2 (U.S. bills only)

Compass is the brainchild of Duncan McDougall (a retired Glasgow policeman and serious plantsman), who obtains seeds from botanic gardens and arboreta all over the world and makes them available to both amateur gardeners and commercial outlets. His activities provide an opportunity for the enthusiastic amateur to obtain unusual and sometimes rare seeds that aren't generally on commercial seed lists.

CRAVEN'S NURSERY

1, Foulds Terrace, Bingley, West Yorkshire, BD16 4LZ United Kingdom | **Phone:** 44 1274 561412 | **Fax:** 44 1274 561412 | **Catalog:** $5

The specialty here is **primula seed**—show and alpine auriculas, many species (including Himalayan and Asiatic), Airedale hybrids, and wandas. The catalog offers beautiful color photos along with lots of primula history, all charmingly related.

EUROSEEDS

PO Box 95, 741 01 Novy Jicin, Czech Republic | **Seed list:** $2 (U.S. bills only)

Mojmir Pavelka specializes in **alpine and bulbous plants and dwarf shrubs,** many of which are quite rare. The seed in his vaults has been collected over a span of ten years from various mountain regions of the world such as Nepal, Turkey, the Balkan peninsula, and the Alps. His prices are most reasonable and his packets generous.

GARDENS NORTH

5984 Third Line Road North, North Gower, Ontario K0A 2T0 Canada | **Phone:** (613) 489-0065 | **Fax:** (613) 489-1208 | **Email:** seed@gardensnorth.com | **Web:** www.gardensnorth.com | **Catalog:** $4 (U.S. and Canada)

In a field of highly passionate people who love to grow plants from seed, Kristl Walek is a star. This is immediately obvious as you begin to peruse her catalog of seeds, generally selected for tougher climates than the one we garden in the Northwest, meaning many of these seeds will grow well here. The range of 1,500-some species she lists covers the gamut; in fact, her catalog is often referred to as "the mother lode" for rare, hardy perennials—the majority of which will be **hardy in Zones 3 to 9.** In the past few years, Kristl has added trees and shrubs to her already impressive list. More recently, she has also become the first commercial seed-house to sell fern spores. Each year, Gardens North features a special collection of seed in addition to the ordinary listings. For 2002, the "True Colors" collection highlights variegated, purple- and yellow-leaved plants that come true from seed. The catalog should be in the hands of any serious plant-lover, for all the effort Kristl has expended tirelessly collecting and seeking out the best, the rare and the unusual, worldwide. Notable features include the historical and cultural information in each seed description, extremely detailed germination instructions on each seed package, and a section in the catalog dealing with Germination News. Exemplary.

ISLAND SEED COMPANY

PO Box 4278, Depot 3, Victoria, BC V8X 3X8 Canada | **Phone:** (250) 744-3677 | **Fax:** (250) 479-0221 | **Catalog:** $2 Canadian ($2 U.S., bills only)

This small company, established in 1960, carries a selection of culinary herb, heirloom vegetable, and old-fashioned flower seeds. Their seeds can be found on seed racks in garden shops or through their catalog.

JIM AND JENNY ARCHIBALD

'Bryn Collen, Ffostrasol, Llandysul, Dyfed, Wales, SA44 5SB United Kingdom | **Seed list:** $3 (U.S. bills only)

Among our friends who take their seed selections very seriously, the names of Jim and Jenny Archibald are much revered. Reading their list will keep you enthralled! They are noted for their forays to far-flung outposts of horticultural interest, and offer reflections from recent expeditions in their newsletter. Each year brings a different selection . . . for example, their first 2001 list offered wild collections from Greece, Russia, Iran, Kyrgyzstan, Georgia, the Western United States, South Africa, New Zealand, and China. Their offerings come from these expeditions and also from their garden in Wales. For Americans, ordering from the extensive list could not be easier. Just print your information clearly and send your personal check in U.S. dollars.

KARMIC EXOTICS NURSERY

Box 146, Shelburne, Ontario L0N 1S0 Canada | **Phone:** (519) 925-3906 | **Email:** androscan@canada.com | **Catalog:** $2 (refundable with first order)

Karmic Exotics is home to probably the **largest collection of rock garden seeds;** this year there are over 800 listings, including 22 androsaces, 35 campanulas, 32 gentians, 41 primulas, just to give you an idea. Although there are a few garden-grown items, they mainly provide wild-collected seed from California, Turkey, Slovakia, Czech Republic, Spain, Bulgaria, Italy, Slovenia, Serbia, Kazakhstan, Caucasus, and Yunnan, China. The collectors are principally Czech experts. Andrew Osyany has distributed seeds this way for 12 years and he reports many enthusiastic repeat customers. Novice to advanced gardeners can specify their needs and leave the choice to Andrew—and get a 20 percent discount to boot!

NATIONAL COLLECTION OF PASSIFLORA

Lampley Road, Kingston Seymour, Clevedon, North Somerset BS21 6XS United Kingdom | **Phone:** 44 1934 833350 | **Fax:** 44 1934 877255 | **Email:** greenholm@lineone.net | **Web:** www.passiflora-uk.co.uk | **Catalog:** Free

The Passion Flower Seed Company has come together with the British National Collection of **Passiflora** to enable these wonderful plants (over 200 of them!) to be purchased, in seed form, online in a secure environment. John Vanderplank is presently engaged in scientific research involving passiflora seed and is closely associated with the Royal Botanical Gardens at Kew, who've enthusiastically supported his unique collection, now internationally renowned. The catalog is really excellent for plant description and cultural information (with minimum temperatures given in Fahrenheit *and* Centigrade). Remember, the *P. caeruleas* are quite hardy for many Northwest microclimates. The website is very well done, with beautiful photos of passion flowers.

PHEDAR (RESEARCH) NURSERY

Bunkers Hill, Romiley, Stockport, SK6 3DS United Kingdom | **Phone and Fax:** 44 161 430 3772 | **Seed lists:** $2 each (U.S. bills only)

Hellebore enthusiasts in the Northwest will probably know the name Will McLewin both for his expertise and from his occasional talks on the subject at the Heronswood Hellebore Open Garden. Mr. McLewin is a world-renowned authority on hellebores and peonies. His nursery in England is, as he states, a means of supporting the work that he does on these two genera. We list him in this chapter because the plants, which he also offers, are not a particularly reasonable option for us here in the United States Fortunately, we can turn to this extraordinary resource for seeds. He points out to us that in almost all cases the supplier of seed is responsible for the incorrect naming of many plants—seed from cultivated hybrid plants usually does not reproduce the parent; cultivated seed of wild species plants is usually hybridized (almost all seed is *seed from* not *seed of*), and the seedlings should not bear the parent name. "Our seed is not like this and we emphasize the point." In other words, look to Will McLewin for very precise seed provenance. The seed lists we reviewed offer peony seed (wild collected, seed from botanic gardens from wild-collected plants, and nursery seed), and a selection of hellebores (over 130 entries), and were, to be completely honest, over our heads technically. However we can say, without reservation, that this should be the first-source choice of serious propagators of **hellebores and peonies.**

PLANTWORLD SEEDS

St. Marychurch Road, Newton Abbot, Devon TQ12 4SE United Kingdom | **Phone and Fax:** 44 01803 872939 | **Catalog:** $2 (U.S. bills only)

Plantworld offers 40 varieties of aquilegias, along with 40 hardy geraniums, lots of campanulas, euphorbias, meconopsis, gentians, tropaeolums (hardy species), and lots of plants with variegated foliage. Seed offered here is almost exclusively from plants grown at the nursery, collected fresh and sent on to eager customers. Additionally, Ray Brown is an avid collector abroad, and sent us a newspaper clipping relating details of a recent trip he made to Chile from which he brought back 200 species not yet in cultivation elsewhere. "From the distant Andes of South America come previously unheard of peacock-hued alstromerias in all sizes. And from half a world away, South Africa sends us unbelievable, new alpine dwarf dieramas. Almost unobtainable kiringeshoma, the new fragrant *Corydalis smithiana....*" Who could possibly resist these? The catalog will completely satisfy seedaholics.

RICHTERS

Goodwood, Ontario, L0C 1A0 Canada | **Phone:** (905) 640-6677 | **Fax:** (905) 640-6641 | **Email:** orderdesk@richters.com | **Web:** www.richters.com | **Catalog:** Free; also online

The Richters' website is just packed with useful information, and you can order online—they send their plants and seeds worldwide! They have a very impressive catalog of over 800 **herb seeds** (plants and starts like comfrey roots are sold as well). By all means get the catalog; it has many color photos and is loaded with herb-related information, as well as offering a huge book selection.

SALT SPRING SEEDS

PO Box 444, Ganges, Salt Spring Island, BC V8K 2W1 Canada | **Phone:** (250) 537-5269 | **Web:** www.saltspringseeds.com/ | **Catalog:** $2

Dan Jason established Salt Spring in 1986. Today, the company continues to offer organically grown, untreated vegetable seed, specializing in **high-protein dried beans** (100 varieties!), grains, garlic, and flowers. Dan still grows his own seed and in 2001 there were over 100 new seed offerings. Check out his new book, *Living Lightly on the Land: Self-Reliance in Food and Medicine* (see catalog or website for further information). Visits by appointment.

SCENTS OF TIME GARDENS

PO Box 402, 11948 207th Street, Maple Ridge, BC V2X 1X7 Canada | **Email:** scentsoftimegardn@mailcity.com | **Web:** www.scents-of-time-gardens.com | **Catalog:** $10 | **Biannual seed list:** $4

Scents of Time Gardens deals in authentic varieties of heritage seeds. In their catalog/growing guide one will find over 200 types of flowers, vegetables, and herbs, all of which have been grown by gardeners for at least 100 years or more, including 17 varieties of **fragrant antique sweet peas** that were grown in Colonial and Victorian times. They are hardy, reliable, tried and true, having been grown for generations. The catalog includes Latin and common names, botanical information, dates of introduction, color photos, garden lore, and recipes. Their website offers several samples of listings from the catalog/growing guide.

SEEDS OF DISTINCTION

PO Box 86 Station A (Etobicoke), Toronto, Ontario M9C 4V2 Canada | **Phone:** (416) 255-3060 or (888) 327-9193 | **Email:** seeds@seedsofdistinction | **Web:** www.seedsofdistinction.com | **Catalog:** Free; also online

This unique collection of seed is not just for the advanced gardener, but also for those who wish to try the more novel varieties. The company caters to purveyors of **unusual or hard-to-find seeds** and has sorted through thousands of varieties of flowering seed, selecting only the best from top European and American trials and from among the world's most outstanding botanical gardens. The picks of the season would include *double Auriculasi primula, red shades* of helleborus for the collectors, and *Crazy Daisy* for all gardeners.

SEEDS TRUST (SEE HIGH ALTITUDE GARDENS)

SILVERHILL SEEDS

PO Box 53108, Kenilworth, 7745 Cape Town, South Africa | **Phone:** 27 214 762 4245 | **Fax:** 27 214 797 6609 | **Email:** rachel@silverhillseeds.co.za | **Web:** www.silverhillseeds.co.za/ (updated weekly!) | **Catalog:** $2

Rod and Rachel Saunders bring us seeds from the ultra-rich **South African plant world,** collected from the Zambezi River to Cape Point, with over 2,000 species of South African native plants offered in their ever-changing catalog. Peek into the life they lead through the chatty "Welcome" newsletter in the introduction. Seeds are organized in categories (with brief but useful descriptions) as annuals, perennials, trees, shrubs, bulbous plants, carnivorous plants, Geraniaceae, Orchidaceae, Proteaceae, Restionaceae, as well as grasses and succulents (no cacti). Conveniently, prices in the catalog are in U.S. dollars.

UNIVERSITY OF BRITISH COLUMBIA BOTANICAL GARDEN

6804 SW Marine Drive, Vancouver, BC V6T 1Z4 Canada | **Phone:** (604) 822-3928 | **Fax:** (604) 822-2016 | **Email:** botg@interchange.ubc.ca | **Web:** www.ubcbotanicalgarden.org

Seed is collected from the UBC gardens and made available at the garden gift shop. *Germination information is not included,* so you may wish to ask for specifics on the really unusual stuff that will be tricky (like the *Cardiocrinum giganteum*).

VANDUSEN BOTANICAL GARDEN

5251 Oak Street, Vancouver BC V6M 4H1 Canada | **Phone:** (604) 878-9274 | **Fax:** (604) 266-4236 | **Web:** www.vandusengarden.org (garden info only; no seed info) | **List:** $1

A listing of 500 selections collected from the garden is offered at the garden or by mail. The list is $1 U.S., packets are $1.50 Canadian, and postage is added based on the number of packets ordered. Also note that VanDusen hosts a great event each year in late February called "Seedy Saturday" where you can exchange or buy seeds, hear speakers, network, pick up information from displays, and tour the gardens.

WEST COAST SEEDS

206-8475 Ontario Street, Vancouver, BC V5X 3E8 Canada | **Phone:** (604) 482-8800 | **Fax:** (877) 482-8822 | **Email:** mark@ westcoastseeds.com | **Web:** www.westcoastseeds.com | **Catalog:** Free; also online

West Coast Seeds have been available to Canadians since 1983, and since then have extended their services to include the United States. They offer an excellent, well-tested selection of **vegetables,** including Oriental and European varieties, and work closely with local market gardeners and commercial growers to find the best restaurant and market quality varieties. They list an assortment of **open-pollinated and hybrid varieties** because they believe that the vigor of hybrids often improves disease resistance and production in this climate. Therefore, they hope to encourage more gardeners to garden organically, or at least to use fewer pesticides and fungicides. When choosing herbs and flowers, they seek out particular varieties that will attract beneficial insects and butterflies to the garden. Their new varieties are all grown at their Zone 8 trial grounds just outside of Vancouver, BC, and are then selected specifically for outstanding performance in their unique West Coast climate. At their demonstration garden, they showcase

existing varieties and organic growing techniques for home gardeners.

SEED TRUSTS / EXCHANGES

If you are active in the world of seed saving, these may just be your old friends and we may offer little you aren't already familiar with. What we hope is that this listing will also reach someone out there who will be inspired to investigate further, and for whom it will open new doors. Refer to Chapter 2, "Clubs, Societies & Volunteer Opportunities," and Chapter 4, "Northwest Native Plants," for complete addresses (if not shown below) and further details. Most organizations will require that you join to participate, but typically this is a small price to pay for the opportunity to access so many rare and unusual seeds, many not available commercially at any price.

ALPINE GARDEN CLUB OF B.C.

Noted as one of the best and most extensive exchanges in the world.

ALPINE GARDEN SOCIETY

AMERICAN PRIMROSE SOCIETY AND THE WASHINGTON CHAPTER OF THE APS

AMERICAN HORTICULTURAL SOCIETY

AMERICAN RHODODENDRON SOCIETY

BERRY BOTANIC GARDEN

THE CENTER FOR PLANT CONSERVATION

PO Box 299, St. Louis, MO 63166 | **Phone:** (314) 577-9450 | **Web:** www.mobot.org/CPC

A network of organizations that collect seeds and cuttings of some 3,000 endangered American native plant species to be preserved in botanical gardens.

FLOWER AND HERB EXCHANGE

3076 N Winn Road, Decorah, IA 52101 | **Phone:** (312) 382-5990

This exchange is offered through the **Seed Savers Exchange.** 2002 will be the 13th year for this innovative, grassroots seed exchange. The yearbook is assembled annually (your entries are due by late January) for a large listing of almost 300 members offering over 2,000 varieties of seeds. The hope is that one will offer special, heirloom, and antique flowers and herbs to share around the country and the world. There are members in the United States, Canada, Italy, Japan, Slovakia/Czech Republic, Denmark, Hungary, and the United Kingdom. There are so many unusual flowers and herbs that it is every bit as daunting as it is alluring! There's also a listing of almost 100 small specialty nursery sources specializing in antique, heirloom, and unusual flower and herb seeds. One very specialized niche some of their sources fill is for restoration or historically correct garden rejuvenation project specialists. Annual membership is $10; $12 in U.S. funds for Canadians.

HARDY FERN FOUNDATION

HARDY PLANT SOCIETY OF GREAT BRITAIN

HARDY PLANT SOCIETY OF OREGON

NATIVE SEEDS/SEARCH

526 N 4th Avenue, Tucson, AZ 85705-8450 | **Phone:** (520) 622-5561 | **Fax:** (520) 622-5591 | **Email:** info@nativeseeds.org | **Web:** www.nativeseeds.org | **Open:** Tuesdays and Saturdays, 10 a.m.–5 p.m.

This nonprofit organization is dedicated to preserving traditional crops of the Southwest United States and northern Mexico. The seed listing has more than 300 varieties of corn, beans, squash, sunflowers, and many other crops grown by Native Americans. They are listed here because they are one of the most prominent groups in the seed conservation movement.

NORTHWEST HORTICULTURAL SOCIETY

NORTHWEST PERENNIAL ALLIANCE

NORTH AMERICAN ROCK GARDEN SOCIETY

Find an overwhelming selection from their catalog, which goes on for pages and pages of itty-bitty type, offering over 6,000 selections, many rare and not otherwise available. Several rock-gardening groups are participating in an exchange of seed with short viability, including our Northwest chapter of NARGS.

ROYAL HORTICULTURAL SOCIETY

One of the unexpected membership benefits for us was the arrival of a seed catalog from their Wisley garden, offering 30 packets of our choice, free to overseas members!

SCOTTISH ROCK GARDEN CLUB

SEED SAVERS EXCHANGE

3076 N Winn Road, Decorah, IA 52101 | **Phone:** (319) 382-5990 | **Fax:** (319) 382-5872 | **Web:** www.seedsavers.org

No discussion on the topic would be complete without mention of this most valuable organization, home to the **Flower and Herb Exchange** as well. This grassroots exchange began in 1975 with 29 members concerned with preserving heirloom and heritage seeds, particularly of food crops. The membership now numbers over 8,000 and they have established a substantive center on a 170-acre farm, where you may visit to see 18,000 endangered vegetable and 650 nineteenth-century apple varieties displayed. An informative color catalog is free; membership is $30 ($35 Canadian), for which you receive several publications over the year.

SINO-HIMALAYAN PLANT ASSOCIATION

81 Parlaunt Road, Slough, Berks, SL3 8BE United Kingdom | **Phone and Fax:** 44 1753 542823

Membership includes a seed exchange and their newsletter, which has recently added color photographs, with lots of plant information from this region. Chris Chadwell is the Association Secretary. U.S. subscription is $18.

SEED SOURCE SOURCEBOOKS & INTERNET SOURCE LISTS

ANDERSEN HORTICULTURAL LIBRARY ONLINE WEBSITE SERVICE

Andersen Horticultural Library, Minnesota Landscape Arboretum, 3675 Arboretum Drive, PO Box 39, Chanhassen, MN 55317-0039 | **Email:** plantinfo@jaws.umn.edu | **Web:** plantinfo.umn.edu

Unlike the paper version of this plant-finding index, the Web version adds over 150,000 citations to current plant literature, where one can find approximately 75,000 different plants and access illustrations and concomitant information. Over 150 currently received serials are indexed as received, and many important monographs in botany and horticulture are indexed. Website subscription service is $59.95 per year for institutional/commercial subscription; $39.95 per year for individual subscription.

Cornucopia II: A Source Book of Edible Plants

Stephen Facciola (Kampong Publications, 1998, 713 pp.; $40 plus $5 s&h to U.S.); 1870 Sunrise Drive, Vista, CA 92084 | **Phone:** (760) 726-0990

This is the authoritative reference book for locating sources (1,350) for edible plants and plant seeds. It covers approximately 3,000 species of food plants and 7,000 varieties—including fruits, vegetables, herbs, wild edibles, mushroom spawn, hard-to-find nut trees, baby vegetables, even sprouting seeds, salad mixes, and starter cultures. Mr. Facciola has compiled another astounding edition of his plant finder, with more user-friendly features and expanded categories.

Plants: A Journal for Plant Enthusiasts

Dirk van der Werff, 2 Grange Close, Hartlepool, TS26 0DU England | **Phone:** 44 1429 423165 | **Fax:** 44 8700 940180 | **Email:** dirk@plants-magazine.com | **Web:** www.plants-magazine.com | **Subscriptions:** Subscribe online in U.S. funds, $72 for six issues.

The (London) Sunday *Times* says it all: "The latest details on new plant varieties from around the world, the people who created them and the nurseries that sell them." *Plants* is a quarterly journal created by the intrepid Dirk van der Werff, who tracks down new plant introductions, gets their photographs, and lets the reader know about the explorers, nurseries, and growers we can thank. It appeals to the gardening enthusiast and to plantaholics who seek leading-edge information about the efforts of plant explorers, including leaders from the Northwest (like Dan Hinkley from Heronswood in Kingston, Washington) and plant breeders (like Dan Heims from TerraNova Nursery in Portland). Although this journal emanates from the UK, it really covers the entire world, with subscribers and correspondents (thanks to the Internet) from around the globe. Every issue is stimulating and makes you want to track down the sources of plants and seeds alike. A tremendous resource. (Dirk also sells his back issues online . . . a great addition to your reference library.)

SEED SAVERS EXCHANGE

3076 N Winn Road, Decorah, IA 52101 | **Phone:** (319) 382-5990 | **Fax:** (319) 382-5872 | **Web:** www.seedsavers.org

This organization, described earlier in this chapter under "Seed Trusts / Exchanges," publishes the following three books:

Fruit, Berry, and Nut Inventory

Kent Whealy (Seed Saver Publications, 2001, 528 pp.); $24 softbound, $30 hardcover, plus $4 shipping.

The current (no pun intended) edition inventories 277 mail-order nurseries listing 6,471 fruit, berry, and nut varieties! What a remarkable job of research and indexing! As we gardeners become more adventuresome or are searching out special heirloom varieties not commonly found, such resources are heaven-sent.

Garden Seed Inventory, 5th edition

Kent Whealy (Seed Saver Publications, 2000, 808 pp.); $26 softbound, $32 hardcover, plus $4 shipping.

This is an inventory of 254 U.S. and Canadian mail-order garden seed catalogs, with varietal descriptions and ordering information for 7,300 standard (nonhybrid) vegetables. The very recent fifth edition lists nearly 1,900 newly introduced varieties, many of which are heirlooms obtained through The Seed Savers Yearbook or from Heritage Farms seed collections. Vegetable gardeners are using this inventory to locate commercial sources for favorite varieties, and to purchase endangered varieties while sources still exist.

Seed Savers Yearbook

Seed Saver Publications

This invaluable book (over 300 pages) is published each January; it contains the addresses of more than 1,000 SSE members and includes 11,000 listings of members' rare and unusual vegetables offered to other gardeners. Annual membership is $30 U.S., $35 (U.S. funds) Canada.

The Seed Search, 4th edition

Karen Platt, 35 Longfield Road, Crookes, Sheffield S10 1QW England | **Email:** k@seedsearch.demon.co.uk | **Web:** www.seedsearch.demon.co.uk | **U.S. orders:** Joshua Schneider, c/o Mourning Dove Farms, 1204 East Oak Street, Mahomet, IL 61853-2709 | **Phone:** (217) 586-7645 | **Fax:** (217) 586-2478 | **Email:** mdovel@aol.com

A top seed-sourcebook published by a talented English nurserywoman, this book connects you with more than 40,000 seeds and where to buy them worldwide. This useful reference provides contacts for 500 seed suppliers who sell seeds from all types of flowering plants and more than 7,500 vegetables. Some listings are extensive,

such as 800-plus tomato varieties and 450-plus eucalyptus. Karen Platt is also the author of *Growing from Seed,* a good companion to *The Seed Search.*

LITERATURE ON SEEDS & GROWING FROM SEED

Botany for Gardeners

Brian Capon (Timber Press, 1990, 220 pp.)

Master Gardener training awakens an interest in the science of gardening, but admittedly may not take one's education very far beyond the preliminaries. Thank heavens for botany professor Brian Capon, who has reached out to the serious and curious gardener with an excellent book, written in lay language, that helps to explain the inner workings of the plant world. In his words: "Most gardeners have a limited knowledge of the plants they work with. They know how to grow them, but they don't know how they grow. They learn to prune a tree to make it branch but don't know why it responds to the surgery. They know that they must provide water and fertilizers but have no idea of what happens to the water and minerals once they are inside the plant. This book is meant to give new meaning to many gardening practices by looking at them from the plant's point of view."

Burpee Seed Starter

Maureen Heffernan (Macmillan, 1997, 224 pp.)

A handbook for starting flower, vegetable, and herb seeds indoors and out. From one of this country's most venerable seed companies, this book is a comprehensive seed-starting guide. It includes excellent introductory material, covering all the aspects of seed sowing, thinning, transplanting, fertilizing, hardening off, and transplanting, with all kinds of troubleshooting help and experts' tips, clear illustrations, and sharp color photography. One of the best features is the detailed encyclopedia covering 33 of the author's well-chosen annuals, perennials, vegetables, and herbs, profiling each plant's growing needs and propagation requirements. As a Burpee book it favors their products, but on the whole it is well balanced and very well written.

Creative Propagation

Peter Thompson (Timber Press, 1989, third edition printed 1992, reprinted 1993, 1994, 220 pp.)

This is a fabulous grower's guide, with solid information on all manner of propagation skills and techniques, as well as comprehensive and well-drawn illustrations and a plethora of propagation and germination data not found elsewhere and easily read by the avid hobbyist. It has become our number one book on the subject. Especially valuable is the extensive propagation table listing over 600 genera of plants with data on how to propagate them. Since many seeds come to you without this information, having this source can make your success more certain and the process less frustrating.

Easy Plant Propagation
Nancy J. Ondra (Houghton Mifflin, 1998, 122 pp.)

From the Taylor's Weekend Gardening Guide series, this handsomely illustrated book is written for those of us who like the idea of filling our gardens with new plants—inexpensively, and meanwhile having an enjoyable and rewarding experience accomplishing this magic. The areas of plant propagation covered include seeds, cuttings, divisions, and layers. Avid propagators will be interested in how well the author bridges what is essentially a most approachable introduction to the topic with information that those with more experience can use, too. Both botanical and common names are included. Another feature that makes the book easy to peruse is the use of sidebars to break out supplementary information in digestible chunks. One of the best of these is the "Troubleshooting" sidebar for each propagation method. Practical and well considered, these tips finger the culprit when things go wrong.

Garden Flowers from Seed
Christopher Lloyd and Graham Rice (Timber Press, 1994, 312 pp.)

Now in paperback! Originally published in England (as one might expect), this book is now readily available in this country thanks to Timber Press. Get set to nestle in for a good (serious yet humorous) read with one of your soon-to-be-favorite horticultural curmudgeons and his friendly adversary as they discuss (written in dialog form) the pros and cons of germinating and flower-growing techniques. It's reassuring to find, as with so much of gardening, that there's no pure black and white.

Greenhouse Gardener's Companion
Shane Smith (Fulcrum Publishing, 1992, 544 pp.)

This monstrous volume is an acknowledged "bible" on the subject and you'll enjoy chapters such as "How to Plant the Very Tiny Seeds" and "Integrated Pest Management." It's a terrific resource, particularly for the novice greenhouse gardener.

Growing Vegetables West of the Cascades
Steve Solomon (Sasquatch Books, 5th edition, 2000, 340 pp.)

Organic Gardening West of the Cascades
Steve Solomon (Pacific Search Press, 1985, 172 pp., out of print)

From the man who launched Territorial Seed Company in 1979, these books are scholarly without becoming too serious. He offers lots of tables and charts to back up his opinions and shares invaluable insights on seed varieties for this area, plant physiology, insect control, and irrigation. As more of us turn to organic gardening, we're fortunate to have this author as our regional (but nationally recognized) authority on gardening organically.

Making More Plants: The Science, Art, and Joy of Propagation
Ken Druse (Clarkson Potter, 2000, 256 pp.)

Here is an elegantly photographed book deserving of the coffee table—but you'll want to wrap it in a huge Ziploc bag to take to the potting bench. Ken Druse has indeed packaged a passion for propagation, including growing plants from seeds, into his lovely book. He covers seed sowing, hunting, harvesting, conditioning, and germinating, advocating for the benefits of "making more plants." The photos might look like they belong in a fashion magazine, but they are clear, instructive, and serve to walk the reader through a progression of steps to grow plants from seeds.

The New Seed-Starters Handbook
Nancy Baubel (Rodale Press, 1988, 385 pp.)

We're not sure if the title actually refers to the fact that this is a new edition of her highly respected book, or if it is also meant to encompass new seed-starters, but in any event we can attest to the value of Nancy's clear and comprehensive approach. Well-illustrated.

Saving Seeds
Marc Rogers (Storey Publishing, 1990, 185 pp.)

First published as *Growing and Saving Vegetable Seeds* (Garden Way Publishing, 1978), this classic has been expanded upon by the author to include the best ornamental plants to grow for seeds. There are many compelling reasons to consider saving seed, and this thoughtful book explores them all, from the aspect of frugality to the hotbed of political policies concerning the influence of large-scale agribusiness and the self-interest of large seed companies. Whether you're drawn to saving seeds for philosophical reasons, as a rewarding hobby, or as a practical necessity, you'll find this handbook provides valuable insights into the specifics of a broad range of plants, from the Liliaceae family (asparagus, chives, onions) to ornamentals like hollyhocks and chrysanthemums. With the proliferation of heirloom variety sources, this is an especially important book.

Secrets of Plant Propagation
Lewis Hill (Storey Publishing, 1985, 168 pp.)

This book was voted one of America's 75 Best Gardening Books by the American Horticultural Society in 1997. It is easy to see why this popular book has won high praise and a national award of excellence. The text covers a very broad range of propagation techniques, all supported by clear illustrations. It also offers lots of information on various grafting techniques, growing evergreens from seed, the author's top choice for a misting system, a chapter on tissue culture, and a quick overview of propagation choices with details for many specific plants. This would be an excellent choice for a serious beginning gardener, but even those who are more experienced will give it a look because there are techniques and approaches even old hands will find enlightening.

Seed Germination Theory and Practice, 2nd edition

Norman C. Deno, 139 Lenor Drive, State College, PA 16801; self-published, 2nd edition June 1993; First Supplement, March 1996; Second Supplement, January 1998; $20 for the 2nd edition and an additional $15 for each of the two supplements.

For the more serious seed-growing fanatic, this is the "bible," and those who refer to it just say, "According to Deno . . . " It is based on his extensive experiments dealing with the factors affecting seed germination, seed collections, storage, and longevity, as well as research on the use of gibberellic acid to stimulate germination. His theory is that "every species has some mechanism for delaying germination until after the seed is dispersed. The science of seed germination is the discovery and description of such mechanisms and the development of procedures for removing them so the seeds can germinate." Be sure to check out his seed sources section at the back of the book! The 2nd edition covers 4,000 species and 805 genera. The First Supplement updates the 2nd edition and adds 40 new plant families, 518 new genera, and 1117 new species. The Second Supplement is the final one in the series and covers bamboo, garden herbs, Iridaceae and Lilaceae from South Africa, Australian rushes, and sedges.

Seed Sowing and Saving

Carole B. Turner (Storey Publishing, 1998, 217 pp.)

Subtitled, "Step-by-Step Techniques for Collecting and Growing More Than 100 Vegetables, Flowers, and Herbs," the book is part of the Storey's Gardening Skills Illustrated series. If you have been toying with the idea of saving seed, collecting it in the wild, and/or propagating plants from seed but feel the least bit intimidated about making the first move, this is the book for you! It is as straightforward an approach as we've seen, yet as simple and approachable as the format is, the book is just packed with excellent information and great advice. It's all right here. Get this book, go forth and propagate!

Seed to Seed

Suzanne Ashworth (Seed Saver Publications, 1991, 224 pp.; available through Seed Savers Exchange, listed above).

This is the most comprehensive handbook on the topic of saving seeds of crop plants, both common and uncommon varieties.

Seeds: The Definitive Guide to Growing, History, and Lore

Peter Loewer (MacMillan, 1995, 230 pp.)

Peter Loewer could not be a more engaging, knowledgeable and capable companion. His pen-and-ink illustrations are divine, his conversational style is agreeable, and his approach to the subject pleasantly anecdotal. He gives a very human side to the seed business, as he leads the reader through the history of the big seed houses and the lives of seed mongers otherwise known only through the pages of their lovingly crafted seed catalogs. Meet Jerry Black from Oregon Exotics Rare Fruit Nursery and Jan Blum of Seeds Blum, Ed Rasmussen of The Fragrant Path, and Joe Seal of Burpee Seed. It's hard to choose a favorite part of this book if you love seeds, but be sure to read the chapter on "Seed Nurseries, Seed Exchanges, and Some Great Sourcebooks" (it lists far more than we can here, for instance).

Seeds of Woody Plants in North America

James and Cheryl Young (Timber Press, 1992, 414 pp.)

The most comprehensive source you'll find for information on collecting, handling, and germinating seeds of woody plants. For the serious seed collector and those who come upon uncommon seed, this is an enlarged and expanded revision of the old USDA Handbook #450.

WEBSITES

This section attempts to point you to seed-specific Web resources, but we encourage you to check Chapter 4, "Northwest Native Plants," and Chapter 11, "Gardening on the Internet," for other great resources.

www.backyardgardener.com/tm.html

Here is the *Thompson & Morgan Successful Seed Raising Guide* with a searchable seed propagation database giving details on 810 species.

www.eSeeds.com

This website is gorgeous! Covering well-known and well-loved garden favorites such as cosmos, zinnias, and pinks as well as more unusual varieties such as astrantia, catanache, and eryngiums, eSeeds carries seeds from familiar, high-end, brand-name suppliers, exclusive boutique nurseries, and botanical / research gardens from around the world, all available for purchasing directly online, in one place. Many of the seed companies you've found in this chapter are conveniently located at eSeeds, so if you're a fan of one-stop shopping, this is a great site for it. They also have a wide selection of gardening books, including many on seeds.

www.gardennet.com

This site offers a lot of general gardening information, including a Q&A service, lots of great links to various seed websites, and specific gardening websites, but we were most impressed by their "E-books" section (though the name is a bit misleading, they aren't downloadable books)—it's a giant listing of garden book reviews, catalogs, information, and more, including a hefty seeds section.

www.rainyside.com/resources/faq_seeds.html

From Travis Saling at the Rainy Side Gardeners site, here are some useful FAQ (frequently asked questions) on growing from seed, seed saving, and his recommended best books on the topic.

eesc.orst.edu/agcomwebfile/garden/seeds/

At the Oregon State University Extension Service site, here's a Fact Sheet of interest to download: "FS 220, Collecting and Storing Seeds from Your Garden." There are also several free articles about collecting and germinating seeds, published by Oregon State University Extension Services.

FURTHER SEED INFORMATION AND RESOURCES

* Greenhouses: See Chapter 8, "Emporiums: Gardening Shops"

* Native seed sources: See Chapter 4, "Northwest Native Plants"

* Propagation classes and workshops: See Chapter 3, "Educational Opportunities for Adults and Children"

* Propagation supplies: See Chapter 9, "Products, Materials & Professional Services"

PLANT SALES

Seasonal Sources & Events

Oregon Plant Sales

Washington Plant Sales

Plant sales are familiar harbingers of spring, but luckily they increasingly signal fall's arrival as well. Most events are sponsored by garden clubs, societies, and foundations as fund-raisers for their own activities or for other causes. In any event, you will usually be given access to the treasures of established growers or the bounty of experienced gardeners (often both) so you'll find unusual varieties not often available in nurseries. It's great to regularly attend a couple of the "better known" sales. If you arrive an hour or so before opening, you'll be among a healthy crowd of dedicated plant hounds milling anxiously, waiting for the "gates" to open. Fair warning (and happy hunting!).

We encourage you to patronize the fall sales as this is indeed the best season for adding plants to the landscape. Here, we've endeavored to list the consistent and reliable plant sales. Rather than provide specific dates, though (they change with each year), we've highlighted the month during which the sale typically occurs. If you'd like to receive advance notice, please call the sponsoring organization or association to be added to the mailing list. Also, look in newsletters and journals for plant sale announcements. In early spring, you're likely to find notices at the Northwest Flower and Garden Show, in area garden publications, and, of course, your local newspaper. Two of the very best such sources are the *Seattle Times* Sunday garden calendar (which runs in the Real Estate/Home section) and the Portland *Oregonian* Thursday and Sunday papers, veritable gold mines of plant sale dates. The Northwest Gardens section of the *Seattle Post-Intelligencer* (Thursday) has finally resumed its Garden Calendar, so let them know you appreciate it. See "Garden Clubs" in Chapter 2 for a list of plant-specific organizations, many of which have sales.

For the first-time plant-sale attendee, a word of advice: This is not like shopping in a specialty retail nursery. For one thing, this is a place where you usually can talk with the grower, in person—what a treat to learn about a new variety or some choice introduction long awaited by local gardeners. Good behavior is also required. When the King County Master Gardeners Foundation planned its sale in 2001, the group actually printed these "plant sale survival tips" on fliers:

❋ Plan ahead: Make a list of the plants that interest you. Or simply let gardening abandon overwhelm you.

❋ Wear comfy shoes, dress for the weather, and pray for sunshine.

❋ Keep cash, checkbook, and credit card in a fanny pack or backpack so that your hands are free to explore the plants.

❋ Avoid the morning shopping frenzy and shop midday or in afternoon hours.

❋ Keep up your strength: Bring a water bottle and snacks.

❋ Bring your own wagon or boxes for transporting plants.

❋ Take time to "talk plants" with the many enthusiasts, growers, and experts you meet. You'll probably learn about some wonderful new variety that will wow you.

❋ Take a chance and buy something you've never grown before.

And we pass along this tip from some friends who have seemingly found the secret to "getting *more* great plants." Volunteer! If you are passionate about the types of plants offered at a sale (such as an event that brings in wonderful native plants or one that's widely known to attract the best growers), add your name to the sponsoring group's list of much-needed volunteers. If you help with setup, you'll enjoy a wonderful preview of plants as they arrive from the car, the van, or the off the nursery truck. Many groups allow their volunteers to "shop" the sale prior to the public opening as thanks for their time. That sounds like a horticultural win-win situation!

Abbreviations used in this chapter

CUH = Center for Urban Horticulture, 3501 NE 41st Street, Seattle (just east of University Village); see www.urbanhort.org for directions.

GVC = Graham Visitor Center, Washington Park Arboretum, Seattle; see www.wparboretum.org for directions.

PGC = Portland Garden Club, 1132 SW Vista Avenue, Portland.

SPNS = Sand Point Naval Station, 7400 Sand Point Way NE, Seattle.

VDBG = VanDusen Botanical Garden, Vancouver, BC (generally held in the Floral Hall).

❋ = Editor's choice and "heavy hitters."

OREGON

Here are some places to get information about gardening-related events in Oregon:

❋ *Garden Showcase* magazine; see the "Events Calendar."

❋ *The* (Portland) *Oregonian*, weekend edition and Thursday garden section, and on the Web at www.oregonlive.com.

❋ www.slugsandsalal.com, a great gardening site from Victoria, B.C., that offers events, classes, and more for all the Northwest, including Oregon.

❋ *The Garden Tourist*, once a book listing gardening events nationwide, now has gone digital at www.gardentourist.com. The website lists state-by-state events.

❋ Chapter 2, "Clubs, Societies & Volunteer Opportunities," has more listings of shows and plant sales within the entries for specific organizations. Have a favorite plant? Peruse that section in the chapter with your calendar and a sharp pencil.

Oregon Plant Sales

OREGON CONSERVATION DISTRICT NATIVE PLANT SALES

Nearly every western Oregon county has a Conservation District Office, and each year they hold sales—via catalog and on-site—of plants that have conservation value. These are well-attended sales since the plants are *very reasonably priced*. The following website gives you a directory to each of the county's conservation district websites, many of which list plant sale dates and inventory: http://nacdnet.org/resources/OR.htm

MASTER GARDENERS

Master Garderners often offer super plant sales (and classes, workshops, etc.). Launch off the statewide website to the home pages of each county MG office for information and event details. Web: http://osu.orst.edu/extension/mg/

April

BERRY BOTANIC GARDEN—SPRING PLANT SALE ❋

This annual sale, held at the Cedar Hills Recreation Center in Beaverton, Oregon, is renowned for an outstanding selection of choice, unusual, difficult-to-find, and must-have perennials, shrubs, and trees. Nursery stock from over 15 specialty growers and Berry's own plants will be on hand. Look, too, for a good selection of gardening books and hypertufa troughs. Call (503) 636-4112, email bbg@rdrop.com, or see www.berrybot.org for details.

CLARK PUBLIC UTILITIES HOME & GARDEN IDEA FAIR ※

Fairgrounds, Ridgefield, Washington. The best Portland- and Vancouver-area nurseries and growers around the area sell their freshest and finest! Several of the fairgrounds buildings are filled with displays from area plant societies and landscapers, plus you can take in demonstrations and an excellent roster of speakers. This is a dandy event to get you into the gardening spirit. Free, with a nominal parking fee. Call (360) 992-3368 or see www.clarkpud.com for details.

EARLY RHODODENDRON SHOW AND PLANT SALE

Crystal Spring Rhododendron Garden, 28th and Woodstock, Portland; usually held the first Saturday in April. Call Bob MacArthur at (360) 356-2522 or email ltcmac@teleport.com for details.

FRIENDS OF BUSH GARDENS ANNUAL PLANT SALE

At Bush's Pasture Park, Salem, Oregon; three-day sale, last weekend in April. Find old roses, organic tomato starts, unusual annuals, perennials, choice trees and shrubs, and native plants. Call Gretchen Carnaby at (503) 588-2410 for details.

HARDY PLANT SOCIETY OF OREGON SPRING PLANT SALE ※

Held at the Washington County Fair Complex, across from the Hillsboro Airport on Cornell Road. Always the second weekend of April. This is a BIG SALE (70 vendors) and very well thought of! We know people who come from as far as San Francisco and Bellingham *every year* for it. Native plants are included in the sale. Call (503) 224-5718 or see www.hardyplant.com for details.

LEACH BOTANICAL GARDEN SALE

Held at Floyd Light Middle School, Portland. Features about 20 vendors selling a good selection of trees, shrubs, and hardy perennials. Call (503) 823-9503 or (503) 761-9503; or see www.portlandparks.org/Parks/LeachBotanicalGar.htm for details.

MEDFORD ROSE SOCIETY AND JACKSON COUNTY MASTER GARDENERS PLANT SALE

Jackson County Exposition Center (fairgrounds), Central Point, Oregon. Choose from all kinds of roses, especially miniature varieties, plus a wide array of perennials, annuals, bulbs, and vegetable starts. Call (541) 773-2954 for details.

OSU MASTER GARDENERS OF MARION COUNTY— HOW-TO GARDEN FAIR AND PLANT SALE

Annual sale, held at the Oregon State Fairgrounds, 2330 17th Street, Salem. Call (503) 373-3770 or see http://osu.orst.edu/extension/marion/mg/ for details.

PORTLAND DAHLIA SOCIETY TUBER SALE

Second Tuesday of April at Rose City United Methodist Church, 5830 NE Alameda, Portland. Call Teresa Bergman at (360) 274-8292 for details.

YAMHILL COUNTY MASTER GARDENER ANNUAL SPRING PLANT FAIR

McMinnville Armory, McMinnville, Oregon. Call (503) 434-7517 or see http://osu.orst.edu/extension/yamhill/mgsite/ for details.

May

CLACKAMAS COUNTY MASTER GARDENERS SPRING FAIR AND PLANT SALE

Clackamas County Fairgrounds, Canby, Oregon. Held the first weekend in May. Hanging baskets, bedding plants, annuals and perennials, vegetables and herbs, shrubs and trees, and garden ornamentation, plus free pH soil tests. Master Gardeners are on hand to answer questions. Call (503) 655-8631 or see http://community.oregonlive.com/cc/clackamascomg?display=fundraising for details.

DESTINATION IMAGINATION ANNUAL PLANT SALE ※

Alton Baker Park, Eugene (formerly Odyssey of the Mind). Many great specialty nurseries participate in this worthy sale to benefit youth enrichment and education programs (including Trans-Pacific Nursery, Curry Native Plants, Carter's Greenhouse & Nursery, Trillium Gardens, and others) You'll find great choices in Northwest native plants, Japanese maples, plants for water gardens, and more. Contact Sheila Klest at (541) 937-3073 or email info@trilliumgardens.com for details.

MOTHER'S DAY RHODODENDRON SALE

Crystal Springs Rhododendron Garden, 28th and Woodstock, Portland. Call Bob MacArthur at (360) 356-2522 or email ltcmac@teleport.com for details.

MOUNT PISGAH ARBORETUM WILDFLOWER FESTIVAL AND PLANT SALE ※

Held in the Eugene area, Oregon. Call (541) 747-3817, email mtpisgah@efn.org, or see www.efn.org/~mtpisgah for details.

NORTH AMERICAN ROCK GARDEN SOCIETY

Eugene Fairgrounds. The RGS Emerald Chapter (Eugene/Corvallis) Mother's Day Plant Sale. Contact Louise Parsons at parsonst@peak.org. or see www.peak.org/~parsont/emerald/ for details.

POLK COUNTY MASTER GARDENERS PLANT SALE

Dallas, Oregon. Usually held Mother's Day weekend. Call Neil Bell at (503) 623-8395 for details.

WILLAMETTE VALLEY HARDY PLANT GROUP ❀

A combination event, including the Eugene Hardy Plant Group and the Emerald Chapter of the North American Rock Garden Society. This huge plant sale draws 11 vendors to the Lane County Fairgrounds near Eugene. You'll also discover garden artists selling their wares. Call Diana Learner at (541) 342-6696 or email dglearner@ aol.com for details.

June

CONNIE HANSEN GARDEN, FESTIVAL OF GARDENS

Lincoln City, Oregon, at 1931 NW 33rd Street; includes garden walks, speakers, and a plant sale. Call (541) 994-6338 or see www.conniehansengarden.com for details.

SALEM PLANT SALE AND TOUR

Salem area gardens. Sale and tour benefit A. C. Gilbert's Discovery Village, Salem. Call (503) 371-3631 or see www.acgilbert.org for details.

July

PACIFIC NORTHWEST CHAPTER OF THE AMERICAN BAMBOO SOCIETY

Portland-area sale, third weekend in July (location varies). Call Erika Harris at (206) 242-8848 or email clintonbamboo@sprynet.com for details.

SALEM ART FAIR AND PLANT SALE

Third weekend in July; co-sponsored by the Salem Art Association and Friends of Bush Gardens. Call Gretchen Carnaby at (503) 588-2410 for details.

September

BERRY BOTANIC GARDEN FALL PLANT SALE

Cedar Hills Recreation Center, Beaverton, Oregon. This event draws specialty nursery vendors and features a good selection of horticultural books. Call (503) 636-4112, email bbg@rdrop.com, or see www.berrybot.org for details.

HARDY PLANT SOCIETY OF OREGON FALL PLANT SALE ❀

Held at the Washington County Fair Complex, Hillsboro, Oregon (always second weekend in September). A BIG SALE (70 vendors) and very well thought of, too! It's not quite as large as the spring event, but is very well attended, with vendors going out of their way to provide fresh and glorious stock. Call (503) 224-5718 or see www.hardyplant.com for details.

LEACH BOTANICAL GARDEN FALL PLANT SALE

Floyd Light Middle School, 10800 SE Washington, Portland. Shop many vendors, with an emphasis on native plants. Call (503) 823-9503 or (503) 761-9503; or see www.portlandparks.org/Parks/LeachBotanicalGar.htm for details.

SALEM HARDY PLANT SOCIETY FALL SALE

Polk County Fairgrounds, Rickreall, Oregon (on Hwy 99W), second weekend in September. You'll find lots of specialty nursery vendors, native plants, and free seminars. See www.open.org/~shps for details.

October

FALL RHODODENDRON SALE

This sale benefits Crystal Springs Rhododendron Garden in Portland's Eastmoreland District (sale location varies). Call Bob MacArthur at (360) 356-2522 or email ltcmac@teleport.com for details. Web: http://www.parks. ci.portland.or.us/Parks/CrysSpringRhodGar.htm.

HOYT ARBORETUM ANNUAL WOODY PLANT SALE

At the Hoyt's Visitor Center, Portland, with many rare treasures that are extras from Arboretum propagation, plus a reliably good selection of native plants. The sale also features nursery donations of choice plants and selections from the North Willamette Experimental Station. Call (503) 228-8733 or see www.hoytarboretum.org for details.

MOUNT PISGAH ARBORETUM MUSHROOM FESTIVAL AND PLANT SALE

Eugene, Oregon, area. A fun(gus)-filled fall event! Call (541) 747-3817, email mtpisgah@efn.org, or see www. efn.org/~mtpisgah for details.

December

HOLIDAYS AT HOYT

This Greens Sale, at the Hoyt Arboretum Visitor's Center, features fresh-cut greens, garlands, wreaths, and also holiday crafts. Held the first two weekends of December. Call (503) 228-8733 or see www.hoytarboretum.org for details.

WASHINGTON

Here are some key places to look for information about gardening-related events, including plant sales, in Washington:

❀ *Garden Showcase* magazine; see the "Events Calendar."

❀ *Northwest Garden News*; see the calendar.

❀ *Seattle Homes & Lifestyles*; see the "Garden Planner."

❖ *Seattle Times*, gardening news and columns in Friday and weekend editions.

❖ Center for Urban Horticulture. The quarterly calendar covers CUH, Northwest Horticultural Society, and Washington Park Arboretum classes, events, and tours.

❖ www.slugsandsalal.com is a website from Victoria, B.C., that covers Washington events, too.

❖ The Miller Horticultural Library maintains a list of spring plant sales. Call (206) 543-0415 for information, or view the website: www.millerlibrary.org.

❖ *The Garden Tourist*, once a book listing gardening events nationwide, now has gone digital at www.garden-tourist.com. The website lists state-by-state events.

❖ Chapter 2, "Clubs, Societies & Volunteer Opportunities," has more listings of shows and plant sales within the entries for specific organizations. Have a favorite plant? Peruse that section in the chapter with your calendar and a sharp pencil.

Washington Plant Sales

SOUTH PUGET SOUND COMMUNITY COLLEGE PLANT SALE

Completely planned and organized by the students, this sale benefits the program while teaching the students the ins and outs of the industry. Call (360) 754-7711, ext. 5219 or 5594 for information and dates. Web: www.sp-scc.ctc.edu/programs_of_study/horticulture_ata_de-gree.html

WASHINGTON PARK ARBORETUM

In Seattle, the Plant Donations Department at the Pat Calvert Greenhouse is open for sales throughout the year, with a lighter winter schedule. Plants sold here are grown from seeds or cuttings, mostly taken from trees and shrubs growing in the Arboretum. Call (206) 325-4510 or see www.arboretumfoundation.org for times and details.

WESTERN WASHINGTON CONSERVATION DISTRICT NATIVE PLANT SALES

Nearly every western Washington county has a Conservation District Office that each year holds a sale via a catalog of plants (largely trees and shrubs) that have conservation value and will be used specifically for that purpose. Many of the districts also hold sales, open to the public, of plants not pre-ordered through the catalog. (See a detailed description in Chapter 4, "Northwest Native Plants.") The website gives you a directory to each county's own conservation district website, and many of these list plant sale dates and inventory: http://nacdnet.org/resources/WA.htm

March

ANNUAL TREE & PLANT EXTRAVAGANZA

Fairhaven District, Bellingham. This friendly event draws lots of the best nurseries and growers and benefits local causes. Call (360) 671-3389 for details.

MEERKERK RHODODENDRON GARDENS SPRING PLANT SALE

Greenbank, on Whidbey Island. Find a grand selection of rhododendrons and companion plants, enhanced by a tour of the early blooming gardens. Call (360) 678-1912, email meerkerk@whidbey.net, or see www.meerkerkgardens.org for details.

NORTHWEST FUCHSIA SOCIETY SPRING PLANT SALE

CUH, Seattle. Meet the experts and choose your starts for the season. Call (206) 364-7735 or email will@savvy-diner.com for details.

OLYMPIA ROSE SOCIETY ANNUAL ROSE SALE

At the Centennial Rose Garden of the Schmidt Mansion, in Tumwater. Call (360) 459-0169, email deborah@oly-rose.com, or see www.olyrose.com for details.

PUGET SOUND DAHLIA ASSOCIATION TUBER SALE

Faith Lutheran Church, NE 82nd Street at 18th Avenue NE, Seattle. Expect to find more than 300 varieties of dahlias with more than 10,000 tubers to choose from! The association also provides free handouts and expert advice. Call the hotline at (425) 836-4487 or see www.pugetsounddahlias.org for details.

WSU TRI-CITIES COOPERATIVE EXTENSION SALE

Washington State University Tri-Cities campus, Richland, Washington. Enjoy a series of gardening classes offered throughout the day; plus shop a great selection of gardening books. Call (509) 735-3551 for details, or email ophardtm@wsu.edu.

WESTERN CASCADE FRUIT SOCIETY ❋

Puyallup area, held at varying locations. An annual scion wood, rootstock, and fruiting plant sale. The event also features grafting workshops. Great prices, and experts to answer your questions. See www.wcfs.org for details.

WHATCOM COUNTY FARM FORESTRY ASSOCIATION

Held at the Northwest Washington Fairgrounds, Lynden. The annual seedling sale (bare root) here gives you a chance to choose from 13 varieties of upwards of 25,000 two-year conifer seedlings (at 50 cents apiece). Fair warning: Lines form early, and they sell out! Call Mel and Henry Reasoner at (360) 595-2618 for details.

ZOO DOO FECAL FEST ❋

Woodland Park Zoo's popular sale of zoo manure is now held only by mail requests, due to the overwhelming interest jamming phone lines. For details on the annual "lottery," call (206) 625-POOP or mail your request, *before* mid-March, to Zoo Doo, Woodland Park Zoo, 5500 Phinney Avenue, Seattle, WA 98103-5897. Find more details at www.zoo.org/zoo_info/special/zoodoo.htm.

April

African Violet Show and Plant Sale

Sponsored by the Seattle African Violet Society and Puget Sound Gesneriad Society, this spring sale will expand your horizons and introduce you to the amazing variety of African violets (going well beyond the standard florist's fare). The sale is usually held at CUH. Call (206) 282-2748.

Arboretum Foundation BIG FLORabundance ❋

The Arboretum's Spring Plant Sale, now indoors in a lovely large area at Sand Point Naval Air Station, Building 30, Seattle. Features more than 50 specialty nursery vendors—and includes native plants, a chance to talk to experts, abundant and free parking, food vendors, and book signings. Call (206) 325-4510 or see www.arboretumfoundation.org for details.

Benton-Franklin Master Garden Foundation Spring Plant Sale

Mid-Columbia Library/Master Gardener Demonstration Garden, 1620 S Union, Kennewick, Washington. Shop a wide array of Master Gardener-propagated perennial flowers, herbs and vegetables; miniature roses; gardening books and more. Call (509) 735-3551 for details, or email ophardtm@wsu.edu.

Children's Hospital Garden Sale

Held at the hospital, 4800 Sand Point Way NE, Seattle. Here's a chance to shop for interesting plants propagated by the hospital's talented grounds crew and from other local sources. Call Linda Shaw of the Marna Bloom Fleetwood Guild for times and details (425) 222-3776.

Clark County Master Gardener Plant Sale

Washington State University Research Station, Vancouver, Washington. Meet the growers and choose from a great selection of plants for the landscape and garden. Call (360) 397-6060, ext. 7718, 7724 or 7725 for details. Web: http://gardening.wsu.edu/text/clark.htm.

Clark County Public Utilities Home & Garden Idea Fair ❋

At the fairgrounds in Ridgefield, Washington. Here's where the best Portland- and Vancouver-area nurseries and growers around will be selling their freshest and finest! Several of the fairgrounds buildings are filled with displays from area plant societies and landscapers, plus you can take in demonstrations and an excellent roster of speakers. This is a dandy event to get you into the gardening spirit. Free, with a nominal parking fee. Call (360) 992-3368 or see www.clarkpud.com for details.

Early Bloomers Plus Sale

Pat Calvert Greenhouse and the Plant Donations Department, Washington Park Arboretum, Seattle. This event features plants that bloom early in Northwest gardens, with hundreds of unusual and favorite selections. Call (206) 325-4510 or see www.arboretumfoundation.org for details.

Evergreen Chrysanthemum Association Sale

Swanson's Nursery, 9701 15th Avenue NW, Seattle. Choose from 1,000 mum plants and more than 125 cultivars. Call Curtis Jacobs at (425) 481-4763, email cejacobs@msn.com, or see www.mytown.koz.com/community/ evergreenmums for details.

Festival of the Trees

Port Townsend, Washington. This fundraiser for Jefferson Land Trust includes tree and plant sales, speakers, and festival atmosphere with music and food at the Jefferson County Fairgrounds. Call Jefferson Land Trust at (360) 379-9501, email admin@saveland.org, or see www.saveland.org for details.

King County Master Gardener Foundation Plant Sale ❋

CUH, Seattle. Lots and lots of plants for sale (Northwest natives, unusual and standard vegetable starts, herbs, ornamental trees and shrubs, fruit trees, and lots of perennials), garden-related items, special children's events, speakers, demonstrations, and plant diagnoses—so bring your plant problems for authoritative advice. Call (206) 296-3425, tape 118, or (206) 205-8616; or see http://gardening.wsu.edu/text/king.htm for details.

Lake Washington Technical College Spring Plant Sale

11605 132nd Avenue NE, Kirkland, usually held the last weekend of April and the first weekend of May. This student-run "Seed to Sale" helps fund the school's environmental horticulture programs and gives students experience in planning, planting, growing, and sales. Call (425) 739-8279 or email don.marshall@lwtc.ctc.edu for details.

The Little Puyallup Spring Fair

Puyallup Fairgrounds. Flower and gardening tips are part of this weekend version of the BIG FAIR. Visit the Spring Plant Expo & Sale in Expo Hall, featuring a sale of rhododendrons, primroses, orchids, bonsai, and more. Call (253) 841-5045 or see www.thefair.com for details.

Meerkerk Rhododendron Gardens April Arbor Plant Sale

Greenbank, on Whidbey Island. The sale features treeform rhododendrons, with a select offering of companion trees. Call (360) 678-1912, email meerkerk@whidbey.net, or see www.meerkerkgardens.org for details.

Northwest Perennial Alliance Plant Sale ❋

Sand Point Naval Station, Seattle. Recently opened to the public after years as a members-only event. Fabulous collectors' plants and new introductions for the perennial garden from Northwest growers, divisions from the famous NPA border at the Bellevue Botanical Garden, and plants from NPA members' own gardens; held at SPNS Building #3. Call (425) 413-1410 or see www.northwest-perennialalliance.org.

Pierce County Master Gardeners Plant Sale ❋

Held at the WSU Demonstration Garden, 7711 Pioneer Way, Puyallup. Find a large selection of plants from area growers and local Master Gardeners. The event features eductional displays on environmentally friendly garden practices, water conservation, worm and yard composting, Square Foot Nutrition and more. You can also tour the expanded display garden. Call (253) 798-7180 for details.

Puget Sound Fuchsia Society Spring Plant Sale

West Seattle Senior Center. Call Irene Bergum at (425) 742-2606 for details.

Rhododendron Species Foundation Spring Sale ❋

Federal Way. With thousands of hard-to-find plants, especially species and hybrid rhododendrons and azaleas, plus Japanese maples, heathers, hostas, ferns, natives, ornamental trees and shrubs, rock garden plants, perennials, bonsai, rare collectibles, and bulbs. There are even Phytosanitary Certificates for plants crossing the Canadian border, and the Botanical Garden is open for *free* this day. The proceeds from the sale help to fund the Garden and the Foundation's educational and conservation efforts. Call (253) 838-4646 or see www.rhodygarden.org for details.

Seattle Audubon Spring Plant Sale

SAS Nature Shop at 8050 35th Avenue NE, Seattle. Call (206) 523-8243 or see www.seattleaudubon.org for details.

Seattle Rhododendron Society Show and Sale

Wells-Medina Nursery, 8300 NE 24th Street, Medina, WA. The sale features rhododendrons and great companion plants, plus expert advice from SRS's members. Call (425) 481-9075 for details.

Skagit Valley Dahlia Society Annual Tuber Sale

Skagit Valley Gardens, Mount Vernon, Washington. Call (360) 855-1357 or email csell@pioneerdahlias.com for details.

Snohomish Dahlia Society Tuber Sale

Legion Hall, 145 Alverson Boulevard, Everett. See www.scdahlias.org for details.

Sno-King Fuchsia Society Spring Plant Sale

Country Village, Bothell. Call Salcha Earley at (425) 290-9232 for details.

WSU Master Gardeners of Grays Harbor & Pacific County Lawn & Garden Show

Grays Harbor County Fairgrounds, Elma, Washington. Call Don Tapio at (360) 482-2934 for details.

Yakima Area Arboretum "The Arbor Festival" and Spring Plant Sale

At the arboretum, and featuring plants from Yakima-area growers and nurseries. Call (509) 248-7337 or see www.ahtrees.org for details.

May

Bellevue Botanical Garden Society Plant Sale ❋

12001 Main Street, Bellevue. Enjoy an amazing array of over 30 specialty nursery vendors (varieties of tomatoes, black-flowered annuals, hellebores, lewisias, and cyclamen!). Master Gardeners are in attendance. Activities for children, lectures, tours, and gifts. Call (425) 451-3755 or see www.bellevuebotanical.org for details.

Botanica Wallingford Neighborhood Sale

Corner of Corliss Avenue and N 40th Street, Seattle. If you've shopped the big sales, like the King County Master Gardeners or the Northwest Horticultural Society Sale, you've seen the interesting, diverse, and very healthy plants propagated and grown by Botanica. This sale offers even more of the same. Call (206) 534-1370 for details.

Clallam County Master Gardener Plant Sale

Master Gardener Demonstration Garden, 2711 Woodcock Road, Sequim, Washington. Shop from a great selection of plants, from grasses to trees (plus, you'll find some great bargains at the "white elephant" table). The sale also features garden art and tours of the 2½ acre garden. Call (360) 417-2279 for details, or email astro@olypen.com.

Friends of the Conservatory ❋

Volunteer Park Conservatory, 1247 15th Avenue E and E Galer Street, Seattle. Select from blooming orchids, bromeliads, and larger-sized cactus. Also featured are a collector's corner (jasmines, desert succulents, vines, and passifloras) as well as tropical foliage plants, hardy perennials, herbs, lilies, tree peonies, sedums, bananas, and carnivorous plants. What a luscious array! Usually held the Saturday before Mother's Day. Call (206) 322-4112 for details.

Fuchsia Fanciers Spring Plant Sale

At the Levi's Outlet Mall in Centralia, Washington. Call Salli Dahl at (360) 736-8470 for details.

Greater Seattle Fuchsia Society Spring Plant Sale

12735 1st Avenue NW, Seattle. You'll find lots of fuchsias, perennials, annuals, and tomatoes at this event. Call Will Gibbs at (206) 364-7735 for details.

Island County Master Gardeners Plant Sale

Held in conjunction with the Coupeville Water Festival, along Front Street in downtown Coupeville. Many wonderful plants are offered, plus it's a fun day trip to Whidbey Island. The sale features annuals, perennials, vegetables, grasses, shrubs, ground covers, houseplants, and advice from Master Gardeners. Call (360) 679-7327 or see www.island.wsu.edu for details.

Kubota Garden Foundation Spring Plant Sale

At the garden, Renton Avenue South and 55th Avenue South, Seattle. Call (206) 725-5060 for details or see www.kubota.org.

Lake Bay Fuchsia Society Spring Plant Sale

At the Vaughn Civic Center, Vaughn (Pierce County, near Tacoma). Call Sharon Miller at (253) 884-2536 for details.

Lewis County Master Gardener Annual Plant Sale

Yardbirds Mall, Chehalis, Washington (Exit 79 off I-5). Choose from a wide variety of plants raised by Master Gardeners, including vegetable starts, annuals, perennials, herbs, shrubs, trees, houseplants and more. Call (360) 740-1216 for details, or email burrisd@coopext.cahe.wsu.edu.

Meerkerk Rhododendron Garden's Purple Passion Rhodie Sale

Greenbank, on Whidbey Island. An event featuring rhodies in every shade from red-violet to black-purple, with companion perennials and ground covers. Call (360) 678-1912, email meerkerk@whidbey.net, or see www.meerkerkgardens.org for details.

MsK Rare Plant Nursery, Mother's Day Sale

20312 15th Avenue NW, Shoreline. A once-a-year chance to shop this specialty nursery's fascinating inventory. Call (206) 546-1281 for details.

Olympic Peninsula Chapter of American Rhododendron Society Show and Sale

At the Chapel at Fort Worden State Park, near Port Townsend. Cheer your friends who are racing or walking in the "Rhody Run," and then shop for a wide array of rhododendron plants (usually the third weekend of May). Call Peggy Middleton at (360) 385-9994 for details.

The Orca at Columbia School Garden

3528 S Ferdinand Street, Seattle. The students, parents, and many volunteers grow veggies, herbs, and garden plants in the elementary school playground-garden. Master Gardeners are on hand to answer questions, so help support this neat project! The sale is usually held the Saturday before Mother's Day. Call Alan Moores at (206) 722-3620 or email acmoores@home.com for details.

Puget Sound Bonsai Association Spring Show and Sale

This two-day event showcases beautiful bonsai creations from the region's best bonsai artists. You'll have a chance to buy bonsai starts, supplies, and more. CUH; call (206) 781-9790.

Seattle Rhododendron Society Annual May Show & Plant Sale ❋

GVC, at the Arboretum, Seattle. Enjoy displays and competition of mid-season blooming rhododendron trusses, foliage, and plants; meet the experts; and purchase great rhododendron plants. Call (425) 481-9075, email dking4@gte.net, or see www.seattlerhododendronsociety.org.

Seattle Tilth Edible Plant Sale ❋

Good Shepherd Center, 4649 Sunnyside Avenue N, Seattle. The largest edible/organic plant sale in the Seattle area, and arguably THE BEST source for tomatoes! Lots of informational booths, plant vendors, food—come early for this one! Call (206) 633-0451 or see www.seattletilth.org for details.

W. W. Seymour Botanical Conservatory Plant Sale

316 S G Street, Tacoma. An annual event held in the cozy Conservatory, where you can buy potted bulbs and primroses for spring, foliage plants, cacti, and miniature roses. Call (253) 591-5330 or email wwseymour@tacomaparks.com for details.

Skagit County Master Gardener Foundation Plant Faire

WSU Mt. Vernon Research and Extension Unit, 16650 S.R. 536, Mount Vernon, Washington. Shop thousands of tomato plants, vegetable starts, annuals, herbs, perennials, shrubs, bulbs, and specialty plants and garden art from area vendors. Master Gardeners are on hand to address plant questions, diagnose problems and provide educational resources. Call (360) 428-4270 for details, or email denisem@co.skagit.wa.us.

Snohomish County Master Gardener Plant Sale ✳

McCollum Park, 600 128th Street SE, in South Everett. Find a great lineup of local growers, plus knowledgeable Master Gardener advice. The sale features perennials, trees, shrubs, vegetable starts, ground covers, Mother's Day fuchsia baskets, and more. Call (425) 357-6010 for details.

South King County Arboretum Foundation Plant Sale

22520 SE 248th Street, Maple Valley. New selections of rhododendrons, trees and shrubs, perennials, native plants, and more. Call (206) 366-2125 or see www.skcaf. org for details.

South Seattle Community College Garden Center

Spring Plant Sale, West Seattle, with 25 percent off all plants, including a great selection propagated by students in the landscape horticulture program. Call (206) 764-5323 for details. For directions, see www.southseattle.org/campus/map.htm.

Thurston County Master Gardener Foundation Plant Sale

DirtWorks, Alta Drive, at Yauger Park, Lacey, Washington. Shop Master Gardener-grown and propagated plants, annuals, biennials, and perennials. Choose from several free gardening workshops. Call (360) 786-5445, ext. 7908 for details, email mastergardener@email.com, or see http://thurston.wsu.edu.

Washington Native Plant Society Sale ✳

Bellevue Botanical Garden, 12001 Main Street, Bellevue. Find a large selection of native trees, shrubs, and herbaceous plants, as well as gardening and other botanical books. In addition, take one of the native plant walks or see the slide presentations. Call (206) 527-3210 or see www.wnps.org for details.

Whatcom County Master Gardener Plant Sale

Hovander Homestead Park, Ferndale, Washington. Shop a wide array of plants for the garden. Master Gardeners are on hand to answer plant questions; Master Composters sell composted manure (a hot commodity!) and more. Call (360) 384-3444 for details.

June

Hardy Fern Foundation Fern Festival and Plant Sale ✳

CUH, Seattle. A wonderful source for diverse ferns and companion plants (including Japanese maples, natives, and dogwoods), plus a lecture by a featured expert. Call (206) 870-5363 or see www.hardyferns.org for details.

Seattle Bamboo Festival and Plant Sale

At CUH, hosted by the PNW Chapter of the American Bamboo Society. A sale for bamboo, including an auction of rare bamboo. This is a great time to expand your horizons about bamboo! Call (206) 242-8848 or (206) 781-9790, or see http://www.halcyon.com/abs/ChapterPages/PNWChapterInfo.html for details.

Sorticulture ✳

Evergreen Area Arboretum, Legion Park, Everett. This hip event combines great plants from area growers and fine northwest garden arts and crafts with demonstrations, live music, food, and lectures on gardening. What does "Sorticulture" mean? Some say it's a hybrid term for "sort of" and "horticulture." Be sure to visit and decide for yourself! Call (425) 257-8389 or see www.ci.everett. wa.us/Everett/parks/eprd for details.

South Seattle Community College Garden Center

End-of-the-Year Sale. Enjoy 30 percent off all plants, including a great selection propagated by students in the landscape horticulture program. Call (206) 764-5323 for details. Directions: http://www.southseattle.org/campus/map.htm.

August

Fronderosa Frolic at Fancy Fronds ✳

Gold Bar, Washington. Fern expert extraordinaire Judith Jones gathers together her specialty nursery friends, Northwest garden artists, and hundreds of temperate ferns for a weekend party, fest, and sale. Call (360) 793-1472 or see www.fancyfronds.com for details.

September

Fall Fecal Fest

Woodland Park Zoo's popular fall sale of zoo manure and "zoo brew" compost tea is now held only by mail requests, due to the overwhelming interest jamming the phone lines. For details on the annual lottery, call (206) 625-POOP or mail your request, *before* September, to Zoo Doo, Woodland Park Zoo, 5500 Phinney Avenue, Seattle, 98103-5897. Find more details at www.zoo.org/zoo_info/special/zoodoo.htm.

Friends of the Conservatory Fall Plant Sale ✳

Volunteer Park, 1247 15th Avenue E and E Galer Street, Seattle. A great selection of perennials for fall planting, plus colorful bromeliads, orchids, cactus dish-gardens, and many tropical plants similar to those on display in the Conservatory. Call (206) 322-4112 for details.

Kubota Garden Foundation Fall Plant Sale

At the Kubota Garden, Seattle. Call (206) 725-5060 or see www.kubota.org for details.

Northwest Horticultural Society Plant Sale

CUH, Seattle. This is a BIG sale with lots of this area's finest specialty nurseries bringing plants. Meet the growers and learn more about this great organization. Call (206) 527-1794 or see www.northwesthort.org for details.

Odd Plant Show & Sale ❄

Held at Sky Nursery, 18528 Aurora Avenue N, Shoreline, Washington 98133, typically the second weekend in September, and sponsored by the Cascade Cactus and Succulent Society and the Carnivorous Plant Society. Call (206) 546-4851 or see www.skynursery.com for details.

PlantAmnesty Annual Plant Sale and Fall Festival ❄

SPNS, Seattle. You'll discover new, used, slightly abused, native, and extra-large plants donated by individuals and nurseries. Visit the Collector's Corner of choice plants, ornamental grasses, and rare and specimen trees and shrubs; the Stump the Experts panel of plant and pest diagnosticians; and see pruning demonstrations. Winners of the annual Ugly Yard Contest are announced; and there's an auction of gardening-related stuff. This is the major fund-raiser for this worthy organization, so GO! Call (206) 367-0863 or see www.plantamnesty.org for details.

Rhododendron Species Foundation Fall Plant Sale ❄

Federal Way. Look for hard-to-find plants, species and hybrid rhododendrons and azaleas, plus Japanese maples, heathers, hostas, ferns, natives, ornamental trees and shrubs, rock garden plants, perennials, bonsai, rare collectibles, and bulbs. Phytosanitary Certificates are here for plants crossing the Canadian border, and the Botanical Garden is open for *free* this day. Proceeds from the sale help to fund the Garden and the Foundation's educational and conservation efforts. Call (253) 838-4646 or see www.rhodygarden.org for details.

W. W. Seymour Botanical Conservatory Annual Fall Sale

At the Conservatory, 316 S G Street, Tacoma. Sale features a wide array of cacti, foliage plants, and more. Call (253) 591-5330 or email wwseymour@tacomaparks.com for details.

South King County Arboretum Foundation Fall Plant Sale

22520 SE 248th Street, Maple Valley. New selections of rhododendrons, trees and shrubs, perennials, native plants, and more. Call (206) 366-2125 or see www.skcaf.org for details.

October

Seed & Bulb Sale

At SPNS, Seattle, sponsored by the Central Puget Sound Chapter, Washington Native Plant Society. This new sale is becoming a popular fall event. Call (206) 527-3210 or see www.wnps.org for details.

Yakima Area Arboretum Bulb Sale

At the Arboretum, Yakima. Call (509) 248-7337 or see www.ahtrees.org for details.

Arboretum Foundation Bulb and Plant Sale ❄

At Washington Park Arboretum, Seattle. Members receive a listing in advance to study and help plan, especially because this sale encompasses many bulbs that are quite rare or uncommon. If you have to miss the sale, leftover bulbs are subsequently sold at the Arboretum's Graham Visitor Center. Call (206) 325-4510 or see www.arboretumfoundation.org for details.

Tacoma Nature Center Native Plant Sale

1919 S Tyler Street, Tacoma. There is a wide array of native trees, shrubs, and perennials for the Northwest garden; experts will be on hand to answer your native plant questions. Call (253) 591-6439 or email tnc@tacomaparks.com.

Meerkerk Rhododendron Gardens Hybrid Test Garden Plant Sale

Greenbank, on Whidbey Island. Find field-grown mature rhododendrons here. Staff members are on hand to answer rhododendron questions. The sale is by invitation only; request notification through the website at www.meerkerkgardens.org or call (360) 678-1912.

Western Cascade Fruit Society Fall Fruit Show and Sale

Tukwila. The event features fruit tasting and a sale of fruiting plants. See www.wcfs.org for details.

December

Greens Galore! ❄

At GVC, Washington Park Arboretum, typically held the first weekend in December. A sale with festivities; here's where you can find a fabulous selection of fresh holiday greens, cones, wreaths, and garlands, as well as demonstrations. Call (206) 325-4510 or see www.arboretumfoundation.org for details.

chapter

EMPORIUMS: GARDENING SHOPS

Garden Centers

Cyber-Shopping

Emporiums in British Columbia, Oregon, and Washington

Garden Art and Artists

Conservatories, Greenhouses, Sheds, Sunrooms, and Accessories

As our appreciation of and passion for nature's botanical riches increase, we're on the lookout for ways to decorate, adorn, and embellish our indoor and outdoor living spaces. Luckily, an increasing number of similarly minded retailers are responding to this urge, opening up galleries, emporiums, and stores dedicated to garden ornaments, fine gardening tools, nature-inspired gifts, home accessories, garden furnishings, and "found" objects that seem fitting additions to the landscape.

Every sort of thing—from artisan objects to garden antiques and farm implements—is offered for your perusal. On the more practical end of the spectrum, there are outlets that specialize in unique products like Adirondack chairs, greenhouse supplies, and stonework. Here's a full array of some of the many unique retail outlets in our region. If you don't see your favorite local haunt in this chapter, let us know! We hope this chapter lures you to undiscovered destinations, whether for gift-giving or decorating your own garden spaces. And when the choice is just too tough, gift certificates provide a thoughtful gift as well.

GARDEN CENTERS

There was a time, not long ago, when the local garden center supplied all our needs—from vegetable starts to the trowel we'd use to dig places for them; from the straw hats to protect us from the sun to the rubber boots to protect us from the damp; from the fertilizer to make things grow each spring to the green manure seeds for fall planting . . . completing the cycle by rejuvenating the soil for *next* year's planting season.

Since the early '90s, the advent of specialty garden shops and small nurseries, along with the proliferation of mail-order and online gardening sources, has presented the consumer with a vast range of choices. As a result, we've not only enjoyed a far greater selection of plants and gardening products, but also an amazing year-round availability for everything we need and think we must need to be happy and successful gardeners. There is even an entire industry for gardener wanna-be's, and that's good news for all of us. These outlets appeal to folks who may someday become avid gardeners . . . they just need to be lured into gardening through the back door! The bottom line is this: Follow your heart's desire and you'll find everything from the must-have garden basics to the rarest of plants.

In Chapter 5, "Nurseries," look for this symbol ❋ to find garden centers and larger nurseries with full lines of gardening supplies and products. Most have excellent selections of accessories (from indoor and outdoor pots and containers to supplies for ponds, water gardening, and water features), soils and amendments, seeds, bulbs, and plants of all sorts, tools large and small, garden garb, books and magazines on horticultural subjects, botanical gifts and, for when you've just had enough of puttering around in the p-patch, outdoor furniture, from benches to fully outfitted patio sets, barbeque and all.

CYBER-SHOPPING

One of the most significant changes you'll see in this edition of *Northwest Gardeners' Resource Directory* and in the region's entire gardening world is the vastly expanded presence of the Internet. Growers and nurseries have found their way to the Web. They've taken the steps to develop their own domain name, website, and in many cases an online store, and with them the garden world is indeed "wired." The good news is that with the skyrocketing costs of printing and postage, not to mention the excessive use of paper, the Internet provides nurseries, growers, and garden shops an attractive alternative to share their goods and services with us. Here's a way to take a virtual tour of the best our region has to offer.

The ability to place an order online using a credit card, without having to worry about the security, has also improved tremendously. Still, some feel uncomfortable with purchasing in this fashion. For them, a visit to the website serves as a fine introduction, but the good, old-fashioned, in-person, on-site visit, phone, or mail-in order is still their *modus operandi.*

Here are a couple of online sites with a regional/ Northwest focus:

❋ **www.GardenNet.com** GardenNet was started in 1994 by Port Townsend, Washington–based Cheryl Trine, with the idea of combining garden information and Internet services on a single website. This "gateway" for all things garden-related is a great resource for any search you might have. It is information-heavy and gardener-focused, and includes links, descriptions, and contact information for thousands of gardening companies, mail-order catalogs, associations, websites, services, products, events, and more.

❋ **www.gardenshoponline.com** Garden Shop Online is a hybrid venture shared between a longtime garden-store book and gift buyer, Vickie Haushild, and Peter Punzi, "Horticulture Guy," who runs a separate garden Q&A website (www.horticultureguy.com). Both have established ties to Tacoma's Lakewold Gardens, one of the region's best small, private estate gardens. At this relatively new site, you can be assured that the remedies, tools, and resources are time-tested. Vickie and Peter recommend and sell only what they've used in their own backyards. The site specializes in wonderful garden books, supplies, and great garden gear.

EMPORIUMS

So what is an "emporium" and how does it differ from a "garden center"? There actually is a similarity, as both tend to cater to a broad range of needs a gardener might have. Perhaps the difference is in scale, with the emporium being a smaller, more intimate shop, sometimes with a specialty (like garden nostalgia or classic statuary), but often just offering a different range of gardening goods, generally without any plants offered. Or at least only a smaller plant offering than one would find in a typical garden center. Emporiums often cater to gardeners who are on a serious hunt for special details for the garden, or perhaps the very best quality tools, which may be imports and thus more expensive. They are more likely to seek out and support local artisans who make unique garden products, or to take the time to poke around auctions, rummage sales, and foreign markets for antiques or one-of-a-kind details like old gates or charming picket fences. So we have collected a bevy of such shops that caught our fancy.

British Columbia Emporiums

Start with these great sources of information to help you ferret out interesting BC garden shops:

❋ *Garden City: Vancouver,* by Marg Meikle and Dannie McArthur (Polestar, 1999), an excellent gardener's resource guide to Vancouver and the immediate area. Well-researched!

❋ *GardenWise Directory,* published annually by the BC Landscape and Nursery Association; (800) 663-0518 or

(604) 574-7772 or www.gardenwise.bc.ca. This is a great source for finding Lower Mainland and Vancouver Island garden centers and retailers, landscape professionals, and local garden club activities.

❋ Attend the Annual **VanDusen Botanical Garden Flower and Garden Show,** held in early June, which takes place right in this glorious garden. You'll meet sources for the most artistic and innovative garden ornaments, accessories, gifts, and more. For dates, call (604) 878-9274 or visit www.vandusengarden.org.

❋ Attend the **Victoria Flower and Garden Show,** held in early July (see www.flowerandgarden.net for details).

THE AVANT GARDENER

1460 Marine Drive, West Vancouver, BC V7T 1B7 Canada | **Phone:** (604) 926-8784 | **Fax: (604) 926-1427** | **Second location:** 2235 W 4th Avenue, Vancouver, BC V6K 1N9 | **Phone:** (604) 736-0404 | **Fax:** (604) 736-1283 | **Email:** avantgardener@telus.net | **Web:** www.avantgardener.com | **Open:** Daily

As the name implies, The Avant Gardener offers everything new and special in the world of gardening . . . finding the best in trends whenever possible. Owner Darlene Sanders, an avid old-rose gardener, conceived of this venture 13 years ago, letting her passion for gardening drive her search for home and garden products to entice you. The shops are brimming with an enticing collection of **functional and creative goodies**—tools, books, seeds, bulbs, stationery, bird feeders, furniture, and glorious pots, along with fine giftware and fragrant bath products. Clever, useful, unique, inspiring—we can almost guarantee you'll not leave empty-handed! The original location, in West Vancouver, is charmingly ensconced in an old house where you are invited up to discover treasures in the attic and out into the backyard where there are, in season, clematis and mini-roses (of course!) and other horticultural treasures. With options from trellises to tools, the serious gardener will find quality, not to mention a good pinch of romance. Special items include Jolly's Clogs from Germany, and Bosbags, trugs, and croquet sets from England. The newer shop is located in a trendy neighborhood, and its penchant for style is reflected in the assortment of gardening gifts and gear for the urban *avant gardener.* For seeds, find West Coast, Cedar Creek, and Nature's Garden (wildflowers). In the spring, you can find Darlene's favorite clematis, miniature roses, organic herbs; year-round, she has potted myrtle available.

Find a good parking spot, you'll want to spend some time exploring. (Here's a tip: One hour free parking under the building—entrance by Capers on Vine Street.)

PS: As an added service, Darlene offers U.S. and Canadian prices for all goods shown online. Join the Smart Points program to accumulate points every time you shop . . . which translate into future discounts. Plus,

take in the anniversary sale, usually the last week of September.

BETTER GNOMES & GARDENS

3200 Quadra Street, Victoria, BC V8X 1G2 Canada | **Phone:** (250) 386-9366 | **Fax:** (250) 386-9368 | **Email:** bettergnomes@home.com | **Open:** Daily (closed Mondays)

Laurie McKay spent 25 years as a government bureaucrat, but she pined for a career that would encompass her love of gardening. In 1997, she found a "funky little building where I could renew my soul" outside downtown Victoria and opened this whimsical shop with a clever name. Indoors and out (there is a **1,000-square-foot display garden**), you'll find statuary, garden ornamentation, great ideas for planting and garden design, plus a great lineup of **perennials, annuals, and small ornamental shrubs** for the beginner or connoisseur. Better Gnomes has a strong emphasis on **tropicals, orchids, and tender perennials** for the conservatory (or for seasonal trips from the garden to the sunny kitchen window). Laurie took a gold medal for her "A Garden Medley" display at the 2001 Victoria Flower and Garden Show, so it's no surprise that she's developed a passionate following.

CHINTZ & COMPANY

Vancouver location: 950 Homer Street, Vancouver, BC V6B 2W7 Canada | **Phone:** (604) 689-2022 | **Fax:** (604) 689-2055 | **Victoria location:** 1720 Store Street, Victoria, BC V8W 1V5 | **Phone:** (250) 381-2404 | **Email:** info@chintz.com | **Web:** www.chintz.com | **Open:** Daily

At this home accessories store *par excellence,* you'll find the garden is one of the rooms the talented staff at Chintz & Co. will help you furnish with style—with beautiful blooms, stately statuary, timeless teak, and a treasure-trove of accessories all included. The store is a lovely and inspiring **design resource for garden and garden-style home interiors.** You'll also find benches, unique patio furnishings, terra-cotta pots, and an array of amazing cement urns! Garden and floral design offerings include topiaries, bouquets, wreaths and garlands, centerpieces, and grand arrangements. Chintz also offers quality wooden market umbrellas (or just the frames, so that you can custom-select a favorite fabric and have it assembled). Register online for notices on special sales, events, and new product announcements.

DIG THIS—GIFTS & GEAR FOR GARDENERS

Several BC locations: | 102-45 Bastion Square, Victoria, BC V8W 1J1 Canada | (250) 385-3212 | 10-1551 Johnston Street, Granville Island, Vancouver, BC V6H 3R9 | (604) 688-2929 | **Corporate mailing address:** PO Box 5668, Station B, Victoria, BC V8R 5S4 | **Email:** digthisHO@home.com | **Web:** www.digthis.com | **Open:** Daily

A perennial stop for many garden enthusiasts, Dig This started in 1984 in Victoria; Robyn Burton and Roger Harper purchased Dig This in 1990 and since 1993, they've franchised the idea. The chain has expanded considerably from two Victoria stores and a shop at Vancouver's Granville Island Market to a total of nine stores throughout Canada. You'll find **wide selections of fine tools for working, materials for seeding, reference books for planning, clothing for protection,** gadgets for gardening, products for making water features, garden gifts, furniture and ornaments for outdoor living, products for indoor gardening, floral arranging materials, and items for attracting birds to the landscape. Products are organically oriented and environmentally sensitive. And you'll find spirited staff that know lots about gardening.

FOXGLOVE FARM EVERLASTING FLOWERS

6741 224th Street, Langley, BC V2Y 2K5 Canada | **Phone:** (604) 888-4140 | **Fax:** (604) 888-0740 | **Email:** rebeccaeblack@cs.com | **Open:** Tuesday–Saturday

Located in the heart of the Fraser Valley, 40 miles east of Vancouver, 15 miles north of the Aldergrove crossing at Lynden, this little jewel came to our attention through a kind reader who called about an article in *Victoria* magazine that featured Foxglove Farm. We have since thoroughly enjoyed poking through the ancient, tiny gatehouse and adjacent conservatory for the perfect wire basket and everlasting floral supplies. Proprietor Rebecca Black stocks **natural (not dyed or processed) everlasting and dried flowers,** ornamental grasses, seedpods, freeze-dried roses, pomegranates, pepperberries, and preserved greenery, with lots of glorious selection. You can buy finished arrangements or all the ingredients to create your own wreaths and baskets. Rebecca offers dried floral arrangement classes on request. During the holidays, her fresh Christmas wreaths combine greenery and twigs. If you want to make your own, she'll teach you how.

GARDENSTONE

3150 Celtic Avenue, Building 2, Vancouver, BC V6N 3X7 Canada | **Phone:** (604) 221-6760 or (800) 209-0917 | **Fax:** (604) 221-6760 | **Web:** www.gardenstonestatuary.com

Here's a new discovery: GardenStone manufactures and sells cast-stone planters, pedestals, urns, statuary, wall fountains, plaques, and other **decorative stone garden art.** Crafted in the European style, with a wide array of hand finishes, GardenStone pieces are durable and suitable for damp Northwest winters. The hand-rubbed finishes have great names, like Tuscan Amber, Old Roman, Dark Bronze, Black Iron, and of course, Natural. Founder Bob Naymie works with local sculptors and artists to develop his product line, and combines their artistry with proven construction techniques. There are lots of great photos on the website to inspire you.

HOBBS

2129 41st Avenue W, Vancouver, BC V6M 1Z6 Canada | **Phone:** (604) 261-5998 | **Fax:** (604) 261-5979 | **Open:** Daily

If you are drawn to the genius of Thomas Hobbs in providing luscious temptations for gardens indoors and out,

you will happily lose yourself among the tasteful wares and elegant details offered by Tom and partner Brent Beattie at "Hobbs." They have created this wonderful emporium (adjacent to Tom's former florist shop) in European style, and with a gardener's sensibility. The merchandising and displays are classically and artfully presented, just as you'll find at their specialty nursery, Southlands (see Chapter 5, "Nurseries").

Browse among statuary cherubs, faux lead window boxes, an amazing selection of fountains, English country china, framed botanical prints, wirework plant stands, and **an unequaled selection of gifts with a horticultural motif.** Always on hand is a sumptuous display of books (including, of course, Tom's own book, *Shocking Beauty*). If you're decorating the home, you'll love the selection of accessories, dinnerware, tabletop throws, and trays, plus bath and other linens. The garden isn't ignored, as there are always containers and garden furnishings to choose from. French soaps, potpourri, and the fragrant herbal bath line from Thymes are also featured.

LEE VALLEY TOOLS LTD.

1180 SE Marine Drive, Vancouver, BC V5X 2V6 Canada | (604) 261-2262 | **Fax:** (604) 261-8856 | **Mail-order catalog for American customers:** | PO Box 1780, Ogdensburg, NY 13669-6780 | (800) 267-8735, customer service; (800) 871-8158, orders | **Email:** customerservice@leevalley.com | **Web:** www.leevalley.com | **Open:** Daily, except Sunday

This has been a frequent stop over the years for avid woodworkers, but gardeners will be pleased with the high-quality tools offered for their hands, because Lee Valley has an equally impressive array of quality **gardening tools and all manner of related gardening gear.** The expansive list includes supplies for composting, harvesting and preserving, watering and weeding, and more. You can also find garden apparel and footwear, all sorts of gadgets and accessories, and unusual tools for specific garden tasks. There are wonderful **garden-inspired gifts** here, too, including a Victorian plant stand, garden books, sundials, tool totes, and floral design supplies. Stop by, or request their **tempting catalog.** In-store seminars are offered for woodworkers, but call during the gardening season if you're interested in possible garden workshops.

PINKS: A GIFT SHOP FOR GARDENERS

4235 Dunbar Street, Vancouver, BC V6S 2G1 Canada | **Phone:** (604) 222-3772 | **Fax:** (604) 222-3775 | **Open:** Daily

Nancie Ottem opened this shop, close to the University of British Columbia campus in the west part of the city, in 1998. She carries **garden-related and floral-themed products,** everything from gloves and tools to books, candles, notepads, pot stands, wreaths, and more. You'll find a collection of unique garden accessories: ornaments, chimes, stepping-stones, lanterns, containers, and seeds from Cedar Creek and Mr. Fothergill's, to name just a bit of what you'll discover on your visit. She makes a special effort to bring in Canadian-made products, too.

THE POTTING SHED ANTIQUES & GARDEN

1706 152nd Street, White Rock, BC V4A 4N4 Canada | **Phone:** (604) 541-6100 | **Fax:** (604) 541-9114

Jason and Sheralynn Oliver created The Potting Shed three years ago when they found this great location just 17 blocks from the U.S.–Canada border. In fine weather, when they open the huge garage doors of this former glass studio, their wonderful garden wares spill onto the sidewalk. This place is a discovery unique enough to lure any U.S. gardening enthusiast over the border . . . and it will be a guaranteed detour for BC gardeners heading south. In addition to the clever **containers, salvaged garden antiques, vintage home décor, and indoor and outdoor furniture,** you can talk with a staff horticulturist and choose from unusual perennials, annuals, and herbs. The shop has garnered a following from as far away as Vancouver, especially since The Potting Shed has won The VanDusen Flower Show's "best of show" for the structures and features booth category for three years running. Where do they get all these nifty finds? Jason says the salvaged goods come from barns and farmyards in Europe, the eastern United States and Canada, and even local sources. The shop offers garden and courtyard design consults, as well.

ROMANOFF HOME AND GARDEN

1816 Government Street, Victoria, BC V8T 4N5 Canada | **Phone:** (250) 480-1892 | **Email:** romanoffhome@home.com | **Open:** Daily

Recently profiled in *Home* magazine as one of British Columbia's best sources for accessories and design, Romanoff Home and Garden is a great place to discover when you're visiting Old Town Victoria. The store wants to decorate your indoor and outdoor "rooms" from top to bottom, offering a wide array of **exclusive lines,** including the clay- and silica-based Farrow & Ball interior and exterior paints, along with lamps, furniture, jewelry, accessories, tapestries, reproduction pieces, and more. The garden will welcome **ornamentation and adornments** from Romanoff—urns, topiaries, and a mix of antiques and contemporary accessories.

SHOP IN THE GARDEN & PLANT CENTRE

6804 SW Marine Drive, Vancouver, BC V6T 1Z4 Canada | **Phone:** (604) 822-4529 | **Fax:** (604) 822-1514 | **Open:** Daily | **Email:** ubcbotgdn@hedgerows.com | **Web:** www.hedgerows.com

Located at the entrance to the University of British Columbia Botanical Gardens, this is a sunny, well-appointed shop, with a **particularly well-stocked book selection** (. . .but with *so much more!*). Very interesting and often hard-to-find seeds collected from the Gardens are sold here (over 300 varieties from the Gardens alone), plus exotic and uncommon plants (many propagated from the Gardens). While small, the Plant Centre offers a wide selection of perennials and small shrubs, es-

pecially **rare and unusual species featured in the Gardens.** There is always a good selection of Pacific Northwest native plants. The shop stocks lovely botanical cards, gardening accessories, substantive gifts, outdoor pots and statuary, and more. Classes and workshops are frequently offered, so call for details. Operated by volunteer "friends of the garden," the shop is a great place to visit when you come to special Botanical Garden events, including the October Apple Festival and the Perennial Plant Sale each May.

TUSCAN FARM GARDENS

24453 60th Avenue, Langley, BC V2Z 2G5 Canada | **Phone:** (604) 530-1997 | **Fax:** (604) 532-0350 | **Email:** heather@tuscanfarmgardens.com | **Web:** www.tuscanfarmgardens.com | **Open:** Seasonal and by appointment

This 80-acre family estate and B&B in the heart of the Fraser Valley gets you away from the urban setting. Inhale the fragrance of lavender and stroll through the fields. Visit the Shop in the Farmhouse and have tea and biscotti in the garden. The shop features **aromatic and herbal products for skin and bath,** including Tuscan Farm's own Echinacea Tincture and Throat Spray. Special events include a Lavender Fair in June and a late-July celebration of the beautiful and useful herb, Echinacea.

TWIGS & PETALS CONCRETE GARDEN ORNAMENTS

330 Mulgrave Place, West Vancouver, BC V7S 1H1 Canada | **Phone:** (604) 925-8677 | **Fax:** (604) 925-8697 | **Email:** twigsandpetals@home.com | **Open:** By appointment | **Catalog:** Free, upon request; wholesale and retail.

Susan and Chester Brewster started their careers in floral and garden design, but changed direction when they became enchanted with **old English concrete ornaments.** Chester studied with an Italian master who not only taught him the techniques, but sold Twigs & Petals his molds, most of which came from a group originating in Bath, England. Call ahead to order a catalog or schedule a visit to peruse urns, statuary, wall plaques, birdbaths, and more.

VANDUSEN BOTANICAL GARDEN GIFT SHOP

5251 Oak Street, Vancouver, BC V6M 4H1 Canada | **Phone:** (604) 257-8665 | **Web:** www.vandusengarden.org | **Open:** Daily

The gift shop is located adjacent to the garden's main entrance. Here you will find **garden-theme gifts and a good selection of books.** There are many mementos to remind visitors of their visit to this splendid Garden.

Some Favorite Oregon Emporiums

We've listed some wonderful places, but here are some other sources of information to help you discover interesting Oregon garden shops:

❋ *Garden Showcase* magazine and the *Oregonian's Homes and Gardens of the Northwest* (a weekly supplement published on Thursday) are very supportive of the horticultural community.

❋ The annual **Yard, Garden, and Patio Show** and the two Portland **Home and Garden Shows** (spring and fall) also attract some great exhibitors who have retail garden-inspired shops you can visit.

ARBUTUS GARDEN ARTS

119 West Main Street, Carlton, OR 97111 | **Phone:** (503) 852-6530 | **Fax:** (503) 852-6570 | **Email:** jaczav@europa.com | **Web:** www.arbutusgarden.com

Located in the heart of Yamhill County's wine country, Arbutus Garden Arts offers local gardeners and wine enthusiasts a great destination for botanical and garden art, tools, books, and gardening supplies, PLUS noteworthy landscape plants. Deb Zaveson and Norm Jacobs operate a small farm and nursery near Yamhill and opened Arbutus Garden Arts in a historic brick building in downtown Carlton two years ago. They represent **local and national artists** working in metal, ceramics, fiber, wood, and glass, whose creations will add beauty both indoors and out. There is a special selection of **hardy plants,** grown at the owners' nursery, with an emphasis on texture-rich shrubs, small trees, and perennials for year-round interest. The tools here are chosen for function and durability, and range from stainless-steel border forks and shovels to a wide selection of pruning and arborist tools. (Ask about the "tool rehab" service for refurbishing or sharpening your own tools.) Heirloom and organic vegetable starts are offered each spring. **Garden furniture and structures**—including gliders, swings, benches, arches, and gates—will inspire your own garden planning. Visit the reading room where you can enjoy tea and cookies and always purchase books and magazines at 15 percent off the publisher's list price.

COBBLESTONES

416 NW 12th Avenue, Portland, OR 97209 | **Phone:** (503) 796-9255 | **Fax:** (360) 835-8963

Renee Verdies sells antiques, **vintage décor,** and gifts in the heart of Portland's trendy Pearl District. Here you'll find vintage garden gates, garden statuary, iron tables and chairs, garden ornaments, architectural elements, and much more . . . from her "secret" sources in England, France, and America.

COURTYARD LIVING GALLERY

65 SW First Avenue, Portland, OR 97204 | **Phone:** (503) 223-6168 | **Fax:** (503) 223-7950 | **Open:** Wednesday, Saturday, and Sunday, or by appointment

Connie Grenfell specializes in **Sierra Mirage iron garden architecture,** arbors, trellises, and topiary frames. She also carries Northwest-made garden products and you'll find them all in this 1,500-square-foot shop in the new Market Theater building (adjacent to Portland's Saturday Market).

DOWN TO EARTH

532 Olive Street, Eugene, OR 97401 | **Phone:** (541) 342-6820 | **Fax:** (541) 342-2261 | **Second location:** 2498 Willamette Street, Eugene, OR 97405 | **Phone:** (541) 349-0556 | **Web:** www.home2garden.com | **Open:** Daily

There is the feeling of an old-fashioned (down to earth?) mercantile business here, both at the shop housed in the historic old Farmer's Union Marketplace on Olive Street and in the new location. You'll find a large selection of **organic garden goods** from fertilizers to pest controls to bulk amendments. The tools include everything from a miraculous looking scythe to sturdy Spear & Jackson weeders from England, and to go with them you'll find lots of books and magazines, and many large pots and containers. Look for the Chinese hand-built ceramic pots, wood fired and glazed—they come with no drain holes but would make elegant water-garden features. The "home store" offers a wide array of bath and personal care items, candles, kids stuff, and more. There is a choice nursery and a large selection of **earth-friendly furnishings and goods for the home and garden.**

DIG

425 NW 11th Avenue, Portland, OR 97209 | **Phone:** (503) 223-4443 | **Fax:** (503) 223-8424 | **Email:** dreamingrn@aol.com | **Open:** Tuesday–Sunday

Patty Hines and Peter Kallen have run this wonderful garden emporium in Portland's Pearl District for nearly three years. In addition to providing garden design services, dig is the perfect downtown retail getaway for gardeners and those who want to "bring the outdoors in." The 1,600-square-foot store is housed in a turn-of-the-century building, complete with 14-foot ceilings and industrial skylights. The setting is inviting and perfect for urban and suburban gardeners in search of **design ideas for small spaces, roofs, and decks.** Patty describes it as "a real mix in modern forms and vintage things . . . a little eclectic." You'll find furniture, ornamentation, pots, ironwork, vases and more.

HOLLYHOCKS GARDEN ESSENTIALS

2707 SE Belmont Street, Portland, OR 97214 | **Phone:** (503) 872-8672 | **Fax:** (503) 234-6609 | **Email:** hollyhocksge@earthlink.net | **Open:** Tuesday–Sunday

Holly Hood has a background in landscaping and garden design, but after more than a decade in the business she was drawn to the idea of sharing her taste with other garden lovers. "I just got this wild hair to start this store," she jokes. Her own name inspired the store's name, Hollyhocks, which has operated in Portland's Belmont neighborhood for a few years now. Holly specializes in **local garden art,** much of which comes from recycled "finds." Ironworkers make trellises, arbors, topiary forms, and whimsical plant stakes. Another artist makes arbors and trellises in copper. You'll also find garden shrines made from recycled barnwood. Holly took the initiative and recruited English wares from **Whichford Pottery** to her store. To date, she's the only Portland-area dealer to carry these wonderful containers, which offer a ten-year frostproof guarantee. The shop also carries locally produced white terra-cotta pots, Garden Gear clothing (from another Portland vendor), and useful English and stainless-steel hand tools. Holly continues to offer garden design services, which is a fun way to put all this art to work.

HOYT ARBORETUM GIFT SHOP

4000 SW Fairview Boulevard, Portland, OR 97221 | **Phone:** (503) 228-8733 | **Fax:** (503) 823-4213 | **Email:** haffdir@ci.portland.or.us | **Web:** www.hoytarboretum.org | **Open:** Daily

Have you visited the shop at the Hoyt Arboretum yet? For one thing, if you're looking for horticultural titles from Portland's Timber Press Books, this place is a sure bet. The gifts selection is garden-inspired, and your purchases help support the Arboretum and its programs.

THE LAWN CENTER

11925 S.E. 22nd Avenue, Milwaukie, OR 97222 | **Phone:** (503) 654-6725 | **Web:** www.lawncenter.com | **Open:** Daily (closed Sundays)

Opened in 1991, The Lawn Center is part retail store and part equipment rental facility; it also maintains numerous turf research plots where staff try out new products and new techniques for lawn care. What a cool idea, especially for those of us in search of good lawn-care practices and new grass varieties. The store serves both professionals and home gardeners, so look for everything from "golf course–quality" seed mixes to specialty seed mixes for various applications. Proven soil amendments, professional-grade garden and garden tools, fertilizers specially formulated for Oregon lawns, a "soil analysis station," landscaping supplies, and irrigation systems. There is usually a pot of coffee, jar of candy, and a friendly smile to greet you. Take note of the useful website with fact-sheets and FAQs on just about any lawn concern you might have (lawn problem-shooting, aerating, de-thatching, ecology lawns, installation, and more). The Lawn Center is not an all-organic store (read: they do stock chemical pesticides and herbicides), but it's a great place to learn more about your lawn and how to care for it.

LEACH BOTANICAL GARDEN GIFT SHOP

6704 SE 122nd Avenue, Portland, OR 97236 | **Phone:** (503) 823-9503 | **Fax:** (503) 823-9504 | **Web:** www.portlandparks.org/Parks/LeachBotanicalGar.htm | **Open:** Daily (closed Monday)

LBG members receive a 10 percent discount. Here you will find gardening supplies, books (including many specifically for children), bird and bat houses, plant teepees and trellises, plant labels, bird and squirrel feeders, and gift items on botanical themes, like tea pots. At the beginning of December there's a big Holiday Bazaar the volunteers put a great deal of effort into. They go to great lengths to collect mountain-fresh greens that will enliven your home with the finest holiday fragrance around.

MAX & HILDY'S GARDEN STORE

19350 NW Cornell Road, Hillsboro, OR 97124 | **Phone:** (503) 645-5486 | **Fax:** (503) 645-5680

A drive out to Max & Hildy's will reward you with the pleasure and diversion the shop provides. Naturally you can expect to find an excellent range of **quality tools** (both domestic and imported), the goods needed to care for one's garden, seed from a wide array of companies (Territorial, Thompson & Morgan, Shepherd's, Botanical Interests, Ed Hume, and Renee's Garden), and an excellent book department. But you'll also find lots of merchandise aimed at **attracting wild creatures** (a birdbath warmer, wild bird seed) or discouraging them (squirrel bafflers). The gift and accessories department offers a fun lineup of goodies for you or others: soaps, vases, decorative pots, Asian containers and lamps, water features and fountains, statuary, bronze, garden footwear, garden fairies, decorative garden art, and plant stands, not to mention window art, screens, bonsai tools and supplies, and wind chimes.

NORTHWEST GARDEN AND TOPIARY

(see Urban Gardener)

OUTDOOR ENVIRONMENTS

7529 SW Barber Boulevard, Portland, OR 97219 | **Phone:** (503) 293-5755

This is a place to head if you are on the hunt for special fountains or containers, trellises and ironwork, or the custom services of expert tent and awning makers. The selection here isn't enormous, but what they offer is gorgeous.

POPPYBOX GARDENS

Tigard location: 7295 SW Dartmouth Street, Tigard, OR 97223 | **Phone:** (503) 968-8804 | **Fax:** (503) 968-7223 | **Portland location:** 3433 NE 24th Avenue, Portland, OR 97212 | **Phone:** (503) 280-1228 | **Fax:** (503) 280-1299 | **Email:** listen@poppyboxgardens.com | **Web:** www.poppyboxgardens.com | **Open:** Daily (extended holiday hours)

Sisters Cheryl Krane and Allison O'Connor founded this innovative new garden shop in 1998, bringing a fresh perspective to garden retail. Guided by the principle **"of the garden, for the garden,"** poppybox was named after Cheryl's two favorite plants—poppies and boxwood. The items offered here are sought out for their integrity, function, design, quality, aesthetics, and value. Garden furniture, plus containers and ornaments from Europe, Asia, and local craftsmen are chosen for simple designs and natural materials like wood, metal, glass, and stone. Tools are selected for enduring design and ease of use. The newest and most unique varieties of plants are offered and presented in combinations to inspire gardeners. Colorful indoor plants are potted in exclusive containers, making it easy to give the beauty of the garden as a gift.

Free classes and events are held at both stores every weekend; look for details in a free copy of *Grow,* poppy-box's bimonthly newsletter.

PORTLAND NURSERY

5050 SE Stark Street, Portland, OR 97215 | **Phone:** (503) 231-5050 | **Fax:** (503) 231-7123 | **Second location:** 9000 SE Division Street, Portland, OR 97266 | **Phone:** (503) 788-9000 | **Fax:** (503) 788-9002 | **Web:** www.portlandnursery.com

This is the place Portlanders seek out for all their **gardening basics**—from a really excellent selection of plants to the same for seeds (Territorial, Thompson & Morgan, Shepherd's, Ed Hume, Burpee, Lilly Miller, and some from Europe), pots and water-feature equipment and supplies, pest and disease controls, garden-related books (at the Stark Street store), and of course, tools galore. Gift certificates are a very popular item (especially for brides and grooms, we're told), but the gift shop here also carries garden-inspired products, candles, gnomes, and art from local craftspeople.

RAVENNA GARDENS

Pioneer Place, 340 SW Morrison Street, Portland, OR 97204 | **Phone:** (503) 224-4771 | **Email:** ravennagard@earthlink.net | **Web:** www.ravennagardens.com | **Open:** Daily

This wonderful plant and products outlet is dedicated to serving urban gardeners in Portland (plus two locations in Seattle). The creation of veteran retailer Gillian Mathews and a group of retail experts, Ravenna Gardens offers you a plant-buying treat. This store is devoted to quality—in both **plant material and well-designed accessories for the home and garden.** You'll find a delightful assortment of objects in a creative presentation, thanks to Gillian's own active involvement in the Northwest horticultural scene, and thanks to her talented managers and buyers. In the spirit of a shop you'd see on the corner of a vibrant European city, Ravenna Gardens' plant racks, tables, and pots spill outdoors onto sidewalk space. The masterful product selection includes hand-picked antique and vintage finds combined with textiles, pottery, frames, candles, vases, and gifts. You'll also find a well-edited inventory of good-quality tools, garden ornaments, and hard goods. The displays are thoughtfully and creatively executed and that's enough to make you want to visit—and succumb to a tempting plant or two.

REJUVENATION HOUSE PARTS

1100 SE Grand Avenue, Portland, OR 97214 | **Phone:** (503) 238-1900 | **Fax:** (503) 230-2656 | **Email:** store@rejuvenation.com | **Web:** www.rejuvenation.com | **Open:** Daily

Most widely known for the reproduction lamps and fixtures sold by parent company Rejuvenation Lamp & Fixture Co., this is where savvy sleuths head in a wink to survey 35,000 square feet filled with an overwhelming selection of architectural cast-offs, salvaged ornaments, great finds, period pieces from long ago, and funk from our childhood era. Rejuvenation House Parts promises that this is a "store that is way behind the times" and you won't be disappointed. This is an **unbelievable place** for those with a creative spirit and just the right spot for an English chimney pot. Have you yearned for some **decorative ironwork** to set "just so" into a wooden gate? Or maybe an arc of classic pillars for your climbing rose? Look here. Rejuvenation also carries garden furniture made precisely to its specifications, along with some very handsome Reproduction Stickley pieces for your indoor spaces.

RESTORATION HARDWARE

315 NW 23rd Avenue, Portland, OR 97210 | **Phone:** (503) 228-6226 | **Fax:** (503) 228-8488 | **Web:** www.restorationhardware.com | **Open:** Daily

Here you'll find an array of all those classical garden details that add just the right touch—from a smashing selection of hardware (for your gate, garden shed, patio structures), to stately weather vanes, birdbaths, sundials, watering cans, and plant stands, and on to potting benches, hand tools, floral buckets and vases, trellises and arbors, some fountains and furniture, craftsman lighting—and a small but discerning selection of books.

THE ROSE GARDEN STORE

850 SW Rose Garden Way, Portland, OR 97201 | **Phone:** (503) 227-7033 | **Fax:** (503) 227-8462 | **Web:** www.rosegardenstore.com | **Open:** Daily

Built by the City of Portland and operated by the Portland Rose Festival Association in the heart of Washington Park, this store looks and smells sweet, thanks to more than the roses in its name. When you shop here, you'll enjoy a **wonderful array of rose-themed merchandise,** including stationery, greeting cards, jewelry, watches, candles, framed art, pottery, china and tea sets, garden accents, bath products, and goodies for the rose gardener, like thorn-resistant garden gloves, stepping-stones, trellises, and garden accents. You'll also find a great selection of rose books for beginners and veterans. Then see the "fabulous fakes," silk roses that fool even the bees! The store also caters to the Rose City's tourist biz, with film, disposable cameras, sunscreen, and sun and rain hats. Rose Garden T-shirts and postcards are always on hand. The good news is that shopping here helps provide financial support for the Portland Public Rose Gardens. When you arrive, you'll be greeted with a **complimentary cup of rose tea**—enjoy it while you shop.

SMITH & HAWKEN

30 NW 23rd Place, Portland, OR 97210 | **Phone:** (503) 274-9561 | **Fax:** (503) 274-9634 | **Web:** www.smithandhawken.com | **Open:** Daily

As one might expect, the home of this well-known firm is a snazzy site in an old brewery with a classic greenhouse structure on the back terrace that cossets a small, elegant display of plants. The store is flanked by a beautiful Amdega conservatory, filled with wonderful color and texture and seasonal fragrances. Located just a few steps from a woodland trail network that leads to the city's historic Forest Park and Washington Park Wild Area, this urban gardeners' refuge is a retail paradise. Count on S&H for a good selection of **garden-hardy and dressier garments and** a great **garden footwear** department. Of course, there's also a handsome array of pots, books relating to the garden, some tools, and botanically themed gifts. Call for special events listings.

TUALATIN RIVER NURSERY & CAFÉ

65 S Dollar Street, West Linn, OR 97068 | **Phone:** (503) 650-8511 | **Fax:** (503) 638-9908 | **Web:** www.tualatinrivernursery.com

Among the highlights of the cafe are the fresh greens, herbs, and edible flowers grown in five raised beds at the nursery—so be sure to plan your foray here around lunch (great salads and soup) or a rejuvenating espresso and pastry. In addition to a great plant selection, the nursery offers garden art, pottery, gloves, tools, soaps, lotions, and such. If you are on the mailing list you will hear about TRN's many classes and workshops, and events such as their Summer Concert Series, held Friday evenings beginning after the Fourth of July.

URBAN GARDENER (FORMERLY NORTHWEST GARDEN AND TOPIARY)

805 NW 23rd Avenue, Portland, OR 97210 | **Phone:** (503) 222-9939 | **Fax:** (503) 222-5033 | **Open:** Daily

Retailer Katie Parsons has taken over this shop to bring a "hip, urban," design-oriented style to the garden world. Since the 23rd Avenue area is such an appealing destination these days, a visit to this shop is a must.

UWAJIMAYA

10500 SW Beaverton-Hillsdale Highway, Beaverton, OR 97005 | **Phone:** (503)643-4512 | **Web:** www.uwajimaya.com | **Open:** Daily

"Irasshaimase" means "welcome," and this is the feeling you'll get when you visit Uwajimaya, the largest Asian grocery and gift market in the Pacific Northwest. Uwajimaya offers a wide product mix that includes items from China, Japan, Korea, the Philippines, and other Asian countries. If you are looking for great baskets, pottery, and porcelain urns, the selection at Uwajimaya is exciting . . . especially because you'll find **an out-of-the ordinary selection not likely to show up in your local garden shop.** We also like the great choices of tumbled stones, glass marbles, and other "by the scoop" pieces that are perfect to fill trays for bulb forcing or to put in the bottom or vases.

VICTORIAN STATION

3816 Rocky Ridge, Hood River, OR 97031 | **Phone:** (541) 386-5159 | **Fax:** Same | **Email:** fishett1@aol.com | **Open:** By appointment

Billie and Larry Fisher design and manufacture cast, **fired-clay pottery of all kinds for gardens.** Enjoy their whimsical, romantic, and classical styles. They also specialize in birdhouses and bird feeders. You can usually see their wares at the larger flower shows, but if you're in the Hood River area, call for an appointment.

WEST COAST PLANT COMPANY

1825 NW Vaughn Street, Portland, OR 97209-1823 | **Phone:** (503) 227-6500 | **Fax:** (503) 227-0213 | **Open:** Tuesday–Saturday

In spite of the nursery-esque name, this shop specializes in accessories for the home and garden. Greenery is available here, though it consists chiefly of indoor tropicals and a small but select choice of outdoor plants. For example the nursery offers **a wonderful array of "formal garden" plants,** including boxwood, juniper, arborvitae, and formed topiaries. If you are on the hunt for a wide variety of containers and fountains, make a beeline for the stone yard. Polish off the visit by considering their stylish home accessories in the "garden room." You'll find finials, lamps, small indoor pots, ball decorations, faux fruit, faux plants, tables, and candlesticks, among many seasonal goodies.

Washington Emporiums

For other sources of information to help you ferret out interesting Washington garden shops, find information at these events and sources.

* The **Northwest Flower & Garden Show,** held in Seattle in February, and other Home and Garden Shows throughout the state will put you in touch with hundreds of flower and garden specialists.

* A variety of local newspapers and magazines focus their editorial content on gardening, often featuring articles about or referencing garden shops (it's not a bad idea to pay attention to the great advertisers in these publications, too). Look for *Pacific Northwest Magazine* in the *Seattle Times* on Sunday, and the annual Home and Garden special issues in the *Seattle Weekly,* in spring. *Seattle Magazine* has recently launched a twice-yearly NW Homes & Gardens supplement to its pages, while *Seattle Homes & Lifestyles* magazine is a good source for design-oriented retailers. The *Seattle Post-Intelligencer* publishes a weekly Northwest Gardens section on Thursdays; in Snohomish County, look for *The Herald,* which publishes a weekly Home & Garden section on Thursdays. Finally, *Garden Showcase* magazine and *Northwest Garden News* both frequently mention local garden shops along with their gardening features.

A GARDEN OF DISTINCTION

5819 Sixth Avenue S, Seattle, WA 98108 | **Phone:** (206) 763-0517 | **Fax:** (206) 762-2002 | **Email:** gardenpots@aol.com | **Web:** www.agardenofdistinction.com | **Open:** Monday–Saturday

Located one building south of the Seattle Design Center on the corner of Sixth and Fidalgo, A Garden of Distinction will transport you to the raw materials that dreams are made of. You might need to save your pennies for a $600 vintage French olive oil jug or a $2,000 rustic café set, but there's plenty else here to simply inspire the best in garden décor and ornamentation. Gail Hongladarom skillfully selects **the best from small French artisans, dealers, and village markets** on her twice-yearly trips to Europe. She loves to discover sources previously unknown to the U.S. garden enthusiast or collector (THIS is where you'll first find special French soaps, a wonderful collection of enamel pitchers, or vintage wine racks—then, eventually, these goodies will show up in the pages of national design and garden publications). Gail has also gravitated to **impressive, large-scale signature items.** She might return from a buying trip having grabbed a farm sleigh, a long-pole boat, large ceramic jars for trees or shrubs, chandeliers, and bistro tables.

The store was named by *Garden Design* magazine as "One of the best garden shops in America"—and that was several years ago! Gail hasn't hesitated to expand her vision and passion for great products since then. Her "set design" approach to display makes **this 10,000-square-foot emporium a perfect destination** for those who yearn to see the garden with a new set of eyes. There is a large selection of high-fired, frostproof, ash-glazed containers in many sizes from gargantuan to petite. The Barnwood Collection of custom-structured objects, handcrafted just for this shop—potting tables, garden benches, magical garden sheds—has created a strong following, as consignments back up for months. The always popular book selection continues to grow, too; currently, there are upward of 600 titles in a newly outfitted "library" of sorts with comfy chairs, large tables piled with books for you to peruse. The eclectic combination of garden and home books and titles on "everything French" is delightfully inviting on a sunny (or rainy) afternoon.

A LOT OF FLOWERS

1212 11th Street, Bellingham, WA 98225 | **Phone:** (360) 647-0728 | **Open:** Daily

Located in Bellingham's Fairhaven District, this **charming little shop** sells elegant garden-related gifts, glorious fresh-cut flowers, an especially tempting collection of planters and pots (terra cotta, cast concrete, and wooden), and many other accessories for the garden and home. This special shop is a cozy, welcoming spot on a tiny urban corner.

ARBORETUM BOOK AND GIFT SHOP

Graham Visitors Center, 2300 Arboretum Drive E, Seattle, WA 98112-2300 | **Phone:** (206) 543-8800 | **Web:** www.arboretumfoundation.org | **Open:** Daily

Here, right in the Arboretum, you will find books and botanical gifts designed to charm the garden lover and nature enthusiast alike. This is a great place to pick up a hostess gift, lovely piece of jewelry, or recently released garden title. Arboretum members enjoy a 10 percent discount, which makes it even more appealing to stop here. Not only is there a great selection of children's books

here, but also garden-themed toys for young Arboretum visitors.

AW POTTERY

21031 76th Avenue W, Edmonds, WA 98026 | **Phone:** (425) 778-2292 | **Email:** awpot@gte.net | **Open:** Saturdays only

This "best-kept secret" is a small, out-of-the-way retail outlet run by the importers of large **outdoor and indoor decorative and rustic pots from Asia.** Because there are many seconds, prices are very good. If you are shopping for a large pot for a tree or water garden/feature, plan a visit.

BAMBOO GARDENS OF WASHINGTON

5016 192nd Place NE (196th Ave NE and Hwy 202/Redmond-Fall City Road), Redmond, WA 98074 | **Phone:** (425) 868-5166 | **Fax:** (425) 868-5360 | **Email:** bamboo@blarg.net | **Web:** www.BambooGardensWA.com | **Open:** Daily

The plants here are not available through the mail, but you can request a free brochure listing other bamboo products that are. This is an **excellent source for architectural bamboo poles** (split and solid), fencing materials; bamboo water features and spouts, and circulating pump systems; plus the bamboo digging devices called "slammers." The nursery has many inspiring detailed plantings in place, ready for you to inspect and hopefully emulate. You'll also find a small selection of bamboo-compatible garden art.

BAMBOO HARDWOODS

Home store: 6402 Roosevelt Ave. N.E., Seattle, WA | **Phone:** (206) 529-0978 | **Open:** Daily | **Warehouse:** 510 S. Industrial Way, Seattle, WA | **Phone:** (206) 264-2414 | **Open:** Wednesday-Saturday | **Web:** www.bamboohardwoods.com

We love bamboo in our gardens, so it's no wonder this alluring plant is used for everything from furniture and flooring designs to fencing and arbors.

The popularity of bamboo in our lives is growing exponentially, says Bamboo Hardwood's Doug Lewis, who with his mother, Daphne Lewis, imports bamboo furniture, and building materials. "There are so many good virtues of bamboo. It's an environmentally sustainable product, and people are realizing we're not going to be able to use wood timber forever. This is a good alternative." Visit the home store in Seattle's Roosevelt neighborhood to view a showroom of custom and ready-made furniture, gifts, and accessories. You can also see samples of bamboo flooring here. The warehouse stocks building materials for do-it-yourselfers who want to create bamboo panels, trellises, and fencing. The company also provides design and installation services.

BASSETTI'S CROOKED ARBOR GARDENS

18512 NE 165th Street, Woodinville, WA 98072 | **Phone:** (525) 788-6767 | **Email:** leanettebassetti@aol.com | **Web:** www.bassettisgardens.com | **Open:** Seasonal and by appointment

At Bassetti's, besides the well-regarded botanical fare, you will find garden sculpture both large and small by Pacific Northwest artists, hypertufa troughs for alpine/rock gardens, birdbaths, wrought-iron plant hangers, and other garden art. This retail nursery (dwarf conifers and alpine plants) and display garden on 3 acres is only 2 miles from downtown Woodinville, and makes a lovely spot for a wedding (or you can rent it for a group picnic or luncheon spot). The display gardens include a perennial border, several types of arbors, a shade garden, sculpture garden, container garden, a pond area, a kitchen garden, and various garden "rooms." Bassetti's is also famous for its popular Annual Garden Sculpture Opening and Sale, usually in late June (call for dates and to add your name to mailing list for announcements), which features many local artists (sculptors, blacksmiths, ceramicists, photographers, and more) along with growers from specialty nurseries who are invited to sell their plants in this festive country setting.

BELLEVUE BOTANICAL GARDEN GIFT SHOP

12001 Main Street, Bellevue, WA 98005 | **Phone:** (425) 451-3755 | **Web:** www.bellevuebotanical.org | **Gift Shop Open:** March–December, 10 a.m.–4 p.m.

Call for current information on special events, such as the Garden D'lights holiday display. The Botanical Garden's Visitor's Center is open daily; the garden itself is open 7:30 a.m. until dusk (see Chapter 13, "Gardens to Visit"). After a stroll through the borders and along the paths, pop into the Visitor's Center, where you will find the Gift Shop. It's not large, but you'll find it filled with an **excellent selection of garden books and gifts with a botanical theme.** Run by volunteers to help support the Garden, the shop offers a carefully selected lineup of horticulturally inspired gifts, from the whimsical to the unique. Find a small treasure in the children's corner, or try out gardener-tested tools and gloves. The shop also features an **extensive selection of the popular "flower fairies," inspired by the original Cicely Mary Barker books.** Speaking of books, you can order any title through the BBG Gift Shop—and your purchase will benefit the Garden's programs.

CAPE COD COMFYS

114 N 36th Street, Seattle, WA 98103 | **Phone:** (206) 545-4309 | **Fax:** (206) 545-4520 | **Email:** info@capecodcomfys.com | **Web:** www.capecodcomfys.com | **Open:** Daily

Located in Fremont, on the main drag driving north from downtown and west toward Ballard, Cape Cod Comfys offers the **finest Adirondack furniture** around, especially at these prices. Each piece is made in the traditional manner (by hand), bearing the maker's marks. Fine cedar, great design, honest workmanship all combine to give you great garden seating (and not only that but tables, rockers, swings, and other garden furnishings). Stylish interpretations on the classic model, these "comfy" pieces come natural or painted, in teak or cedar. Owner Dwight Jacobson likes to drop the "who's who" of Cape Cod Comfy clients on his website, so it's clear you'll be in good company if you shop here.

CAROLYN STALEY FINE JAPANESE PRINTS

314 Occidental Avenue S, Seattle, WA 98104 | **Phone:** (206) 621-1888 | **Fax:** (206) 621-6493 | **Email:** info@carolynstaleyprints.com | **Web:** www.carolynstaleyprints.com

This Pioneer Square gallery has changed its emphasis from antique prints to Japanese woodblock prints. While you'll still occasionally find **antique botanical prints,** such as a group featuring reichenbachia orchids, Carolyn now focuses primarily on Japanese work. You'll find woodblock prints, paintings, drawings, and illustrated art books from the late-18th to mid-20th centuries that feature **native Japanese flora of all kinds.** Many of the pieces feature botanical subjects, so keep an eye out for the chrysanthemums, peonies, and an occasional scroll of flower paintings.

CHUCKANUT BAY GALLERY & GARDEN SHOP

700 Chuckanut Drive, Bellingham, WA 98226 | **Phone:** (360) 734-4885 | **Fax:** Same | **Email:** info@chuckanutbaygallery.com | **Web:** www.chuckanutbaygalley.com | **Open:** Daily

Don and Carol Salisbury have been hard at work gathering an impressive selection of handcrafted and **unique garden-related art**—utilitarian, whimsical, decorative, and contemplative—from lyrical fountains to gourmet bird-feeders, handsome patio torches to enchanting chimes. Don is an accomplished potter, so you'll find his work here, along with that of 400 artists represented by the gallery. Visit the **outdoor sculpture gallery garden,** situated in a well-landscaped spot to showcase artwork to its best advantage. This is a great stop along breathtaking Chuckanut Drive and is only a 4-minute drive south of the Fairhaven District of Bellingham. Besides, there's an espresso bar to boost your shopping endurance levels! Make sure you've added your name to the mailing list for special openings and events.

CITY PEOPLE'S GARDEN STORE

2939 E Madison Street, Seattle, WA 98112 | **Phone:** (206) 324-0737 | **Fax:** (206) 328-6114 | **Web:** www.citypeoples mercantile.com | **Open:** Daily

If you live in the area, you already know about this delightful destination for all things botanical. If you're visiting the Washington Park Arboretum, this is a **must-visit nearby emporium and nursery.** Serious gardeners will love the excellent book department, quality tools, garden ornaments, organics and such; gift-buyers will be enchanted by the extensive array of home and garden accessories, card and stationery selection, gifts to give, and items you'll buy with the best of intentions . . . for yourself or a friend. Each fall, City People's collaborates with Pratt Art Center to host a show of concrete garden ornaments made by local artists. Call for dates.

CITY PEOPLE'S MERCANTILE

5440 Sand Point Way NE, Seattle, WA 98105 | **Phone:** (206) 524-1200 | **Web:** www.citypeoplesmercantile.com

True to the images conjured by the name, this "general purpose" **old-fashioned hardware store** is bursting with character, and such a nice neighbor for a city dweller who'll find everything from light bulbs to laundry baskets. For gardeners there is a generous selection, from bagged potting soil to goatskin garden gloves. CPM carries on the theme of an updated, old-fashioned, neighborhood-oriented mercantile, where the gardening department is an important part of the whole mix, including a good selection of garden plants in season (always top-notch vegetable and herb starts). You'll find the same personality and a like-minded product mix akin to the one that's offered in the gift and accessories area of City People's Garden Store: good design combined with urban practicality.

Cottage Flowers & Company

387 Birch Bay Lynden Road, Lynden, WA 98264 | **Phone:** (360) 354-6908 | **Fax:** Same | **Open:** Tuesday–Saturday

Norma Bosman's downtown fresh-flower shop has been transplanted into a charming little spot set at the outskirts of town, behind a pink picket fence and along a flower-filled pathway. Inside the cheery little building you'll find **home and garden accessories, topiaries,** and (in season) a nice selection of old-favorite perennials, herbs, and annuals. If you are casting about for a trellis or a bent-willow bench to spruce up your garden consider stopping here for a look. Norma features European soaps and potpourri, and she has an amazing array of **French ribbon and organza ribbon** of all sorts, in all sizes, colors, and styles. "We're hooked on ribbons," she enthuses.

Country Garden Antiques

6451 Yakima Valley Highway, Wapato, WA 98951 | **Phone:** (509) 877-4644 | **Fax:** Same | **Open:** By chance, or by appointment | **Directions:** From I-82, located 6.5 miles south of exit 40, and 4 miles north of exit 50.

Located in the carriage house of the Old Sawyer mansion, this wonderful shop is a destination worth remembering if you are anywhere in the Yakima vicinity—or make a special day trip of it with friends. Pat and Fred Erickson seek out, import, and specialize in **garden ornament and antiques** in addition to English country furniture, Victorian linens and jewelry, and elegant decorative items for your home. Recently they have added Emma Bridgewater Pottery for your table. You can often find Country Garden Antiques at the Northwest Flower and Garden Show, but be sure to get on the mailing list so you can plan a memorable foray east of the mountains when a shipment laden with **Whichford Pottery, rustic garden furniture, Victorian chimney pots, statuary,** and other antiques comes in from the UK. The inventory is always fully stocked with a good selection in every season, with some objects on display in the surrounding garden, which you're welcome to visit.

The Country Store and Gardens

20211 Vashon Highway SW, Vashon Island, WA 98070 | **Phone:** (206) 463-3655 | **Email:** tcsag@centurytel.com | **Web:** www.vashoncountrystore.com | **Open:** Daily

Located "7.5 miles from any ferry" and perhaps the catalyst for a day away in the country, this is a place where you'll discover the charm of a bygone era. The Country Store stocks garden décor and gifts alongside herbs and unusual perennials. Choose from many **excellent gifts from gardens here,** be they packets of perennial seeds or culinary treats (owner Vy Biel also operates www.goodjam.com, a source of homemade treats). Check out the comfortable **natural fiber clothing and hard-working footwear** department. This country gem, true to the name, will surely take you back in time to a simpler era, and if you're too young to remember, then that's another good reason to come! There is honest nostalgia in this wonderfully homey place. (Check the website for a ferry coupon offer.)

DIG Floral & Garden

19028 SW Vashon Highway, Vashon Island, WA | **Phone:** (206) 463-5096 | **Fax:** (206) 463-4048 | **Open:** Daily (November to December, weekends only, or call for appointment); see Chapter 5, "Nurseries," for directions.

This gal has the eye of an artist (and in fact, the idea for DIG germinated while she was a student at the School of the Art Institute of Chicago). Work in the Big City floral world gave her images and experience she has brought to her Northwest nursery, where the **accessories that mingle with plants** are an important part of what makes DIG big. Sylvia Matlock has **garden furniture ranging from antique Indonesian benches to metal tables and chairs,** BIG pots, wire topiary frames from France, and concrete garden gargoyles and other fauna for your flora. She features the work of **two wonderful mosaic artists,** Claire Dohna and Elaine Summers, combining their colorful forms with plants in a delightful and alluring manner in small vignettes throughout the grounds here. The Richard Frombach–designed arbor is worth visiting to get ideas for your own landscape.

Dig It

3526 Fremont Place N, Seattle, WA 98103 | **Phone:** (206) 547-2044 | **Fax:** Same | **Email:** jodyseibel@hotmail.com | **Open:** Tuesday–Sunday

Tucked into a tiny nook on an exuberantly colorful mosaic plaza (directly in the shadow of Fremont's stolid bronze statue of Lenin) find "fresh ideas for garden living" where Jody Seibel and Craig Nixon specialize in **small-scale gardening, featuring unusual plants and containers for courtyards, patios, rooftops, window ledges, porches, balconies, and other intimate urban gardening sites.** The couple discovered Dig It "through serendipity while shopping for a gift for a friend," Jody said. She and Craig bought the business and have changed it from a shabby-chic style to a place thoroughly

Asian in sentiment. There's an Indonesian flair, with painted exotic hardwood furniture from India, pots, and indoor and outdoor plants. The new Dig It features garden-themed gifts like decorative wine plugs, lamps, jewelry, and lots of bamboo gates and benches. The courtyard entry is filled with furniture and outdoor design ideas.

DREES

524 S Washington Street, Olympia, WA 98501 | **Phone:** (360) 357-7177 or (866) 228-8266 | **Fax:** (360) 357-7208 | **Email:** dreesinc@aol.com | **Open:** Daily

Housed in a 1890s brick building that's on Olympia's historic register, Drees was founded in 1929 by A. P. "Jimmie" Drees. This landmark store is now owned by Ruthann Goularte, who has created a destination worth stopping at when you're heading north or south on the Interstate. She carries an extensive line of home furnishings and accessories for the tabletop, gift-giving, and more. You'll see linens, fine paper, gourmet foods, personal-care products, and exquisite seasonal finds. The gardener is not overlooked here, as many products are **garden- and botanically themed.** The store stages several special events throughout the year, and is a regular participant in the Junior League of Olympia "Gift and Garden" event each April. Add your name to the mailing list for newsletter announcements of Ruthann's great product introductions and events.

EMERY'S GARDEN

2829 164th Street SW, Lynnwood, WA 98037 | **Phone:** (425) 743-4555 | **Fax:** (425) 743-0609 | **Web:** www.emerysgarden.com | **Open:** Daily

As this enterprising nursery has grown in size and scale, it has continued to upgrade its offerings of specialty gifts and accessories. Emery's has also passionately devoted more square footage to **garden gear, fine tools, candles, pottery, linens, water features, containers, ornamentation, gifts, stationery, and aromatic and herbal body-care products.** Where once you'd find soil amendments, you'll now find a delightful collection of botanically inspired items for the indoors and out too. Stop by for a cup of tea, a cookie, and a fun shopping excursion.

ENVIRONMENTAL HOME CENTER

1724 4th Avenue S, Seattle, WA 98134 | **Phone:** (206) 682-7332 | **Email:** customerservice@built-e.com | **Web:** www.built-e.com | **Open:** Monday–Saturday

You'll be delighted to learn about this terrific resource for **environment-friendly home and garden goods.** EHC has gone to a lot of effort to seek out small companies who recycle waste products not only into useful objects, but also very **classic building materials, products, and decorative ornaments.** These run the gamut from sustainable-harvested tropical wood and recycled materials for decks, benches, and raised planter beds to handcrafted pavers for patios, and on to paints in a rainbow of stunning colors for interior and exterior use. The store has just imported a new product from Germany that is a non-toxic, plant-based wood preservative. Put some stop-in time here on your agenda soon. You'll find lots of free off-street parking just south of Safeco Field.

FOUND COLLECTIONS

7354 35th Avenue SW, Seattle, WA 98126 | **Phone:** (206) 923-1553 | **Open:** Tuesday–Saturday and by appointment

Jane Milford has turned a lifelong love of old things—especially textiles—into a charming destination for like-minded collectors and decorators, one that she calls "a vintage boutique for the home and garden." The sidewalk in front of her West Seattle storefront is usually filled with **architectural finds, from café chairs converted to planters to pot racks and window frames.** Indoors, she's designed a space that makes you feel like you've entered her own home . . . in one corner you'll find the "bedroom," in another, the "living room." Her vignettes are inspiring and offer great new ideas for displaying beloved collectibles while also showcasing her wares. Goods for the garden include **wrought-iron fencing and beds that you can convert to "trellis" treatments,** architectural pieces for indoors and out, cupboard doors with garden-inspired paintings and phrases, old corbels cut into lamps and candlesticks, vintage hand tools, and potting shed accessories. Found Collections also offers interior restyling consultations for your home, using your own furniture and accessories. The shop serves two English high teas during the year, at Mother's Day and Christmas.

GARDEN OF STONE

14706 Hwy 99, Lynnwood, WA 98037 | **Phone:** (425) 743-7923 | **Open:** Wednesday–Sunday or by appointment

For five seasons Jack Fletcher has sold **fine stone statuary, elegant garden ornaments, and planters for any garden.** He escaped a long career in the health-care profession to pursue a love of statuary, teaching himself how to make original molds for casting his own designs (recent creations include migrating salmon, mermaids, fish, chickens, pigs, and finials). Jack travels to Asia to cultivate great import sources, including pieces from Indonesia and Thailand. He's also tracked down sources for Roman and Greek pedestals and statuary reproduced from the originals, centuries-old (say, 600 years) Chinese antiquities, and more. Garden of Stone recently relocated to a two-block location near the Mukilteo Speedway; here, Jack has created **a landscaped display garden** where you can see trees and shrubs planted among the statuary and pots. "I didn't want it to look like a concrete cemetery," he confesses. Take advantage of some great pricing on "firsts" and be sure to ask Jack about special deals on "chips and dents."

GARDEN GEAR

102 5th Avenue N, Edmonds, WA 98020 | **Phone:** (425) 778-6112 | **Fax:** (425) 774-5829 | **Email:** gardeng@premier1.net | **Web:** www.garden-gear.com | **Open:** Daily

Lili Hall has operated this delightful shop that carries "Gifts and Gadgets for Gardeners" in downtown Edmonds since 1996. Lili specializes in **English and Japanese garden items.** You'll be drawn into her little shop that's filled with an abundance of, well, Garden Gear: statuary, tools, books, fountains, wind chimes, bird feeders, birdbaths, and birdhouses, weather stations, watering cans (many types, including Haw's and ones made of brass or copper), seeds (Mr. Fothergill's Seeds), gardener's clogs, Felco pruners (and replacement parts), and so much more. She has **Ikebana supplies** too, and represents the popular Tom Torrens Sculpture Garden Bells. Check the website for Ikebana classes and other garden-related events.

THE GARDEN ROOM / SCHWIESOW & DRILIAS

1006 Harris Street, Suite 120, Bellingham, WA 98225 | **Phone:** (360) 734-9949 | **Fax:** (360) 734-9716 | **Open:** Daily

Susan Schwiesow and Chris Drilias display their design talents with **glorious container plantings** to celebrate the best flora of the season. Sharing space with their landscape design firm, this elegant little shop specializes in **fine appointments for the indoor and outdoor garden, the sunroom, and throughout the home.** The Garden Room is a truly stylish shop located in the historic Fairhaven District, showcasing fashionable pieces of home décor with antique chests and large imported pots, a nice selection of Chinese and teak furniture, mirrors, and accent tables. New are Italian writing journals, lots of unusual dried foliage and pods, bell jars, and French linen. You will still find quality garden tools and ornaments, many imported from England, practical work gloves, and an eclectic assortment of tropical trees and flowering houseplants. You'll find the book selection, while small, remains well chosen by a professional with an eye for a tasty read.

GARDENS AND SUN SPACES GALLERY

15611 Main Street NE, Duvall, WA 98019 | **Phone:** (425) 788-9844 | **Email:** gssart@oz.net | **Mailing address:** PO Box 598, Duvall, WA 98019 | **Open:** Daily

Sunny Ruthchild opened this wild and wonderful avant garde(n) shop 12 years ago. She focuses on **indoor (new) and outdoor art** that may include anything from giant metal found-object weather vanes to captivating blown-glass pieces. "We blend architecture, art, and nature with furnishings that play on the intermingling of spirited interiors and special interest gardens," she says. Here you may find screening devised from a composition of layered plants or the more traditional elements of wood, stone, or metal—or perhaps a marriage of elements. When your life has just become a little too stolid, take a walk on the wild side and come to Duvall to meet Sunny. She loves to cater to the senses, perhaps most importantly of all, one's sense of humor! Lately, the gallery has been carrying **garden icons that may have personal or spiritual significance** for gardens, including saints, Buddhas, crosses, Celtic symbols, and more. Quarterly shows featuring original art are sure to pique your imagination.

THE GARDEN SPOT

Wallingford Center, 1815 N 45th Street, Seattle, WA 98103 | **Phone:** (206) 547-5137 | **Fax:** (206) 547-4409 | **Open:** Daily

J. J. and Marian Jarosz have brought fresh energy to this favorite Seattle hangout since they bought this neighborhood shop in 1998. You'll find **all manner of urban gardening goods,** from the best in seeds to organic soil-builders. Find that special pot you have searched for, peruse the gardening books, and check out a top-notch selection of interior and exterior plants on the terrace, where you will be enchanted by ironwork artist Jonathan Ward's beguiling garden fence, and Bellingham artist Chris Pauley's arbor and entry gate (worth a stop in and of themselves). The Garden Spot features luscious fresh-flower exotica and everlastings for bouquets. There's also a huge gift selection, **floral-oriented products, benches, garden furniture, indoor plant stands, and more.** The shop is also known for its outstanding, year-round selection of simple, **good gardener's hats** (seasonally appropriate, of course), including everyday hats for men.

THE GARDEN SPOT NURSERY

900 Alabama Street, Bellingham, WA 98225 | **Phone:** (360) 676-5480 | **Fax:** (360) 738-4730 | **Email:** marcy@garden-spot.com | **Web:** www.garden-spot.com | **Open:** Daily (except January)

Warm and personal is the hallmark of this wonderful little nursery shop, open year-round with the exception of January. Come by especially on a drab and drizzly day—your spirits are sure to rise. Marcy Platner works her unique magic in skillfully ferreting out the most **marvelous details for the garden,** and displays them with real flare in this cozy and rustic shop and throughout the garden as well. There is obvious heart here. She features **garden-related and inspired gifts, both practical and whimsical,** along with gardening hats, tools, supplies, books, and magazines. (See also Chapter 5, "Nurseries.")

GLENN RICHARDS

964 Denny Way, Seattle, WA 98109 | **Phone:** (206) 287-1877 | **Fax:** (206) 287-9025 | **Email:** info@glennrichards.com | **Web:** www.glennrichards.com | **Open:** Tuesday–Sunday

Located between I-5 and the Seattle Center (park behind the building and use the rear entry), Glenn Richards is a family-owned business opened in 1997. Owners John and Laurie Fairman have traveled to China, Japan, and the Philippines on average four times a year for more than two decades. John was born and raised in Asia and comes from a family of fine-antique art dealers with three generations of experience (his family still owns and operates

Honeychurch Antiques in Hong Kong). This 15,000-square-foot warehouse features room after room packed to bursting with antiques and accessories from China, Japan, India, Thailand, the Philippines, and Indonesia. Of particular interest are the **new and antique hand-carved granite Japanese lanterns, millstones, and water stones.** If you are looking for furniture that will turn heads (unique chairs, trunks, cabinets, tables, screens, and the like), this is the spot. Elegant bamboo fencing is also of interest for landscape designs. You'll find some great ideas in the small Asian-inspired display garden accented with stone lanterns, stepping-stones, and granite basins. When you come, allow time to browse, and ask to be added to the mailing list for periodic shows and exhibits. Shipping is available worldwide.

Go Outside

111 Morris Street, La Conner, WA 98257 | **Phone:** (360) 466-4836 | **Fax:** Same | **Mailing address:** PO Box 216, La Conner, WA 98257 | **Open:** Daily

This distinctively outfitted store will stir your creative juices and certainly warrants a drive to La Conner. Find just the **quality tools** you would expect, gardening books, and special terra-cotta pots. There's a selection of **garden sculptures** in the Go Outside open-air Gallery, well-crafted, **hand-forged iron plant and pot hangers,** rugged yet handsome garden togs, English teak benches and tables, elaborate (definitely high-rent district) birdhouses (condominiums?), glorious Italian wall tiles, English and Japanese hand tools—you get the picture. A special place. Mark Epstein also carries a special Adirondack chair created for the shop. Don't overlook the practical **French garden footwear** here—olive green or black rubber slip-ons. As for plants, Go Outside features potted topiary, plus Shepherd's Seeds (if you want to grow your own plants).

Herban Pottery & Patio

Pottery store: 3220 First Avenue South, Seattle, WA 98134; (206) 621-8601 | **Patio store:** 3200 First Avenue South, Seattle, WA 98134; (206) 749-5112 | **Web:** www.herbanpottery.com (under construction) | **Open:** Daily

Alison Rae and Dan Bockus are an amazing, lively couple who have created not one, but **two stores devoted to good design** and that are great sources for garden lovers. Two years ago, they moved a small Herban Pottery shop from Seattle's Wallingford district to a 7,000-square-foot warehouse south of Safeco Field. The setting is spacious and gracious, elegant and rustic at the same time. Here, you can find terra-cotta pots—in all sizes from teeny tiny to triumphant, in styles from classical to contemporary (representing 18 domestic artists), and from the craftsmen of more than 30 countries to boot. So you thought this might be a pot shop only? How about rhubarb forcers, horseradish pots (as featured in *Sunset* magazine), birdbaths, garlic roasters, pot feet, wall plaques, fountains, baking pans, candle lanterns, sculptures,

sconces, picture frames, classical columns, seed pans, patio fireplaces, amphoras—there, convinced? **Lots of pots, and lots more!** For those unable to move pots in and out of our sometimes harsh Northwest winter conditions, Alison and Dan can help choose the most frost-resistant variety and can provide you with a sealant that helps protect pots as well. They are knowledgeable, energetic and pride themselves on customer service.

And as if this wasn't enough to dazzle Northwest gardeners, last summer the couple took on an adjacent warehouse space to launch **Herban Patio, which may soon be the definitive source for garden furnishings of all materials and makes.** The airy and inviting building is filled with iron, wood, metal, and wicker chairs, plus tables, benches, and chaise lounges, and all sorts of accessories for dining al fresco.

Indoor Sun Shoppe

911 NE 45th Street, Seattle 98105 | **Phone:** (206) 634-3727 | **Email:** staff@indoorsun.com | **Web:** www.indoorsun.com | **Open:** Daily

The original urban garden store, and a Seattle landmark, the Sun Shoppe has an **overwhelming selection of unusual indoor plants and tropicals** (running the gamut from carnivorous to cactus, herbs to orchids), a terrific selection of seeds (Thompson & Morgan, Territorial, Shepherd's and Lake Valley Herb Seeds), garden books/magazines, a wide array of plant lights, pottery, beneficial bugs, specialty soils and fertilizers and 30 years of experience giving out free advice. (See also Chapter 5, "Nurseries.")

Karma Place Japanese Garden, Nursery & Antiques

3533 Chuckanut Drive, Bow, WA 98232 | **Phone:** (360) 766-6716 | **Fax:** (360) 336-1526 | **Email:** smorgan@fidalgo.net | **Web:** www.karmaplace.com | **Open:** Tuesday–Sunday

What a surprise! Here's a discovery shared by veteran garden writer and nurserywoman, Nancy Davidson Short . . . **a Japanese display garden, antiques store, and emporium** rolled into one. Founded by Deymian LeSar, Karma Place features a private Japanese garden and koi pond that you're invited to tour ($2 per guest, with group tours and teas also offered). In the garden shop, discover everything you'd need to design and plant a bonsai tree, grow orchids, and incorporate Asian pottery, stonework, and bamboo into the garden. **Pots, books, tools, planters, birdbaths, fountains and chimes, screens, and stepping-stones are among the offerings.** Outdoors, the nursery features more than 50 varieties of bamboo, as well as sculpted Japanese pines, Japanese maples, and more. Classes are offered in bonsai; check the website for details.

Lakewold Gardens Shop

12317 Gravelly Lake Drive SW, Tacoma, WA 98499 | **Mailing address:** Friends of Lakewold, PO Box 39780, Lakewood, WA 98439-0780 | **Phone:** (253) 584-4106 or (888) 858-4106 | **Fax:**

(253) 584-3021 | **Email:** info@lakewold.org or gardenshopping@aol.com | **Web:** www.lakewold.org | **Open:** At times when the Gardens are open; call ahead or check the website.

There are garden shops and there are garden shops. This is one you should make an effort to visit. Among other things, you'll be impressed with the large selection of excellent gardening books. Manager Vickie Haushild works hard to make her **magazine selection the most comprehensive in the region** and in addition, for her literary gardening section, she seems to find the **best mysteries and novels with botanical themes.** Vickie has also sought out and added **videos for the traveling gardener** . . . so if you are off to Ireland or the British Isles, she can provide the preview. This cheery shop is plumb full of botanical temptations, and you'll appreciate the effort and enthusiasm that's been expended in gathering gardening goods that are innovative, useful, of high quality, and durable. Vickie commissions unique pieces of garden furnishings and travels far and wide through the region to assemble her small but exceptional collection of plants. (See also Chapter 13, "Gardens to Visit.")

LAVENDER HEART BOTANICALS

2812 East Madison Street, Seattle, WA 98122 | **Phone:** (206) 568-4441 | **Open:** Tuesday–Saturday (some Sundays, call first)

Take a little city trip and discover Holly Henderson's **warm and inviting shop** (near Cafe Flora and City People's Garden Store); you'll enjoy every nook and cranny at this "gallery" **of botanical art, with its topiaries, French hedges, wreaths, and sculptural pieces** that are on the cutting edge of design, yet classical in their spirit. Holly has a loyal following and a fantastic reputation throughout the region for original pieces that are fresh and provocative. This shop is always in motion, so come back frequently to see what inventive botanical creations will do to spark your imagination. Holly has discovered and collected a great selection of French personal-care items (eight lines of soaps, lotions, and scented candles)—inhale and luxuriate. She's always bringing in new sources, like the truckload of fabulous lavender, or pee gee hydrangea from a little country grower who shows up on her doorstep. Next thing you know, you'll see these everlastings have been dried and shaped into an enormous wreath or arrangement. Stop, shop, and then drop over to Cafe Flora for an innovative lunch or pick-me-up afternoon tea or rosemary lemonade.

LAVENDER HEART BOTANICALS

4233 N DeGraff Road, Deception Pass, WA 98277 | **Phone:** (360) 675-3987 | **Open:** Seasonally (call the Seattle store for details) | **Directions:** Located on the north end of Whidbey Island 2 miles south of the Deception Pass Bridge (7 miles north of Oak Harbor), just a block off the main highway.

You'll find this **rustic little shop** on the periphery of the family holly farm surrounded by 200, 70-year-old English Blue Stem holly trees, where artist Holly Henderson grew up. You can tell the moment you drive up that this is going to be a scintillating visit, for everywhere your attention is drawn to subtle and delightful details, but it is not until you enter the shop that your eye falls on the sophisticated pieces Holly is known for across the country, featured on the pages of *Sunset, Victoria, Better Homes & Gardens,* and *Northwest Best Places.* She is a master at creating distinctive topiaries, wreaths, and French hedges, an innovative artist and skillful craftsman. Her work is just plain glorious. This alluring shop also offers stunning decorative items like special candles and candelabra, French milled soaps, herbal bath sachets, and (in season) a choice assortment of lavender plants.

LEFT BANK ANTIQUES

1904 Commercial Avenue, Anacortes, WA 98221 | **Phone:** (360) 293-3022 | **Fax:** (360) 299-8888 | **Email:** seeus@leftbank antiques.com | **Web:** www.leftbankantiques.com | **Open:** Daily

If you're a regular at the Northwest Flower and Garden Show, you know Ron and Donna Radtke, purveyors of this enormous Anacortes shop. Make a trip to this 10,000-square-foot emporium ("the Antique shop you always hoped to find") when searching for **garden ornamentation** and you'll find everything from English chimney pots to Belgian pumps. The Radtkes are brilliant antique hunters, and return from twice-yearly trips with containers from all over Europe and the UK. **Fabulous iron gates, wheelbarrows, birdbaths, English hay racks, French bee skeps, sundials, watering cans, garden edging, very old stone fountains, plant stands,** and such esoterica as saddle stones, harrows, and glass flycatchers. Get on the LBA mailing list for an invitation to the container-unloading parties . . . or search them out at the next Flower Show to find something just right for your home or garden. If you're in search of something specific, email Ron and Donna and they'll search it out for you, too.

LITTLE AND LEWIS

1940 Wing Point Way NE, Bainbridge Island, WA 98110 | **Phone:** (206) 842-8327 | **Fax:** Same | **Web:** www.littleandlewis.com | **Open:** By appointment only

If you are searching for a water feature with a stunning presence, a wall fountain that is well-crafted and very special, or perhaps want to add unique columns with a sense of antiquity, then you must take a journey to visit this remarkable garden, conservatory, and in-situ gallery tucked away on Bainbridge Island. David Lewis and George Little **are two talented artists and water-garden aficionados who have garnered a national reputation for their design work.** You may have seen their stained-concrete garden forms, fountains, and vessels in such magazines as *Horticulture, Garden Design, Sunset Garden Guide, Fine Gardening, House and Garden, Gardens Illustrated, Martha Stewart Living,* and *Traditional Home,* as well as in numerous garden books. As there is not much to ponder in garden statuary that speaks to individuality at the high level their work does, this lush country garden setting is genuine magic.

LUCCA STATUARY

7716 15th Avenue NW, Seattle, WA 98117 (and see second location below) | (206) 789-8444 | **Fax:** (206) 789-0623 | **Email:** info@luccastatuary.com | **Web:** www.luccastatuary.com | **Open:** Daily

Lucca Statuary is indeed a great destination for **fountains and cast-stone garden ornaments.** Francine Katz and Peter Riches have more than doubled their display space, now at 20,000 square feet, to handsomely house hundreds (thousands?) of classical pieces—urns, pedestals, pots, and statuary, all carefully selected from around the country, and with recent shipments directly from England. Look here for the Northwest's largest selection of **Italian poured-stone statuary,** and a reliable selection of tasteful, endearing, and durable pieces for home, garden, and patio. You'll find stylized birdbaths festooned with lion's heads, formal benches, troughs for a water garden, and traditional Italian fountains. Lucca has greatly expanded its array of smaller gift and interior pieces, so pay a visit even if you are not in the market for a more stately ornament. The best news is that Lucca's own artisans manufacture (and custom-stain) the store's own exclusive line of statuary, containers, and fountains, using classic, old-world designs.

LUCCA, GREAT FINDS (SECOND LOCATION)

5332 Ballard Avenue NW, Seattle, WA 98107 | **Phone:** (206) 782-7337 | **Fax:** (206) 782-1626 | **Web:** www.luccastatury.com | **Open:** Daily

Opened in early 2001, the **newest Lucca venture is gift and home décor–oriented.** Francine Katz says she wanted to give customers "Essential personal objects and vintage furnishings for indoors and out," and that's a great reason to visit this Old Ballard destination. You'll find **European designs and vintage goods** (chandeliers and birdcages are a specialty) to charm and delight; many of Lucca's own pieces are here, as well as ephemera and paper accessories (prints, illustrations, letterpress cards, ink bottles, silver pens, French postcards, black-and-white postcards). There is an inviting display garden and patio that showcase plants, planters, and a Lucca fountain. If you recall Francine's fabulous al fresco courtyard from the 2000 Northwest Flower and Garden Show, this will renew your memories. Visit when you can take in the flavor of this vibrant cultural and arts community. Old Ballard now sponsors a "redlight shopping on Thursday nights" event (when retailers like Lucca turn on their red lights to signal the shop is open) and the Second Saturday Artwalk.

MAISON ET JARDIN

404 Commercial Avenue, Anacortes, WA 98221 | **Phone:** (360) 299-2500 | **Fax:** (360) 299-1243 | **Web:** www.mjcatalog.com

For the past five years Lonna Hogan and her parents, Jim and Hazel, have operated this **wonderful emporium in downtown Anacortes,** in the town's old brick bank (shared with a restaurant and apartments). "I could just move in," is a feeling often expressed here. Like its name, the concept of the store—the whole range of choices from furniture to plants—has proven to be incredibly successful, bringing together a loyal customer base from near and far. Lonna likes to "shop as you live," gathering possessions as you go along, blending together the old and new and displaying them in the store as you would in your own home. The Hogans design their own lines of furniture, soft goods, and much of the home accessory line. You'll also find **custom tile and stonework, garden art, sculpture and fountains, and holiday décor.** Design services for home interiors or the landscape are offered too.

MOLBAK'S GREENHOUSE AND NURSERY

13625 NE 175th Street, Woodinville, WA 98072-8559 | **Phone:** (425) 483-5000 | **Web:** www.molbaks.com

Under the roof of this highly respected nursery and garden center there is a vast selection of **everything garden-related** to be found. So much so, that even though this chapter is largely devoted to the smaller specialty shops, we recommend a visit to acquaint yourself with the breadth of **quality choices in outdoor furniture, garden pots and statuary, water feature equipment and supplies, books, gardening tools,** and other supplies—it is all here and in a fun place to shop!

MOONROSE PERENNIALS

114 N Second Street, La Conner, WA 98257 | **Phone:** (360) 466-0338 | **Mailing address:** PO Box 847, La Conner, WA 98257 | **Open:** Daily

Laura Campbell has moved, yet again, to a charming turn-of-the-century house where every room is filled with a **splendid array of antiques, primitive furniture, farm, garden, and architectural salvage, wrought iron, period lighting, and garden art,** including handmade pieces by local craftsmen. Among the cache of vintage artifacts you will find a small but thoughtful selection of garden books, tools, gloves, pots, and more. Surrounding the house is a fenced yard with display gardens (a work in progress). You'll be inspired by the creative effects with **container gardening and primitive pieces;** also, take in a pleasing array of unusual perennials, vintage roses, trees, and shrubs for the garden. Garden design services are offered.

NICHOLS BROS. STONEWORKS

20209 Broadway, Maltby, WA 98296 | **Phone:** (800) 483-5720 | **Fax:** (425) 483-5721 | **Email:** enquiries@nicholsbros.com | **Web:** www.nicholsbros.com | **Open:** Weekdays

If you are shopping for fine, **European-styled garden accessories—urns, pedestals, pots, benches, or massive stone tables—**you may have seen the work of this quality company. Available in a variety of subtle shades, the reconstituted sandstone pieces have a silky-smooth finish and are winter hardy. Nichols Bros. has taken on the **exclusive reproduction of garden ornaments designed by Frank Lloyd Wright.** If you visit the shop/manufacturing site/sales yard, you will see the largest selection of what they carry and also have the opportunity to look over the discounted seconds (at 50 percent reduction). Cast-concrete beasties also populate the yard, from rabbits and hedgehogs to toads and plump pigs. The Stoneworks creates a wide assortment of the ever-popular gargoyles in a variety of finishes and you'll find several beautiful tabletop and floor-sized fountains and birdbaths as well.

OVER THE FENCE

112 E Washington Street, Sequim, WA 98382 | **Phone:** (360) 681-6851 | **Mailing address:** PO Box 2680, Sequim, WA 98382 | **Email:** otf@olypen.com | **Open:** Daily

Jeri Sanford offers her customers an **upscale and unique collection of garden furnishings** and accessories. You'll find the shop in downtown Sequim—look for the planters on the roof and potted lavender along the storefront. Indoors, be inspired by displays of pottery and furnishings year-round. She carries Plants of Distinction seeds from England (which you won't find readily elsewhere), the finest gardening tools, containers of all sizes, fountains, whimsical garden ornaments, and whatever else she's excited about for the home or garden, especially the original and distinctive.

OVER THE FENCE

1401 Commercial Street, Bellingham, WA 98225 | **Phone:** (360) 738-4100 | **Fax:** (360) 738-4102 | **Email:** overthefencebellingham@hotmail.com | **Open:** Monday–Saturday

In 2001, Emily and Scott Underwood (Jeri Sanford's daughter and son-in-law) opened Chapter Two of "Over the Fence" in an old building in downtown Bellingham. Classy and sophisticated in feel, it's a shop, as Emily says, where "we carry my mom's best stuff." Having worked with Over the Fence in Sequim for three years, Emily knows what she likes and she has kept an eye out for new lines. In addition to the signature offerings of high-quality pottery, this new shop offers a fine range of home and garden décor, including **mirrors, desks, lamps, clocks, ornamental iron trellises, garden benches, rose towers, bamboo benches and tables, screening, and ladders.** There's also a collection of recycled glass accessories.

PALAZZI GARDEN ARTISTRY

1531 S Central Avenue, Kent, WA 98032 | **Phone:** (253) 520-5788 | **Fax:** (253) 520-5814 | **Email:** markwin@telisphere.com | **Web:** www.mypalazzi.com | **Open:** Tuesday–Saturday (Sundays during spring and summer)

Mark Winward has "imported" the talents of the Mendunis, an Italian craftsman family living in Australia, whose work allows him to offer Northwest retail and wholesale customers a broad selection of **classic European garden statuary, fountains, pots, and urns.** The Menduni artisans are known for the authentic look they give to cast concrete, with an unusual patina finish. Palazzi also specializes in weather-resistant, powder-coated iron arbors, gazebos, and patio furniture. Whether you're looking to dramatically grace a home entrance with a fountain and columns, or you simply desire beautiful, unique pots and urns for the garden, you will find many choices in this downtown Kent location—and great images on the website, too.

THE PALM ROOM

5336 Ballard Avenue NW, Seattle, WA 98107 | **Phone:** (206) 782-7256 | **Email:** Brandon@thepalmroom.com | **Web:** www.thepalmroom.com | **Open:** Wednesday–Sunday or by appointment

The name suggests a 1930s nightclub, but The Palm Room is the creation of Brandon Scott Peterson, a Seattle garden designer who's brought his talents to the retail scene, treating this eclectic space as a garden design studio. "My mission is to share my knowledge," he says. Not surprisingly, clients and friends gravitate here to visit and share in garden talk, plus shop for urban plants for indoors and out. The Palm Room features **containers, dwarf plants, outdoor furniture, and garden accessories.** One of Brandon's specialties is designing "little lands," backyard landscapes for children that feature dwarf trees, bonsai, and small-scaled plantings. He has also gathered some fantastic interior plants to serve apartment and patio gardeners. Check the website for upcoming classes and events.

THE PERFECT SEASON

918 Water Street, Port Townsend, WA 98368 | **Phone:** (360) 385-9265 | **Fax:** (360) 385-9710 | **Open:** Daily

Longtime friends Catherine Persun and Regina Siefried were part of a women's gardening group that met each Friday at a different member's home to work in her garden. Filled with a sense of accomplishment (and inspiring ideas), the two realized they wanted to create a place where other gardening enthusiasts could go to find **unique accessories and tools for projects and gift-giving** . . . and so The Perfect Season was born two years ago. The shop is located in downtown Port Townsend, where Catherine and Regina carry unusual and high-quality tools, gifts, and accessories for garden and home. They like to say the shop is a place "where passion for gardening meets creativity in design." **Antique, reproduction, and contemporary objects complete the inventory.** Pots, garden plaques, fountains, and works from local artists are also on display here. You'll even discover seasonal plants and indoor topiary, as well as seed kits. Garden-themed soaps, salts, and balms nurture the gardener's body; books nurture her mind. Ornaments nurture the garden. It's all here and worth a stop just for a friendly visit with these two women. (The shop is located on the left, across from the Port Townsend–Keystone ferry dock.)

PIRIFORMIS

1031 N 35th Street, Seattle, WA 98103 | **Phone:** (206) 632-1760 | **Fax:** (206) 632-5682 | **Web:** www.piriformis.com | **Open:** Daily

Until she injured her piriformis—the formal name of the digging muscle—Tory Galloway was a successful landscape contractor, specializing in paving and low-maintenance plants. Now, in her tiny shop and nursery she offers **rare and wonderful drought-tolerant, low-water-demanding plants** (and good advice) but also has an appealing offering of garden art—especially for the urban garden—including **locally crafted pieces, antique garden funk and junk, handsome stepping-stones, new and used tools, potting soil, compost, and fertilizers.** Piriformis carries lots of wonderful forged trellises made by local artisans. If you loved the giant painted bathing-beauties from the gold-medal-winning Piriformis display garden at the 2001 Northwest Flower and Garden Show, you can find them here, too. Tory even offers classes.

PLAIN HARDWARE HOME & GARDEN

18636 Beaver Valley Road, Plain, WA 98826 | **Phone:** (509) 763-3836 | **Fax:** (509) 763-2204 | **Open:** Daily

If any town can claim that its local hardware store is the "heartbeat" of the community, the residents of Plain, Washington, are certainly good candidates. We discovered this charming general store on a visit to Lake Wenatchee, about 15 miles east of Stevens Pass heading toward Leavenworth. There's everything you'd want to find in a hardware and lumber store "out back," but the inviting entrance is decorated with birdhouses, wooden benches, metal art, and other garden ornamentation. Inside, there's **a nice selection of garden-inspired gifts, bird and wildlife food and feeders,** Plain Hardware Home & Garden sweatshirts and Ts in great colors, hand tools, and practical gardening supplies. The buyers know their customers—locals and folks from the big city who love to come to the mountains summer and winter alike. They've been busy finding all sorts of **very cool, useful, and fun stuff to stock the shelves** (to please all ages). There are great garden events each season, such as the Plant a Pansy Day (bring in the kids for a free pansy, pot, and soil) in the spring. Locally grown vegetable starts also arrive in the spring, and you can get all the best organic amendments anytime. Add your name to the mailing list to receive *Plain Talk,* the twice-yearly newsletter that sorta seems like *the* local news source around here.

PRICE ASHER GARDEN & HOME

970 Denny Way, Seattle, WA 98109 | **Phone:** (206) 254-9226 | **Fax:** (206) 254-1199 | **Email:** sheilab@priceasher.com | **Open:** Daily

The former Price-Ragen has been reincarnated into two shops as the former partners in design parted ways for independent endeavors (see Ragen & Associates, below, for the more of the story). Elizabeth Price Asher moved into a warehouse space near Denny and Westlake in 2001, gathering together an **extensive lineup of select furnishings, plants, and accessories for the urban home** or commercial environment. When you arrive here, take note of the entrance, adorned with a series of outdoor "plant vignettes." Indoors, there are tropical and temperate plants in bloom year-round, including bromeliads, orchids, ferns, indoor/outdoor trees, ivies, and perennials. Well known for her expertise in landscape and interiors (as well as special event design), Elizabeth has had her work featured in *Seattle Homes & Lifestyles* and *Sunset* magazine. Noted for her **"matchless" holiday-event design and accessories,** Price Asher is booked well in advance for decorating homes and parties. The shop also offers interior and exterior plant maintenance, orchid and blooming programs, fresh flowers, seminars, and exterior landscape design. When you visit, you'll be charmed and seduced by the **exotic and elegant containers and baskets,** textiles, personal care products, scents and candles . . . and an endless variety of beautiful finds to delight and inspire. **Garden accessories** include gazebos, arbors, furniture, art, and even the basics for plant care. Call for details on occasional seminars and the famous holiday event schedule.

PRICE ASHER "ISLAND LIVING"

635 Spring Street, Friday Harbor, WA 98250 | **Phone:** (360) 370-5880 | **Fax:** (360) 370-5884 | **Email:** sheilab@priceasher.com | **Web:** www.priceasher.com | **Open:** Daily

This is a smaller and more intimate San Juan Island version of the Seattle store, offering a **global collection of furniture and accessories for the garden and home.** You'll find exceptional quality plants, silks and floral arrangements, containers imported from around the world, and full-service interior and exterior design programs.

RAGEN & ASSOCIATES

517 East Pike Street, Seattle, WA 98122 | **Phone:** (206) 329-4737 | **Fax:** (206) 329-9926 | **Email:** Annette@ragenassociates.com | **Open:** Tuesday–Saturday or by appointment

For more than 15 years, Chip Ragen has not only designed wonderful Seattle-area gardens, he's supplied gardeners and homeowners with a **great selection of high-quality planters and pots.** Now that he's gone solo, Chip is continuing the business with Italian terra-cotta pottery, as well as pottery and glazed containers from Vietnam and China—bold, outsized pieces that make a dramatic statement in the garden or on your patio. Outdoor garden accessories are naturally a priority here, including a wonderful selection of frost-hardy cast pots from Italy. Design services are offered; when you visit, you're likely to see some of Chip's best ideas on display in seasonal containers.

RATTAN INTERIORS

1191 Andover Parkway, Seattle, WA 98188 | **Phone:** (206) 575-2201 | **Fax:** (206) 575-0604 | **Second location:** 1024 116th Ave NE, Bellevue, WA 98004 | **Phone:** (425) 455-1500 | **Open:** Daily

Here's where to find **an extensive selection of wicker furniture and rattan** for interior use, plus the Brown Jordan and Lloyd Flanders all-weather wicker product line and other outdoor furniture (in teak, wrought iron, wrought aluminum, cast aluminum, and tubular aluminum), along with sturdy market umbrellas, all of which stand up to the demanding conditions in the Pacific Northwest.

RAVENNA GARDENS

2201 Queen Anne Avenue N, Seattle, WA 98119 | **Phone:** (206) 283-7091 | **Second location:** 2580 NE University Village, Seattle, WA 98105 | (206) 729-7388 | **Web:** www.ravennagardens.com | **Open:** Daily

Gardeners love the masterful wand that conjured up these elegant shops and their wares. There are two elements at work here that make this a destination that builds a loyal following. The first is **ambiance—relaxed, with pleasant background music and a rustic/sophisticated decor** that suggests ideas to try in one's own garden. The other is the careful balance of merchandise—from the practical (a wonderful selection of seeds and bulbs, basic but quality tools, and potting soil) to the ethereal (garden-related bath and body products, beautiful cards, and paper goods). A distinguished selection of annuals, perennials, trees, shrubs, and vines is available from early spring to mid-fall. Not only is it evident we are in the company of dedicated gardeners, but ones who have made their reputation on seeking out the **unique, the well-crafted, the whimsical, and the truly useful for our own garden plots and homey nests.** You'll especially love the frequently-changing displays that inspire one's own home decorating.

RHODODENDRON SPECIES BOTANICAL GARDEN GIFT SHOP

2525 S 336th Street, Federal Way, WA 98003 | **Phone:** (253) 661-9377 | **Fax:** (253) 838-4686 | **Email:** rsf@rhodygarden.org | **Web:** www.rhodygarden.org | **Open:** Seasonal; call for hours or check the website.

This shop is really packed with great finds. Look for an extensive selection of **horticultural books, garden and Bonsai tools and supplies, apparel, unique botanically themed gifts,** and a plant pavilion that offers unusual and hard-to-find plants, including species rhododendrons, ferns, natives, alpines, and perennials.

RIVERROCK GARDEN & DECK

Country Village | 720 238th Street, Suite D, Bothell, WA 98021 | **Phone:** (425) 402-7163 | **Fax:** Same | **Email:** riverrock garden@yahoo.com | **Web:** www.riverrockgarden.com | **Open:** Daily

Since late 1997, Karen Will Johnson and Dennis Johnson (with canine assistants Shammy and Noche) have brought enthusiasm and expertise to their business. Spend a few minutes conversing with them and you know they just love what they are doing. In a setting of river-rock planters and twig shelves, you'll find a varied

assortment of **handsome accessories for your garden—** inner sanctums as well as outdoor living spaces—including birdhouses and feeders, stylish weather vanes, sundials, bell-tower wind chimes, English garden tools, copper and iron arbors, trellises and gates, custom address plaques in rock, slate, wood, or cast metal, unique indoor fountains, and **all the components to help you assemble your own one-of-a-kind water feature.** For outdoor fountains they carry Brass Baron fountains and statuary (in brass, of course!) and feather-light, granite-appearing fiberglass ponds. **Practical necessities,** such as good garden gloves, small hand tools, and a nice selection of garden books for the dreamer and pragmatist are tucked into this lovely shop, snug behind a splashing fountain and a compact herb garden in the popular Country Village, a complex of 45 specialty antique and interiors shops and restaurants north of downtown Bothell. If you're charmed by the store but still at a loss for what to give your favorite gardener, may we recommend one of Karen's custom garden gift baskets (variety of sizes and prices) or a RiverRock Garden & Deck gift certificate on lovely botanical stationery?

ROOZENGAARDE, A DIVISION OF WASHINGTON BULB CO., INC.

15867 Beaver Marsh Road, Mt. Vernon, WA 98273 | **Phone:** (800) 732-3266 (store) or (800) 488-5477 (toll-free orders) | **Fax:** (360) 424-3113 | **Email:** info@tulips.com | **Web:** www.tulips.com | **Open:** Daily (closed Sunday, except for special events).

Noted for its splendid display garden at the height of the annual Skagit Valley Tulip Festival in April, and then on throughout the year, Roozengaarde has an inviting shop, too. This is a place to take a moment to browse for **gifts of a botanical nature, and for home décor.** You can order fresh flowers shipped by mail, year-round. Request the catalog, which features 200-plus varieties of spring flowering bulbs.

SECRET GARDEN STATUARY

11061 Pacific Highway S, Seattle, WA 98169 | **Phone:** (206) 764-7150 | **Fax:** (206) 768-0544 | **Web:** www.seattlesecretgarden.com | **Open:** Daily

Open since 1995, Secret Garden Statuary is now located in a 35,000-square-foot display yard 1 mile south of the King County Airport at Boeing Field. Considered to have one of the region's largest and **most varied selections of garden ornamentation,** Secret Garden endeavors to carry everything from classic Italian to modern, with all styles in between. Fountains are the forte here. In an adjacent facility, the company manufactures custom-design fountains, countertops, and fireplaces as well as **architectural elements for the home and garden, including balustrades, paving stones, and garden furniture.**

SEATTLE TILTH STORE

4649 Sunnyside Avenue N, Seattle, WA 98103 | **Phone:** (206) 633-0451 | **Fax:** (206) 633-0450 | **Email:** tilth@seattletilth.org | **Web:**

www.seattletilth.org | **Open:** Weekdays, 10 a.m.–2 p.m.; Saturdays, 10 a.m.–3 p.m.

Merchandise sales at this store help support the Seattle Tilth programs, so you'll feel great shopping here. You can find **compost bins in various sizes,** plus a selection of worm bins, and even a composting video by Howard Stenn. If you have wondered where to get Red Wrigglers for your vermiculture composting bin, this is your place (see worm adoption hours in Chapter 9, "Products, Materials & Professional Services"). You can also meet with Master Composters, who are at the fabulous Tilth Compost Demonstration Site (check the website for hours) to sell worms and answer questions. Other organic gardening supplies on hand here include **gloves, slug and snail barriers, floating row coverings and clips, Felco pruning shears, and Walt's Organic Fertilizers (several products).** You'll also find a great book selection, including Tilth's *Maritime Northwest Garden Guide,* Mason Bee blocks, T-shirts, hemp shopping bags, and some posters.

SMITH & HAWKEN

12200 Northup Way, Bellevue, WA 98005-1914 | **Phone:** (425) 881-6775 | **Web:** www.smithandhawken.com | **Open:** Daily

The S&H brand is synonymous with bringing American gardeners **high-quality English gardening tools and handsome teak garden benches.** The national chain, catalog, and online store are well-known for stocking durable, attractive clothing selected with a gardener's rigorous needs as well as after-work relaxation or entertaining in mind. At the retail store, find essentially what you've come to expect in the catalogs, with the addition of a small selection of garden books, some seeds, a few plants, and soil and organic amendments for the urban gardener. The Bellevue store is inviting and welcoming, engulfed in a vine-covered arbor that surrounds great plant displays and a full line of garden furniture.

STICKS & STEMS FLORAL AND GIFT SHOP

189 Hummel Lake Road, Lopez Island, WA 98261 | **Phone:** (360) 468-4377 | **Fax:** (360) 468-4378 | **Mailing address:** PO Box 694, Lopez Island, WA 98261 | **Email:** sticksandstems@rockisland.com | **Open:** Monday–Saturday (Wednesday–Saturday during winter months).

A quick walk from the marina and a 4-mile trip from the ferry landing, Twanette Porter's elegant shop serves Lopez residents with unique gifts, fresh flowers, U-cut flowers (perennials), full-service floral design, including weddings, and a nursery of garden perennials. She also carries **whimsical yard and garden art, metal ornaments and stakes, hand tools, gloves, amendments, and basic garden supplies, not to mention gardener's soaps and lotions.**

THE SUMMER BEAM CO.

PO 25043, Seattle, WA 98125 | **Phone:** (206) 381-3726 | **Email:** thesummerbeam@mindspring.com | **Web:** www.thesummerbeam.com | **Open:** By appointment

A "summer beam" is a horizontal beam supporting the ends of floor joists or one that rests on posts and supports the wall above. The surprisingly relevant term is the name of a **great source for architectural elements that you can invite into your own home and garden,** giving these eclectic (and often once utilitarian) pieces a new life. Kji Kelly has assembled a "virtual" store filled with architectural antiques, recycled building materials, and more. Much of his inventory is consigned through a variety of salvage and antique stores in Seattle. You can see a great selection on his website—from **doors, fences, and gates to porch parts and terra cotta**—just contact him if you have any questions.

THROUGH THE GARDEN GATE

15774 McLean Road, Mount Vernon, WA 98273 | **Phone:** (360) 424-0195 | **Open:** Thursday–Sunday (April–October) or by appointment

Interior designer Pat Love and her daughter Molly Williams have run this shop, situated in a former milk-can storage outbuilding on 4 acres of Pat's farm, since 1997. Set in the heart of Skagit Valley, this **attractive little shop features an eclectic mingling of decorative and functional accessories for home and garden with an emphasis on arbors and trellises, topiaries, and pots.** The women seek out local artists and craftspeople whose work is showcased in the outdoor gallery that surrounds the rustic shop. There is an imaginative display garden out back, and inside you can order coffee, tea, or baked treats to comfort you as you make the difficult decisions among so many wonderful garden goods beckoning you to make them yours. One of the best times to visit is during the April Tulip Festival, when Through the Garden Gate is open seven days a week, or in June, when the antique roses are especially lovely. When the shop is open, the garden is too, and you're welcome to "bring your own picnic."

U.S. CLUBHOUSE GARDEN COLLECTION

3810 Airport Way S, Seattle, WA 98108 | **Phone:** (206) 287-1500 | **Fax:** (206) 287-1520 | **Open:** Daily, except Sunday

Yes, it looks like a random bunch of huge pots filling the parking lot of a giant warehouse south of downtown Seattle, but once you slow down, park, and wander inside the gate, you'll be wowed by the **great selection of large-scale containers for indoors and out.** Peter Norris, who owns a commercial landscaping firm called Camden Designs, decided to sell a container of irregular pots "to the public" in 2000. The inventory blew out the door proving that there was much enthusiasm for the rusted iron urns (some as dramatically large as 6-feet high), faux stone containers (deceptively convincing even though they're made in fiberglass), and glazed pots from several Asian countries. Look for the "seconds" corner for even better bargains.

WINSLOW HARDWARE & MERCANTILE

240 Winslow Way E, Bainbridge Island, WA 98110 | **Phone:** (206) 842-3101 | **Email:** whaminc@msn.com

About six years ago, Mary Hall and Ken Nelson bought the local hardware store in downtown Winslow on Bainbridge Island, setting out to transform it into a **country mercantile and emporium** that meets the needs of the modern home and garden owner. Today, "WHAM," as it's fondly called, provides important home improvement goods and services, including those very useful things like fishing licenses, lamp and screen repair, blade and knife sharpening, pipe cutting and threading, and recharging of fire extinguishers (it's a full-fledged member of the True Value Hardware family).

But the "M" stands for Mercantile, and this is where garden and home emporium-lovers will find a delightful and intelligent selection of goods: linen guest towels, bath accessories and milled soaps, Rowe Pottery, farm baskets, great pots, comfy chairs, and more. The store carries Shepherd's Garden Seeds, Renee's Garden, Lilly Miller, and **sweet pea seeds from two English sources:** Robert Bolton & Sons and S&N Brackley. Speaking of sweet peas, these fragrant flowering vines are a favorite of Mary's, so much so that she's launched an annual Sweet Pea Festival in July (prizes awarded for the best customer bouquet, with all bouquets donated to shut-ins at the end of the day). Likewise, there's a nifty "Painted Furniture" contest in the fall! Pick up some new skills when you take a class here (like faux-finish painting techniques or other how-tos). The sidewalk is decorated with lively and whimsical containers each spring and summer, so this is a welcoming gardeners' destination. P.S.: Get on the mailing list for a great, info-packed newsletter.

GARDEN ART AND ARTISTS

For many of us, gardening is a means of expression, an art form in and of itself. For most of us, plants are the major, if not the sole means of expression. Yet for others, the integration and play of plants with non-plant elements is vital to their creativity. Listed here are businesses, artists, and crafts(wo)men who do not necessarily maintain shops to market their work but nonetheless rely on reaching customers who are, in fact, searching for unique embellishments or structures for their distinctively personal gardens. We hope this section will help you find each other. Please call first to make an appointment. These are not retail outlets, but artists' studios and private homes/gardens.

Note: One of the best ways to find artisans is to visit area plant sales and major garden shows, which are increasingly providing space for garden art that complements our region's horticultural riches.

In **Oregon,** the Hardy Plant Society has successfully added a Garden Art Fair to its already popular Fall Plant Sale. Many of the artists are members of OHPS and avid gardeners themselves. For details on future Garden Art Fairs, call (503) 224-5718 or visit www.hardyplantsociety.org. Look for garden art-makers from **Western Washington** and beyond at Sorticulture Garden Art Show, sponsored each June by the City of Everett Parks & Recreation Department. This is a fun event that attracts great artists who know the patrons appreciate their whimsy, artistry, and unique offerings. For details on future Sorticulture events, call (425) 257-8300 or email wbecker@ci.everett.wa.us.

Make sure to attend Bassetti's Crooked Arbor Gardens' annual **Plant Sale & Garden Sculpture Show,** usually the weekend before July 4th at this Woodinville nursery. In addition to discovering that this is a good place to meet specialty growers, you'll be wowed by the dozens of large-scale garden art by talents such as Judy Thomas (who crafted a giant pair of pears for a recent show). For details on future shows, contact the Bassetti nursery at (425) 788-6767 or check www.bassettisgardens.com.

Another source for one-of-a-kind ornamentation is the Annual Garden Art Sale, sponsored by **Pratt Fine Arts Center** in Seattle, usually held in August. There is a swanky opening-night party and auction, followed by a free weekend show featuring hundreds of hand-crafted works made for, or inspired by, the garden. Call Pratt to request an invitation: (206) 328-2200, email events@pratt.org, or check the website at www.pratt.org.

A related show, **"Concrete Art from Pratt,"** follows the garden art sale, usually in September and October at Seattle's **City People's Garden Store.** Curated by the talented sculptor Lynn DiNino, this popular event showcases concrete sculpture, water bowls, seating, and ornamentation created by local talent. City People's displays the pieces in and among its nursery stock—to the delight of plant-lovers and art patrons alike. This is not your ordinary concrete! A recent show featured giant Dorothy-inspired ruby slippers by Robyn Crutch and Greg Skei, as well as an elegant garden "love seat" and matching architectural pylons created by Buffalo McGillvray. Contact Pratt at (206) 328-2200 or City People's at (206) 324-0737 to inquire about future show dates.

FRANCIE ALLEN & CO.

8243 Wallingford Avenue N, Seattle, WA 98103 | **Phone:** (206) 522-8582

Francie is a fine artist and sculptor who lived for 15 years on Vashon Island, and much of her animal imagery comes from living with the creatures of the forest, meadows, and neighboring frog ponds. She has moved her studio and gallery to Seattle, where she creates garden sculptures. Her pieces feature the decorative use of animal and figurative imagery: rain bowls, fountains, pedestals, and "protective guardians" in cast stone are designed for outdoor

use (as it weathers well and strengthens over time). Frogs and salamanders factor into many designs as do Francie's amazing faces (nymphs, Buddhas, and the Green Man), which seem to float in water or among plants in her shallow sculpted dishes.

ART IN STONE

(425) 640-5888 | **Email:** khinch@foxinternet.net | **Web:** www.artinstone.com

Ken Hinch is an Everett-based artist who has been sculpting garden statuary for more than a decade. The Green Man, gargoyles, planters, foliage bowls, and other garden icons influence his cast-stone pieces, many of which are tinted in rich, organic shades. You can find Ken selling his pieces at The Best of the Northwest art show, Sorticulture, the Northwest Flower & Garden Show, and other area crafts events. View much of his collection online or call/email him for a free brochure.

GARDEN ARCHES

PO Box 4057, Bellingham, WA 98227 | **Phone:** (800) 947-7697 or (360) 398-1587 | **Fax:** (360) 398-9856 | **Email:** info@garden arches.com | **Web:** www.gardenarches.com | **Catalog:** $2

Rick Anderson is gaining a reputation across the United States for his well-crafted wood (and now also copper) **garden structures,** and has expanded into custom design work. He started with (and continues to offer) do-it-yourself plans, complete with a full materials list and step-by-step instructions. He also offers well-designed and built pieces that can be shipped for assembly at your home (be it a condominium/apartment balcony, five-acre estate, or something in between.) The traditional Rose Garden Arch is his most popular piece. The catalog features a modular trellis system (you mix and match to meet your needs/inspiration); a line of gates and headers (for those with the fence but in need of an elegant entry point); pyramids and obelisks (to gussy up your kitchen garden); lots of planters (which come with heavy duty plastic liners), casters optional. Garden Arches now also offers copper **arbors, trellises, and gazebos** as well as a line of hand-forged iron arbors and trellises.

IMAGE CUSTOM IRON WORK

6631 Ellis Avenue S, Seattle, WA 98108 | **Phone:** (206) 767-2629 | **Open:** Weekends, or by appointment

Georgetown artist Rickey Cabine makes **trellises, arbors, pyramids, and smaller ornamental iron and rebar garden pieces.** You can stop by his studio (near Julius Rosso Nursery in South Seattle) during weekends or call for an appointment.

LANI AND COMPANY

11844 22nd Avenue SW, Seattle, WA 98146 | **Phone:** (206) 439-8132 | **Email:** laniandcompany@home.com | **Open:** By appointment only

Lani is a talented nurserywoman who can't stop creating. It's in her blood. It's a must. She has combined a love of horticulture and a talent for crafting stained glass (with a lot of artistry) to **pressed botanical and floral designs.** Some are framed traditionally; others are incorporated into leaded and stained glass panels; hydrangea, larkspur, salvia, sweet peas, scabiosa, a basketful of leaf forms, hellebores, and countless other plants appear in her colorful work. Some local nurseries (including her alma mater, West Seattle Nursery) carry Lani's very affordable framed designs. You can make an appointment to shop at Lani's home studio or inquire about commissions and her small group, pressed-flower classes.

OLYMPIC TOPIARY LIVING SCULPTURES

370 Guiles Road, Sequim, WA 98382 | **Phone:** (360) 683-8702 | **Fax:** Same | **Email:** oliver@olympictopiary.com | **Web:** www.olympictopiary.com | **Open:** By appointment only

Oliver and Penny Strong handcraft the **most extraordinary topiaries.** We're not sure if the delightful description of "living sculptures" in the name refers to the tiny ivy that nattily clothes the topiary or to the life-like poses captured in a dog running or deer leaping, but there's no argument that the Strongs' work inspires good old-fashioned marvel. The frames are strongly welded and forms are cleverly plumbed from within for more effective watering. They also fashion the human form and work effectively in **large scale on custom pieces, and in boxwood.** Special effects are created with the use of ornamental grasses, yellow-eyes grass, woolly thyme, and blue star creeper. The Strongs offer monthly workshops in topiary at their working greenhouse and will travel to groups/garden clubs. You are welcome to visit their working greenhouse by appointment.

RED STEP STUDIO

PO Box 63, Bremerton, WA 98337 | **Phone:** (206) 226-2642 | **Email:** paulagill@redstep.com

Terra cotta artist Paula Gill crafts precise squares and rectangles of tile, embellishing them with delightful icons from the garden, home, and nature. Paula carves her graphic birds, watering cans, wheelbarrows, trowels, fruit, and houses, wood-cut style, into the clay; then she glazes and fires the slabs. These are substantial pieces that you'll want to add to the front porch or across a fireplace mantle (or give as gifts). You can often find Paula at major garden events, such as the flower shows, Bainbridge in Bloom, and Everett's Sorticulture. She has expanded her repertoire by adding clay birdbath "bowls," patterned with the imprints of everything from star shapes to buttons. These baths rest on custom-made iron bases, which allows them to sit nicely in the landscape.

ROSEBAR

20640 Skagit City Road, Mt. Vernon, WA 98273 | **Phone:** (360) 445-2294 | **Fax:** (360) 445-4414 | **Email:** contact@rosebar.net | **Web:** www.rosebar.net

Artist and welder extraordinaire Mary Taylor has set high standards in the area of **hand-crafted metal garden art, both structural and ornamental.** Her widely available work includes arbors, arches, armillories, gates, towers, trellises, and freestanding whimsical figures. Her skill and attention to detail are superb, not to mention her rich sense of humor. One of her characteristic embellishments is a small wire nest with a little bird or two curiously poking their heads up. It's an exciting experience to visit her studio on Fir Island to see her in action, suited up in welding garb, sparks gracefully flying from her busy hands. In 1998 Mary installed a lovely garden adjacent to her workspace, professionally designed and with a great assortment of unusual plants. Throughout the garden she displays a wide variety of her work so you can see it in context. Add Rosebar to your travel plans next time you are cruising the Skagit Valley on a botanical expedition.

Snohomish Arts

1614 4th Street, Snohomish, WA 98290 | **Phone:** (360) 568-7258 | **Email:** snohomisharts@cs.com | **Web:** www.snohomisharts.com

C. K. Dunlap is a painter and ceramic artist with a lot of talent and vigorous sense of humor. Her booth at the Flower and Garden Show in Seattle always gathers passers-by in need of a spontaneous smile, who linger to admire the craftsmanship and detail in **fountains, wall plaques, tiles, a garden bench, and, for the birds, colorful houses and bird baths.**

Steel Shadows Inc.

4266 King Mountain Road, Bellingham, WA 98226 | **Phone:** (888) 253-5379 or (360) 671-5146 | **Fax:** (360) 647-7689 | **Email:** info@steelshadow.com | **Web:** www.steelshadow.com

Frank and Deborah Malone's family-owned business reflects this wisdom: "Everyone dances in the garden." Steel Shadows' dancing characters are rumored to keep away slugs and weeds . . . at the very least, they will make you smile. Artist Deborah and steel-wizard Frank (he cuts each piece using an oxygen acetylene torch) turn **common steel into dancing and whimsical hearts, carrots, dog bones, stars, and chili peppers** . . . adorned with fused glass accents. We also enjoy the full-sized sunflowers with fused glass faces. The 10-gauge steel pieces are mounted on stakes, which makes it easy to tuck them into a dull corner of the garden and liven things up. You can check the website for show dates and custom ordering information.

Sue Skelly Wattle Works

24329 NE Snow Hill Lane, Poulsbo, WA 98370 | **Phone:** (360) 598-5447 | **Open:** By appointment

Sue Skelly is a wattle worker, weaving Northwest native Western red cedar into **fences, arbors, gates, trellises, foundation skirting, railings, chain-link camouflage, spandrels, and screens.** These pieces are made to last in the rainy Pacific Northwest, that's why Sue works 100 percent with the red cedar. The majority of her work is custom made. Be imaginative—what about a headboard or hurdle to hide the compost heap?

The Topiary Store (formerly In and Out of the Garden)

16307 115th Avenue SW, Vashon Island, WA 98070 | **Phone:** (866) 567-5047 or (206) 567-5047 | **Email:** topiarysales@cs.com | **Web:** www.topiarystore.com

Visitors to the display gardens at the Northwest Flower and Garden Shows flock around the beautifully crafted topiary created by Cindy Morrison. If you have stood transfixed by her work, have you been left with the lingering feeling that what your garden needs is a bit of whimsy? Bunnies, dogs, people (Mr. Macgregor), elephants, and many charming flora and fauna will grow on you! All of The Topiary Store's products are **planted, living sculptures . . . not just moss-covered forms.** Make an appointment to visit Cindy's working studio and greenhouse to see her many creatures or come to purchase topiary supplies. Cindy offers **frames,** mossed and planted **topiary,** herbal topiary, **custom design services** for commercial and residential clients, **workshops and classes,** and hundreds of styles. Her website is a great source for everything topiary, from forms and tools to essential plants. Wholesale and retail.

Wilburton Pottery

PO Box 40161, Bellevue, WA 98015 | **Phone:** (425) 455-9203 | **Web:** www.wilburtonpottery.com | **Open:** By appointment (sales twice a year)

Bob and Iris Jewett have achieved their vision to make distinctive winter-hardy pots, recalling the past in patina and design, but with "the spirit of modern day life." Using **Italian Renaissance methods in creating each tile and container,** the Jewetts and daughters Laura and Leonora hand-build and glaze their distinctive collection, now boasting over 300 designs to choose from. See their work photographed on page 155 *Further Along the Garden Path* (Ann Lovejoy) and find their work in garden shops throughout the region and at shows. If you come to the studio, you'll be able to view more than 150 of their pots, filled with common and rare plants.

Woodlands Garden Pottery

2122 N. 117th Street, Seattle, WA 98133 | **Phone:** (206) 362-5424 | **Open:** By appointment only

Lynda Ann Nielson sculpted pottery proves that one does not need applied color to create an eye-catching piece of art. Using floral themes, Lynn starts with hand-rolled slabs of stoneware to create containers, wall pockets, garden boxes, and botanical plaques—applying her hand-shaped flowers and critters to the surfaces. The result: a three-dimensional, but monochromatic bas-relief that uses shadows and light to its advantage. Lynn Ann works with Vashon orange stoneware (a warm, buttery orange with fabulous texture) or Klamath red stoneware (a deep plum-brown with casts of shimmery black). Choose from a garden of flowers—dogwood, hollyhock, morning glories, trillium, and more! We loved seeing

Lynn Ann's work in one local garden, where the real perennial grew against the wall on which hung its stoneware mirror-image.

CONSERVATORIES, GREENHOUSES, SHEDS, SUNROOMS, AND ACCESSORIES

Here are a few resources well known in the greenhouse world. Attend the **Northwest Flower and Garden Show,** the **Home and Garden Shows** and **Fairs** to view greenhouses and pick up literature to study.

HOBBY GREENHOUSE ASSOC.

8 Glen Terrace, Bedford, MA 01730-2048 | **Phone:** (781) 275-0377 | **Email:** jhale@world.std.com | **Web:** www.hobbygreenhouse.org

This national nonprofit organization publishes a **directory of greenhouse manufacturers,** with a good discussion of the features to look for and factors to consider in choosing a greenhouse. HGA lists nearly 50 manufacturers, and includes the address/phone numbers (many have toll-free numbers), catalog costs, the product lines sold, a general description of the construction details, and in many cases, price ranges. This compendium is updated frequently and costs $2.50. You can also join HGA ($19 for one-year membership; $36 for two years). Members receive a discount on greenhouse products as well as a subscription to *Hobby Greenhouse Magazine,* a quarterly publication on greenhouse gardening. Non-members can order a sample copy for $3.50.

ADVANCED GREENHOUSE MANUFACTURING LTD.

140-6165 Hwy 17, Delta, BC V4K 5B8 Canada | **Phone:** (800) 656-7477 or (604) 940-1820 | **Fax:** (604) 940-1830 | **Web:** www.greenhouse.bc.ca

Advanced Greenhouse designed and built the first "Therma-Gro®" greenhouse, adapting some of the same principles used by commercial growers to the home greenhouse market. Using 8mm double-walled material, the system helps save up to 66 percent on heating costs and registers a 30 percent increase in crop yield (when compared to glass greenhouses). These systems also have full-length roof venting, fully automatic vent openers, and imported solar-control systems. Check the website for dealers in the United States and Canada.

ARCHITECTURAL GLASS

4260 23rd West, Seattle, WA 98199 | **Phone:** (206) 284-6947 | **Fax:** (206) 284-0774

Architectural Glass is the manufacturer of the "Renaissance" Greenhouses and Conservatories. Built according to traditional European design, these structures incorporate durable aluminum framework, insulated glass and operable roof, and side vents, with a choice of custom colors.

B.C. GREENHOUSE BUILDERS LTD.

A5-19327 94th Avenue, Surrey, BC V4N 4E6 Canada | **Phone:** (604) 882-8408 | **Fax:** (604) 882-8491 | **Email:** inquiries@bcgreenhouses.com | **Web:** www.bcgreenhousebuilders.com

This 50-year-old full-service firm specializes in greenhouse, solarium, and conservatory design and installation. You can order the catalog or go online to learn more about the wide array of choices, including glass, polycarbonate, and combination greenhouses, custom designs, and even commercial-scale systems.

CASCADE GREENHOUSE SUPPLY

214 21st Avenue SE, Auburn, WA 98002 | **Phone:** (800) 353-0264 or (206) 282-1356 | **Web:** www.cascadegreenhouse.com | **Catalog:** Free

This company offers the full range of greenhouse equipment and supplies, including greenhouses from Eden and the highly respected English manufacturer, Halls, in kit form ready for assembly (shipping available). The shop displays everything listed in the catalog, has demonstration greenhouses, a special section of orchids and specialized products for orchid growers, ornamental pots, gifts for gardeners, greenhouse-related books, and much more.

CHARLEY'S GREENHOUSE SUPPLIES

17979 Memorial Hwy (SR 536), Mt. Vernon, WA 98273 | (800) 322-4707 or (360) 428-2626 | **Fax:** (800) 233-3078 | **Email:** cgh@charleysgreenhouse.com | **Web:** www.charleysgreenhouse.com | **Catalog:** $3 | **Orders:** Order online or visit the appealing shop

All across the country, this company is a (green)household word for the complete line of supplies and array of greenhouses they offer. If you are considering a greenhouse (or even a mini-propagator the size of your kitchen sink), then a trip to Charley's will make you feel like a kid in the proverbial candy store! Here there are 14 standing models of greenhouses (with over 75 custom greenhouses available) and most of the paraphernalia to get you started and keep you going, including an excellent selection of books for all levels. Get the 80-page color catalog, packed with everything in the store and more.

DAYBREAK GARDENS

25321 NE 72nd Ave, Battle Ground, WA 98604 | **Phone:** (360) 687-5641 | **Open:** Hours vary; call in advance

Dave and Donna Burnett carry Sky Bright molded fiberglass greenhouses, available in a variety of sizes with various options, delivered assembled. They have operating watering systems and working models of Sky Bright greenhouses for your inspection. Classes for bonsai, general pruning, and greenhouse growing are offered in season.

GARDEN SOLUTIONS

14435 Woodinville-Redmond Rd., Woodinville, WA 98072 | **Phone:** (800) 839-1584 | **Email:** info@gardensolution.com | **Web:** www.gardensolution.com | **Open:** Daily

Michael Gruskin builds greenhouses, but we also love his creative garden sheds, unique garden buildings, arbors, gazebos, weathervanes, and cupolas. In fact, Garden Solutions does just what its name says: creates any outdoor garden structure you can think of. In business since 1986, this is the largest independent seller of garden buildings in Washington. Garden Solutions is not to be missed, as it operates from a charming cluster of display sheds just a stone's throw from Woodinville's wine country (you can see Chateau Ste. Michelle and Columbia Winery out across the back field); and anyone whizzing along Woodinville–Redmond Road slows down a bit to eye those colorful, architectural, and whimsical structures in the outdoor showroom. You can customize a variety of building styles or bring in your own sketch or photos, and Garden Solutions will build your "dream" structure. Good ideas fill the website, so take a look.

MOORE/LAWRENCE GREENHOUSE MFG. INC.

PO Box 1924, Clackamas, OR 97015 | **Phone:** (503) 761-6026

Standard features on Moore/Lawrence products include double-strength glass and clear acrylic glazing, clear Western red cedar framing, aluminum doors, easy-opening roof hatches, and cedar siding. From a 2-by-5-foot cold frame and attachable sunrooms to freestanding greenhouses, this manufacturer will design, construct, and install your system. Free delivery and setup within 50 miles of metropolitan Portland. Accessories for greenhouse gardeners also available.

RAIN OR SHINE

13126 NE Airport Way, Portland, OR 97230 | **Phone:** (800) 248-1981, (503) 255-1981 | **Fax:** (503) 255-9201 | **Email:** rainorshine@malloryco.com. | **Web:** www.rain-or-shine.com

Specializing in hobby greenhouses and products for serious gardeners, this shop offers quality tools, a huge seed selection, pond and pump supplies, drip and other irrigation supplies, and fertilizers/pest control supplies, featuring systems from Sunshine GardenHouse, Rainbow Mini Greenhouses, and Hall's Greenhouses. You'll also find arches and gazebos, propagation supplies, and even Radio-Flyer wagons for garden chores.

SEATTLE SUN SYSTEMS, INC.

1701 1st Avenue S, Seattle, WA 98134 | **Phone:** (206) 343-2822 | **Fax:** (206) 343-7559 | **Email:** seasun@seanet.com | **Web:** www.seattlesun.com

Seattle Sun's very large showroom is filled with solariums, sunrooms, and conservatories. The firm's systems offer fine wood interiors and aluminum clad exteriors. You can also order do-it-yourself kits, kits delivered and assembled on site by Seattle Sun's crew, as well as a full-service design-build program.

STEUBER DISTRIBUTING COMPANY

3rd and Pine Streets, Snohomish, WA 98290 | **Phone:** (800) 426-8815 or (360) 568-2626; Seattle: (206) 632-8724 | **Fax:** (360) 568-8960 | **Open:** Monday–Friday, 8 a.m.–5 p.m.; Saturday 8 a.m.–noon (March–July 4, Saturday to 2 p.m.)

This wholesale greenhouse and greenhouse grower's supply store sells retail to the public. If you're in Snohomish to visit the antique shops, make a stop here and poke around Steuber's facility (what it lacks in stylish details it makes up for in stock on offer). This is a working profes-

sional's store where you can expect to find an enormous array of growing supplies (indoor and outdoor).

STURDI-BUILT GREENHOUSE MFG. CO.

11304 SW Boones Ferry Road, Portland, OR 97219 | **Phone:** (800) 722-4115 or (503) 244-4100 | **Email:** catalog@sturdi-built.com | **Web:** www.sturdi-built.com. | **Catalog:** 16-page catalog free

Quality redwood greenhouses in a variety of sizes and shapes, greenhouse accessories (separate catalog, free). This is a family business building greenhouses on a customer-by-customer basis for forty years. The website has great photos of all Sturdi-built's designs.

SUNSHINE GARDENHOUSE

PO Box 2068, Longview, WA 98632 | **Phone:** (888) 272-9333, (360) 636-5750 | **Fax:** (360) 577-4244 | **Email:** greenthumb@gardenhouse.com | **Web:** www.gardenhouse.com

These well-designed greenhouses come in a sizes from 6x8 to 8x12, with a 4x8 lean-to style (and cold frame). They are constructed with an attractive redwood frame, have double-wall polycarbonate glazing, an automatic venting system, are durable, easy to assemble and economical.

THE YARD WORKS

15919 Highway 99, Lynnwood, WA 98037 | **Phone:** (800) 369-8333, (425) 787-6603 | **Fax:** (425) 741-0603 | **Email:** info@theyardworks.net | **Web:** www.yardworks-greenhouses.com

Ron and Carol Calendar offer many options for a greenhouse or cold frame (pre-assembled, as a kit or the materials for a do-it-yourself project). Come to see demonstration models from a wide variety of manufacturers, including the Sunshine GardenHouse (see above). This is also home of the highly respected Halls of England and Therma-Gro® Greenhouses in a wide range of sizes. Benchworks potting bench and worktable systems, accessories, supplies, and books are sold here, too.

chapter

9

PRODUCTS, MATERIALS & PROFESSIONAL SERVICES

Even avid gardeners will at some time rely on professionals to help design, renovate, maintain, or procure specialized materials for their landscapes. Maybe certain family members have declared mutiny, leaving you at the mercy of a professional landscaper—or perhaps you're just not the kind of do-it-yourselfer who *relishes* hauling two-man rocks up 30 steps! You may even feel a sense of relief knowing that someone gifted in the art and science of gardening will lend a fresh perspective to the project.

If you are not familiar with what points to consider when hiring expert help, perhaps this advice will answer some of your questions.

Treat the "search" process of recruiting someone to work in your garden with the same care as you would in hiring a remodeler to work on your house. Some of the best sources you'll find are personal references from friends, neighbors, and colleagues, as you'll hear the accolades and warnings alike. Beyond that, you can turn to the telephone directory, which offers listings under such headings as "Gardeners," "Landscape Architects," "Landscape Contractors," and "Landscape Designers."

Most garden and landscape professionals are happy to provide free estimates, so be sure to discuss the work with more than one company. You can make the bidding for the job easier if you provide the prospective vendor with something in writing that outlines the scope of your project. This not only helps them in fairly appraising the work involved, but it also gives you the chance to organize your thoughts and articulate some more difficult concepts, such as your philosophy of gardening (for example, your feelings about the use of pesticides or the degree of pruning you feel is healthy for trees), or your dreams and aspirations (as in the degree of formality / informality you envision in your landscape or the degree of perfection you expect from your lawn).

Hiring a landscape professional is often like hiring a relative. Depending on the complexity of your project, this is a person or crew who will be in and out of your private world over a period of time. Make sure there is a good camaraderie and mutual agreement on the goals of your project. Then take advantage of hiring that stonemason, arbor builder, or garden designer and learn as much as you can from them!

WHO'S WHO

ARBORISTS

Anyone can claim to be an arborist or tree surgeon. The key to finding someone who has proven qualifications to prune large or challenging trees is to hire someone *certified* by the **International Society of Arboriculture** (ISA), a professional and educational organization with several good regional members in Western Oregon and Washington and British Columbia. An ISA-certified arborist has passed a rigorous exam to demonstrate an understanding of tree biology and current tree-care practices.

Contact the Pacific Northwest Chapter of the ISA (PO Box 811, Silverton, OR 97381; phone: (503) 874-8263 or (800) 335-4391; fax: (503) 874-1509; email: info@pnwisa.org; web: www.pnwisa.org). This site has an excellent discussion on **"How to Hire an Arborist"** and one called **"Tree Care Information"** discussing tree myths, the truth about topping, how to save trees, along with a guide to pruning techniques. They can provide you with a list of all the certified arborists in Washington, Oregon, and British Columbia, and with additional literature on preserving and protecting trees. Also, see the Friends of Trees (Portland) website: www.friendsoftrees.org for their piece on "Why Hire an Arborist."

We've known a number of *very* unhappy homeowners who have hired a company to prune or thin trees while they were at work, only to return home to find irreplaceable trees, shrubs, and hedges butchered or destroyed. It is best to be very clear in your communication if such work is to be accomplished unsupervised. In general, your interview when making contact with someone will indicate to you whether your philosophy and theirs will be compatible. You can consult with the regional chapter of the ISA for help in formulating what questions to ask. PlantAmnesty and the Master Gardener offices in Seattle also have lists of trained arborists.

BANKERS / CONTRACTORS

If you are applying for a loan to finance renovations or construction of a new home, discuss your need for a sufficient budget to encompass landscape design and installation services and materials. Bankers are increasingly receptive to this concept and if you wait until the day you walk in the front door of your new dream home to address this expensive situation, you may have missed an important opportunity. Forethought during the construction phase will save money. At the very least, *insist* that your site be carefully considered during construction, as restoration is expensive, difficult, and unnecessary. Make sure you and your contractor are like-minded when it comes to "saving" that precious oakleaf hydrangea from an unaware or sloppy subcontractor who drops a ladder on it!

GARDENERS

A landscape gardener's specialty is **maintenance**—beginning with lawn care and including installation, mowing, fertilizing, thatching, and weeding. Tree and shrub pruning and maintenance is another major aspect of the gardener's business. These professionals often have good sources for soil, bark, and manure, and will take care of ordering, delivery, and installation. Most work is on an hourly basis. If you choose to establish an ongoing service contract, many are willing to bill you monthly. No special training is required for most work, so do check references. (Pesticide application usually requires certification.)

Word of mouth is one of the best methods of finding competent help. Many more gardeners (with years of experience) are available than you'll find listed with a classified ad in the yellow pages. Some of the best don't need to advertise because they have as many happy customers as they have time to serve. If you don't know of anyone to ask, then keep your eyes peeled for a contract gardener at work—most have signs on their trucks that may be their only form of advertising. Then, if you like what you see, write down their phone number!

HOME REPAIR / CONSTRUCTION SERVICES

Having your roof power-washed? Painting the exterior of the house? Adding a playroom? All these activities have an impact on the garden that surrounds your house. Don't neglect to express your concern that the workers will need to protect your plantings as they accomplish the tasks they are hired to perform. Perhaps putting something in writing about costs of plant replacement would provide an inducement to consider this factor. Otherwise you may be among those amazed and dismayed by the lack of concern non-gardeners have for your carefully tended borders, trees, and shrubs.

LANDSCAPE CONTRACTORS

A landscape contractor is involved in the **installation** aspect of the business. These professionals should be bonded, licensed, and insured, although many aren't. Call the **Washington State Department of Labor & Industries Contractors Hotline,** (800) 647-0982. The Washington State Nursery and Landscape Association has a certification program, that calls for experience, testing, and continuing education. The Washington Association of Landscape Professionals conducts an extensive training program, which awards a Certified Landscape Technician designation (participants specialize in Installation, Maintenance, Irrigation, and Advanced Horticultural Management). It is important to always ask for references; ask to see a portfolio or even drop by the site of a previous client, because the quality of work can vary. Get estimates from more than one vendor, but provide them all with a proper plan so each will be able to bid fairly on the same components, and you can compare the results.

LANDSCAPE DESIGNERS

Landscape designers work with you to embody your vision and move your ideas into reality. The work of a landscape designer involves analysis, planning, design, creation and/or construction of exterior spaces utilizing plant materials, as well as choice of appropriate hardscape elements including incidental paving and building materials. A good landscape designer spends time learning about your lifestyle and how you plan on using your garden spaces, along with evaluating your site. The designer may draw plans to scale, prepare plant lists and indicate proper plant placement, and is often involved in plant installation.

A good source to begin with is the Association for Professional Landscape Designers, which was formed in the late 1980s. The APLD has members in British Columbia, Oregon, and Washington (see www.apld.org for a list of certified designers in your area). As the group is expanding its membership of qualified designers, there are still many good professionals who have yet to obtain this designation. Be aware, though, that almost anyone may hang out a shingle and take to calling themselves a garden designer.

This profession requires a great deal of technical knowledge and aesthetic sense, so protect your interests by selecting your designer carefully. There are many knowledgeable and experienced individuals practicing landscape design. Find out about their training, as several community colleges have excellent one- and two-year landscape-design degree programs. Ask to see a

portfolio of work, make sure to check references of past clients, and talk with more than one firm.

Some design firms are willing to work on a consultation basis, which allows you to pay for a few hours of time while getting a feel for their qualifications, the range of their capabilities, and their ability to communicate well with you. While most work on an hourly-fee basis, some will provide a fixed fee for a specific job. Not all firms are able to both design and then *install* all that is required in the plan. If your designer will not be responsible for this most important phase—getting the stones set and plants planted—find out who will. Make sure to ask these questions: Is it up to you to hire someone? Are there serious site problems such as drainage, tree removal, rock work, or the need for site preparation using heavy equipment? Assess your property and the difficulty of the work you require as you choose what kind of professional help you will need.

LANDSCAPE ARCHITECTS

The American Society of Landscape Architects defines the profession as the art and science of analysis, planning, design, management, preservation, and rehabilitation of the land. The scope of the profession includes site planning, garden design, environmental restoration, town or urban planning, park and recreation planning, regional planning, and historic preservation. The professional society provides a referral service at www.asla.org.

The landscape architect is a professional who has had a great deal of training. In order to be able to use the title, landscape architects must have graduated from an accredited university with a Master's Degree in Landscape Architecture, worked several years in the profession, and then passed a difficult certification exam. Their training covers the aesthetic side of garden design, the technical requirements of soils engineering, and such hardscape elements as decks, arbors, patios, driveways, and retaining walls. Their fee is based on an hourly rate. Some will consider working on a consultation basis. A landscape architect will oversee the installation of a garden but will not be involved in construction. While many who practice landscape architecture work on commercial jobs, you may find you need this level of service for your residential setting. As you interview candidate firms, follow the same process as with landscape designers and contractors: ask for references, view their past work, and make sure you choose a professional with whom you can be aligned philosophically. Read tips on hiring a landscape architect at: http://www.asla.org/nonmembers/publicrelations/selectla.htm.

NURSERY AND LANDSCAPE PROFESSIONALS

The nursery industry uses a certification process to designate professionals who have passed an exam the industry devises and administers. To qualify for the exam one must have practical and/or institutional experience as well. See listings below for professional organization offices in British Columbia, Oregon, and Washington. Note: Many Certified Nurserymen are employed at the retail specialty nurseries you'll find listed in Chapter 5, "Nurseries."

PEST-CONTROL SERVICES

To advertise as a professional in this field a sprayer must pass a state exam (or in B.C., a provincial pesticide applicators permit), and be recertified every several years to retain the license (which calls for a required number of hours of continuing education). As with most fields, there are good and bad practitioners. Especially with environmental and personal safety questions in mind, it is very important to interview a sprayer and get an estimate (generally free). Solicit recommendations from someone knowledgeable about this highly charged subject (see Chapter 1, "Organizations That Help Gardeners"). Many workshops and classes are given on common-sense pest and disease control, so you may also want to check sources listed in Chapter 3, "Educational Opportunities." Think about it like you would in taking first-aid classes to avert a human crisis—it's wise to be prepared with some background on the subject of pest control before a horticultural crisis arrives. In B.C., the Ministry of Water, Land, and Air Protection offers IPM (integrated pest management) manuals, brochures and other publications online at www.gov.bc.ca/wlap (click on "Integrated Pest Management" from the list of key words).

PROFESSIONAL ORGANIZATIONS

If you are a professional or about to become one, these organizations are worth your time to check out. If you are a horticulture student, you might consider contacting them about their scholarship offerings, certification program, or student membership rate. (When you run across references to a "Certified Nursery Professional" or "Certified Landscaper," you have found someone who has undergone horticultural training and work experience and then passed an administered examination.) If you are a member of the plant-buying public, ask if these organizations publish any materials to help you reach members. For example, the Washington State Nursery and Landscape Association puts out a free, annually updated *Retail Nursery Guide,* which lists member nurseries and includes locator maps.

ASSOCIATION FOR WOMEN IN HORTICULTURE (AWH)

PO Box 75093, Seattle, WA 98125-0093 | **Phone:** (206) 781-7741 (Info Line); (206) 781-3827 (Gardeners Referral Service, where you, the potential client, can find qualified landscape professionals to help you with projects large and small) | **Email:** info@awhort.org | **Web:** www.awhort.org

This very active, nonprofit organization began as the Association for Women in Landscaping and has in recent years changed its name to reflect the broader membership of professionals in education, government, botanical gardens, and nurseries, as well as in landscaping. AWH is especially good for professionals networking with one another. It offers a great introduction for those new to the profession, too. Meetings feature an educational speaker (nonmembers welcome for $5 fee), and an annual conference and regular projects offer opportunities to involve members, such as displays at the Northwest Flower and Garden Show. Check the a bimonthly newsletter, called *Leaf* and find out about ongoing scholarships to women pursuing studies in the horticulture / landscaping profession.

BRITISH COLUMBIA LANDSCAPE & NURSERY ASSOCIATION (BCLNA)

#101 - 5830 176A Street, Surrey, BC V3S 4E3 Canada | **Phone:** (604) 574-7772 or (800) 421-7963 | **Web:** www.canadanursery.com/bclna/

The BCLNA has over 500 member companies, representing nursery, landscape, retail, education, supply, service, and government organizations working in the landscape horticultural industry. The website allows you to browse for plant sources, landscaping services, and supplies in BC's Lower Mainland, Interior, and Island areas. This site is mostly geared to the trade, but savvy gardeners will enjoy the resources here too.

OREGON ASSOCIATION OF NURSERYMEN, INC. (OAN)

2780 SE Harrison Street, Suite 102, Milwaukie, OR 97222 | **Phone:** (503) 653-8733 or (800) 342-6401 | **Fax:** (206) 653-1528 | **Email:** info@oan.org | **Web:** www.nurseryguide.com

The OAN's extensive membership yields a hefty *Directory and Buyer's Guide.* You'll appreciate the **online Buyer's Guide** because it allows visitors to search by plant name, by company name, or by types of services and supplies. You can order the 500-page directory that catalogs Oregon's expansive horticultural industry for a mere $10 ($15 Canadian), by phone or on the website. While it's geared to the wholesale plant buyer, the guide lists numerous sources that also sell to retail customers. The directory lists 30,147 plant, service, and supply listings from vendors in 4,327 different categories. There are 4,107 separate plant categories and 422 service/supply categories. Take advantage of this resource! OAN also stages the annual **Yard, Garden, and Patio Show** in late February (see Chapter 12, "Flower & Garden Shows, Festivals & Events").

WASHINGTON ASSOCIATION OF LANDSCAPE PROFESSIONALS (WALP)

1723 100th Place SE, Suite C, Everett, WA 98208 | **Phone:** (425) 385-3333 or call in-state toll-free (800) 833-2186 | **Fax:** (425) 385-3344 | **Email:** info@walp.org | **Web:** www.walp.org

This is an industry-based organization representing members of the landscape profession. Order the free

WALP membership directory, which lists members by profession (members include landscape architects, contractors, designers, and educators) by calling the state office. On the website, there's a great feature that allows you to search for professionals in your city by category. WALP offers a certification program (CLT or Certified Landscape Technician and CLP or Certified Landscape Professional). If you are interested in becoming certified they have a Study Guide (in English or Spanish) you can buy. There are also regional chapters, which provide a forum for professional development, networking, and informal continuing education. The annual awards program recognizes excellence in residential landscape design. If you're looking for an award-winning design, contracting, or installation firm, check to see which WALP members have participated in the program.

WASHINGTON STATE NURSERY AND LANDSCAPE ASSOCIATION (WSNLA)

PO Box 670, Sumner, WA 98390 | **Phone:** (253) 863-4482 or call in-state toll-free (800) 672-7711 | **Email:** wsnla@nwrain.com | **Web:** www.wsnla.org

This association publishes the hefty *Washington State Nursery and Landscape Association Directory and Buyer's Guide,* which prints WSNLA bylaws, lists members, provides information on each chapter, lists affiliate associations, and gives a run-down on schools offering horticulture and related courses; it also references a large buyer's guide of nursery stock / supplies and equipment offered by association members. While the directory is primarily geared to wholesalers and the trade, the WSNLA website allows visitors to search member retail nurseries and landscaping firms by county. Click on "News & Information" to download some useful articles, including a few that outline the human and financial benefits of landscaping, along with tips for healthy water use and landscaping.

GARDEN PRODUCTS

Gardeners everywhere are fortunate to have access, through the Web, to the Oregon Association of Nurserymen members' database. On this site you can search not only for plants but also for services and products. The website is at **www.nurseryguide.com/index.html,** and gives you access to more than 200 categories of services and supplies (from arbors and pergolas to wreath frames). Since not all companies are members, you won't have the whole enchilada to choose from. But for you avid researchers, this resource provides a nifty way to find companies in the vast world of horticulture—and often their informative websites. Those looking for employment might use this as a scouting tool.

Soil / Amendments

We like to say "get the dirt on your dirt." Before you buy just any soil, take the time to research what you're getting. You'll save money, time, and unnecessary work. A savvy consumer makes it a point to personally inspect the product before delivery or to condition the sale on your approval of the material *at time of delivery.* You and your plants are going to live with this stuff for a long time! Common problems (unfortunately not readily apparent) are weed seeds (which may come from incompletely composted manures), an overabundance of soluble salts, incompletely composted wood products (which rob nitrogen from plants), and too much debris or too many rocks. There has also been a problem with latent herbicides that don't decompose in compost. Ask the soil company about the percentage of "ingredients" in mixes, as topsoil is often sold as a three-way or five-way mix. Will your new topsoil be used throughout the garden, including the vegetable patch? If so, you will want to ask if sewage sludge (which may be contaminated with heavy metals) is part of the mix. The City of Portland has devised a (voluntary) **Earth-Wise Compost** program (see below) that sets stringent standards for consumer protection. In addition, the *Maritime Northwest Garden Guide* published by Seattle Tilth has a county-by-county list (Oregon and Washington) of verified compost sources.

Questions about compost? Call your local Master Gardener office (listed in Chapter 1, "Organizations That Help Gardeners"), the **Seattle Compost Hotline** (206) 633-0224, or the **Portland Metro Recycler/Composter Hotline,** (503) 731-4104. In B.C., contact the **Delta Recycling Society** at (604) 946-9828 (ext. 315) or www.drsociety.bc.ca for information on composting and organic gardening workshops.

Your success in the garden may hinge on the quality of your soil. Fortunately, over time one can improve even the worst soil. Aeration and the continued addition of organic matter of whatever form will gradually transform clay muck into the stuff that crumbles in your hand. Saintlike qualities of patience and perseverance are the keys! Here is a very good website to visit for the other materials: www.mastercomposter.com.

Soil / Amendments: Oregon

COVENTRY GARDENS ORGANIC PLANT FOOD PRODUCTS

Earth Conscious Co., 7737 NE Killingsworth Street, Portland, OR 97218

Their bagged products are readily available in nurseries and garden centers. Educational brochures about their products are available at many nurseries.

EARTH-WISE COMPOST DESIGNATION PROGRAM

Metro Regional Environmental Management Department, 600 NE Grand Avenue, Portland, OR 97232 | **Phone:** (503) 797-1674 | **Fax:** (503) 797-1795

This program recognizes how curbside collection of yard debris benefits everyone, by redirecting waste from landfills into productive reuse. The program also offers processors a means of obtaining certification, and consumers a means of assessing a safe composted product. Processors pay a fee of $1,000 (within the tri-county region) to cover the costs of the testing, which is wholly voluntary. The objective is to measure chemical, physical, and biological characteristics of compost, using a standard test. The goal is to provide potential consumers a standard to use in selecting compost of consistent quality.

LANE FOREST PRODUCTS INC.

PO Box 1431, Eugene, OR 97440 | **Phone:** (541) 345-9085 | **Fax:** (541) 461-2427 | **Email:** lane@pond.net

Compost products (including recycled yard debris compost), custom soil mixing, soil amendments, soil mixes, bark products, sod, and turf.

REXIUS FOREST BY-PRODUCTS, INC

PO Box 2276, Eugene, OR 97402-0105 | **Phone:** (541) 342-1835 or (800) 285-7227 | **Fax:** (541) 343-4802 | **Email:** dans@rexius.com | **Web:** www.rexius.com | **Sales yards:** 750 Chambers Street, Eugene | 4490 Main Street, Springfield; (541) 747-8575 | 17750 SW 63rd Avenue, Lake Oswego; (503) 635-5865

Planting mix and soil amendments products include Fertile Mix, Garden and Chicken Compost, Orchid Bark, Transplant Soil, Organic Planting Soil, Custom Mixes, Steer Plus, and Compost Tea. Rexius currently composts many different types of materials. Specifically for yard waste, the firm has established recycling centers in the Eugene/Springfield area. Rexius currently has a yard-waste compost product on the market called Garden Compost, available delivered, u-haul, and bagged. Recycling centers or "drop-off depots" are located at 1250 Bailey Hill Road, Eugene, (541) 345-2174, and 4490 Main Street (45th and Main), Springfield, 747-8587. Open daily 8 a.m.-5:30 p.m.

WHITNEY FARMS

PO Box 70, Independence, OR 97351 | **Phone:** (800) 531-4411 | **Email:** info@whitneyfarms.com | **Web:** www.whitneyfarms.com/

Whitney Farms is a leading producer of potting soils, soil amendments, and natural organic fertilizers for the western gardener. Located outside Salem, the firm operates the largest composting site in the Northwest—a minimum of 50,000 cubic yards of **agricultural by-products** are processed annually at the company's 67-acre site. You can find bagged WF products at nurseries, garden centers, and feed and hardware stores in the Northwest. This is a wholesale company but we list them here so you can look for their products by name, and also because they have an informative newsletter and website (which will direct you to a nearby retail outlet). Order a 45-page organic Garden Guide, free, online.

Soil / Amendments: Washington

BAILEY COMPOST

12711 Springhetti Road, Snohomish, WA 98296 | **Phone:** (360) 568-8826 | **Email:** baileyc1@gte.net | **Open:** Monday-Friday, 8 a.m.-5 p.m.; Saturdays (mid-March to September), 9 a.m.-4 p.m.)

Here's a grass-roots company that has a loyal and growing following in Snohomish County. Fourth-generation dairy farmers, Don and Barb Bailey in the mid-1990s began mixing their cow manure-and-yard waste compost to sell locally. They come from a passionate gardening family, so Bailey Farm Blend has increased in popularity through enthusiastic word-of-mouth marketing. Get it direct from the source! Your garden will thank you. If you have a truck, they'll load the compost for $15/yard. If you want it delivered, there is a 6-yard minimum, with delivery charges ranging from $30 (locally) to $70 (Bellevue/Eastside).

CARPINITO BROTHERS FARM

1148 Central Avenue N, Kent, WA 98032 | **Phone:** (206) 623-8103 | **Fax:** (253) 854-2158

Products include Steergro compost, chicken manure, compost and soil conditioners, bagged potting mix, bark, play chips, and peat moss. They deliver or you pick up.

CEDAR GROVE COMPOSTING

17825 Cedar Grove Road SE, Maple Valley, WA 98038 | **Phone:** (425) 432-2395 or call toll-free order line: (877) SOILS 4U | **Web:** www.cedar-grove.com

Since 1989 Cedar Grove and the City of Seattle have collaborated through the **Clean Green Program** to divert garden waste from landfills to a completely composted soil amendment ready to return to the garden, sold bagged or bulk throughout the Northwest in nurseries and garden centers. You can pick it up in bulk or have the company deliver, by the yard. You can also order 1-cubic-foot bags shipped, via UPS, anywhere in the world. They're now offering a nifty blower service, too, which allows you to have dry amendments (including GroCo or bark) blown into hard-to-reach gardens, like ones at the top of a hill. (Who wants to carry all that mulch up steps when that cool blower can do the trick?)

DEJONG'S SAWDUST AND SHAVINGS

11818 184th Avenue NE, Redmond, WA 98052 | **Phone:** (425) 885-1821; Everett telephone (425) 252-1556 | **Alternate pick-up yard:** 3413 Old Hartford Road, Lake Stevens

Chicken and Chips is the product for which these folks have gained admiration among aficionados of mulch. They also offer Fertilemulch.

HENDRIKUS ORGANICS / SOIL DYNAMICS

14461 Tiger Mountain Road Southeast, Issaquah, WA 98027 | **Mailing address:** P. O. Box 1289, Issaquah, WA 98027 | **Phone:**

(425) 392-1200 | **Fax:** (425) 392-4335 | **Email:** soilinfo@soildynamics.com | **Web:** www.hendrikusorganics.com or www.soildynamics.com

Award-winning landscape designer Hendrikus Schraven was far ahead of the industry when he began preaching the importance of organically based landscape practices. With more than 40 years of experience working with nature, soils, crops, and gardens, his firm's approach is rooted in the philosophy that "the whole is greater than the sum of its parts." This concept is essential for gardeners who wish to re-establish the life and balance of their soils. In 2001, after years of selling his organic mixes to the landscaping trade, Hendrikus launched a line of soils, fertilizers, compost teas, brewers, and soil amendments for the consumer. You can buy the Hendrikus Organics line at several Oregon and Washington specialty nurseries and garden centers (check the website for a current list). A sister company called Soil Dynamics sells EssentialSoil™, an all-organic blend of topsoil that that has fantastic properties for use in erosion control, landscape installations, and structural soil applications. When amending the existing soil is not practical or an option, EssentialSoil™ provides a fantastic growing medium.

KELSEY CREEK FARM DOO

Bellevue Parks & Community Services Dept., PO Box 90012, Bellevue, WA 98009 | **Phone:** (425) 452-7688

From unwanted waste produced by the animal barn at Kelsey Creek to "gold for your gardens," here is a product as popular as Zoo Doo (see below). Farm Doo donors include the many resident cows, pigs, horses, sheep, and geese of this miniature farm. The waste is composted and mixed with grass clippings and leaf material and sold to the public during fall and spring events on a first-come, first-served basis. Add your name to the Farm Doo list by calling the number above. Gardeners load their own material (!) so dress accordingly and bring a shovel and pickup truck (or cans and trash bags). Bellevue residents are given preference.

MANUFACTURER'S MINERAL

1215 Monster Road SW, Renton, WA 98055 | **Phone:** (425) 228-2120 | **Fax:** (425) 228-2199 | **Web:** www.manufacturersmineral.com

Especially recommended for their bulk or bagged **grits** and **sands** for potting soil mixes, for all ye who start from seed or grow rock garden plants.

MYSTIC LAKE DAIRY

Located 6 miles east of Redmond | **Phone:** (425) 868-2029

For composted goat manure; call first to receive specific directions. They load!

PACIFIC TOPSOILS

Mill Creek: 14002 35th Avenue SE, Bothell, WA 98012 | (425) 337-2700 or (800) 884-SOIL (7645) | **Kenmore:** 7500 NE 175th Street, Bothell | (425) 485-0701 | **South End:** S 216th Street & 44th Avenue S, Kent | (253) 872-7431 | **Eastside:** 17723 NE 70th Street, Redmond | (425) 882-9194 | **Northgate:** 1212 N 107th Street, Seattle | (206) 418-13001 | **Open:** Daily; call the location you'll be visiting for retail hours, which vary seasonally | **Web:** www.pacifictopsoils.com

A comprehensive source for **landscape materials,** such as topsoils (including a special mix for vegetable gardens), bark, compost (they are a recycle center and manufacture their own), cow manure, sand and gravel, sod and grass seed, a full line of fertilizers, peat bales, and railway ties. PacTopsoils also sells tools such as lawn rollers, fertilizer spreaders, and landscape rakes, and rents some equipment. Inquire about dropping off your garden and clean wood waste (also brush and stumps, manure, soil and sod, concrete, and asphalt). Not every site accepts all kinds of materials so call first to confirm. For really BIG jobs, they rent, deliver, and pick up an on-site container.

RAINIER WOOD RECYCLERS

27529 Covington Way SE, Kent, WA 98042 | **Phone:** (253) 630-3565 | **Fax:** (253) 631-3032

This firm's mulch is 100% recycled from clean wood waste and comes in a variety of chip sizes—coarse, medium, and fine.

SAWDUST SUPPLY COMPANY

15 S Spokane Street, Suite A, Seattle, WA 98134 | **Phone:** (206) 622-4321 or (888) 622-4321 | **Fax:** (206) 622-9661 | **Open:** Weekdays 7:30 am-5 p.m., and March-June, Saturday 8 a.m.-4 p.m. | **Web:** www.sawdustsupply.com

Manufactures "Steerco" and "GroCo," the former a composted steer manure and the second a by-product of Metro's water treatment plant, composted under high temperatures and mixed with sawdust. Their signature product since 1912 has been sawdust, which is useful as a garden mulch, soil amendment, pathway material, and as pet bedding. Buy it bagged or in bulk, you pick up or they deliver.

SMITH BROTHERS DAIRY

27441 West Valley Highway, Kent, WA 98032 | **Phone:** (253) 852-1000 or (206) 682-7633

Far and wide, gardeners sing the praises for Smith Brothers' wonderful washed dairy manure. Just ask Ann Lovejoy, who is utterly "mad about manure" and frequently writes about the Smiths.

SUNLAND BARK AND TOPSOILS COMPANY

12469 Reservation Road, Anacortes, WA 98221 | **Phone:** (360) 293-7188 | **Fax:** (360) 293-1355 | **Email:** edwardalittle@aol.com | **Open:** Mon.-Fri. 8 a.m.-4:30 p.m. in winter, Mon.-Sat. 8 a.m.-5 p.m. in summer.

Sunland is able to boast about their incredible soils, and the professional designers we know in this area back that up when they turn to Sunland for its special mixes—with marvelous results. You will find a variety of **topsoils** for different types of sites, screened compost and bark in three grades, wood chips for children's play areas, and a selection of rock (lava, crushed, and drain rock). They deliver (to three counties, including the San Juans) or pick up at their yard.

Zoo Doo

Woodland Park Zoo, Seattle, WA | **Phone:** (206) 625-POOP | **Web:** http://www.zoo.org/zoo_info/special/zoodoo.htm

The product here is in such hot demand there's a lottery for it, and the prize for the winners is a chance to buy elephant poop. Twice a year the Zoo holds its bulk compost sale, known as the Fecal Fest. The only way to buy this sweet-smelling doo is to send in a postcard during the lottery "open" dates. Calling the Poop hotline in August will get you the exact dates and deadlines for the Fall Fecal Fest, as will calling in February for the Spring Fecal Fest. Demand always exceeds the supply, so this event is a perennial sellout. Dr. Doo will randomly pick the winners from the postcards received before the deadline and contact them. The winners also get to pull on the boots and gloves and load and haul their own lottery booty. This is the most exotic compost in the Pacific Northwest, containing multispecies feces from ten nonprimate herbivores at the Woodland Park Zoo. The ZooStore (at the South gate) sells the compost year-round in 2-gallon and pint-sized buckets for those who missed out on the bulk sale. While you're at the store you can grab a Fecal Fest T-shirt and a gallon of Dr. Doo's latest ZooBroo compost tea. Also, look for bags of Woodland Park Zoo Doo Rose Mix at select local nurseries and garden centers.

Lawns / Grass Seed

Hobbs & Hopkins

1712 SE Ankeny Street, Portland, OR 97214 | **Phone:** (503) 239-7518 | **Fax:** (503) 230-0391 | **Email:** info@protimelawnseed.com | **Web:** www.protimelawnseed.com

This specialty seed company has watched the trends in lawn sensibilities change, and thankfully, as times have changed, has provided a wide array of nontraditional choices for the residential lawn. Products here include Ecology Lawn Seed Mixtures (such as "Fleur de Lawn"), Wildflower Seed Mixtures ("Meadow Bouquet"), Low-Growing Grass Cover Crops, and more. Visit the website for useful tips on lawn care, including articles like these: "Managing Your Wildflowers," "What Is an Ecology Lawn and Why Would I Want to Plant One, Anyway?" and "Soil Enrichment - The Key to a Beautiful Healthy Lawn."

Peaceful Valley Farm Supply

PO Box 2209, Grass Valley, CA 95945 | **Phone:** (530) 272-4769 | **Email:** contact@groworganic.com | **Web:** www.groworganic.com

This earth-friendly company offers a huge assortment of seeds, including custom mixes, wildflowers, and many lawn and native grass-seed mixes, as well as perennial and annual cool and warm weather cover-crop seeds. Spring and fall catalogs are free.

SOIL TESTING

EarthCo.

PO Box 50084, St. Louis, MO 63105 | **Phone:** (314) 994-2167 | **Web:** www.earthtest.com

EarthCo. is a soil-testing service for gardeners where tests are designed for horticultural crops and lawns. The reports offer easy-to-follow recommendations. This Internet-based company allows you to order a soil-testing kit from its website; once you submit your soil sample in a prepaid mailer, EarthCo. will mail, fax, or email you a detailed graphical report with a prescribed fertilization plan for your garden. Test prices range from $20 to $55 and services include custom tests for specific nutrients. Check the website for the "Ask Dr. GoodEarth" feature, where you can obtain answers to specific lawn and garden questions.

Integrated Fertility Management

1422 N Miller Street, #8, Wenatchee, WA 98801 | **Phone:** (509) 662-3179 or (800) 332-3179 | **Email:** phil@agricology.com | **Web:** www.agricology.com

Offers soil tests for both professionals and home gardeners.

Master Gardener / Cooperative Extension

In Oregon and Washington, check your county's MG program for a listing of local soil-testing sources. (See Chapter 1 "Organizations That Help Gardeners," for county-by-county contact information.)

❀ Order a free fact sheet—Number 6: "Soil Qualities: Testing & Improvement"—from WSU Cooperative Extension offices (at http://king.wsu.edu).

❀ Call DialExtension for free recordings on soil topics: (206) 296-3425, tape 144 "Soil Testing." (If you live outside King County, call (800) 325-6165 during normal business hours and ask the operator to connect you with DialExtension.)

❀ Check the Oregon State University "Gardening Information" website to see articles on soils (http://eesc.orst.edu/agcomwebfile/garden/hints.html).

❀ Two publications worth checking out here include "Soil Quality Card," EM 8711, and "Guide," EM 8710, at: http://eesc.orst.edu/agcomwebfile/edmat.

Peaceful Valley Farm Supply

PO Box 2209, Grass Valley, CA 95945 | **Phone:** (503) 272-4769 | **Web:** www.groworganic.com

The catalog and website offer a wide array of soil-testing tools, supplies, and analysis services.

Ribeiro Plant Lab Inc.

10744 NE Manitou Beach Drive, Bainbridge Island, WA 98110 | **Phone:** (206) 842-1157 | **Email:** fungispore@aol.com | **Web:** www.ribeiroplantlab.com

Founded by Dr. Olaf K. Ribeiro, this lab has been in business since 1984 serving the agricultural, horticultural, arboricultural, and turf industries diagnosing plant health problems. RPL offers on-site consultations for homeowners who want diagnosis for plant and tree health problems. The lab also provides soil and compost analysis to ensure that the material you're using in the landscape is pathogen-free. You can have a complete pathogen analysis done for under $100. Send for a brochure listing services and charges and inquire about upcoming all-day workshops on plant health. While RPL typically serves landscape and nursery professionals, Dr. Ribeiro is a great resource for your local horticultural society or garden group, too.

Soil Foodweb, Inc.

1128 NE 2nd Street, Suite 120, Corvallis, OR 97330 | **Phone:** (541) 752-5066 | **Fax:** (541) 752-5142 | **Email:** info@soilfoodweb.com | **Web:** www.soilfoodweb.com

This company offers a very interesting and educational website. Our favorite part is the Image Gallery, where you can see pictures of what the scientists see under the microscope as they are analyzing your soil sample. The images are extraordinary and the explanations are remarkably clear and readily understood. You'll never think about the creatures in your soil the same way again!

Woods End Research Laboratory

PO Box 297, Mount Vernon, ME 04352 | **Phone:** (207) 293-2457 or (800) 451-0337 | **Email:** info@woodsend.org | **Web:** www.woodsend.org

Woods End is an environmental testing source, offering compost, soil, and related testing materials, and they also do consulting. The Solvita compost maturity test kits available here are aimed primarily at commercial and industrial buyers. For the home gardener, Woods End has a nifty new product: the Garden Care Kit, which tells you how much compost your soil needs for "full fertility," and enough tests for one growing season ($23.50 plus s&h).

MATERIALS / STONE

First: Need wood chips? *Lots* of wood chips? Like a minimum dropoff of 12 to 15 yards? Puget Power may be able to help you beyond your wildest dreams. Call (800) 321-4123 (talk to a customer service rep) for information on their "free chips, delivered" program. There may be some time constraints, so call early in your planning process, as delivery depends on where the tree-limbing crews are clearing around power lines. This, by the way, is a working mulch, *not* decorative bark—but, hey, the price is right, and it might be just the ticket for your big project!

Alpine Rockeries, Inc.

23711 63rd Avenue SE, Woodinville, WA 98072 | **Phone:** (425) 481-3456 or (425) 788-1000 | **Email:** rockalpine@aol.com | **Web:** www.alpinerock.com

Located on the west side of the confluence of SR 9 and SR 522, and obvious thanks to its vast yard of large rock selections, everything from a massive rock outcropping for your new rock garden to the flagstones for a patio. There are many types of landscape materials here, rock and stone are the main features.

Holmquist Hazelnut Orchards

9821 Holmquist Road, Lynden, WA 98264-9537 | **Phone:** (360) 988-9240 or (800) 720-0895 | **Web:** www.holmquisthazelnuts.com

In our opinion, cracked hazelnut pathways are among the most handsome we've ever seen. Go to the source! Although the product inside that shell is the main focus here, the nuts do generate a pile of pathway potential in the form of crunchy, deep-brown shells, so call to find out about coming by to see what they have, by the truckload or by the bag.

Interstate Rock Products (Oregon locations)

Oregon City: 15903 S Park Place Court, Oregon City, OR 97045; (503) 655-3323 | Salem: 6242 Portland Road NE, Salem, OR 97305; (503) 390-6337 | Tualatin: 18480 SW Pacific Drive, Tualatin, OR 97062; (503) 625-3258 | **Email:** info@interstaterock.com | **Web:** www.interstaterock.com

Find a huge variety—over 60 types—of stone for walls, water features, paving, landscape features, and for interior and exterior use. They will custom cut stone to your specifications. They deliver and set stone and gladly offer advice for DIYs.

Interstate Rock Products (Washington locations)

Seattle: 23711 63rd Avenue SE, Woodinville, WA; (425) 481-1117 | Vancouver: 9921 N.E. 72nd Avenue, Vancouver, WA 98686; (360) 573-3410; (800) 596-3616; from Oregon: (503) 285-4142 | **Email:** info@interstaterock.com | **Web:** www.interstaterock.com

An immense selection of stone for walls, water features, paving, landscape features, and for interior and exterior use. They will custom-cut stone to your specifications; they also deliver and set stone and gladly offer advice for DIYs.

Lakeview Stone and Garden

4647 Union Bay Place NE, Seattle, WA 98105 | **Phone:** (206) 525-5270 | **Open:** Monday-Fri. 9 a.m.-5 p.m. (check for extended hours during spring and summer months)

For urban Seattleites, Lakeview is located conveniently behind the University Village shopping center. This source for stone stocks over 200 different varieties of landscape and interior materials. The sales yard offers a display pathway constructed of a variety of formal and informal stones and pavers for you to "test drive." Lakeview's specialty is paving stone (six kinds of flagstone, plus sandstones, quartzites, cobblestones, river rock, and pebbles, plus stone benches). You can tell this place caters to gardeners by the playful streetscape garden planted along the front fence.

Marenakos Rock Center

30205 SE High Point Way, Issaquah, WA 98050 | **Phone:** (425) 392-3313 | **Web:** www.marenakos.com | **Open:** 7:30 a.m.-4 p.m. Monday-Fri., 8:30 a.m.-3:30 p.m. Sat. (closed Saturdays during winter). | **Directions:** Heading east, take exit 22 off I-90 at Preston (on the north side of the freeway), turn left on High Point Way, watch for the Marenakos sign.

If you are in the market for stone, both for small and more ambitious projects—footpaths, patios, water features, or walls and such—this is one source you will absolutely want to visit. This is a "working yard," so wear sensible shoes. Marenakos has an attractive demonstration area that provides inspiration and education on many aspects of using stone in the home landscape. Custom stone services provided.

MUTUAL MATERIALS

605 119th Avenue NE, Bellevue, WA 98005 | **Phone:** (425) 455-2869 | **Mailing address:** PO Box 2009, Bellevue, WA 98009 | **Open:** Generally Monday-Friday 7 a.m.-5 p.m. | **Web:** www.mutual materials.com | **Other locations:** Auburn (253) 939-7854; Bremerton (360) 377-3939; Everett (425) 353-9677; Redmond (425) 881-6700; Port Orchard (360) 876-1845 and (360) 474-0885; Olympia (360) 357-3343; Vancouver (360) 693-4766

For almost a century Mutual Materials has provided masonry products for the Pacific Northwest. They are a manufacturer of clay brick and brick pavers, concrete block, stepping-stones, lawn edging, Keystone Retaining Wall Systems, and stair tread materials.

NORTHWEST LANDSCAPE SUPPLY

14904 Smokey Point Boulevard, Marysville, WA 98270 | **Phone:** (360) 651-2144 | **Fax:** (360) 651-2312

These are hardscape specialists with lots of choices. If you're looking for Japanese garden details like stone lanterns and fountains, they have them, plus patio planters and paving materials galore! Also a source for water feature and pond materials, supplies, and products.

ORNAMENTAL STONE INC.

East 101 North Bay Road (PO Box 641), Allyn, WA 98524 | **Phone:** (360) 275-4241 or (800) 446-4241 | **Web:** www.ornamental stone.com

If you're in search of highly-durable exposed aggregate containers, tables, benches, urns, and more, visit this outlet located west of Tacoma. These products are indestructible and the containers come in an attractive array of forms, from rectangle and square planters, to shallow bowls for rock gardens.

PACIFIC STONE CO. INC.

3826 Rucker Avenue, Everett, WA 98201 | **Phone:** (425) 258-1911 or (888) 722-7866 | **Email:** pacstone@email.msn.com | **Web:** www.pacificstoneco.com

Between them, Timothy Gray and Lloyd Glasscock have several decades of stone experience, combining an excellent knowledge of product and a design sense that makes your project successful. At Pacific Stone's display yard near downtown Everett, you'll find samples of natural and manufactured stone materials for patios, paths, walls and more (such as statuary and containers). The company sources basalt, granite, sandstone and slate from

Northwest quarries and beyond. Check out the nifty "wall display" behind the store, where you can see how stacked drystone walls size up to interlocking manufactured stone blocks, among other examples.

RHODES, RAGEN & SMITH

2011 East Olive Street, Seattle, WA 98122 | **Phone:** (206) 709-3000 | **Email:** info@rhodes.org | **Web:** www.rhodesragensmith.com

Rhodes, Ragen & Smith offers antique and handcrafted building products, providing a combination of traditional European masonry design with access to wonderful stone supplies from around the world. The company offers full design, drafting, and consulting services and fabulous handcarved, custom stone products. The website (with its elegant photography) gives you a peek at the architectural ornaments and objects, new and antique stone materials, and oddities, like "Fossil Stone," but if you're in search of really special pieces, you'll want to schedule an appointment to visit the showroom. Through relationships developed by co-founder and CEO Richard Rhodes and others, RRS has been salvaging, reclaiming, and importing stone artifacts from China's Yangtze River (including millstones, urns, steps, vineyard posts, and more—each of which bears the intriuging marks of everyday wear-and-tear by their original users).

TERRAZZO AND STONE SUPPLY COMPANY

13162 SE 32nd Street, Bellevue, WA 98005 | **Phone:** (425) 644-5577 | **Open:** Weekdays 7:30 a.m.-4 p.m., and Saturdays 7:30-10 a.m. in summer

The company offers displays of stone in both landscape and architectural settings and one of the nicest selections of stone in this area. You'll find a huge assortment of native and imported stone for many uses, including Montana travertine, Vermont slate, Mica slates, Arizona stone, feather stone, granite river stones, and more. No minimum; pick up or let them deliver.

BENEFICIAL INSECTS, ORGANIC FERTILIZERS, PEST CONTROLS

GARDENS ALIVE!

5100 Schenley Place, Lawrenceburg, IN 47025 | **Phone:** (812) 537-8651 | **Email:** gardener@gardens-alive.com | **Web:** www.gardens alive.com

Environmentally responsible products for gardeners—natural, chemical-free, and organic pest and disease controls, fertilizers, soil amendments, beneficial insects, drip irrigation supplies, and other gardening equipment especially for the organic gardener, such as row covers, slug baits, insecticidal soaps, and weed barrier mats. Very informative free catalog.

INTEGRATED FERTILITY MANAGEMENT

333 Ohme Gardens Road, Wenatchee, WA 98801 | **Phone:** (509) 662-3179 or (800) 332-3179

For more than 15 years this company has been in the business of supplying organic products, fertilizers, and pest and plant disease controls, agricultural blankets, weed barriers and netting, herbicides, and books. They also do soil testing and leaf-tissue analysis. Stop by their shop, near Ohme Gardens. Free catalog; reasonable prices.

KITSAP E-Z EARTH

PO Box 5030, Bremerton, WA 98312 | **Phone:** (360) 377-3989 | **Email:** ez-info@kitsapezearth.com | **Web:** www.kitsapezearth.com

Finding meaningful employment opportunities for people with disabilities has been a real challenge in Kitsap County. To remedy this situation, two innovative non-profits, Holly Ridge Center and Peninsula Services, developed Kitsap E-Z Earth. Their collaboration is now a business enterprise centered around manufacture and distribution of vermicompost and other environmentally friendly products. The product line includes red worms (in limited quantities), vermicompost (worm castings), worm bins, and other supplies. Vermicompost is also a main ingredient in brewing "worm tea," a natural substitute for pesticides and environmentally harsh fertilizers. You can print an order form off the website for E-Z Earth organic fertilizer, "worm tea," and red worms ($18/pound). If you'd rather visit a retail specialty nursery to pick up your E-Z Earth, the website also lists Kitsap area outlets. You'll feel great supporting this earth-friendly company!

KNOX CELLARS

1607 Knox Avenue, Bellingham, WA 98225 (Brian Griffin) or 25724 NE 10th Street, Redmond, WA 98074 (Lisa Novich) | **Phone:** (425) 898-8802 | **Fax:** (425) 898-8070 | **Email:** brian@knoxcellars.com or lisa@knoxcellars.com | **Web:** www.knoxcellars.com. (Here you'll view the fun online newsletter, *The Urban Farmer.*)

This is the place for orchard mason bees, safely sleeping in comfortable homes built expressly for them by bee buddy Brian Griffin and his clever daughter Lisa Novich. Also, homes for homeless OMBs, "Humble Bumble Homes," and "Canned Bees." Newly on offer are nesting boxes for Aphid Eaters, a native, nonaggressive solitary wasp that feasts on aphids! Also a source for informational books (see Chapter 10, "Literature & Periodicals"), audio tapes, and a video about the hard-working OMB and other bees from this nationally recognized authority and tireless promoter of nature's premier pollinators. You can find most of these products at specialty nurseries and garden centers in the Northwest, or look for the great booth at the Northwest Flower and Garden Show (that's when you'll be seduced by Brian and Lisa's enthusiasm for these great pollinators).

NATURE'S CONTROL

PO Box 35, Medford, OR 97501 | **Phone:** (541) 899-8318 | **Fax:** (800) 698-6250 | **Email:** kathy@naturescontrol.com | **Web:** www.naturescontrol.com

This is a great resource for beneficial insects and biological controls for garden, greenhouse, and home. Mail-order catalog is free.

PLANTEA

Plantamins, PO Box 1980, Kodiak, AK 99615-1980 | **Orders:** (800) 253-6331 (VISA and MC) or (907) 486-2500 | **Fax:** (907) 486-2686 | **Email:** marion@plantea.com | **Web:** www.plantea.com

Organic and Master Gardener Marion Owen has created a great product designed to give indoor plants the same benefit of organic fertilizers that your garden plants enjoy. Simply put, PlanTea is an organic fertilizer sealed in handy little tea bags. Made entirely from all-natural and organic ingredients, PlanTea is brewed like Lipton tea to make a nutrient-rich, liquid concentrate that you can pour over your potted plants. PlanTea contains blended kelp, fish bone meal, rock phosphate, carrots, beets, onions, parsley, and other dried vegetables, herbs, and flowers. "It might sound like an odd combination, but the important thing is that the ingredients work beautifully together to support the whole plant, and not just make it look pretty," Marion says. Included in her kits are 12 generous PlanTea bags, an informative booklet, soil/moisture indicator check sticks, and a packet of quartz crystal powder ($12.95). This makes a swell gift! By the way, Ed Hume Seeds offers handy packets of PlanTea on seed racks throughout the region. If you'd like a free sample of PlanTea, send a self-addressed, stamped envelope (2 stamps please) marked, "Free Sample."

SOILSOUP INC.

9792 Edmonds Way #247, Edmonds, WA 98020 | **Phone:** (206) 542-9304 or (877) 711-7687 | **Email:** services@soilsoup.com | **Web:** www.soilsoup.com

If you've heard of compost tea, SoilSoup is one of the leading-edge ways to incorporate this "wickedly-good" brew into your garden. In the simplest of terms, the concept starts with a huge vat of water and a jumbo "blender" that incorporates oxygen into a mixture of high-quality compost and organic, molasses-looking "juice" (actually beneficial bacteria and millions of healthy soil biota ready to work their magic on your garden plants).

Organic gardening advocate and writer Ann Lovejoy predicts that in five years every nursery (and many gardens) will have a compost tea-making system like the one she uses at Bainbridge Gardens, where customers show up with gallon milk jugs to buy fresh SoilSoup each Saturday. "Using SoilSoup is like adding several inches of compost to the soil," she says. Among other attributes, SoilSoup's makers point out that this cutting-edge technology gives you the benefits of compost without dealing with space and weight requirements. You can spray your roses to reduce mildew; attack your clay soil to improve its overall health, and pour SoilSoup directly onto plants. The 6.5-gallon backyard SoilSoup Compost Brewing Systems contain everything necessary to begin making your very own aerobically brewed SoilSoup (approximately $330). You can order the full system and supplies online or see a list of local nurseries and dealers.

Walt's Organic Fertilizer Co.

PO Box 31580, Seattle, WA 98103-1580 | **Phone:** (206) 783-6685 | **Email:** sales@waltsorganic.com | **Web:** www.waltsorganic.com

We're sure you'll agree: If there is anything in the garden that one really struggles with, it's fertilizers. We recently came upon a handy Product Information and Application Guide from Walt Benecki on the organic products he has created with the Northwest gardener in mind. We've found it to be very useful as a reference.

Recycled Materials / Architectural Salvage

2nd Use Building Materials

Seattle: 7953 2nd Avenue S, Seattle, WA 98108 | **Phone:** (206) 763-6929 | **Open:** 9 a.m.-5 p.m. daily | **Olympia:** 210 Thurston Avenue, Olympia, WA 98501 | **Phone:** (360) 709-2769 | **Web:** www.seconduse.com

Used and discounted lumber, doors, windows, brick, building block—that kind of stuff—which could be a gold mine if you are out to create a unique, less expensive greenhouse or cold frame, garden shed, or one-of-a-kind ornamental garden feature.

Bedrock Industries

1401 W Garfield Street, Seattle, WA 98119 | **Phone:** (206) 283-7625 | **Fax:** (206) 283-0497 | **Email:** bedrockind@qwest.net | **Web:** www.bedrockindustries.com

The motto here is "specializing in trash beautification." Bedrock transforms glass and stone waste into elegant and fun tiles and hardscaping products for the home and garden. A recent foray to their facility (near the Magnolia Bridge) impressed us with many creative possibilities. Bedrock offers statuary seconds and tumbled glass, and if you time your visit right you may find classical cast-stone ornaments from owner Maria Ruano's secret source (available to you here, cheap, by the pound!). A cool place to find unusual stone and tiles.

Hooplah!

9182 Holly Farm Lane, Bainbridge Island, WA 98110 | **Phone:** (206) 842-7053 | **Web:** www.hooplahgarden.com

Lindsay Smith is an artist and avid gardener whose fabulous creations start with the most basic of industrial material: steel rebar and copper screening. Lindsay has developed an innovative "rebar bending" system that allows you to twist, turn and curl ordinary 5/8-inch wide rebar into lovely garden stakes. This is the stuff that's used to stabilize concrete in construction projects so you know it's durable. Now, create cages, supports, and decorative stakes to hold those floppy hollyhocks and peonies and to display vines that need a bit of height to show off their blooms. Contact Lindsay to find out where she's teaching Hooplah! classes, usually offered at nurseries throughout Western Washington and Oregon. She also teaches garden clubs and horticultural societies and will host group classes at her garden on Bainbridge Island. You'll love the class—it's generally small (8–10 people)—and you'll bring home a few curly stakes to "plant" in your own borders. You can also purchase the Hooplah! Kit (a 20-minute how-to video and the nifty "bender"), which allows you create an imaginative and unending supply of garden supports at home. The cost is $65, plus shipping. Call Lindsay or check the website for details.

And if the rebar idea wasn't innovative enough, Lindsay has added a second project in her class series. Her Copper Mesh garden lanterns are elegant and delicate, made from origami-like folds of copper screening material. Imagine how beautiful they'd look hanging from branches of trees, holding a small votive and lighting the garden at night (or, you can make some great Hooplah! rebar stakes to hold the lanterns). Inquire about local classes in your area or get a group together and invite Lindsay to your neighborhood.

King County Commission for Solid Waste

201 S Jackson Street, Room 701, Seattle, WA 98104 | **Phone:** (206) 296-4466 | **Fax:** (206) 296-4475 | **Web:** http://dnr.metrokc.gov/swd/ | **Open:** Weekdays 8 to 5

While many people rush into the Northwest Flower and Garden Show each year to see what horticultural wizardry has been worked, a few of us go to see what King County Commission for Solid Waste's "garbage mongers" have designed, magically using recycled materials Society's cast-offs, garbage, and waste products are transformed into beautiful, earth-friendly gardens by a team of designers sponsored by King County's waste reduction and recycling programs. You'll be awed to think the translucent, jade-green tiles from Bedrock Industries or the graceful forged-steel trellis created by IXL evolved from products destined to fill our already overflowing landfills. King County has taken the lead in helping to organize these resources so that they truly become viable alternatives in homes, gardens, businesses, and communities. Check the user-friendly website the commission has designed to put you in touch with projects, companies, and activities promoting the use of recycled products. Their list keeps changing, so be prepared to see new sources in the future.

Rejuvenation Lamp and Fixture

1100 SE Grand Avenue, Portland, OR 97214 | **Phone:** (503) 238-1900 | **Fax:** (503) 230-2656 | **Web:** www.rejuvenation.com

A source perhaps most widely known for their lamps and fixtures. The savvy sleuth heads here first for an overwhelming selection of architectural cast-offs, salvage, great finds, period pieces from long ago, and funk from our childhood era. This is an unbelievable place for those with a creative spirit and just the right place for an English chimney pot. Have you yearned for some decorative ironwork to set *just so* into a wooden gate, or an arc of classic pillars for the Paul's Himalayan Musk rose you plan for the patio? Rejuvenation even has some garden furniture made to their own specifications, along with some very handsome current Stickley pieces for your den.

RESOURCE WOODWORKS

627 Fourth S, Tacoma, WA 98134 | **Phone:** (253) 474-3757 | **Fax:** (253) 474-1139 | **Email:** rwtimber@aol.com

Re-milled lumber for great garden construction projects.

SEATTLE MUSIC HALL FACADE

Contact: Mike O'Dell | **Phone:** (206) 770-1191 | **Email:** modell@tradermick.com | **Web:** www.tradermick.com

Here's a splendid opportunity for anyone in search of a monumental piece of Seattle's history, in the form of an element salvaged from the demolition of a downtown landmark in 1991. The demolition contractor, McFarland Wrecking Corporation, chose to save and preserve the exterior cast stone artwork of the elegant Music Hall, circa 1928, with its elaborate cast-stone embellished facade. Nearly 1,000 pieces from this ornamental Spanish Baroque facade are now for sale, on display at auctioneer Mike O'Dell's website or in person, by appointment. The artifacts now cover an acre of ground where they are stored, waiting to be discovered by interested people for use in homes, gardens, or landscape.

RED WORMS

Vermicomposting, the art of using red worms to create wonderful, rich compost for the garden, calls for some of those little wigglers. Here are some sources.

KITSAP E-Z EARTH

(See listing under Organic Fertilizers, above.)

SEATTLE GARDEN CENTER

1600 Pike Place, Seattle, WA 98101 | **Phone:** (206) 448-0431 | **Web:** www.molbaks.com

SEATTLE TILTH

4649 Sunnyside Avenue N, Room 1, Seattle, WA 98103 | **Phone:** (206) 633-0451 | **Open:** Weekdays, call for hours. | **Web:** www.seattletilth.org

The price for the red wigglers is $10, which includes an ample supply of worms, baby worms, and worm eggs to get your worm bin off to a super start. Master Composter volunteers are present at the Tilth Compost Demonstration Site to answer questions and sell worms on certain days (call for more info). They have three worm bins just for the purpose of "growing" worms and will gladly accept "worm donations" from our friends that have *extra* red wigglers!

SKY NURSERY

18528 Aurora Avenue N, Seattle, WA 98133 | **Phone:** (206) 546-4851 | **Fax:** (206) 546-8010 | **Web:** www.skynursery.com

YELM EARTHWORM & CASTING COMPANY

14741 Lawrence Lake Road, Yelm, WA 98597 | **Phone:** (360) 894-0707 (farm); (206) 352-9565 (office) | **Email:** mail@yelmworms.com | **Web:** www.yelmworms.com

Not only can you order red wigglers, the "Cadillac" of earthworms, but a visit to the website will also introduce you to the fabulous (online) Earthworm Store, which offers compost tea, worm bins, and more.

MAIL-ORDER GARDEN SUPPLIES

While we strongly advocate buying local to support businesses in our Northwest "neighborhood," we have to admit that these catalogs provide some products and brands we simply can't find nearby.

DULUTH TRADING CO.

170 Countryside Drive (PO Box 409), Belleville, WI 53508 | **Phone:** (800) 505-8888 | **Web:** www.duluthtrading.com

This is essentially a catalog for carpenters, but the high quality of the tools, equipment and work clothing will impress discriminating gardeners. We learned of this cool source when a house guest sent a "thank you" gift that only a gardener could love: The Garden Bucket Caddy Plus ($20.99), everything you need to turn a plain old 5-gallon bucket into the ultimate garden tool organizer. There are several pages of more nifty landscaping products, like the Birkenstock Knee Cushion ($37.99), which fits your knees as snugly as your favorite pair of "birkies" fit your feet.

GARDENERS' SUPPLY COMPANY

128 Intervale Road, Burlington, VT 05401 | **Phone:** (800) 833-1412 | **Email:** info@gardeners.com | **Web:** www.gardeners.com

Order a free catalog or check the one online with over 2,000 products (the website includes a "bargain basement" for sale items). Also on the Web you can ask gardening questions and read gardener Katherine LaLiberte's knowledgeable insights about growing techniques. If you're one of those setting up a greenhouse, you will probably come to rely on the Gardener's Supply patented seed-starting system called APS. This organically sensitive company offers quality supplies, equipment and tools, a mix of the traditional (like Spear & Jackson's guaranteed-for-life tools from England) and innovative (like their self-watering patio garden system).

PEACEFUL VALLEY FARM SUPPLY

PO Box 2209, Grass Valley, CA 95945 | **Phone:** (503) 272-4769 | **Web:** www.groworganic.com

Find a great selection of organic fertilizers (soil building and foliar), pest controls, beneficial insects, Bt's, traps, lures and soaps, pyrethrins, rotenone, neem, deer and bird controls, tools and equipment, irrigation and watering supplies, and many season extenders (including cold frames, greenhouse kits, row covers, etc.). This source also sells open-pollinated vegetable seeds, bare-root fruit trees, and fall bulbs.

WOMANSWORK

18 Grandview Lane (PO Box 65), Sharon, CT 06069 | **Phone:** (800) 639-2709 | **Web:** www.womanswork.com

Womanswork started as a source for women who needed work gloves that, quite simply, FIT! For more than 15 years, founder Dorian Winslow has sold her fabulous original work glove from suede pigskin (long cuffs are a great feature, as is an optional Thinsulate lined version). Now, the expanded catalog features other sensible supplies for women who work (and garden), including a gardening hat, tool holster, hand salves, workboots, "muck" shoes, gardening socks, professional tools and a work apron. This is a cool, woman-owned company worth supporting. The catalog and website offer important hand-measuring tips so you can ensure a perfect glove fit.

LITERATURE & PERIODICALS

The reading gardener has myriad areas to choose to cultivate, as the ongoing emergence of new publications devoted to gardening and horticultural topics continues at a brisk pace, complete with dazzling photography, feature stories on hot topics, historical evaluation of choice plants, and more. What better way to devour the best of the garden world's news that to find it in your mailbox (or library or newsstand) each month?

JOURNALS & MAGAZINES

Helpful Tips

❀ If you have access to a copy machine, photocopy the table of contents of every magazine you want to keep as it arrives, then file the pages in a three-ring binder. Make notes in the margins of these sheets for reference later.

❀ So many worthy magazines and horticultural journals never make it before the eye of the public in libraries or on the newsstand. Word-of-mouth or advertising will eventually bring them to your attention. Check Garden Literature Press to see an annual index of magazine articles about plants and gardens. Editor and publisher Sally Williams is in her tenth year of this amazing cataloguing endeavor (details on page 230).

❉ Many periodicals offer online versions or selected excerpts for you to try. For an example, try this website: www.plants-magazine.com.

The American Gardener

7931 E Boulevard Drive, Alexandria, VA 22308-1300 | **Phone:** (703) 768-5700 | **Fax:** (703) 768-7533 | **Web:** www.ahs.org | **Subscriptions:** Bimonthly, $35/year for new members, $4.95 cover price

As the official publication of The American Horticultural Society, this magazine comes with your membership and is available to the public on newsstands, at many libraries—and is now online. For keen gardeners who also love to read, this is a stimulating, provocative, and insightful publication. You will look forward to each issue, and keep them on hand too. (Russell Graham Nursery, Heronswood nurseryman Dan Hinkley, and Portland's venerable Timber Press have been featured here, and the memorable article on David Douglas in the a recent issue rekindled our interest in the fascinating history of plant exploration, in this case, throughout the Pacific Northwest.) One of our favorite features is their "Pronunciations" page, an attractive inclusion for those of us whose botanical Latin lacks luster.

Arboretum Foundation Bulletin

Washington Park Arboretum Foundation, 2300 Arboretum Drive E, Seattle, WA 98112-2300 | **Phone:** (206) 325-4510 | **Subscriptions:** $25/year, $5 cover price at Graham Visitors Center Gift Shop

This is the official publication of the Arboretum Foundation. Become a member and receive this highly respected journal. Quality photography accompanies the subject matter, illustrating the knowledgeable yet very approachable articles. This is a premier publication for the Pacific Northwest gardener, written by some of our most eminent horticulturists about topics pertinent to this region.

Avant Gardener

PO Box 489, New York, NY 10028 | **Web:** www.avantgardener.org | **Subscriptions:** $20/year, $2 sample copy

While not geared directly to the Northwest, this unique news service brings late-breaking, practical information on "new plants, products, techniques (with sources) plus feature articles and special issues" to gardeners everywhere. It has been awarded the prestigious Garden Club of America award and recognition by the Massachusetts Horticultural Society. Every issue offers some irresistible resource, from tissue culture (DIY) kits to Italian (to die for) raspberries. How can you go wrong with an outlay of only a couple of dollars for a sample copy?

Aquascape Lifestyles

1200 Nagel Boulevard, Batavia, IL 60510 | **Phone:** (877) 206-7035 | **Email:** email@aquascapedesigns.com | **Web:** www.aquascapedesigns.com | **Subscriptions:** Quarterly, $19.95/year

Water gardens are the fastest growing trend in the "Green Industry" today and are the newest rage with homeowners. Whether you're an up-and-coming wannabe, a rookie, or a veteran, this magazine is for you. It covers all the various aspects of owning and maintaining ponds.

Country Living Gardener

PO Box 7335, Red Oak, IA 51591 | **Phone:** (800) 888-0128 | **Web:** www.countryliving.com | **Subscriptions:** Monthly, $24/year, $2.95 cover price

There are so many gardening magazines on the market today that one's subscription budget can be eaten up lickety-split. However, it doesn't take many issues purchased regularly off the newsstand shelf to figure out that it makes sense to subscribe! Look forward each month to the contributions from excellent gardener/writers Sharon Lovejoy, Rob Proctor, Lauren Springer, and many others, and watch for the excellent book review column. We feel that western gardeners are well represented in this publication.

Fine Gardening

The Taunton Press, 63 S Main Street, Box 5506, Newtown, CT 06470-5506 | **Phone:** (800) 283-7252 | **Fax:** (203) 426-3434 | **Email:** fg@taunton.com | **Web:** www.taunton.com | **Subscriptions:** Bimonthly, $29.95/year

This profusely illustrated (color photos and educational diagrams) publication—from the publishers of *Fine Woodworking, Fine Homebuilding, Fine Cooking,* and *Threads*—shares information from reader-experts on propagation, design, planting and maintenance, gardening news, and trusty tips from real gardeners. There are book reviews, a question-and-answer section, and a slew of well-chosen feature articles in every issue. Each profiles a wide range of ornamental plants and home gardener–friendly techniques in design and building projects.

The Garden

Bretton Court, Bretton Centre, Peterborough PE3 8DZ UK | **Phone:** (01733) 264666 | **Fax:** (01733) 282655 | **Email:** thegarden@rhs.org.uk | **Web:** www.rhs.org.uk | **Subscriptions:** Monthly, $50/year membership

It's available on better newsstands and by subscription, but we think the best way to get the official publication of the Royal Horticultural Society is to join. Membership will bring you a smashing (free) seed exchange, and if you happen to be visiting Britain, entrance into gardens and events throughout the UK. The quality and focus of the horticultural writing is, for any serious garden and plant lover, well worth the price of admission in its own right. The features cover practical garden design ideas, plant profiles, and outstanding gardens, large and small. Every month, RHS scientists address seasonal problems in the advice column, and Hugh Johnson, under his nom de plume of Tradescant, offers a gardener's view of the world. (See Chapter 2 under "Garden Clubs" for membership information.)

The Gardener

30 Irene Street, Torrington, CT 06790 | **Phone:** (877) 257-5268 | **Email:** custserv@whiteflowerfarm.com | **Web:** www.thegardenermagazine.com | **Subscriptions:** $24 for 6 issues (published quarterly)

Backed by the folks at White Flower Farm, this new publication likes to think of itself as "public radio with dirt under its nails" because there is no advertising between the covers. As a magazine for active gardeners, *The Gardener* features great plants, stimulating designs, and techniques that remain useful long-term. It is edited by Tom Cooper, longtime editor of *Horticulture* magazine. The first issue debuted in Fall 2001, and *The Gardener* promises to be a strong, new presence among garden periodicals. Subscription includes a $20 merchandise credit for shopping at White Flower Farm.

Garden Design

PO Box 420325, Palm Coast, FL 32142-0235 | **Phone:** (800) 513-0848 | **Fax:** (904) 447-2321 | **Web:** www.gardendesignmag.com | **Subscriptions:** Bimonthly $23.95/year

Garden Design covers topics of broad horticultural interest. Designed to appeal to the boomer generation, GD zeros in on hot, environmentally friendly topics, (upscale) design, a worldwide view, eye-popping photography, and handsome illustrations. How-to articles are interplanted as features and sidebars, there are always lots of sources and resources (thank you, thank you), and the plants are generally given their botanical names. When it arrives, turn first to their kraft-paper insert entitled "Leaves" that looks to our rich heritage, often excerpting notable garden literature, and embellishing each piece liberally with luscious botanical illustrations.

Gardens Illustrated

US Agents: 3330 Pacific Avenue, Suite 404, Virginia Beach, VA 23451-2983 | **Phone:** (888) 428-6676 | **Fax:** (757) 428-6253 | **Subscriptions:** $59.95/year for 10 issues, or $5.99/issue on newsstands (check for subscription discount coupon)

If you are new to this publication, the name aptly describes it, as this elegant magazine is both stimulating to the eye (with quality photography) and to the mind (with articles by and about leading garden writers, designers, and plantsmen, as well as gardens past, present, and future). Each issue also brings garden touring and gardening course information that the footloose American gardener will find appealing and useful. There's a liberal sprinkling of artists' gardens and garden art as well as the plant profile pieces where you will often find something you can't live without (and sources to help you find your heart's desire, often with U.S. nurseries, too). While GI is essentially not a "how-to" publication, that doesn't mean is it devoid of insights from wise veterans. Just look for the "Know How" feature, which brings the wisdom of Penelope Hobhouse, Anna Pavord, and Mary Keen, and "Sowing the Seed," practical advice on propagating from seed from head gardener Fiona Crumley.

Garden Showcase

PO Box 23669, Portland, OR 97281-3669 | **Phone:** (503) 684-0153 or (800) 322-8541 | **Fax:** (503) 639-0179 | **Email:** info@gardenshowcase.com | **Web:** www.gardenshowcase.com | **Subscriptions:** $19.95/year for 10 issues (subscriptions@gardenshowcase.com)

This tabloid-size, color-illustrated, almost-monthly publication for gardeners of Western Oregon and Western Washington is just packed to bursting with information and inspiration on a remarkable number of timely gardening topics. A number of features here will make gardening and visiting in the area far more pleasurable, such as the considerable gallery of nurseries, listed along with locator maps. It includes regular monthly columns by Ann Lovejoy, Dan Hinkley, Lucy Hardiman, Ed Hume, Mike Darcy, Jolly Butler, and Ray McNeilan, as well as articles by other skilled Northwest writers, appealing to both beginning and intermediate gardeners. Features of the magazine include "Plant Sources," to help readers locate the plants discussed in the articles; a "Hitting the Road" map, to help readers find their way to local nurseries; and an "Events Calendar," which describes classes, sales, and happenings of interest to gardeners. In 2001, this magazine changed to an all-glossy publication, allowing for better color reproduction and making a good magazine even better and more beautiful.

Gardens West

Cornwall Publications, PO Box 2680, Vancouver, BC V6B 3W8 Canada | **Phone:** (604) 879-4991 | **Fax:** (604) 879-5110 | **Email:** grow@gardenswest.com | **Web orders:** www.gardenswest.com | **Subscriptions:** $23.50 (US), $32 (Canadian) for 9 issues

This is a newsy and informative publication, with the majority of articles pertinent to all Puget Sound gardeners and ads that provide sources for products and services. "Grapevine," a calendar of events, apprises you of flower shows, sales, meetings, workshops, and more.

Garden Wise

Canada Wide, 4th floor, 4180 Lougheed Highway, Burnaby, BC V5C 6A7 Canada | **Phone:** (800) 663-0518 or (604) 299-2116 | **Fax:** (604) 299-9188 | **Web:** www.canadawide.com | **Email:** cwm@canadawide.com or subscriptions@canadawide.com | **Subscriptions:** Bimonthly; $21.35 Canadian or about $14 US

Previously called *The Coastal Grower*, this publication emanates from Vancouver Island and is our favorite regional gardening magazine. It is well read throughout western Washington and the lower mainland as well. If your local garden center or newsstand doesn't carry it, ask for it!

GreenPrints "The Weeder's Digest"

PO Box 1355, Fairview, NC 28730 | **Phone:** (800) 569-0602 | **Subscriptions:** Quarterly, $19.95 US, $26 Canadian

Funny, tender, and heartfelt, this journal for gardeners covers the human, not the how-to, side of gardening. A jazzy mix of essays, lighthearted illustration, literary tidbits from readers, and some topical ads (always fertile ground for a resource sleuth). Pat Stone spent 11 years as garden editor of *Mother Earth News* and has now settled into this innovative niche. This magazine is available ever more widely on newsstands. A literary bumper crop is yours in the form of an anthology containing 40 of their best pieces, thoughtfully harvested from the magazine's back issues, including 60 of their characteristic and appealing illustrations ($15.95 plus $3 s&h).

The Growing Edge

PO Box 1027, Corvallis, OR 97339 | **Phone:** (541) 745-7773, subscriptions (800) 888-6785 | **Email:** tom@growingedge.com | **Web:** www.growingedge.com | **Subscriptions:** Bimonthly, $26.95/year, also available on newsstands

Primarily aimed at those interested in hydroponic growing techniques, this is an excellent resource in which to find advertising by merchants active in this innovative horticultural arena. Larger concerns than the techniques themselves, however, make up the philosophy behind the publication, as with issues related to our world's attitude toward sustainable and efficient agriculture. Even if you haven't ventured into hydroponic growing, the selection of fascinating feature articles will make you want to read each issue cover to cover. (Examples: an article on hardy fruit varieties that can extend our choices beyond the obvious; an article on tissue culture, an important technique opening many options to the adventurous home propagator; the windowsill herb garden; and an excellent series on understanding plant breeding.) Pick a copy up at the newsstand or visit their website. If you like what you see, you can find a collection of past articles in *The Best of the Growing Edge* (New Moon Publishing, 256 pp.) at the above address, and now the sequel, *The Best of Growing Edge II*.

The Herbalist

Herb Society of America, 9019 Kirtland Chardon Road, Kirtland, OH 44094 | **Phone:** (440) 256-0514 | **Fax:** (440) 256-0541 | **Email:** herbs@herbsociety.org | **Web:** www.herbsociety.org | **Subscriptions:** $12/annual issue

This handsome academic journal has been published by the Herb Society of America since 1935. It provides information on the latest findings, and writings on herbal history, cultivation, science, and lore.

The Herb Companion

Herb Companion Press, PO Box 7714, Red Oak, IA 51591-0714 | **Phone:** (800) 456-6018 | **Fax:** (970) 663-0909 | **Subscriptions:** Bimonthly, $24/year

This lovely magazine does a very nice job of bridging the many aspects of herbs, from culinary to medicinal to ornamental, and from good, practical, how-to information for the kitchen and garden to resource research. The publication title is aptly chosen—as you read it, you feel you have a companion sitting with you, chatting about herbs over a cup of tea.

Herbs for Health

Herb Companion Press, PO Box 7714, Red Oak, IA 51591-0714 | **Phone:** (800) 456-6018 | **Fax:** (970) 663-0909 | **Subscriptions:** Bimonthly, $24/year

In recent years, interest in the broader ramifications of herbs for health has settled in as a field of personal interest for a growing number of people. If you want to make informed decisions about your health, here is a helpful advisor. Use it to help you through that perennial winter cold or flu, or even for your overall health.

The Herb Quarterly

PO Box 689, San Anselmo, CA 94979 | **Phone:** (800) 371-HERB | **Web:** www.herbquarterly.com | **Subscriptions:** Quarterly, $20/year

Our area offers a nurturing climate to herb enthusiasts. This publication is devoted to the culture of these plants, as well as garden design, recipes, and the folklore and history of herbs, in well-illustrated articles. Consider giving a subscription as a gift—it has that feel to it.

Horticulture

PO Box 51455, Boulder, CO 80323-1455 | **Phone:** (800) 234-2415 | **Fax:** (617) 367-6362 | **Email:** horteditorial@primediasi.com | **Web:** www.hortmag.com | **Subscriptions:** $28/year for 8 issues

Northwest gardeners will glean a great deal of pertinent information from this "Magazine of American Gardening." For one thing, our "voice" is heard through Dan Hinkley, a regular contributor, as well as through Marty Wingate, Ann Lovejoy, Lucy Hardiman, and Richard Hartlage, with Valerie Easton and Portland garden transplant Ketzel Levine of NPR fame (as the Doyenne of Dirt) represented via the "Northwest Field Notes" column.

HortIdeas

750 Black Lick Road, Gravel Switch, KY 40328 | **Email:** gwill@mis.net | **Web:** www.users.mis.net/~gwill | **Subscriptions:** $25/year; $2.50 single issue ($3.50 air mail), or receive 12 issues of HortIdeas OnLine for $15, sent via email in Adobe Acrobat PDF format

Greg and Pat Williams are shameless sleuths in their relentless search for the latest in research, tools, plants, books, and techniques for flower, vegetable, and fruit gardeners, gathered from sources worldwide. It's a treat to read—you can be out grubbing in the herb garden and let them slave away as your "personal clipping service."

Hortus

The Bryansground Press, Bryan's Ground, Stapleton (near Presteigne), Herefordshire, LD8 2LP, United Kingdom | **Phone:** 44 1544 260001 | **Fax:** 44 1544 260015 | **Email:** all@hortus.co.uk | **Web:** www.hortus.co.uk | **Subscriptions:** Quarterly, $65/year; on the website you can order back issues for $8 each, postpaid. Also onsite, see the table of contents for each issue, which lets you select the ones that appeal most.

This beautifully printed and exquisitely illustrated (wood engravings, line drawings, and stunning black-and-white photographs) literary journal contains articles on gardens, plants, people, and books, as well as history, design, and ornament. Find conversations with the great figures of present-day horticulture, essays, notes, and thoughtful reviews of new and reissued books. These lovely volumes, each of 128 pages, will be a valued addition to your library. Collections from past issues are now available in book form.

Northwest Garden News

PO Box 18313, Seattle, WA 98118 | **Phone:** (206) 725-2394 | **Fax:** (206) 721-5335 | **Email:** norwesgard@earthlink.net | **Web:** under construction at press time, but check the column the publication has on www.nwcn.com (Northwest Cable News/Gardening) | **Subscriptions:** $20/year for home delivery, otherwise available at no cost

This newspaper-format publication is packed with lots of timely and newsy bits about gardening in this area. It is distributed free in many communities from Portland north to the Canadian border through garden centers, bookstores, and horticultural organizations, although guaranteed delivery is available by subscription. If you don't find it at your favorite nursery, ask them to call to be placed on the distribution list. There is a broad spectrum of subject matter from contemplative to constructive, including a monthly gardening almanac, classified ads, and a calendar of gardening events. This is a great place to look for or publicize club and plant society events, tours, and classes. They sponsor Tours to Puget Sound gardens/nurseries. (See Chapter 14, "Travel Opportunities.")

Organic Gardening

Rodale Press, 33 E Minor Street, Emmaus, PA 18098 | **Phone:** (610) 967-5171 | **Web:** www.organicgardening.com | **Subscriptions:** $15.96/year for 6 issues

This magazine is a classic on the subject of gardening the natural way, with useful comparative articles on equipment (on tillers or riding mowers, for instance). The advertisements provide great resources for products, services, and other ideas. There's an emphasis here on growing vegetables (particularly tomatoes), with some features on flowers. Each issue includes tips for specific USDA hardiness zones. They also make a point of providing sources for everything they reference in their articles (always including something for their Canadian readers as well), which you'll find most helpful. The January issue features the annual "Cream of the Crop" Seed Suppliers resource list.

Pacific Horticulture

Pacific Horticultural Foundation, PO Box 680, Berkeley, CA 94701 | **Phone:** (510) 849-1627 | **Fax:** (510) 883-1181 | **Web:** www.pacifichorticulture.org | **Subscriptions:** Quarterly, $25/year

This scholarly—yet very readable—publication provides serious gardeners with a range of stimulating articles in a handsome and approachable format. Gardeners from throughout the western region look forward to and, quite naturally, treasure their collections of this highly respected magazine. Recent issues have included fine articles by Northwest luminaries Dan Hinkley, the late Gerald Straley, Richard Hartlage, Lee Neff, Ann Lovejoy, and Duane Dietz. Back issues and a complete index are available by mail from the office. See Chapter 14, "Travel Opportunities," for tours with Pacific Horticulture editor Richard Turner.

Pond and Garden, Creating Backyard Havens

1670 S 900 E, Zionsville, IN 46077 | **Phone:** (317) 769-3278 | **Fax:** (317) 769-3149 | **Email:** hnash@pondandgarden.com | **Web:** pondandgarden.com | **Subscriptions:** $20/year or $5 per issue

Pondkeepers have a great resource in this publication, with its 96 to 114 full-color pages per issue! The editors have conscientiously sought far and wide to find the most respected writers and present a very complete range of editorial content (from pond-care concerns, plant features, design profiles and considerations, to book and video reviews, and how to involve children in making and keeping ponds, and much more). Although this magazine sells over the counter at selected garden centers around the United States and Canada, it is primarily available by subscription.

Sunset

80 Willow Road, Menlo Park, CA 94025. | **Subscriber assistance:** PO Box 64206, Tampa, FL 33662-4068 | **Phone:** (650) 321-3600 | **Fax:** (650) 324-1532 or (800) 777-0117 | **Email:** subsvcs@sunset.customersvc.com | **Web:** www.sunset.com | **Subscriptions:** Quarterly, $21/year in Western states, or $4.50 cover price

Sunset is a staple of virtually every Western gardener's reading regimen, no doubt about it. While not devoted entirely to topics near and dear to our Northwest hearts, it will forever provide inspiration and solid, basic advice on all aspects of gardening both to the novice and the veteran. The Pacific Northwest team does a particularly good job of featuring gardens to visit, out-of-the-ordinary resources, and profiles of down-to-earth gardeners who accomplish feats in their gardens that are worthy of emulation and deserving of recognition. If for some reason you don't subscribe, consider the Annual compilation of all the year's gardening articles into one bound edition—a volume that's very helpful as an easy-to-use reference (and much easier to thumb through than your lifetime collection of back issues).

Magazine Article Retrieval

If your collection of gardening magazines is as mind-boggling as that of most garden junkies (you know, the stacks of magazines are starting to make your shelves bow under their weight), how do you find that one obscure article you recall reading once? Those of us who, time and again, remember having seen an article on a particular topic, person, plant, nursery (or whatever), and then waste a phenomenal amount of time in the frustration of thumbing from issue to issue now have several helpful alternatives. In the "Tips" listed in the "Magazine" section above, we've included one way to meet that challenge. Here are a couple of additional tools to use as you research and retrieve information.

Andersen's Horticultural Library, online website service

Andersen Horticultural Library, Minnesota Landscape Arboretum, 3675 Arboretum Drive, PO Box 39, Chanhassen, MN 55317-0039 | **Email:** plantinfo@jaws.umn.edu | **Web:** plantinfo.umn.edu | **Website subscription service:** $59.95/Institutional/Commercial per year, $39.95/Individual subscription per year

Unlike the paper version of this plant-finding index, the Web version adds over 150,000 citations to current plant literature; here, one can find approximately 75,000 different plants, and access illustrations and concomitant information too. Over 150 currently received serials are indexed as received, along with many important monographs in botany and horticulture.

Garden Literature: An Index to Periodical Articles and Book Reviews

Garden Literature Press, 398 Columbus Avenue, Suite 181, Boston, MA 02116-6008 | **Phone:** (617) 424-1784 | **Fax:** (617) 424-1712

Publisher Sally Williams sells back issues of *Garden Literature* (1992, 1993, and 1994 editions), an annual author and subject index to articles about plants and gardens. Her accumulation covers a diverse range of more than 100 English-language periodicals. You can purchase these indices for $49.95 each, plus s&h; contact Garden Literature Press for discounts on purchasing the three years together.

Beginning with 1994, *Garden Literature* began producing a less extensive, less expensive version called *SPROUT,* an index that covers a dozen of the top gardening magazines published in the United States and the United Kingdom. *SPROUT,* Volume 10, has just been released, featuring articles published in 2001. Each index is $29.95, plus s&h.

You can read more of Sally Williams at the GardenNet where she evaluates a slew of resources for gardeners, from International Plant Finders (Australia, New Zealand, Canada, Belgium, France, U.K., U.S.), and Guides to Nurseries, to B&Bs in beautiful Australian and East Anglian gardens, and much more.

Sunset Western Garden Annual

Leisure Arts, Inc., 5701 Ranch Drive, Little Rock, AR 72212-9630 | **Phone:** (800) 526-5111 | **Web:** www.sunset.com | **Subscriptions:** $21.95 plus s&h.

This 320-page hardbound compilation brings together all the year's *Sunset* magazine gardening and outdoor living articles, and conveniently includes down-to-earth, hands-on articles packed with the magazine's characteristically thorough presentation. Find inspirational photos, how-to illustrations, shopping sources, and easy-to-understand charts. Even if you keep all of your old Sunset magazines, you will still really appreciate having the information in this practical format for quick reference.

Vegetables and Fruits: A Guide to Heirloom Varieties and Community-Based Stewardship, Volumes I, II, and III

Alternative Farming Systems Information Center, National Agricultural Library, Room 304, 10301 Baltimore Avenue, Beltsville, MD 20705-2351 | **Phone:** (301) 504-6559 or (301) 504-5724 | **Fax:** (304) 504-6409 | **Email:** afsic@nal.usda.gov | **Web:** www.nal. usda.gov/afsic | **Ordering:** Available without charge (also available on cassette diskette and accessible from the AFSIC website)

This series focuses on the published literature, organizations, and other informational resources pertaining to heritage varieties of fruits and vegetables. Volume I is an annotated bibliography on the topic, with a particularly good introduction to heirloom varieties—what they are, why they are important, and who is actively working to save, disseminate, and garden with them. Suzanne De-Muth has compiled the extensive annotated listing here, which will be of tremendous value to anyone with even the slightest interest in heirloom fruits and vegetables (researching them, seeking seeds, looking for advice). This volume cites relevant publications, including books, journal and magazine articles in current periodicals, videos, and Internet resources, broken down by topic and by specific crop ("Corn," "Peppers," "Potatoes," etc.). It is a researcher's or enthusiast's dream. If you want to go further in your research, consider Volume II, devoted to resource organizations and Volume III, a plant and seed source supplement (see "Plant-Finding Sourcebooks," below).

Calendars

Dahlia Fascination

Lauren Morley Bullock, 127 Willowbrook Lane, Suite 127, West Chester, PA 19382-5571 | **Phone:** (484) 356-0520 or (800) 660-2324 | **Fax:** (484) 356-0521 | **Email:** b-bullock@mindspring.com | **Ordering:** Prices not yet set; call to check.

For several years, Laurie has turned a personal fascination with dahlias into a one-woman promotional venture through her colorful and informational calendar. She recently relocated from Bothell, Washington, to points east, but that hasn't stopped her publishing plans. Contact her if you wish to be notified of the 2003 edition, due out in late 2002. Much of the photography for this month-by-month journey through dahlia fields originates in Oregon and Washington. The project is a wonderful "resource directory" for all things dahlia, with helpful advice on cultivation, pointers to special topical Internet sites, and words of wisdom from gardeners.

Pacific Northwest Gardener's Guide

Fulcrum Publishing, 16100 Table Mountain Parkway, Suite 300, Golden, CO 80403 | **Phone:** (303) 277-1623 or (800) 992.2908 |

Email: fulcrum@fulcrum-books.com | Web: www.fulcrum-books.com | Ordering: $11.95, plus s&h.

This region-specific calendar is designed to help you garden successfully throughout the year, using environmentally safe techniques and tips. The colorful calendar covers Oregon, Washington, British Columbia, and northern California. The text offers month-by-month instructions for the cultivation and care of all your plants, both indoors and outdoors. Also included are helpful design ideas, and spaces for recording plant information like first blooms and last fall colors, rainfall, and frost dates.

Susanne Lewis Calendars

Tide-Mark Press, PO Box 280311, East Hartford, CT 06128-0311 | Phone: 888-461-4619 | Email: customerservice@tide-mark.com | Ordering: $11.95 each, plus s&h

Eugene, Oregon-based photographer Suzanne Lewis produces two beautiful floral calendars annually for Tide-Mark Press. You can find each new year's editions of "Antique Roses" and "Bouquets" at better bookstores, or you can order them directly from the publisher or through the calendar section of Amazon.com. In "Bouquets," Lewis not only gathers together glorious floral arrangements, she identifies each flower, so you can acquire and grow them in your own garden. In "Antique Roses," she shares a passion for collecting and growing heirloom roses, taking the time to tell of their origins. Imagine enjoying a larger-than-life photograph of a 'Mutabilis' or 'Duchesse de Brabant' antique rose on your wall each month.

BOOKS

There are a number of books written specifically for the Pacific Northwest gardener and many others that are mainstays in the home library of any gardener anywhere. Listed here are several from the former category and some great ones from the latter. Many of the most comprehensive or liberally illustrated references may be too expensive for a home library but are generally found in your local library.

A particularly well-endowed library open for your use is the Elisabeth C. Miller Horticultural Library at the University of Washington Center for Urban Horticulture in Seattle. The library is currently in temporary, significantly smaller, digs at CUH, as the efforts to rebuild Merrill Hall and the Miller Library complex continue after the May 2001 terrorism that firebombed it. (See the section on libraries in Chapter 1, "Organizations That Help Gardeners," for details). Regardless, the library staff has endeavored to make available much of its collection, as well as online reference cataloging, while in this interim stage. There are still easy access, easy parking, and very helpful librarians—what more could you ask! Also, if you are trying to locate books on a particular topic, such as "gardening with children," "gardening in the Northwest," or "starting and running a horticultural business," then ask for one of the thoughtfully prepared book lists, which also include relevant periodicals.

If you are looking through this listing and can't find a particular book, such as Dr. Art Kruckeberg's *Gardening with Native Plants,* then look under the more specific literature listings on the topic, such as Chapter 4, "Northwest Native Plants," Chapter 6, "Seed Sources," and Chapter 14, "Travel Opportunities."

Finally, we want to say that compiling this list is an excruciating experience, because we could fill this whole book with suggestions of "favorites." It's as bad as asking an avid gardener to give you a short selection of favorite plants, and it just won't do! Nevertheless, here we highlight Northwest garden writers, even if the books speak to a national audience, because there is generally a Northwest bias or flavor that we certainly appreciate. Also included are other garden writers whose books address gardening concerns and sensibilities pertinent to our area. Sprinkled throughout the list are books that we hope to introduce to friends and readers. Consider this list, then, a good start.

Good Reads

From the Ground Up
Amy Stewart (Algonquin Books of Chapel Hill, 2001, 261 pp.)

There's nothing Northwest about this book, but the recommendation to read it comes from Judith Chandler, one of the Northwest's stellar experts on booking authors for lectures (Third Place Books, Lake Forest Park, WA). When she said the book was heart-warming, we had to read it. Texas native Amy Stewart wrote *From the Ground Up* as a journal documenting her first garden in Santa Cruz, California. There's something very endearing and charming about Stewart's self-effacing writing voice. She truly wants us to experience the same emotional highs and lows, the essential passion of gardening, that she lives through. It's a wonderful late-night read . . . pick it up as an alternative to moonlight gardening.

Gardening with Friends
George Schenk (Houghton Mifflin Co., 1992, 218 pp.)

George Schenk invites us along on his travels, as he finds himself a most welcome guest, always anxious to nip out to the garden for a go at the pruning, planting, dividing, or whatever needs doing. This is a man lost without a garden to tend, having retired from his (much respected) nursery and his own garden in 1977, in favor of wandering the world. Mr. Schenk is on the most amazing (and enviable) yearly cycle, gardening four months each year in the Philippines, then heading for New Zealand, and finally back to Vancouver, BC, and then Seattle. None of these gardens belong to him in the strict sense of land ownership, but in each he is heartily welcomed back annually, both by dint of his personal friendship with the actual landowners and by the plants he has long tended lovingly. This delightful, witty, and talented man shares his adventures and love of gardening in an unmistakable and enchanting style.

In a Country Garden
Noel Richardson (Whitecap Books, 1996, 208 pp.)

We're among those readers who have gotten to know (trust and follow) Noel Richardson's sage advice and felicitous musings on her life and gardens at Ravenhill Farm on Vancouver Island, shared through her two cookbooks and monthly columns in Vancouver's *CityFood* magazine. This beautifully illustrated little book shares her love of cooking and the idyllic rural herb-farm setting she and husband Andrew Yeoman (himself author of *A West Coast Kitchen Garden*, Whitecap, 1995), have nurtured over the past 20 years. Written to follow the cycle of the seasons month by month, the vignettes on their life and surroundings are generously sprinkled with gardening tips (such as how to extend the basil harvesting period), and sumptuous recipes (egg, tomato, and rosemary soup; chicken breasts in plum sauce; lemon thyme cake).

Merry Hall (1951), Laughter on the Stairs (1955), Sunlight on the Lawn (1956)
Beverley Nichols (Timber Press, 1998-1999, 264 pp.)

Of the 53 or so books written by Beverley Nichols, his 1950s treatises on gardening are among the most popular. Thanks to Timber Press, those of us with a penchant for just about anything British, horticultural, and humorous are served up a memorable cast of characters, an intermingling of opinionated gardening advice, and a delicious setting featuring the quintessential English country estate. This widely available, recently reprinted trilogy will undoubtedly leave many of you hungry for more Nichols, so look at the end of this chapter for the list of bookshops specializing in out-of-print and old gardening books.

Perennials: Toward Continuous Bloom
Edited by Ann Lovejoy (Capability's Books, 1991, 287 pp.)

The subtitle reveals a great deal of the spirit of this anthology, as we grope to express what is evolving across this country through the work of gardeners often influenced by traditions and philosophies imported from abroad who nonetheless give form to gardens solely their own. With the hand of an experienced garden-maker and the eloquence of a word-meister, Ann Lovejoy quilts the thoughts of gardeners from across the country into a well-crafted whole, neatly stitched together with her own commentary. From this region you'll find the elegant essays of Sue Buckles, the late Jerry Sedenko, Mark Houser, Judith Jones, Peter Ray, Amber Karr, Margaret Ward, Daphne Stewart, Pat Bender, and the late Kevin Nicolay.

Plant This!
Ketzel Levine, with illustrations by Rene Eisenbart (Sasquatch Books, 2000, 224 pp.)

Ketzel's voice and wry attitude are familiar to NPR audiences, thanks to her ongoing reports about gardening, plants, and related topics. It's nice to know she's in our neighborhood now, gardening in her own Portland backyard and writing about her favorite plants. But this is no ordinary compilation of plant profiles. This is a book you continue to page through, reading Ketzel's short essays with joy, taking notes or highlighting the varieties she admires, and chuckling at her frank asides on 100 plants that perform throughout the season in her garden. She makes it easy to devour otherwise serious botanical information, with such help as pronunciation tips (Salvia guaranitica, she says, sounds like "Salvia swore, admit it, suh!"), and choice pieces of information that make each of these plants unforgettable. Rene Eisenbart's wonderful watercolor-like illustrations are little works of art in themselves.

Soul Gardening: Cultivating the Good Life
Terry Hershey (Augsburg Fortress, 2000, 161 pp.)

Vashon Island–based garden designer and speaker Terry Hershey is a former Protestant clergyman who turned to the soil in search of his soul. This slim volume offers meditations on what the garden teaches our spirit. Terry's musings, meditations, and quiet advice help to put a voice to the things we know deep down about why we garden. There's even a sizable dose of garden advice sprinkled throughout.

The 3,000 Mile Garden
Leslie Land and Roger Phillips (Viking, 1996, 330 pp.)

This isn't a new book, but it is a favorite on the shelves of many gardeners who yearn for the camaraderie exuded by these two garden writers. Leslie writes from her home in New York and Roger writes from his in London, and by sharing in their correspondence we join their friendship, gardening highs and lows, passionate discussions, and more. Leslie shares recipes; Roger shares planting schemes. The book is a delight and one that offers a peek into the psyche of gardeners around the globe. These highly personal letters exchanged between friends resonate with a certain familiarity and are extremely gratifying to read. This was the companion volume to a six-part TV series on PBS.

The Year in Bloom (1987, 264 pp.); The Border in Bloom (1990, 280 pp.); The Garden in Bloom (1998, 275 pp.)
Ann Lovejoy (Sasquatch Books)

"Time is the gardener's friend; there is no hurry about making a garden, for the process, rather than the product, is the point." So advises Ann Lovejoy, a remarkably prolific and energetic author, columnist, public speaker, teacher, mother, and Northwest gardener. With an engaging, often humorous, style that nonetheless expresses her own strong views, she heartily encourages you to expand your horizons and get on to developing your own personal style of gardening. Each of the three "In Bloom" books offers a delightful collection of articulate and knowledgeable essays that offer year-round inspiration for gardeners of all abilities. For the non-gardener, the books offer a great read; you'll appreciate Ann's witty, highly personal prose. Because what she writes begins with her own experiences gardening here in the Northwest, readers can identify with many of her anecdotes— on places we know, nurseries we have visited, inside jokes we share as a regional community. Each book shares a familiar Lovejoy voice, yet each addresses gardening at a particular time. In The Garden in Bloom, she touches on timely topics of the late '90s, from "Tropicalismo for Temperate Gardens," to "Bellevue's Beautiful Borders," to "Bio-Cool Gardening Boosts Productivity." New cultivars are explored, and hot resources referenced in handsome sidebars.

This Rambling Affair: A Year in a Country Garden
Des Kennedy (Sasquatch Books, 2000, 256 pp.)

Des has a passionate following among British Columbia gardening enthusiasts, and now the rest of the Northwest is discovering his charming style. Join this gardener and humorist as he pays tribute to the glorious art of gardening. Des introduces the reader to his rambling 11 acres and drops gardening hints appropriate for both the novice and master gardener. In 52 essays (one for each week of the year), you'll laugh and learn about a variety of subjects, ranging from the virtues of growing garlic to the difficulties of avoiding the outside world (this one is called "Born to Hedge"). Funny, literate, and even useful!

The Beginner's Bookshelf

You'll generally find two main types of books that give new gardeners advice: those that are step-by-step skill builders that focus on the practical aspects of garden-making (often illustrated with easy-to-interpret line drawings), and those that interweave philosophy and down-to-earth advice (melding articulate text with inspirational photos). We think it is necessary to select some from each camp to add to your horticultural library shelf as you balance perspectives on garden-making with the hand and with the heart.

Most certainly, no self-respecting West Coast gardener's library would be complete without our recognized "Bible," Sunset's *Western Garden Book*, described below. And if we were given the responsibility to help build this new gardener's book collection, we would also include Seattle Tilth's *Maritime Northwest Garden Guide*. Here, we offer some other suggestions for rock solid basics.

200 Tips for Growing Flowers in the Pacific Northwest, 200 Tips for Growing Beautiful Roses, and 200 Tips for Growing Beautiful Perennials
Barbara Ashmun (Chicago Review Press, 1996, 1998, 1998 respectively.)

Barbara Ashmun has a series of books that are aimed particularly at the novice. These small-format, inexpensive little books make perfect gifts for budding gardeners. The solid tips, loosely organized around topics such as "Coping with the Weather," "Designing with Roses," and "Perennial Partners," are a useful blend of the author's personal opinions, recommendations, and (longtime) experience, combined with tips and suggestions, a few of which may seem self-evident to the old hand but which are nonetheless so valuable for a beginner. Each book includes a short but well-considered reading list and nursery sources.

Barbara has also capitalized on her years as a garden designer in her valuable book, *The Garden Design Primer* (1999, 2nd edition, 240 pp.). In this practical handbook she speaks authoritatively to gardeners of many stripes, whether you hanker for the naturalistic landscape and wish to make your garden meld into it, or you're a plant collector trying to figure out how to make some sense of how to organize lots of plant treasures that don't seem to have a common "theme." Barbara's style is to recommend favorite cultivar suggestions, and her mix of common plant names with botanical ones is something we think is essential for gardeners of all persuasions.

Easy Answers for Great Gardens
Marianne Binetti (Sasquatch Books, 2000, 212 pp.)

Marianne is a Northwest garden columnist, TV and radio personality, and a master in the art of identifying shortcuts and tips to make gardening easier, quicker, more enjoyable, and more rewarding. In this book, she compiles everything from the painfully obvious (except you didn't think of trying it) garden tips to far-out and wacky (but tested and verified) things you can try in your own landscape while addressing the recurring themes that face all of us. She loves to share "outlandish ideas" throughout the book, which is a well-designed reference with lots of clues to the topic on any given page (look for graphic markers that indicate facts about selecting, siting, care, and problems). There are 500 tips and techniques worth trying yourself.

Gardening from Scratch
Ann Lovejoy (Macmillan, 1998, 164 pp.)

Ann Lovejoy is one of the best-known (and by a long shot the most prolific) of Pacific Northwest garden writers. In this book, subtitled, "How to Turn Your Empty Lot into a Living Garden," beginning gardeners will discover many good ideas. While she speaks with the voice of authority, having successfully begun and developed many gardens by now, Ann has the gift of articulating dreamy, do-able solutions to distressing design problems, starting with the most disheartening of all, the compacted blank slate of earth left for most new home owners by ignorant construction crews.

Shortcuts for Accenting Your Garden

Marianne Binetti (Garden Way Publishing, 1993, 202 pp.) Order this book ($12) from the author at PO Box 872, Enumclaw, WA 98022.

With this collection of "Over 500 Easy and Inexpensive Tips" in hand, home owners and renters, urban dwellers in apartments and condominiums and those who live in suburban neighborhoods, and those with little time and scanty budgets for landscaping details will thank Marianne Binetti many times over (at least 500 times) for all the clever ideas she presents.

Storey's Gardening Skills Illustrated

Includes Pruning Made Easy / Secrets to Great Soil / Seed Sowing and Saving, by Elizabeth Stell (Storey Publishing, 1998).

This series from Storey's is a real standout. The well-illustrated, step-by-step guides, while aimed primarily at novices, cover the topics broadly, with tips for gardeners of all abilities. Of the three, the one we turn to most frequently is *Secrets of Great Soil*. From the standpoint of soil, many Northwest gardens are forced to grow on a foundation of heavy clay, lousy drainage, or dry shade. Author Elizabeth Stell does an admirable job of covering the topics of composting, mulching, testing, soil building, lawn tending, and dealing with all types of environmental concerns (shade, sun, dry, wet) and soil types (clay, sand, contaminated, thin, stony—the works!). Find out answers to questions like: "Soil polymers, are they worth the cost?" and "How to prevent compacted soils." The Storey booklist continues to expand, so refer to this reliable publisher and "country living resource" for a wide variety of garden titles.

Tips for Carefree Landscapes: Over 500 Sure-Fire Ways to Beautify Your Yard and Garden

Marianne Binetti (Garden Way Publishing, 1990, 168 pp.) Order this book ($12) from the author at PO Box 872, Enumclaw, WA 98022.

Many Puget Sound gardeners know Marianne as the person they turn to weekly for advice in her newspaper columns. Thousands more gardeners nationwide turn to her for advice and clever tips through this popular book. If you love having a satisfying garden, but find the tasks of creating and maintaining it are just not high on your list of favorite relaxing activities, this book's for you!

General Gardening (Skill & Confidence Builders)

The Organic Garden Book

Geoff Hamilton (Crown Publishers, 1994, 288 pp.)

This is an essential book for beginning gardeners who want technical advice (terrific photos and illustrations) and explanations of such things as soil amendments and nutrients. This manual explains how to grow naturally better-tasting fruits and vegetables and cultivate healthy plants in healthy soil (with excellent dialog on making that healthy soil). The late Geoff Hamilton was one of Britain's most respected gardeners. His untimely death left the country's gardeners in shock. Thank heavens his books carry on the legacy of his expert advice.

Passport to Gardening: A Sourcebook for the Twenty-first Century Gardener

Katherine LaLiberte and Ben Watson (Chelsea Green Publishing, 1997, 310 pp.), or look for this book at the website, www.gardeners.com

This book seems like a natural cross between a garden resource directory and the Whole Earth Catalog—you'll see lots of photos, illustrations, sidebars, charts, guest expert essays, soul-stirring quotes, and resources, all intermingled yet well organized and easy to use. The book is set up around six well-considered topics ("The Basics of Ecological Gardening," "Edibles," "Ornamentals," "Broader Gardening Horizons," "Gardening in Harmony with Nature," and "Gardening Beyond Your Own Backyard") that are further subdivided into 32 chapters. Each chapter becomes a little world to explore. For instance, the book starts with "Building Healthy Soil," and within that topic you find the basics of this important and often misunderstood subject supplemented with a guest essay from expert Grace Gershuny, several appropriate book reviews and (in boxes) excerpts from the best writing on soils, diagrams of soil elements, a test for identifying your soil type (and test lab sources), profiles of pertinent websites, informative sidebars on testing your soil and correcting soil pH, and a list of frequently asked questions. The whole wonderful book is like this. Gardener's Supply Company provided sponsorship for this publication, and many of their products are profiled within its pages.

Rodale's All-New Encyclopedia of Organic Gardening

Rodale Gardening (1992, 690 pp.)

This is an indispensable resource book for gardeners of all persuasions and all levels of expertise. Encyclopedic in format, this authoritative guide is very easy to use and read, includes many helpful illustrations, charts, and sidebars elaborating on each topic. What you'll find here is a book that covers all the basics—so, for instance, you'll find an informative entry on "Hellebores" that will give you a good general description, but won't go much beyond the basics in terms of providing the latest strains you're now able to buy. On the other hand, because the overall emphasis here is on vegetables, under "Tomatoes" you will find cultivar-specific advice.

Seattle Tilth's *Maritime Northwest Garden Guide*

Tilth Store, Good Shepherd Center, 4649 Sunnyside Avenue N, Room 1, Seattle, WA 98103 | **Phone:** (206) 633-0451 | **Email:** tilth@speakeasy.org | **Web:** www.seattletilth.org | **Orders:** By phone or email; $10 plus tax

Tilth has been a prime resource, educating the Seattle gardening community (and so by extension the whole maritime Northwest) in the techniques and benefits of organic gardening for the past 21 years. This 82-page guide, updated in 2000, is a detailed almanac for year-round organic gardening, with facts gleaned from the organization's experience in building and tending their wildly successful demonstration garden at the Good Shepherd Center in Seattle. In a deceptively simple way (airy layout, lots of handsome illustrations, charts, and lists), the authors have provided a remarkable handbook, well written and packed with pertinent details. Look here for a maritime Northwest climate zone map; how to extend the growing season; revised and updated vegetable, fruit, and herb variety recommendations; recipes for the soil mixes they use themselves when sowing seeds or transplanting seedlings; and advice on how to beat common plant diseases organically. It's all accurate, practical, and not overwhelming. One way to describe this guide: A godsend for the novice, read and respected by veterans as well.

Sunset's *Western Garden Book*

(Sunset Publishing Corporation, 2001, 7th edition, 768 pp.)

It's pretty certain that many readers of this *Directory* will already know this authoritative guide to Western gardening. For many of us, it is the definitive reference, the mainstay of a gardener's library. We include Sunset's *Western* here for obvious reasons. Information is conveyed through the liberal use of color photographs, carefully designed quick-reference charts, and their proprietary climate/zone maps, combined with discussions of contemporary issues now facing conscientious gardeners in the West, visual guides that help you identify common pest and disease problems (along with treatment suggestions), and a new and helpful resource directory. The newest edition now features color illustrations in the meaty plant section; while small, they are a huge improvement over the previous black-and-white line drawings.

Garden & Plant Problems

Field Guide to the Slug

David George Gordon (Sasquatch Books, 1994, 48 pp.)

Know thine enemy! The best defense is a good offense. Not a gardener in the Pacific Northwest is spared a relationship with this voracious gastropoda. We all have our favorite hunting regime (or if not, we are desperately looking for one that will work for us). Understanding the life cycle and particular habits of these marvels of adaptive behavior will help you formulate your approach. Did

you know slugs can slide along a razor blade's sharp edge unharmed? (So much for crushed eggshell edging around our vulnerable borders!) And do you know which slugs are native to this area and pose no threat to your garden plants but, on the contrary, are considered beneficial to the ecology of the forest? This little volume could be an excellent stocking gift for your favorite gardener (right size, right price).

Northwest Weeds: The Ugly and Beautiful Villains of Fields, Gardens and Roadsides

Ronald J. Taylor (Mountain Press, 1990, 177 pp.)

You may gravitate to this book in search of the names of the monsters who have invaded your garden uninvited, only to discover that many of the plants you treasure are also classed as "weeds"! Great photos add to the usefulness of this book, in a genre that often merits only nice line drawings.

Plants for Problem Places

Graham Rice (1988; in paperback 1995 from Timber Press, 184 pp.)

While you may think Graham Rice must have written this book specifically for you, every gardener will identify with at least some of the conditions this valuable and well-written book addresses. For some, he speaks of damp shade and waterlogged soils; for others, it is stony soil or a windy setting. Whether you're coping with a hot, dry site, a seaside garden, clay soil, or dry sandy shade, this blessed author has come to our aid with a sympathetic heart and real solutions. This is a down-to-earth, how-to (and can-do) primer with line illustrations and color photos to illustrate points made in the text. Though it is easy to feel overwhelmed, with Graham Rice at hand we needn't feel doomed when Mother Nature has dealt the awkward card of too much shade or not enough water.

Sunset's *Western Garden Problem Solver*

(Sunset, 1998, 320 pp.)

This is the invaluable companion to your indispensable Sunset's *Western Garden Book*. As always, Sunset provides the combination of excellent color photos and detailed text, offering easy-to-find help for the distressed gardener who has just come face to face with an ominous growth on a prized specimen tree or who suffers the heartbreaking loss of the best season's crop of plump, juicy strawberries. As the title suggests, this is a garden problem-solver, so not only does it address the full range of challenges you face in keeping all the elements of the garden healthy, it arms you with the most powerful tool of all—a sound understanding of how to work closely with nature to keep the ecosystem in balance, taking the approach of prevention. This book provides successful alternatives to the heavy-handed use of chemicals while also teaching us better skills that lead to healthy gardens.

WASHINGTON STATE UNIVERSITY COOPERATIVE EXTENSION PUBLICATIONS

View or order these and other reference guides at the WSU College of Agriculture and Home Economics Publications website: http://pubs.wsu.edu/scripts/PubOrders/webcat.asp.

WSU has produced a number of manuals to help gardeners in the Pacific Northwest identify and diagnose landscape-plant problems (cultural, pest, and disease), to treat the problem, and to do something about preventing those problems in the future. These books were originally destined for use by Master Gardeners and professionals helping home gardeners. They are now available for us to use in expanding our own skills in coping with the challenges of maintaining a healthy garden.

❖ *Landscape Plant Problems: A Pictorial Diagnostic Manual.* Ralph S. Byther (Washington State University Puyallup, 1996). This manual offers 500 color photographs covering shade trees, conifers, shrubs, fruit trees, and flowers afflicted with disease, insects, herbicide injury, and cultural or environmental problems. It's important to have a good hand lens to examine your specimen for tell-tale signals; this book then gives the steps in making a diagnosis and helps you make it.

❖ *The Pacific Northwest Plant Disease Control Handbook.* (Extension Services of WSU, Oregon State University, and the University of Idaho) Published each year with information current to December, and specifically geared to the Northwest, this book serves as a reference for control measures for the more important plant diseases found here. It's well organized, with supportive charts that provide control data, as well as a helpful glossary of plant pathology terms.

❖ *The Pacific Northwest Landscape IPM Manual.* Van Bobbitt and others (WSU Cooperative Extension, 1996). IPM is Integrated Pest Management, and this manual addresses the approach to landscape maintenance known by those initials. If you arm yourself with knowledge of your plants' cultural needs, gain a thorough understanding of pest organisms, learn to accurately diagnose plant problems, and then carefully consider pest-management options, you'll reduce pesticide misuse and environmental degradation.

❖ HortSense | **Web:** http://pep.wsu.edu/hortsense/. If the IPM topic interests you, then check out HortSense, a website designed to provide users with both cultural and chemical remedies for the most common yard and garden plant problems occurring in the Pacific Northwest.

Reference Books

Black Magic & Purple Passion

Karen Platt (Karen Platt Publishing, 2000, 128 pp.) If you can't find this locally, see the website: www.seedsearch.demon.co.uk.

We first discovered this book through Lorene Edwards at Fremont Gardens, a real seed and plant sleuth if there ever was one. Like Lorene, we're among those gardeners fascinated with "black" plants (the color really is a continuum that starts at dark red, moves through all hues of deep purple, and ends at black mondo grass). Thanks to Karen Platt, a prolific English writer and the only woman to have run a nursery specializing in black plants, we can learn about the exquisite choices (in foliage and flower) available to accent the garden. Plant portraits and cultural information give instant reference to dark plants in the conservatory or border. Platt is also the writer and publisher of "The Seed Search," "Plant Names A-Z," and "Growing from Seed," all of which are on the website.

Botanical Latin

William T. Stearn (Timber Press, 4th edition, 1996, 546 pp.)

As we stretch our limits as gardeners, seek out plants of specialists, order seeds from the massive lists of garden societies, and work harder at learning and remembering Latin names of the plants we fall in love with, the need for a really serious yet approachable text on these plant names becomes painfully obvious. Learn to fully appreciate the horticultural riches at your disposal with this great resource. For the historical background on the development of this system of naming plants alone, the book is of great value.

The Color Encyclopedia of Ornamental Grasses

Rick Darke (Timber Press, 1999, 325 pp.)

To satisfy our passion for ornamental grasses in the landscape, Timber Press has brought us two outstanding books on the topic that complement each other beautifully (see *Gardening with Grasses* in the "Garden Design" listing below). This one is the first authoritative text gardeners can now turn to in understanding how to grow and use these appealing plants. Mr. Darke covers the territory thoroughly and expertly so that your questions about fertilization, watering, cutting back, dividing, and siting will be clearly answered. He includes 500 color photos from his collection of 15,000 grasses, accumulated over the 20 years he has studied ornamental grasses the world over. But the heart of the book is an extensive illustrated encyclopedia of important ornamental grasses, sedges, rushes, restios, cattails, and selected bamboos. Thankfully, many of them are photographed in more than one season, an element of great importance in selecting and adding these plants to your garden.

The Explorer's Garden: Rare and Unusual Perennials

Dan Hinkley (Timber Press, 1999, 350 pp.)

Plant enthusiasts and fans of Dan Hinkley's mesmerizing enthusiasm for the plant kingdom have been drawn to this book, which has been wildly successful. The ultimate setting for this tale is Heronswood Nursery and Garden on the Kitsap Peninsula. The characters whose essences are explored and profiled here are hundreds of species, varieties, and cultivars from the 75 genera of herbaceous perennials Dan deems worthy of greater consideration by curious, adventuresome, awestruck, and thoughtful plant aficionados. The richly crafted text, characteristic of Hinkley's boundless energy and encyclopedic knowledge, is illustrated by 251 color photos, captured thanks to the magic eye of Lynne Harrison. In 28 chapters, we are introduced to the lesser-known relatives of familiar friends, from thalictrums to aralias, helonias to hardy geraniums, rheums, and the climbing aconites. The plot for each plant's story involves amazing tales of its origin that we glimpse through the tasty details of this avid plant explorer's ambitious trips to China, Japan, Korea, Nepal, Mexico, Chile, and the wild places of the American West. We are then given plump descriptions of the cultivated behavior of these botanical immigrants from the author's experience testing them in the Heronswood gardens. Steeped in detail, the book is strong on taxonomic relationships, cultural requirements, propagation methods, and hardiness recommendations. And it makes a choice companion for your dog-eared Heronswood nursery catalog.

Gardening in Vancouver
Judy Newton (Lone Pine Publishing, 1992, 176 pp.)

Judy, the education coordinator at University of British Columbia Botanical Gardens, offers her easy-to-follow advice to create the garden of one's dreams, drawn from one of Canada's best places to grow plants.

Taylor's Dictionary for Gardeners
Frances Tenenbaum (Houghton Mifflin, 1997, 351 pp.)

Compiled by one of this country's most respected horticultural editors (and a fine gardener), Frances Tenenbaum provides us with exactly the reference we all need to master the language of horticulture. With more than 2,000 entries and 286 illustrations, this is a useful reference tool you'll find yourself consulting often. If you've heard the term but are not quite sure what a "herbaceous perennial" is, or are confused by such words as "hybrid," "cultivar," "strain," "species," and "variety," then this is just the book for you! Our favorite entry is "iffy." Get the book and turn to page 160 for a good chuckle.

Time-Tested Plants: Thirty Years in a Four-Season Garden
Pamela J. Harper (Timber Press, 2000, 351 pp.)

Pamela Harper takes us on a walk through a lifetime of gardening. Season by season, in good conditions and bad, she describes the plants that did not live up to expectations, as well as those that exceeded every expectation. Above all, Pamela focuses her attention on the trees, shrubs, and perennials that have earned her trust and af-

fection for a decade or more, offering inspiration for new and veteran gardeners alike. The photography, the majority of which is from her own garden, adds an authentic presence to her text.

The Tropical Look
Robert Lee Riffle (Timber Press, 1998, 428 pp.)

Dedicated to Diane Laird, a local loco Tropicalismo kinda gal, this extensive encyclopedia of dramatic landscape plants will be the "Bible" for gardeners infected with a fancy for fantastical foliage, sublime fragrance, and otherworldly bloom. Although primarily aimed at USDA zones 8-10, even in the zone 7 Northwest there is much we can incorporate from this plant palette, whether as half-hardy, annual, or conservatory plants. Many examples of tropical-looking plants for year-round use are also described here. Visit Linda Cochran's garden on Bainbridge Island or shop Jungle Fever in Tacoma if you're in doubt or in need of inspiration. Bless Bob Riffle for all the information he has packed into this monumental effort—including how to pronounce botanical names, plant zone facts, meaty plant descriptions, cultural requirements, and propagation details. What's more, the book is accessible to a wide range of plant lovers. There are lots of excellent color photos and, one of my favorite features, many "Landscape Lists" of plants that grow in or are tolerant of various conditions, like bogs, near saltwater, in droughty conditions, and in shade.

The Well-Tended Perennial Garden
Tracy DiSabato-Aust (Timber Press, 1998, 269 pp.)

If you are at a loss about pruning, cutting back, deadheading, and maintaining perennials in your garden, this book will be a great inspiration. Tracy DiSabato-Aust has devoted years of study to creating showplace gardens that need minimal maintenance. Her advice helps us care for and salvage the potential of the vast number of perennials that make their home here with us. The book is filled with methods of pruning and shaping perennials and tips on producing more flowers, encouraging lush new growth, discouraging pests, staggering bloom times, and maintaining vigorous health of your garden favorites. You might find this book's greatest value in its encyclopedia section, where you can locate advice on when and how to prune and maintain perennials for improved appearance and better performance. For the Northwesterner, though, her experience as a Midwest-oriented, cold-winter gardener is not always appropriate.

Garden Design

The American Mixed Border
Ann Lovejoy (Macmillan, 1993, 240 pp.)

This Northwest author has drawn heavily on area gardens to illustrate points she makes regarding companion planting, border building, and border care and culture.

While addressing a national audience and seeking to articulate the elusive defining characteristics of an American garden style, she really speaks from the heart of a passionate practicing gardener and from her experience in transforming a rugged rural site on Bainbridge Island to the lusty mixed borders she gardened until a recent move to a new site where she has begun afresh. We are the climatic beneficiaries of her anecdotes.

Artists in Their Gardens

Valerie Easton and David Laskin, photographs by Allan Mandell (Sasquatch Books, 2000, 160 pp.)

Here's a private look into the landscapes that reflect the artists who work and live in them. Valerie and David teamed up to find ten creative, unconventional, sometimes outrageous gardens made by painters, glassblowers, collage artists, and sculptors. Their uncommon approaches provide fresh ideas and inspiration for all gardeners who are ready for a change from the ordinary. The writers have let the artists' voices come through in the stories they tell about making art in such beautiful settings.

Bold Visions for the Garden

Richard Hartlage (Fulcrum Publishing, 2001, 160 pp.)

Richard is well-known for his lectures on garden design and the use of fabulous plants in the landscape. He is also a very talented photographer and writer, and he's brought together his passion for "going bold" in his first book. *Bold Visions* is devoted to the practice of adventuresome garden design, but for Richard, great design is most inspiring when "thoughtful garden architecture and deft horticulture converge to create a unique place." There's a strong Northwest thread in his text and photos, although this well-traveled curator of the Elisabeth C. Miller Botanical Garden in Seattle also manages to share with us some of his favorite landscapes in the East and Southwest.

Color by Design

Nori and Sandra Pope (in the United States, SOMA Books, 1998, 160 pp.)

To the casual passer-by, this sumptuous tome might appeal as a lushly photographed collection of gorgeous plants, organized in a progression of intense and arresting colors. If you know of Hadspen House Gardens in Somerset, England, then you know that the Popes' work there has gained them a revered following for their skill as colorists and superb plantsmen. As accomplished artists, they use plants as their medium, sort of the Jacqueline du Pré and Daniel Barenboim of the botanical world. We are fortunate that they also have a masterly command of the English language and are able to articulate their understanding of this complex world of color theory and how it can be manipulated on an ever-changing garden canvas. This remarkable book cannot help but stretch your mental muscles and inspire you to at least dabble in this seductive horticultural art-form.

The Complete Shade Gardener

George Schenk (Houghton Mifflin Co., 1991, 278 pp.)

This is the classic work on this common and troublesome topic, and it offers a knowledgeable presentation from a wise plantsman and gardener intimately experienced with the Northwest who knows we have good reason to seek such advice. For so many of us who experience the agony of coping not only with shade but shade in less than ideal soil, the remedies are calmly and expertly addressed here. One situation so many of us struggle with is a narrow strip alongside the house or garage that begs for attention. This challenge too is addressed with stylish and practical specifics. Shade or not, George Schenk is an affable author, and always a good read.

Fragrance in Bloom

Ann Lovejoy (Sasquatch Books, 1996, 160 pp.)

As elusive as fragrance is, in description or use, the ever-observant Ann Lovejoy once again brings her readers insights into the very nature of scent, from the scientific aspects to the spiritual ones. What you'll find most endearing is Ann's creative treatment of the subject, beyond the excellent plant descriptions. She ventures into an alluring discussion of designing fragrant plant combinations for scent ("Creating Fragrance Effects"), a variation on the more familiar commentary on color in design. Lovely illustrations by Jean Emmons and a small but elegant portfolio of photos round out a beautifully crafted volume on this heady topic.

Further Along the Garden Path

Ann Lovejoy (Macmillan, 1995, 248 pp.)

Luscious is the word that comes to mind the moment you have delved into the rich prose and luminous photography of this passionate "coffee table" book by the prolific Ms. Lovejoy. However, behind the opulence lies the solid horticultural advice and erudite analysis her readers have come to expect, respect, and rely upon. For Northwesterners, the use of many familiar regional garden settings creates a special bond with this author. Ann wants to help beginning and intermediate gardeners walk further along the path on which she's already journeyed. She considers each month of the year, offering invaluable information, advice, and instruction geared to seasonal themes. The plethora of specific plant names will send you rushing to a your favorite plant-source reference to learn where you can purchase Ann's favorite botanical specimens.

Gardening with Grasses

Michael King and Piet Oudolf (Timber Press, 1998, 152 pp.)

With the increased popularity and availability of ornamental grasses, novice and expert gardeners alike are experimenting with their use in a number of garden and landscape situations. These two internationally recognized experts on the topic have used these plants to stunning effect in public and private gardens for many years. The great value of this book is in their wise and elegant plant combinations. These give not only inspiration through many color photos of breathtaking uses of these grasses, but also the benefit of their understanding of design principles and their experience with cultural demands that lead to successful plantings. (See also *The Color Encyclopedia of Ornamental Grasses* in the "Reference Books" listing.)

Journeys Through the Garden
Paddy Wales (Whitecap Books, 1998, 134 pp.)

A spirited and keen-eyed professional garden photographer, Paddy Wales has emerged as an equally inspired writer whose own skill and passion as a gardener are reflected in this sumptuous book. Paddy has photographed locations throughout the Pacific Northwest, and has kindly identified the gardens and garden owners who have provided the appealing horticultural vignettes that demonstrate the points she makes in her well-written, often humorous text. She focuses on topics near and dear to Northwest gardening hearts and intersperses each chapter with an eclectic and interesting sprinkling of sidebar comments, be they on the importance of a garden mentor, the etiquette of garden touring, hints on forcing branches into bloom, or tips on taking care of the most precious garden tool, the gardener her or himself. For many of us this is a new voice you'll want to meet.

Making Gardens Works of Art
Keeyla Meadows (Sasquatch Books, 2002, 128 pp.)

If you don't know the name Keeyla Meadows, once you've viewed her vibrant garden designs, you'll never forget her influence in the landscape. Meadows won the Best in Show at the 2001 San Francisco Flower and Garden Show for the color- and artifact-infused decorative garden that had crowds fighting to view, sketch, or photograph. In her first book, Meadows reveals how her training as a fine artist and sculptor greatly influence the garden, which she views as a blank canvas ready to be painted. She's photographed much of her own garden and those of her clients' to illustrate how to harmonize and contrast hues, organize shapes in space, and place garden features to transform an ordinary patch of ground into a magical oasis. The book includes tips that you can use in your own garden, including a recipe for "Keeyla's Secret Soil Mix."

Natural Landscapes
John Brookes (DK Publishing, 1998, 190 pp.)

Inspired by a series of fascinating garden case-histories, John Brookes explores ways to combine native vegetation and materials with exotic plants. He shows how to produce such effects in your own landscape while remaining true to your own locale. The book provides indispensable advice on how to work in harmony with nature at every stage of your garden's development, from basic design to selection of materials, plants, and garden art. There's a very nice overview on the history of landscaping, as well as John's own definitions for natural gardening.

Northwest Garden Style: Ideas, Designs and Methods for the Creative Gardener
Jan Kowalczewski Whitner, photographs by Linda Q. Younker (Sasquatch Books, 1996, 192 pp.)

For those who want a peek at the garden created by the late Stephanie Feeney and her husband Larry Feeney, turn to this book by Jan Whitner that profiles 22 Northwest gardens. The Feeney garden is featured in "Designing Gardens with Hardscapes," illustrating the many trellises and pathways Stephanie and Larry built as major organizing elements in their Bellingham garden. The book begins: "Gardening, like politics, is the art of the possible; in both fields the most successful practitioners are flexible problem solvers who are able to maintain an ultimate vision, even as they encounter difficulties along the way." How true, and how well this theme has been developed throughout, dealing with concerns for integrating our gardens into a natural habitat (and vice versa), attracting wildlife, waterwise planting or adding the element of a water feature, small-space gardens, gardening on a slope, and using roses in Northwest gardens. This is a meaty book, with over 100 colorful photographs, a number of site plans, numerous plant lists from the gardens, complementary sidebars that explore the topics, and handy checklists. (See "Videos on Pacific Northwest Themes" in this chapter for details on the companion video.)

Organic Garden Design School
Ann Lovejoy (Rodale Books, 2000, 280 pp.)

Ann enthusiastically introduces us to her many practical gardening and design themes from The Sequoia Center for the Healing Arts, her former school and current residence on Bainbridge Island, Washington. Her philosophy is the antithesis of formal, controlled landscape design. Ann likes to ask plants what they do best in the landscape, thinking about what the plants' own desired roles may be. Her method of garden design incorporates five essential "senses," including welcome, enclosure, entry, flow, and place. Each is well illustrated in the book. You'll enjoy her small essays and asides, shared in a personal voice. Organized as a primer of sorts, this is one useful reference book.

Plant Life: Growing a Garden in the Pacific Northwest
Valerie Easton, with photographs by Richard Hartlage (Sasquatch Books, 2002, 240 pp.)

Readers who've faithfully clipped (then misplaced) Valerie Easton's insightful weekly column, "Plant Life," from the *Seattle Times Pacific Northwest* magazine will be delighted to find more than 100 of her best essays compiled in this highly personal book. Organized around the 12 months, Easton's book covers such themes as her favorite plants (especially the unappreciated ones), garden design, gardening practices, and more. Some pieces are highly instructive, others more philosophical in nature. The photographs from Seattle author and popular lecturer Richard Hartlage are exquisitely framed and show his familiarity and friendship with the author's garden in North Seattle.

Shocking Beauty, Tom Hobbs' Innovative Garden Vision

Tom Hobbs (Raincoast Books, 1999, 160 pp.; through C. E. Tuttle in the United States)

Whenever Tom Hobbs is in town speaking on this his favorite topic, crowds of loyal fans flock to the meeting hall for an evening of horticultural hijinks and breathtaking beauty as only Mr. Hobbs can dish it out. His first book is as thought-provoking and luxuriantly illustrated as are his lectures. Using examples (and 200 photos) from innovative gardens worldwide, including, of course, his own riveting, warm-toned landscape in Vancouver, British Columbia, he lures us on to free up our thinking, to throw off conventional bonds of design precepts, and to look to nature (or alternatively nature through Tom Hobbs's quirky eyes) for color, texture, and detail in plant combinations that will invigorate a garden's visual appeal.

Sunset's Western Landscaping

(Sunset Publishing Corporation, 1997, 416 pp.)

Designed as a companion to the indispensable Sunset's *Western Garden Book,* this monumental volume covers 11 western states, from the plains to the Pacific. Northwest gardeners will find hundreds of design considerations directly aimed at solving concerns unique to this region, including climate, soil, and the topographical challenges we face. One of this book's greatest assets is the balance between hundreds of lush photos depicting beautiful gardens, brilliant garden ideas, and the hundreds of clearly illustrated, step-by-step, do-it-yourself building instructions on everything from popping in ponds, pouring pathways, and protecting against pests to capturing soil and avoiding erosion.

Urban Sanctuaries: Peaceful Havens for the City Gardener

Stephen Anderton (Timber Press, 2001, 144 pp.)

This is one of the newest design books to focus on the unique needs of smaller urban spaces. Stephen Anderton presents examples of innovative designs from both private and communal inner-city gardens all over the world, inviting us to create an inspiring outdoor haven even in very limited conditions. He offers ideas for low-maintenance minimalist gardens, family-friendly havens, gardens with soothing water features, roof terraces and balcony retreats, and indoor-outdoor garden rooms. Designs and practical tips are given to create each of these different styles.

Plant Monographs

The Cattleyas and Their Relatives

Carl Withner (Timber Press); Vol. I, The Cattleyas (1988, 147 pp.); Vol. II, The Laelias (1990, 160 pp.); Vol. III, Schomburgkia, Sophronitis, and Other South American Genera (1993, 180 pp.); Vol. IV, The Bahamian and Caribbean Species (1996, 198 pp.); Vol. V, Brassavola, Encyclia, and Other Genera of Mexico and Central America (1998, 242 pp.); and the final volume, Vol. VI, The South American Encyclia Species (2000, 222 pp.)

Carl Withner, now retired and ensconced in Bellingham, is a world-renowned expert on orchids, as is evidenced by his extensive research, study, and experience. He has spent more than a decade compiling these excellent reference books. This series on the cattleya alliance brings his readers an unparalleled range of information, in lengthy descriptions filled with both the precision of an academic and his personal enthusiasm for the subject. This series is useful as a botanical/horticultural reference. Note: Volume VI, the most recently published, includes taxonomic and nomenclature changes affecting species covered in earlier volumes, as well as additions and changes to the text of each of the five earlier books.

My Experience Growing Hardy Geraniums

Phoebe Noble (Trio Investments, PO Box 20154, Sidney, BC V8L 5C9 Canada; 1994, 36 pp.) $8.95 postage paid, no credit cards. Order directly from the publisher: (250) 656-2463, Fax (250) 655-3993.

This well-known British Columbia gardener provides solid information about favorite cultivars for the Northwest. Phoebe Noble is a great proponent of these "ultimate in easy care garden plants," especially ones good for a low-maintenance, handsome, weed-choking ground cover. The book is illustrated with leaf silhouettes of the varieties. The 1994 edition has been updated with new information about modern cultivars.

Peonies

Allan Rogers (Timber Press, 1995, 384 pp.)

You'll enjoy 143 color plates here, along with a detailed history of the peony and cultural information on these captivating plants. As co-founder of the highly respected Caprice Farm Nursery (now handed over to his daughter and son-in-law Cindi and Charlie Turnbow, who have relocated from the original location to Aumsville, Oregon), Allan has been in the international vanguard in propagating and popularizing peonies as they enjoy a renaissance of popularity. In Appendix III, landscape designer Linda Engstrom provides garden plans that feature peonies and suggests appropriate companion plants.

Scented Geraniums: Knowing, Growing, and Enjoying Scented Pelargoniums

Jim Becker and Faye Brawner (Interweave Press, 1996, 96 pp.)

Fragrance in the garden is not exactly anything new, yet it seems the selection of plants with fragrant foliage has increased dramatically in the past few years. Scented geraniums are an extra delight for their texture, for selections with variegated foliage, and for their color effects—not to mention the culinary uses to which the leaves and delicate little flowers can be put. Looking for a guide to the botany and culture of these fascinating plants? Who better to turn to than Jim Becker (who with his wife, Dotti, owns Goodwin Creek Gardens in Williams, Oregon), and co-author, Faye Brawner, a geranium breeder and owner of a mail-order geranium nursery in West Virginia.

The Tulip: The Story of a Flower That Has Made Men Mad
Anna Pavord (Bloomsbury, 1999, 439 pp.)

This definitive tome on the tulip and its history is a captivating read for students of both culture and horticulture. Anna has woven a compelling lineup of characters, protagonists, and drama of an era through this book as she describes the tulip mania that swept Europe, driving prices for certain bulbs to outrageous levels during the 17th century. While such a remarkably thorough history may seem somewhat intimidating, you'll find her story most captivating. The tulip devotee or garden historian will cherish this book, especially during the fall, winter, and early spring while waiting for the tulips to emerge.

Wild Plants of Greater Seattle
Arthur Lee Jacobson (2001, 496 pp.) To order call (206) 328-TREE or email: alj@consultant.com. $24.95 plus handling.

For those of you who equate Seattle's venerable horticultural historian Arthur Lee Jacobson with trees, here's something that might surprise you: before he was swept away by the idea of writing several tree books, he was first into wild plants—some would call them "weeds." "I just got sidetracked into trees," he says. Arthur Lee started work on this book 20 years ago and he's just published it. You'll find reliable accounts and finely detailed drawings of more than 500 trees, shrubs, weeds, vines, wildflowers, and grasses that grow not only in Seattle's gardens, but in alleys and vacant lots. Think campanulas, Welsh poppies, and that ubiquitous Centranthus ruber (red valerian), not to mention salal and countless "volunteer" ferns. Uniquely focused on our region, this book has an annotated checklist of 1,270 species and varieties. It will tell you not only where to find and how to identify species, but also offers appealing notes on the edibility, toxicity, or medicinal role of each plant.

Wisterias: A Comprehensive Guide
Peter Valder (Timber Press, 1995, 160 pp.)

Here's Australian horticulturist Peter Valder, with an infuriatingly seductive book on the wisteria genus, in which he describes over 60 kinds of this elegant vine that hails from China and Japan. It is the first authoritative book on the subject in any European language and thor-oughly covers everything from the history of the vine to its cultivation, pruning, propagation, diseases, and pests.

Woody Plants (Trees, Shrubs, Hedging)

Conifers, The Illustrated Encyclopedia
D. M. van Gelderen and J. R. P. van Hoey Smith (Timber Press, 1996, reprinted 1997; Vols. I and II, 706 pp.)

This set encompasses the most complete collection of photographs (2,347) of conifers ever assembled. Sixty-five genera are represented, covering familiar as well as less-well-known and new cultivars. Compiled by two of the world's most respected authorities, this book may be of greatest use to a professional. However, it can be of great benefit in identifying conifers in public and private gardens, and as you select conifers for your own landscape.

Dirr's Hardy Trees and Shrubs
Michael Dirr (Timber Press, 1997, 493 pp.)

This is an illustrated encyclopedia of woody plants, principally those for the cooler climates of zones 4-6, but allowing for the fact that most species will also grow in zones 6 and 7 too. The book portrays more than 500 species (with an additional 700 cultivars and varieties described), and is illustrated through 1,600 photographs from the author's collection. A renowned expert in the field, Michael Dirr has spent a quarter century in "pursuit of the perfect plant specimen." For most principle species featured in this book, several photos give the reader a view of the plant's habit, along with close-ups showing essential ornamental characteristics (bark, flower, or foliage). The text is brief but includes essential details as to habit, foliage characteristics, flower, fruit, bark, noteworthy seasonal characteristics, size, zones of adaptability, and native habitat. (A CD version offers 7,500+ high-resolution tree, shrub, and vine images along with the advantage of a searchable database.)

Japanese Maples
J. D. Vertrees and Peter Gregory, revised and expanded by Peter Gregory (Timber Press, 3rd edition, 2001, 332 pp.)

With its 312 color photographs, this is considered the definitive work and standard reference to these exquisite denizens of the Northwest landscape and garden. Keen amateurs and professionals alike consider the book a staple in the horticultural library. All cultivars of *Acer palmatum* and related *Acer* species are covered, with extensive information on identification, culture, and use in the garden or landscape. Since J. D. Vertrees's death in 1987, Peter Gregory, chairman of the International Maple Society, has added to this valuable resource. In this edition, there are 100 important new maple hybrids and selections, bringing to nearly 400 the total number of plants described.

North American Landscape Trees

Arthur Lee Jacobson (Ten Speed Press, 1996, 722 pp.). To order, call (800) 841-2665 or visit the Web at www.tenspeed.com.

In 1997 Arthur Lee was awarded the prestigious American Horticultural Society Book Award for this book. Pacific Northwesterners with any affinity for our wealth of landscape trees will know of Arthur Lee Jacobson, author of several books on the subject. His love and great knowledge of trees, married with his interest and scholastic achievements in history, have shaped this arboreal tour de force. With close to 5,000 different trees listed, this resource is more complete and exhaustive than any other single volume on the subject, covering 72 families, 198 genera, 950 species, 36 subspecies, 159 varietals, and 3,540 cultivars. Featuring cold-hardy North American landscape trees, the book also provides 288 color photographs and 514 detailed line illustrations of leaves, flowers, and branches. In his characteristic style, Arthur Lee comments on favorable and unfavorable characteristics, growth habits, remarkable specimens, historical tidbits, and taxonomic details and anomalies. After sitting with this massive tome a short while, you'll see that each description is a personally crafted biography, written with the same respect afforded our human ancestors.

Success with Rhododendrons and Azaleas

H. Edward Reiley (Timber Press, 1992, 314 pp.)

There is hardly a gardener or citizen of the Pacific Northwest who does not have an appreciation for our wealth of rhododendrons and azaleas. It's obvious, judging by the large number of organizations and societies, specialist nurseries, and gardens open to the public devoted to these ubiquitous stalwarts, that a large proportion of our population is actively involved in growing, promoting, and appreciating them. If you are looking for an excellent primer covering the successful selection, growing, care, and propagation of rhododendrons and azaleas, you could not ask for a more comprehensive guide. Well illustrated with photographs and useful line drawings, the book is also packed with very specific listings of the best species and hybrids to select for this area, deer-proof, disease- and pest-resistant selections, and show-quality favorites. The author's story is one of an amateur turned professional, and Mr. Reiley alerts his readers, with a knowing smile, that their casual interest may turn to passion and the garden may turn into a nursery!

Trees and Shrubs for Pacific Northwest Gardens

John and Carol Grant; 2nd edition revised by Marvin Black, Brian Mulligan, and Joseph and Jean Witt (Timber Press, 1990, 456 pp.)

First published in 1943, this popular classic now addresses those plants that have come into cultivation over the past 50 years. It is refreshing to note that the authors have chosen only those plants that are actually available through a nursery (though some may require a bit of a search), are hardy, and are not unreasonably difficult to grow. This book holds its place as a standard reference in the libraries of this region's serious gardeners.

Tree and Shrub Gardening for British Columbia; Tree and Shrub Gardening for Washington and Oregon

Alison Beck and Marianne Binetti (Lone Pine Publishing, 2001, 360 pp.)

Part of a series that also includes guides for annuals and perennials, these very easy-to-read reference books are great for anyone who wants a quick overview of the best plants from which to choose for the Northwest garden. The authors, including syndicated gardening columnist Marianne Binetti, give each specimen a thorough inspection, offering their advice on best features, and describing seasonal color, location and siting, soil and sunlight requirements, plus maintenance and pest/disease troubleshooting.

Trees of Greater Portland

Phyllis C. Reynolds and Elizabeth F. Dimon (Timber Press, 1993, 216 pp.)

The authors correctly note that a history of trees is also a history of the people who planted them, and this compendium of 132 greater Portland area trees provides the stroller, bicyclist, and casual driver with directions to find a rich heritage. This unique guide to the city's significant trees provides 196 color photographs; detailed descriptions of 22 native and 100+ introduced trees (blessedly including pronunciation); addresses of where to view the trees; nine tree tours with simple maps; a brief historical note about the area and tree identification; and a month-by-month listing of best tree-viewing times. This is the kind of book you might pick up casually but not be able to put down.

Trees of Seattle

Arthur Lee Jacobson (Sasquatch Books, 1989, 432 pp.)

While out of print, this tree-finder's guide to Seattle's 740 varieties of trees, which includes tips on choosing and caring for yard and garden trees, is still available at libraries (or if you're lucky, perhaps you can find it used). There is a special section with tree location maps for Washington Park Arboretum and the Carl S. English, Jr. Gardens at the Chittenden Locks in Ballard. It's an amazing resource, and Arthur Lee promises that it will be updated and re-released in the future. Check his website for details at www.arthurleej.com. Also by this author, see the self-published volume, *Trees of Green Lake, Seattle's Favorite Park* (1992), which can be ordered from the author by writing 2215 E Howe Street, Seattle, WA 98112.

The Trees of Vancouver

Gerald B. Straley (University of British Columbia Press, 1992, 232 pp.)

It is impossible to think of Vancouver without images of the vast diversity of mature trees that provide a rich tapestry throughout this lovely city. To learn more about them, see this book, written to appeal to experienced horticulturists and inquiring novices alike. In addition to creating the text, the late Dr. Straley, for many years a respected botanist and horticulturist at the University of British Columbia, has lent his talent as a botanical illustrator, with nicely crafted line drawings of representative leaves. Locator maps of the University of British Columbia campus and The Crescent provide users with a useful guide to designated species. If you have an appreciation of beautiful trees but wish your identification skills were better developed, learning within the context provided here is a most sensible approach.

The Year in Trees, Superb Woody Plants for Four-Season Gardens

Kim Tripp and J. C. Raulston (Timber Press, 1995, 274 pp.)

Well-written, thoughtfully considered, and tested through years of professional experience complimented by sheer skill, this book also provides a most enjoyable read and a guide to making the tough decisions that put wonderful woodies into your garden and/or landscape. You will find portraits of 150 woody plants, from the familiar to the obscure; for each, the authors comment on the plant's virtues, give cultural and propagation information, and mention creative gardening possibilities.

Pruning

Complete Guide to Landscape Design, Renovation and Maintenance

Cass Turnbull (F & W Publications, 1991, 192 pp.). PlantAmnesty, (206) 783-9813 or www.plantamnesty.org.

You can still find this essential guide to using your secateurs and more at libraries, even though it's out of print. What's more, if you join PlantAmnesty, the group founded by Cass Turnbull, as a "CyberMember," you can access her guide free online. We recommend it, as the annual dues are $50 and you'll receive the e-version of this book and so much more. An outspoken advocate for thoughtful and knowledgeable pruning practices and founder of PlantAmnesty, Cass calls upon her broad experience as a professional landscape gardener in this comprehensive guide, which is copiously and clearly illustrated, personable, professional, and approachable. It's very much like having Cass drop over for a friendly chat about your garden or landscape questions and problems. She offers sound advice on new landscapes, installation decisions, and a section on renovating the overgrown yard (now what could that be?).

The Pruning of Trees, Shrubs, and Conifers

George E. Brown (Timber Press, 1995, 354 pp.)

Timber Press is to be congratulated for returning to print this essential classic, which provides in-depth coverage of thousands of woody plant species and cultivars. Mr.

Brown offers us the benefit of his decades of experience as assistant curator at the Royal Botanic Gardens at Kew, in charge of the extensive arboretum. He is a keen arborist with a wealth of experience in observing and working with one of the world's most extensive collections of plants. The text is very approachable, even for the lay reader, and you'll appreciate that great care has been taken to convey advice down to the minutest details. This extends from the pruning advice that makes up the body of the book to an Appendix that carefully and thoroughly describes the care and use of tools and equipment. It's well illustrated too, and provided with a forward and updated nomenclature by John Bryan.

The Edible Garden (Fruits and Vegetables)

Creative Vegetable Gardening: Accenting Your Vegetables with Flowers

Joy Larkcom (Abbeville Press, 1997, 208 pp.; also released by Artabras, 1999, 204 pp.)

We have been introduced to and inspired by the European idea of a potager, or kitchen garden, wherein beautifully grown vegetables mix with the beauty of ornamental and edible flowers. Joy's book is beautifully illustrated with inspirational photos, but it is the sage advice of this experienced gardener that really makes this a superior text. A couple of the sticky wickets she explores are small-space gardens and how to cope with planting a winter garden in the midst of a productive summer season! She also addresses lots of design considerations here, packs in considerable garden maintenance advice, and then provides an extensive encyclopedia of the best vegetables and herbs (and edible flowers, covering their decorative qualities too), with advice on how to grow them successfully.

Gardening Under Cover

William Head, Amity Foundation (Sasquatch Books, 144 pp.)

Easy-to-follow instructions and great illustrations show the Northwest gardener how to construct coverings that will protect plants from the elements, bringing the satisfaction of year-round gardening. Also, you will find a helpful listing of varieties that flourish under cover and do well in this climate, sowing timetables, and advice on transplanting and watering.

Growing Vegetables West of the Cascades

Steve Solomon (Sasquatch Books, 5th edition, 2000, 340 pp.). By the same author: *Organic Gardening West of the Cascades* (Pacific Search Press, 1985, 172 pp.; out of print).

From the man who launched the Territorial Seed Company, based in Cottage Grove, Oregon, these books are scholarly without becoming too serious. Steve Solomon offers lots of tables and charts to back up his opinions, and shares invaluable insight on seed varieties for this area, plant physiology, insect control, and irrigation. As more of us turn to organic gardening, we're fortunate to have this author as our regional (but nationally recognized authority) on gardening organically.

Movable Harvests: Fruits, Vegetables, Berries: The Simplicity & Bounty of Container Gardens

Chuck and Barbara Crandall (Chapters Publishing, 1995, 128 pp.)

There are many books about container gardening, most of them of the ornamental and decorative ilk. But this one addresses the cultural peculiarities of growing edibles in containers. In particular, pest and disease problems are discussed, and an excellent selection of container-worthy plants is provided. This book should also appeal to urban gardeners with minimum planting spaces (like balconies), and those with limited mobility for whom gardening in raised containers makes the pleasure of gardening accessible.

The Northwest Herb Lovers' Handbook

Mary Preus (Sasquatch Books, 2000, 256 pp.)

Mary's background has combined innkeeping on Washington's Kitsap Peninsula with a passionate interest in culinary, medicinal, and ornamental herbs, and the combination has led her to craft this lyrical guide to herbs and how to use them. With handsome photography by the author (another of her many talents), this engaging book offers detailed instructions on how to grow 50 of the most popular herbs. You'll want to adopt an "herb lovers' lifestyle" for yourself after reading Mary's delicious recipes and using her tips on crafts, gifts, landscaping, aromatherapy, and more.

Winter Gardening in the Maritime Northwest

Binda Colebrook (Sasquatch Books, 1998, 164 pp.)

This widely recognized professional landscape consultant specializes in native habitat restoration and design, landscaping for wildlife, and environmental interpretation. However, when she began gardening in Washington in 1977 she specialized in edibles, emphasizing the potential for year-round vegetable gardens in the maritime Northwest. Her book has been a best-seller for over two decades, educating and encouraging multitudes of diehard gardeners on how to reap the benefits of their vegetable and herb plot through the challenging seasons of fall and winter. This new edition offers updated sources and resources, as well as new information on pests and diseases, food safety, and organic gardening techniques. The warm, conversational text is supplemented with illustrations, charts, and useful lists. You will be captivated by her enthusiasm and successes in cultivating myriad tantalizing, healthful edibles through the cool and drizzly winter months.

Pollination (Gardens, Bees, and Butterflies)

Butterfly Gardening: Creating Summer Magic in Your Garden

Xerces Society and The Smithsonian Institution, introduction by E. O. Wilson (1998, revised, updated 2nd edition, 208 pp.)

This is a rich and gloriously beautiful book on gardening to attract butterflies and other invertebrates for the ecological value their conservation brings to the Earth, for the biological diversity their presence in a garden fosters, and for the sheer delight of having them as companions as we work or relax in our gardens. This book groups together a number of individual essays that broadly and specifically cover the topic, from the pens of writers, photographers, scientists, amateur lepidopterists, and gardeners. They are each and every one a fascinating good read and the photography is utterly riveting in its detail and incredible color. This book will influence the selection of plants you make, encouraging you to include more varieties that attract these important pollinators and gentle creatures.

Humblebee Bumblebee: The Life Story of the Friendly Bumblebees and Their Use by the Backyard Gardener

Brian Griffin (Knox Cellars Publishing, 1997, 112 pp.). Order from Knox Cellars Publishing, 1607 Knox Avenue, Bellingham, WA 98225 | **Phone:** (425) 898-8802 | **Fax:** (425) 898-8070 | **Email:** lisa@knoxcellars.com | **Web:** www.knoxcellars.com

If you think you know all there is to know about bees, you're wrong. Pick up Brian Griffin's delightfully engaging and enormously enlightening little book on this creature that's every gardener's best friend. A great storyteller, Brian sparks an interest in natural history and instills a respect for the complex interrelationships among the plants, insects, humans, and even the seasons in the life of a healthy garden and the greater environment. There is just the right balance of science, history, and anecdotal information here. As a bonus, Brian has added detailed color illustrations and a field guide to North American Bumble Bees (the Bombus of America). After reading this popular and timely book, you'll never look at bumblebees the same way again, and you'll think of a raft of friends you'll want to pass the book along to as a gift.

The Orchard Mason Bee

Brian Griffin (Knox Cellars Publishing, 2nd edition, 2000, 70 pp.) (See ordering information under Humblebee Bumblebee above.)

What began a few years ago as a poorly pollinated espaliered "Belgian" fence made up of 40 varieties of apples and pears, and a subsequent Cooperative Extension Bee Bulletin, has become a burgeoning business and never-ending stream of educational encounters for Brian Griffin, as he introduces fascinated gardeners to their longtime neighbor and newly recognized friend, the Orchard Mason Bee. The charmingly written and illustrated little book covers "the life history, biology, propagation, and use of a truly benevolent and beneficial insect." This updated version is twice as large as the original, with more illustrations and information about bees and their propagation in tubes as well as blocks. This is a must if you want to raise and nurture these fantastic little pollinators in your own backyard. (It's also now available on cassette tapes, read by the author, and there's a video, too!)

Famous Gardens

Chapter 14, "Travel Opportunities," offers an excellent listing of titles to help guide you on your journeys beyond the Pacific Northwest. The books listed below refer to specific Northwest destinations.

The Bloedel Reserve: Gardens in the Forest

Lawrence Kreisman (The Arbor Fund, 112 pp.) The Bloedel Reserve, 7571 NE Dolphin Drive, Bainbridge Island, WA 98110-1097 | **Phone:** (206) 842-7631. $14.95 paperback.

This stunning book, with its 103 color photographs, was published to celebrate the public opening of one of the Northwest's most beautiful gardens, located on Bainbridge Island not far from Seattle. The book reflects on the historical context from which this important landscape emerged, describing how the efforts of architects, landscape architects, botanists, grounds crews, and the vision of the Bloedels came together to create this extraordinary property. (See also Chapter 13, "Gardens to Visit.")

Human Nature: The Japanese Garden of Portland, Oregon

Bruce Taylor Hamilton (Japanese Garden Society of Oregon, 1996, 150 pp.) $21.95 at the Japanese Garden Society Gift Store.

The Japanese Garden in Portland is a favorite of Northwest fans and tourists alike, no matter what the season or weather. This book addresses the history of the garden, but in addition serves as a very fine guide for anyone interested in deepening the experience of meandering through the five main gardens that make up this exquisite destination. One hundred fifty ravishing color photos set off Mr. Hamilton's engaging text. We recommend this book for anyone who plans a visit here, and for those who wish to take away with them a memorable keepsake.

Washington Park Arboretum Guidebook

Kimberly Mills (Arboretum Foundation, 1998, 49 pp.) $5 at the Graham Visitors Center Gift and Book Shop, Seattle | **Phone:** (206) 325-4510.

This dandy, handsomely illustrated, spiral-bound guidebook is an indispensable tool for understanding and exploring the Arboretum. From descriptions of the major collections and major points of interest to seasonal walking tours, there's something in this Guidebook for first-time visitors and frequent visitors alike. You'll delve into the rich history of the Arboretum, discover how the collections are cared for, and decipher the language of

plants. The book is endowed with a number of annotated maps, too.

The Woody Plant Collection in the Washington Park Arboretum

(Arboretum Foundation, 1994, 143 pp.) $9.95 at the Graham Visitors Center Gift and Book Shop, Seattle | **Phone:** (206) 325-4510

The WPA has one of the finest collections of woody plants in North America. The first revision of this title since 1977, this book backs up the Guidebook and brings up-to-date a more fully representative listing of the current collection, providing names and locations of nearly all the 4,300 plant types (10,000 plants) in the 200-acre Arboretum. A fold-out map makes the use of this valuable resource more convenient and enjoyable. Plants are listed in alphabetical order by scientific name, followed by common name, geographic range (or "garden origin"), and known location(s) in the Arboretum (by grid coordinates tied to the map). Once you've identified it, queries for additional information about a particular plant can be directed to Arboretum staff at the Graham Visitors Center. And remember—you may request propagation of something special from the Arboretum through the kind efforts and skill of volunteers at the Pat Calvert Greenhouse on the grounds.

Plant-Finding Sourcebooks

Andersen Horticultural Library's Source List of Plants and Seeds

University of Minnesota, Andersen Horticultural Library, Minnesota Landscape Arboretum, 3675 Arboretum Drive, PO Box 39, Chanhassen, MN 55317-0039 | **Phone:** (952) 443-1405 | **Email:** plantinfo@jaws.umn.edu | **Web:** plantinfo.mnu.edu | **Price:** $39.95, 5th edition

The Andersen Horticultural Library uses two formats for the dissemination of its plant-finding information. One is through a hefty book, which, in the current edition, lists more than 59,000 different plants and seeds (trees, shrubs, vines, perennials, annuals, bulbs, herbs, and vegetables) from 450 U.S. and Canadian mail-order sources. This book is a cousin in spirit to the British Plant Finder, though less ambitious. Due to various limitations, Andersen is on a three- to five-year update cycle, which means that if you want to find the very latest source for something, you might find the volume has only referenced the 1994 catalog (as they have for Heronswood Nursery in the current edition, for example). In this case, Heronswood now has an online version of its catalog. Nonetheless, the Andersen Plant Source guide is a phenomenal effort, and it's well cross-referenced by state and by common names (botanical names are also listed). You can also subscribe to the online version, where you will find more than 1,000 nursery sources in the database (each profiled with contact information and hot links where there is a website) and a listing of over 60,000 plants. You can search for specific plants by common or scientific name; for sources by nursery name, state, or whether they sell retail or wholesale; by nursery specialty; or any combination of these. In addition, the website indexes over 150 current journals in the "Plant Citation" database.

Cornucopia II: A Source Book of Edible Plants

Stephen Facciola (Kampong Publications, 1998, 713 pp.) 1870 Sunrise Drive, Vista, CA 92084 | **Phone:** (760) 726-0990 | **Price:** $40 plus $5 s&h to the U.S.

For edible plants and plant seeds, this is the authoritative reference book for locating sources, of which there are 1,350. Through them, approximately 3,000 species of food plants and 7,000 varieties—including fruits, vegetables, herbs, wild edibles, mushroom spawn, hard-to-find nut trees, baby vegetables, even sprouting seeds, salad mixes, and starter cultures—can be found. Mr. Facciola has compiled another astounding edition of his plant finder, with more user-friendly features and expanded categories.

GardenNet.com/GardenLiterature/index.htm

The Queen of Indexing, Sally Williams, lists "International Plant Finders and Guides to Nurseries" and "Selected Sources of U.S. Gardening Information" with valuable commentary and contact details. The website is periodically updated, revised, and expanded. Planning a trip to Australia? Sally has posted helpful garden-touring information from her current on-site travels. (See other cyber gardening information in Chapter 11, "Gardening on the Internet.")

Gardening by Mail: A Source Book

Barbara Barton (Houghton Mifflin Co., 1997, 5th edition)

GBM is similar to this *Resource Directory* in spirit, but with a scope that is national—and even international—focusing primarily on mail-order nursery and seed sources of every imaginable stripe. Well cross-referenced and passionately researched by Ms. Barton, it is a remarkably thorough reference guide. For many, this is an indispensable component of the gardening library and a fascinating companion so easy to nestle down with for hours at a time! Since 1997, Barton has updated the book annually (there is information on ordering the inexpensive updates in the back of her book). Even if this doesn't sound like a book you would pour over, do give it a perusal. We think you'll be pleasantly surprised and intrigued.

The Pacific Northwest Gardener's Book of Lists

Jan and Ray McNeilan (Taylor Publishing, 1997, 208 pp.)

Throughout the Northwest we know the McNeilan name for the many years these two have dedicated to helping identify and prescribe cures for the ills of every gardening problem imaginable through their work with the Oregon State University Cooperative Extension Master Gardener Program. It makes a lot of sense to harness the knowledge of both regional and international gardeners

with their own. Collected in this dandy volume are many, many (over 200) lists of specific plant recommendations to help in the often frustrating task of selecting just the right variety or cultivar for a challenging site. This means that if you are perplexed by soggy soils or deep shade, determined to find a thornless rose for the entry garden or to seek the honest truth about overly vigorous vines, this book has lots of wisdom to convey.

The Pacific Northwest Plant Locator

Susan Hill and Susan Harizny (Black-Eyed Susans Press, 2nd edition, 2000, 336 pp.) | **Phone:** (503) 245-8049 for orders | **Web:** www.blackeyedsusanspress.com | **Price:** $20 plus shipping

This amazing book holds a listing of 40,000 plants and the nurseries in Oregon, Washington, and Idaho that carry those plants. There is a common name/botanical name index, too, so if you don't know the botanical name of the plant you're looking for, you can look its garden name up first. Then you look up the plant, and you'll find the coded names for the nurseries that carry it. The 320-plus nurseries are listed in the back of this book. The two Susans have researched every plant name in order to be as correct as possible, and indicate in the listing when they couldn't verify the name or if it's questionable. New nomenclature information and details on ordering this extremely valuable reference are on the website.

Vegetables and Fruits: A Guide to Heirloom Varieties and Community-Based Stewardship, Volume III

Alternative Farming Systems Information Center, National Agricultural Library, Room 304, 10301 Baltimore Avenue, Beltsville, MD 20705-2351.

There are three volumes in this series. (See above under "Magazine Article Retrieval" for more details.) Volume III features an extensive listing of plant and seed sources (both in the United States and Canada) for heirloom vegetables and fruits. It's a publication that is similar to this *Directory*, although expanded to cover a broader range of climate beyond the Pacific Northwest.

Books in Series

Annuals for British Columbia, Perennials for British Columbia, Annuals for Washington and Oregon, and Perennials for Washington and Oregon

Alison Beck and Marianne Binetti (Lone Pine Publishing, 2001)

These handy guides in the Lone Pine Gardening series are packed with great photographs and user-friendly text, making them good "starter" books for any new gardener's library. The best thing about these books is that you can page through them and instantly know whether a plant is right for the environment, soil, conditions, and personality of your own garden.

21st Century Gardening Series

Brooklyn Botanic Garden, 1000 Washington Avenue, Brooklyn, NY 11225 | **Phone:** (718) 623-7200 | **Web:** http://www.bbg.org/

A couple of years ago, these dandy little guides began to appear on our horticultural bookshelves in places like Molbak's and Flora and Fauna Books (the specialty bookshop in Seattle's Pioneer Square). They are absolutely terrific! Well-written and illustrated, they are comprised of the collected essays of leading experts (the whole range, from academia to garden writers and practitioners), with many useful sidebars and helpful resources. One benefit of membership in the Brooklyn Botanical Garden is the opportunity to be a "Subscribing Member" at $35/year, and receive four of these books each year (a $30 value in itself). For more information, see "Horticultural Societies" in Chapter 2, "Clubs, Societies & Volunteer Opportunities.")

Of their many publications, here are two of our favorites.

✿ *The Natural Lawn & Alternatives.* "Life is too short to be spending purposeless moments mowing your lawn." Such declarations will catch and hold your attention through 100 pages of innovative ideas to consider as alternatives to great expanses of grassy lawn. In conjunction with these ideas, and knowing most of us will cling to areas of turf nonetheless, there are essays on better lawn-seed selection, care techniques, and renovation strategies.

✿ *Soils.* If you've been craving a book that would really get down to specifics in this complex topic, look no further. While soils are covered to some degree in most books on gardening, this liberally illustrated guide packs a lot of nitty-gritty information into its 100 pages, with detailed discussions of fertilizing, soil building, soil organisms, soil testing, watering techniques, lead in soils, and more such topics. While this may not be as sexy as a lush, full-color, coffee-table book on garden design, reading this interesting little volume can do so much more to create a happy relationship between you and your garden.

Bootstrap Guides

Lee Sturdivant, San Juan Naturals, PO Box 642, Friday Harbor, WA 98250 | **Phone orders:** (800) 770-9070 | **Fax:** (360) 378-2584 | **Email:** naturals@bootstraps.com | **Web:** www.bootstraps.com | **Ordering:** See prices below; add $2 postage for one book and $.50 for each additional book; WA residents add 7 percent sales tax.

These books are valuable and compelling for many reasons; they are packed with the real-life stories of dozens of small growers and businesses who are making a living from the flowers and herbs they grow; the books are creatively and extensively researched resource guides to everything from seed sources to supply houses and offer heaps of practical business advice; and there's plenty of cultural information on growing flowers and herbs to start you off right. Introduce yourself to these guides—they may inspire you to grow for sale what you love to grow for yourself and friends.

✿ *Flowers for Sale: Growing and Marketing Cut Flowers, Backyard to Small Acreage.* (1992, 225 pp., $14.95) Have you ever been interested in entering the cut-flower market? Then take this book home and read every word. You will have a greater understanding of the fascinating life led by the people who have chosen this line of work.

✿ *Herbs for Sale, Growing and Marketing Herbs, Herbal Products, & Herbal Know-How.* (1994, 250 pp., $14.95)

✿ *Profits from Your Backyard Herb Garden.* (2nd edition, 1995, 120 pp., $10.95)

✿ *Medicinal Herbs, In the Garden, Field, and Marketplace.* Lee Sturdivant and Tim Blakley (1999, 336 pp., $24.95) This book is difficult to put down once you begin to poke through it. You will find it both provocative and educational on many levels. It also provides a clearer perspective of the industry by detailing stories of the people who work within it. Every aspect of the medicinal herb business is explored (including U.S. regulations, organic growing regulations, herb safety, herb standardization, cultivation advice, machinery, tools and equipment used to process herbs, and tons of useful resources). A large encyclopedia lists appropriate herbs to grow, each with a plant description, followed by propagation, planting, cultivation, harvesting, processing/drying, and selling information. Even if you are not interested in starting such a business, this book helps in considering how herbs might enter your health-care decision-making, and gives you sources to turn to for advice and products.

Royal Horticultural Society Gardening Series

Bless Timber Press (web: www.timberpress.com) for making these volumes available to us as a series extracted from the massive "Mother" four-volume Royal Horticultural Society Dictionary, which, at around $800, exceeds the literary budgets of most recreational gardeners. These spin-off titles include all the material on a respective plant group found in the Dictionary, and more. Especially if you are propagating or are a serious collector or grower, this series—with its detailed cultural information, species descriptions, natural history, and excellent line drawings—will be a valued addition to your library.

✿ *Manual of Climbers and Wall Plants.* (Timber Press, 1995, 304 pp.) If you are an avid grower of vines, this is your book. You'll find this book especially useful if you grow out-of-the-ordinary plants like *dioscorea, sollya,* and *schizophragma* that are not well covered in the popular press on vines.

❀ Other manuals in this royal series include the *Manual of Bulbs* (446 pp.), *Manual of Orchids* (448 pp.), and the *Manual of Grasses* (219 pp.).

Cascadia Gardening Series

Sasquatch Books, 615 Second Avenue, Suite 260, Seattle, WA 98104 | **Phone:** (206) 467-4300 or (800) 775-0817 | **Fax:** (206) 467-4338 | **Email:** books@sasquatchbooks.com | **Web:** www.sasquatchbooks.com

❀ *Growing Herbs.* Mary Preus (1995, 104 pp.) For years Mary Preus operated Silver Bay Herb Farm on Washington's Kitsap Peninsula. She has vast experience in selecting the best herbs to grow in this region. Along with profiles of 24 first-rate herbs to grow here, you will find lots of tried-and-true advice on organic approaches to gardening, from mixing your own manure-tea fertilizers to organic pest and disease management. There are excellent herb garden combination suggestions, lists of herbs for freezing or drying, container gardening ideas, and resources for putting it all together.

❀ *North Coast Roses.* Rhonda Massingham Hart (1993, 96 pp.) Written specifically for gardening conditions in the Northwest, this handy little book provides newcomers and those unfamiliar with roses an excellent base to begin from. There's also good advice that will help you select the best performers in this climate.

❀ *Water-Wise Vegetables.* Steve Solomon (1993, 96 pp.) Whether you come to this book concerned by a tenuous water supply (drought years in the Pacific Northwest or a dwindling or expensive supply) or a tedious irrigation regime, you will be fascinated by the work that led Steve Solomon to develop what he calls "dry-gardening." Several years of astute research in his own subsistence-inspired rural Oregon vegetable garden have provided the basis for his theories, and the results are shared in his book. Be prepared to find some controversial notions, as he decries the use of conventional mulches and favors setting plants farther apart to obtain highest yields. The seed selection suggestions are particularly helpful.

❀ *Winter Ornamentals.* Dan Hinkley (1993, 96 pp.) Dan Hinkley is widely known in serious gardening circles for his horticultural dexterity. Here, the literary gardener will also appreciate Hinkley's gift for prose, as his infectious enthusiasm for his subject captures your own imagination. The Northwest is particularly blessed with conditions that allow garden elements to be enjoyed from within as one looks out on a wintry scene, but it also a benefits from a climate that allows forays through the garden for a peek at the stalwarts that are at their best during this season. Today there are a number of winter gardens open to the public, and more area nurseries (such as Hinkley's Heronswood) now feature winter beauties. Tuck this handy little book, a notebook and pen, and a thermos of hot-spiced cider in your tote, then sally forth in search of ideas gleaned from shared resources. (We think you too will enjoy the Foreword by Rosemary Verey, who expresses genuine delight in her wintertime visits to the Pacific Northwest and the gardens and gardeners she has spent time with here.)

❀ *Seasonal Bulbs.* Ann Lovejoy (1995, 96 pp.) In this book, Ann Lovejoy takes you through four seasons of blossoms, from the first winter snowdrops to the final autumn crocus. You'll discover the pleasure of off-season bloomers, expand your plant palette with easy-to-please exotics, grow glorious blooms in borders or containers, and combine blossoms with companion plantings for spectacular displays all year long.

Patrick Taylor Gardening Guides

Timber Press, Portland, OR | **Web:** www.timberpress.com

In his inimitable fashion, Patrick Taylor has compiled several indispensable plant guides, but apart from his expertise, it is his prose that makes this English gardener endearing. His command of expression allows him to gracefully capture the essence of things.

❀ *Gardening with Bulbs: A Practical and Inspirational Guide* (1996, 256 pp.) This book covers a broad range of bulbous plants (including true bulbs, corms, rhizomes, and tubers) in all seasons and for a broad spectrum of growing situations. It's written in a narrative style, interlaced with the opinions of a knowledgeable plantsman, yet also has a nice balance of cultural information—to give us a clue about whether this is the uvularia of our dreams, or a eucomis destined for that glorious pot on the pedestal. You could say this range of plants is painfully glorious, as bulbs tends to be quite an investment. But now that they are more readily available than ever before, it is essential to have a trusty reference to guide our decision-making. As always, the photography sparkles.

❀ *Gardening with Roses: A Practical and Inspirational Guide* (1995, 256 pp.) In this hefty guide, Mr. Taylor has taken on the endearing rose—easy to love but not always easy to grow. His 200 color plates are of exceptional quality, often featuring a close-up view of a rose or cluster of roses and the foliage (though alas not the overall shape or form, which he covers in prose). The text provides a straightforward introduction to the many types of roses (generally so confusing), and then proceeds with an extensive directory of specific roses in each category. If we have a criticism it would be that he tends to romanticize a rose without fully divulging weak points or annoying characteristics. But for pure inspiration and much practical advice, this is a handy, handsome book.

Sunset Books

We could easily take each and every one of the Sunset Garden Book Series and write it up, but just don't have the space. Instead, we have singled out some of our favorites. For the full catalog of Sunset titles, see www.sunset.com/books/books.html.

❈ *Trellises and Arbors and Vines* and *Ground Covers* are two titles released in 1999. All the plants are well described, even unto the warnings about rambunctious growth habits. The Trellis and Arbor book covers its topic well, from inspirational ideas to plant selection to the nuts and bolts of the building skills you'll need. It is also well illustrated.

❈ Sunset has also given a nod to the burgeoning passion for "bringing the garden indoors" and turning gardens into outdoor living spaces. *Ideas for Great Garden Décor* (2000) illustrates artful ways to ornament the garden with decorative accessories. *Garden Style Decorating* (2001) shows how to create a peaceful interior décor that can bring a sense of being in the garden into any room in the home.

❈ Also published by Sunset Books: *Annuals and Perennials; Attracting Birds; Azaleas, Rhododendrons & Camellias; Basic Gardening Illustrated; Bonsai; Bulbs; Complete Patio Book; Container Gardening; Garden Pools, Fountains & Waterfalls; Greenhouse Gardening; Landscaping for Small Spaces; Lawns; Orchids; Perennials; Pruning Handbook; Roses; Trees & Shrubs;* and *Vegetable Gardening.*

Audio Books

The Writer in the Garden / The Writer in the Garden II

Produced by Jane Garmey (HighBridge Company, 1000 Westgate Drive, St. Paul, MN 55114 | **Phone:** (800) 755-8532 | **Web:** www.highbridgeaudio.com | **Ordering:** WIG (1996), and WIG II (1998) each run about 3 hours on 2 cassettes, and cost $17.95 plus shipping.

In these sensitively produced audio books, you'll feel the inner voice of each of the writers beautifully evoked, providing new dimensions of appreciation for the words and work of such literary greats as Vita Sackville-West, Henry Mitchell, Louise Beebe Wilder, Ken Druse, Russell Paige, Mary Keene, Colette, Beverley Nichols, Gertrude Jekyll . . . and the list goes on and on. Your time in the car will fly gloriously by, and you'll have the added benefit of meeting garden writers whose work has not yet graced your shelves or lap!

Computers in the Garden

The Gardener's Computer Companion

Bob Boufford (No Starch Press, 1998, 295 pp.)

Bob's book is an easy-to-use, comprehensive source, covering the basics for anyone new to computers and intimidated by the lingo and seeming complexity of the whole cyber world. One-third of the book is strictly devoted to making sense of computers for the novice, and also looks at the rather complex area of programming, hardly directed to that same audience. However, this book provides a solid base for anyone who wants to explore all the possible (and viable) ways in which the computer can be a useful tool, adding a new dimension to enjoying the act of being a gardener. The book shows gardeners how to plan and design a garden using computer software and ways to choose and research plants using CD-ROM reference databases and online resources. The enclosed CD gathers much material that's otherwise free on the Internet, but does bring you the convenience of someone else's effort in accomplishing the hunting and gathering. The software offers garden simulation, space for journal entries, and more.

"Gardens of the Pacific Northwest," Computer Screen Saver

Purchase online from www.impulsegifts.com; $14.95 plus shipping.

This spellbinding, high-resolution photo and screen saver features our very own Northwest gardens, and will walk you through a desktop garden tour. With images by Paddy Wales, a well-known garden photographer, this beautiful computer accessory invites you to bask among radiant rudbeckia, be transported to the dazzling Laburnum Walk at VanDusen Botanical Garden, meander along a beckoning path at the Northwest Perennial Alliance's Bellevue Borders, gaze at the glorious fall color of maples in the Washington Park Arboretum, and sit transfixed by close-up photos of a magenta-flecked pink hellebore and a field of golden yellow daffodils.

Videos on Pacific Northwest Themes

Videos offer a convenient way to communicate the nuts and bolts about a plant specialty or a gardening technique. They can also be a means of sharing your visit to a special place with others, and they make a fine gift to someone who will be visiting or moving here. They also provide a means of recalling a special place you've enjoyed from the comfort of your cozy armchair in any season, or can help you prepare for a special trip.

Bloedel Reserve

7571 NE Dolphin Drive, Bainbridge Island, WA 98110-1097 | **Phone:** (206) 842-7631 | **Ordering:** $10

This 14-minute video (romantic photography set to music, without narration) features the large former estate with its woodlands, meadows, and a series of lovely formal gardens, along with lots of shots of their famous swans.

Lakewold, Where the Blue Poppy Grows

12317 Gravelly Lake Drive, Lakewood, WA 98499 | **Phone:** (888) 858-4106 | **Web:** www.lakewold.org | **Ordering:** $25

If we could offer you one heartfelt piece of advice about visiting the estate gardens at Lakewold (just south of Tacoma) besides urging you to go often, it would be to view this video beforehand (or upon arrival, in their lovely sunroom). That's because this video captures the essence of the place so skillfully. It will give you a deeper appreciation not only for the significance of the garden itself, but also of the historical context of Northwest estate gardens, and the eminent professionals like Thomas Church who worked with the Wagners over the years, and the role Lakewold is playing today in growing and conserving endangered species from around the world.

Northwest Garden Style: A Regional Tour of Private Gardens

Produced by PBS KCTS/9 Public Television and Puddle Duck Productions, $19.95. Available through KCTS.

Created by Jan Kowalczewski Whitner, this 80-minute video invites you to visit 20 private gardens in the Northwest, from the Willamette Valley of Oregon through Western Washington to British Columbia. Each of the gardens represents the personal style of the garden-maker(s), who chat with host Maria LeRose as they meander through their gardens, sharing bits of gardening philosophy or reflecting on favorite cultural and design tips. You can get a glimpse into the lives of these amazing gardeners, including the late Stephanie Feeney and her husband Larry Feeney, whose garden on the shores of Lake Whatcom is one of those featured. This is an entertaining and educational garden tour, to be enjoyed from your cozy couch! See also the companion book, *Northwest Garden Style*, described under "Garden Design" in this chapter, also written by Whitner, and with garden photographs by Linda Q. Younker.

Six Solutions to the Overgrown Yard, and Plant It Right

Plant Amnesty, PO Box 15377, Seattle, WA 98115-0377. Two separate videos on one 120-minute cassette; $20 plus shipping.

The indefatigable Cass Turnbull, originator of Plant-Amnesty and queen of Arboreal Activism, provides stunning examples of how not to do it—horror after sad horror—along with experienced advice on ways to avoid these ugly and harmful mistakes. Sale of these two videos brings greatly needed funds to help this nonprofit organization (featured elsewhere in this *Directory*) keep doing its good work in teaching us all to be more educated in our pruning decisions.

BOOKSTORES

ARBORETUM FOUNDATION BOOK AND GIFT SHOP

Graham Visitors Center, 2300 Arboretum Drive E, Seattle, WA 98112-2300 | **Phone:** (206) 543-8801 | **Open:** Daily, year-round, 10 a.m.–4 p.m.

The selection here has been very well considered. Look for gardening, nature, outdoors (especially the Pacific Northwest), crafts, birds, wildflowers, mushrooms, and the like. The children's section is renowned locally for books and children's games, activities with a nature or botanical theme, and kits. Members receive a 10 percent discount.

FLORA AND FAUNA BOOKS

121 First Avenue, Seattle, WA 98104 | **Phone:** (206) 623-4727 | **Fax:** (206) 623-2001 | **Open:** Monday–Saturday, 10 a.m.–6 p.m.

In the Northwest there is no greater selection than that found in this charmingly packed shop off Pioneer Square. If you haven't been, do go! Plan time to peruse their many fine collections (down a short flight of steps). They publish a book list and have on hand an extensive array of both rare and out-of-print, as well as new books hot off the press on gardening and related subjects (a very fine selection of natural history subjects, for instance). This is an excellent source for hard-to-find horticultural books and titles imported from Great Britain, many personally selected by proprietor David Hutchinson. They appear at some of the large Flower and Garden Shows and plant sales with a booth exhibiting their botanical bounty nicely set up for serious browsing. Come also for their selection of audio cassettes and CDs of bird song and some botanical and historical prints.

FORTNER BOOKS

9631 Summerhill Lane NE, Bainbridge Island WA 98110 | **Phone:** (206) 842-6577 | **Fax:** (206) 842-0683 | **Email:** books@fortnerbooks.com | **Web:** www.fortnerbooks.com | **Open:** By appointment (and on the Web, database updated daily)

Robert and Nancy Fortner house their cozy shop adjacent to their home. "The concept of a used bookstore 'at home' is not one that is common around here, but they are all over New England. It is nothing to travel down a deserted country road and find someone's book barn at the end of it. We have loved the concept since the first one we saw," says Nancy. We guarantee this shop, which extends into the attic above, is as charming and inviting as their former place in Winslow. It is toasty on cool days, heated with a gas stove, and surrounded by gardens. Their literary specialty is used and out-of-print books in all fields, with a very fine gardening section. They have a special talent for tracking down first editions, elusive and obscure titles. They also have a good eye for current gardening books, intermingling the old and the new. On their website, you are able to search the database by author, title, keyword, or by "catalogue," such as gardening, photography, etc.

THE GARDEN SHOP

2525 S. 336th Street, Federal Way, WA 98003-9996 | **Phone:** (253) 661-9377 | **Open:** Year-round March–May, 10 a.m.–4 p.m., closed Thursdays; June–February, 11 a.m.–4 p.m., closed Thursdays and Fridays

This is the gift shop of the Rhododendron Species Botanical Garden, at the entrance to the Garden. There is an excellent horticultural book selection here, with a marvelous selection on rhododendrons, as you would expect!

LAKEWOLD GARDENS SHOP

12317 Gravelly Lake Drive SW, PO Box 98092, Lakewood, WA 98498 | **Phone:** (888) 858-4106 (the Gardens Shop is located just inside the entrance in the Carriage House) | **Email:** info@lakewold.org | **Web:** www.lakewold.org | **Open:** April–September, Thursday–Monday, 10 a.m.–4 p.m., except Friday, 12 p.m. –8 p.m.; October–March, Friday–Sunday, 10 a.m.–3 p.m.

There is an obvious bookworm on the premises, with a penchant for excellent gardening related books, audiotapes, and magazines. Now Vickie Haushild has expanded her selection to include novels and mysteries with horticultural plots and has worked like a demon seeking out videos of gardens and garden touring across the United States and abroad. Anyone en route to South Africa? Australia? Great Britain?

THE NEWSTAND

111 E Magnolia, Bellingham, WA 98225 | **Phone:** (360) 676-7772 | **Open:** Daily 7 a.m.–7 p.m.

This is a terrific source of gardening periodicals from all over the world, including Australia, Great Britain, and France. For travelers, this newsstand is the best in the Puget Sound.

POWELL'S BOOKS

1005 W Burnside, Portland, OR 97209 | **Phone:** (800) 878-7323 or (503) 228-4651, TDD (206) 226-2475 | **Fax:** 228-4631 | **Web:** www.powells.com | **Open:** Everyday 9a.m.–11p.m.

If you are in the Portland area, you'll not want to miss an opportunity to browse the extensive selection of gardening and related books, with the gardening section located in the Ann Hughes Coffee Room at the corner of Burnside and 10th. Their total collection of over a million new and used volumes (plus they'll look for rare and out-of-print books for you) takes up not only a huge city block (on several floors in a literary labyrinth), but with additional outposts as well—including Powell's Books for Cooks and Gardeners at 3747 SE Hawthorne, Portland, OR 97214; phone: (800) 354-5957 or (503) 235-3802; fax: 230-7112. Dedicated solely to books on gardening and cooking! (Open Monday–Saturday, 9 a.m.–9 p.m.; Sunday, 9 a.m.–8p.m.; book-buying hours: daily 10a.m.–5:30p.m.)

R.R. HENDERSON, BOOKSELLER

116 Grand Avenue, Bellingham, WA 98225 | **Phone:** (360) 734-6855 | **Open:** Wednesday–Saturday 9 a.m. 6 p.m., Sunday 11 a.m.–6 p.m., closed Mondays and Tuesdays

For locals and visitors alike who thrive on "great finds," this shop offers a substantive, beautifully exhibited, and well organized collection including a very noteworthy gardening book section. You may wish to cull through your library, as Henderson's will reward you fairly with cash or credit, as you desire.

THIRD PLACE BOOKS

Lake Forest Park Towne Centre, 17171 Bothell Way NE, Lake Forest Park, WA 98155 | **Phone:** (206) 366-3333 | **Fax:** (206) 366-3338 | **Open:** Monday–Thursday, 8 a.m.–10 p.m.; Friday–Saturday, 8 a.m.–11 p.m.; Sunday 8 a.m.–8 p.m.

Located in a small mall that feels like a bustling town center (the local library and a ballet school reside here, too). Third Place Books could not have come up with a better concept. First, the name refers to the idea that everyone has three essential places to be: home, work, and that "third place." The bookstore itself occupies a very large space that adjoins a food court (including the famous Honey Bear Bakery). Comfortable seating areas are interspersed throughout and there is a large and active performance stage for music, speakers, book readings, and such. The books, you ask? This is the part where your heart will sing. New and used books are intermingled, with a very nice selection of gardening books and a commitment to provide patrons with presentations from local and visiting garden writers. Cull your home library, bring them in for cash or credit, and then nestle in to what will no doubt become your "third place."

THE UNIVERSITY (OF WASHINGTON) BOOKSTORE

4326 University Way NE, Seattle, WA 98105 | **Phone:** (206) 634-3400 or (800) 335-READ | **Email:** bookstore@u.washington.edu | **Web:** www.ubookstore.com | **Open:** Monday–Friday, 9 a.m.–9 p.m.; Saturday, 9 a.m.–6 p.m.; Sunday, 12 p.m.–5 p.m.

This well-loved bookstore is dedicated to carrying a large selection of horticultural books. They are especially supportive of authors who write for gardeners in this region, mostly because a number of the staff garden themselves. Also watch out for opportunities to meet authors and hear them speak on their books. The gardening section is located on the mezzanine level of the main (University) store. They offer free shipping, free gift-wrapping and validation for their parking lot conveniently located behind the store (whether you make a purchase or not). Also visit their wonderful store (a terrific gardening book section) at 990 102nd Avenue NE, Bellevue, WA 98004; phone (425) 462-4500; free parking beneath store (half block north of Bellevue Square).

VILLAGE BOOKS

1210 11th Street, Bellingham, WA 98225 | **Phone:** (360) 671-2626 or (800) 392-BOOK | **Fax:** (360) 734-2573 | **Email:** books@villagebooks.com | **Web:** www.villagebooks.com | **Open:** Monday–Saturday, 9 a.m.–10 p.m.; Sunday, 10 a.m.–8 p.m.; in the historic Fairhaven District

Not only one of our favorite places to wile away the hours, but a destination many out-of-towners call "home" in Bellingham. The atmosphere is welcoming and there is an in-house cafe for a great Mugga Mocha Moo after you've found that great little book on Gertrude Jekyll you've looked for everywhere! They have quite an extensive gardening book selection and carry most of the periodicals concerned with the topic. Drop in also to check out the Bargain Book Basement with an excellent selection of discounted and used books. They can also help locate hard-to-find books.

Books by Mail and/or Internet

Amazon.com

www.amazon.com

Does anyone (cyber shopper or not) not know about this company? You can find almost any new gardening book through this site. Your only proviso is to consider the shipping charge when you weigh an order online compared to a local book source. If your order is a large one then the convenience may be a deciding factor.

Carol Barnett Books

3562 NE Liberty Street, Portland, OR 97211-7248 | **Phone:** (503) 282-7036 | **Email:** cbarnettbooks@webtv.net.

Gardening books by mail, request a free catalog, issued 3 to 4 times per year covering the topics of garden history, design and practice, and plant sciences. Carol has a particular interest in "those 'eminent' Victorian garden writers, trying to make their work available in its original form or in modern reprints." She also offers many modern authors' work.

Fortner Books

www.fortnerbooks.com

If you cannot visit the Fortners' used bookstore on Bainbridge Island (housed adjacent to their home; see "Bookstores," above), then try their searchable database, which is updated daily.

The Garden Book Club

3000 Cindel Drive, Delran, NJ 08370 | **Web:** http://gbc.booksonline.com/gbc/

If you haven't become a member of the Garden Book Club yet, just let that fact slip at a gathering of local gardeners and you will enjoy an immediate rise in popularity. For heaven's sake, don't join on your own when you can make a friend for life by having a present member sign you up. Not only do you get your bonus books at an earthshaking discount, but the lucky duck who signs you up gets bonus books, too!

Quest Rare Books

774 Santa Ynez, Stanford, CA 94305 | **Phone:** (650) 324-3119 | **Email:** questbks@batnet.com | **Open:** By appointment

Gretl Meier specializes in out-of-print and antiquarian garden/landscape books. She welcomes visitors since her catalog/lists offer only a small part of the collection. $5 for annual catalog.

Raymond M. Sutton, Jr. Books

430 Main Street, Williamsburg, KY 40769 | **Phone:** (606) 549-3464 | **Fax:** (606) 549-3469 | **Email:** suttonbks@2geton.net | **Web:** www.suttonbooks.com; | **Open:** Monday–Friday, 9 a.m.–5 p.m.; weekends by appointment or chance

This company offers an extensive selection: rare, used, and new on botany, floras, cryptograms, trees and shrubs, gardening, landscaping and garden history, herbals, birds, mammals, fishes, reptiles and amphibians, insects, mollusca, marine and freshwater biology, geology, palaeontology, travel, bibliography and color plate book, and original art.

Sasquatch Books

615 Second Avenue, Ste 260, Seattle, WA 98104 | **Phone:** (800) 775-0817 | **Fax:** (206) 467-4301 | **Web:** www.sasquatchbooks.com

This press is a favorite regional publisher, with a specialty in gardening books. Sasquatch has been influential in bringing new writers and new titles to the Northwest gardening enthusiast, covering topics such as garden art, design, and practical tips. Indeed, it's thanks to Sasquatch that *The Northwest Gardeners' Resource Directory*, 9th Edition, the very book you hold in your hand, has been published. You can order direct at their website.

Suite 101

www.suite101.com/userfiles/79/books.htm.

Website for book sources. This site, as it offers an excellent launch pad, links to book sources, even some abroad.

Timber Press

Timber Press, 133 SW 2nd Ave., Ste. 450, Portland, OR 97204 | **Phone:** (800) 327-5680 or (503) 227-2878 | **Email:** info@timberpress.com | **Web:** www.timberpress.com

Portland's publishing riches are generously shared with the rest of us, as Timber Press passionately delivers "better books for gardeners." Timber's online bookstore allows you to read reviews, book excerpts, and interviews with writers—plus learn about new releases. You can order books (check for occasional discounted specials), request a catalog, download horticultural screen savers, compete for monthly awards, and subscribe to the e-newsletter. This is a garden-friendly site and you'll enjoy receiving the monthly updates.

Wide World Books and Maps

4411A Wallingford Avenue N, Seattle, WA 98103 | **Phone:** (206) 634-3453 or (888) 534-3453 | **Fax:** (206) 634-0558 | **Email:** travel@speakeasy.net | **Web:** www.travelbooksandmaps.com/ | **Open:** Monday–Saturday 10 a.m.–9 p.m.; Sunday, 10 a.m.–7 p.m.

A knowledgeable staff and a wide choice of books, maps, and gear to help prepare traveling gardeners for your journey abroad or across the country. Great website!

chapter

11

GARDENING ON THE INTERNET

Why do sweet peas fail to thrive in my garden? What does the cone of an Alaskan cedar look like? Are forsythia pods edible? Does Ciscoe Morris' dog Kokie really like brussel sprouts?

To find the answers to such questions, inquisitive gardeners once had to spend hours in a library or quiz their peers over backyard fences. Today, innumerable horticultural volumes and the advice of a legion of gardeners are available online, but that doesn't necessarily mean finding answers is any quicker. At times, the Internet seems to be an information quagmire instead of an information superhighway. Type the words "forsythia pods" into a search engine and you'll be presented with hundreds of websites. You'll be able to read haikus about the pods or look at paintings of your subject or even get ideas for using them in floral arrangements, but where's the answer to your question? Probably somewhere on the 262nd site. Thus the technology that was supposed to get you out of the library and back into the garden more often than not keeps you chained to the computer.

There are resources that can make navigating the Web easier. Often times the best solution is to turn to the sites of your fellow gardeners. (Check out Kokie's page on Ciscoe's site, for example.) Many amateur gardeners and professional horticulturists have started their own sites to share their hard-earned wisdom. It can be fun to follow the progress of others' gardens—and to borrow ideas from them. Many of these sites also include a list of great links to the most useful gardening sites on the Web. In other words, the work of searching has been done for you.

The key to making the Internet work for you is experimentation. Take a few hours on a rainy afternoon and find a few favorite links. Start with those in this chapter: You might find some that cover all the topics you're interested in or others that link you to the perfect site. Many Web authors update their sites regularly, so checking back periodically can be helpful. Once you've identified your favorite sites, you should be able to spend less time searching for answers on the computer and more time in the garden putting your newfound knowledge to use. And isn't that the whole point?

—Jessica Campbell

About This Chapter

As we updated this 9th edition of *The Northwest Gardeners' Resource Directory*, the single most compelling change noted in the world of gardening is the proliferation of websites. Even the smallest mom-and-pop specialty nursery or the youngest volunteer-run plant society has taken the on-ramp to the Information Superhighway. This is great news for those of us who need to communicate quickly and track down information that we can't get in person. Online gardening has never been better. In this chapter, we have endeavored to highlight general, regional, and specialty gardening resources found on the Internet. However, we have added hundreds of new web addresses throughout the book, so keep an eye out for specific addresses to nurseries, emporiums, gardens, organizations, and societies in their respective chapters. Log on and dig in! And as you wonder about new links and updates to this edition, visit the author's website at www.debraprinzing.com.

Websites with Gardening Links

The following websites offer lists of links that can be helpful in navigating the very large quantity of online garden information. Some of the sites also feature articles and other information.

www.backyardgardener.com

In addition to a beefy links section, gardener and Web author Duncan McAlpine offers tip-filled articles on a variety of garden topics and an archive of articles written by garden columnists Elisabeth Ginsburg and Jennifer Moore. Topics that are covered in depth include alpine, rock, and trough gardens. The site, which is affiliated with plantideas.com, contains a plant finder that offers several ways to find specific plants on the Web, as well as links to catalogs and retail stores.

www.botanique.com

Planning a trip? Love to garden? Enjoy the fruits of someone else's labor in the landscape? Marvel at the way flora and fauna co-exist naturally? Botanique lists many places that represent the botanical gems of our planet. This site is meant to be a pleasure to lose yourself in. The site is a portal to more than 2,300 gardens, arboreta, and nature sites in North America. Select the destination and you'll be linked to the appropriate list of destinations in a specific city or region, with its hyperlink if available. There is also an updated calendar of events and resources, plus a great search program.

www.botany.net/IDB/

The Internet Directory for Botany was created by an international team of experts: Anthony R. Brach, Raino Lampinen, Shunguo Liu, and Keith McCree. Their compilation of botany-related links, which number in the thousands, is more scientific than recreational but does include many sites relevant to Northwest gardening. The site can be searched alphabetically or by subject.

www.digital-librarian.com

New York librarian Margaret Vail Anderson catalogs the best websites devoted to subjects ranging from activism to yurts. Her gardening page offers hundreds of links to gardening sites in categories including History, Ethnobotany, Images, News, and Research Centers. The low-tech site is essentially one long list of links, but it is a good starting point for a Web search.

http.garden-gate.prairienet.org

Master Gardener Karen Fletcher made one of the first and best attempts to organize the tangle of gardening destinations. Categories on her site include: The Gardener's Reading Room (links to magazines, catalogs, and books), The Teaching Garden (glossaries, special-topic websites, databases, and collections), the Garden Shop ("Shop till your mouse goes belly-up"), Sun Room (houseplants, tropicals, and greenhouse plants), Down the Garden Path (botanical gardens, greenhouses, and gardens around the world), Mailing Lists, Newsgroups and Web Forums, and a Holding Bed (a potpourri of newly discovered sites that have not yet been incorporated into their appropriate categories). The site's index is useful for finding specific information quickly.

www.gardeninglaunchpad.com

Jim Parra, of Zilker Botanical Gardens in Austin, Texas, updates his prodigious list of links weekly. In addition to thousands of links in nearly a hundred categories, the home page has a featured article, a featured site, and a tip of the week. Northwest gardeners will be particularly interested in the Regional Sites category, which features several Northwest-specific sites.

www.gardennet.com

Washingtonian Cheryl Trine blends information and commerce in this directory, which includes plants, plant groups, equipment and products, gardening types, information, travel and events, and services. In addition to the links directory, the site includes a guidebook for planning garden travel, a garden shop, a chat room, and a catalog request service. The What's New page features ideas and products Trine recommends.

www.gardenweb.com

The GardenWeb hosts forums, garden exchanges, articles, contests, and a plant database, with the overall goal of providing comprehensive gardening information. Based in New Jersey, the site hosts a calendar of garden events that frequently lists horticultural festivals and tours in the Northwest. There is also a helpful, large garden-related glossary (at last count it offered 4,400 terms relating to botany, gardening, horticulture, and landscape architecture) and links to online catalogs.

www.hedgerows.com

We were all set to delete Hedgerows from the 9th edition of this *Directory*, as it hadn't been updated since April 2001 and our sources in British Columbia said creator Mala Gunadasa-Rohling had disappeared from the local gardening scene. But as luck would have it, we caught up with Mala via (what else?) the Internet, where she wrote from her new home in England. Mala has juggled this recent international move, the birth of a third child, and the launch of her other project, **www.eSeeds.com**, so she has fallen behind on updating Hedgerows Garden Tapestry. At its peak, this site was a central element to Vancouver's rich horticultural scene, and Mala could be counted on for listing every plant society even, large or smal— a free community webpage service for gardens and garden clubs. With the new nanny coming for her children, Mala promises to "reintroduce" www.hedgerows.com as soon as possible, so we wish her the best of luck in the endeavor.

www.hortiplex.com

Actually a part of GardenWeb (see above), HortiPlex is a nexus of useful plant information on the Web—and you can go to it directly at the address here. As the site explains, typing "lily" into a general search site is as likely to bring up links to a cutting-edge rock star as a plant of the genus *Lillium*. By organizing HortiPlex around plant names, and carefully selecting the sites they link to, this plant database will help you find relevant information about plants without having to sift through the clutter! You'll find 97,941 plant listings; 4,212 images, and more than 75,000 links to useful information, images, and plant vendors (at last count, but growing!). The site also serves as a community exchange, where you can share opinions, experiences, and your own plant images, which will clearly only serve to improve HortiPlex as time progresses.

www.ICanGarden.com

This Canada-based site is Tom and Donna Dawson's ambitious collection of articles, links, forums, and more. The visitor who takes the time to navigate the dense site will be rewarded with topical essays, book reviews, garden tours, and ideas for gardening with kids. Through forums, links, newsletters, and email pals, the site also connects visitors with an international community of gardeners.

www.nwgardening.com

Landscape designers Marie McKinsey and Susan Rafanelli share their thoughts on gardening topics as well as their reading lists. They also maintain a list of links to sites on Northwest gardening, medicinal plants, new ornamentals, and more.

www.Suite101.com

The motto of this site is "real people helping real people." The site allows people to share their interests with others by becoming an editor, and posting articles and links relevant to their chosen topic. Gardening is just one of hundreds of topics covered by the site, and there are dozens of garden editors who address everything from bulbs to xeriscaping.

www.timberpress.com

This well-organized site offers access to the publications of Portland-based Timber Press, providing short excerpts from a variety of plant- and flower-oriented books and online shopping. Its selection of links reflects the range of horticultural topics covered by Timber Press publications, and includes associations, garden societies, garden writers, electronic gardens, botanical images, online references, and Pacific Northwest specialties.

www.usda.gov/news/garden.htm

This is a great, very easy-to-navigate site that offers a little bit of everything for the beginning or veteran home gardener. Check links to topics on backyard conservation, landscaping, organic vegetable gardening, and the USDA Plant Hardiness Zone Map. This site also links you to the very enticing website for the U.S. National Arboretum.

Websites for Pacific Northwest Gardeners

www.binettigarden.com

Enumclaw, Washington-based Marianne Binetti is a familiar face and name among garden enthusiasts who follow her great (and very humorous) advice in the *Seattle Post-Intelligencer* each Thursday. Now that she has her own site, check here for expanded information on her column's most popular advice, see the garden "tips of the month," see photos of Marianne's own garden, plus view a calendar of Marianne's lectures and appearances. You can also order her books here and send this witty garden expert a question or two of your own.

www.ciscoe.com

Ciscoe Morris (aka Mr. Brussel Sprouts) is as entertaining online as he is on his KIRO 710 AM radio show broadcast from Seattle. His site includes some of his gardening secrets, his speaking schedule, and his radio-show lineup, with contact information for his guests. On the site, Morris also writes about plants, bugs, and other horticultural topics. For fun, he's included a page about his dog Kokie and one devoted to brussel sprout recipes. Links to Morris's favorite websites are also included on the site, most of them offering information of interest to Northwest gardeners.

www.Country-Lane.com/yr/

Yesterday's Rose, Andrew Schulman's site dedicated to old and old-fashioned roses, features glorious photos, substantive content, excellent links to other rose-related sites, book reviews, a rose finder, and more. Schulman is a Seattle-based landscape architect and rose enthusiast who writes frequently for *Fine Gardening* magazine.

http://eesc.orst.edu/agcomwebfile/garden

This is the central site for all gardening information compiled and published by the Oregon State University Extension & Experiment Station. You can search by a topic, such as "beneficial insects" or "fruit and nut growing," or check the online gardening calendar. You can link to Oregon's Master Gardener Program, listen to audio programs of "Northwest Gardens," and read a lengthy archive of gardening articles. Also view clips and schedules for Northwest Gardening, a weekly half-hour television program hosted by Portland horticulturist Mike Darcy.

gardening.wsu.edu

The Washington State University Cooperative Extension's site enables you to ask Master Gardeners about your most perplexing plant, pest, pruning, planting, pesticide, or propagation problems. The library links you to expert publications written by WSU faculty and staff. The site also features frequently asked questions, links, success stories, local opportunities, a calendar, Mary Robson's regional gardening column, and pointers on Northwest native plants, stewardship gardening, lawns, landscape plants, basic gardening skills, composting, vegetables, tree fruit, berries, solutions to plant problems, indoor plants, weeds, insects, and house pests.

www.millerlibrary.org

The Elisabeth C. Miller Horticultural Library is affiliated with the Center for Urban Horticulture and is open to the public, despite the setback its collection faced due to the fire set by terrorists in May 2001. While many of the periodicals and books suffered from smoke damage, the wonderful library staff has continued to serve the public at a smaller, temporary site at CUH in Seattle. The catalog for its extensive collection of books on gardening topics is available on its website—thankfully, the fire couldn't hurt the online catalog. Questions about library usages and questions frequently asked of the librarians are also answered on the site. Users can email the library's Plant Answer Line or access links to recommended gardening sites. Local plant sales and garden tours are also featured.

www.npr.org/programs/talkingplants

NPR's "Doyenne of Dirt" and the Pacific Northwest's horticultural humorist, Ketzel Levine, loves to juggle her botanical expertise with her flair for quick quips. Listen to Levine's past radio broadcasts, ask her a question, check out her plant profiles, or read up on her background. Levine's articles, diary, and progress updates on her personal garden are also included.

www.orst.edu/instruct/for241/

If you need a crash course in tree identification, this is the URL for the home page of "Trees of the Pacific Northwest," a tree ID page hosted by Oregon State University's College of Forestry. You can skip through the pages to learn more about specific genera or try your hand at identifying a tree specimen with a user-friendly dichotomous key. If you click on Yew, for example, the site offers you the botanical name (Taxus), plus the tree's needle, fruit, and bark description and a color photograph. If you want to order a printed version of this valuable reference, the website tells you how to do so.

www.rainyside.com

Debra Teachout-Teashon and Travis Saling, two Washington gardeners, expound on topics such as Northwest native plants, organic gardening, and growing edibles and ornamentals. This top-notch site is packed with substance for active gardeners, and peppered with a bit of good humor. There is a good selection of Northwest events and organization contact info, an excellent list of nurseries with links to those with their own sites, a weed ID test, virtual garden tours of Teachout-Teashon and Saling's gardens in progress, and tons of terrific stuff for kids.

www.slugsandsalal.com

Helen Chestnut, an established garden writer, and Lois Sampson created the site to address gardening issues in Washington, Oregon, and British Columbia. They maintain a list of organizations, events, and shopping resources. Chestnut's columns and photos of local gardens are included. A searchable plant directory, book reviews, projects and techniques, seasonal task lists, and a chat room round out the site.

www.tardigrade.org/natives

Pacific Northwest Native Wildlife Gardening, created by Allyn Weaks, offers resources for gardeners interested in native plants and wildlife. The simple, straightforward site lists books, organizations, nurseries, and events related to the subject. Readers are encouraged to contribute to the site.

www.weather.com/activities/homeandgarden/regionalreports/IP.html

This regional site on weather.com is especially favored by amateur farmers and orchardists who are concerned with how climatic changes in our region affect their crops (it is compiled by the National Gardening Association). But everyone who gardens will enjoy the highly personal voice of Patt Kasa, the horticultural extension coordinator in Kitsap County for Washington State University. Patt files reports such as "Dealing with Deer and Other Garden Raiders" and "Putting Your Garden to Bed for Winter." P.S., this is the site to visit when you want to track temperature trends (see the Precipitation and Soil Moisture maps) and to look up information like average dates of first freeze for your region.

Websites About Horticultural Therapy

www.ahta.org

The American Horticultural Therapy Association's site includes professional information, educational opportunities, and a listing of publications.

www.botanicgardens.org

The Morrison Horticultural Demonstration Center at the Denver Botanical Garden is used to demonstrate, teach, and research the theory and practice of horticultural therapy. They offer a certificate program in horticultural therapy. The site profiles their program and the Morrison Center. (The DBG is the current home of the American Horticultural Therapy Association.)

www.chicago-botanic.org

The Chicago Botanic Garden is in the forefront when it comes to horticultural therapy, and this site reflects their commitment. Find out about the professional services of the Chicago Botanic Garden's internationally acclaimed Horticultural Therapy Department and read essays on related topics.

www.cityfarmer.org

The site includes information on books, organizations, educational opportunities, links, and excerpts from their handbook, *Gardening with People with Disabilities*.

www.hort.vt.edu

The Virginia Tech Department of Horticulture site addresses human issues in horticulture, including therapy. It includes research and theory abstracts from professional publications, including the *Journal of Therapeutic Horticulture*. The department provides information on HT programs worldwide, plus links to botanical gardens and arboreta offering training in horticultural therapy and institutions offering internships.

Websites About Gardening with Children

www.garden.org

The National Gardening Association's site offers information for teachers, as well as community partners interested in using plants and gardens to enrich learning. It includes lots of resources and links.

www.raw-connections.com/garden/

The Kid's Valley Garden gives good basic gardening information to kids in an appealing format. It addresses planning, planting, and growing kid-friendly flowers, herbs, shrubs, and veggies. It was originated for the Pakenham Junior Horticultural Society in Arnprior, Ontario, Canada.

telegarden.aec.at/index.html

The Telegarden allows users to use a robotic installation to view and interact with a remote garden filled with living plants. Visit the site, go through the demonstration, then become a member. You will be allowed to actually plant, water, and monitor the progress of seedlings via the movements of an industrial robot arm that you control from your computer.

www.treetures.com

On the Treetures site, you'll meet the tiny guardians of our forests: the Treeture Teachers, Tree Twirlers, Leaf Turners, Tree Doctors, Smoke Detectors, The Sun Beam Team, Rooters, Sap Tappers, Blight Fighters, Protectors of the Heartwood, Keepers of the Crown, Ring Counters, Sprig Wigs, and more as they encounter The Forest Fiends and The Mudsters. The Treeture family teaches kids about the importance of tree care and tree planting.

www.urbanext.uiuc.edu/gpe/index.html

The Great Plant Escape introduces kids to Detective Le Plant and his partners Bud and Sprout. Detective Le Plant has discovered that one plant can produce many other plants. He needs you to help him find out how this happens. If you solve this case, you're well on your way to becoming an official Junior Plant Detective.

BRIAN THOMPSON:

VISITING THE "INTERNET GARDEN"

There was a time, not too long ago, when the Internet was a fantastic new vision that offered gardeners promises way beyond the most exaggerated seed catalog. Horticultural magazines and mail order catalogs were full of the latest electronic tools to enhance your backyard experience, and so was almost everyone you talked to. We would browse the Web rather than the bulb bins and use "spiders" to search for our favorite plant society rather than fight their latest infestation in the potting shed. Who needed a real garden when you could go virtual?

The pace of this frenzy has slowed. Now, like everyone else, gardeners have made the Internet an integral part of their lives. E-mail has reconnected long-lost family and friends, and made links to new ones who share common interests from Alpines to Apples. Almost every mail-order nursery has a website, and that means you needn't wait until the latest edition of the print catalog appears in your mailbox (although I still get excited when they do!).

But we've also become less dazzled by the show. We won't wait 30 (or even 3) seconds for the image of the latest rose cultivar to pop onto our screen. Yet we've all, at least once, descended into the black hole of "it's gotta be here somewhere, it's *gotta* be here" while outside the bindweed is smothering the tomatoes. So when and why should the average gardener use the Internet? When is it best to go back to the old faithful book, or favorite magazine? And when is it best to get back to the dirt and rely on our own experience?

First of all, consider the reasons a website exists. If you understand the purpose of the person or group who created it, you have a key to how valuable, complete, timely, and useful the information could be. Nurseries, public gardens, and garden societies want your attention. They want you to buy, to visit, to join—and they know (or should know) your hassle tolerance when Web surfing goes slowly. That's why sites like these are in general well engineered, have accurate information, and are incredibly useful. Keep in mind, though, that there may be some fall-off for smaller entities that may lack funds or staff for website development and maintenance.

Another vast category of sites exist simply to share information, with little concern for financial return. These include research, archival, or outreach entities that have always made their collections available to interested parties, but who now have a means to extend that service well beyond their physical space. While nothing will replace the hands-on information you receive at your local Master Gardener clinic, you can now supplement that with the bulletins, newsletters, and other publications from Cooperative Extensions across the state or the country. Extensive databases, like the International Plants Name Index (www.ipni.org), the New York Botanical Garden Library (www.nybg.org/bsci/libr/), or the USDA's Plants Database (plants.usda.gov/) are examples of the serious research opportunities now available and open to all of us.

A great way to expand your personal list of key websites is to check out the horticultural or botanical directories, gateways, and portals listed in the Chapter 11, "Gardening on the Internet." These locations, whether commercial, institutional, or someone's labor of love, can sort the myriad options into clear-cut categories, and introduce you to possibilities you'd never find with a search engine. Instead of doing a general keyword search on "iris" and finding yourself awash in selections that include astronomy and even mythology, you'll learn how to rid yourself of iris borer and that a whole society shares your delight in Pacific Coast Hybrids.

Not every tasty tidbit on the Internet lunch-counter is free. There are some excellent offerings that ask for a reasonable amount of money up front, and then provide you with a login and password so you can enter the site. Many such sites are available through libraries. Plant Information Online (plantinfo.umn.edu/arboretum/default.asp), from the University of Minnesota's Andersen Horticultural Library, is just such a service, and provides access to plant sources throughout North America along with an index by plant name to both periodicals and book publications. This is incredibly useful to the serious plant collector who is looking for a source, or perhaps for information on a newly discovered but obscure treasure. Plant Information Online is available at no charge when you visit the Elisabeth C. Miller Library (see the listing for the library under "Libraries and Media" in Chapter 1) at the University of Washington's Center for Urban Horticulture.

If these are some of the pros of the Web, what are the cons? Nothing will replace good writing and, most good writers still want to be rewarded financially for their efforts. To date this means you'll continue to turn to print publications for the reflective and richly rewarding reading that will stimulate your creativity and take your thinking down paths you haven't considered. In print, the review and editorial process is typically more rigorous, and that allows you to place more confidence in the accuracy and authority of what you've read.

After all, much about gardening is picked up through your own trials and errors, or from the wisdom shared by a mentor with extensive expertise. Remember too that the most cleverly crafted website will never design your yard or prune your trees as well as a professional. At its best, the Internet is now simply one of the many great tools in a gardener's repertoire.

So enjoy cyberspace when you want to, and by all means take advantage of its amazing ability to hunt down bits and pieces of discrete information. But also be sure to turn off the computer and go delve in the dirt!

Brian Thompson gets plenty of opportunities to surf the Net in his role as Systems and Technical Services Librarian at the Elisabeth C. Miller Library at the Center for Urban Horticulture, and he invites you to visit the library's website (www.millerlibrary.org) for more tips and recommendations. At home in north Seattle, he's quite happy to curl up with the latest low-tech catalog and although he could take his laptop into the herb garden, so far he's stayed organic.

chapter

12

Flower & Garden Shows, Festivals & Events

The Big Flower & Garden Shows:

Portland, San Francisco & Seattle

Vancouver & Victoria, B.C.

Garden Tours and Open Houses

Competitions

While the Pacific Northwest is blessed with a mild climate, we find the march of the seasons nonetheless requires all but the most ardent of year-round gardeners to cool their heels through more than one holiday—roughly Thanksgiving through President's Day. Then, just as we begin to weary of counting the subtle shades of brown, gray, and green, our senses are shaken into a full alert by the magical appearance, overnight, of magnolias and roses in full bloom, heady jasmine-clad arbors, and brilliant masses of hyacinths, luscious lettuce, and frilly fennel. Annually, in February, we of the Northwest catapult ourselves from calm to chaos as the Northwest Flower and Garden Show opens the season (and its doors) to invite us into a dreamy, hypnotic realm.

Properly inspired and imbued with renewed energy, we march forth into the garden and perform our own brand of magic, participating in the transformation of sleeping borders, waking up from under warm winter mulches. It is in this season that the first of the early "Show and Tell" events begin, with early truss shows from rhododendron-ophiles. The parade continues right on until the last chrysanthemum of fall takes its curtain call. We hope you will have time on your busy calendar to take in these events, to enjoy the beauty, and to be where passionate specialists are so willing to share their vast knowledge and obvious love of growing a particular type of plant.

NEWS AND INFORMATION ABOUT NORTHWEST GARDENING EVENTS

www.slugsandsalal.com

Based in Victoria, B.C., this website covers current gardening events throughout the Pacific Northwest, including those in Oregon, Washington, and British Columbia.

www.rainyside.com

Two rainy-side gardeners (based in Western Washington) keep abreast of regionwide events.

www.gardentourist.com

Formerly a book, *The Garden Tourist* evolved in 2002 into a valuable online guide to gardens and garden events in the United States, Canada, and abroad. At www.gardentourist.com, garden enthusiasts can do simultaneous searches of gardens and garden events by state or province—an unique tool for travel planning. Listings link to garden and event websites for more information. You are even invited to add your own review of gardens, events, and shows. In the "Northwest" section, you'll find information on most major events and some lesser-known garden gatherings of our region.

British Columbia

* *Vancouver Sun* on Saturday
* *Vancouver Province* on Sunday
* *Gardens West* magazine; look for the column "Grapevine."
* *GardenWise* magazine; look for the column "What's Up."

Oregon

* *Garden Showcase* magazine; look for the "Calendar."
* *The Oregonian* (Portland); see the weekend edition, garden events calendar in the Thursday "Homes and Gardens of the Northwest," and find more information online at www.oregonlive.com.

Washington

* *Northwest Garden News*, published ten times a year. Mary Gutierrez includes a monthly "Calendar" in this widely distributed free publication.
* *Seattle Times*; see the Sunday Home/Real Estate section.
* Center for Urban Horticulture, Seattle. Quarterly calendar covers CUH, Northwest Horticultural Society and Washington Park Arboretum classes, events, and tours (on the Web see www.urbanhort.org).
* Miller Horticultural Library, Seattle; call (206) 543-0415 or see www.millerlibrary.org.

Specialty Shows and Events

Chapter 2, "Clubs, Societies & Volunteer Opportunities," provides additional listings of shows and special events within the entry for each organization. Have a favorite plant? Peruse that section in Chapter 2 with your calendar and a sharp pencil, and you're likely to learn about a specialty show or competition staged by other enthusiasts.

MAJOR NORTHWEST SHOWS

Note: Because the dates change slightly from year to year, we have listed only the month during which the show typically falls. If you plan to attend, please visit the show's website, or call in advance to get specific dates (the producers often list dates for several upcoming years, as well).

NORTHWEST FLOWER AND GARDEN SHOW / FEBRUARY

Venue: Washington State Convention Center, downtown Seattle | **Show hot line:** (800) 229-6311 | **Produced by:** Salmon Bay Expositions, 1515 NW 51st Street, Seattle, WA 98107 | **Phone:** (206) 789-5333 | **Fax:** (206) 784-4545 | **Web:** www.gardenshow.com

If you have any soil coursing through your veins where mere mortals run on blood, you will find it impossible to escape the fever to get out and garden after one morning or afternoon spent meandering under the influence of this event. Now **North America's third-largest** (and arguably the best) spring flower show, this event jump-starts the gardening season with five days of gardens, exhibits, seminars, and more. Show founder Duane Kelly and president Grant Dull and their amazing crew of show-makers never stop trying to improve on the original success of this show. In 2002, an expansion of the Convention Center added 3 acres to the show's original 5 acres, allowing visitors to enjoy **8 acres of fragrance, color, blossoms, and gardening inspiration.** In short, this show is better than ever. Yes, all the talented growers, nurserymen and women, and garden designers are still playing tricks and forcing Mother Nature and her plants to bloom early, but there's also a good dose of reality here. The show acts as a catalyst to move us from the dream world of winter "gardening" to the high-energy phase required of early spring. Each year, nearly 30 large and small nurseries, landscape designers, and horticultural groups pull out the stops in designing and miraculously bringing to flower **dazzling display gardens and major exhibits.** Five days of free seminars and hands-on demonstrations, sponsored by *Sunset* magazine, vie for one's time at the show, presenting recognized experts of regional, national, and international repute. Over **300 commercial exhibitors** offer everything from tools and supplies to greenhouses and garden ornaments, every imaginable plant society vies for membership support, and dozens of public garden and horticultural organizations bring representatives anxious to answer questions and disseminate armloads of free literature. New exhibits and features, such as a garden club competition, a specialty nursery plant sales area called the "Cool Plant Corner," a new-plant introduction area titled "Meet the Plants," and other special offerings keep us coming back year after year.

Tips: Advance tickets are available from late November, so order yours to avoid wasting valuable time standing in line to buy a (more expensive) ticket! Or consider grabbing the affordable All-Show pass. Buy them through nurseries and garden shops area-wide, by mail from the show office, or from the website, which also has a great section entitled Frequently Asked Questions (like: Is photography allowed? and, Is there a place to leave plants during the day?). If the seminars interest you, request a copy of the brochure or pick one up the week before the show—they're printed by the *Seattle Times* (another show sponsor). Round-trip shuttle buses run from Northgate Shopping Center, departing every 20 minutes for the 15-minute trip in to downtown. Park at the mall for free and pay only $3 for the round trip to the show! Kids under 11 ride free with an adult.

Note: The show brochure and website give information on hotel discount rates and additional transportation.

PORTLAND YARD, GARDEN, AND PATIO SHOW / FEBRUARY

Venue: Oregon Convention Center, 777 NE Martin Luther King Jr. Boulevard, Portland, OR (Near the spot where I-5 and I-85 converge, just across the Willamette River to the east of downtown Portland. For your landmark, look for the Center's distinctive pair of glass spires.) | **Show hot line:** (800) 342-6401 | **Produced by:** Oregon Association of Nurserymen, 2780 SE Harrison Street, Suite 102, Milwaukie, OR 97222 | **Phone:** (503) 653-8733 | **Email:** info@oan.org, | **Web:** www.ygpshow.com

Gardeners, growers, and professional landscapers welcome spring with this three-day show that puts the emphasis on outdoor living, from plants to garden accents, landscape supplies, and much more. More than 200 unique exhibitors are on hand, from full-service garden centers and specialty merchants to designers and craftsmen. The event showcases a number of **larger display gardens**, as well as smaller garden vignettes. Free with show admission are **educational seminars** from the best horticultural authors, lecturers, and designers. It is truly a celebration of Oregon's vibrant horticultural industry, the largest in the nation when it comes to growing and exporting nursery stock. Here's where you'll meet the plants of your dreams, and gain inspiration for new ways to garden.

GMC PORTLAND HOME AND GARDEN SHOW / FEBRUARY

Venue: Portland Expo Center (located on NE Marine Drive, just off I-5 exit 307, north of downtown Portland) | **Produced by:** O'Loughlin Trade Shows, PO Box 25348, Portland, OR 97298 | **Phone:** (503) 246-8291 | **Fax:** (503) 246-1066 | **Web:** www.oloughlintradeshows.com/ots-shows-hg-pdx.html

The GMC Portland Home and Garden Show is one big place where you can shop, explore new products, goods, and services—even plan entire **home and garden improvement projects** under one roof. It's a combination home show and garden show lasting five days, and with a little bit of everything. At the heart of this show are more than **20 showcase gardens** in full bloom during the middle of winter, and sure to spark new ideas for your garden. The **Pacific Northwest Orchid Show and Sale** is also held here, as are countless displays and flower arrangements from the **Oregon State Federation of Garden Clubs**. A **huge plant sale** offers nursery stock from many of the region's best growers, with proceeds going to benefit the Portland Habilitation Center. Nearly 1,000 booths fill more than 300,000 square feet of exhibit space, including the newly remodeled main hall (the show fills a number of adjacent buildings at the Expo Center, too). The show organizers also produce the Portland Fall Home & Garden Show in October.

SAN FRANCISCO FLOWER & GARDEN SHOW / MARCH

Venue: Cow Palace, 2600 Geneva Avenue, San Francisco, CA | **Show hotline:** (800) 829-9751 | **Produced by:** Salmon Bay Expositions, 2183 Greenwich Street, San Francisco, CA 94123 | **Phone:** (415) 771-6909 | **Fax:** (415) 771-9724 | **Web:** www.gardenshow.com

Every year, nearly 60,000 people searching for inspiration for their gardens visit the San Francisco Flower & Garden Show, the sister show to Seattle's (with the same great producers). Many come to be awestruck by the beauty and magnificence experienced while walking through the show's display gardens, while others come to stock up and make purchases for spring garden projects. Californians know this is the place to go for gardens, gardening accessories, and garden know-how.

San Francisco's Cow Palace draws visitors from around California (and lots of Northwesterners), who take great ideas for their own gardens from it. Talented top landscaping teams design and plant more than **20 full-scale display gardens**. There are more than **450 commercial exhibitors**, offering garden tools, books, accessories, decorations, and lots more. In addition, the 6-acre show features a 21,000 square foot **Orchid Pavilion**, a free, world-class seminar series with top-name horticulturists and other experts, an outdoor-living area, a garden vignette area, and other displays. Recently, this event has also encompassed the popular **California Koi Show**.

Note: The show brochure and website give information on hotel discount rates and additional transportation.

VanDusen Flower and Garden Show / June

Venue: VanDusen Botanical Gardens, 5251 Oak Street at West 37th Avenue, Vancouver, BC V6M 4H1 Canada | **Produced by:** VanDusen Botanical Gardens Association, 5251 Oak Street, Vancouver, BC V6M 4H1 Canada | **Phone:** (604) 878-9274 | **Fax:** (604) 266-4236 | **Web:** www.vandusen.org

This spectacular, 55-acre urban botanical garden is the setting for a festive four-day show that celebrates the emerging summer gardening season. Set under marquee tents and throughout 11 acres of the Garden's grounds, this is without a doubt the horticultural highlight of the province—and beyond. Exhibitors offer an **exquisite array of plants**, garden furnishings, equipment, supplies, and horticultural sundries. Pavilions house a broad range of educational gardening resources and plant-oriented organizations, and show botanically themed art. Major nurseries and designers display their skills through garden vignettes that invite the public to enjoy them in the **real outdoors**. That makes this a completely different kind of party from the indoor shows, leading many to compare the VanDusen event to London's famed Chelsea Garden Show.

Be sure to save time for the excellent lectures and demonstrations, meeting garden-book writers at the **Author's Corner**, and listening to the CBC Radio One live broadcasts, and then judge for yourself which design should win the Hanging Basket Competition. Refreshments, including those available in the vintners' tent, are sold to fortify garden enthusiasts for "one more round" through the show. Come early to this very popular event, then escape the crowds and stroll through the glorious Gardens beyond. For an extra treat, take in the **Gala Preview Party** the night before the show opens, and relish the time to meander, a glass of wine in hand, to tête-à-tête with friends over extraordinary hors d'oeuvres, peruse the exhibits, and peak in on vendors' booths (not open for sales this evening) in the glorious ambience of twilight (tickets to this event are sold separately).

Victoria Flower & Garden Show / July

Venue: Historic Hatley Castle grounds, part of the 640-acre site of Royal Roads University, Victoria, BC, Canada, 15 minutes from downtown Victoria | **Produced by:** Victoria Flower & Garden Show | **Phone:** (250) 381-1139 | **Fax:** (250) 381-1195 | **Web:** www.flowerandgarden.net

The historic Hatley Castle provides a magical setting for this three-day **outdoor summer garden show**. The grounds are festooned with lush, elegant floral displays as show guests enjoy a wide array of presentations by authors and gardening experts, sales of plants (including new introductions), demonstrations and lectures, a hanging basket and flower arrangement competition, an artists' and sculptors' garden, and more. Islands of creativity, musical entertainment, and sheer beauty are interspersed throughout the castle's grounds. Friends of Hatley Castle docents lead tours of Hatley's permanent gardens (including an Italian garden and a Japanese garden), plus tours of the castle itself. Area garden societies and clubs participate as well. For your culinary delight, enjoy a meal in the Vienna Gardens (while enjoying breathtaking views of the Straight of Juan de Fuca and the snowcapped Olympic Mountains). Then take in strawberry tea on the terrace of the castle. The show has partnered with The Land Conservancy of British Columbia and the Horticulture Centre of the Pacific, two nonprofit organizations that advocate for preserving and promoting research in the region. There is a Gala Preview Party the evening prior to the show's opening to benefit The Land Conservancy.

Garden Tours and Open Houses / Open Garden Days

The joy of seeing private residential gardens that have been lovingly planned, planted, and cared for is one reason to love the gardening lifestyle. Many of the most rewarding tours provide an opportunity to meet those involved in a garden club or society. That's when (we tell you from first-hand experience) one enjoys a real sense of open camaraderie. The questions tend to fly fast and furious, and occasionally there may be a generous offer of cuttings of this, a promise of divisions of that, and an invitation to return in another season.

❋ Organizations. Join an active regional group like the **Hardy Plant Society of Oregon** and/or the **Northwest Perennial Alliance** to take advantage of one of the many benefits of membership: touring each other's gardens. These groups provide members with a fat annual directory of *Open Gardens*, inspired by the British "Yellow Book" scheme. You'll see which individuals will open their garden gate for you to visit, usually in spring or summer. And if you're planning to travel during the garden-touring months, treat yourself to a copy of **The Garden Conservancy's** *Open Days Directory*, a guide to the several hundred private gardens that open their gates to visitors as part of a national effort to support the Conservancy's work (you can order the book in January of each year). The Garden Conservancy is preserving America's exceptional gardens around the country. You can order the directory for $15.95 and join the Conservancy as a member to receive a discount. Call (845) 265-2029, write: The Garden Conservancy, PO Box 219, Cold Spring, NY 10516, or see their website, at www.gardenconservancy.org.

❋ Volunteering. Working as a volunteer on a garden tour is satisfying in and of itself, as you watch hundreds of smiling, happy people meander through a residential setting on a single Sunday afternoon. Perhaps this is why we do what we do.

❀Dates. Tour dates change from year to year, so please note that we provide only the month during which the tour generally takes place. You will also want to check Chapter 2, "Clubs, Societies & Volunteer Opportunities," and Chapter 13, "Gardens to Visit," where you can read about ongoing special festivals, garden parties, open houses, and fairs unique to the many public gardens and plant societies in our region.

British Columbia

BOWEN ISLAND HOME AND GARDEN TOUR / JULY

Sponsored by the Bowen Island Memorial Garden Society and the Bowen Island Historians | **Phone:** (604) 947-2655

Aptly called "People, Plants, and Places," this tour offers a chance to meander through some of this lovely island's historic homes and gardens to get a feeling of life here, both from another era and today.

VANCOUVER PRIVATE GARDEN TOUR / JUNE

Sponsored by the Vancouver Park Board, 2099 Beach Avenue, Vancouver, BC V6G 1Z4 | **Phone:** Terri Clark at (604) 257-8400 | **Web:** www.parks.vancouver.bc.ca.

This is an annual tour. Tickets must be purchased in advance and they come with a map. Call in early May.

VICTORIA CONSERVATORY OF MUSIC ANNUAL GARDEN TOUR / MAY

Victoria Conservatory of Music, 907 Pandora Avenue, Victoria, BC V8V 3P4 Canada | **Phone:** (250) 477-4114 or (250) 384-0594 | **Fax:** (250) 386-6602 | **Email:** info@vcm.bc.ca

Visit ten gardens, including a tea garden with music from students of the Conservatory—and a plant sale!

Oregon

BERRY BOTANIC GARDEN

11505 SW Summerville Avenue, Portland, OR 97219-8309 | **Phone:** (503) 636-4112 | **Email:** bbg@rdrop.com | **Web:** www.berrybot.com

Ongoing tours of public and private gardens are sponsored by Berry Botanic Garden. Members are often allowed to register for these events in advance of opening them to the public. Twice each year the Berry itself hosts Open Houses, during which free tours of the garden are led by volunteer docents and staff.

PORTLAND METRO NATURAL GARDENING TECHNIQUES TOUR / JULY

Metro Recycling Information | **Phone:** (503) 234-3000

Take a tour of healthy home gardens grown using natural gardening methods. Metro, the Portland Bureau of Environmental Services, and the East Multnomah County Soil Conservation District sponsor this event.

SALEM GARDEN TOUR / JUNE

Phone: (503) 371-3631 | **Email:** info@acgilbert.org | **Web:** www.acgilbert.org

This annual tour of gardens features several gardens located in south and west Salem. It benefits the A. C. Gilbert Discovery Village, a museum for young people. The tour runs in conjunction with a big three-day plant sale!

SPRINGFIELD MUSEUM ANNUAL GARDEN TOUR / JUNE

Contact: Kathy Jensen, at Springfield Museum, (541) 726-3677

The Springfield Museum holds its annual garden tour the first Sunday of June in support of programs for the museum. You can pre-register for a guided bus tour that will ease parking difficulties and walking time.

Washington

BAINBRIDGE IN BLOOM GARDEN TOUR / JULY

Bainbridge Island Arts and Humanities Council, 261 Madison Avenue S, Bainbridge Island, WA 98110 | **Phone:** (206) 842-7901 | **Web:** www.artshum.org

This is a marvelous opportunity to visit six private residential gardens and capture the flavor of life on one of Puget Sound's most garden-filled islands. The organizers have packed the event with activities to educate, entertain and refresh their visitors, with a garden art and crafts fair, book and plant sales, a gourmet luncheon, and informative lectures. Order your tickets in advance to avoid missing this sellout event, which benefits the Bainbridge Island Arts and Humanities Council.

COLUMBIA CITY GARDEN TOUR / JUNE

Garden Tour, 3931 S Ferdinand Street, Seattle, WA 98118

This vibrant South Seattle Community is home to some energetic gardeners, a fabulous Farmer's Market, and one of the best school gardens around (Orcas Elementary School). You can see all of the above, plus some delightful residential gardens, during the annual tour.

ENUMCLAW COUNTRY GARDEN TOUR / MAY

Contact: Debbie Handugan, (360) 802-3282

This tour benefits the Enumclaw Community Hospital and features several outstanding and unique gardens; it promises to be a wonderful country excursion. The garden of popular writer Marianne Binetti is frequently on this tour. Guests of the tour enjoy speakers, garden vendors, and a plant sale, too.

EVERETT GARDENS OF MERIT TOUR / JUNE OR JULY

Phone: (425) 257-8583 | **Web:** www.evergreenarboretum.com

This event helps raise funds for the Evergreen Arboretum and Gardens at Legion Park and is co-sponsored by the Snohomish County Master Gardeners. Visit everything from a city-size backyard with sweeping views of Puget Sound to mature suburban landscapes filled with ornamental displays. The tour frequently includes the lovely Master Gardener Perennial Bed at Legion Park, a 250-foot display of several styles of gardening (you'll also enjoy the adjacent Arboretum).

GARDEN RHAPSODIES TOUR / JULY

Contact: Environmental educator Jennifer Johnson, (360) 754-4111, ext. 7631

Take a tour of earth-friendly private gardens in and around Olympia, sponsored by the Thurston County Environmental Health Department.

GEORGETOWN / MAPLE HILL GARDEN WALK AND ART TOUR / JULY

PO Box 80021, Seattle, WA 98108 | **Phone:** (206) 763-9895

Visit more than 30 private gardens and many artist studio-galleries in a part of Seattle that's quickly emerging as a tiny pocket of innovation, creativity, and horticulture. This tour can usually be done on foot and one of the local churches joins in to serve a pay-what-you-can barbecue lunch in its parking lot. Pretty good city-folk fun!

GIG HARBOR GARDEN TOUR / JUNE

Phone: (253) 851-3776 | **Web:** www.tacoma.ctc.edu/ghc/gardentour.shtm

Stroll through the beautiful gardens of Gig Harbor, a community located near Tacoma on the shores of Puget Sound. The tour showcases local gardens, features vendors and artists with garden-related products, and offers a lunch for a nominal charge. The event is a benefit for the Peninsula Adult Education Program, a literacy program for adults in Gig Harbor and the Peninsula area.

KITSAP PENINSULA SUMMER SPLENDOR TOUR / JULY

Silverdale Chamber of Commerce | **Phone:** (360) 692-6800

Some of Kitsap County's most creative gardeners and their gardens are the highlights of this tour. You can even extend a visit to the Peninsula into a weekend excursion, and add your own side trips to several area specialty nurseries.

LAURELHURST GARDEN TOUR / MAY

Phone: (206) 526-8604 | **Email:** tdbarden1@attbi.com

The Friends of Laurelhurst School Foundation holds an annual tour of gardens in Seattle's Laurelhurst neighborhood. You'll enjoy varied landscapes, from the stately to the cozy in character.

MERCER ISLAND SUMMER CELEBRATION GARDEN TOUR / JULY

Phone: (206) 236-7285

Visit a variety of gardens, from small cottage cutting gardens to expansive waterfront landscapes.

PACIFIC NORTHWEST ART COUNCIL ARTISTS' GARDEN TOUR / MAY

Sponsored by the Pacific Northwest Art Council. Tickets can be purchased in advance through the Seattle Art Museum box office. | **Phone:** (206) 654-3121

Visit the gardens of artists throughout the Seattle area to see how they've creatively integrated art and horticulture. This popular tour gives you a chance to see the work of some famed artists in their home settings.

PORT TOWNSEND MASTER GARDENER TOUR OF SECRET GARDENS / JUNE

Phone: (360) 379-5610

You will be treated to an "insider's" walk through several picturesque gardens, and frequently these include those around the area's historical homes. The Jefferson County Master Gardener Foundation sponsors the tour. Tickets are sold at nurseries in the area and the Port Townsend Chamber of Commerce Visitor's Center.

SECRET GARDENS OF MEDINA / AUGUST

Phone: (425) 454-9451

This is the most exclusive garden tour in town, thanks to the addresses in Medina, a tiny community on the shores of Lake Washington, just outside Bellevue. Visit these ordinarily secluded gardens in Medina and enjoy a light lunch and plant sale at St. Thomas Episcopal Church.

SKAGIT VALLEY ROSE SOCIETY GARDEN TOUR / JUNE OR JULY

Phone: (360) 766-6483

Enjoy rose gardens in all their glory as you visit gardens in and around Mount Vernon in Skagit Valley, a community widely known for its great gardening conditions.

SNOHOMISH GARDEN TOUR / JULY

Phone: (360) 568-9581

For a *terrific* tour, with many generously planted country gardens and gardening related shops/studios featured, take a trip to the country and enjoy the well-designed gardens and all the other horticultural riches.

TOUR OF GARDENS-WOODINVILLE GARDEN CLUB TOUR / JULY

Woodinville Garden Club, PO Box 1764, Woodinville, WA 98072 | **Phone:** (425) 481-6127

This popular tour showcases several wonderful gardens created by members and friends of the Woodinville Garden Club. You'll see acres of beautiful landscapes, woodland settings, water features, and creative design. Ticket holders are invited to a wine-tasting reception after the tour at Willows Inn. Order tickets by mail at the above address.

VASHON ISLAND BLUE HERON GARDEN TOUR / JUNE

Blue Heron Arts Center | **Phone:** (206) 463-5131

Visit several "hidden" country gardens that feature not only plants but sculpture and other garden art. You'll also find a book sale, workshops, and lectures, and box lunches are sold at one of the gardens.

THE WASHINGTON ARBORETUM FOUNDATION'S WINNING GARDENS SUMMER TOUR / JUNE

Arboretum Foundation | **Phone:** (206) 325-4510 | **Web:** www.arboretumfoundation.org

Here's your chance to see into the backyards and step through the garden gates of some of the Seattle area's most cherished gardens. The Arboretum organizes a tour each summer to showcase some of the winning designs in the Pacific Northwest Garden Competition. PS: Occasionally there's an autumn edition of this tour, such as a recent one focusing on great gardens in the communities of Snohomish and Monroe.

WEST SEATTLE'S "ART OF GARDENING" TOUR / JULY

Information: (206) 938-4566, or the ArtsWest Gallery, (206) 938-0339

This fun event involves all of West Seattle, and invites you into the enchanting western-facing gardens of the community. You'll be inspired by everything from ponds and bird habitats to garden architecture and great planting ideas. Volunteers and Master Gardeners are on hand to answer questions and help identify plants. Proceeds benefit ArtsWest, the community-based nonprofit arts organization, and several other local causes.

WHATCOM HORTICULTURAL SOCIETY GARDEN TOUR / JUNE

Whatcom County Visitors Bureau | **Phone:** (360) 671-3990

Held in the Bellingham area, an annual tour of private gardens benefits this nonprofit, education-oriented society. There are generally six private gardens on the tour, which may be seen over a two-day period if you'd like to linger in the area over the weekend.

WHIDBEY ISLAND GARDEN TOUR / MAY OR JUNE

PO Box 164, Freeland, WA 98249 | **Phone:** (360) 321-4191 | **Email:** wigt@whidbey.net

Visit six lovely private gardens to benefit a worthy Whidbey cause selected by the organizing board. Each year this tour draws a tremendous sellout response, so we advise you to order your tickets well in advance!

WHITE CENTER HOME GARDEN TOUR / JULY

Contact: Peggy Weiss, (206) 767-6337 | **Web:** www.mindspring.com/~wcgt/

A self-guided tour of home and community gardens gives visitors a chance to enjoy the "real" White Center, a vital and diverse community. The organizers continue to stage this as a *free* event, inviting guests to learn more about the benefits of living here. In addition to residential gardens, the tour often includes the nearby Seattle Chinese Garden and the Elda Behm Garden / Highline Botanical Gardens.

WOODINVILLE SPRING GARDEN OPEN HOUSE / APRIL

Phone: (425) 483-9104, ext. 302

Sponsored by the Water District, this free tour showcases low-water-use gardens and offers lectures on drought-tolerant landscaping practices and water-wise lawn care.

COMPETITIONS

EDMONDS IN BLOOM

This summerlong festival of gardens in the waterfront community of Edmonds, north of Seattle, includes a spring garden festival in May; a garden design competition in June (followed by a fabulous tour of the participating gardens); and a floral competition in July. For details, call the Edmonds in Bloom Association at (425) 771-2631.

PACIFIC GARDENS COMPETITION

This is an annual garden design competition, sponsored by the *Seattle Times' Pacific Magazine,* the Northwest Flower and Garden Show, and the Arboretum Foundation, and it's open to residential gardeners in King, Pierce, and Snohomish Counties. Entry deadline is typically in June, with judging in July. The grand prize is a trip for two to London and its famed Chelsea Garden Show, and there are many prizes for other entrants as well. You don't have to enter your whole property; it can be a front or back garden, or other special spot. For entry forms, call the Arboretum Foundation at (206) 325-4510 or look for a form at area nurseries. There is also information on the Web at www.arboretumfoundation.org.

SEATTLE'S TRAFFIC CIRCLE ROUNDUP

This new competition, sponsored by the City of Seattle's Transportation Urban Forestry Landscape Services, recognizes the creativity of neighborhood volunteers who plant and care for the ubiquitous traffic circle. (If you can't beat 'em, join 'em and turn that annoying distraction into a miniature garden for that puts smiles on the faces of drivers.) The City looks for "circle gardens" with heart and soul. For details, call Liz Ellis at (206) 684-5008 or email liz.ellis@ci.seattle.wa.us.

WHATCOM COUNTY IN BLOOM FRIENDLY GARDEN COMPETITION

Sponsored by the Whatcom County Parks Department, this competition has for nearly 20 years been recognizing many categories of great gardens—residential, but also business and community plantings. There are special categories to applaud categories like chemical-free gardens and children's gardens. The entry period typically begins in May. For an entry form, write Dana Hanks, 2600 Sunset Drive, Bellingham, WA 98225, or call (360) 733-6897.

chapter

GARDENS TO VISIT

**Public Gardens in
British Columbia,
Oregon & Washington**

**Private Gardens
Open to View**

As you travel through the Pacific Northwest, be it a quick trip to the grocery store or to points beyond, try to fit in an excursion to one or more of these lovely gardens. Some are large and filled with mature plants; a few are small and emerging in significance. Some are very urban, others very rural, some are as American as apple pie, others are striking because of their "foreignness." Perhaps circumstances will conspire to allow you a few unplanned minutes stolen from a busy schedule or a long journey to wander down a garden pathway. You may plan ahead, or make slipping into gardens a regular habit and become an addict, as happened to us in researching this book. Either way, garden interludes like these will go a long way to perking up a flagging day.

START YOUR TOUR HERE!

Guidebook Companions

Visiting gardens has much in common with touring art museums—some people like to visit gardens alone in order to set their own pace and concentrate on details of design, plant combinations, or gardening technique (or at the very least, to capture the atmosphere of the place unencumbered by the necessity of making conversation). Others wouldn't think of setting out on a garden foray without a friend or two in tow. No matter what inspires the event or how it is organized, a welcome companion to touring is a well-researched and entertainingly written guidebook to the gardens of the Pacific Northwest. Here are

266

some suggested authors and books who have been trusty companions during the many research trips and journeys on which this *Resource Directory* has led us over the years.

Garden Touring in the Pacific Northwest

Jan Kowalczewski Whitner (Alaska Northwest Books, 1993).

Though a little dated now, this book nevertheless covers the topic and area very well. Jan makes a convivial guide, providing an overview of the garden or park, historical details, design and plant descriptions, and practical details like directions and best viewing seasons. The useful appendix lists gardens by type: "Gardens of Winter Interest," "Gardens for Picnicking," "Rose Gardens," "Asian Gardens," and "Native Plant Collections," for example.

Green Afternoons: Oregon Gardens to Visit

Amy Houchen (Oregon State University Press, 1998).

For anyone touring through Oregon this book is a *must have*. Amy has done her research and ferreted out a broad range of gardens and other places of interest to touring gardeners—parks, arboretums, college campuses, and experiment stations—all are well-described with lots of detail, including historical information and botanical and common names of noteworthy plants. Clear maps and directions (including bus information where appropriate) are a blessing for those from afar.

Garden City: Vancouver

Marg Meikle and Dannie McArthur (Polestar Book Publishers, 1999).

This resource guide parallels many of the topics in *The Northwest Gardeners' Resource Directory*, but instead of covering a region it covers a city, Vancouver, British Columbia, and very thoroughly. Essentially a handy guide for locals, it also makes a useful planner for a gardening-themed trip to this beautiful place. You'll find it a useful complement to this *Directory* as you hone in on the gardens and shops to visit, events and classes to take in, and follow helpful hints on special opportunities not to miss.

Guide to Portland Area Gardens

Berry Botanic Garden (see contact information under "Gardens to Visit: Oregon" below).

The Berry Botanic Garden staff has produced this excellent brochure, which is packed full of useful information on many of the Rose City's beautiful public and private gardens. The publication includes descriptions of a number of Portland's neighborhood gardens that we couldn't include in this chapter but which may spark interest in visitors who want to garden-hop while seeing Portland's larger gardens. The brochure lists addresses, phone numbers, limited directions (including Tri-Met public transportation routes), hours and days of operation, entry fee costs, and brief descriptions of the gardens. Call or write Berry Botanic Garden for a free copy.

Join a Club or Society

If you are particularly keen to visit small, private residential gardens, two alternatives come readily to mind. First, join a garden club, foundation, or society, most of which schedule members-only garden tours each year. Some of the most interesting gardens you'll ever visit are accessible only through such an opportunity. The intimacy of the group often leads to an ease of discussion, especially with the garden creator(s). For those covetous of the British system of "Gardens Open," the Oregon Hardy Plant Society and the Northwest Perennial Alliance offer quite extensive listings in their respective "gardens open" directories, specifying dates, details, and directions to choice landscapes—for members only.

Local Garden Tours

Take advantage of garden tours. There are dozens throughout this region, primarily in the spring and early summer. Many are major fundraisers, like the annual July **Bainbridge in Bloom** (which provides major funding for several Bainbridge Island arts and humanities programs), the Bellingham area's **Whatcom Horticultural Society Tour**, which helps fund horticultural activities, and the **Salem Garden Tour**, which benefits the A. C. Gilbert Discovery Village for children. Check Chapter 12, under "Flower and Garden Shows," for details.

Other chapters that highlight gardens to visit: Chapter 4, "Northwest Native Plants," lists gardens that emphasize design with native trees, shrubs, and perennials; Chapter 14, "Travel Opportunities," lists tours of private and public gardens.

Gardening on the Internet

Many societies have websites with links to public and private gardens that relate to their interests, such as the wonderful site of the American Rhododendron Society at www.rhododendron.org, which includes great references to regional rhododendron gardens. Some listings provide only basic information; others offer more elaborate profiles or links to the actual home pages of a public garden. Here are some sites that are the heavy hitters, and that offer the largest number of gardens, with the most information, color photos, and (often) maps.

ELISABETH C. MILLER HORTICULTURAL LIBRARY

www.millerlibrary.org

When you go to "Web Resources" here and click on "Arboreta, Gardens and Herbaria," you'll find an excellent list of links to national and regional gardens. The site leads you to the American Association of Botanical Gardens and Arboreta (and its member gardens), plus more than 25 Pacific Northwest gardens and several international sites.

L. R. FORTNEY

www.phy.duke.edu/~fortney/tours/tours.html

This is a quirky site, but we're glad that Dr. Lloyd R. Fortney, a physics professor at Duke University, loved to travel, take photos of gardens, and share them with others via his website. He's an enthusiastic guide, offering great photos and commentary from his tours around the Seattle area and beyond to Vancouver, BC. Visit the Bellevue Botanical Garden, Wells Medina Nursery, Little and Lewis Water Gardens and Linda Cochran's garden, the UBC Botanical Garden, and VanDusen, for instance.

Notes to the Listings

* The term "wheelchair accessible" is used to indicate the general level of ease with which anyone with a walking difficulty can navigate the garden or facility.

* Traveling from a distance to one of these areas? When a garden listed here offers a brochure, send them a self-addressed stamped envelope (SASE) and request one. Better yet, visit the website and send an email with any questions about special events or unexpected holiday schedules. You'll be better prepared when you arrive—and have a wonderful sense of anticipation as you look for those plants and garden features deemed remarkable.

GARDENS TO VISIT: OREGON

BERRY BOTANIC GARDEN

1505 SW Summerville Avenue, Portland, OR 97219 | **Phone:** (503) 636-4112 | **Fax:** (503) 636-7496 (office open weekdays 9 a.m.-4:30 p.m.) | **Email:** bbg@rdrop.com | **Web:** www.berrybot.org | **Directions:** From downtown Portland, take Front Ave or First Ave S and follow signs for the Ross Island Bridge (being careful to avoid driving onto the bridge). Take the Lake Oswego exit and proceed south on Macadam Ave, which turns into SW Riverside (Hwy 43) to SW Military Road. Turn right onto Military Rd and continue to Summerville. Turn right and follow to the garden. From I-5, take the Terwilliger exit 297 and follow Terwilliger Blvd to just before Lewis & Clark College; follow signs to the college, which puts you on Palatine Hill Road. Continue on Palatine Hill Rd 1/4 mile past college to Military Road. Turn right on Military and continue to Summerville. Turn right and follow to the garden. | **Open:** Daylight hours, by appointment. Open Houses scheduled during April, May, and October. Check website for specific dates. | **Entry fee:** Adults $5, children under 12 free, members free. | **Tours:** By prior arrangement; often included on the itinerary of organized tours of Portland gardens; tours on Open House days. | **Accessibility:** Partially accessible for those with walking difficulties. Visitor Center is wheelchair accessible. | **Support organization:** The Berry Botanic Garden (a nonprofit organization) founded 1977.

Originally the home and garden of Rae Selling Berry (1881-1976), who was deeply dedicated to acquiring and propagating species plants from around the world for growing in the Pacific Northwest. From the early 1930s, she actively subscribed to plant-hunting expeditions in China, the Himalayas, and Tibet to receive seed of plants she would then grow on her wooded site. On this 6.5-acre site, visitors will find splendid species collections of rhododendrons, primulas, and alpine plants, along with many valued Northwest natives, specimen trees and shrubs, woodland plants, and unusual perennials. The garden is nestled in a residential area among the hills of southwest Portland. Berry Botanic Garden is a peaceful woodland setting with trails that meander through a number of microclimates established to nurture native and exotic plants alike. Outstanding perennials, ferns, shrubs, and trees provide context and structure. Along with preserving and enhancing flora, the garden is also noted for its conservation programs of native endangered plants, playing a major role as the Pacific Northwest affiliate garden for the National Center for Plant Conservation: The Berry is home to the Seed Bank for Rare and Endangered Plants of the Pacific Northwest, with the largest collection of seeds of rare plants in the region. Besides membership, consider supporting the garden through its plant sales, and request information on an outstanding lineup of workshops, nursery and garden tours, classes, and lectures. Seed exchange for members.

BUSH'S PASTURE PARK

600 Mission Street SE, Salem, OR 97302 | **Phone:** (503) 588-6261 or (503) 363-4714 | **Web:** oregonlink.com/salem_parks | **Directions:** From I-5 traveling south, take the Salem Parkway exit 260 and continue south on Commercial St. Turn left onto Mission St. From the south, take the Hwy 22 exit 253 west, which becomes Mission St. Continue west over the overpass to High St, turn left on High St, and take the first left into the park. | **Open:** Daily, year-round. Located within a lovely 90-acre park, with picnic facilities. | **Tours:** Self-guided; Rose Identification brochure is available. | **Brochure:** Free; historic and modern photos of house, shop, Bush Barn Art Center, gardens, and the surrounding park. A map is included as well. | **Accessibility:** Limited wheelchair access. | **Support organization:** Friends of Bush's Pasture Gardens; became a city park in 1953.

Bush's Pasture is a neighbor of Salem's Deepwood Estate, so plan to stop at both gardens while in the area. This is a lovely park that spans 100 acres, complete with picnic facilities. Of particular note at Bush's is the Tartar Old Rose collection. Many of the roses are from early pioneer days, and are set in a lovely Victorian garden complete with a new period gazebo and "modern" roses. The collections are labeled. The property is blessed with many flowering trees, including crabapples. Of special interest to many will be the 1882 conservatory, the oldest example of its type in the Northwest. It houses a collection of tender treasures, while a number of small gardens feature herbs, spring bulbs, annuals, and perennials. Of historical interest, the apple trees were planted over a century ago by Father Leslie on the original Donation Land Claim. In about 1927 the revered landscape architects Elizabeth Lord and Edith Schryver, who lived nearby, helped in an informal, neighborly sense with some of Sally Bush's planting decisions in the orchard . . .

adding ornamental cherries, crabapples, and plums. Later they were involved professionally with some of the rose beds housing old and species roses donated from the Mae M. Tartar collection. The handsome Victorian Bush House, built in 1877, is open to the public as a museum and gallery run by the Salem Art Association (Adults $4, seniors and students $3, children 6-12 $2, and children 5 and under free), and the historic barn houses the Bush Barn Art Center.

BUTTERFLIES FOREVER

260 Bay Street, Astoria, OR 97103 | **Phone:** (503) 738-3180 | **Email:** bforever@bforever.org | **Web:** www.oregonbutterflies.org | **Mailing address:** PO Box 604, Astoria, OR 97103-0604 | **Directions:** Traveling north or south on I-5, take the Longview/Ocean Beaches exit and follow signs to the Oregon Bridge and Oregon Hwy 30. Follow Hwy 30 West for 60 miles to Astoria. Stay on the highway, past downtown, until you reach Bay St. Turn right, and directly ahead you will see Butterflies Forever. Or follow Sunset Hwy 26 from Portland through Seaside (100 miles) and follow the Hwy 101 directions. | **Open:** Daily for self-guided tours; Memorial Day weekend through Sept. 30, 10 a.m.-6 p.m. (5 p.m. closing after Labor Day). | **Entry fee:** $4.50 adults, $3 seniors, children (4-12) $1.50, children (3 and under) free. | **Accessibility:** Wheelchair accessible.

Come and view the butterflies flying freely in the 4,000 square foot enclosed butterfly garden filled with gorgeous blooming plants. Butterflies Forever's nonprofit Live Butterfly Garden in Astoria allows you to walk among over 300 butterflies that fill this enclosed garden. Created to celebrate the short but beautiful life of butterflies, the gardens are planted with trees, shrubs, and flowers that naturally attract these fluttering creatures. The horticultural surroundings have been designed to meet butterfly needs for food and shelter in both the larval and adult stages. The garden is planning to build a permanent glass conservatory in 2003, able to house 1,000 butterfly varieties from around the world.

CECIL & MOLLY SMITH RHODODENDRON GARDEN

5065 Ray Bell Road, St. Paul, OR; Mail: PO Box 86424, Portland, OR 97286-0424 | **Phone:** (503) 590-2505 (no phone at the garden). | **Email:** red@hardy-orchids.com | **Web:** www.arsportland.org/pdx-csg1.htm (maintained by the Portland Chapter of the American Rhododendron Society). | **Directions:** Take 99W (Pacific Hwy) south to Newburg. At the first traffic light, turn left onto Springbrook Rd and go 2 miles, jog right, then turn left (south) onto SR 219 (St. Paul Hwy) and travel 1 mile; cross the Willamette River and then take the next right onto Champoeg Rd; 0.8 mile after leaving the junction of SR 219 and Champoeg Rd, go straight onto Ray Bell Rd to the third house on the right. Parking is on the shoulder of the road. | **Open:** Third Saturday in March, first and third Saturdays in April and May, 10 a.m.-4 p.m; plants (especially rhododendrons) for sale on days the garden is open, propagated from the garden by volunteers. | **Entry fee:** $3 (free to members of the ARS). | **Tours:** By appointment; call (503) 590-2505. | **Accessibility:** Partly wheelchair accessible—very limited as garden is on a hillside. Restroom facilities, but handicap access is limited. | **Support organizations:** Owned by the Portland Chapter of the American Rhododendron Society; with support from the Willamette, Tualatin, and Yamhill chapters.

This is a private garden now owned by the Portland Chapter of the American Rhododendron Society. Almost half a century has passed since Cecil and Molly Smith began introducing rhododendrons into this peaceful rural woodland setting of 5.5 acres. Along with species grown from seed collected from afar, Mr. Smith's legacy as an internationally recognized rhododendron hybridizer is still much in evidence. Today over 400 species and hybrid rhododendrons mingle artfully among prolific underplantings of ferns, hellebores, trilliums, cyclamen, and many other woodland bulbs and wildflowers. Carefully selected trees such as paperbark maples (*Acer griseum*) and Japanese umbrella pine (*Sciadopitys verticillata*) weave among the native Douglas firs.

CLACKAMAS COMMUNITY COLLEGE

19600 S Molalla Avenue, Oregon City, OR 97045 | **Directions:** Travel south of Portland on I-205 to Oregon City, take the Park Place exit (#10), and follow south on SR 213 to and onto Beavercreek Rd, then turn left into the campus of Clackamas Community College.

❋Horticultural Department Gardens

Contact: Elizabeth Howley, Dept. Chair | **Phone:** (503) 657-6958, ext. 2389 | **Email:** ehowley@clackamas.cc.or.us | **Directions:** After arriving at the campus, bear right and follow Douglas Loop and the signs for Clairmont Hall. | **Open:** Daily, 8 a.m. to dusk. | **Entry fee:** Free. | **Accessibility:** Wheelchair accessible on level ground, handicap parking nearby. | **Support organization:** Clackamas Community College, Horticulture Department.

These gardens, some of which date back 15 years, exist for student development as well as community enjoyment. There are a number of different established garden areas here. If you garden, you are no doubt aware of the All-American Selections that are featured by the American Gardening Bureau, and one feature garden here has been established just to display these promising plants. You will find separate displays of dwarf conifers, ornamental grasses, herbs, herbaceous perennials, and a garden devoted to annuals that students (of course) replant annually. The rose garden was recently installed to commemorate and celebrate the successful joining of the Hardy Plant Society of Oregon, the nursery industry, and benefactors who've donated funds for much-needed improvements (totaling over $1 million!) to the Horticulture program facilities.

❋John Inskeep Environmental Learning Center

Contact: (503) 657-6958, ext. 2351 (weekdays) | **Email:** elc@clackamas.cc.or.us | **Web:** www.clackamas.cc.or.us/elc/. (Here you'll find a map for a self-guided tour, with photos. You'll also find their calendar of events and information about classes.) | **Directions:** Follow as above to Clairmont Hall, but continue on to the sign for the ELC and turn right (go past the recycling center). | **Open:** Daily, 8 a.m. to dusk. | **Brochure:** Yes. | **Accessibility:** Wheelchair accessible, about a mile on a gravel trail. | **Support organization:** Clackamas Community College, Horticulture Department.

This Environmental Education Center is startling proof of the power of reclamation as the area was once the industrial site of a jam factory. The three major buildings (a viewing pavilion, an observatory, and an educational hall) all stand as an impressive testament to the power of creative scrounging. The 5-acre nature center is now housed among ponds and creeks, and also houses a Metro Composting Demonstration site. The center features displays and demonstrations geared to a more sensitive and environmentally friendly approach, not only to gardening but also to the entire impact we have on the fragile ecosystem. You'll also find a solar-heated greenhouse, a plastics recycling demonstration area (including a sturdy bridge made from recycled plastics), and a recycled materials sculpture garden. If you are concerned with stream-bank and upland restoration, there's a demonstration site here for that here too. About 250 native plants, along with ornamentals for wetlands and wildlife habitat grow here, and there is a nursery where plants are offered for sale.

❀ Home Orchard Society Arboretum

Contact: Jim Cox | **Phone:** (503) 234-3559 | **Mailing address:** The Home Orchard Society, PO Box 230192, Tigard, OR 97281-0192 | **Web:** www.wvi.com/~dough/HOS/HOS8.html | **Open:** Saturdays, April through October, 8 a.m. to 3 p.m., or by appointment. | **Accessibility:** Wheelchair accessible. | **Support organization:** The Home Orchard Society.

Located on 1.6 acres of Clackamas Community College land, this demonstration orchard was designed, installed, and is maintained by the Home Orchard Society. It features edible plants, with mature fruit trees, shrubs, vines, and espaliers providing an excellent source of cultural information. You'll find sections of the arboretum dedicated to apples, pears, stone fruit, small fruit, unusual fruit, edible landscaping, grapes, blueberries, and historic varieties. Part of what makes this such a valuable destination for the home orchardist or gardeners interested in adding fruit to their site is that a number of tests are always in progress, whether they are directed at fruit-variety testing (both old favorites and newer varieties), examples of different rootstocks, training methods, watering techniques, plant combinations, ground covers, pest-control methods, harvest timing, or countless other fascinating inquiries.

❀ Pauling Center Native Garden

19600 S Molalla Avenue, Molalla, OR 97045 | **Contact:** Joan Harrison-Buckley | **Phone:** (503) 657-6958, ext. 2383 | **Email:** joanh@Clackamas.cc.or.us. | **Accessibility:** Wheelchair accessible. | **Entry fee:** Free. | **Support organization:** Life Science Dept., Clackamas Community College.

The Pauling Center Native Garden is home to 14 separate plant beds, housing approximately 100 different plant species native to the Pacific Northwest and the southern Oregon Siskiyou Mountains. Of these, about 10 are rare and endemic to specific locations. The garden is designed to showcase our native flora as being valuable to the home landscape, while the garden's central pond serves as a native wetland system and provides safe haven for native frogs. Also featured in the garden is the "Geologic Walk Through Time," reminding us of the immense time periods that have passed during Earth's existence, and the very brief period we humans have been here. Adjacent to the native garden is the "Oregon Tree Transect." Here visitors can feel as though they are emerging from Eastern Oregon to the Pacific Coast as they observe the sequence of evergreen trees that one would naturally encounter on such a trip. Additionally, the garden often takes on the role of an outdoor art gallery.

PORTLAND CLASSICAL CHINESE GARDEN

NW 3rd at Everett, Portland, OR 97208 | **Contact:** PO Box 3706 Portland, OR 97208 | **Phone:** (503) 228-8131 | **Email:** glee@portlandchinesegarden.org | **Web:** www.portlandchinese garden.org | **Directions:** Between NW 2nd and 3rd and NW Flanders and Glisan in downtown Portland's Old Town/Chinatown district. The garden can be reached from I-405 by taking the Everett Street Exit and turning east. | **Support organizations:** The Chinese Garden Society, the City of Portland, the City of Suzhou, and the Classical Chinese Garden Trust. | **Open:** Nov.-March, 10 a.m.-5 p.m; April-Oct., 9 a.m.-6 p.m. | **Entry fee:** Adults $6; Seniors and Students, $5; Children (5 and under), free.

The genesis of this garden goes back to 1985, when a delegation from Portland traveled to Suzhou, China, to develop a relationship that resulted in sister-cities status in 1988. A year later, the Classical Chinese Society was formed. A major effort in 1993, spearheaded by then-Mayor Vera Katz, led to the acquisition of land in the heart of Portland—in Chinatown—occupying one entire city block. In keeping with the mission to develop a traditional Suzhou-style garden, the principal design work was accomplished in China (with collaboration of a Portland architectural firm). The result of all of these efforts is the largest authentic, urban Suzhou-style garden ever created outside China. Within this enclosed garden serpentine walkways, a bridged lake, and open colonnades will guide you through a meticulously arranged landscape of rock groupings, delicate trees and shrubs, lattice screens, and pavilions. All told the gardens encompass nine pavilions and buildings, including a teahouse and a gift shop. With nearly 100 mature specimen tress, hundreds of rare and unusual shrubs, water plants, orchids (and more), nature puts on a show year-round at the garden. Visit the website for a schematic drawing of the walled, 40,000 square foot enclosed garden; look too for events listings, news, history, a description of the garden, and tour information.

CONNIE HANSEN GARDEN

1931 NW 33rd Street, Lincoln City, OR | **Phone:** (541) 994-7174 | **Email:** conniehansengarden@hotmail.com | **Web:** www.conniehansengarden.com | **Mailing address:** PO Box 776, Lincoln City, OR 97367 | **Directions:** From Hwy 101 go west on either NW 34th or NW 33rd to the garden, which is between the two at NW Oar St. | **Open:** Daily, 9 a.m.-5 p.m; Tuesday and Saturday hosts are on-site, and library, gallery, gift shop, and handicapped restroom are open. | **Entry fee:** No admission fee but donations are appreciated. | **Tours:** For groups by appointment. |

Brochure: Free, general information. | **Accessibility:** Partially wheelchair accessible. | **Support organization:** Connie Hansen Garden Conservancy.

This is an Oregon coastal wetland residential garden of great diversity, just over an acre in size—the garden of the late Connie Hansen, a botanist, hybridizer, and plant collector. The garden is filled with the **botanical treasures** she collected and grew from seed over a span of 20 years until her death in 1993 at age 83. The garden's impressive magnificence sparked interest in the media, and it has been featured in *Sunset*, *Better Homes and Gardens Quarterly*, and *Fine Gardening* magazines. Hansen was noted for her avid participation in seed exchanges and for growing the unusual. This site is shady and moist, characteristics she capitalized on in her love of primulas, Siberian and Japanese irises, and rhododendrons (both species and hybrids). Many lovely specimen trees and shrubs grow here, including viburnum, magnolias, Japanese maples, and stewartia, to name a few. Now under the care of a group of dedicated friends and volunteers, Connie Hansen's home and garden have it all, with a horticultural center including a library (horticultural and literary), meeting space, classroom, gallery, and gift shop.

CRYSTAL SPRINGS RHODODENDRON GARDEN

SE 28th and SE Woodstock Boulevard, Portland, OR | **Contact:** PO Box 86424, Portland, OR 97286 | **Phone:** (503) 771-8386 | **Web:** www.arsportland.org/pdx-cyst.htm | **Directions:** From downtown Portland travel east on Ross Island Bridge (Hwy 26), keeping right to exit from the bridge onto 99E. Again, keep to the right and exit 99E onto Holgate Blvd. Proceed east on Holgate to SE 28th, and turn right (south) on SE 28th to the garden, at Woodstock Blvd. (Reed College campus is across the street. From SE Powell Blvd (Hwy 26), turn south onto 26th Ave. Turn left on Holgate Blvd, then right on SE 28th Ave. The garden parking lot is 0.7 mile on the right. | **Open:** Thursday-Monday, March-Labor Day, 10 a.m.-6 p.m | **Entry fee and events:** $3 (under 12, free). You may avoid paying the fee by coming before 10 a.m. or after 6 p.m. Rhododendron Show and Plant Sale held on first Saturday of April and Mother's Day weekend. | **Accessibility:** Wheelchair accessible. | **Support organizations:** Friends of Crystal Springs, Portland Chapter of the American Rhododendron Society, and Portland Parks.

Crystal Springs is a 7-acre garden featuring some 2,500 hybrid and species rhododendrons, first planted here in 1950. This original garden area, now called "The Island," was designed by landscape architect Ruth Hansen, a Rhododendron chapter member. The portion of the garden known as "The Peninsula," showcasing additional display gardens, was designed by Wallace K. Huntington, a well-known Portland landscape architect. This area was dedicated in 1977. In the early years, The Island was the site of a rhododendron test garden to check hybrids for local adaptability. It was one of only three ARS test gardens in the country, though it is no longer used for that purpose. Companion woody plantings of azaleas, magnolias, dogwoods, Japanese maples, and 140 different choice ornamental trees meld with the underplantings of perennials, ferns, and woodland ground-covers.

The site borders Crystal Springs Lake and thus has the added feature of waterfowl. The Audubon Society has recorded 94 species of birds in the garden. At the Jean Martin Entrance Garden, at the North Lagoon area beneath the parking lot, and at The Island rock garden, you will find cascading waterfalls. Or picnic on a grassy swath on the south end of The Island, a glorious spot.

While in this vicinity, take advantage of the lovely grounds of **Reed College**, where mature beech, oak, and maple trees mingle with exquisite conifers. Make sure to bring along your copy of *Trees of Portland* (see Chapter 10 under "Literature").

DARLINGTONIA BOTANICAL WAYSIDE

Address: 84505 US Highway 101 S, just north of Florence, OR | **Phone:** (800) 551-6949 | **Open:** Year-round; the plants emerge between March-September, but are best viewed for flowering in April, May, and June. | **Tours:** Self-guided. | **Accessibility:** Forest path to viewing from a wooden deck.

The Darlingtonia Wayside just north of Florence is a tourist stop just off Highway 101 and is the natural habitat of the native carnivorous plants *Darlingtonia californica* and *Drosera rotundifolia*. They fit marvelously into the marriage of the exotic and the native, a theme we see often these days in cultivated Northwest gardens, but these live here quite happily at the dictate of Mother Nature herself. It is a beautiful place and the plants are seen by walking underneath the canopy of incense cedar and rhododendrons.

DEEPWOOD GARDENS

1116 Mission Street SE, Salem, OR 97302 | **Phone:** (503) 363-1825 | **Web:** www.oregonlink.com/deepwood/index.html | **Directions:** From I-5, take exit 253 west on Mission St SE. Turn left (south) on 12th St for 1 block to Lee St SE. | **Open:** May-Sept, Noon-5 p.m., Sun.-Fri. (closed Sat.); Oct.-April, 1-4 p.m. Sun., Mon., Wed., and Fri. | **Entry fee:** The gardens are free; there is a small charge to tour the house. | **Brochure:** *Historic Deepwood Gardens* is packed with fascinating information, historical photos, and a plan of the garden. | **Accessibility:** Partial wheelchair accessibility. | **Support organizations:** The Friends of Deepwood, City of Salem.

The genius and genesis of this relatively small (2 acre), historic estate garden come from the partnership of landscape architects Elizabeth Lord and Edith Schryver, hired in 1929 by Alice Brown Powell to create a sophisticated garden befitting her 1894 Queen Anne style home. The influence of European structure is seen in the skilled use of clipped boxwood, holly, and yew in the background, and in the border hedging and topiary details. The integration of an elegant wrought-iron gazebo (brought from the 1905 Lewis and Clark Exposition in Portland), wrought-iron fencing, and vine-covered arbors all heightens the overall feeling that one has somehow been transported to a lavish European garden. The substantive border designed to follow a Gertrude Jekyll-esque color progression (created in 1982 by the Volunteer Deepwood Gardeners) just heightens the effect. At the south end of the property, find the William S. Walton

Greenhouse, installed by the City of Salem, which is filled with plants and is open to the public for an admiring look. In addition to a number of formal gardens, one has the opportunity to follow a steep path into a woodland area, the 2-acre Ruth Steiner Fry Nature Trail. This forested walk is very pleasant on a hot day, with its stream and abundance of native flora and bird life.

ELK ROCK, BISHOP'S CLOSE

11800 SW Military Lane, Portland | **Phone:** (503) 636-5613 | **Mailing address:** PO Box 69244, Portland, OR 97201 | **Directions:** From downtown Portland follow the signs for the Ross Island Bridge, being careful to avoid driving onto the bridge; take the Lake Oswego exit and proceed south on Macadam Ave, which turns into SW Riverside (Hwy 43), to SW Military Rd, three lights south of Sellwood Bridge. Turn left, then immediately right onto Military Lane and drive to the end. | **Open:** Daily, 8 a.m.-5 p.m. | **Entry fee:** Free, although donations are appreciated. | **Tours:** Available to groups, with a guide; call for reservations. | **Brochure:** Free; provides historical information, a plan, and a detailed "walk" through the garden. | **Accessibility:** Partial wheelchair access on lawn and gravel pathways. | **Support organization:** An endowment, and Friends of Elk Rock Garden (you can join!)

A private garden of the Episcopal Diocese, Elk Rock welcomes the public to visit and experience the beauty and serenity of this setting, home to a celebrated collection of rare and interesting plants. Elk Rock has expanses of formal and informal lawn and woodland garden areas, and a richly planted stream tumbling over outcroppings of stone down the hillside, and its uncommon plants will delight enthusiasts. Originally, in the early 1890s, the property was home to three bachelors (dubbed the "Cliff Cottage Club"), of whom Scotsman Peter Kerr was one. By 1914, Mr. Kerr was the remaining partner on the property. After he married and started a family, the cottage gave way to a larger house. The garden evolved over many years as Mr. Kerr, an avid gardener, collaborated with John Olmsted of the prestigious and prolific Olmsted Brothers Landscape Architects firm. After Mr. Kerr's death in 1957 at the impressive age of 95, his daughters Jane Platt and Anne McDonald (well-respected garden-makers in their own rights) gave and endowed the garden to the Episcopal Bishop of Oregon, with the stipulation that visitors be welcome. Perched on a high bluff overlooking the Willamette River, the garden exploits the solid bones of native Douglas firs, western dogwoods and madrone, and incorporates many rare specimen trees, which have been expertly planted among the natives. Amble along the terraces, through the woodland area, and in the more formal areas closer to the imposing stone house. There is an especially fine collection of mature magnolias—22 different species and varieties are represented.

GEORGE OWEN MEMORIAL ROSE GARDEN

Eugene Public Works Maintenance, Parks Services Division, 1820 Roosevelt Boulevard, Eugene, OR 97402 | **Phone:** (541) 682-4800 or (541) 682-4845 | **Web:** www.ci.eugene.or.us/pw/parks/vip.htm |

Directions: Located at North Jefferson, along the south bank of the Willamette River (accessible on the river bike path system). From downtown Eugene, drive north on Washington St, turn left on 1st Ave, and then right on Jefferson St. | **Open:** Daily, 6 a.m.-11 p.m. | **Entry fee:** Free. | **Accessibility:** Accessible on level lawn.

A public-spirited lumberman and philanthropist, George Owen, donated this 8-acre riverside tract to the City of Eugene in 1950; subsequently, an All-American Rose Test Garden was born. At its inception, the rose donations came from the Eugene Rose Society and other rose enthusiasts. The collection now numbers over 4,500 individual rose plants, representing over 400 varieties. The garden includes "modern" roses (newer than 1867) as well as species and old-fashioned roses. The collection in this latter category is what makes this garden unique. Take note of the bermed island bed of mixed plantings, with many daring and striking combinations of unusual perennials. A venerable feature of the site is a hundred and forty year old Tartarian (or Black Republican) cherry tree, a remnant of a very old orchard, and the largest of its type in Oregon. Come in April when it is laden with delicate white blossoms.

HENDRICKS PARK RHODODENDRON GARDEN

Address: Eugene Public Works Department, Parks Services Division, 1800 Skyline Boulevard, Eugene, OR 97403 | **Contact:** (541) 682-5324 or 682-4800 for reservations | **Email:** michel.j.Robert@ci.eugene.or.us | **Web:** www.ci.eugene.or.us/pw/parks/hendricks/index.htm | **Directions:** From W Franklin Blvd (Hwy 99), turn south onto Walnut St to Fairmount Blvd, then turning east onto Summit Ave. | **Open:** Daily, dawn to dusk. | **Tours:** Head gardener Michael Robert offers the following: Wildflower Tours, Sundays at 11 a.m., March 24-May 5. Rhododendron Tours, Sundays at 1 p.m., April 7-May 19. Meet at the picnic shelter, and if you're a large group, call ahead to schedule an appointment. | **Brochure:** See the excellent color brochure with wonderful historical information and a map/plan of the park. | **Accessibility:** Limited wheelchair accessibility. Wear practical shoes to walk the groomed gravel paths of the hillside garden.

After spending one afternoon here picnicking and basking in the flush of bloom, one is forced to decide that Eugene must be a heavenly place to live (or at the very least worth a visit in the height of spring!). The 5,500 woody ornamentals include an enviable collection of over 2,500 rhododendrons and azaleas. What is significant is that in the early years of the 1950s, when this garden developed through the volunteer efforts of the newly formed Eugene chapter of the American Rhododendron Society, this area was the hotbed (outside of Great Britain, of course) for rhododendron collection and hybridizing. For many years the plants in this woodland garden have come solely as donations, with many rare and treasured contributions. There are trilliums, ferns, and other native plants throughout. The garden covers 15 acres of the 77-acre forested park. Over the past few years, there has been a concerted effort to plant the area in layers, with an emphasis on enlarging the collection of ground covers, bulbs, and perennials, and they've labeled most plants throughout for your edification. Hendricks Park is festooned with ornamental trees (stewartias, *Davidia involucrata*), an impressive collection of nearly 300 magnolias (many daphnes and viburnums), and a stand of native Oregon white oaks (*Quercus garryana*) and 200-year-old Douglas firs. Appealing ribbons of lawn invite a leisurely stroll or perhaps a longer stay to linger on the trusty Pendleton blanket you cleverly stowed in the trunk for such opportune moments.

HOYT ARBORETUM

Address: 4000 SW Fairview Boulevard, Portland, OR 97221 | **Phone:** (503) 228-8733, Fax: (503) 826-4213 | **Email:** haffdir@ci.portland.or.us | **Web:** www.hoytarboretum.org | **Directions:** Located adjacent to Washington Park; from downtown Portland, take I-405 west to Hwy 26W, then take the Washington Park Zoo exit and follow the signs to the Arboretum. Or take W Burnside, turn south onto SW Tichner Lane, and follow the signs. | **Open:** Daily in daylight hours; Visitor's Center open daily 9 a.m.-4 p.m. | **Entry fee:** Free. | **Tours:** Free one-hour guided tours, offered every Saturday and Sunday at 2 p.m., April through October. Leave from the Visitor's Center. Self-guided tour booklet, maps, and seasonal tour information available at the Visitor's Center. | **Accessibility:** The Bristlecone Pine Trail and the Oregon Vietnam Veterans Memorial Trail are wheelchair accessible, other areas are partially accessible. | **Support organization:** The Friends of the Hoyt Arboretum (same address and phone as the Visitor's Center).

Portland's Urban Forest of 175 acres provides city dwellers and visitors with 10 miles of scenic hiking trails to explore (connecting to the more extensive 40-mile loop through Portland's west hills). With 950 species of trees and shrubs (5,000 of them labeled), this is a Mecca for those of us intent upon learning more about their identification, along with cultural information on a wide range of woody plants. Here you will find, as one would expect, our Northwest natives—but also unique plants from six continents. Make the Visitor's Center your starting point and follow trails bearing the names of arboreal collections you will find along the way. Take the Oak Loop for example, featuring collections of quercus as well as other deciduous trees, notably magnolias and maples. Or try the Redwood-Spruce Trail along which you will find Oregon's own Brewer's weeping spruce (*Picea breweriana*), which is very rare. Spring is an especially fine time to find the understory plantings of trilliums and many species of wildflowers in bloom. The Hoyt offers lots of classes, walks, events for the family, and a sale of rare and unusual trees and shrubs in late October.

JACKSON & PERKINS

Address: 2518 S Pacific Highway, Medford, OR 97501 | **Phone:** (541) 864-2121 | **Web:** www.jacksonandperkins.com | **Directions:** From the north on I-5, take the South Medford/Barnett Rd exit, follow to Hwy 99S, and go about 1.5 miles. From the south, take the Phoenix exit and travel north on Hwy 99S about 3 miles. | **Open:** The best times are late April through September, when the roses are in bloom, but the gardens are open daily from dawn to dusk. | **Entry fee:** Free. | **Accessibility:** Wheelchair accessible.

It is easy for most of us living outside the immediate area to think of Jackson & Perkins roses thanks to the prominent place they are given in garden centers, and from their beautiful full-color mail-order catalog. But did you know they also have a dazzling display of roses at their headquarters in Medford, Oregon? It was created in 1971, and today you will be able to see the full array of hundreds of roses in a 43,000 square foot garden (many of the photographs in their color catalog are shot here). You are able to assess the whole collection for color, form, scent, and season of bloom—all in one place. You'll especially appreciate that everything is labeled and easy to identify! At the information kiosk you'll find a self-guided tour brochure, historical information about the company, and catalogs. The company horticulturist is likely to be out in the gardens working and you'll not find a better source for pruning advice or information on proper planting techniques. Nearby you'll find a smaller and less formal test garden, including perennials, where the most promising candidates for the All America Selections are evaluated (about 400-450 varieties).

JENKINS ESTATE

Address: 8005 SW Grabhorn Road (Grabhorn Rd at 209th and Farmington Rd, Hwy 10), Aloha, OR | **Phone:** (503) 642-3855 | **Fax:** (503) 591-1028 Web: www.thprd.org/Facilities/Jenkins/jenkins_estate.htm | **Mailing address:** PO Box 5868, Aloha, OR 97006 | **Directions:** From Portland head west on Hwy 26 to the 185th St exit; travel southwest on 185th to Farmington Rd (Hwy 10). Turn right and follow Farmington Road. Just before 209th St, turn left onto Grabhorn Rd and carry on a short way to the entrance. | **Open:** Grounds are open weekdays 8 a.m.-5 p.m. (on weekends, restricted to functions by appointment). | **Tours:** Self-guided tour brochure; guided tour by prior arrangement. | **Entry fee:** Free. | **Accessibility:** Limited wheelchair accessibility. | **Support organization:** Tualatin Hills Parks and Recreation District.

This 68-acre estate was once the sporting retreat of Ralph and Belle Ainsworth Jenkins, who would come out to the country from turn-of-the-century Portland as a getaway from their busy lives in the city. In 1913 they moved permanently to the property, built their hunting-lodge style home, and began establishing formal English-style gardens. After a sad period of neglect following Mrs. Jenkins' death, the Estate was purchased by the Tualatin Hills Parks and Recreation District. Today it is proudly listed in the National Registry of Historic Places, and a cadre of volunteers are helping with the maintenance and restoration of the gardens. Come for the wonderful herb garden, the historic plantings of rhododendrons, perennials (a half acre), rare specimen trees and shrubs, and the ponds. Much of the garden exists near the house but there are also woodland paths to wander (2.7 miles, paved) in search of rockeries and lilac borders. The Rose Garden features species that were available to gardeners in 1913, the year the Jenkinses moved to their estate. You'll also find a teahouse, a greenhouse, and a water tower.

LEACH BOTANICAL GARDEN

6704 SE 122nd Avenue, Portland, OR 97236 | **Phone:** (503) 823-9503 | **Fax:** (503) 823-9503 | **Email:** pkweb@ci.portland.or.us | **Web:** www.parks.ci.portland.or.us/Parks/LeachBotanicalGar.htm | **Directions:** Located 20 minutes southeast of downtown Portland. Follow Powell Blvd to SE Foster. Turn right and follow all the way to NE 122nd (you'll pass under I-205). Turn right (south) on 122nd Ave and continue south for about an eighth of a mile to the Garden entrance at Johnson Creek. Parking is just across the bridge. From I-205, exit on Foster Rd and travel east to 122nd Ave. Turn right (south) and follow directions above. | **Open:** Tuesday-Saturday, 9 a.m.-4 p.m., Sundays 1-4 p.m., closed Monday. | **Entry fee:** Free, although donations are greatly appreciated. | **Tours:** Curator's tour on the first Wednesday of the month, year-round, at 2 p.m; weekly tours Saturdays at 10 a.m. and Wednesdays at 2 p.m., March through November. Self-guided tour brochures are available (volunteers are often there to answer questions as you wander the grounds); guided group tours by appointment. | **Accessibility:** Access for wheelchairs to Manor House displays and restroom, limited area around the Visitor Center; trails are steep. | **Support organizations:** Leach Garden Friends (join!) and the Portland Bureau of Parks and Recreation.

The Leach Garden represents Portland's first public botanical garden, a gift in 1979 of John and Lilla Leach. It is the home and beloved 5-acre woodland garden they called Sleepy Hollow. In 1984, an additional 4 acres were added to the land that they had first purchased in the 1930s. As the Leaches traveled extensively to the backcountry of Oregon and Washington on collection trips, their own garden reflected the natural habitats from which treasured botanical prizes had come. We are all richer for *Kalmiopsis leachiana*, a small rhododendron-like plant, and *Iris innominata*, a native yellow iris, two of Lilla's discoveries. Throughout the 9-acre grounds over 2,000 different species, hybrids, and cultivars are labeled and grouped by habitat, from rock garden to bog, streamside to woodland (along 1.5 miles of trails). Other plants on display throughout the garden include ground covers, camellias, viburnums, wildflowers, a noteworthy Trillium Collection, a very broad range of ferns, bamboo, winter-interest plants, and native iris. Trained as a botanist, Lilla Leach was very active in her search for garden-worthy native species; many are displayed here today. The volunteers have begun a Penstemon Collection, and the Oregon Fuchsia Test garden is also located here. A centerpiece for the Garden is the Colonial Revival manor house, which serves as a visitor's center, gift shop, library, and meeting rooms. The Friends are very active in schools, community education, and fund-raising efforts.

MARTHA SPRINGER BOTANICAL GARDENS

Willamette University, 900 State Street, Salem, OR 97301 | **Contact:** Dean Wentworth, Curator | **Phone:** (503) 370-6143 | **Web:** www.willamette.edu/cla/biology/ | **Directions:** From I-5, south of Salem, take exit 253, Mission St, and proceed west on Mission, following the signs for City Center through the light at 12th St onto Bellevue St. The first right past 12th on Bellevue is into the University parking lot. The Botanical Garden is north of the lot behind the first brick building to the east, and borders 12th St. | **Open:** Private garden open to the public, daily. | **Tours:** By appointment.

The gardens, on the campus of this private liberal arts institution founded in 1842, are the fulfillment of the inspiration and hard work of a group of professors headed by Dr. Susan Kephart and students. Planning began in 1986 with planting the following year. The gardens were dedicated in 1988 to Martha Springer, professor emeritus, who inspired students for over 30 years with her enthusiasm for botany. The gardens are divided into 12 areas of interest, with theme gardens featuring Herbs, an Alpine Rock Garden, a Butterfly Attracting Garden, educational beds featuring examples of plant families, and Ethnobotanical plantings. More than a third of the garden area is dedicated to Oregon native plants, and seeks to recreate the environments of the coast, western Cascades, Willamette Valley, and southern Oregon. Also of interest on the Willamette University campus, and located off State Street across from the Capitol, is the **Sesquicentennial Rose Garden**, planted in 1992 to commemorate the 150 year anniversary of the founding. Initially, 150 roses were planted, but over 150 more roses have been added so the garden now includes floribundas, grandifloras, hybrid teas, climbers, English, albas, gallicas, rugosas, Chinas, moss, damask, and patio types. This is a popular spot from the promise of the first rose in April until winter's frost. There is also a small teaching garden with several examples of Japanese Garden styles.

MOUNT PISGAH ARBORETUM

33735 Seavy Loop Road, Eugene, OR 97405 | **Phone:** (541) 747-3817 | **Fax:** (541) 747-3817 | **Email:** mtpisgah@efn.org | **Web:** www.efn.org/~mtpisgah/ (very nice website) | **Directions:** Located 5 miles southeast of Eugene, from the east end of the I-5 overpass at the 30th St/LCC exit, go 1 block left, turn right at the gas station. Take the first left onto Seavy Loop Rd and drive about 2.2 miles, go over the one-lane bridge, and into the Recreation Area. | **Open:** Daily, dawn to dusk, year-round. | **Tours:** Weekly guided hikes emphasize seasonal ecology for the public (with a suggested donation of $3 ($2 for MPA members) and many opportunities for schoolchildren. | **Accessibility:** Limited wheelchair access. | **Support organization:** Friends of Mount Pisgah Arboretum. You can join!

The Arboretum covers 208 acres of diverse ecological habitats—riparian meadow, oak savanna, open plateaus, forested hillsides, and waterways. The history of the arboretum reaches back to 1969, when the mayor of Eugene called for the establishment of an international arboretum featuring trees from around the world. Within a decade the 2,300-acre Howard Buford Regional Recreation Area, a Lane County Park, was established. The site for the Arboretum was leased within its boundaries, bordering the Coast Fork of the Willamette River. During the 1980s staff was hired, trails were built, education programs were set up to serve thousands of area schoolchildren, and public natural history-related events were held. Mt. Pisgah Arboretum includes a specialty 2-acre garden planted with 37 families, 70 genera and 112 species of native trees, shrubs, ferns, perennials, and annuals, and is particularly noted for its wildflowers. An entrance garden features 89 species of woody plants, including 57 rhododendron species (mostly Asian) and 13 native and introduced tree species. There are over 7 miles of groomed trails and a Visitor Center offers interpretive displays and a gift shop. Weekend workshops are planned for adults, children, and families. Picnic areas are provided as well.

THE OREGON GARDEN

Westfield Street and Main Street, Silverton, OR | **Phone:** (503) 874-8100 or (877) ORGARDEN (877-674-2733) | **Email:** jim@oregongarden.org | **Web:** www.oregongarden.org | **Mailing address:** The Oregon Garden Foundation, PO Box 155, Silverton, OR 97381-0155 | **Directions:** In Silverton, about 15 miles east of Salem. From I-5 northbound, take exit 260 (Keizer exit); from I-5 southbound, take exit 263 (Brooks exit). Signs guide you 15 miles east to the garden. | **Open:** Daily, 9 a.m.-6 p.m. (March 1-Oct. 31), and 9 a.m.-3 p.m. (Nov. 1-Feb.). | **Tours:** For information on the garden, tram tours, concerts, lectures, and other events, call (877) 674-2733 or (503) 874-8100, or visit the website. | **Entry fee:** Adults $7, seniors $6, students $5, children (8-13) $3, children (7 and under) free; members free. Tram Tour, $2. | **Accessibility:** The Oregon Garden is ADA compliant.

For decades, thoughts of a major botanical garden in western Oregon's horticultural paradise inspired local visionaries to dream and to muse. Now a reality, The Oregon Garden opened in the summer of 2001 with this mission: "To be a botanically challenging, world-class facility which will showcase the wealth and diversity of plant material in a visually compelling manner. It will be a landscaped approach to plant display, resulting in a garden that is a skillfully arranged environmental laboratory for education, research and public enjoyment.".

Phase I of the Garden encompasses 60 acres (financed through public and private funds), although ambitious plans set the ultimate size at 240 acres. Located near Silverton (approximately 45 miles south of Portland), the garden is a result of a collaborative effort that includes the Oregon Association of Nurserymen taking a leading role, but also involves educators, horticultural professionals, organizations, communities, and the public in the planning process. The gardens are educational and over the next several decades will grow to become a world-class destination for garden lovers. Write for a color brochure and for information on how you can become involved as a member and/or as an active volunteer.

PACIFICA: GARDEN IN THE SISKIYOUS

14615 Watergap Road, Williams, OR 97544 | **Mailing address:** P.O. Box 1, Williams, OR 97544 | **Phone:** (541) 846-1100 | **Web:** www.pacificagardens.org | **Directions:** Pacifica is located 2.3 miles south of Williams, on Watergap Road, off Hwy 238 (between Murphy and Applegate Roads). To reach Williams, travel south on I-5 to Grants Pass (about 4–5 hours south of Portland). At Grants Pass, exit onto US 199 South, then onto SR 238 (the sign reads:

"Jacksonville Hwy./Medford"). | **Open:** Approximately 2 miles of trails are open at the nature center for self-guided tours. If you are interested in visiting, call in advance to schedule a tour.

Pacifica is a nonprofit botanic garden, nature center and educational facility all peacefully ("pacifically") woven together on 500 rolling, secluded acres in the lovely Siskiyou Mountains of southwest Oregon. This ambitious project is well on its way to becoming a must-visit destination, especially for garden lovers who are visiting nearby Ashland, on their way to or from San Francisco, or shopping at some of the region's nearby cool nurseries (Forestfarm and Siskiyou Rare Plant Nursery, to name two great spots). Pacifica is beginning a long-range plan, so we encourage you to visit, tell your friends, and consider financially supporting this wonderful regional effort. The organization has also established (in partnership with Forestfarm Nursery and the Australian Horticultural Correspondence School) "Pacifica's School of Practical Horticulture," which provides 600 hours of practical horticultural study leading to a certificate. For information on the program, call Peg at (541) 846-9230 or Forbes at (541) 846-9807 or via email: forbes@pacificagarden.org.

PORTLAND'S JAPANESE GARDEN

611 SW Kingston Avenue, directly above the Washington Park International Rose Test Garden | **Phone:** (503) 223-1321; Gift Shop (503) 223-5055 | **Email:** japanesegarden@japanese garden.com | **Web:** www.japanesegarden.com | **Mailing address:** PO Box 3847, Portland, OR 97208-3847 | **Directions:** From I-405 in downtown Portland follow signs for Hwy 26W. Take the Oregon Zoo and Forestry Center exit, bearing right after the exit and following signs for the Forestry Center. Continue up hill and turn right on Kingston Dr, where you will see a wood sign for the Japanese Garden and Rose Garden. Follow Kingston Dr for just under 2 miles through Washington Park to garden entrance. | **Open:** April-Sept., 10 a.m.-7 p.m. (Monday 12-7); Oct.-Mar., 10 a.m.-4 p.m. (Monday 12-4). | **Tours:** Daily guided tours, April-Oct. at 10:45 a.m. and 2:30 p.m. To schedule a tour, call (503) 223-9233 or email: tours@japanesegarden.com. | **Brochure:** Free, with garden highlights, map. (We highly recommend the book *Human Nature: The Japanese Garden of Portland, Oregon* by Bruce Taylor Hamilton, which provides, in fabulous color photographs and detailed, sensitive text, the story of this beautiful garden. If you plan a trip to Portland consider ordering this book in advance to prepare for your visit to the garden.) A full video of the garden is available as well. | **Entry fee:** Adults $6, seniors 62+ $4, students (college and ages 6-17) $3.50. | **Accessibility:** Partial wheelchair accessibility. | **Support organization:** Japanese Garden Society of Oregon; (503) 223-1321 (with wonderful events for members).

This is one of the country's most highly respected Japanese Gardens. Designed by the distinguished Japanese landscape architect Professor Takuma Tono and completed in 1967, the Garden masterfully incorporates a number of traditional styles while effectively utilizing the hilly, wooded site. Entry into the garden is through a magnificent gate of the Daimyo Period. There are five traditional gardens set on 5.5 acres, impeccably maintained in all seasons. Footpaths wind their way from one to the next, with invitations to stop, reflect, and relax throughout. The structural elements of gates and fences, the traditional tea house, bridges and huts, the granite stepping-stones and hand-carved stone lanterns are all masterpieces of craftsmanship. Many events are scheduled through the year that provide insights into Japanese culture and the elements of design utilized in an authentic Japanese garden style.

PORTLAND ROSE GARDENS

400 SW Kingston Avenue, Portland, OR | **Phone:** (503) 823-3636 or (503) 823-3635 | **Email:** pkweb@ci.portland.or.us | **Web:** www.ci.portland.or.us/parks/RoseGardens.htm (this website links to a short profile, often with color photo of Portland's parks) | **Mailing address:** Portland Rose Society, PO Box 515, Portland, OR 97207 | **Phone:** (503) 777-4311 | **Email:** generalinfo@portland rosesociety.org | **Web:** www.portlandrosesociety.org.

Portland, the **City of Roses**, maintains three municipal rose gardens (each described below): the International Rose Test Garden, Ladd's Addition Rose Blocks, and the Peninsula Park Rose Garden.

❁ International Rose Test Garden

400 SW Kingston Avenue, Portland, OR | **Directions:** From downtown Portland take W Burnside west to SW Tichner Lane, turn left on Tichner at the blinking yellow light, and follow onto Kingston to the Washington Park Rose Test Garden. | **Open:** Daily, 7 a.m.-9 p.m. | **Entry fee:** No entry fee is required, but donations are accepted. | **Accessibility:** Partially wheelchair accessible on service road; parking accessible, restrooms accessible. | **Support organizations:** Portland Parks and Recreation Bureau; Portland Rose Society.

Talk about a Room with a View! From the three terraces set on 4.5 acres, visitors have breathtaking vistas out across the skyline of Portland to Mt. Hood beyond, with 130-acre Washington Park as a backdrop ... ultimate sublimity. Here rose-lovers will find over 10,000 roses of over 500 labeled varieties and an official testing site for the All-America Rose Selections. Peak bloom is June and July but bloom carries on through September and October. Nearby, find a Shakespeare garden of mixed plantings representing the references from this botanically literate bard.

❁ Ladd's Addition Rose Blocks

SE 16th and Harrison, Portland, OR | **Directions:** From downtown Portland, cross the Hawthorne Bridge and travel east to SE 16th, then turn right. | **Open:** Daily, 7 a.m.-9 p.m. | **Entry fee:** No entry fee is required, but donations are accepted. | **Accessibility:** Partially wheelchair accessible; parking accessible; no restrooms. | **Support organizations:** Portland Parks and Recreation, Portland Rose Society, Friends of Ladd's Addition Gardens (503) 233-5451.

A good way to understand the Ladd Addition is to look at a map of Portland. Just east of the Hawthorn Bridge you'll see an eight-block square removed from the conventional grid pattern and replaced with a criss-cross pattern, with the Ladd Circle garden in the very center. There are four rose gardens (the Squares) within this historic Hosford-Abernethy neighborhood, centered around a garden of rhododendrons, azaleas, and camel-

lias (Ladd's Circle). You'll find over 4,000 roses; both old and new varieties are represented. Park near the Circle Garden, in 1909 originally named the Central Garden, and walk to the others, originally referred to as East, West, North, and South parks. It's at Ladd Circle that one will find the longest range of bloom, beginning in spring with the rhododendrons and camellias and carrying on with hydrangeas, iris, ornamental grasses, and other perennials.

❁ Peninsula Park Rose Garden

N Ainsworth between Kerby and Albina Streets, Portland, OR | **Directions:** From downtown Portland, cross the Willamette River on one of the bridges and connect onto I-5 North. Take the Portland Blvd exit #304 and proceed east on Portland Blvd to N Albina. Turn right, then left on Ainsworth; this is the south entrance to the rose garden. | **Open:** Daily, 7 a.m.-9 p.m. | **Entry fee:** No entry fee is required, but donations are accepted. | **Accessibility:** Not accessible by wheelchair; parking accessible; restrooms accessible. | **Support organization:** Portland Parks and Recreation Bureau.

Peninsula Park is the site of Portland's first community center and formal rose gardens, dating to 1909. Today it houses nearly as many individual rose shrubs (over 8,900 plantings on a 2-acre site) as the larger and more visible International Rose Test Garden. What characterizes this sunken garden is the formality of the design, the broad brick pathways, box-edged beds, the color blocks of modern roses, and the wonderful 1913 era octagonal bandstand that overlooks the garden.

SEBRING ROCK GARDEN

Located near the entrance to Alton Baker Park, Centennial Boulevard, Eugene, OR | **Email:** parsontnospam@peak.org | **Web:** www.peak.org/~parsont/emerald/ (for details and photos of Sebring Rock Garden) | **Directions:** From I-5, exit at I-105 (Beltline West), turn left at the exit, and travel south on Coburg Rd toward downtown Eugene. Take a quick left onto Centennial Rd going toward Autzen Stadium, then take an immediate right onto Country Club Road. Turn left into Alton Baker Park entrance. The rock garden is adjacent to the parking area. | **Open:** Daily, dawn to dusk. | **Entry fee:** Free. | **Accessibility:** Wheelchair accessible; no restroom facilities on premises, but nearby. | **Support organization:** Emerald Chapter of the North American Rock Garden Society.

This garden was constructed in 1996 by the Emerald Chapter of the North American Rock Garden Society, using massive basalt rock from the Oregon Cascades. Seven beds, totaling 6,000 square feet, display nearly 1,000 species of dwarf shrubs, perennials, and bulbs from most of the world's mountain regions. See the separate collections representing the Pacific Northwest, the Mediterranean basin, and the Southern Hemisphere.

SHORE ACRES STATE PARK BOTANICAL GARDEN

10965 Cape Arago Highway, Coos Bay, OR 97420-9647 | **Phone:** (541) 888-3732 or (541) 756-5401 | **Web:** www.shoreacre.com | **Directions:** Located 13 miles southwest of Coos Bay. Take the Empire-Coos Bay Hwy exit from Hwy 101 west to the coast, turn south on Cape Arago Hwy (Hwy 14) through Charleston, and past Sunset Bay State Park approximately 1 mile. Follow signs for Shore

Acres State Park. | **Open:** Daily, dawn to dusk (exact times vary by season). | **Brochure:** Call (541) 888-3778 for a color brochure about the history of the property. | **Entry fee:** $3 per vehicle day-use permit fee (buses and motorcycles included). | **Accessibility:** Wheelchair accessible. | **Support organizations:** Oregon Parks and Recreation Department; Friends of Shore Acres, Inc.

One could not ask for a more gloriously romantic and visually stimulating destination. Originally the extravagant seaside estate and summer home of wealthy timber baron Louis J. Simpson and his family, these gardens have survived their tenure (from the heydays of the early 1900s to the hard times of the 1930s and 1940s), including the loss of the two baronial mansions built here (one to fire, one to neglect). The estate at one time kept several gardeners busy maintaining the formal, boxwood-hedged borders, expanses of lawn, a Japanese Garden, pond, and great stretches of trail through the adjacent forest. As the family fortunes turned, the expense of keeping up the estate could not be supported, and in 1942 the Oregon Parks Department purchased the property. By the 1970s, the gardens were in near ruin but work then began to return them to their former glory, perhaps with an eye to interpreting that era as well. Now a 7-acre botanical garden with a mix of original features reclaimed and new features skillfully integrated, Shore Acres makes a stunning destination for garden and nature lovers alike. The Friends of Shore Acres work with the Parks staff, providing funding for various projects from the purchase of plants to the installation of interpretive signs. A fountain brings a much-needed focal element to the structured plantings. Plant aficionados will find much of interest here, including specimens representing every continent, and particularly the Pacific Rim. The setting is spellbinding, with the juxtaposition of the forested backdrop, magnificent Monterey pines and cypress of great character, the cliffs looking out on the wild Oregon coastline, and hidden, protected within, a botanical treasure. You can also visit the greenhouse, filled with tender tropicals. During the period between Thanksgiving and New Years, the garden is decorated as an illuminated wonderland with over 250,000 lights for the "Holiday Lights at Shore Acres" display. The historic gardener's cottage is open for visitors, and free refreshments are available. Lights are on each evening from 4 to 10 p.m. during the run of the show.

GARDENS TO VISIT: WASHINGTON

ANDERSON GARDEN

Enumclaw, Washington | **Email:** Enumclaw@eskimo.com | **Web:** www.eskimo.com/~enumclaw or for view of the garden, www.rhododendron.org | **Directions:** Provided when you schedule a visit. | **Open:** To the public, Sundays in May or by appointment; open anytime to members of the American Rhododendron Society. | **Entry fee:** Donations accepted to benefit the Autism Society of Washington.

In the 1940s and '50s, Bob and Betty Anderson hand-crafted a large stone house and created an 8-acre rhododendron park in Summit, New Jersey. But Bob had read about the Pacific Northwest climate that was ideal for cultivating a wider variety of his favorite plants. He rode a Greyhound bus from New York City to Seattle, took the local transit to the end of the line, and arrived in Enumclaw, walking the rest of the way to Buckley (which he'd heard had rich, black, loamy soil). He loved the dirt but couldn't find the site he was looking for and returned to Enumclaw discouraged. While waiting for the bus, he wandered around and found the same world-famous loam. The following year, he returned and bought a 5-acre hayfield at the edge of town.

When Bob and Betty were 50, they packed everything they could fit into their nursery truck and headed to the Pacific Northwest for good. They built a home, designed a garden and settled here in 1962, beginning the work on their second rhododendron park. Today the garden features influences of northeastern, southeastern, and northwest styles, with a smattering of British and Japanese elements. The color patterns reflect Bob's training in oil and watercolor painting, using an extensive palette. Over the years, word has spread from person to person as visitors from all around the country asked to tour the Anderson garden. The American Rhododendron Society brought several busloads of rhododendron enthusiasts during two national conventions in the 1990s. In 1996 (Bob died in 1994), the gardens passed on to John and Doreen Anderson, the next generation. Take special note of the wonderful garden furniture designed and crafted by John, much of it using old rhododendron logs.

ARBORETUM OF THE CASCADES (FORMERLY THE PRESTON ARBORETUM)

29700 Southeast Highpoint Way, Preston, WA 98050 (Greenbank Farms building) | **Mailing address:** P.O. Box 512, Preston, WA 98050 | **Phone:** (425) 888-3162 | **Email:** sbond@nwlink.com | **Open:** Environmental Learning Center operated by appointment only. Call for scheduling details.

In the works for several years as a 300-acre arboretum dedicated to native trees, shrubs, and habitat, The Preston Arboretum changed its name in early 2002 as it began to implement Master Planning with the King County Parks Department. The Arboretum is located north of I-90 near Preston. A 6-acre wetland restoration garden is in the design phase, with an anticipated opening in 2003. The Arboretum of the Cascades is supported by more than 160 dues-paying members and by funds raised through major special events. As this fabulous idea for a regional native plants arboretum begins to take shape, executive director Susan Bond reports that the Arboretum of the Cascades is working with well-known Seattle landscape architectural firm Charles H. Anderson Architects (which also designed the Mount St. Helens visitors' center and is designing the Seattle Art Museum sculpture garden). "We're actively looking for volunteers and people to be part of our Master Planning process, so give us a call," she says.

BELLEVUE BOTANICAL GARDEN

12001 Main St., Bellevue, WA 98005 | **Phone:** (425) 452-2750 | **Web:** www.bellevuebotanical.org | **Mailing address:** PO Box 40536, Bellevue, WA 98015-4536 | **Directions:** The Garden is located between SE 124th and SE 118th Aves on Main St. From I-405, take the NE 8th St EAST exit to 120th Ave NE; turn south (right) and go to the first light at Main St, then turn east (left) for 3 blocks. | **Open:** Daily, 7:30 a.m. until dusk; Visitor's Center open 10 a.m.- 4 p.m; Gift Shop open daily 10 a.m.-3:30 p.m. mid-March through Nov. and 4-10:30 p.m. in Dec. during Garden D'Lights. Call (425) 452-2750 for current information. | **Entry fee:** No admission charge but a donation is greatly appreciated. | **Tours:** For group and/or children's tours call (425) 451-3755. | **Accessibility:** Partial wheelchair accessibility. | **Support organization:** Bellevue Botanical Garden Society.

This 36-acre botanical garden opened in 1992. Docents are available to answer questions Sundays Noon-3 p.m. In the Visitor's Center you'll find informational pamphlets about the various gardens, about the supporting organizations, and general leaflets on such topics as waterwise gardening. The site on Wilburton Hill was, from 1947, the home of Harriet and Calhoun Shorts. They created a garden, designed as a rhododendron glen of 7 acres, which displayed a treasury of natives and unusual ornamental trees underplanted with rare shrubs and ground covers (as you'll find in the Shorts Ground Cover Garden). In 1980 they donated the property to the community. The Bellevue Parks and Community Services Department, along with a dedicated group of volunteers, spent countless hours to prepare for opening the garden to the public. In 1996, *Garden Design Magazine* selected BBG for a feature article as one of the Top 34 Public Gardens in the United States. The editors gave special praise to the Northwest Perennial Alliance's Perennial Border (see below), rating it third in the nation. A beautifully simple and sophisticated water feature, The Stanley Smith Rill, greets visitors entering from the parking area. Water spills from a large granite boulder at one end of the Entry Plaza along a narrow rill cut in the stone of the Plaza and empties into a small pond. Many area Garden Clubs contribute gardens here: colorful dahlias are planted each year near the exquisitely crafted cabin (ca. 1920); there are two Fuchsia Display and Test Gardens with nearly 100 varieties in the ground, including many hardy varieties. Look for the useful plant labels throughout the BBG, placed to educate visitors at all levels of expertise. A large outcropping of stone has sprung up along the Plaza, with 250 tons of rock forming the base for the Alpine Rock Garden, a cooperative effort of the Bellevue Parks and Community Services Department and the BBG Society. The alpine garden features many plants from the Cascade and Olympic mountain ranges native to the Northwest. Accompanying these natives are their showy relatives, species from around the world, as well as additional small and dwarf plants selected for their form and beauty. Just beyond, you'll find the Waterwise Demonstration Garden, featuring a diverse selection of plants that thrive in the Northwest. Look here for inspiration from common plants used in uncommon ways. Take note of the attractive shelter that cleverly collects water from the clear roof and routes it to a 1,000 gallon cistern buried nearby. During dry months, the on-site reservoir can serve the drip irrigation system. This garden is the cooperative effort of Bellevue's Utilities and Parks Departments and is supported by a self-guided tour and displays, and waterwise gardening workshops in the Visitor's Center. The Yao Garden, representing Phase I of the Eastern Garden, is named for Bellevue's sister city in Japan. Basalt quarried in Oregon and hand-picked by the architect was imported to form the foundation. Ultimately the Eastern Garden sequence, of which the Yao Garden is a part, may encompass approximately 2 acres. Take a stroll along the Garden Loop Trail, a fully wheelchair-accessible walk that winds through much of the garden, through many native plants and trees, a new Native Plant Garden, and a wetland area. A number of the specimens in the Rhododendron Garden are over 40 years old and reach heights of 20 feet. The original plantings have been augmented with newer additions, along with appropriate companion underplantings. A major feature is the imposing double gate, with a beautiful copper adornment at its peak. Once you've discovered it you will want to make many visits to the BBG through all the seasons. It will surely become a favorite retreat from the urban scene so close at hand! Have you taken in the Garden D' Lights, with over 135,000 lights decorating the Garden in a festive holiday/botanical theme during the month of December? Make it an annual tradition! Other events include a May plant sale, with plants from the border and area specialty nurseries; the Mother's Day Open House; and summer events such as concerts and tours.

Northwest Perennial Alliance (NPA) Border: A major draw for many locals and visitors from afar and abroad to the Bellevue Botanical Garden is its extensive mixed perennial border, designed, created, and maintained by volunteers—members of the Northwest Perennial Alliance. Integrated beautifully into the garden as a whole are a 12,000-square-foot mixed perennial border, a 6,000-square-foot mixed border dedicated to shade conditions, and a 4,000-square-foot shrub border on the west side of the path. Sheer exuberance and great skill in plantsmanship will captivate a serious gardener for hours on end, in virtually any season. A printed plant list, while never quite comprehensive due to the dynamics of this vast garden, is nonetheless helpful in identifying many of the hundreds of unusual varieties and forms of perennials, bulbs, annuals, ground covers, ornamental grasses, shrubs, and small trees used in this mixed border setting. While the scale is monumental, any observant gardener will come away with inspirations for texture and form, sophisticated color combinations, and design fundamentals. The national and international horticultural press have discovered these exemplary plantings and have featured them with heaps of praise! You can become a volunteer helping to maintain these borders for all to enjoy; just join NPA and donate a few hours (second and fourth Sundays and first Thursdays and third Tuesdays; call Bob Lily at (206) 324-0179 to volunteer), for others, and for yourself! The borders are partially wheelchair accessible.

Big Rock Garden Park

2900 Sylvan Street, Bellingham, WA 98226 | **Contact:** c/o Parks Operation Center, 1400 Woburn Street, Bellingham, WA 98226 | **Phone:** (360) 676-6801. Email: Steve Nordeen at snordeen@ cob.org or Marcia Wazny at mwazny@cob.org | **Directions:** From I-5 North, take Exit 254, turn right (east) on Iowa St, then left (north) on Woburn St. Turn right (east) on Alabama St. Go up the hill to Sylvan St, and turn left (north) on Sylvan St to the top of the hill. Turn right into Big Rock Garden Park. From I-5 South, take the Iowa St exit, immediately turn right (north) on King St, turn right (east) into Iowa St. Turn left (north) on Woburn St, then turn right (east) on Alabama St and travel up hill to Sylvan St. Turn left (north) on Sylvan S, then turn right into Big Rock Garden Park. | **Open:** Daily, 8 a.m.-dusk. | **Brochure:** Simple brochure provides park and garden histories; map included. | **Accessibility:** Limited wheelchair accessible (please call (360) 676-6801 for more information on accessibility or individual accessibility needs). | **Support organizations:** Bellingham Parks Department, the Big Rock Garden Committee, and Whatcom Parks & Recreation Foundation.

For several years operated as a nursery and gallery of outdoor fine art, this property was purchased by the City of Bellingham in 1992 and opened as a public park in 1993. As a nursery, it made a wonderful park, and as a park it makes a fabulous place to stroll in any season, in any weather. This 2.7-acre woodland setting features pleasant pathways weaving through towering Douglas fir, hemlock, and cedars underplanted with Northwest natives, hostas, nearly 100 varieties of hardy ferns (donated by the Hardy Fern Foundation), and hundreds of varieties of rhododendrons, azaleas, and Japanese maples. The art gallery has been retained and new collections added. Currently there are 22 permanent pieces of art in the park. An annual International Art Exhibit, including sculptures from regional and internationally renowned artists is in the garden from mid-May to mid-October. Quiet strolls through the park provide visitors with a sense of discovery and a lovely view to Lake Whatcom. The Big Rock Garden Committee was formed to help provide direction and address maintenance needs. In 2001, a final Master Plan for the park was created and adopted. The Whatcom Parks & Recreation Foundation has granted funds to Bellingham City Parks for a Horticultural Therapy Program and handicap accessibility resources.

Bloedel Reserve

7571 NE Dolphin Drive, Bainbridge Island, WA 98110-1097 | **Phone:** (206) 842-7631 | **Fax:** (206) 842-8970 | **Web:** www.bloedelreserve.org | **Directions:** Located on the northeastern tip of Bainbridge Island, the Reserve is reached from Seattle by the Seattle-Winslow Ferry or from the Olympic or Kitsap Peninsulas by the Agate Pass Bridge. From Hwy 305 there are directional signs to the Reserve. | **Open:** By reservation; call (206) 842-7631 (TDD equipped); 10 a.m.-4 p.m., Wednesday-Sunday, except Federal holidays. | **Entry fee:** Adults $6, seniors (over 65) $4. | **Tours:** Docent-led tours are available for groups of six or more; arrange at the time you book your reservation. | **Brochure:** Free; describes the history and development of the Reserve. | **Accessibility:** The Bloedel Reserve has received national recognition for its dedication to making the gardens as accessible as possible through a number of thoughtful gestures: ramps replace steps as is practicable; trails are maintained to remove overly exuberant brush; wheelchairs and a printed tour-guide booklet are available on loan at the Gate House. | **Support organization:** The Arbor Fund, a nonprofit foundation, now owns and maintains the Reserve. A Bloedel Reserve membership is $35 per year, and among other benefits the pass admits the member (and up to three guests) to unlimited visits to the Reserve for the year.

From the time Prentice and Virginia Bloedel acquired this 150-acre property in 1951, they began a sensitive courtship aimed at marrying the designing hand of man with the natural attributes of the woodland setting. Over a period of 30 years, and with the commissioned partnerships of wisely selected professionals (Fujitaro Kubota, for help with the Japanese Garden, and landscape architects Thomas Church, Richard Haag, and the firm Environmental Planning and Design), Prentice Bloedel orchestrated the development of many garden rooms set in the varied landscape of second-growth hardwood and conifers, meadow and wetlands, glens and gullies. While incorporating influences from the Japanese and European gardening traditions, a respect for the natural attributes of the land prevailed and pervaded. There are now about 84 acres of second-growth forest and 66 acres of altered landscapes. The result: a native woodland crisscrossed with shady paths, meadows, and a broad selection of formal and informal gardens. In the Bird Refuge, the water and plantings both attract and display a wide range of birds; red-winged blackbirds, ducks, geese, and swans are among the many who find food, shelter, and safety among the cattails, dogwood, spirea, and moosewood viburnum. In late spring and early summer vast numbers of rhododendrons cast great drifts of color through the understory of the forest. As they fade, the floral display is taken up by thousands of wildflowers, perennials, and bulbs, and, most notably, more than 15,000 cyclamen plants carpet the forest floor; it's one of the largest plantings in the world. A unique and lush woodland Moss Garden opens onto the Reflection Pool, a startling juxtaposition of the soft, wild, and almost brooding elements of the former with the strict formality and reverent aura of the latter. Rosemary Verey writes admiringly of her winter's-day visit here with nurseryman, writer, and teacher Dan Hinkley in the introduction to his book *Winter Ornamentals*. A visit in any season is rewarding, both botanically and spiritually. (See Chapter 10 under "Literature" for this book.).

CENTER FOR URBAN HORTICULTURE

3501 NE 41st St., Seattle, WA | **Phone:** (206) 543-8616 | **Web:** www.urbanhort.org | **Mailing address:** PO Box 354115, Seattle, WA 98195-4115 | **Directions:** Located 0.5 mile east of Husky Stadium. From I-5, take the NE 45th St exit 169 east, and drive past the University of Washington. After descending the steep hill, turn left at the stoplight. Just past University Village mall, turn right at the 5-way stoplight onto Mary Gates Memorial Dr, and travel about 2 blocks. Free parking is available at the Center. | **Open:** Gardens are open daily, dawn to dusk; offices are open 8 a.m.-5 p.m., Mon.-Fri. | **Accessibility:** Wheelchair accessible. | **Support organizations:** Northwest Horticultural Society, Seattle Garden Club, Puget Sound Mycological Society, The Arboretum Foundation, Hugh and Jane Ferguson Foundation, Molbak's Nursery and Garden Center, and many other horticultural and environmental organizations.

The McVay Courtyard is snugly surrounded within the protective "arms" of this horticultural haven, harboring drifts of ornamental grasses and plants with grasslike foliage, vines, small shrubs, and trees. Come especially for the marvelous use of the hardscape—stones, pavers, and cleverly worked concrete paths meander amid the undulating raised beds that invite you to just plunk down for a good look. This will easily become a favorite tiny courtyard garden for anyone who visits. The Seattle Garden Club Entry Court creates a botanical "foyer," displaying an enviable ground cover garden in shade, under a canopy of stripe bark maples. This tiny space is well worth your while to visit if you've fretted over a similarly difficult growing site in search of a brilliant approach! The newest (Fall of 1998) installation is an idea garden, the Orin and Althea Soest Herbaceous Display Garden. This one-half-acre site with eight display beds provides gardeners with a demonstration of 280 different herbaceous plants grown in a variety of conditions (varying soil, light, water needs) so that you can select plants to grow in similar conditions at home. There is a Robert Hestekind–designed fountain and the paths are paved for full accessibility.

Also on this Union Bay campus, find the 50-acre Union Bay Natural Area, with wetlands, natural prairie restoration demonstrations, and bird-watching. Major changes recently brought new signage, trails and supporting programs. The Goodfellow Grove displays native woody plants in a landscape setting. Before you leave the area, have a look at the streetscape plantings that feature new cultivars of crape-myrtle as well as native plants, and check out the container gardens. There are plant lists available for most of the CUH gardens. You'll surely seek them out with gratitude.

Although you may or may not be accustomed to the Center's old entrance in Merrill Hall and the many associated internal resources—including the Miller Horticultural Library (the largest in the Northwest), the Hyde Herbarium, a year-round Master Gardener Clinic, the Washington Rare Plant Care and Conservation Program, and various offices and labs—a devastating arson fire on May 21, 2001, destroyed most of the facility. This fire, set by a terrorist organization that placed a bomb in one of the labs, while destroying Merrill Hall, fortunately did not damage the gardens surrounding the Center. In 2004, a new building will open that not only replaces Merrill Hall and its associated programs, but will celebrate urban horticulture in the Pacific Northwest. It is hoped that a better, larger, and more exciting facility will be created to serve the gardeners of the Pacific Northwest as well as those interested in all aspects of horticulture, from ecological restoration applications to the management of public gardens and parks. If you would like to contribute toward making this vision a reality, please contact the Center for Urban Horticulture at (206) 543-8616, or University of Washington development officer Linda Kaye at (206) 543-9505.

THE CHASE GARDEN

Located in Orting, WA; directions given at time of appointment confirmation | **Phone:** (206) 242-4040 | **Web:** www.chasegarden.org | **Mailing address:** PO Box 98553, Des Moines, WA 98198; for information, send SASE. | **Open:** Spring tours, by appointment only; guided tour fee is $5 per person; slide presentation available in King and Pierce Counties. | **Support organizations:** The Garden Conservancy, a national nonprofit organization (www.garden conservancy.org); Friends of the Chase Garden.

When Emmott and Ione Chase met with Tacoma landscape architect Rex Zumwalt in 1962, they requested a design for their 4.5-acre garden that would suggest the simplicity of a Japanese garden. Over the years they have developed that garden, keeping in mind Ione's belief that the act of gardening consists in creating beauty in natural surroundings. With this in mind the Chases have established a carefully groomed woodland of second-growth native trees carpeted with trillium, vanilla leaf, and other wildflowers. Two small reflecting pools near the house are surrounded by raked pea gravel, contributing to the Japanese garden effect. Pathways meander through drifts of colorful ground-covers in the meadow, reminiscent of an alpine setting. An open vista of forested foothills overlooking the Puyallup River valley provides an impressive view of Mount Rainier. In their early nineties now, the Chases have accepted a conservancy easement and have guided the formation of a local nonprofit organization, Friends of the Chase Garden, to take over management of the plantings. When you visit, take special note of the Northwest native wildflowers in "the woods border," "the woods interior" and "the moss garden," three special areas planted with the simple elegance of small, woodsy plants from our region.

CRESCENT MOON ROSE GARDEN

1911 Zylstra Road, Oak Harbor, WA 98277 | **Phone:** (360) 679-1799 | **Email:** bweakly@asd103.org | **Directions:** From Hwy 20 on Whidbey Island, just at Penn Cove, there is a sign alerting you to the turn for Hummingbird Farm, which is also on Zylstra. Crescent Moon Rose Garden is a few miles up the road, on your left, before you reach Hummingbird Farm. | **Open:** By appointment, and by chance most days April-Sept. | **Tours:** By appointment. | **Accessibility:** Wheelchair accessible on lawn and bark pathways.

Tina Weakly, one of this area's finest and most enthusiastic rose growers, and her husband, Bruce, have created an impressive country garden with nearly 800 varieties of roses, including many unusual ones you're not likely to have yet discovered. The garden at Crescent Moon Roses is set in 5 peaceful woodland acres, cleared to allow for sun, but with a strong undisturbed background of trees. Tina is justly proud that she grows in her garden every variety of hybrid musk available in the United States and Canada, plus over 50 varieties of David Austin English roses, both as freestanding shrubs and climbers. While once one could say this is essentially a rose garden with some happy companions, it has grown beyond that as Tina expands her plant palette to include many more perennials, vines, and shrubs. For instance, she now displays 20 buddleia varieties to enhance the midsummer roses. Many rose- and vine-covered arbors and metal sculptures (by Bruce) are key features among the companion plants Tina loves to intertwine through her first love, the roses. When you visit, take note of the 150-foot-long, hourglass-shaped pond with a handsome bridge finished in Bruce's characteristic metalwork. A wide range of water plants flourish at the edge, and waterfowl visit as though this pond had existed forever. New also is a greenhouse bursting with another of Tina's new passions—tropicals. Fragrance, repeat bloom, and disease resistance are always top priorities for this exacting gardener. So, if you are a plant lover, and especially if you are a rose aficionado, you have an invitation to visit.

DISCOVERY GARDEN

Mt. Vernon/WSU Research & Extension Unit, 16602 Memorial Hwy., Mt. Vernon, WA | **Contact:** WSU/Skagit County Cooperative Extension Master Gardeners, 306 S First, Mt. Vernon, WA 98273 | **Phone:** (360) 428-4270 | **Web:** www.skagitcounty.net/wsu.htm | **Directions:** From I-5, take exit 226 into downtown Mt. Vernon, turn right on 3rd St, and cross the bridge over the Skagit River, heading west on SR 536. | **Open:** Daily, dawn to dusk. | **Brochure:** Informational brochure provides a map, with descriptions of the many garden spaces and the garden themes. | **Tours:** Self-guided; however, during the growing season seminars are held at the site for the public. | **Accessibility:** Wheelchair accessible. | **Support organizations:** WSU/Skagit County Cooperative Extension/Skagit County Master Gardener Foundation.

This multidimensional demonstration and display garden includes an Enabling Garden, stressing the therapeutic and economic benefits that can be derived from gardening for people with varying abilities; a Naturescaping Garden demonstrating the transition from yard to wildlife sanctuary; A Garden for Children with examples and ideas for making a garden child-friendly; an Ethnobotany/Herb Garden with a focus on historical use of plants, including plants used by settlers, indigenous peoples, and today's herbalists; a Vegetable/Small Fruit/Test garden demonstrating the most effective growing techniques and tests of new varieties; a Composting Demonstration area; an Ornamental Garden area with several themes (Cottage Garden, Alternatives to Turf, Water-Wise Gardening, Landscaping to Deter Crime, Japanese Garden, Easy Care Garden, Fall and Winter Garden, Cool Color Border, Hot Color Border, and Shade Garden); and examples of Screens/Hedges/Espaliered Fruit Trees used to protect plantings and define areas of the garden. There is even a Garden of Weedin,' which identifies weeds you are likely to be familiar with but may not know much about, and an educational Pavilion and toolshed. A wide variety of ecologically sound pest-management methods are demonstrated, and adjacent to the Discovery Garden area plant societies are installing display gardens too. Look for gardens from the Skagit Valley Rose Society, the Koma Kulshan Chapter of the Washington Native Plant Society, and the Skagit Valley Dahlia Society. There is a great deal of community support for the Discovery Garden, with generous gifts from area businesses and many individuals. As this is an area deeply involved in commercial agriculture, there's a natural partnership here, and one that will lead you to better understand issues of how one type of gardening may impact another.

Added in 2001, **The Skagit Veg Trials and All American Selections** is a project set up to identify the best available vegetable varieties and cultural practices for the Puget Sound maritime climate. Sponsored by the Skagit Men's Garden Club, the project helps trials of varieties that emerge in cool soils and have a range of maturities—early, mid, and late. This allows the commercial or home grower to plant at one time and harvest over a long period. In 2001 alone, the trials included 45 varieties of peas and a staggering 185 varieties of corn. About 26 varieties of spinach and 30 varieties of tomatoes are tested each year, too. The All-American Selections is a national testing program of newly developed varieties that is conducted by a nonprofit consortium of seed companies. When you visit, you may see the AAS award-winning vegetables (17) and flowers (23) from the past several years, growing in a border along Memorial Highway. Trial results are posted to the project's Website: www.mtvernon.wsu.edu/SkagitVegTrials. For further information, you may also call Nancy Liggett at (360) 848-6129 or email: liggett@wsu.edu.

WESTERN WASHINGTON FRUIT RESEARCH FOUNDATION (WWFRF)

See Discovery Garden, above, and contact info below.

Formed in 1991, WWFRF is an all-volunteer organization that helps to fund fruit research in the region, supporting the WSU/Mount Vernon Research & Extension Unit staff work of testing and discovering the best fruit varieties for the unique Western Washington climate. WWFRF's 5-acre display garden showcases several groups, from a Kiwi and Grape Vineyard to a Nut Orchard, an Unusual Variety and Small Fruit area, an Antique Apple Orchard, as well as Organic Orchard, Cider Apple Orchard, and Rootstock Trial areas. Currently in planning are a fruit garden using only organic growing methods, and an area in which wine and table grapes, kiwis, and other vines can be grown. Other possibilities include a section for berries, unusual fruits such as figs and pawpaws, rootstock trials, and special pruning methods. In its beginning stages, the basic framework is in place, thanks to an extensive planting of mature trees in 1999. Join the WWFRF and take advantage of ongoing harvests, where you can sample and pick some of the bountiful seasonal fruit grown here. For more information, write WWFRF, PO Box 9716, Seattle, WA 98109, or see: www.wwfrf.org. To volunteer at the display garden, contact Kim Siebert at (425) 334-0387 or kjjsiebert@aol.com.

E. B. DUNN HISTORIC GARDEN TRUST

PO Box 77126, Seattle, WA 98177 | **Contact:** (206) 362-0933 (for information or a reservation) | **Email:** info@dunngardens.org | **Web:** www.dunngardens.org | **Directions:** Given at the time a reservation is secured. | **Open:** By reservation only; tours are Thursdays at 2 p.m., Fridays and Saturdays at 10 a.m. and 2 p.m., April-Sept; limited to 12 adults/7 cars. | **Entry fee:** $7 per person, with discounts to seniors and students. | **Accessibility:** Sloping lawns, woodland paths, some steps. | **Support organization:** E. B. Dunn Historic Garden Trust.

The Dunn family estate was built in 1915. The plans for the grounds were laid out by the revered Olmsted Brothers landscape architectural firm of Brookline, Massachusetts. While the original house is gone and the property now divided among the Dunn children, their homes have sympathetically melded into the site. The original plan has changed little, and has matured along the lines for which the Olmsteds were famous—with diagonal view corridors, natural outlines, and informal plantings. Ed Dunn was a devoted collector of rhododendrons (including many fragrant Loderi hybrids) and woodland bulbs, with a particular interest in erythroniums. The 2.7-acre garden, with 4 additional acres of lawn and landscaped grounds, is undergoing renovation to accommodate the many now-shady beds on the site. The garden features walks among the mature rhododendrons in a woodland setting, the pond garden, woodland glade, perennial border, and specimen trees set in the "great lawn." In 2001, thanks to the support of donors and friends of the Dunn Garden, construction began on the Barbara Leede Bayley Garden Classroom, an ambitious undertaking that will enable the garden to accommodate demand for its growing education programs.

ELANDAN GARDENS

3050 W State Highway 16, Bremerton, WA 98312 | **Phone:** (360) 373-8260 | **Email:** dianerobinson@prodigy.net | **Web:** http://elandangardens.8m.com | **Directions:** From Tacoma, drive past mile marker 28 on Hwy 16. From Bremerton, stay on Hwy 16 past Gorst, take the Tremont exit, go under the freeway, and return on Hwy 16 to Elandan, directly off the highway. | **Open:** Tuesday-Sunday, 10 a.m.-5 p.m. (closed Mondays and the month of January). | **Entry fee:** Adults $5, children under 12 $1; special group rates available. | **Accessibility:** Limited; some steep trails.

Dan and Diane Robinson started Elandan Gardens in 1993 when they realized they could no longer handle the busloads of bonsai fans coming to see their ancient and unique collection of bonsai. The garden is located on a 6-acre chunk of land, a former landfill sheltered in a saltwater inlet on Puget Sound. Never developed past its refuse origins, the land had seemingly waited for them to dream and plan a public bonsai garden. They added 30,000 cubic yards of sandy fill dirt and moved 800 tons of granite boulders to the site. Diane coined the name from *élan*, which means "courageous" in French, and then added Dan's name. Visually, the garden is like a condensed 20-mile walk in an alpine zone, offering discoveries of ancient gnarled trees, silvery deadwood, and monuments of stone encrusted with moss and lichen. Wide pathways encompass bonsai displays as you walk 10 to 15 feet below the earthen ridges that force you to look up toward the trees. More than 200 trees are rotated through the outdoor museum, including a Rocky Mountain juniper approaching 1,500 years old (Dan found it in Wyoming at a place called "Nick's Ledge"). You'll also see a 34-inch-high, 245-year-old black pine, and hundreds of other ancient trees. Or walk the shores of Puget Sound among 2.5 acres of huge rhododendrons and Japanese maples. You can also visit the sculpture garden, Elandan Gallery, and the Avalon Exotic Nursery.

CARL S. ENGLISH, JR. BOTANICAL GARDEN (AT THE HIRAM M. CHITTENDEN LOCKS)

3015 NW 54th Street, Seattle, WA 98107 | **Phone:** (206) 783-7059 | **Directions:** From downtown Ballard in north Seattle, go west on Market St to NW 54th St, then turn left to the Hiram M. Chittenden Locks; the gardens are near the Lake Washington Ship Canal in Seattle. | **Open:** Garden open daily, 7 a.m.-9 p.m; Visitor's Center open daily, May 15-Sept. 15, 10 a.m.-6 p.m; and Sept. 16-May 14, Thurs.-Mon., 10 a.m.-4 p.m. (closed Tues./Wed.). | **Entry fee:** Free. | **Accessibility:** Paths through the gardens are mostly wheelchair accessible. | **Support organization:** Managed by the Seattle District of the U.S. Army Corps of Engineers.

This 7.5-acre botanical garden supports an extensive and impressive collection of exotic trees, shrubs, and herbaceous plants, in all numbering about 800 species of native and exotic plants. The garden is named after one of the Northwest's leading horticulturists, Carl S. English, Jr. (1904-1976). In charge of the development of the grounds adjacent to the Government Locks over a career of 43 years, this botanist obtained much valuable seed and plant material from his acquaintances in botanical and horticultural positions worldwide. Through his ambitious efforts, an amazing array of trees is represented. In his book *Trees of Seattle*, Arthur Lee Jacobson cites 175 different kinds of trees ("and there are others"). With a copy of this book or the self-guided tour map available at the Locks from the Visitor's Center, one can locate and identify many mature specimens of great interest. There is something of interest year round. Be sure to have a look at the Fuchsia Test Garden, where the Greater Seattle Fuchsia Society is demonstrating and monitoring hardy varieties, and where they hold an annual show in August. A daylily demonstration bed has also been added, thanks to the efforts of the Puget Sound Daylily Club.

ERNA GUNTHER ETHNOBOTANICAL GARDEN

NE 45th Street at 17th Avenue NE, Seattle, WA | **Contact:** Box 353010, University of Washington, Seattle, WA 98195-3010; 24-Hour Information: (206) 543-5590 | **Email:** recept@u.washington.edu | **Web:** www.burkemuseum.org/ events.html (for events) | **Directions:** Northwest corner of the University of Washington campus at NE 45th St and 15th Ave NE. From I-5, exit east onto NE 45th St. Travel east on NE 45th St to 17th Ave NE. The museum is on the right. Parking free in adjacent lot Saturday afternoons and Sundays, otherwise by fee. | **Open:** Daily, dawn until dusk. | **Accessibility:** Wheelchair accessible.

Appropriately adjacent to the entry of the Burke Museum of Natural History and Culture, this relatively small (100+ species) but well-labeled collection of native plants offers insight into the use of plants by Pacific Northwest indigenous peoples. Plants have been used for thousands of years for food and medicine, and as the raw materials for houses, canoes, clothing, ceremonial artworks, and myriad tools and utensils. While the Gunther Garden can stand alone as an attraction, this outdoor exhibit is an integral part of the indoor displays, building on them and reinforcing their messages. Visit the *Life and Times of Washington State* exhibit, with its message of stewardship, for information on plant habitats and land use. In the *Pacific Voices* exhibit, discover how Northwest and other Pacific cultures used plants in their lives. Reference works, including *Plants of the Pacific Coast* (by Pojar and Mackinnon) and *Ethnobotany of Western Washington* (by Erna Gunther) are available in the Museum Store. An annual guided garden tour is offered in early May.

Note: Dr. Erna Gunther studied the plant lore of several tribes in western Washington. Gunther was a longtime museum director, much-loved educator, and social activist.

EVERGREEN ARBORETUM AND GARDENS

Legion Memorial Park, Alverson Avenue and West Marine View Drive, Everett, WA | **Mailing address:** PO Box 13014, Everett, WA 98201 | **Phone:** (425) 257-8300 or (425) 257-8597 | **Email:** info@evergreenarboretum.com | **Web:** www.evergreen arboretum.com | **Directions:** From the north, take I-5 exit 194. Turn right on Everett Ave and continue to Broadway. Turn right (north) on Broadway and exit onto Marine View Dr (just before the bridge over the Snohomish River). Turn left from the exit ramp onto Marine View Dr. The entrance to the golf course is 0.4 mile on the left. The road to the park is 0.7 mile on the left. From the south, take I-5 exit 195. Turn left at the bottom of the exit ramp onto E Marine View Dr. Continue on this street as it curves around the north end of Everett and becomes W Marine View Dr. The golf course is on the left. To reach the Arboretum, continue to the next intersection (Alverson Ave) and turn left. | **Open:** Daily, dawn to dusk. | **Entry fee:** Free. | **Tours:** Upon request; call (425) 257-8597. | **Accessibility:** Limited wheelchair access. | **Support organizations:** Evergreen Arboretum and Gardens Society; Snohomish County Master Gardeners.

Founded over 30 years ago, the Arboretum is tucked into the west side of Everett's Legion Park and remains undiscovered by many county residents. It is now enjoying a resurgence of interest thanks to the regional fascination in landscaping and gardening. Already planted with a Woodland garden, a Water Conservation garden, Perennial border, Conifer garden, Japanese Maple grove, and Dahlia garden, the Arboretum offers ideas pertinent to today's gardener, as well as a peaceful, beautiful setting. Some wonderful sculpture is on display here as well. As you enter the Arboretum, take note of the Master Gardener Perennial Garden, within which are planting vignettes featuring bulbs, cottage garden styles, shade plants, exotic varieties, a corner pathway garden, a scented garden, and a formal white garden. There are excellent, free plant lists available to help you take a self-guided tour. To get involved, join the Evergreen Arboretum and Gardens Society, which holds frequent meetings and sponsors the "Garden of Merit" tour of Everett's finest gardens each June.

FORT VANCOUVER HISTORICAL GARDENS

1000 East Fifth Street, Vancouver, WA 98661 | **Contact:** (360) 696-7655, ext. 17 | **Web:** www.nps.gov/fova | **Directions:** From I-5 in Vancouver, head north; take exit 1C and follow signs. | **Open:** Daily, 9 a.m. to 5 p.m. | **Entry fee:** $2 fee includes access to the entire fort. | **Accessibility:** Partially wheelchair accessible. | **Support organizations:** National Park Service; Fort Vancouver National Historical Society.

In 1825 the Hudson's Bay Company established Fort Vancouver, a critical supply post along the Washington side of the Columbia River. Early settlers there grew fresh vegetables, medicinal herbs, flowers, and ornamental trees and shrubs. Recently, a group of volunteers have restored (and maintain) a 1-acre garden that represents historical plants and gardens. Visit the site to see how early kitchen gardens and crops were grown, including agricultural techniques that the Fort's original residents used, such as crop rotation, sustainable methods, cover crops, and composting. You'll see heirloom vines, vegetables, flowers, and herbs. When you visit, pick up packets of seeds harvested at the fort to try in your own garden; just leave a donation in the watering can.

FRAGRANCE GARDEN

(See "Tennant Lake Park," below)

FRENCH LAKE CONSERVATION DEMONSTRATION GARDEN

French Lake Park, 31531 1st Avenue S, Federal Way, WA | **Contact:** PO Box 4249, Federal Way, WA 98063 | **Phone:** (253) 941-1516 | **Web:** www.lakehaven.org/conservation.htm | **Directions:** From I-5, take the exit at Federal Way onto S 320th and head west. Turn right on 1st Ave S. | **Open:** Daily, dawn until dusk. | **Accessibility:** Wheelchair accessible. | **Support organization:** Lakehaven Utility District

This relatively new water-wise garden at French Lake Park demonstrates techniques that allow gardeners to have lush green gardens without expending the energy and resources required by water-hungry gardens. The concept of *xeriscaping* is demonstrated, and you can pick up free handouts explaining the garden. There is a broad mix of plants here, from ground covers to shrubs and trees, ornamental grasses to perennials. Stone walls and arbors add handsome structure to this peaceful wooded setting in the park. You'll find the garden inviting year-round. It's a residential scale garden most of us can identify with!

GOOD SHEPHERD CENTER

4649 Sunnyside Avenue N, Seattle, WA 98103 | **Web:** www.historicseattle.org | **Directions:** Easy access from I-5; go west on N 50th St NE, about 4 minutes. Turn left onto Sunnyside Ave. | **Open:** Daily, dawn to dusk. | **Tours:** Guided tours arranged with Gil Schieber, head gardener; fee by donation, call (206) 547-8127. | **Accessibility:** Partial (lawn and uneven paths). | **Support organization:** Historic Seattle Public Development Authority; managed by Seattle City Parks Department.

This 12-acre site is owned by Historic Seattle P.D.A. Located in a quiet Wallingford neighborhood, Good Shepherd's gardens feature mixed borders, 2 to 15 feet deep, filled with a tapestry of unusual and uncommon plants. The sizable area, once home to an old orchard, is now a City of Seattle park called Meridian Playfield. The orchard dates back to the building's origins (from 1906 to 1973 it served as a home for women run by the Sisters of the Good Shepherd community). The site is also home to the Seattle Tilth offices, demonstration gardens, and composting demonstrations, offering great synergy.

GREEN LAKE PARK

7201 E Greenlake Drive N., Seattle, WA | **Contact:** Green Lake Park Alliance, 8061 Densmore Avenue N., Seattle, WA 98103 | **Phone:** (206) 985-9235 or (206) 684-0780 | **Open:** Daily, dawn to dusk. | **Tours:** Self-guided walking tour, outlined in a "Trees of Green Lake" brochure. | **Entry fee:** By donation, at the Green Lake Community Center desk, or by sending a SASE to the Alliance at the above address. | **Accessibility:** Paved and gravel paths.

Over 170 different species of trees grace the 400 acres of the Green Lake Park landscape in North Seattle. The trees here have been specifically planted over time for their beauty, appeal, suitability for an urban park, and worldwide diversity. Begin your tour at the Sierra Redwood tree, located near the concession stand at the northeast corner of the lake, and stroll counterclockwise around this popular destination. Use the guide to locate 129 noteworthy trees on and off the path, identified with small tags.

HOVANDER HOMESTEAD PARK

5299 Nielsen Road, Ferndale, WA 98248 | **Phone:** (360) 384-3444 | **Contact:** Whatcom County Parks Department, 3373 Mount Baker Highway, Bellingham, WA 98226 | **Phone:** (360) 723-2900 | **Directions:** Exit I-5 heading west toward Ferndale; turn left after the railroad trestle on Main St. A large sign on the right will direct you to the Park, which is managed by the Whatcom Parks and Recreation Department. | **Open:** Daily, dawn to dusk. | **Entry fee:** Admission is $3 per car for non-county residents, in-county residents park free. | **Accessibility:** Wheelchair accessible. | **Support organizations:** Whatcom County Parks Department; WSU/Whatcom County Cooperative Extension Master Gardeners/Master Composters.

A traditional homestead, now a National Historic site, provides the setting for a fruit, vegetable, and herb demonstration garden maintained by volunteers in the Master Gardener program. A compost demonstration and weed ID bed are combined with the large planted area, all of which exists for public educational purposes. The flower and shrub garden at the front and side yards of the Victorian farmhouse and the orchards surrounding the property provide a fitting setting for the wandering peacocks who strut freely among the visitors. A grape arbor was erected in memory of the many generous hours, days, and years of dedicated service of longtime Master Gardener Al Anderson, who died in 1991. Annual Master Gardens/Fragrance Garden plant sale (the Saturday before Mother's Day), 9 a.m.-2 p.m.

THE JUNTUNEN GARDENS

Mount Vernon, WA | **Phone:** (360) 856-1447 | **Email:** juntunent@ncia.com | **Web:** www.ncia.com/~juntunen/ | **Directions:** Provided when you schedule a visit. | **Open:** The garden is best viewed April-June; by appointment. | **Entry fee:** Donation accepted.

This family garden project located in the Skagit Valley includes 5 acres of grass, shrubs, flowers, and fruit trees. Charles and Sue Juntunen began landscaping the gardens in 1979 and have several types of plant collections, including hostas, daylilies, rhododendrons, and fruit trees. A grape arbor supports three varieties of grapes and is surrounded by fig trees that bear fruit each August. When you visit, take note of the wonderful carved wood and soapstone sculptures created by Charles and peek inside his art studio, also on the grounds, where you may see some of his landscape paintings on display. There are occasional events held here, so contact Sue by email to add your name to the mailing list. Ask about her special moss basket designs, available each spring by custom order.

KENMORE RHODODENDRON PARK AND GARDEN

6910 NE 170th (Simonds Road and Juanita Drive), Kenmore, WA 98011 | **Web:** www.metrokc.gov/parks | **Open:** Daily, dawn to dusk. | **Entry fee:** Free. | **Tours:** Guided park tours are offered in

April and May; call (206) 296-2973 for details. | **Support organizations:** King County Park System; American Rhododendron Society.

The "old garden" features the Reginald Pearce Plant Collection. Most of the trees and shrubs in this garden are over 50 years old. Mr. Pearce was an Englishman who immigrated to the Pacific Northwest at the turn of the century. From 1920 to 1960 he owned and operated State Flower Nursery, one of the region's leading producers of rhododendrons. Pearce was well known for hybridizing techniques that developed a number of beautiful and rare, one-of-a-kind varieties ('Pinky Pearce', 'Pearce's Golden Jubilee', and 'Pearce's American Beauty' are products of his hybridizing). Mature specimens of these and other unique plants can be enjoyed at the park, as well as remnants of the original family home, garden, and nursery. Warren F. Timmons III and his wife, Diane M. Timmons donated the "new garden" in 1995. They collected many of these plants while operating a small nursery, Warren Gardens. The displays include many of the newer rhododendron and azalea hybrids, as well as many companion trees and shrubs: conifers, Japanese maples, and heather, among others. Warren and Diane, along with members of the American Rhododendron Society and other patrons, continue to donate to the collection. When you schedule a tour, you'll have a chance to talk with Warren, a passionate rhododendron expert.

KING COUNTY / WSU MASTER GARDENERS URBAN DEMONSTRATION GARDEN

15680 SE 16th Street, Bellevue, WA | **Phone:** (425) 644-9601 | **Directions:** Heading east or west on I-90, take the 148th Avenue SE exit, following signs to Bellevue Community College. Continue north on 148th to SE 16th St and turn right. The demonstration garden is on the left at the bottom of the hill, just before to the 4-way stop at 156th. Look for signs; there is ample parking. The garden is located within the Bellevue Parks Department Community Garden. | **Open:** Daily, dawn to dusk. Master Gardeners staff the garden April-Oct., 9 a.m.-1 p.m., Wednesdays and Saturdays. Free workshops at 10:30 a.m., every Saturday, Jan.-Sept. | **Tours:** Guided tours available upon request. Call (425) 644-9601. | **Entry fee:** No admission fee. | **Accessibility:** Most paths are wheelchair accessible, on asphalt, crushed gravel, or packed wood chips. Master Gardeners have recently collaborated with the City of Bellevue Parks Department to install wheelchair access "switchbacks" that meander through a new retaining-wall garden. | **Support organization:** King County Master Gardeners Foundation; (206) 205-3122.

This is a fabulous working demonstration garden, and a lush, inviting place to visit, located just blocks from the hustle and bustle of I-90. A series of raised beds, and retaining-wall gardens, with display areas in full sun and deep shade offer gardeners successful ideas for their smaller, urban backyard spaces. There is an extensive dahlia test garden here, and the MGs are often the first to get their hands on new (or rescued heirloom) seed varieties to test. When you visit at the peak of summer, check out the myriad tomato staking ideas, the great strawberry patch, the Asian vegetable beds (showing how to grow those exotic greens and vegetables that you spend a fortune buying at the specialty grocer), and excellent ideas for composting. New displays include bog plants and the less-than-sexy "weed" garden, that helps visitors identify the backyard weeds they love to hate. All produce grown here is donated to local food banks. In addition to the free workshops, the garden hosts a Children's Fair in June, an Open House in August, and a Harvest Festival in September. Check garden events calendars in the Seattle-area newspapers for specific dates, or pick up a free schedule of lectures and events when you visit the garden.

HULDA KLAGER LILAC GARDENS

115 S Pekin Road, Woodland, WA | **Phone:** (360) 225-8996 for information on the garden and open house | **Web:** www.lilacgardens.com | **Directions:** Located about one mile off I-5, southwest of Woodland; take exit 21 north or south and follow the signs. | **Open:** Dawn to dusk, year-round, but plan your trip for lilac bloom in late April/early May. | **Entry fee:** Donation requested at gate. | **Accessibility:** Paved walkways, wheelchair accessible. Wheelchairs, including a child's chair, are available for visitors during Lilac Days Open House. | **Support organization:** The Hulda KLG Society, PO Box 828, Woodland, WA 98674.

Plan your trip for late April through early May to soak in the heavenly lilac scent of your childhood, emanating from over 42 hybrid varieties lovingly propagated by Hulda Klager from about 1910 until her death in 1960 (plus 30 newer additions). Now a national historic site, the arboretum setting, with its many kinds of trees, shrubs, and beds, makes a visit rewarding any time of the year. The Victorian farmhouse has been restored and is open during the two special Opening Weeks, late April through Mother's Day, otherwise by appointment. The old red barn of the historic property houses a quaint gift shop featuring lovely lilac gifts, arts and crafts, and lilac starts from over 70 varieties (40 of which are Hulda Klager originals), available during the Lilac Celebration. Enjoy tables and picnic benches around the grounds for an impromptu outdoor meal. Call for details on mail order and shipping of bare-root lilacs.

THE KRUCKEBERG BOTANIC GARDEN

20066 15th Avenue Northwest, Shoreline, WA 98177 | **Phone:** (206) 542-4777 | **Web:** www.kruckeberg.org | **Tours:** By appointment only, typically held 10 a.m. to Noon. Tours normally are offered for groups of 6 to 15 persons; the fee is $15 per person. To schedule, contact KBGF at the number above. The cities of Shoreline and Edmonds also sponsor tours of the garden, offered for a fee through their respective parks departments. To inquire about current dates, call the City of Shoreline at (206) 546-3772 or the City of Edmonds at (425) 771-0227 | **Membership:** $35 (student, senior and benefactor levels also offered). The garden is open to "members only" at least once a year. Mail dues to Kathie Morino, Treasurer, KBGF, 958 Walnut, Edmonds, WA 98020.

The Kruckeberg Botanic Garden is located in Shoreline's Richmond Beach area, about 15 minutes north of Seattle.

The four-acre garden and plant collection have long been the home and nursery of Mareen and Arthur Kruckeberg, two of our region's horticultural pioneers. (Art, author of *Gardening with Native Plants of the Pacific Northwest* and other books, retired from the University of Washington in 1980 as a Professor Emeritus of Botany; Mareen operates the MsK Rare Plant Nursery on the property.)

The family has lived here since 1958, when the couple bought the land and a circa 1903 farmhouse. They introduced plantings of unusual, rarely cultivated species from other regions and worked to preserve and enhance the native plant collection under a canopy of old-growth Douglas fir. The garden includes many different species: exotic conifers (larches, sequoias, pines, firs, spruces, and hemlocks); hardwoods, especially oaks and maples; rhododendrons, magnolias, the unique "wingnut," and a host of other woody plants. The displays of ferns, cyclamens, wood sorrel and inside-out flower are distinctive. The landscape is a mix of native species and choice specimens from other lands, mostly China and Japan. Mareen—devoted fans continue to enjoy MsK Rare Plant Nursery's annual Mothers' Day open house and plant sale, a custom that began in the late 1980s. The Kruckeberg Botanic Garden Foundation was formed in 1999 with the objective of buying and preserving the Kruckeberg land and plant collection in perpetuity, as a garden, open space and horticultural learning center.

KUBOTA GARDEN

Renton Avenue S and 55th Avenue S, Seattle, WA | **Mailing address:** PO Box 78338, Seattle, WA 98178-9998 | **Phone:** (206) 684-4584 (Garden), (206) 725-5060 (Foundation) | **Web:** www.kubota.org | **Directions:** Located in the Rainier Beach area of South Seattle between 51st Ave S and 55th Ave S; turn west off Renton Ave So onto 55th Ave. | **Open:** Daily, dawn to dusk. | **Entry fee:** No admission fee | **Tours:** Every consecutive fourth Saturday and Sunday at 10 a.m., April-October, or ask about arranging a tour for your group of eight or more; (206) 725-5060. There is no charge. | **Accessibility:** Limited wheelchair access. | **Support organization:** The Kubota Foundation, established in 1989 as a nonprofit corporation to provide support for future development, maintenance, and operation of the garden, as well as to promote informational and cultural programs. Seattle Parks Department Adopt-a-Park volunteers come here to work on the third Sunday, April-October, 8 a.m.-noon.

Owned by the City of Seattle since 1987 and designated as a City of Seattle Historic Landmark, the garden began life in 1927 as the hobby of Fujitaro Kubota. It developed into a full-time profession as his landscape design business grew, and the garden was used both as a working nursery and a demonstration of the blending of traditional Japanese garden concepts with native Northwest plants. This stunning 20-acre setting of hills and valleys is crisscrossed with streams, waterfalls, ponds, rock outcroppings, and a marvelously rich and complex collection of specimen plants. Traditional details of Japanese garden design are found throughout, such as the brilliant red Moon Bridge and statuesque Kasuga-style stone lantern. Pines were the signature plants of the Kubota Company. In traditional Japanese gardens, the sharp-needled Japanese black pine and the softer-needled red pine were often planted together, as they are here, to represent male and female energy. Fine examples of other trees include an extraordinary 32-foot-long weeping blue Atlas cedar, a 37-foot-tall weeping Norway spruce, a forest of threadleaf cypress, and a grove of Yellow Groove and Black Groove bamboo. The newest portion of the garden opened in 2000 as the Tom Kubota Stroll Garden, a level, accessible strolling garden that encompasses 4 acres. Every year there is a popular Pine Pruning Workshop, where you can prune with the experts and learn about tool use and selection, pine tree styles, artistic concepts, and thinning and shaping techniques (call for dates; the workshop is typically held in May). Plant sales are held in May and September.

LA CONNER FLATS

15920 Best Road, Mt. Vernon, WA 98273 | **Phone:** (360) 466-3190 | **Email:** bobhart@fidalgo.net | **Directions:** From I-5, take the Hwy 20 exit going west, and travel 5 miles to Best Rd; turn left and proceed about 2 miles. The garden is just past Christianson's Nursery, on the right. | **Open:** March-October, Tuesday-Sunday, daylight hours, daily in April. | **Entry fee:** Free, but a donation is greatly appreciated. | **Accessibility:** Wheelchair accessible on grass.

Old friends of Margie and Bob Hart know all they have brought to Skagit Valley gardeners over the many years. These days you will find them still hard at work next door to their former passion, now Christianson's Nursery. Their traditional English garden is planted to provide interest over a span of eight months, with a rose arbor, an orchard, a white garden, and a sunken garden, along with the perennial border. Wander through the outdoor "rooms" and allées bordered by enviable "bones" (those statuesque structural evergreen hedges this expansive setting displays so gracefully). These gardens have matured over the years and continue to provide viewers with a sense of having stepped from the Pacific Northwest into the horticultural heritage of the British Isles, if only for a brief stroll. There's a new gazebo placed perfectly in the center of the rose garden, with a bench generously offered for you to sit and enjoy a picnic or just the view. During the Skagit Valley Tulip Festival—in fact, throughout the entire month of April—Margie sets up a small cafe with a menu offering soup and sandwich lunches. She also serves afternoon tea (by appointment). Seek out Bob or Margie when you visit; they're probably puttering in the garden and have a wealth of information to share.

LAKE WASHINGTON TECHNICAL COLLEGE ARBORETUM

Located on the college campus, 11605 132nd Avenue NE, Kirkland, WA 98034-8506 | **Phone:** (425) 739-8356 | **Email:** don.marshall@lwtc.ctc.edu | **Directions:** From SR 405, take the Redmond / Kirkland exit and head east toward Redmond. Turn north (left) at the 132nd Ave NE exit, a little less than 2 miles. |

Open: Daily.

Created as a learning tool for the environmental horticulture program of the college, the arboretum is organized by plant family and encompasses virtually every tree, shrub, vine, and ground cover on the Washington State Nursery and Landscape Professional exams. This arboretum, open to the public, is worth a side trip for its educational value. Don't miss the "Seed to Sale" student plant sales, held in April and May (call for dates).

LAKEWOLD GARDENS

12317 Gravelly Lake Drive SW, Lakewood, WA 98499 | **Phone:** (253) 584-4106 or (888) 858-4106 | **Web:** www.lakewold.org | **Directions:** From I-5 just South of Tacoma, take exit 124 (Gravelly Lake). Travel west about 1 mile; the gardens are only about 5 minutes off I-5. | **Open:** April-September, Thursday-Monday, 10 a.m.-4 p.m. (closed Tuesday and Wednesday); October-March, open Friday-Sunday, 10 a.m.-3 p.m. The fabulous Garden Shop is open when the garden is open (you can visit without paying to enter the garden). | **Entry fee:** General admission $5; seniors, students/military $3; children under 12 free. From October-March, Saturdays are Family Day; one family, in one car, is admitted for one low price of $5. | **Tours:** Guided tours are offered by appointment for groups or individuals, so call early to avoid disappointment. For more information or to arrange a tour, call (253) 584-4106, ext. 106. The house is available to rent for retreats, weddings, and special events. | **Brochure:** Brochures have color photos, a map, and general garden information. | **Video:** You may also want to purchase *Where the Blue Poppy Grows*, the very interesting and informative video history of the garden (available through the Garden Shop). We recommend beginning your visit in the Sunroom to view this excellent video on Lakewold (or order it in advance of your trip). It will add much to your visit. | **Accessibility:** Limited wheelchair access. | **Support organization:** The Friends of Lakewold, Box 39780, Lakewood, WA 98439-0780 | **Phone:** (253) 584-4106. Why not join?

What is known as Lakewold Gardens today was originally the site of a summer cabin purchased in 1908 by Emma Alexander. The landscape of towering Douglas firs and Garry oaks, with their understory of native woodland plants, remains intact. During the next 30 years two other owners developed the framework for what we see today at the garden. One of the most dramatic architectural elements of the garden is a sweeping brick pathway laid out in a herringbone pattern leading from the house to the domed latticework tea house, an inviting destination covered in June with the profusely blooming, old-fashioned musk rose, 'Kathleen'. The stone walls, iron fences, and gates we see today are the originals. Over the years some of the tree canopy gave way to the formal gardens and rolling lawns, which provided the palette on which the ultimate private owners would begin their life's love affair with Lakewold. In 1938, Corydon and Eulalie Wagner began growing collections of their beloved rhododendrons, Japanese maples, roses, and rare rock and alpine plants. They designed, developed, and maintained what has become one of the Pacific Northwest's landmark estate gardens, combining the essence of European formality, Asian simplic-

ity, and Northwest splendor in their 10-acre estate. The couple worked for many years with the renowned landscape architect Thomas Church to establish this treasure above the oak-lined shores of Lakewood's Gravelly Lake. The Hardy Fern Foundation has installed a display garden here also. Though Lakewold is open year-round, perhaps its best viewing period begins in early April, with the magnificent show of the justly famous rhododendron collection, set amid sophisticated selections of trees and shrubs, and continues through the final burst of color in September, provided by Japanese maples and other deciduous trees chosen for their autumn show, including the brilliant foliage of *Viburnum tomentosum* along the lakeside fence. The **Carroll O'Rourke Library** is open for reference use to the public. Wonderful programs are offered throughout the year, so check the website for details.

LITTLE AND LEWIS

1940 Wing Point Way, Bainbridge Island, WA 98110 | **Phone:** (206) 842-8327. Web: www.littleandlewis.com | **Directions:** Given at the time an appointment is set. | **Open:** By appointment only. | **Accessibility:** Partially wheelchair accessible.

It is appropriate to find watermeisters George Little and David Lewis hidden unassumingly on a back road of an island, because as you pass through the shrubbery that encircles the garden you will feel you have passed into another world, perhaps another time. These aqueous Pied Pipers play their alluring tune of gently falling water and soon you, too, will fall under its magical spell. And theirs. Throughout this small but lush garden gallery are the creations of a classicist and a sculptor, most predominantly their signature columns, Tuscan, Doric, or Egyptian, water oozing ever so gently from the cap, drip, drip, dripping to the little pool beneath. The elements of cast stone and water are set in the context of a garden where unusual varieties of perennials in beds and borders contend for one's attention. Aquatic plants, some ensconced in garden vignettes, some as water gardens per se, may be focal pieces of garden art or planted in among the ornamental grasses or billowing perennials, from mirror-perfect reflecting basins to the fantastical cast leaves of the giant gunnera. The garden continues to evolve as David and George incorporate new installations, such as varying garden "rooms," changes of level, and paths that lead to and from the central courtyard. Large, colorful stucco walls display their signature plaques, paintings, and cast leaves. Additionally, the studio where much of the work is conceived is often open for viewing (especially inspiring if you are shopping for a Little and Lewis piece for your own Eden). Throughout the garden you are invited to sit awhile and meditate, perhaps dreaming of taking refuge forever from a less romantic world beyond. No wonder Little and Lewis have received much national acclaim. The evidence can also be seen in a number of articles featuring their unique creativity and sumptuous garden, such as the recent stories on the work of Little and Lewis featured in *Gardens Illustrated*, *Martha Stewart Living*, and *Traditional Home*.

MAGNUSON COMMUNITY GARDEN

7400 Sand Point Way NE, Seattle, WA 98115 | **Email:** magnuson garden@hotmail.com | **Web:** www.cityofseattle.net/magnuson garden | **Directions:** From I-5 north or south take the the NE 45th St. exit and head east. Continue through the University District and down the hill. (Do NOT veer to the right and go to University Village on 25th!) Take a left turn at the stop light and go past University Village. Follow the signs to "Children's Hospital." You will find yourself on Sand Point Way NE. Enter Sand Point/Magnuson Park at the main gate (7400 Sand Point Way/east side of the street) to the old Navy station. | **Open:** Dawn to dusk.

This emerging garden is a byproduct of Seattle's Comprehensive Plan, which designated Community Gardens in its Open Space Network goals. The gardens at Magnuson Park are being developed as multipurpose space as the city takes over the vast acreage of the former Sand Point Naval Station. The 4-acre site east of the Community Activities Center was created through a public design process facilitated by Barker Landscape Architects. Various committees are working on components of the Community Garden, such as a children's garden area, a conservation area, a native plant nursery, orchard, P-Patch Plots (approximately 150 plots, including some designated for persons with physical disabilities), a tranquil garden, and a composting area. Space has also been designated for public art and a public gathering/amphitheater. A 2000 Seattle Parks bond issue and a 2001 "Small and Simple" grant for design development have helped nurture this emerging garden. The coalition website will update you on the project and offer involvement opportunities. Since so many gardening and horticultural organizations are now holding plant sales and events at Sand Point (PlantAmnesty, The Arboretum Foundation's FlorAbundance Plant Sale, and more), you should make it a point to see this new garden while visiting them.

DELBERT McBRIDE ETHNOBOTANICAL GARDEN

Washington State Capitol Museum, 211 West 21st Avenue, Olympia, WA 98501 | **Phone:** (360) 753-2580 | **Email:** srohrer@wshs.wa.gov | **Open:** Museum open Tues.-Fri., 10 a.m.-4 p.m.; Sat., noon-4 p.m. Closed Sundays, Mondays and state holidays. Garden grounds are open dawn to dusk. | **Brochure:** A free informational brochure about traditional plants can be supplemented with a substantive 72-page booklet, *Respecting the Knowledge: Ethnobotany in Washington*, by Angel Lombardi. | **Accessibility:** On a crushed-rock path and woodland forest path (there are several benches throughout the garden). | **Support organization:** Washington State Historical Society.

Located on the grounds of the Washington State Capitol Museum, this is a living exhibition of plants American Indians in western Washington found important as food, medicine, and tools used for everyday living. The garden is named for Delbert McBride, an expert on the subject and Curator Emeritus of this Museum.

MEDICINAL HERB GARDEN

Botany Department, Box 355325, University of Washington, Seattle, Washington, 98195-5325 | **Phone:** (206) 543-1126 | **Web:** http://nnlm.gov/pnr/uwmhg/index.html | **Directions:** Located generally in the southwest quadrant of the campus, adjacent to Stevens Way, bordered by the Botany Greenhouse to the west (across Stevens Way) and Benson Hall to the north. The Chemistry and the Forestry Buildings are nearby. | **Open:** Daily. | **Admission:** Free; free brochure. | **Accessibility:** Partially accessible, with a few stairs. | **Support organization:** Friends of the Medicinal Herb Garden, funded solely by donations and memberships.

Established in 1911 by the School of Pharmacy, this historic garden has covered as much as 8 acres with 836 different species of medicinal plants from around the world. The fate of this garden, at turns the recipient of attention and serious neglect, turned for the better in 1984 with the formation of (you guessed it) the Friends of the Medicinal Herb Garden. Their goal is to preserve, maintain, and improve the present 2 acres of beds in six areas with an inventory of 630 plants. The free brochure will provide you with a map of the gardens, information on their history, and membership data. Also of interest here are 125 different kinds of trees. Arthur Lee Jacobson profiles 50 specimens of note in his book *Trees of Seattle*. Among these you will find *Magnolia acuminata*, cucumber tree; *Cornus officinalis*, Chinese cornelian cherry; *Eucommia ulmoides*, hardy rubber-tree; *Podocarpus andinus*, plum-fruited yew; *Quercus mongolica*, Mexican blue oak, and *Asimina triloba*, pawpaw (to mention a few of the numerous rare trees.) The intriguing Botany Greenhouse adjacent to the garden is also open.

MEERKERK RHODODENDRON GARDENS

3531 S Meerkerk Lane, Whidbey Island, WA | **Contact:** PO Box 154, Greenbank, WA 98253 | **Phone:** (360) 678-1912 | **Email:** meerkerk@whidbey.net | **Web:** www.meerkerkgardens.org | **Directions:** Located on Whidbey Island, south of Greenbank, WA, off Hwy 525. From Seattle, take I-5 north to the Whidbey Island / Mukilteo Ferry, and travel to Clinton. From Clinton (about a 20 minute ferry crossing), take Hwy 525 north approximately 15 miles, turn right on Resort Rd, and left onto Meerkerk Lane. From the north, take Hwy 20 south to Hwy 525; about 1.5 miles south of Greenbank, turn left onto Resort Rd and then left to Meerkerk Lane. | **Open:** Daily 9 a.m.-4 p.m. year-round, with an emphasis on spring bloom; wonderful fall color, too. The Plant Nursery is open weekends in spring, weather permitting, selling rhododendrons, companion plants, and Meerkerk gift items. | **Entry fee:** Adults $3; children under 12 are admitted free when accompanied by an adult. Special events admission varies. No pets permitted on the garden grounds. | **Tours:** Guided group tours for groups of ten or more may be scheduled by calling at least two weeks in advance (or call to make arrangements for visitors with special needs); contact garden manager Kristi O'Donnell; (360) 678-1912. | **Accessibility:** A mix of accessibility, on paving, grass, mulch, and gravel. | **Support organizations:** Friends of Meerkerk; Seattle, Cascade, Pilchuck, Komo Kulshan and Whidbey Island chapters of the American Rhododendron Society; WSU Island County Master Gardeners; and local garden clubs.

Known as Whidbey Island's peaceful woodland garden, this 53-acre site originates from the estate of Max and

Ann Meerkerk. Created as a private garden in 1963, the preserve now rests in the hands of the Seattle Rhododendron Society as an endowed gift from Ann Meerkerk. Meerkerk Rhododendron Gardens operates as a private, nonprofit garden open to the public, supported by admissions, plant sales, and memberships. Plantings showcase more than 1,800 rhododendron varieties (species and hybrid) and include examples from many well-respected local breeders, as well as English and Dutch hybrids. In the 10-acre display gardens, large-leafed species and hybrids of the Grande and Falconeri series grow well in this woodland setting alongside many plants from the American Rhododendron Seed Exchange, the University of Washington Arboretum Society, and several of Ann Meerkerk's own unnamed hybrids. The International Hybrid Rhododendron Test Garden here is expanding to be the largest collection on the West Coast. It was established to "give an impartial and consistent rating to hybrids grown here," under carefully controlled garden conditions. Highly respected plant collector Warren Berg has been hard at work planting an Asian garden to show his rare species rhododendrons, many propagated from seed he collected in China, Tibet, and Bhutan, in their native setting. The peak bloom period for the rhododendrons is mid-April through May, so there are many activities planned during that time for visitors. In addition to rhododendrons, however, many companion plants enhance the collection. You'll find magnolia, dogwood, katsura, and beech trees, along with many unique specimens of Diamond Bark maple, Dove Tree, Empress Tree, Monkey Puzzle Tree, and sequoias. A stately 43-acre evergreen forest of cedar, hemlock, and Douglas fir shelters the display garden, and a 5-mile nature trail wends its way through the forest past wildflowers, huckleberries, ferns, salal, and other NW native woodland plants. There are many ongoing special events, including the an annual Opening and Plant Sale in late March, when you'll find rhododendrons (consider the source and get there early!) and companion plants. Take in the Mother's Day Concert in the gardens for a special treat (check the website for details).

ELISABETH C. MILLER BOTANICAL GARDEN

Contact: PO Box 77377, Seattle, WA 98177 | **Phone:** (206) 362-8612 | **Web:** www.millergarden.org | **Directions:** Provided at the time you schedule a visit. The garden is located approximately 10 miles north of downtown Seattle. | **Open:** By appointment only, March-Nov. 14, Wednesdays and Thursdays, 10 a.m. and 2 p.m. | **Tours:** Call to schedule your tour on a first come, first served basis. Reservations for the upcoming year are taken after Feb. 15. Group tours are limited to 15 persons. Parking is extremely limited and carpooling is required for all groups. The garden is unable to accommodate vehicles larger than a 14-passenger van. | **Entry fee:** Free. | **Accessibility:** Gravel paths and steps make the accessibility limited.

The Elisabeth C. Miller Botanical Garden was the private home and garden of Elisabeth and Pendleton Miller.

The garden is known for its exceptional collection of fine trees and shrubs in addition to an expansive collection of woodland herbaceous perennials. The Millers purchased the 5-acre piece of land north of the Seattle city limits on a bluff above Puget Sound in 1948. The site commands spectacular views of the Sound and the Olympic Peninsula, and offers unique microclimates for growing plants. There are in excess of 3,600 taxa, or different kind of plants, in the 3 acres of gardens. Once you meet the spirit of Betty Miller in the garden, you'll have a keen appreciation for her legacy to all Northwest gardeners. Her garden was the refuge and basis for all her work in the community. She received many honors and medals for her advocacy of horticulture. Two of the more notable awards are the Liberty Hyde Bailey Medal, awarded to her in 1988, and the Natalie Peters Webster Medal from the Garden Club of America. She was a member of the elite Rare Plant Group of the Garden Club of America. She spearheaded the plantings along the Lake Washington Ship Canal, the founding of the Elisabeth C. Miller Horticultural Library at the Center for Urban Horticulture, and assembled the plant list for Freeway Park in downtown Seattle.

THE MUKAI FARM AND GARDEN

c/o Island Landmarks, PO Box 13135, Burton, WA 98013 | **Phone:** (206) 463-2445 | **Email:** mukai@centurytel.net | **Directions:** Provided when you schedule a visit. | **Open:** Select Saturdays in May during cherry tree bloom season, and by appointment. | **Entry fee:** Free. | **Support organizations:** The Garden Conservancy (www.gardenconservancy.org) and Vashon Island Landmarks.

The Island Landmarks group is working to save this site, which represents a chapter in the early Japanese-American experience. In the middle of her family's prosperous strawberry farm, a first-generation Issei woman created this Japanese-style garden, replete with "islands" and waterfalls, and surrounded by pools filled with koi and water lilies.

DAVID F. NEELY HOMESTEAD GARDEN

5311 S 237th Place, Kent, WA | **Phone:** (253) 856-5000. | **Open:** Daily, dawn to dusk | **Directions:** From I-5, take the Kent-Des Moines exit and head east. Turn left on Meeker Ave(where you'll see the River Bend Golf Course entrance); then turn left on Russell Rd, and left on Lakeside E (at the entrance to "The Lakes" development). Turn left at Lakeside Blvd W and follow this to River Place. Turn left on River Place and look for the Neely Homestead historical marker. You can't miss the large white Victorian home. | **Entry fee:** Free. | **Tours:** By arrangement through King County Master Gardeners; (206) 205-3122. The home is available for rental through the City of Kent Parks Department; (253) 856-5000. | **Accessibility:** Wheelchair accessible. | **Support organizations:** King County Master Gardeners Foundation; City of Kent Parks Department.

Thanks to a dedicated group of committed Master Gardeners, the grounds and gardens surrounding this circa 1884 house have been restored. Originally the first general store and post office in the White River Valley near

Kent, the homestead grew to become a 360-acre dairy farm. The Neely family maintained the residence for a century, after which they donated the site to the City of Kent in trust. As a demonstration garden, the homestead is a living museum of sorts. The home stands on 1.5 acres, and the residential garden is maintained as it would have been at the turn of the century in 1900. There are vegetable and herb gardens, a rose bed, a mixed border, perennials, grape and hop arbors, foundation beds, and the remnants of a fruit orchard. All plant material predates 1900 and you can pick up a useful list of heirloom varieties to try in your own gardens (some charming selections include amaranth 'Elephant Head'; 'Black Valentine' beans, 'Blue curled Scotch' kale, 'Deer tongue' lettuce, and countless other discoveries). Check with Kent Parks for seasonal classes and demonstrations. There are plenty of volunteer opportunities here, as well: Work parties are held the first and third Saturdays of the month, called "weed and feed," because, according to chief volunteer and chef Kate Bean, "you weed and we feed you!"

OHME GARDENS

3327 Ohme Road, Wenatchee, WA 98801 | **Phone:** (509) 662-5785 | **Web:** www.ohmegardens.com | **Open:** Daily, April 15-Oct. 15. Spring: 9 a.m.-6 p.m. (before Memorial Day weekend); summer: 9 a.m.-7 p.m; fall: 9 a.m.-6 p.m. (after Labor Day weekend) | **Directions:** Just north of Wenatchee near the junction of Hwys 2 and 97A. | **Entry fee:** Adults $6, ages 7-17 $3, children 6 and under, with adult, free. | **Brochure:** Includes color photos, garden history and information, and a map. | **Support organizations:** Washington State Parks, managed with Chelan County. | **Accessibility:** Be forewarned this is a difficult garden to traverse. Wear sturdy, rubber-soled, low-heeled shoes. Those with walking difficulties will not be able to negotiate most of the garden / terrain, but can enjoy the upper gardens and the magnificent view.

This garden has received a revival of national attention recently and with good reason. A family effort, achieved over 60 years, has transformed a once-barren hill overlooking the parched Wenatchee Valley into a lush 9-acre alpine paradise. What distinguishes this phenomenal accomplishment is the success the Ohmes have had in creating what would appear to be a completely natural, rich alpine environment. Through the years they planted hundreds of evergreen trees and covered the arid slopes with a blanket of low-growing alpine plants. Literally hundreds of tons of rock have been gathered, moved, and hand placed to form winding pathways and to create crystal-clear pools. Groves of trees provide shady glens. A visit in spring is particularly rewarding as the brilliantly colored ground-cover carpets provide a warm welcome from winter's gloom. This is a highly recommended foray, and can be accomplished as part of an ambitious scenic circle route over Highway 20 (The North Cascades Highway) and Highway 2 (Stevens Pass). Bring a picnic—tables are provided just outside the garden entrance in a pleasant setting.

THE PACIFIC RIM BONSAI COLLECTION

33663 Weyerhaeuser Way South, Federal Way, WA 98003 | **Phone:** (253) 924-5206 | **Email:** david.degroot@weyerhaeuser.com | **Web:** www.weyerhaeuser.com/bonsai/ | **Directions:** Located off I-5 about 23 miles south from Seattle; take exit 143, Federal Way / S 320th St, turn left and cross over the freeway, then turn right on Weyerhaeuser Way S and follow the Weyerhaeuser directional signs. If you are coming from Tacoma, travel north on I-5 about 8 miles and take exit 142-A, Hwy 18 East, and stay in the far right lane. This becomes the exit lane to Weyerhaeuser Way S. At the stop sign turn left (north) and cross the overpass, following the directional signs to the garden parking area. | **Open:** Year round; March-May, 10 a.m.-4 p.m., closed Thursday; June-February, 11 a.m.-4 p.m., closed Thursday and Friday. | **Entry fee:** No admission fee. | **Tours:** Guided tours of the collection Sundays at noon (inquire at the Garden Shop). The collection can be viewed year-round; remember that this is an outdoor exhibit and bring your umbrella on a rainy day. To schedule group tours, call (253) 924-3153. | **Accessibility:** Wheelchair accessible. Parking at front gate, also anyone with restricted walking ability can be let off at the front gate. | **Support organization:** Weyerhaeuser Corporation.

Weyerhaeuser Corporation created the Pacific Rim Bonsai Collection in the fall of 1989 in honor of its trade relations with Pacific Rim nations and as a tribute to the Washington State Centennial. Nestled within the forest at Weyerhaeuser Corporation Headquarters, the collection features more than 50 examples of bonsai art from the Pacific Rim nations of Canada, China, Taiwan, Korea, Japan, and the United States. Some are hundreds of years old.

This is one of the only permanent bonsai collections on the West Coast; plants were selected for year-round interest, with bright autumn berries (pyracantha), colorful foliage (maples), and delicate spring flowers (apples). The landscape architects commissioned to design the site have won enormous praise for their innovation in displaying the bonsai collection outdoors, each one in relative isolation like individual works of art, and in juxtaposition with trees of great scale. Descriptive signage will greatly enhance your viewing pleasure. (Facilities exist for the special needs of groups, so consider putting together a tour with your garden club, society, or foundation.) Don't miss a visit to the conservatory for the tropical bonsai collection. During spring and through the fall lectures and demonstrations are offered, along with special exhibits (check website for details).

PACIFIC SCIENCE CENTER / TROPICAL BUTTERFLY HOUSE

Ackerley Family Exhibit Gallery in the Pacific Science Center (Seattle Center), 200 Second Avenue N, Seattle, WA | **Phone:** (206) 443-2001 | **Web:** www.pacsci.org | **Directions:** From I-5 north or south, take Mercer Street exit 167; turn right on Fairview Ave N and take an immediate left at the first light. At Denny Way, turn left; continue to Second Ave and turn right; the Science Center is on the right. Some street parking; also ample lots serve the Seattle Center. | **Open:** Tues.-Fri., 10 a.m.-5 p.m; Sat.-Sun., 10 a.m.-6 p.m; closed Monday. | **Entry fee:** Adults $8, seniors and ages 3-13 $5.50. Seniors admitted free on Wednesdays; Science Center members receive unlimited free admission. | **Accessibility:** Wheelchair accessible; for inquiries, contact visitor services at (206) 443-2844.

Opened in 1998, the Tropical Butterfly House is a welcome retreat on a chilly day. You're invited to walk among a thousand gracefully gliding and fancifully fluttering butterflies in a brightly lit enclosure kept at a balmy 80 degrees and nearly 80 percent humidity. Tropical trees, shrubs, and other flora provide a luxurious habitat for the more than 40 species of Lepidoptera (with some beautiful moths represented as well). This attractive exhibit makes an ideal place to come observe these spellbinding creatures as they pupate (seen through a window, up-close in the emergence room), as they dry their wings before first flight, and as they soar from the tops of trees to the feeding stations set out with fresh fruit (to the delight of many visitors young or old, the butterflies often land on a shoulder or head of *Homo sapiens* and visitors must be "brushed off" prior to exiting). Outside the Tropical Butterfly House is the Insect Village, where you can watch bees busily at work in their hive, take in an Insect Slideshow, and, at the Insect Zoo, hold giant millipedes, and—dare we suggest it?—cockroaches, too.

POINT DEFIANCE PARK

5400 N Pearl Street, Tacoma, WA | **Contact:** Metropolitan Park District of Tacoma, Marketing and Community Relations, 4702 S 19th Street, Tacoma, WA 98405-1175; MPD Marketing office: (253) 305-1070; TDD (253) 305-1006 | **Web:** www.tacomaparks/parks& gardens/gardens.htm | **Directions:** From I-5, take the Bremerton exit (Hwy 16) west, then the exit for the Point Defiance Zoo and Aquarium (going north). | **Open:** Daily, dawn to one-half hour after sunset. | **Entry fee:** The Park is open free to the public. | **Tours:** Call (253) 564-0990; Tacoma Garden Club members conduct tours of the Northwest Native Garden from 10 a.m.-noon, on second Mondays each month from July-October (by advance arrangement). There are also special Herb Garden events in June and September; call MPD for dates. | **Accessibility:** Wheelchair accessible. | **Support organization:** Metropolitan Park District of Tacoma.

Along with its world-renowned zoo, PDP provides many horticultural opportunities for visitors. The **All-American Rose Selection Display Garden** is supported by the Tacoma Rose Society. As the focal point of Point Defiance Park, there is more than an acre of rose gardens, the oldest of which was established in 1895. The site includes a garden of miniature roses, arbors of climbing roses, a picturesque wishing well, and quaint gazebos. From June through September, 1,500 rose bushes provide a fragrant rainbow of color. Members of the Society host a rose-pruning demonstration at the Display Garden in March, with educational materials and refreshments.

Dedicated in 1992, in cooperation with the Pierce County Iris Society, the **Iris Garden** contains 101 tall bearded iris, 80 Pacific Coast iris hybrids, and 26 *Iris tectorum*. Established in 1983, the **Perennial, Medicinal Herb, and Kitchen Gardens** were planted and are main-

tained by a small but devoted group of volunteers and offer 140 different types of herbs to see and study. Tucked into the convergence of two paths are a couple of welcome benches that invite you to rest as you enjoy the long border planting and the small niche bed between the seats. The Horticultural Study Group of the Tacoma Garden Club offers a free information program on herbs here in mid-September. The **Rhododendron Garden** is less like a garden than a nearly 5-acre natural planting of rhododendrons in a setting with native stands of bigleaf maple, western hemlock, Douglas fir, red alder, western red cedar, and many native understory plants. Established in 1968 in cooperation with the Tacoma Chapter of the American Rhododendron Society (which continues to lend its support), this area boasts 115 cultivated and 29 species rhododendrons. The **Northwest Native Garden**, a project undertaken by the Tacoma Garden Club in 1963, demonstrates the unique range of biodiversity in the Pacific Northwest. Within the 1.5-acre site, the plant habitats range from a coastal forest of moist woodland to the arid yellow pine forest of the Eastern Cascades. Also represented are the High Alpine and Scree regions, with rock and alpine plantings; a Subalpine Region of alpine fir, Alaska cedar, and white pine; the San Juan Region with madrona and Garry oaks; and a wetland and bog area planted with rushes and sedges, water lilies, and spirea. The **Dahlia Trial Garden** displays hybrid dahlias at least three years old and grown from seed by growers from all over the world. Using a point system, local judges rate the blooms labeled only by number for anonymity. Dahlia entries earning 85 of a possible 100 points are available the next year for sale. Dahlia Society members are available to answer questions in the garden every Tuesday from 8-11 a.m. from mid-July through September. The **Fuchsia Test Garden** is supported by the Tahoma Fuchsia Society; here you will find around 20 hardy shrub and trailing fuchsias in a raised bed. The **Japanese Garden** provides all the elements one would hope to find, from the delicate cherry blossoms of spring to the splendid Torii Gate and Shinto Shrine, gifts to the City of Tacoma from its sister city of Kitakyushu, Japan, in 1961. The Capitol District of the Washington Federation of Garden Clubs helped to establish this garden in 1965, and continues to support it.

POWELLSWOOD

430 South Dash Point Road, Federal Way, WA | **Mailing address:** 29607 8th Avenue S, Federal Way, WA 98003 | **Phone:** (253) 529-1620 | **Email:** monte@powell-homes.com | **Directions:** From Seattle, take I-5 to S 272nd S, and exit to right. Proceed west to Pacific Hwy S. Turn left and proceed south to the stoplight at Dash Pt Rd (Shell station on corner). Turn right and continue for 1 mile; driveway is on right. From Tacoma, take I-5 to S 320th St, and exit to left. Proceed west to Pacific Hwy S and continue as per above directions. Extensive directions are also provided when appointment is scheduled. | **Open:** Spring and Summer Open Garden dates, or by appointment, Thurs.-Sat. | **Accessibility:**

Partially accessible on lawn paths. | **Entry fee:** Open Days are free; $5 per person for scheduled tours. The garden is frequently a featured stop on the Federal Way Symphony Garden Tour.

Monte and Diane Powell have spent six years converting this vacant, overgrown lot into a 2-acre private garden (the first two years of which involved clearing brush and amending the soil before they could begin planting). They worked with landscape architect Ned Gulbran to design a number of garden rooms; local perennial expert Sue Buckles also added her finesse. Every time the Powells opened their garden several hundred people appeared, prompting the family to formalize the tour program in the late 1990s for select dates and special seasonal classes in the garden. Powellswood includes a total of 40 acres, much of which has been left natural. The gardens are graced with more than 1,000 trees, shrubs, and flower plants, walking paths, and a meandering manmade stream.

Puget Gardens

3204 N Ruston Way, Tacoma, WA | **Contact:** Metropolitan Park District of Tacoma (see Point Defiance Park, above) | **Phone:** (253) 305-1070 | **Web:** www.tacomaparks/parks&gardens/gardens.htm | **Directions:** Located at the corner of Alder St and Ruston Way; from downtown Tacoma travel north on N Ruston Way to Alder St and turn left. The park is on the left. | **Open:** Daily from dawn to one-half hour after sunset. | **Accessibility:** Moderate on pathways; not accessible by wheelchair. | **Support organization:** Metropolitan Park District of Tacoma.

This 3-acre woodland site was once the private garden of Clara and John Skupen. Nestled back from Ruston Way, it's a destination you'll find appealing on a hot summer day. The shady retreat includes several ponds, a stream, picturesque foot bridges, and a wooded ravine. Established drifts of candelabra primroses, many rhododendrons, flowering cherries, and azaleas make early spring a prime viewing time. Ferns, perennials, and roses provide summer interest.

Rhody Ridge Arboretum Park

17415 Clover Road, Bothell, WA 98011 | **Phone:** (425) 743-3945 | **Web:** www.co.snohomish.wa.us/parks/rhody.htm | **Directions:** From I-5, take exit 183, going east on 164th, passing Martha Lake. Turn right on 2nd Ave W (North Rd) and continue 1 mile. Turn left on Gravenstein / 174th St SE (both names listed on post) and drive 1 block. Turn left at the "T," drive 1 block, then take first sharp right onto Clover Road. Rhody Ridge is a short distance on the left. Park along the fence and enter through wooden gate on the driveway. Park sign (not very easy to see) is on lamppost inside gate. Be sure to close the gate. | **Open:** Daily, 10 a.m.-7 p.m. or dusk. No need to call ahead, though the Park may be closed occasionally. | **Entry fee:** Free. | **Tours:** Caretaker Fir Butler is available to help you locate plants. It's best to call ahead to arrange a group tour as Fir is a delightful guide and her company and knowledge will enhance your visit enormously. | **Support organization:** Snohomish County Parks, (425) 388-6600.

This is one of the loveliest surprise discoveries in the Northwest for those who hold a walk among breathtaking trees to be one of life's most exalting experiences.

Hidden in a quiet neighborhood is this secret arboretum, the horticultural legacy of one couple's love affair with woody plants. Rhody Ridge, the 11-acre private garden and arboretum of Fir and Merlin Butler since 1960, is now a living trust owned by the Snohomish County Parks system. The Butlers reside on the property as caretakers and continue to lovingly maintain the property and their impressive assemblage of species rhododendrons, and the vast collection of trees, shrubs, and ground covers. For artful plantsmanship, superb pruning techniques, and ideas concerning their meticulous maintenance program to battle the inevitable pest, disease, and weather challenges, this arboretum-like park provides an exceptional opportunity for observation and inquiry. A wide, well-maintained bark path meanders down a gentle slope through the 11-acre garden, with diversions off-trail into the surrounding woodland. Many of the plants are identified with their botanical name. In spring you'll find the short detour (just a few minutes off I-5) rewarding for the extensive collection of rhododendrons and crabapples in bloom; in fall there's a glorious display of foliage color and spectacular berries; and in winter an impressive array of tree and shrub bark and the opportunity to study branching structure. The park is quite hidden, so you'll have that extra bonus of discovery when out on a day of exploration.

Rhododendron Species Botanical Garden

2525 S 336th Street, Federal Way, WA 98003-9996 | **Mailing address:** PO Box 3798, Federal Way, WA 98063 | **Phone:** (253) 661-9377 | **Email:** rsf@rhodygarden.org | **Web:** www.rhodygarden.org | **Directions:** Driving directions are the same as those given for the Pacific Rim Bonsai Collection, above. | **Open:** March-May, 10 a.m.-4 p.m., closed Thursday; June-February, 11 a.m.-4 p.m., closed Thursday and Friday. | **Entry fee:** Adults $3.50; students and seniors $2.50; free to members, school groups, and children under 12. Call for reduced group rates. | **Tours:** Guided tours for groups of ten or more, with advance registration. | **Accessibility:** Partially wheelchair accessible; handicapped parking at the entry. | **Support organization:** Rhododendron Species Foundation.

This 24-acre botanical garden features one of the largest collections of species rhododendrons and azaleas in the world. Over 2,000 varieties of 435 species are displayed in a mature woodland setting. There is a wide bloom season (spring and fall), which is certainly an inducement to schedule a visit, but the spectacular foliage of these plants is perhaps best appreciated when they are not in bloom. Information-packed self-guided tour materials are available free to guide you through the best of the season. Special features you'll come upon as you meander the gravel and wood-chip pathways include the Alpine Garden, where literally hundreds of rhododendrons and companion plants native to high mountain regions are planted among more than 200 tons of granite; a large natural pond garden, and study gardens specially planted to demonstrate comparative displays of rhododendron foliage, form, and bloom. Make your way to the large gazebo for an overview of much of the garden. Among the vast collections of the RSF, you will find Hardy Fern Foundation displays, as well as significant plant collections donated and cared for by the Cascade Heather Society, the Northwest Chapter of the American Bamboo Society, and the Pacific Northwest Carnivorous Plant Club. Your visit here will no doubt begin and end with a look through the well-stocked Gift Shop, with its year-round plant sales pavilion. Call in spring and fall for advice on best bloom time, and note that a visit in the "quieter season," November through February, is rewarding for the rich, woody collection of outstanding trees—and entry is free! While here, it would be a shame not to also visit the exceptional exhibits of the Pacific Rim Bonsai Collection, located adjacent to the garden (see the listing above).

ROOZENGAARDE

15867 Beaver Marsh Road, Mt. Vernon, WA 98273 | **Phone:** (360) 424-8531 or (800) 732-3266 | **Email:** info@tulips.com | **Web:** www.tulips.com | **Directions:** From I-5, take exit 226 (Kincaid St), and go west on Kincaid. At the first stoplight turn right and follow through the next stoplight and over the Division St Bridge. Continue to the first stoplight after the bridge and turn left on Wall St, which makes a quick right turn and becomes McLean Road. Continue down McLean Rd about 3 miles, turn left onto Beaver Marsh Rd, and continue to the garden. In the height of the viewing season, parking is in a large field-lot across from the gardens. | **Open:** Daily, March-May; June-February, Monday-Saturday (closed Sunday). | **Accessibility:** Wheelchair accessible. | **Support organization:** Washington Bulb Co., Inc.

This is a 3-acre display garden, and a veritable cornucopia of bulbs: tulips, daffodils, crocuses, hyacinths, iris, and on and on, at its peak during the tulip blooming season through April and May. The pathways offer easy accessibility as they meander around many flowering borders packed with planting combinations to emulate. A camera and notepad would be sorely missed if forgotten at home. The history of the Roozen family reveals they've been involved in growing bulbs for almost three centuries. They are the largest bulb grower in the Skagit Valley and the largest commercial grower of tulips, daffodils, and iris in the United States. You will find that a friendly, country atmosphere pervades their garden and shop. You will also, of course, be treated to the spellbinding sight of acres of color swaths from their growing fields as you drive, cycle, or walk throughout the Valley. There are a few picnic tables alongside the old windmill, reminiscent of the Roozen family heritage. Order your bulbs on the spot as you note blooms in the garden that you'd like to duplicate in your own beds, or take home a colorful mail-order catalog to ponder at leisure.

THE SEATTLE CHINESE GARDEN

Located at the South Seattle Community College Arboretum, 6000 16th Avenue SW, Seattle, WA | **Mailing address:** 2040 Westlake Avenue N, Suite 306, Seattle, WA 98109 | **Phone:** (206) 282-8040

| **Web:** www.seattle-chinese-garden.com | **Directions:** Only 10 minutes from downtown Seattle; travel west on the West Seattle Bridge (from I-5 or Hwy 99), and take the Delridge Way SW exit. On Delridge Way, drive south to the third light and turn left onto SW Oregon St. At the top of the hill, veer right onto 21st Ave SW. Turn left onto Dawson and continue on 16th Ave SW. After 0.25 mile, turn left into South Seattle Community College's north parking lot. | **Open:** Dawn to dusk, Monday-Saturday (guided tours available by calling garden offices). | **Support organization:** Seattle Chinese Garden Society; you are welcome to join.

In China, the creation of a garden—with pavilions, stone, water, and plants—is considered one of the highest forms of art. Here, only minutes from downtown Seattle, lies the Song Mei Pavilion and Demonstration Garden, a preview of the expansive Sichuan-style garden soon to be built in West Seattle. Visit the Song Mei Pavilion, designed and fabricated in Seattle's sister city, Chongqing, China, and assembled on-site by a team of Chinese artisans. The first of many planned structures in the 6-acre garden, Song Mei (meaning "pine" and "plum") is surrounded by more than 100 varieties of Chinese plants. The Seattle Chinese Garden Society offers free guided tours during spring and summer. There is a real need for volunteers, while membership in the Seattle Chinese Garden Society brings many benefits, not the least of which is the satisfaction of helping bring this unique educational and cultural resource to our community.

SEATTLE TILTH GARDENS

4649 Sunnyside Avenue N, Room 1, Seattle, WA 98103 | **Phone:** (206) 633-0451 | **Email:** tilth@seattletilth.org | **Web:** www.seattletilth.org | **Directions:** From I-5, take the NE 50th St exit and go 0.5 mile west to Sunnyside Ave N, then turn left. Park on the street or in the lot (second driveway on right) of the Good Shepherd Center. The garden is located at the south end of the grounds. | **Open:** Daily, dawn to dusk; office open Monday-Saturday 10 a.m.-3 p.m. | **Accessibility:** Only moderately wheelchair accessible on (fancifully embellished) paved pathways. | **Support organization:** Seattle Tilth—Become a member.

A visit here should top the list of every imaginative urban gardener! Seattle Tilth was founded in 1978 to provide a resource for urban dwellers who wanted to raise their own food. Ideas abound for backyard organic food production, from tried-and-true techniques to varietal testing. Here you will also find the home of the Master Composter program and one of this area's best composting demonstration sites, where many different composting systems are displayed with informational signage (and handouts available). Whether you come on your own to have a look, take one of the informative on-site classes, or offer your time as a volunteer, there are many lessons to be gleaned at Seattle Tilth. There's a full-size solar greenhouse to explore and even a weed bed (as in weeds labeled for identification). The Children's Garden is the site of a great deal of activity in the form of a hands-on horticultural "classroom" for area schoolchildren, who take part in a well-respected program especially designed to inspire, inform, and educate our youngest gardeners. The medicinal herb bed has been recently renovated by volunteers. And every year hundreds of savvy Seattleites put Tilth's Edible Plant Sale (the first Saturday in May) and the Organic Harvest Fair (early September) on their calendar in red letters: "Be There!" Seattle Tilth offices are located at the gardens (or vice versa). You'll find lots of free advice from the volunteers, staff, and through educational pamphlets—or consult the excellent reference library.

Bradner Demonstration Garden

29th Avenue S and S Grand Street, Seattle, WA

Seattle Tilth's newest demonstration garden is located in the city's Mount Baker neighborhood, where the organization is developing a series of raised beds to accommodate gardeners with disabilities.

SEATTLE UNIVERSITY

900 Madison Street, Seattle, WA 98122 | **Contact:** You'll find a general map of the campus on their website: www.seattleu.edu/general/sumap.htm. | **Directions:** On Capitol Hill; Seattle University is 8 blocks east of I-5 (uphill and east of downtown) at Madison St and Broadway. | **Tours:** Group tours can be arranged by calling (206) 296-6440. | **Accessibility:** Partially wheelchair accessible (wheelchair accessibility routes are marked on the campus map).

Here you will find a 53-acre urban campus that in 1989 gained official designation as a Washington State Wildlife Refuge. The recently-retired campus horticulturist Ciscoe Morris can be thanked for this accolade, as he led the efforts to lovingly and tirelessly develop, defend, and care for the grounds and many pocket gardens here. If you are at all skeptical about keeping up a large horticultural domain organically, just look at the evidence. As with many college campus landscapes, Seattle University is fortunate to have some pretty darned impressive old trees. In this case, many of the most revered specimens date to the early 1900s, when Seattle nurseryman Fujitaro Kubota planted seeds of trees that he brought with him from Japan. As you are exploring the grounds you will find many, many examples of unusual trees and shrubs, like *Parrotia persica*, *Styrax obassia*, and *Franklinia alatamaha*, not to mention the much sought-after, curiosity variegated devil's club, *Aralia elata* 'Variegata'. Take your time and wander throughout the campus, because Ciscoe was here a long time, working his botanical magic in every nook and cranny. Poke into the Secret Garden between the Casey Building and Loyola Hall, where you will also find the Priest's Garden. Before you leave the campus, be sure to pay a visit to the Chapel of St. Ignatius. Architect Steven Holl chose "A Gathering of Different Lights" as his guiding theme in creating this truly spiritual place. A few minutes of contemplation here provide a fitting conclusion to a Seattle University walkabout.

W. W. SEYMOUR BOTANICAL CONSERVATORY

316 South G Street, Tacoma, WA 98405 | **Phone:** (253) 591-5330 | **Email:** wwseymour@tacomaparks.com | **Web:** www.tacomaparks.com | **Directions:** From I-5, take exit 133 to signs that read "705 N / City Center" then follow signs for 705 N / Schuster Parkway; get in the right lane and take the Stadium Way exit. Turn right at the stoplight onto Stadium Way, then turn left on 4th St. Follow 4th to G St and turn right into Wright Park. | **Open:** Daily, 10 a.m.-4:30 p.m. (except Thanksgiving and Christmas); Plant sales in mid-February and mid-September. Plant and gift shop open from 11 a.m.-4 p.m. daily. | **Entry fee:** Free. | **Tours:** Available at nominal fee for groups; call ahead to schedule. | **Accessibility:** Wheelchair accessible. | **Support organization:** Metropolitan Park District of Tacoma.

This beautiful Victorian-style glass conservatory (one of only three remaining on the West Coast) was constructed in 1908. It features a 12-sided central dome and more than 12,000 panes of glass. The Conservatory contains a superb, year-round collection of exotic tropical and flowering plants, with more than 500 species on permanent display. You will find fruit trees (including ornamental figs), bird of paradise, orchids, cacti, and bromeliads. The water feature pond contains colorful goldfish. As displays change monthly, visits throughout the year will find something new of seasonally-related interest, particularly at the holidays. Stop by to visit the wonderful shop, where you can buy rare and unusual plants, reasonably priced (2-, 4-, and 6-inch pots generally), books, and botanically inspired gifts. The conservatory is available for (small) weddings, and group tours can be arranged. This is one delightful destination that will brighten your day with a sensory explosion of colors, scents, and textures.

SOUTH KING COUNTY ARBORETUM

22520 SE 248th Street (225th Avenue SE at SE 248th, adjacent to Lake Wilderness Center) | **Contact:** PO Box 72, Maple Valley, WA 98038-0072 | **Phone:** (206) 366-2125 or (425) 413-2572 | **Email:** arboretum@skcaf.org | **Web:** www.skcaf.org | **Directions:** From I-405, take the Maple Valley Hwy 169 exit and drive south. After passing under SR 18, watch for Witte Rd and turn left. | **Open:** Daily, dawn to dusk. | **Entry fee:** Free. | **Accessibility:** Forest trails. | **Support organization:** South King County Arboretum Foundation.

Located in the heart of Maple Valley, adjoining the Lake Wilderness County Park, the Arboretum encompasses approximately 40 acres, with foot trails to hike in native forests, paths winding through plantings of identified species in the public gardens, and a specialty nursery area providing for the perpetuation of future stock. You'll find mosses, lichens, mushrooms, and native plants on a self-guided nature trail. Featured is the Smith/Mossman Western Azalea Display Garden, the largest selection of wild-collected *Rhododendron occidentale* in the world. The fragrant azalea blooms, at their peak in May, act as magnets for butterflies. Pick up a brochure at the Lake Wilderness Park office. Educational programs are offered regularly, including opportunities for scouts and schoolchildren. There are annual plant sales the Friday and Saturday of Mother's Day weekend, and the second Saturday of September.

SOUTH SEATTLE COMMUNITY COLLEGE ARBORETUM

6000 16th Avenue SW, Seattle, WA 98106 | **Phone:** (206) 764-5323 or (206) 764-5336 | **Directions:** Located at the northwest end of the campus. From I-5 or SR 99, take the West Seattle Freeway westbound, exiting to Delridge Way SW. Drive south on Delridge Way SW to the third light and turn left onto SW Oregon. Take the arterial to the top of the hill, veering right onto 21st Ave SW. Take the first left, on Dawson, continuing to 16th Ave SW, and follow 16th Ave south for approximately 5 miles to SSCC entrance on left. . | **Open:** Daily, dawn to dusk. | **Tours:** Tours can be arranged by appointment through the Landscape Horticulture program; call (206) 764-5336. | **Accessibility:** Partially wheelchair accessible. | **Support organization:** SSCC Foundation at the above address, or (206) 764-5809.

Evolving on the 12-acre site since 1978 as the cooperative effort of many organizations, this arboretum includes numerous areas that are worth the visit. These include an Entry Garden, Sensory Garden, the Helen Sutton Rose Garden, the Acer Garden (maples), and a Water Conservation Garden. There are also gardens featuring Rhododendrons, Perennials, Dwarf Conifers, and Heather. This is also the home of the Seattle Chinese Garden (see description above).

TENNANT LAKE PARK / FRAGRANCE GARDEN AND CHILDREN'S GARDEN

5236 Neilsen Road, Ferndale, WA 98284 | **Phone:** (360) 384-3064 | **Contact:** Whatcom County Parks Department, 3373 Mount Baker Highway, Bellingham, WA 98226 | **Phone:** (360) 723-2900 | **Directions:** Located 10 miles north of Bellingham, near Ferndale and Hovander Homestead Park. See directions to Hovander Homestead Park (above). | **Open:** Daily, dawn to dusk. | **Accessibility:** Wheelchair accessible; many labels in Braille. | **Support organizations:** Whatcom County Parks Department; also, The Whatcom Community Foundation has established The Fragrance Garden Endowment Fund to ensure long-term care and maintenance of this special garden. To support this initiative, call (360) 384-3064.

Access to the park is by a 1.5-mile loop trail, most of it on boardwalk, to a lake and along its marshy shore. No chemical fertilizers, herbicides, insecticides, or fungicides are used in the park, as the pro-organic staff and ground crew strive to stay free of practices that may harm the environment. Of additional interest to the gardener, however, is the Fragrance Garden, specially designed for the visually impaired (several plant identification tags are in Braille), the wheelchair bound, and others for whom stooping to ground level to release a plant's essential oils for fragrance would be difficult—because the beds are attractively raised to about 36 inches in undulating gray-block planters. Plants, predominately herbs, are meant to be caressed for their fragrance and texture. For anyone with even a passing interest in herbs this wonderful garden will prove a valuable asset. Many area garden clubs are responsible for its development and maintenance. The garden became an IPM (Integrated Pest Management) demonstration garden in 1994. A lovely English Perennial Border provides an educational and inspiring addition to this rural park. The Children's Garden is a great place for young naturalists and budding gardeners to gain hands-on experience in planting, tending a worm bin, and exploring nature.

VOLUNTEER PARK CONSERVATORY

1400 E Galer Street, Seattle, WA 98112 | **Phone:** (206) 684-4743 | **Web:** http://www.ci.seattle.wa.us/parks/parkspaces/Gardens.htm | **Directions:** Northbound from downtown Seattle on I-5, take exit 168A; turn left at Lakeview Blvd E, right on Boston, and follow signs to Volunteer Park. Southbound on I-5, take exit 168-A, turn left on Roanoke, right on 10th Ave, left on Boston, and follow signs. | **Open:** Daily, summer 10 a.m.-7 p.m., winter 10 a.m.-4 p.m., including holidays. Plant sales in May and September. | **Entry fee:** No admission fee, although a donation is appreciated. | **Accessibility:** Narrow aisles, partially wheelchair accessible. | **Support organization:** Friends of the Conservatory, 1402 East Galer Street, Seattle, WA 98112; (206) 322-4112.

A beautiful and useful walking guide, *Volunteer Park and the Conservatory in Volunteer Park*, has been published. Contact the Friends for a copy ($3) so you'll have it for your next visit or to give guests as they follow your prescription and trot on a dreary day to the Conservatory for a psychological pick-me-up, or take a sunny day's glorious walk through the park. You and your guests will be treated to some history and little-known facts that will boost your appreciation of this treasure.

The Conservatory is of particular interest if you want to escape the liquid sunshine of the Northwest and transport yourself rather inexpensively to the tropics! Set within stately Volunteer Park on Capitol Hill, it's is a grand reminder of the master plan designed for the park by the noted Olmsted Brothers landscape architectural design firm in 1904. Construction of this **Victorian-style iron and glass conservatory** (now five glass houses) was completed in 1912. The one remaining original ornamental glass piece, the peacock, has been beautifully restored. Note also the stained glass piece *Homage in Green*, by stained glass craftsman Richard Spaulding, seen in the Palm House vestibule. Among the well-tended hot-house exotica you'll find a respected collection of species and hybrid orchids (the Conservatory is home to the Anna Clise Orchid Collection, begun in 1919), with late fall and early winter considered their finest period of bloom. In late winter and early spring come for the delicate blossoms of the large cacti and succulent collection. A pond is enveloped in the lush company of temperate ferns and an overstory of sago palms. For their wonderful textural complements, visit the westernmost wing for the bromeliads (an exceptionally fine collection) and the staghorn ferns. Recent Palm House renovations have been completed. In 2002, the Bromeliad House will undergo more renovation and will be closed June-Sept.

WASHINGTON PARK ARBORETUM

2300 Arboretum Drive E, Seattle, WA 98112-2300 | **Contact:** Arboretum Foundation/General Information: Events hotline, (206) 726-1954; Foundation office, (206) 325-4510; Graham Visitors Center Gift Shop, (206) 543-8800 | **Email:** gvc@arboretum foundation.org; Educational Programs, (206) 543-8800; Adult Education, Center for Urban Horticulture, (206) 685-8033. Arboretum Web: www.wparboretum.org, which is linked to www.arboretumfoundation.org | **Directions:** From I-5, take exit 168B east (Bellevue / Kirkland) onto Hwy 520, then take the first exit (Montlake Blvd). Cross Montlake Blvd onto E Lake Washington Blvd and turn left onto Foster Island Road. Take the first right onto Arboretum Dr E, parking at the Graham Visitors Center. From downtown Seattle, drive east on Madison St over "Pill Hill," First Hill, and along to Madison Park. Turn left at Lake Washington Blvd E. From east of Lake Washington, follow the Evergreen Point Floating Bridge (Hwy 520) to the first Seattle exit (Lake Washington Blvd S). At the stop sign, turn left and take the next exit left onto Foster Island Rd, and a right onto Arboretum Dr E. | **Open:** Arboretum: Year-round, 7 a.m. until sunset. Graham Visitor Center & Arboretum Gift Shop: Daily, 10 a.m.-4 p.m; volunteers are available to answer questions; selection of plants from the Patricia Calvert Greenhouse for sale, free pamphlets, restrooms. Master Gardeners are on hand to answer questions Sundays, noon-4 p.m. Patricia Calvert Greenhouse: Near the Graham Visitors Center; (206) 325-4510. Maintained by volunteers who propagate rare and unusual plants from the Arboretum collections; plant sales Tuesday, 10 a.m.-noon, first Saturday April-Sept., 10 a.m.-2 p.m. | **Tours:** "Saturdays and Sundays at One" tours are led by experienced volunteers who will focus on an aspect of the Arboretum of particular seasonal interest. Admission is free; one-hour tours begin at 1:00, from the GVC (walks are not offered in December, on holidays, or on Husky home football game days). Also, for families and organized groups of children, find hour-long tours led by trained guides; "Explorer Packs" are available to families and organized groups of kids (K-6th grade) by reservation with a small fee (see more details in Chapter 3 under "Educational Opportunities"). The Arboretum Foundation offers guided group tours with three-week advance notice. Topics include seasonal themes, native plants/ethnobotany, and Foster Island ecology. Fee is $15 per group of 15 or fewer adults; $10 per group for Arboretum Foundation and Study Group members. For all tour information, call (206) 543-. | **Brochure and guidebooks:** Free brochure with map and Arboretum highlights. A serious or very interested student of the collections here would be wise to purchase a copy of the *Woody Plant Collection in the Washington Park Arboretum* for its map and cataloged identification information. The *Washington Park Arboretum Guidebook* makes a valuable companion, with maps, history of the Arboretum, collection highlights, lovely illustrations, solid plant information (the basics of taxonomy and botanical Latin), and a month-by-month guide to "What's in Bloom" (find more details in Chapter 10, under "Literature"). | **Entry fee:** Arboretum, no admission; Seattle's Japanese Garden, $2.50/adult, $1.50/seniors and children. | **Accessibility:** Partially wheelchair accessible. | **Support organization:** Arboretum Foundation; (206) 345-4510 | **Web:** www.arboretumfoundation.org.

This Seattle treasure provides **230 acres of urban green space** within the city with over 4,400 different species and cultivated varieties of woody plants, 124 kinds of trees, 205 varieties of shrubs, and 23 types of vines. Not surprisingly, this is the **second largest collection of its kind in North America.** This is, after all, an arboretum,

a place you would expect to come to see and learn about specimens collected from all corners of the earth—from over 75 countries (including 175 plants on the endangered or threatened species list), here to grow in our mild maritime climate. Some will do better than others, given the location of the property, with conditions ideally suited to the strong rhododendron collection (which is world famous) and the magnolia collection. Other prominent collections include conifers, oaks, hollies, mountain ashes, camellias, maples, firs, witch hazels, cherries and birches. Collections are planted according to the cultural needs of the plants, as for those tolerant of wet soils or heavy shade, and by seasonal interest, as along Azalea Way, a favorite route in spring.

The Joseph A. Witt **Winter Garden**, dedicated in 1988 to the late curator, provides a stunning collection of plants selected to exhibit an enticing range of characteristics at their best in winter. Trees from every continent are represented along with native flora, including 20 species of trees native to Seattle. Another guide to consider would be Arthur Lee Jacobson's *Trees of Seattle*, which includes a fold-out map of the Arboretum and whose text describes many of the trees you will find as you wander through the grounds. While at the GVC, have a look though the **Drought Tolerant Garden** housed on the handsome North Patio and look over the Signature Bed along the west side of the building, where each year a new designer selects a specific theme and volunteers the effort to create it. The ponds in the **Woodland Garden** (with its Japanese Maples Collection a stunner in fall) have been renovated.

In 2001, the Seattle City Council and the University of Washington Board of Regents unanimously approved a new master plan for the Washington Park Arboretum. This long-awaited effort (which began in 1995) will establish 21 new plant collections, restore 30 other plant exhibits, improve park access and facilities, and offer more educational resources to the public. The plan embraces the mission of the Arboretum: Conservation, Education, and Recreation. It is expected to take 20 years or more to complete and to require approximately $46 million in public and private funding support. Beginning in 2002, Seattle Parks and Recreation dedicated $2.3 million in initial Arboretum improvements.

Among highlights of the new plan will be a reorientation of some new plant exhibits along ecological lines, restoration of key areas (including Azalea Way and shorelines), reorientation and/or upgrades of pedestrian trails, the addition of a new pedestrian/bicycle trail along Lake Washington Boulevard, renovation and expansion of the Graham Visitors Center, a new pavilion and entrance at the Japanese Garden, and overall improved traffic flow with safer, more convenient parking. We applaud the Arboretum Foundation for supporting this initiative and encourage you to get involved, show your support, and join the Arboretum.

Seattle's Japanese Garden

1501 Lake Washington Boulevard E, Seattle, WA 98122 | **Phone:** (206) 684-4725 | **Web:** www.seattlejapanesegarden.org | **Directions:** In Washington Park Arboretum, on Lake Washington Blvd at the southeastern end of the Park, just 2 blocks north of E Madison St. | **Open:** Daily, March 1-November 30, 10 a.m. to dusk. | **Entry fee:** Fees are expected to increase slightly in 2002. In recent years, the admission has been $2.50 for adults, $1.50 for seniors and children. Annual passes have been sold at $10/individual, $20/family. Group rates are available to K-12 student groups only with advanced reservations. | **Accessibility:** Partially wheelchair accessible, pathways are gravel; no pets or camera tripods allowed. | **Support organizations:** Japanese Garden Society; The Arboretum Foundation.

This 3.5-acre stroll garden is based on designs popular in the Matojabe period of 1693-1730. The meandering paths are laid out to provide the viewer with alternating intimate scenes and open vistas, transforming even a relatively small site into what would appear to be a larger garden. The garden reflects the traditional elements of beautifully maintained trees, shrubs, and vines along with carefully selected and placed stones, water elements, stone lanterns, and carved granite basins. Spring and fall bring breathtaking displays of flower and foliage. During the fall and winter of 2001, the Japanese Garden pond area was fully renovated to repair eroded portions of the pond system. The ponds, waterfalls, and streams have also been refiltered and recirculated. On each third Saturday of the month (April-Oct.), at 1:30 p.m., the public is invited to observe a free demonstration of the Chado tea ceremony. For details on participating in the Way of Tea, contact The Urasenke Foundation at (206) 324-1483.

WOODLAND PARK ZOOLOGICAL GARDENS

5500 Phinney Ave. N, Seattle WA 98103; Zoo information (206) 684-4800 (TDD (206) 684-4026). Web: www.zoo.org | **Entrance gates:** South: N 50th St and Fremont Ave N (closest to the ZooStore, Visitor Center and Education Center); West: N 55th St and Phinney Ave. N; North: 601 N 59th St and Phinney Ave N (generally closed Oct.-March) | **Directions:** From I-5, take exit 169 onto 50th St NE and travel west to the Zoo entrance at N 50th and Fremont Ave N. | **Open:** Daily, 9:30 a.m.-6 p.m. (4 p.m. closing, Oct. 15-March 14). | **Entry fee:** Adults (18-64) $9; Seniors (65+) $8.25; Disabled and Youth (6-17) $6.50; Preschool (3-5) $4.25; Toddler (0-2) free. Parking $3.50. (A discount from these prices of $.50 to $1 is available to King County residents.). | **Tours:** Plant and animal tours available by prearrangement; call (206) 684-4850. Watch for scheduled, horticulturally focused walks and talks. | **Accessibility:** Wheelchair accessible throughout. | **Support organization:** Woodland Park Zoological Society. Join! Levels are Wolf One (individual) $45; Wolf Pack (family) $65; AquaZoo (family/couple) $95. Membership is good for one year and entitles holders to unlimited admission, 10% discount on ZooStore merchandise, discounts on classes and lectures, *Zoo News* subscription, member appreciation events, and free admission to more than 140 other zoos. Contact Woodland Park Zoological Society at (206) 615-1024.

Woodland Park Zoological Gardens is located on 92 acres of Seattle's Phinney Ridge neighborhood. The area was purchased from the Guy Phinney estate in 1899 for use as a city park, and its many old and towering trees make the name "woodland park" an appropriate one for this institution. The Zoo's notable trees include magnificent stands of European beeches (*Fagus sylvatica*), English elms (*Ulmus minor* var. *vulgaris*), Black locusts (*Robinia pseudoacacia*), and many other rare and interesting varieties of herbaceous plants, trees, and shrubs throughout the extensive grounds—including many native to this area. If you're interested in this extensive horticultural collection you'll be glad to know you can expect to find more identifying labels in the future.

Within specific exhibits, look for the following areas:

* **Australasia Botanical Exhibit**, funded by the Pendleton & Elisabeth Carey Miller Charitable Foundation. This new display features many rare and endangered plants of the region.

* **Tropical Rain Forest**: Transport yourself to the tropics. Opened in 1992, this exhibit zone covers 2.5 acres, displays nearly 700 plant species (both temperate and tropical), contains over 50 birds and 33 species of animals, and was awarded Best New Exhibit of the Year in 1993 by the American Zoo and Aquarium Association. Especially interesting are plants of economic importance (such as vanilla, chocolate, coffee, black pepper), carnivorous plants, endangered orchids, and over 20 species of tropical palms. This lush, diverse exhibit complex takes the visitor from the forest floor to the understory and on up into the tree canopy along a circular pathway, past 25 separate animal enclosures.

* **Temperate Forest and Family Farm**: Notable for its use of plants native to the Seattle area, the Family Farm landscape includes a vegetable garden, composting exhibit, butterfly garden, and apple orchard filled with historical apple varieties. Use the Zoo's South Gate for easiest access.

* **Tropical Asia**: This exhibit contains the Asian Elephant Forest completed in 1989 (chosen as Best New Exhibit of the Year by the AZA in 1990) and the Trail of Vines, completed in 1996. This area contains a large collection of bamboo species and a diversity of plant species in a jungle environment. The Asian Elephant Forest is home to the Zoo's elephants, whose daily baths (with zookeeper commentary and explanations) are open to the public. The elephants are allowed to wander over a 1-acre area, the focal point of which is the elephant pool. The Trail of Vines contains seven waterfalls, with streams running throughout and is home to the Zoo's orangutans, siamangs, and lion-tailed macaques, who display their arboreal skills in the trees within their exhibits. Use any of the Zoo's gates for entry.

❊**Northern Trail**: Seven plant communities of southcentral Alaska are replicated in this 7-acre exhibit complex, from dense white spruce forest to shrubby tundra. Vegetation allows separate exhibits to flow into each other so it appears that the elk are accessible to the wolves and the mountain goats to the grizzly bears. This exhibit garnered the Zoo another Best New Exhibit of the Year award in 1995.

❊**Butterflies and Blooms**: New in 1998, this exhibit was funded again for 2002 (reopening mid-May and running to fall). An additional $1 fee is required to enter the exhibit, open 10 a.m.-6 p.m. daily. There are three parts to this fascinating and very educational exhibit of butterfly ecology that features not only the spellbinding beauty of these creatures, but also their life cycle and interdependence with the plants that attract and nurture them. You make your entry through an outdoor "foyer" called the Life Cycle Landscape, depicting the four distinct life stages of butterflies. Then you enter the Butterflies in Flight house, a bright and airy structure through which the sounds of classical music float, as do hundreds of colorful butterflies. At least 15 different native American species (as opposed to tropical species) are present at any one time, free-flying amid trees, flowering plants, and a small stream. In the Emergence House, you can watch butterflies break free from their chrysalis before your very eyes. The final stage of the exhibit, a demonstration garden outside the structure, provides ideas to take home for your own butterfly garden.

Additional information: The Washington Park Arboretum *Bulletin* (58:3 Summer 1996 devotes an entire issue to a "Plant Guide to the Woodland Park Zoological Gardens." From "Zoo Bamboo" to a story on "The Trail of Vines," and from Dan Hinkley on "Feigning Foreign Flora" to Arthur Lee Jacobson on the Zoo's "Outstanding Trees," you'll appreciate the horticultural side of this world-class treasure-place *far more* with this journal in hand! (Only $5 at the Arboretum!)

Woodland Park Rose Garden

700 N 50th Street and Fremont Avenue N, Seattle, WA | **Contact:** Woodland Park Zoological Gardens, 5500 Phinney Avenue N, Seattle, WA 98103 | **Phone:** (206) 684-4040 | **Web:** www.ci.seattle.wa.us/parks/parkspaces/Gardens.htm | **Open:** Daily, 7 a.m. to dusk. | **Accessibility:** Wheelchair accessible.

This 2.5-acre garden is a special place for rose lovers, who have come here since 1924 to wander among their favorites, old and new—now numbering some 5,000 (representing 260 varieties in 88 beds). The garden is **an official test site for the All America Rose** Selections Committee, who honored it in 1995 as the outstanding rose garden in the United States. Annually, the Zoo and the Seattle Rose Society offer a free rose-pruning demonstration the third Sunday in February, and a free rose-care day the third Sunday in July. The garden has

always a popular place for weddings (call 206-684-4800), and the installation of a gazebo in 1995 has made it even more popular with brides.

YASHIRO PARK

8th Avenue & Plum Street, Olympia, WA | **Directions:** Located adjacent to Olympia City Hall. | **Open:** Daylight hours. | **Entry fee:** Free.

This Japanese Garden in the heart of Olympia is a wonderful oasis of tranquility, visual if not auditory (you do hear traffic sounds). Bamboo, rocks, blossoms, a pagoda, a waterfall, and numerous fish live in peace here. Olympia and the City of Yashiro, Japan, have an active sister-city relationship that inspired this park. Note the gates, built by Japanese artisans using no nails.

ZABEL'S RHODODENDRON AND AZALEA PARK

2432 Bethel Street NE, Olympia, WA 98506 | **Phone:** (360) 357-6977 | **Directions:** From I-5, take exit 105, and follow Port of Olympia signs. Go to the fifth traffic light and turn right onto 4th Ave, a one-way street. Get in the left lane and at the first traffic light proceed up the hill 1 block further and turn left onto Puget St. Go north on Puget 0.7 mile to San Francisco St and turn right; go 2 blocks to Bethel, turn left, go another 0.7 mile, and watch for the "Rhody Tour" sign. | **Open:** Daily in May, 9 a.m.-8 p.m. | **Entry fee:** Free. | **Accessibility:** Level trails will accommodate wheelchair navigation.

Art and Peggy Zabel's Rhododendron and Azalea Park is situated behind their home. For 25 years this couple has generously opened the grounds for a month during peak spring bloom. (Since they first extended their invitation over 100,000 appreciative visitors from around the world have passed through this botanical paradise; in 2001, visitors hailed from all 50 states and 28 countries.) There are over 3 acres of nature trails with around 1,200 rhododendrons and azaleas (many labeled) planted among a large variety of ornamental trees, shrubs, ground covers, and other plants. Benches have been thoughtfully provided for your ease as you wend your way through the woodland.

GARDENS TO VISIT: BRITISH COLUMBIA

British Columbia capitalizes on its mild maritime climate and rich English gardening heritage with a number of outstanding tributes to horticultural excellence. Several major gardens are within a day's round trip or weekend outing from anywhere in the Puget Sound region; see the following information about ferry service. Prices for visiting these gardens are quoted in Canadian dollars.

B.C. Ferries: Information: 7 a.m.-10 p.m. daily; (604) 444-2890 (Vancouver); (250) 386-3431 (Victoria). Web: www.bcferries.com. Tsawwassen, BC, to Swartz Bay on Vancouver Island, approximately 1.5-hour crossing time. There is no ferry service between Vancouver proper and Vancouver Island/Victoria, or Seattle, WA. Pacific Coach Lines (call 604-662-8074 or see www.pacificcoach

lines.com) provides coach service between Vancouver and Victoria (via ferry), otherwise you will need a vehicle to get to Tsawwassen (several miles south of Vancouver and north of the U.S.-Canada border), Check a good map.

U.S. Ferries: Black Ball ferry service between Port Angeles and Victoria; (206) 622-2222.San Juan Islands and Victoria from Bellingham, passengers only, May-October; (800) 443-4552. Seattle to Victoria, BC; ferry service via the *Victoria Clipper*, passenger-only catamaran service between Seattle and Victoria, BC, 2.5 hours each way (with service to some of the San Juan Islands in summer). Call (206) 448-5000 or see www.victoriaclipper.com. Washington State Ferry System, between Anacortes, WA and various San Juan Islands, with frequent service; also to Sidney, BC (with bus service from there to Victoria, BC) crossing in summer twice a day each way (once each way in other seasons). Allow about 3 hours each way; (888) 808-7977 or (206) 464-6400. For those with touch-tone phones the ferry system has devised a very convenient for checking schedule information. Web: www.wsdot.wa.gov/ferries/. There is no ferry service between Seattle and Vancouver at the time of this printing.

ABKHAZI GARDEN

1964 Fairfield Road, Victoria, BC V9E 2H2 Canada; Office (250) 479-8053; Garden (250) 598-8096 | **Email:** abkhazi@conservancy.bc.ca | **Directions:** From downtown Victoria, travel north on Fairfield Road. Abkhazi is at the intersection of Fairfield and Foul Bay Road. The garden is also accessible by public transportation; take Bus Nos. 2 or 7. | **Open:** Feb. 16-Sep. 30, Wed., Thurs., Fri., and Sun., 1-4 p.m. | **Entry fee:** $7.50 (March-June 15); $5 off-peak. | **Support organization:** The Land Conservancy of B.C., a land trust that protects cultural and environmental sites; (250) 479-8053 or www.conservancy.bc.ca.

The Abkhazi Garden is a significant heritage garden property located in Victoria, a city that prides itself as the "Garden Capital of Canada." The garden was begun in 1946 on property purchased by Peggy Pemberton Carter, who came to Victoria after spending more than two years in a Japanese internment camp outside Shanghai. She was soon reunited with Prince Nicholas Abkhazi (a Georgian nobleman) who she had met in Paris in the 1920s. They were married in Victoria and were soon building their garden together. Slightly more than one acre, the property consists entirely of the house and garden built by Prince and Princess Abkhazi. The site is characteristic of the unique Victoria landscape, dominated by native Garry oak (*Quercus garryana*) and given shape and topography by a dramatic outcropping of glaciated rock. Highlights of the garden include rock and alpine plants, ornamental evergreens, pools, a rhododendron copse, woodland garden, and views of the Strait of Juan de Fuca and the Olympic Mountains.

Nicholas died in 1988 and Peggy died in 1994. The property was sold in 1999 for $1 million (Canadian) and was under review by the City of Victoria for development of as many as 12 townhouses, a plan that would have destroyed the garden. The happy ending to this story is that The Land Conservancy, in cooperation with a number of private individuals and organizations, purchased the property in 2000 and began raising funds to pay for it. The rescue and preservation of the Abkhazi Garden in Victoria has captured the support of many who have seen this wonderful creation. Renovations are just beginning, so now is a great time to get involved and show your support. You can also book events here by calling (250) 598-8096.

ARTHUR ERICKSON GARDEN

Contact: Arthur Erickson House and Garden Foundation, PO Box 39042, Vancouver, BC V6R 4P1 Canada | **Phone:** (604) 738-4195 | **Email:** ccooper@interchange.ubc.ca | **Web:** www.arthur erickson.com/tours.html | **Open:** By appointment; guided tours offered May through Sept | **Directions:** Provided at the time when appointment is scheduled. | **Entry fee:** $10 per person. | **Accessibility:** Wheelchair accessible. | **Support organization:** Arthur Erickson House and Garden Foundation.

Open to the public by appointment, this is the Asian garden of renowned Canadian architect Arthur Erickson. If you would like a preview of the garden, find it featured on the video *Northwest Garden Style*. The Erickson Garden is also featured in *Artists in Their Gardens* by Valerie Easton and David Laskin.

THE BUTCHART GARDENS

Contact: Box 4010, Victoria, BC V8X 3X4 Canada | **Phone:** (250) 652-4422, Recorded information (250) 652-5256 | **Email:** email@butchartgardens.com | **Web:** www.butchartgardens.com | **Directions:** The Gardens are located on Vancouver Island approximately 13 miles (21 kilometers) north of Victoria. You can reach Butchart Gardens by taking one of the ferry services: Seattle to Victoria (Victoria Clipper), Anacortes to Sidney (Washington State Ferries); Port Angeles to Victoria (Blackball Transportation); Tsawwassen to Swartz Bay or Horseshoe Bay to Nanaimo (BC Ferries). The route to the Gardens is well signposted from Hwy 17, and bus tours are readily available from Victoria and Vancouver, BC. There is no charge for moorage at the buoys in Butchart Cove, where you can dinghy in to disembark at the wharf. No overnight tying up is available. Dock facilities are restricted to dinghies and may be quite busy in the height of summer. | **Open:** Daily from 9 a.m., with closing times varying by season. | **Entry fee:** Peak season rates are $19.25 for adults (over 18), $9.50 for juniors (13-17), $1.50 for children (5-12). | **Accessibility:** Wheelchair accessible, and wheelchairs available on loan. As a thoughtful gesture to guests, the Gardens also offer cameras, baby push-carts, and umbrellas on loan.

Open to friends and visitors for nearly a century, this 50-acre showplace was originally the estate of Robert and Jenny Butchart, who founded The Gardens in 1904. The Butcharts took the challenge of transforming a worked-out limestone quarry into a series of gardens based on distinct styles: Japanese, Italian, Rose, and Sunken Gardens. As world travelers dedicated to horticulture, they brought many ideas and plants back to their Vancouver Island estate. In the Butcharts' own home, see a historical display of the gardens. In spring, enjoy dozens of flowering shrubs, trees, and over 7,000 bulbs. On summer evenings June 15 to September 15, Butchart Gardens are illuminated and musical entertainment is provided. On Saturday evenings in July and August, a fireworks display with music complements the brilliance of the horticultural displays. And during the Christmas season the Gardens sparkle and glisten with marvelous winterland lights and sounds. This is a very popular destination, so consider arriving during the late-afternoon or early-evening hours when you will find fewer enthusiasts sharing the lovely paths with you. There are restaurants of varying formality, plus a great Seed and Gift Store.

DARTS HILL GARDEN PARK

170th Street and 16th Ave., Surrey, BC | **Mailing address:** 15488 19th Ave., Surrey, BC Canada V4A 7M8 | **Contact:** (604) 501-5665 | **Email:** dartshillgarden@home.com | **Directions:** From I-5 head north to the Blaine Peace Arch border crossing; after entering BC, take Exit 2 (8th Ave.), head east on 8th Avenue to 176th St; travel north to 16th Avenue, west to 170th Street for garden parking lot and entrance. | **Open:** For group tours only, by appointment, March to October. Contact Friends of the Garden at number above and you will be contacted by a volunteer. | **Entry fee:** $3/person ($5/person, commercial tour groups) | **Support organizations:** Friends of Darts Hill Garden Park; City of Surry Parks Department. | **Accessibility:** The garden is not accessible by wheelchair.

Darts Hill Garden Park is a result of a pioneering spirit, interest and dedication. Edwin and Francisca Darts acquired the property in 1943 before it had ever been tilled. It was covered with bush that had regrown after the logging of the original forest cover in the 1800s. Evidence of that activity was seen in the skid roads used to haul logs to the sawmill at the mouth of the Campbell River. The Darts initially developed an orchard planted with fruit trees including apple, pear, apricot, peach and prune, as well as walnut and filbert trees. It was an exhibit by the Alpine Garden Club of BC at the Pacific Northwest Exhibition that stirred their interest and enthusiasm for horticulture. This led to Mrs. Darts involvement in many organizations devoted to the field, including the Royal Horticultural Society, from which she received seeds of many rare and unusual plants, shrubs and trees. Darts Hill became a real plant collector's garden containing countless species and varieties of plants from around the world. Mrs. Darts developed a particular affection for rhododendrons and magnolias, resulting in an outstanding collection.

In 1994, the Darts donated their estate to the City of Surrey, intending the gardens to be a horticultural center for the preservation, enhancement and development of plants. Darts Hill consists of 7.5 acres developed over 55 years: the variety of rare plants, shrubs and trees is extensive. The gardens are contained within a larger 22 acre park site. The City has worked directly with Mrs. Darts in the development of a plan and overall guiding principles for the garden, in order to ensure that the garden will continue to be managed in the future. The City

has built on the Darts' lifetime work on the garden by setting up the framework for a Native Plant Garden. Mrs. Darts has generously welcomed garden clubs, horticultural organizations and other groups to visit her gardens. A dedicated group of volunteers have formed *Friends of the Garden* to help with booking and leading group tours.

DR. SUN YAT-SEN CLASSICAL CHINESE GARDEN

578 Carrall Street, Vancouver, BC V6B 5K2, Canada | **Phone:** (604) 662-3207; Info-line: (604) 689-7133 | **Email:** sunyatsen@telus.net | **Web:** www.discovervancouver.com/sun | **Directions:** Located in Vancouver's Chinatown, at the corner of Pender and Carrall Sts. From the U.S. border or south of Vancouver, take Hwy 99 (which becomes the Oak Street Bridge). Take the East exit onto Marine Dr and follow until Main St. Turn left on Main St and follow all the way into Chinatown. Turn left on Keefer St in Chinatown, and continue to Carrall St, where you'll turn right. (Approximate time from Oak Street Bridge is 15 minutes.) The Garden is located on the right; look for a large, white-walled structure. | **Brochure:** Call, write, or email for a free color brochure. | **Open:** Daily, 10 a.m.-6 p.m., May 6 -June 14; 9:30 a.m.-7 p.m., June 15-August 31; 10 a.m.-6 p.m., September; 10 a.m.-4:30 p.m., Oct. 1-May 5. | **Entry fee:** Adults $7.50, seniors $6, students $5; group rate available with ten or more (groups must book at least one week in advance). | **Tours:** Guided daily; call for a seasonal schedule, offered several times per day. If you are interested in renting the Garden grounds for a private event or are interested in the programs and private "music, tea, and tour evenings," call (604) 662-3207. | **Accessibility:** Wheelchair accessible. | **Support organization:** Dr. Sun Yat-Sen Garden Society of Vancouver.

Named after the first president of the Republic of China, this Ming Dynasty (1368-1644) style garden is the first of its kind built outside China. Artisans from China's garden city, Suzhou, west of Shanghai, created the many intricate structural details the traditional way, using no electrical tools and no nails. Here you can discover the Taoist philosophy behind the Garden's angled corridors, twisted trees, tangled foliage, and distorted limestone rockery, retrieved from the bottom of Lake T'ai in China and transported to Vancouver for the Garden. Deceptively small and tucked behind the Chinese Cultural Center at the edge of Chinatown, this garden unfolds behind tall white walls. A gentle waterfall and tranquil pools, the rustle of bamboo, and other trees and plants of China transform a bustling city corner into a peaceful haven. Make an early morning visit in April when the cherry blossoms and rhododendron trusses are at their best. Summer evenings, come to hear The Enchanted Evening Series offers Chinese music, tea, and a stroll through the Garden under the soft light of handmade lanterns (Friday evenings, July-Sept; additional charge for event). The mid-autumn moon festival in October features lantern displays, myth-telling, and delicious moon cakes. The Garden also celebrates the lunar new year in Jan.-Feb.

The Garden Society is planning an expansion project that includes an educational center, a volunteer resource area, and a kitchen and washroom facilities, as well as a larger gift shop. The 3,814-square-foot building is slated for completion in 2002.

THE GLADES, A WOODLAND RHODODENDRON GARDEN

561 - 172nd Street, Surrey, BC V3S 9R3 Canada | **Phone:** (604) 538-0928 | **Email:** glades@uniserve.com | **Directions:** From the Blaine Peace Arch border crossing traveling north from Washington, take the first exit (8th Ave), going east to 172nd St. Turn right (south) to the garden. From the Pacific Hwy crossing at Blaine traveling north, turn left at the traffic light onto 8th Ave and proceed to 172nd St. Turn left (south) into the garden. From Hwy 99 traveling south, take exit 2 and loop up over the highway, traveling east to 172nd, then turn right. | **Open:** By appointment only to groups, throughout the spring and summer; and without an appointment on Mother's Day for a Tour and Tea, as a fund raising effort for the Peace Arch Hospital Auxiliary.

In 1956, when Murray Stephen and his wife, Lydia, bought the 5-acre property now known as The Glades, it was a tangled tract of brush in an area logged off at the turn of the century. Through an enormous effort they transformed this area into a garden of many exotic trees and shrubs, and in particular rhododendrons and azaleas, their passion. When the property passed to the present owners, Jim and Elfriede DeWolf in 1994, the garden had become very run-down. They have been enthusiastically busy bringing it back "from the wild." The Glades' original plantings cover the entire 5 acres and include over 1,600 mature rhododendrons, azaleas, and companion plants. There is a superb collection of designated Heritage trees, and a wonderful mix of native and non-native ornamental woody plants are intermingled throughout the woodland setting. The acreage supports a wide diversity of environments, from shady groves and sunny lawns to lily ponds and bogs dressed out in massive gunnera. You'll find western red cedar, dawn redwood, tall maples, flowering cherries, clematis, and many other plants. Additionally, it is a sanctuary for wildlife and birds.

GOVERNMENT HOUSE GARDENS

1401 Rockland Avenue, Victoria, BC V8S 1V9 Canada | **Phone:** (250) 356-5139 (garden) | **Directions:** Located about 1 mile from the Inner Harbor. Go east on Fort St to Cook St, turn right (south) to Rockland Ave, then turn left for 5 blocks. | **Open:** Daily, dawn to dusk. | **Entry fee:** No admission charge. | **Tours:** Available on request. | **Accessibility:** Wheelchair accessible. | **Support organization:** Friends of Government House Gardens Society.

The gardens and grounds of Government House, Victoria, encompass nearly 36 acres. The traditions of English garden design have greatly influenced the gardens' creator, landscape architect Robert Savery, who was born and educated in England. In 1991, His Honour, The Honorable David C. Lam, Lieutenant Governor of British Columbia (1989-1995) and his wife Dorothy, initiated the Garden Volunteer Program to enhance the existing gardens and create new gardens for public enjoyment. The Friends of Government House Gardens Society was formally established in partnership with The Lieutenant Governor and the BC Government. Now nearly 300 volunteers support this project.

You'll enjoy an English Country Garden of traditional cottage garden flowers and plants. Two borders have a splendid display of herbaceous perennials and foliage plants. The Victorian Rose Garden was a gift (in 1991) by the Lams to the people of BC. The design is based on the rose garden at Warwick Castle, England. The Sunken Rose Garden has a display of David Austin roses and is wheelchair accessible by a ramp from the Herb Garden. The Demonstration Cut Flower Garden features many sun-loving perennials and foliage plants, and a magnificent London plane tree provides shade for hostas and hellebores. Choice plants from mountainous areas of the world are featured in the Rock and Alpine Garden on a natural rock outcrop. The Heather Garden illustrates that these plants can provide flowers and colorful foliage throughout the year. The Winter Garden has a splendid collection of hardy plants that provide flowers and fragrance from November through April. The grounds feature a great variety of mature trees and shrubs, and several plantings of mature rhododendrons. A waterfall flows down a rock outcrop known as Pearkes Peak, named after Lieutenant Governor George Pearkes who was an avid gardener; the Fountain Pond is the habitat of wild ducks, turtles, and a very interesting variety of birds and pond life. The Rotary Garden of International Friendship is the inspiration of Rotarian Alan Potter. It features a collection of trees, shrubs, and plants representing the countries and regions of the world; a new bed of summer-flowering bulbs and plants is also being developed. The nursery, the Friends Cottage and Garden, swimming pool and flagpole garden, and the Ballroom Terraces are not open to the public, but may occasionally be visited by prior appointment.

In addition to the formal gardens, there is a 22-acre Garry Oak Ecosystem. The mandate of the Friends is to protect, preserve, and enhance this Ecosystem and to provide opportunities for appreciation and education. Access is by prearranged, conducted tours.

HATLEY PARK GARDENS, AT ROYAL ROADS UNIVERSITY

2000 block on Sooke Road, Colwood, about 7 miles west of downtown Victoria | **Contact:** 2205 Sooke Road, Victoria, BC V9B 5Y2 Canada | **Phone:** (250) 391-2511 | **Web:** www.royalroads.ca | **Directions:** Located about 7 miles west of downtown Victoria. From Victoria, take Hwys 1 and 1A west, following the signs for Fort Rodd Hill; take the Colwood exit from Hwy 1, and go for about 1 more mile. | **Open:** Daily, for self-guided tours, dawn to dusk. In July this is the venue for the Victoria Flower and Garden Festival. | **Tours:** Adults $3, students $1. Schedule a castle tour by calling (250) 391-2600, ext. 4456. Group or school tours, call (250) 656-0853. | **Entry fee:** No admission fee. | **Accessibility:** Limited wheelchair accessibility. | **Support organization:** Friends of Hatley Park Society, 2100 Trident Place, North Saanich, BC V8L 5J4 Canada | **Phone:** (250) 656-0853 | **Web:** http://www.royal roads.co/docs/fohps/index.html.

This baronial estate of over 600 acres is the setting of Hatley Castle, now owned by the Canadian government and leased by Royal Roads University. The imposing stone castle itself was completed in 1910 as the retirement home of James Dunsmuir, a Vancouver Island coal mining and rail tycoon who also served as Premier and Lieutenant Governor of British Columbia. Construction of the formal gardens began in 1913 and was completed in 1916. The elegant grounds are open to the public and include a mix of formal gardens and native woodland. Adjacent to the Castle is the walled Italian terrace garden containing many of the Dunsmuir's original urns and statues of the four seasons. English ivy cloaks the stone wall of the Castle, 80-year-old wisteria intertwined with clematis graces the pergola, and pillars and formal clipped box hedges neatly edge the planting beds. Leaving this formal garden through the wrought-iron gateway, encounter some newer plantings, among which are a long mixed border with alpines, and a species geranium collection, a small rock scree, and a collection of small maples. You are then led to a less regimented, 4-acre Japanese Garden along a spring-fed stream that feeds three man-made lakes, which empty ultimately at the Equinalt Lagoon. There are many details that reflect Japanese symbolism, as with Tortoise Island, representing longevity (there is a lovely Atlas cedar planted to the left of the end of the bridge). Also found here are a teahouse, Japanese lanterns, numerous stone groupings, a well, and many appropriate plantings, including the original Japanese cherries, Japanese maples, Japanese umbrella pines, rhododendrons, and azaleas, along with western red and incense cedars, and copper beeches. You can continue on to the lagoon with its waterside garden of primula, hostas, ligularia, gunnera, and others of an aquatic association. Throughout the property there are many outstanding specimen trees. A favored season for refreshing color is spring, when the many Japanese cherries and rhododendrons are in bloom.

The Glen is a rehabilitated original Dunsmuir garden at the intersection of Cottonwood Creek Road and College Drive. It features a large rock garden and a small species rhododendron garden in a natural amphitheater, which is bisected by a stream with some lovely waterfall features.

HORTICULTURE CENTRE OF THE PACIFIC

505 Quayle Road, Victoria, BC V9E 2J4 Canada | **Phone:** (250) 479-6162 | **Email:** hcp.info@hcp.bc.ca | **Web:** www.hcp.bc.ca | **Directions:** Located near Victoria. From Pat Bay Hwy, take the Royal Oak Dr exit (turn left at stop sign if coming from Victoria or right if coming from Swartz Bay), and go to W Saanich Road. Turn right and drive 0.7 mile to Beaver Lake Rd and turn left. Watch for signs. | **Open:** Daily; summer hours: 8 a.m.-8 p.m., winter hours: 9 a.m.-4 p.m. | **Entry fee:** Adults $5, children and HCP members admitted free. | **Tours:** One-hour guided tours may be scheduled with a sliding-scale additional charge ($15 for one guide leading up to 12; $60 for four guides leading 37 to 48 persons). Inquire about custom tours that may include tea, or a lecture,

demonstration, or workshop. | **Accessibility:** Partially wheelchair accessible. | **Support organizations:** Specialty garden clubs and members (this is a great organization to join). There is a membership of 1,300.

Nestled in 100 acres of native habitat and serene wetlands, The Horticultural Centre's 5 acres of gardens reflect the tireless work and skills of many specialty garden clubs, which undertake to show through demonstration gardens what will grow well in this climatic zone. Most plants are labeled—an amazing feat, considering the collection here numbers 10,000 plant varieties. The Winter Garden is especially colorful and of interest in late January through February. The revamped Rhododendron and Hosta Garden is most spectacular in early spring. The Takata Japanese Garden provides a peaceful oasis where visitors may stroll over the lovely curved wooden bridge and others built of stone before returning through the lower Winter Garden, the Heather Garden, and the Hardy Fuchsia Garden. Then head back to the sunny gardens, which include perennial beds, herb gardens, Canada's only Dahlia Test Garden, a kitchen garden, and a wonderful display of eucalyptus trees and ornamental shrubs. The Drought-Resistant Garden is in the forefront of a regional water conservation plan. The wetland attracts migrating and resident waterfowl, and many species of birds make the garden a permanent home or frequent destination. Diligent volunteers are working to preserve endangered native plants. The Centre has a registered training school, based loosely on the British model, for gardeners who wish to earn a ten-month accredited landscape horticulture certificate. There is also a 90-hour Master Gardener course plus courses for the horticultural industry, weekend workshops, and guided tours for schoolchildren and other groups. .

MINTER GARDENS

52892 Bunker Road, in Rosedale, BC, Canada | **Contact:** PO Box 40, Chilliwack, BC V2P 6H7 Canada; April-Oct. | **Phone:** (604) 794-7191; Nov.-March, (604) 792-3799; North America toll free (888) 646-8377 or (800) 661-3919 | **Web:** www.mintergardens.com | **Directions:** The garden is about 75 miles east of Vancouver on the Trans-Canada Hwy 1, off exit 135. The garden is a short distance from exit 135 and is signposted from the highway. | **Open:** Daily, 9 a.m.-dusk, April-October. | **Entry fee:** Adults $12; seniors $10.50; ages 6-18 $6.50; age 5 and under free; $32 for a family (season passes available). | **Accessibility:** Wheelchair accessible on concrete pathways.

This magnificently sited 27-acre property, spread at the foot of 7,000-foot Mount Cheam, is divided into 11 specialty gardens, with sections concentrating on native plants, roses, stream plants, alpines, ferns, meadow flowers, climbers, rhododendrons, and a fragrance garden. The Chinese Garden features a very special collection of rare Penjing rock bonsai. There are three aviaries, and an unusual maze planted with cedar hedging, too. For those who delight in the tradition of brilliantly colored annuals bedded out in creative tapestries, you will appreciate the care that went into the likes of the largest floral flag of Canada and the fanciful Southern belles—a floral sculpture in the style of topiary art. This garden is fully accessible, with a fragrance garden designed especially for the visually impaired. Many wonderful festivals and seasonal events are staged throughout the year; check the website for specific dates. And there's a gift shop, plant shop, wine shop, cafeteria, and restaurant.

PARK & TILFORD GARDENS

440-333 Brooksbank Avenue, North Vancouver, BC V7J 3S8 Canada | **Phone:** (604) 984-8200 | **Directions:** Located in North Vancouver at Main and Brooksbank. Take the Trans-Canada Hwy (Hwy 1) west through Vancouver over the Second Narrows Bridge. Take exit 23A onto Main St and travel west 1 mile to the Park and Tilford Center. | **Open:** Daily 9:30 a.m.-dusk, times adjusted seasonally; Christmas hours 4-9 p.m. | **Entry fee:** No admission fee; free parking including easy bus parking. | **Tours:** Guided tours (for groups of 10 to 25) available upon request. | **Accessibility:** Largely wheelchair accessible. | **Support organization:** Park & Tilford Gardens are one of the few privately owned, nonprofit display gardens in Canada. The site is sponsored by the merchants of the adjacent Park & Tilford Shopping Centre. Students of the Capilano College horticulture department use the gardens as a training ground.

This beautiful, 2.5-acre treasure features nine theme gardens integrated into the natural landscape—rose, native, oriental, white, yellow, herb, townhouse, annual and magnolia/rhododendron display gardens—all hidden in the midst of rapid urbanization that surrounds the site. As public gardens are generally on a grand scale, beyond the scope of most home gardeners, this is a particularly refreshing gem to visit for ideas one can carry back to a residential setting. Here you will find a broad mix of architectural and horticultural details that work together surprisingly well in creating the garden rooms (the whitewashed walls of the Oriental Garden; hedging "bones"; raised beds; pergolas and trellises). Aficionados will appreciate treatment of the rose plantings, where many of the climbers are married with clematis, a reflection of British influences. The formal rose garden is juxtaposed to the little herb garden, where a mix of the traditional and the more exotic will impress those with an eye for the unusual. The pond area makes a splendid structural and textural contribution to the garden as a whole. The Native Garden draws visitors through a bit of urban woodland of native firs. The gardens stage three plant sales each year, in April, June, and October; call for specific dates. The sales offer hardy and herbaceous perennials, unusual and tender exotic plants, and select trees and shrubs, much of them grown in-house or propagated from garden stock. December brings the garden's brilliant display of lights, free each day from 4-9 p.m.

ROYAL BRITISH COLUMBIA MUSEUM, NATIVE GARDEN

675 Belleville Street, Victoria, BC V8W 9W2 Canada (250) 356-7226 | **Directions:** The museum and garden are located at the intersection of Belleville and Government Sts, just 1 block's walk from the Black Ball and Victoria Clipper ferry terminals. | **Tours:** Upon request; call Richard Hebda, the museum's curator of botany and earth history at (256) 356-7226. | **Support organization:** The Victoria Horticulture Society.

Here you will find in excess of 300 native plant species representing coastal forest, dry interior, and alpine regions, planted in a series of microenvironments. Since the elegant Empress Hotel is just a stone's throw from here, make afternoon tea your next stop, or come here afterward.

QUEEN ELIZABETH PARK

Contact: Vancouver Park Board, 2099 Beach Avenue, Vancouver, BC V6G 1Z4 Canada | **Phone:** (604) 257-8400 or (604) 872-5513 | **Web:** www.parks.vancouver.bc.ca | **Directions:** From the U.S. border or south of Vancouver, take Hwy 99 north. After you cross the Fraser River you will be on Oak St. At 41st, turn right (east), then left on Cambie St to Queen Elizabeth Park. The Bloedel Conservatory is atop the hill. | **Entry fee:** Free. | **Accessibility:** Partially wheelchair accessible. | **Support organizations:** Vancouver Park Board; major benefactor, Prentice Bloedel.

This 130-acre park and garden perched on top of Little Mountain (about 500 feet) provides a sweeping view over the city of Vancouver and its magnificent mountainous backdrop. Created from a disused quarry, the property was "rescued" in 1929 by the Vancouver Park Board. The lush civic arboretum offers wide diversity, with sweeping lawns, native woodland, flowering trees and shrubs, and masses of rhododendrons. The formal gardens, transformed from the quarry eyesore and unveiled in the early 1960s, are a major attraction here. There are two Quarry Gardens, an Arboretum, Rose Garden, and other displays. A coffee shop and gift shop are also featured on the grounds, as is the more formal Season's Restaurant (call 604-874-8008, an elegant restaurant with a fabulous view.

Bloedel Conservatory

290 E 51st Avenue, Vancouver, BC V5X 1C5 Canada | **Phone:** (604) 257-8584 | **Fax:** (604) 257-2412 | **Directions:** Located within Queen Elizabeth Park, 33rd Ave at Cambie St, Vancouver. | **Open:** April-Sept., Monday-Friday 9 a.m.-8 p.m., Saturday-Sunday 10 a.m.-9 p.m; Oct.-March, daily 10 a.m.-5 p.m. | **Entry fee:** Adults $3.90, seniors $2.75, youth (13-18) $2.95, children (6-12) $1.95, children under 6 free. | **Accessibility:** Wheelchair accessible.

It is difficult to turn one's back on the majestic view across the cityscape, English Bay, and the mountainous backdrop—but do so nonetheless! Opened in December 1969, the triodesic dome structure, rising to 70 feet, is constructed of 1,500 Plexiglas bubbles, making this North America's second largest conservatory. The 16,000 square foot garden houses a great diversity of exotic flowering plants in three separate climate zones: desert, subtropical, and rain forest. You'll find over 500 species of plants, including palms, tree ferns, gingers, bananas, cycads, and cactus. Some 60 species of free flying birds live here too—colorful parrots and tiny tropical birds that thrive in this temperature-controlled environment, serenading visitors with songs of the Southern hemisphere, while colorful koi swirl around a large rock pool and waterfall.

RIVERVIEW HORTICULTURAL CENTRE, DAVIDSON ARBORETUM

Riverview Hospital, 500 Lougheed Highway, Coquitlam, BC | **Contact:** PO Box 31005, 2929 St. John's Street, Port Moody, BC V3H 4T4 Canada | **Phone:** (604) 290-9910 | **Email:** rhcs@usa.net | **Directions:** Take exit 44 off Hwy 1 (the Trans-Canada), and travel east onto Hwy 7 (Lougheed). Riverview Hospital is located on the west side of Hwy 7, just NE of the Port Mann Bridge. See site directory at the entrance on Holly Dr, or the RHCS kiosk on Pine Terrace. | **Open:** Year-round; TreeFest, a special event to celebrate trees, is held here each September. | **Entry fee:** The grounds are open to the public; no fee for tree tours. | **Tours:** Third Sunday of the month, March-October, at 1 p.m. Call for weekday dates or private tours. | **Accessibility:** Wheelchair accessible in most areas, some difficult walking areas such as Finnie's Garden. | **Support organizations:** The Riverview Horticultural Centre Society; Friends of the Riverview Trees; B.C. Schizophrenia Society.

The Riverview Lands are located about 12 miles east of Vancouver and form a thin crescent of urban greenbelt (244 acres) on a hillside overlooking the Coquitlam River. Many rare and unique specimen trees (native and non-native) survive on this vital link in the chain of urban green spaces. The habitat the Lands support for songbirds, birds of prey, and other animals is important to the ecology of the area and to the historical value this place represents in the horticultural development of Vancouver. In 1911 Prof. John Davidson, as the first Provincial Botanist, was given the task of completing a survey of BC flora and establishing a botanical garden and herbarium of native plants. He was given 2 acres at Riverview Hospital (a mental health facility), where he created the first botanical garden in British Columbia. Within two years, the garden contained over 700 species of native plants, including 35 species of trees from throughout the temperate world. When the Pt. Grey Botanical Garden site (now University of British Columbia) was established in 1916, 25,000 plants were moved to the new site, leaving behind the original arboretum. Today there is a documented inventory of approximately 1,700 heritage trees (70 genera, 160 species).

STANLEY PARK

Contact: Vancouver Park Board, 2099 Beach Avenue, Vancouver, BC V6G 1Z4 Canada | **Phone:** (604) 257-8400 | **Web:** www.parks. vancouver.bc.ca | **Directions:** Located northwest of downtown Vancouver. From Granville St turn left (west) on Georgia St, which will take you directly to the Park. | **Accessibility:** Portions of this very large park, with its many facets, are wheelchair accessible. | **Support organization:** Vancouver Park Board.

This lush 1,000-acre park provides a peaceful oasis for Vancouverites and their visitors. It's sandwiched between the bustle of the city center and the Lion's Gate Bridge leading to North and West Vancouver, and is surrounded on three sides by water—a heavily wooded sanctuary that provides miles and miles of peaceful forested trails and a seawall promenade, the Lost Lagoon bird sanctuary, a bountiful rose garden, a zoo and an aquarium. Of special note is the Ted and Mary Grieg Rhododendron Collection. In 1966 their sizable collection of 7,000 plants and several thousand seedlings was purchased by the Park Board. While much of the collection is on display at Stanley Park with prime spring blooming, a small portion of this legacy has been replanted at VanDusen Gardens.

UNIVERSITY OF BRITISH COLUMBIA BOTANICAL GARDEN & CENTRE FOR HORTICULTURE

6804 SW Marine Drive, Vancouver, BC V6T 1Z4 Canada | **Contact:** General information, (604) 822-9666 | **Email:** botg@ interchange.ubc.ca | **Web:** www.ubcbotanicalgarden.org; Horticultural information, (604) 822-3928 or (604) 822-4208 (Botanical Garden Gatehouse) | **Directions:** From Oregon or Washington, take I-5 to the U.S.-Canada border. Continue north on Hwy 99 to Vancouver. Once over the Oak Street Bridge, take SW Marine Dr westbound directly to the garden. Alternatively, turning left onto 49th or 41st Ave from Oak or Granville Sts will also lead to SW Marine Dr. At the intersection of SW Marine and 41st or 49th, turn right and continue along SW Marine to reach the main entrance to the Botanical Garden. Parking is available on site and in nearby lots. | **Open:** Daily; mid-March-mid-Oct., 10 a.m.-6 p.m; mid-Oct.-mid-March, 10 a.m.-2:30 p.m. Note: Nitobe Memorial Garden is closed weekends during the winter months. | **Entry fee:** Admission charged mid-March-mid-October: $4.75 adult; $6 double entry ticket (Botanical/Nitobe Gardens); $2.50 senior citizens; $2 student (grades 1-7); $2.50 other students; free to UBC students (with card), children under 6 and handicapped guests with 1 accompanying adult. Season pass (to all gardens): $25 adult, $15 senior citizen/student, family $40. Admission to the gardens during winter months is by donation. | **Accessibility:** Largely wheelchair accessible. | **Tours:** tours are offered every Wednesday and Saturday at 1 p.m. with the price of admission; private tours (grades 4 and up) can be arranged by calling (604) 822-9666 (please leave a message). Two weeks notice required for booking or cancellation. | **Support organizations:** FOGS (Friends of the Garden Society). If you are interested in becoming involved as a volunteer, join! Also, UBC Garden Membership—The Davidson Club, was established in 1982. Varying levels of support from $20 to $10,000. Members of both groups enjoy a 10% discount at the Shop-in-the-Garden, located on the site; call (604) 822-4529.

This is the (almost) oldest botanical garden in Canada—a teaching and research site open for public edification and enjoyment. The UBC Botanical Garden started in 1916 with 900 species. By the late 1930s, the Botanical Garden included significant collections of BC natives, willows, alpines, aquatics, and medicinal plants, as well as native and exotic trees in the campus arboretum. Unfortunately, much of the old collections were lost or integrated with campus plantings. The only remnants visible today are some very fine trees in the original arboretum. Today the Botanical Garden collections include those of the Main Garden, the Botanical Garden Nursery, and Nitobe Memorial Garden. The substantive and diverse horticultural menu includes:

* **The E. H. Lohbrunner Alpine Garden.** The largest of its kind in North America, this 2.5-acre volcanic rock and limestone hillside is planted with over 12,000 alpines representing various continents.

* **The British Columbia Native Garden.** Includes 8 acres of native woodlands and meadows, peat bogs and ponds.

* **The Physick Garden.** Behind a trim yew hedge this formal garden typifies a 16th-century herb garden.

* **The Arbour and Food Garden.** Especially interesting for the comprehensive use of climbing vines and espaliered fruit trees, this garden demonstrates for urban gardeners the space-intensive concept of food production. If you have an interest in this area, you will glean tremendous inspiration here. Note the bountiful crops of cantaloupes, eggplants, and other exotica. The espaliered fruit trees are especially enchanting.

* **The David C. Lam Asian Garden.** A 30-acre woodland, the Asian Garden is noted for its unique collection of exotic magnolias, species rhododendrons, climbing roses, and vines, surrounded by drifts of blue Himalayan poppies and meandering plantings of primulas. In season, stop by to see the winter garden planted to demonstrate late fall and early spring potentials.

* **Nitobe Memorial Garden**

Part of the University of British Columbia Botanical Garden & Centre for Horticulture; 6804 SW Marine Drive, Vancouver, BC V6T 1Z4 Canada | **Contact:** (604) 822-6038; open same hours as the Botanical Garden, mid-March-mid-Oct; closed weekends during winter months. | **Directions:** From the main garden entrance, turn left onto SW Marine Dr and travel northwest (it will quickly become NW Marine Dr). Turn right onto West Mall from NW Marine Dr, then turn right onto Memorial Rd and the garden entrance is on the right. Located across NW Marine Dr from the Museum of Anthropology (enter at Gate 4, use Parkade parking spaces). | **Entry fee:** $2.75 adult; $6 double-entry ticket (with Botanical Garden); $1.75 senior citizens; $1.50 students (grades 1-7); $1.75 other students; free admission to UBC students (with card), children under 6, and handicapped. Admission charged mid-March to mid-October; winter admission is by donation. | **Accessibility:** Partially wheelchair accessible.

Created 30 years ago in memory of Japanese educator, scholar, publicist, and diplomat Dr. Inazo Nitobe, this 2.4-acre "island of serenity" provides you with insight into the symbolic nature of a classical Japanese garden. Native plants share the garden with those imported from Japan. As you can imagine, a visit in spring and fall provides an experience rewarding in vivid color and rich texture. Nitobe is an authentic Japanese tea and stroll garden, but also holds a documented collection of Japanese and BC native plants.

VANDUSEN BOTANICAL GARDEN

5251 Oak Street, Vancouver, BC V6M 4H1 Canada | **Phone:** (604) 878-9274 | **Web:** www.vandusengarden.org | **Directions:** Take Hwy 99 north into Vancouver, where it becomes Oak St, and continue to 37th Ave, then turn left. | **Open:** Year-round, from 10 a.m. Closing time varies by season. | **Entry fee:** Adults $6.50, seniors (65+) $4; youth (13-18 years) $5; children (6-12) $3.25. Group rate for adult groups of ten or more, $5.50. All of these entry fees are reduced to half price Oct. 1-March 31. | **Tours:** See below for guided tours for visitors with limited mobility. Note that there are many educational opportunities that take place in the "classroom" of the garden, which is the best kind of tour you can expect. | **Accessibility:** There is a wheelchair route as well as a motorized cart that offers free guided tours of the extensive grounds particularly for visitors for whom walking is difficult (available Easter to Thanksgiving). | **Support organizations:** Jointly operated by the Vancouver Park Board and the VanDusen Botanical Garden Association. VanDusen Botanical Garden Membership: Family $25.68, individual $16.05, youth and seniors $8.56. Benefits vary with level of support. Call (604) 257-8675.

Many programs of interest to serious gardeners happen here (including an informative quarterly newsletter). There are more than 150 events annually, with frequent lectures, seminars, classes and workshops, horticultural demonstrations and shows, and events on the garden grounds (such as the sophisticated VanDusen Flower and Garden Show, the annual Festival of Lights at Christmas, and the May British Field Meet of Classic Cars).

There is an extensive reference library, and a gift shop and restaurant overlook the gardens, which are planned for year round interest. At the front entry a demonstration stand highlights and identifies what is of special interest that day in the gardens.

VanDusen was developed from the Shaughnessy Golf Course beginning in 1971, opened to the public in 1975, and is now in the midst of the great city of Vancouver. Visitors find gently rolling grassy hills, stands of Douglas fir and western red cedar, stately specimen trees standing alone to command your full attention, a massive rock outcropping dissected by a gently falling stream, a large meandering lake fringed in Jurassic-like masses of *Gunnera manicata*, formal rose gardens edged in clipped boxwood, a sweeping laburnum walk dripping in golden chains of bloom in June, and voluptuous perennial borders 12 feet deep. You'll also want to tour the Rhododendron Walk, featuring more than 600 varieties, the largest holly collection in Canada, and an Elizabethan hedge maze (one of only three in North America). These and the many other plant collections, theme gardens, and natural features flow into and out of one another quite unselfconsciously to draw visitors through the 55-acre site on a quest of exploration. In every season there is something of horticultural interest in bloom, berry, or bark. Check the lovely website for further details.

VICTORIA BUTTERFLY GARDENS

West Saanich Road at Keating Cross Road (near the entrance to Butchart Gardens) | **Contact:** PO Box 190, 1461 Benvenuto Avenue, Brentwood Bay, BC V8M 1R3 Canada | **Phone:** (250) 652-3822 or (877) 722-0272 | **Email:** butterfly@victoriabc.com | **Web:** www.victoriabc.com/attract/butterfly.htm | **Directions:** Travel north from downtown Victoria on Hwy 17, following signs to

Keating Cross Rd, where you will turn left to the gardens. | **Open:** Daily, March 1 to mid-May, 9:30 a.m.-4:30 p.m; mid-May to Sept. 30, 9 a.m.-5 p.m; Oct., 9:30 a.m.-4:30 p.m. The garden is closed Nov.-Feb. | **Entry fee:** Adults $8, seniors (55+) and students $7, children 5-12 $4.50, children under 5 with parent free; 10 % discount for family admission. Prices exclude taxes. | **Accessibility:** Wheelchair accessible.

Stroll among hundreds of dazzling, free-flying butterflies in this enchanting indoor tropical garden where flowers always bloom and over 30 species of butterflies soar. The collection includes the brilliant Blue Morpho, the delicately patterned Giant Owl, and the huge Atlas Moth. There are ponds filled with goldfish and koi, and exotic birds fly overhead. Look for the displays that teach you the butterfly's life cycle, bring a camera, and shop a small selection of tropical plants for sale. There is a restaurant and gift shop on site.

chapter **14**

TRAVEL OPPORTUNITIES

Whether you're among those who lament the solitary nature of gardening or find solace in it, it's time for you to shake off that dirt, lay down that trowel, and experience the social side to your hobby. Start up a chat room online, or spend some time just mulling around your local nursery and meeting regulars. The most fulfilling thing we suggest, though, is . . . travel! What better way to socialize than when you are on an educational garden getaway or in a foreign country experiencing new botanical destinations for the first time with other garden enthusiasts. Imagine yourself walking through the islands and highlands of western Scotland, or experiencing the lushness of the south of France with ten of your closest friends. Closer to home, here are some opportunities to make a "getaway" in your own backyard through a range of activities from local garden workshops to gloves-on seminars. Many of the tours offered in this chapter come with their own expert guide. You could even wind up with a local gardening celebrity if you're lucky. Here is an opportunity to gain wisdom from people who have devoted their lives to horticulture. Learn new gardening techniques. Travel to ancient gardens. Share your love of gardening with a travel companion. Going on a tour brings so many benefits, not the least of which is being able to skip the fuss over planning the excursion's many necessary details. Many of the tours offered are prearranged and packed with interesting destination sites. A few tour gurus even tailor gardening trips to your desires. Stop dreaming about English gardens and go visit some!

—Elizabeth Shen

TRAVEL CLUBS

Travel Club operators and charter bus companies provide bus trips to public and private gardens throughout the Northwest as day and overnight excursions. Some of the popular British Columbia destinations include: The University of British Columbia Botanical Gardens, Dr. Sun Yat-Sen Chinese Garden, VanDusen Botanical Gardens, Fantasy Gardens, Butchart Gardens, and Minter Gardens. Oregon destinations include: the Berry Botanic Garden, the Leach Garden, the Jane Kerr Platt Garden, the Japanese Garden in Washington Park, the Bishop's Close, and the Cecil and Molly Smith Rhododendron Garden. In Washington, popular destinations are Lakewold Gardens, Bloedel Reserve, the Washington Park Arboretum, Ohme Gardens, Meerkerk Rhododendron Gardens, the Rhododendron Species Botanical Garden, the Pacific Rim Bonsai Collection, the Northwest Perennial Alliance border at the Bellevue Botanical Garden and the Northwest Flower and Garden Show. Call for information on membership requirements (many companies accept non-members at a slightly higher fee) and request the club's newsletter, which will give detailed descriptions of what's planned for the months ahead. These companies are happy to discuss chartering options on one or multiple day trips for organizations. Find them in the Yellow Pages under "Buses, Charter and Rental."

TOURS TO JOIN

If your ambitions run further afield, a number of magazines carry display advertising for organized garden tours worldwide. The ad will usually give you enough information to determine whether to send for a detailed brochure. Most of these tours are intimate and many feature celebrity escorts. Look especially in these gardening magazines: *American Gardener, Horticulture* (see "The Well-Traveled Gardener"), *Pacific Horticulture,* and such British publications available on our newsstands as *The Garden* (the official magazine of The Royal Horticultural Society), *Gardens Illustrated, Country Life,* and *Country Living.* Garden-related tours are also often advertised in *Bon Appetit, Gourmet, The New Yorker,* and *The New York Times.* There's truly an enormous selection of tours for gardening enthusiasts just now. You should have quite a number to choose from. Some offer terrific value for money on a carefully considered itinerary with a good deal of professional planning to boot. Others are purely opportunistic trips arranged by people who want to have their own way paid by putting together a designated number of paying travelers. Do your homework!

Here are a few tips to think about when making your choice:

*The Sponsor. Who exactly is offering the tour? (An organization you belong to? A publication you subscribe to? A botanical garden you are a member of?) Are they purely the sponsoring organization with no further involvement in your trip? Are they lending their name to the trip in order to raise funds? How did they settle on which tour company to handle "their" tour? (Experience? Price?)

*The Company. What experience does the tour company have in planning and leading a garden tour? Will your escort actually know anything about gardening or the specific gardens you'll visit? Do you care? A company that books and then leads its own tour is more likely to give you value for money as they are not paying out fees to middlemen all along the way (having brokers or local agents handle details is very common).

*The Director. Is this trip led by a celebrity? Are you choosing the trip partially, solely, or not at all because of this personality? If so, does this person have any real expertise that pertains to this trip? Have they ever made the trip before? Do you expect to have any personal interaction with them? Are they offering any special lectures or are they just along for the ride? How much extra are you paying for this association and is it worth it to you?

*Accommodations. Has the company offered this particular tour before? How will your accommodations be selected? Have the operators actually inspected or stayed in them? What do the classifications of accommodations ("deluxe," "first class," etc.) actually mean?

*The Group. How large will the group be? Where has the tour been marketed? How diverse a group is it likely to be? (Age, interests, and nationality are factors to consider depending on your proclivities.)

*The Schedule. Look over the proposed schedule. How much time is spent in transit and how much time actually visiting gardens? Are there too many gardens? (Only 90 minutes at Hidcote would be a travesty!) Will there be a knowledgeable guide or is this meant as a self-guided tour? Perhaps the price will reflect this.

*Advance Preparation. Does your tour director offer a suggested reading list to further prepare the literary among you? To us, this shows a deeper interest in the destination.

All that said, here is a representative array of the *wildly divergent* choices for you to ponder for the next tour season and beyond . . . travel planning for the future—or at the very least, for your dreaming. *Note:* Telephone numbers for British companies are given with the country code 44.

THE AMERICAN HORTICULTURAL SOCIETY

The Leonard Haertter Travel Company | 7922 Bonhomme Avenue, St. Louis, MO 63105 | **Phone:** (800) 942-6666 | **Fax:** (314) 721-8497 | **Email:** info@haerttertravel.com | **Web:** www.haerttertravel.com

This is the firm that annually handles the travel arrangements for the AHS. Tours occur about once or twice a month. Call for dates or check website for more details. On the home front, members of the AHS are sent a lovely state-by-state directory listing of Flower Shows and Public Gardens that offer free admission or entry discount to AHS members. Email for more information about tours.

BOXWOOD TOURS

Boxwood Tours, c/o RHIW | Llanbedr, Gwynedd LL45 2NT Wales, United Kingdom | **Phone:** 44 1341 241 717 | **Fax:** 01341 241 712 | **E-mail:** mail@boxwoodtours.co.uk | **Web:** www.boxwoodtours.co.uk

This is a small, specialist garden-tour company, run by gardeners, with a strong commitment to offering memorable holidays that are sound value for money. We have reviewed their literature and are impressed by the superb destinations, many offering private introductions by owners and gardeners, the time to enjoy a lunch or tea with a garden owner, and quality accommodations of character. Tour leaders are noted as trained professional horticulturists and enthusiastic plants(wo)men. They draw an international clientele, which could make for a lively group of travel companions who share your love of gardens. This company also puts together customized group travel if you are looking for a professional to make arrangements for such a holiday. Check out their website or email them for tour dates.

SUE BUCKLES GARDEN TOURS

10021 48th Avenue NE, Seattle, WA 98125 | **Phone:** (206) 525-6245

Sue, an active member of the Northwest Perennial Alliance, has been leading tours to visit public and private gardens in England and France for the past decade. Her trips are small and intimate (no more than 20 people), usually to Britain in spring and fall. There's clearly an emphasis on visiting traditional English mixed-border perennial gardens, destinations with which Sue is very familiar. Call to add your name to her mailing list for future dates.

CARNABY HALL TOURS

Gretchen Carnaby | **Phone:** (503) 588-2410 | **Email:** theholow@teleport.com

What we like about these visits to the "Highlands and Islands of Western Scotland" and "Northumberland and the Scottish Borders" is that you are settled into one place for a week or so while you are using that comfortable nest as a home base for days out. Hosts are Denis Carnaby (a native Northumbrian) and his wife Gretchen, a garden designer, and their groups are kept to a very cozy limit of ten. Tours include splendid gardens, history

and local culture, and, as you would expect traveling with a (former) "local," in-depth knowledge and special details of the place.

ECOTEACH

PO Box 737, Suquamish, WA 98392 | **Phone:** (800) 626-8992 | **Email:** info@ecoteach.com | **Web:** www.ecoteach.com

This U.S.-Costa Rica–based organization provides educational connections for gardening and environmental travelers. EcoTeach is committed to increased conservation and cultural awareness through study tours, projects, volunteer placements, and advocacy. Both Dan Hinkley (plant explorer extraordinaire, of Heronswood Nursery fame) and radio personality Ciscoe Morris partner with EcoTeach to lead cultural and ecological adventure tours in Costa Rica. *Northwest Garden News* has also joined forces to host a tour with EcoTeach. You can join one of these tours and see for yourself the incredible biodiversity Costa Rica has to offer and learn about the fragile ecosystems that continue to thrive there. Check the website for current details and to see future tour dates.

THE ENGLISH GARDENING SCHOOL

66 Royal Hospital Road, London SW3 4HS, United Kingdom | 44 20 7352 4347 | **Fax:** 44 20 7376 3936 | **Email:** info@English GardeningSchool.co.uk | **Web:** www.englishgardeningschool.com

Founded in 1983 by Rosemary Alexander and based at the Chelsea Physic Garden, the EGS occasionally sponsors one- to two-week tours led either by Rosemary herself or by Al Hort, the Principal of the English Gardening School. New tours are always being planned. Check out their website for dates or email them for more details.

EXPO GARDEN TOURS

33 Fox Crossing, Litchfield, CT 06759 | **Phone:** (800) 448-2685 or (860) 567-0322 | **Fax:** (860) 567-0381 | **Email:** info@ expogardentours.com | **Web:** www.expogardentours.com

Michael Italiaander hosts these garden tours to the United States (including the Pacific Northwest) and abroad. Expo arranges for a local horticultural expert (often the head gardener or garden owner) to accompany the group, offering their unique perspectives. Additionally, Expo includes an indigenous tour guide to provide insight into the local history and culture. For 2002, you'll find trips planned for South Africa, Japan, Holland, France, England, and the Pacific Northwest. Email them or check out their website for dates.

GARDEN GATE TOURS

c/o August Home Tours, LLC, 2200 Grand Avenue, Des Moines, IA 50312 | **Phone:** (800) 978-9631, ext. 7241 | **Email:** gardengate tours@augusthome.com | **Web:** www.gardengatetours.com

The publishers of the hands-on gardening monthly *Garden Gate* have added tours of favorite global garden destinations to their offerings. Tours set for 2002 include two packages to the famed Chelsea Flower Show (one that incorporates spring gardens in the south of England and another that includes Devon and Cornwall gardens), plus the once-in-a-decade Floriade World Horticultural Exhibition in The Netherlands. The parent company, August Homes, offers a wide variety of packages that may also interest garden tourists, including Historic Homes of England; Discovering Antiques and Flea Markets Across France; The Foods and Lifestyles of Provence, and Cooking in Tuscany.

GARDENING GETAWAYS

3626 41st Avenue W, Seattle, WA 98199 | **Phone:** (206) 285-1143 | **Fax:** (206) 282-0297 | **Web:** www.gardeninggetaways.com

These gardening experiences are the brilliant idea of Cindy Combs. You'll note the active nature of the company name, which is to say, you get away to a cozy and comfy inn or bed-and-breakfast. Your raison d'être, though, is to spend the two or three days away attending a gloves-on seminar, working alongside a professional installing a garden designed by author and expert Ann Lovejoy. Have you ever dreamed of having a real pro right there as you wonder if there is an easier way to lift sod? Fret over the proper mixing of soil and amendments when building a new bed? Puzzle about how much to "tease" roots on potted perennials? Cindy has put together the next best thing, with the added benefit of the camaraderie of your compatriots, a full-color garden plan, and a workbook that includes plant lists, diagrams, care instructions, and words of wisdom from Ann. With its personal, professional attention and upscale accommodations this getaway has it all. Getaways are scheduled four to six months in advance. Call for seminar information and reservations.

GARDEN TOURS OF SCOTLAND

26810 County Road 98, Davis, CA 95616 | **Phone:** (800) 757-0404 | **Email:** scotland@gardenvisions.com | **Web:** www.gardenvisions.com

Veteran garden tour director John Gray relies on his many botanical friends and acquaintances throughout Scotland, which introduces you to special private gardens all along the way. Gardens displaying a wide range of plants and planting styles are included, many with rare treasures and major collections. Past itineraries have included Scotland's many public and private gardens, as well as a tour that blends gardens with golf and antiques. In 2002, a tour is set to visit Scotland's west coast, including the Royal Botanic Garden in Edinburgh.

GENTLE JOURNEYS

PO Box 3854, Sherborne, Dorset DT9 3YB, United Kingdom | **Phone:** Toll-free from Canada/USA: 800/873-7145 | **Email:** tours@gentlejourneys.co.uk | **Web:** www.gentlejourneys.co.uk

This family-owned business, operating from Central London, offers a series of one-day and four-day tours. If you find yourself in London and longing for a visit to the countryside, find out about **day tours** to Sissinghurst, Castle Garden in Kent, and Hidcote Manor Garden in the Cotswolds; they also showcase National Garden Scheme Days, Royal Horticultural Society Days, and

Paris and Giverny Days in France. Their four-day tours to Yorkshire, the English Lakes, Wessex, and the Cotswolds offer more extensive gardening adventures. In addition, Gentle Journeys offers packages to the Chelsea and Hampton Court flower shows.

HARDY PLANT SOCIETY OF OREGON

1930 NW Lovejoy Street. Portland, OR 97209-1504 | **Phone:** (503) 224-5734 | **Fax:** (503) 224-5734 | **Email:** admin@hardy plantsociety.org | **Web:** www.hardyplantsociety.org | **Membership:** $25 new membership, $20 renewal first day of March

You may join the HPSO for many reasons, only one of which is their organized tours. Plans are in the works for touring the Secret Gardens of the Cotswolds, Wales, and Ireland in late May–early June 2002. In May 2003, the destination will be the south of France and the Côte d'Azur. Call or email for dates.

Horticulture MAGAZINE GARDEN PROGRAMS

98 N Washington Street, Boston, MA 02114-1913 | **Phone:** (800) 395-1901 or (617) 742-5600 | **Fax:** (617) 367-6364 | **Email:** horteditorial@primediasi.com | **Web:** www.hortmag.com

Horticulture magazine offers an extensive array of in-the-garden **seminars** and **tours** as well as daylong **symposiums** all over the US—including the Pacific Northwest. Tours for 2002 include "Hidden England-the Late Winter/Early Spring Garden" in February; "Spring in Southern Portugal and the Garden Island of Madeira" in March; "Gardens and Islands—Sardinia," "Ischia and the Amalfi Coast," and "Spring Gardens of the Delaware Valley" in April; "Normandy and Brittany" and "Landmark English Gardens and the Chelsea Flower Show" in May; "Private Gardens of Holland and Belgium" in July; and "Secret Gardens of Santa Fe" in August. Call or email for more information on tour dates.

LUCAS & RANDALL

225 30th Street, Suite 300, Sacramento, CA 95816 | **Phone:** (800) 505-2505 or (916) 414-4040 | **Fax:** (916) 414-4044 | **Web:** www.lucasandrandall.com

John Bradfield has operated these first-class, small-group tours to the gardens of Europe since the early 1990s. The tours occur from about April through July. Visits to gardens large and small, private and public, famous and unknown, form the basis of unique itineraries that balance garden visits with comprehensive sightseeing programs. Call for dates or check the website.

CISCOE MORRIS TOURS

Oh la la! Ciscoe Morris, Seattle's popular radio (KIRO-AM) and television (KING 5) horticultural whiz, leads frequent tours to his favorite spots around the globe. You can check his website for the latest details (and future trips he's planning) at www.ciscoe.com.

His June 2002 excursion to the gardens of Normandy and the Loire Valley included Vasterival, Les Bois de Moutiers, and Villandry, as well as the incredible garden exposition/festival in Chaumont. Other highlights: the historical D-Day beaches and, of course, constant sampling of the tasty food and wine that France has to offer. For information about this trip, contact Northwest Travel at (800) 456-6269 or email brad@nwtravel.com.

Ciscoe's March 2002 trip to Costa Rica was an educational adventure tour in which his companions experienced the incredible diversity of the region's flora and fauna. For details on this and future trips, contact Tom McQueen at EcoTeach, (206) 979-2434, or see www.eco teach.com.

SEATTLE CHINESE GARDEN SOCIETY

2040 Westlake Avenue N, Suite 306, Seattle, WA 98109 | **Phone:** (206) 282-8040 or (425) 483-3880 | **Fax:** (206) 282-8194 | **Email:** info@seattle-chinese-garden.org or scscachinatour@yahoo.com | **Web:** www.seattle-chinese-garden.org

Imagine spending springtime in China when the weather is lovely and gardens and rural landscapes are in full bloom. Sounds tempting? Join supporters and docents of the new Seattle Chinese Garden as they tour classical and botanical gardens and cultural treasures of Beijing, Suzhou, Shanghai, Kunming, and Sichuan. The "Gardens & Gorges" tour also visits the Buddhist stone sculptures at Dazu, Seattle's sister city of Chongqing, and concludes with a cruise through the spectacular Three Gorges of the Yangtze. Tour dates: March 30–April 21, 2002. Seattle Chinese Garden docents lead a new tour each year, so if you can't make this one, get your name on the mailing list for future excursions.

SUE MOSS TOURS

529 11th Avenue W, Kirkland, WA 98003 | **Phone:** (425) 828-3005

Sue is a popular Seattle landscape designer who will be a wonderful horticultural person with whom to tour European gardens. If you're interested in getting in on one of these highly personal tours, ask to be on her mailing list for future dates. Current plans are to take a group to Holland and France, visiting private and public gardens and a wonderful array of nurseries you'd never find on your own.

MYRNA DOWSETT, APLD

3045 SW 66th Court, Portland, OR 97225-3116 | **Phone:** (503) 292-2363

Does an intimate garden tour to England or southern France intrigue you? Group size is limited to ten people, Myrna, and a driver. Want to plan a trip with ten of your closest friends? Myrna also tailors tours to interested groups. Call for more details.

Northwest Garden News TOURS

PO Box 18313, Seattle, WA 98118 | **Phone:** (206) 725-2394 | **Fax:** (206) 721-5335 | **Email:** norwesgard@earthlink.net

Northwest Garden News Tours visit private and public gardens across western Washington in the spring and summer. A complete listing of tours and itineraries is published in the February issue of *NWGN*, which is distributed at nurseries, bookstores, and the Northwest Flower and Garden Show. To have tour information mailed direct, please send a stamped, self-addressed postcard with your name, address, and phone number on it.

Pacific Horticulture TOURS

Pacific Horticultural Foundation | **Mailing address:** PO Box 680, Berkeley, CA 94701 | **Phone:** (510) 849-1627 | **Fax:** (510) 883-1181 | **Web:** www.pacifichorticulture.org

Contact information for 2001-2003 tour programs includes: "Natural History of Southern Chile and Argentina," January 2002, led by Rudolf Thomann and Don Mahoney; contact Geostar Travel at (800) 624-6633. "Northern Spain: Gardens, Culture, and Cuisine," June 2002, led by Alvaro de la Rosa and Katherine Greenberg; contact Landmark Travel at (925) 253-2600. "Holland and the Floriade: A Canal Boat Tour," August 2002, led by Richard Turner; contact Landmark Travel at (925) 253-2600. "Wildflowers of Western Australia," September 2002, led by Rodger Elliot and Richard Turner; contact Geostar Travel at (800) 624-6633.

THE ROYAL OAK FOUNDATION

285 West Broadway, New York, NY 10013-2299 | **Phone:** (800) 913-6565 or (212) 966-6565 | **Email:** general@royal-oak.org | **Web:** www.royal-oak.org | **Membership:** $50/individual/one year, $75/family/one year, $750/lifetime membership.

If you are going to be traveling in England or are a dyed-in-the-wool Anglophile you probably belong to the Royal Oak Foundation (it's the American arm of the British National Trust). If you don't, consider a membership, because this worthy organization is responsible for preserving priceless and irreplaceable art, architecture, and gardens. Your membership fee provides entry to many places you no doubt will be visiting and paying a pretty hefty entrance fee for anyway. Another membership benefit is the opportunity to join tours organized by the Royal Oak Foundation. They offer special events, day tours, educational programs, and trip packages. See their website or email them for more information.

TUSCAN FARM GARDENS

24453 60th Avenue, Langley, BC, V2Z 2G5, Canada | **Phone:** (604) 530-1997 | **Fax:** (604) 532-0350 | **Email:** heather@tuscanfarm gardens.com | **Web:** www.tuscanfarmgardens.com

This is not a tour but a destination we really wanted to pass along to you. This bed-and-breakfast is also a commercial lavender farm where they also grow vast fields of echinacea and sunflowers. Can you imagine awakening to the sight of these fields in bloom on an early July morning? Heather and Arleigh Fair are your congenial hosts in their lovely traditional Tuscan retreat in the sylvan countryside of British Columbia, east of Vancouver. There are gardens to stroll through (Secret Garden, Herb Garden, Mediterranean, Moon Garden, Cutting Garden, and Potager) and many top-notch nurseries to explore nearby. Make a virtual visit on their website.

VANDUSEN BOTANICAL GARDEN

5251 Oak Street, Vancouver, BC, V6M 4H1, Canada | **Contact:** Joan Paterson: (604) 263-7378 | **Email:** donjoan@direct.ca | **Web:** www.vandusengarden.com

The destinations of international tours offered here change from year to year, as do the number of tours per year. Call VanDusen for more information on travel lectures and other tours, look in their newsletter (delivered with membership), or visit the website.

VICTORIAN GARDEN TOURS

145 Niagra Street, #2, Victoria, BC, V8V 1G1, Canada | **Phone:** (250) 380-2797 | **Fax:** (250) 383-2846 | **Email:** vicgt@islandnet.com | **Web:** www.victoriangardentours.com

What a welcome option for a botanical visit to Victoria! This company provides small groups with a guided, interpretive tour of many of Victoria's glorious private and public gardens. Private garden tours are led by the individual garden owner and require advance notice. Public gardens that can be toured include Hatley Park Garden, Saxe Point Park, Horticultural Centre of the Pacific (including the marvelous Doris Page Winter Garden), Ravenhill Herb Farm, Government House Gardens, and Point Ellice House. They provide your transportation in comfort from downtown Victoria, narration en route, and with advance notice they can arrange specialty group tours. Tours are available year-round on weekends with 48 hours' notice. During summer, tours run daily. Email them for more information or check out their website.

MARTY WINGATE TOURS

In May 2002, *Seattle Post-Intelligencer* garden columnist Marty Wingate led a tour of England's gardens, including some of Marty's favorite, such as Great Dixter, Wisley, and Hadpsen House, ending with the piece de resistance—the Chelsea Flower Show. If you missed out on this tour, contact the operator for future excursions hosted by this talented horticulturist. For details, contact Northwest Travel at (800) 456-6269 or email brad@nwtravel.com

Out-of-the-Ordinary Travel Alternatives

OREGON EXOTICS RARE FRUIT NURSERY

1065 Messenger Road, Grants Pass, OR 97527 | **Phone:** (541) 846-7578 | **Fax:** (541) 846-8488 | **Web:** www.exoticfruit.com

Travel on a botanical exploration trip with Jerry Black, founder of Oregon Exotics Rare Fruit Nursery. In the past, Jerry has led an "Ethnobotanical Adventure Collection Trip," as well as visits to China, Peru (the Andes), and Nepal (the Himalayas). There are usually places for eight companion travelers on each of his excursions, so call or check the website if this is something that interests you. You'll learn much more about Jerry's philosophy by ordering his nursery catalog (see Chapter 5, "Nurseries") and reading about the ethic connections and flavors these botanical explorations engender.

TRAVEL PLANNING RESOURCES

Travel research can be almost (well almost) as much fun as going. A top-notch resource is the Miller Horticultural Library, at the Center for Urban Horticulture, Seattle. The Miller Library has a large collection devoted solely to helping you plan your travels to gardens abroad. The library also appreciates receiving brochures and pamphlets from gardens you have visited to help others plan their trips. Many garden societies organize tours, and you can learn about them here.

Other sources for books and travel information:

❋ Flora and Fauna Books in Seattle and Powell's Books in Portland have many of the books described below, even the more obscure titles. Flora and Fauna is at 121 1st Avenue S, Seattle; phone: (206) 623-4727. Powell's Books for Cooks and Gardeners is at 3747 SE Hawthorne Blvd., Portland, 97214; phone: (800) 354-5957 or (503)235-3802; fax: (503) 230-7112. Powell's Travel Store is at 701 SW Sixth Avenue, Portland, 97204; phone: (800) 546-5025 or (503) 228-1108; fax: (503) 228-7062; web: www.powells.com.

❋ Wide World Books and Maps in Seattle has a knowledgeable staff and a wide choice of books, maps, and gear to help prepare the traveling gardener for travels abroad or across the country. They have a great website too. They are located at 4411A Wallingford Avenue N, Seattle 98103; phone: (206) 634-3453 or (888) 534-3453; email: travel@speakeasy.net; web: www.travel-booksandmaps.com.

❋ International Reply Coupons (IRC) can be purchased at your local post office.

❋ Visit Sally Williams on the Web (at GardenNet.com/ GardenLiterature/ausbnbs.htm) for her articles on Australian, British, and U.S. bed-and-breakfasts for garden enthusiasts.

❋ The World Wide Web is a wonderful source of garden touring information. Many botanical gardens worldwide are featured in pictures, collection details, opening times, fees, and more. For an interesting example, see www.gardens.com, a San Francisco website that is very similar to the *The Northwest Gardeners' Resource Directory*, but online. Find dates of upcoming gardening events, nursery info, classes, excellent articles—and lots more great stuff. Not traveling there soon? Make a virtual visit!

❋ Join overseas horticultural societies. A membership in the Hardy Plant Society of Great Britain brings with it the offering of a list of members offering bed-and-breakfast accommodations and a booklet of members' Open Garden Days. From the Royal Oak Foundation, you'll receive National Trust publications on B&B accommodations (one of which is on the grounds at Sissinghurst) with another on Gardens of the National

Trust. From the Alpine Garden Society, you'll receive a Gardens Open Directory.

❀ Bed and Breakfast for Garden Lovers: This brilliant idea is an organized group of B&B owners who love gardens, have them, and invite you into them. They have a delightful brochure with pen-and-ink sketches of the houses and enticing descriptions. Write for a brochure: send a self-addressed No. 10 envelope and four international reply coupons for each copy requested to BBLG/Net, Handywater Farm, Sibford Gower, Banbury OX15 5AE, UK. Web: www.bbgardenlovers.co.uk.

Books and Other Information Sources

THE GARDEN CONSERVANCY, *Open Days Directory*

PO Box 219, Cold Spring, NY 10516 | To order toll-free, call (888) 842-2442 or (845) 265-2029 | **Fax:** (845) 265-9620 | **Email:** info@gardenconservancy.org | **Web:** www.GardenConservancy.org | **Admission:** Admission to each garden is $5; the *Directory* is $15.95 plus shipping/handling, $10.95 for Conservancy members (credit card orders accepted).

The Garden Conservancy is known for its effort to raise funds to preserve fine American gardens for posterity. This is the seventh year they have published a directory of gardens open to the public (based on the model of the legendary Yellow Book in England), offering over 400 gardens in 24 states. The Directory provides entrée to "compact city gardens, sprawling country gardens, formal, informal, and everything in between . . . gardens." Look there for the "Shows and Events" chapter under "Garden Tours" for the date and details on the Seattle-area day of open gardens. Also, check out their website or email them for more information about other events and programs.

Garden Open Today AND THE *National Gardens Scheme "Yellow Book"*

Hatchlands Park, East Clandon, Guildford, Surrey GU4 7RT, United Kingdom | 44 1483 211535 | **Fax:** 44 1483 211537 | **Email:** info@ngs.org.uk | **Web:** www.ngs.org.uk | **Price:** About $7 US (plus shipping/handling)

This guide to British private gardens open to the public on specified days each year is a fundraising effort called The National Gardens Scheme (since 1927). This book is a serious garden tourist's dream come true. Detailed maps and garden descriptions will provide the information around which you will form your next trip to the UK. Covering large estates to cottage gardens (over 3,400 of them across England and Wales), this is a prime example of the generosity of true gardeners. Order the "Yellow Book" (updated annually) through your local bookseller, or order online directly from the NGS site and even Amazon.com.

Gardens Illustrated

This smashing British magazine (see Chapter 10, "Literature & Periodicals") has a very nice feature in each issue, entitled "On Tour." Here's where they write up the most tempting trips and tours for garden enthusiasts, describing sites that run the gamut from an ambitious trek to South Africa to a few days off in the English countryside. An appealing column called "Courses Offered" could add a new dimension to a holiday planned in Great Britain, and in "Timely Visits" the well-traveled Patrick Taylor suggests some of the country's best parks, gardens, and nurseries to visit. The often in-depth articles (with beautiful photographs) feature gardens, nurseries, craftsmen, and garden shops you can visit, and details on opening times and location are provided. Watch also for advertisers offering botanically related tours. If you're planning (or dreaming about) a trip to Britain, pick up a copy at better newsstands and ferret out something really special.

Garden Touring in the Pacific Northwest

Jan Kowalczewski Whitner | Alaska Northwest Books, 1993

This erudite guide to 91 public gardens and 56 specialty nurseries in Oregon, Washington, and British Columbia is an essential companion for anyone who savors not only the pleasure of visiting these Northwest treasures, but the added insights of a thoughtful writer as tour guide. Mechanically, the book has merit: good maps, thoughtful traveling directions, and "best viewing times" tips, attractive illustrations, and such, but what really draws us to this book is the author's ability to capture the heart of a garden. What a perfect gift for a newcomer or for a garden lover planning a trip here!

The Garden Tourist

372 Hopper Avenue, Ridgewood, NJ 07450 | **Phone:** (212) 874-6211 | **Email:** mksols@idt.net | **Web:** www.gardentourist.com | **Price:** $12.95 each per regional book; the website is where you will find updates to your print version of the book!

Recently split into five regional editions, this book provides detailed coverage of more than 200 of the region's best events and dozens of great gardens. Lois Rosenfeld logs in details about Gardens Open to the public in every state; Garden Tours (local, national, and international) Garden Days and Weeks (including the opening of private gardens to the public); dates for Flower Shows, Festivals, and Special Events, Plant Sales and Plant Society Exhibits and a listing of Garden Touring Guides. If you have an entry for her Calendar, send it by September for events in the following year.

The Good Gardens Guide

Peter King | Bloomsbury Publishing Ltd, updated annually

Following the setup of its companion *The Good Food Guide*, this hefty tome covers the subject of gardens to visit throughout the British Isles. There's lots of detailed information (covering over 1,000 gardens open to the public) for those planning trips that include stops of a horticultural nature.

Guide to British Gardens

625 N Michigan Avenue, Suite 1001, Chicago IL 60611 or British Tourist Authority, 7th floor, 551 Fifth Avenue, New York, NY 10176-0799 | **Phone:** (212) 986-2266 or (800) GO-2-BRITAIN | **Email:** travelinfo@bta.org.uk | **Web:** www.visitbritain.com | **Open:** BTA offices open weekdays 9 a.m.-6 p.m.

Free *Guide to British Gardens* map folder lists 90 gardens open to the public in England, Scotland, and Wales. This guide gives their opening and closing times and pinpoints their location.

NURSERY SPECIALTIES

ALPINE / ROCK GARDEN PLANTS

Bassetti's Crooked Arbor, Woodinville, WA
Bear Creek Nursery, Bellingham, WA
The Gardeners, Bainbridge Is., WA
The Greenhouse Nursery, Port Angeles, WA
Joy Creek Nursery, Scappoose, OR
Lazy-S-Nursery, Federal Way, WA
MsK Rare Plant Nursery, Shoreline, WA
Mt. Tahoma Nursery, Graham, WA
North American Rock Garden Society Seed Exchange
   (to members only)
Northwest Garden Nursery, Eugene, OR
Nothing But NW Natives, Battle Ground, WA
Plantasia Specialty Nursery, Olympia, WA
Porterhowse Farms, Sandy, OR
Reflective Nursery, Poulsbo, WA
Rhododendron Species Botanical Garden, Federal
   Way, WA
Robyn's Nest Nursery, Vancouver, WA
Siskiyou Rare Plant Nursery, Medford, OR
Skagit Rose Farm, Mt. Vernon, WA
Squaw Mt. Gardens, Estacada, OR
Thorsett Landscape Nursery, Kent, WA
Tower Perennial Gardens, Spokane, WA
Trans-Pacific Nursery, McMinnville, OR
Valley Nursery, Poulsbo, WA
We-Du Nurseries, Marion, N.C.

ANNUALS

A Lot of Flowers, Bellingham, WA
Al's Garden Center and Greenhouses, Woodburn, OR
Avalon Nursery, Snohomish, WA
Bainbridge Gardens, Bainbridge Is., WA
Bakerview Nursery, Bellingham, WA
Bay Hay and Feed, Bainbridge Is., WA
Bayview Farm and garden, Langley, WA
Bloomer's, Eugene, OR
Bonnie's Greenhouse, Sedro-Woolley, WA
Bonsai Northwest, Seattle, WA
Bush's, Arlington, WA
The Book Mine, Cottage Grove, OR
Brown's Rose Lodge Nursery, Otis, OR
Christianson's Nurs., Mt. Vernon, Stanwood, WA
The Country Store and Gardens, Vashon Island
Cornell Farm, Portland, OR
DeLanceys' Garden Center, Ferndale, WA
DIG Floral and Garden, Vashon Island, WA
Edgewood Flower Farm, Edgewood, WA
Emery's Garden, Lynwood, WA
The Flower Lady, Arlington, WA
Flower World, Snohomish (Maltby), WA
Foxglove Farm, Anacortes, WA
Fragrant Garden Nursery, Canby, OR
Fremont Gardens Seattle, WA
The Gardens at Padden Creek Bellingham, WA
Garden Spot, Bellingham, WA
Garden Spot, Seattle, WA
Gray Barn Garden Center, Redmond, WA

The Greenhouse Nursery, Port Angeles, WA
Hart's Nursery, Jefferson, OR
Hayes Nursery, Issaquah, WA
Interstate Garden Center, Vancouver, WA
Johnson Brothers Greenhouses, Eugene, OR
Julius Rosso Nursery, Seattle, WA
Kildeer Farms, Ridgefield, WA
Little Red Farm Nursery, Springfield, OR
Magnolia Garden Center, Seattle, WA
Minter's Earlington Greenhouses, Seattle, WA
Molbak's, Woodinville, Seattle, WA
Moon Rose Perennials, Mt. Vernon, WA
Olympic Coast Garden, Sequim, WA
Pepper's Greenhouse & Nursery, Anacortes, WA
Portland Nursery, Portland, OR
Rainshadow Greenhouse, Sequim, WA
Raintree Garden and Gift Center, Seaside, OR
Saxe Floral & Greenhouse, Seattle, WA
Seattle Garden Center, Seattle, WA
Skagit Valley Gardens, Mt. Vernon, WA
Sky Nursery, Seattle, WA
Smith Creek Nursery, Snohomish, WA
Smokey Pt. Plant Farm, Arlington, WA
So. Seattle CC Garden Center, Seattle, WA
Squak Mountain Greenhouses, Issaquah, WA
Steamboat Island Nursery, Olympia, WA
Sunnyside Nursery, Marysville, WA
Swans Trail Gardens, Snohomish, WA
Swanson's, Seattle, WA
Territorial Seed Company, Cottage Grove, OR
Thompson's Greenhouse, Sedro-Woolley, WA
Thornton Creek Nursery, Seattle, WA
Tillinghast Seed Co., La Conner, WA
Valley Nursery, Poulsbo, WA
Valley View Nursery, Ashland, OR
Wells Medina Nursery, Medina, WA
Willamette Falls Nursery, West Linn, OR
Windy Meadow Nursery, Ferndale, WA
Wintergreen Tree Farm & Garden Shop,
   Snohomish, WA

AQUATIC PLANTS

Avalon Nursery, Snohomish, WA
Bakerview Nursery, Bellingham, WA
Bainbridge Gardens, Bainbridge Island, WA
Bamboo Gardens of WA, Redmond, WA
Christianson's Nursery, Mt. Vernon, WA
Cricklewood, Snohomish, WA
Crystal Palace Perennials, St. John, IN
The Flower Lady, Arlington, WA
Garland Nursery, Corvallis, OR
Gray's Garden Center's, Inc., Eugene, OR
Green Acres Gardens & Ponds, Yelm, WA
Hayes Nursery, Issaquah, WA
Hilliar Water Gardens, Qualicum, B.C.
Hughes Water Gardens, Tualatin, OR
Interstate Garden Center, Vancouver, WA
Johnson's Brothers Greenhouses, Eugene, OR
Jungle Fever Exotics, Tacoma, WA
Lilypons Water Gardens, Buckeystown, MD
Max and Hildy's Garden Store, Hillsboro, OR
Maxwelton Valley Gardens, Clinton, WA
McComb Road Nursery, Sequim, WA
Molbak's, Woodinville, WA
Moorhaven Water Gardens, Everett, WA
Oasis Water Gardens, Seattle, WA
Oudean's Willow Creek Farm, Snohomish, WA
Plantasia Specialty Nursery, Olympia, WA

Ponderings Plus, Medford, OR
Ponds Ôn' Stuff, Victoria, B.C.
Roadhouse Nursery, Poulsbo, WA
The Rhody Ranch Nursery, Port Angeles, WA
Russell Watergardens, Redmond, WA
Soos Creek Gardens, Renton, WA
Skagit Valley Gardens, Mt. Vernon, WA
Sky Nursery, Seattle, WA
Smokey Point Plant Farm, Marysville, WA
Territorial Seed Company, Cottage Grove, OR
Trans-Pacific Nursery, McMinnville, OR
Trillium Gardens, Pleasant Hill, OR
Tsugawa Nursery, Woodland, WA
Tualatin River Nursery, West Linn, OR
Watershed Garden Works, Longview, WA
Willamette Falls Nursery, West Linn, OR
Wisteria, Herbs and Flowers, South Beach, OR

AROIDS (Arisaema, Amorphophallas)

Collector's Nursery, Battle Ground, WA
Enchanted Garden, Seattle, WA
Heronswood Nursery, Kingston, WA
Meadowsweet Nursery, So. Langley, B.C.
Red's Rhodies, Sherwood, OR
Reflective Gardens, Poulsbo, WA
Siskiyou Rare Plants Nursery, Medford, OR
Sky Nursery, Seattle, WA
Tower Perennials, Spokane, WA
Valley Nursery, Poulsbo, WA
Walker Mt. Meadows, Quilcene, WA

AZALEAS / RHODODENDRONS

B & J Nursery, Maple Valley, WA
Bloomer's, Eugene, OR
The Bovees Nursery, Portland, OR
Brim's Farm and Garden, Astoria, OR
Emery's Garden, Lynwood, WA
Fragrant Garden Nursery, Canby, OR
Furney's Nursery, Des Moines, WA
The Greenery, Bellevue, WA
Greer Gardens, Eugene, OR
Hazelwood Gardens, Newcastle, WA
Heronswood Nursery, Kingston, WA
Julius Rosso Nursery, Seattle, WA
Maxwelton Valley Gardens, Clinton, WA
Molbak's, Woodinville, WA
Nelson Rhododendrons & Azaleas, Sedro-
   Woolley, WA
Olympic Coast Garden, Sequim, WA
Pat Calvert Greenhouse, Seattle, WA
Rhododendron Species Botanical Garden, Federal
   Way, WA
The Rhody Ranch Nursery, Port Angeles, WA
Red's Rhodies, Sherwood, OR
Rockyridge Nursery, Olympia, WA
Smokey Pt. Plant Farm, Arlington, WA
Spooner Creek Nursery, Blaine, WA
Star Nursery & Landscaping, Seattle, WA
Swanson's Nursery, Seattle, WA
Sundquist Nursery, Poulsbo, WA
Valley Nursery, Poulsbo, WA
Wells Medina Nursery, Medina, WA
Whitney Gardens & Nursery, Brinnon, WA
Wileywood Nursery, Mill Creek, WA

BAMBOO

Bamboo Gardens of Wash., Redmond, WA
Beauty and the Bamboo, Seattle, WA

Blue Heron Farm, Rockport, WA
Boxhill Farm, Duvall, WA
Clinton, Inc., Seattle, WA
Cloud Mt. Farm, Everson, WA
Colvos Creek Farm, Vashon Island, WA
Dave's Taste of The Tropics, Shoreline, WA
Fairlight Gardens, Auburn, WA
ForestFarm, Williams, WA
Green Acres Gardens & Ponds, Yelm, WA
Jade Mt. Bamboo, Tacoma, WA
Jungle Fever Exotics, Tacoma, WA
Northern Groves, Philomath, OR
Raintree Nursery, Morton, WA
Rhododendron Species Garden, Federal Way, WA
Seattle Garden Center, Seattle, WA
Soos Creek Gardens, Renton, WA
Tradewinds Bamboo Nursery, Gold Beach, OR
Trans-Pacific Nursery, McMinnville, OR
Tsugawa Nursery, Woodland, WA
Tualatin River Nursery and Café, West Linn, OR

BONSAI / PRE-BONSAI

Baltzer's Specialized Nursery, Pleasant Hill, OR
Bonsai Northwest, Seattle, WA
Daybreak Gardens, Battle Ground, WA
Daryll's Nursery, Dallas, OR
Emery's Garden, Lynwood, WA
Garland Nursery, Corvallis, OR
Greer Gardens, Eugene, OR
Hayes Nursery, Issaquah, WA
Lazy-S-Nursery, Federal Way, WA
Max and Hildy's Garden Store, Hillsboro, OR
Mt. Si Bonsai, North Bend, WA
Powerhowse Farms, Sandy, OR
RainShadow Gardens, Freeland, WA
Rhododendron Species Garden, Federal Way, WA
Seattle Garden Center, Seattle, WA
Sky Nursery, Seattle, WA
Tsugawa Nursery, Woodland, WA

BONSAI / WATER

Walker Mt. Meadows, Quilcene, WA

BOXWOOD

Boxhill Farm, Duval, WA

BULBS / Daffodils, Tulips, etc.

Bonnie Brae Gardens, Corbett, OR
Cascade Seed and Bulb, Scotts Mills, OR
The Daffodil Mart (Mail Order)
Grant Mitsch Novelty Daffodils (Mail Order)
McClure and Zimmerman (Mail Order)
Molbak's, Woodinville, Seattle, WA
Old House Gdns., Ann Arbor, MI (Mail Order)
Oregon Trails Daffodils, Corbett, OR
Seattle Garden Center, Seattle, WA
Skagit Valley Gardens, Mt. Vernon, WA
Roozengaarde, Mt. Vernon, WA
Tillinghast Seed Co., La Conner, WA
VanLierop Bulb Farm, Inc., Puyallup, WA
Wooden Shoe Bulb Co., Woodburn, OR

BULBS / Rare, Unusual and Native

Arboretum Foundation Bulb Sale, Seattle, WA
Bear Creek Nursery, Bellingham, WA
Boskey Dell Natives, West Linn, OR
Cascade Bulb & Seed, Scotts Mills, OR
Daffodil Mart, Gloucester, VA
Dancing Oaks Nursery, Monmouth, OR
Magnolia Garden Center, Seattle, WA
McClure & Zimmerman, Friesland, WI
Mitsch Novelty Daffodils, Hubbard, OR
Molbak's, Woodinville, Seattle, WA
Nichols Garden Nursery, Albany, OR

Ravenna Gardens, Seattle
Red's Rhodies, Sherwood, OR
Reflective Gardens, Poulsbo, WA
Rocky Top Gardens, Olga, WA
Russell Graham, Salem, OR
Seattle Garden Center, Seattle, WA
Siskiyou Rare Plant Nursery, Medford, OR
Skagit Rose Farm, Mt. Vernon, WA
Territorial Seed Co., Cottage Grove, OR
Trans-Pacific Nursery, McMinnville, OR
Trillium Gardens, Eugene, OR
We-Du Nurseries, Marion, NC
Windy Meadow Nursery, Ferndale, WA
Van Lierop Bulb Farm, Puyallup, WA

CACTUS

Brown's Rose Lodge Nursery, Otis, OR
Dave's Taste of the Tropics, Shoreline, WA
Enchanted Garden, Seattle, WA
Indoor Sun Shoppe, Seattle, WA
Molbak's, Woodinville, Seattle, WA
Swanson's Nursery, Seattle, WA

CARNIVOROUS PLANTS

Enchanted Garden, Seattle, WA
Indoor Sun Shoppe, Seattle, WA
Molbak's, Woodinville, Seattle, WA
Oudean's Willow Creek Nursery, Snohomish, WA
Red's Rhodies, Sherwood, OR
Rhododendron Species Botanical Garden, Federal
   Way, WA

CONIFERS (also see NATIVE PLANTS)

Alpine Nursery, Renton, WA
Amber Hill Nursery, Oregon City, OR
Arbutus Garden Arts, Carlton, OR
Baltzer's Specialized Nursery, Pleasant Hill, OR
Basetti's Crooked Arbor, Woodinville, WA
Bloomer's, Eugene, OR
Burlingame Gardens, Hoquiam, WA
Cloud Mountain Farm & Nursery, Everson, WA
Coenosium, Eatonville, WA
Collector's Nursery, Battle Ground, WA
Colvos Creek Farm, Vashon Island, WA
DeWilde's Nursery, Bellingham, WA
Duckworth's Nursery, Eugene, OR
Emery's Garden, Lynwood, WA
Evans Farm Nursery, Oregon City, OR
Furney's, Des Moines, WA
Greer Gardens, Eugene, OR
Heronswood Nursery, Kingston, WA
Kent's Garden & Nursery, Bellingham, WA
Kinder Gardens Nursery and Landscaping,
   Othello, WA
Lazy-S-Nursery, Federal Way, WA
Molbak's, Woodinville, WA
MsK Rare Plant Nursery, Shoreline, WA
Mt. Tahoma Nursery, Graham, WA
Olympic Nursery, Woodinville, WA
Plants of the Wild, Tekoa, WA
Pollock and Son's, Battle Ground, WA
Porterhowse Farms, Sandy, OR
Portland Avenue Nursery, Tacoma, WA
Portland Nursery, Portland, OR
Siskiyou Rare Plant Nursery, Medford, OR
Skagit Valley Gardens, Mt. Vernon, WA
Smokey Pt. Plant Farm, Arlington, WA
Stanley and Sons Nursery, Boring, OR
Star Nursery, Seattle, WA
Swanson's Nursery, Seattle, WA
Tower Perennials, Spokane, WA
Tualatin River Nursery, West Linn, OR
Valley Nursery, Poulsbo, WA

Valley View Nursery, Ashland, OR
Walker Mt. Meadows, Quilcene, WA
Wells Medina Nursery, Medina, WA
Wells Nursery, Mt. Vernon, WA

DAHLIAS

Cindy's Plant Stand, Elma, WA
Connell's Dahlias, Tacoma, WA
Dan's Dahlias, Oakville, WA
Sea-Tac Dahlia Gardens, Seattle, WA
Skagit Heights Dahlia Farm, Bow, WA
Swan Island Dahlias, Canby, OR

DAYLILIES

A & D Nursery, Snohomish, WA
Avalon Nursery, Snohomish, WA
B &D Lilies, Port Townsend, WA
Boxhill Farm, Duvall, WA
Caprice Farm Nursery, Aumsville, OR
Cascade Bulb & Seed, Scotts Mills, OR
Cottage Creek Nursery, Woodinville, WA
Enchanted Lily Garden, Redmond, WA
Rosebriar Gardens & Design, Seattle, WA
Wildwood Gardens, Molalla, OR

DROUGHT TOLERANT PLANTS
   (also see NATIVE PLANTS)

Bear Creek Nursery, Northport, WA
Bellweather Perennials, Lopez Is., WA
Colvos Creek Nursery, Vashon Island, WA
Down to Earth, Eugene, OR
Emery's Garden, Lynwood, WA
Forest Floor Recovery Nursery, Lummi Island, WA
Joy Creek Nursery, Scappoose, OR
Maxwelton Valley Gardens, Clinton, WA
Minter's Earlington Greenhouses, Seattle, WA
Northwest Garden Nursery, Eugene, OR
Oakhill Farms Natives, Roseburg, OR
Perennial Gardens, Everson, WA
Piriformis, Seattle, WA
Porterhowse Farms, Sandy, OR
RoseHip Farm & Garden, Coupeville, WA
Siskiyou Rare Plant Nursery, Medford, OR
Skagit Rose Farm, Mt. Vernon, WA
Squaw Mt. Gardens, Estacada, OR
Stone Hollow Farm, Sammamish, WA
Sunnyside Nursery, Marysville, WA
Trillium Gardens, Eugene, OR
Whispering Springs Nursery, Hillsboro, OR

ERICAS

Burlingame Gardens, Hoquiam, WA
Heaths and Heathers, Shelton, WA
Rhododendron Species Botanical Garden, Federal
   Way, WA
The Rhody Ranch Nursery, Port Angeles, WA
Siskiyou Rare Plant Nursery, Medford, OR
Stanley and Sons Nursery, Boring, OR

EVERLASTINGS

Bonnie's Greenhouse, Sedro-Woolley, WA
Cedarbrook Herb Farm, Sequim, WA
The Flower Lady, Arlington, WA
Foxglove Farm Everlastings, Langley, B.C.
Goodwin Creek Gardens, Williams, OR
House of Whispering Firs, Newberg, OR
Hummingbird Farm, Oak Harbor, WA
Smith Creek Nursery, Snohomish, WA

EXOTICS (HARDY) / Temperennials

Dancing Oaks Nursery, Monmouth, OR
Dave's Taste of the Tropics, Shoreline, WA
Down to Earth, Eugene, OR
Heronswood Nursery, Kingston, WA

Jungle Fever Exotics, Tacoma, WA
Raintree Nursery, Morton, WA
Southlands Nursery, Vancouver, B.C.
Sunnyside Nursery, Marysville, WA
Trans-Pacific Nursery, McMinnville, OR
Walker Mt. Meadows, Quilcene, WA
Willamette Falls Nursery, West Linn, OR

FERNS

Barfod's Hardy Ferns, Arlington, WA
Bear Creek Nursery, Bellingham, WA
Bloomer's, Eugene, OR
Boskey Dell Natives, West Linn, WA
Collector's Nursery, Battle Ground, WA
Dave's Taste of the Tropics, Shoreline, WA
Foliage Gardens, Bellevue, WA
Fancy Fronds, Gold Bar, WA
Foliage Gardens, Bellevue, WA
Forest Flor Recovery Nursery, Lummi Is., WA
The Gardens at Padden Creek, Bellingham, WA
Green Acres Gardens & Ponds, Yelm, WA
Greer Gardens, Eugene, OR
Wallace Hanson Native Plants, Salem, OR
Kildeer Farms, Ridgefield, WA
Mountain Meadow Nursery, Kirkland, WA
MsK Rare Plant Nursery, Shoreline, WA
Pepper's Nursery, Anacortes, WA
Plantasia Specialty Nursery, Olympia, WA
Rainforest Gardens, Maple Ridge, B.C.
Reflective Gardens, Poulsbo, WA
Rhododendron Species Garden, Fed. Way, WA
Robyn's Nest Nursery, Vancouver, WA
Russell Graham, Salem, OR
Siskiyou Rare Plant Nursery, Medford, OR
Squaw Mt. Gardens, Estacada, OR
Sundquist Nursery, Poulsbo, WA
Trillium Gardens, Pleasant Hill, OR

FRUIT TREES/VINES/CANES

Al's Garden Center and Greenhouses, Woodburn, OR
Bayview Farm and garden, Langley, WA
Bear Creek Nursery, Northport, WA
Black Lake Organic Nursery, Olympia, WA
Boxhill Farm, Duvall, WA
Burnt Ridge Nursery & Orchards, Onalaska, WA
Cedar Valley Nursery, Centralia, WA
Cindy's Plant Stand, Elma, WA
Cloud Mountain Farm & Nursery, Everson, WA
Earth's Rising Trees, Monroe, OR
Furney's Nurseries, Bellevue, Seattle, WA
Hayes Nursery, Issaquah, WA
Lazy-S-Nursery, Federal Way, WA
Lon Rombough, Aurora, OR
Molbak's, Woodinville, WA
One Green World, Molalla, OR
Raintree Nursery, Morton, WA
Lon Rombough, Aurora, OR
Rosebriar Gardens & Design, Seattle, WA
Sakuma Brothers Farms, Burlington, WA
Smokey Pt. Plant Farm, Arlington, WA
Territorial Seed Co., Cottage Grove, OR
Thorsett Landscape Nursery, Kent, WA
Tillinghast Seed Co., La Conner, WA
Valley Nursery, Poulsbo, WA
Whitman Farms, Salem, OR
Windy Meadow Nursery, Ferndale, WA

FUCHSIAS / HARDY FUCHSIAS

Bloomer's, Eugene, OR
Brown's Rose Lodge Nursery, Otis, WA
Bush's, Arlington, WA
Delancy's Garden Center, Ferndale, WA
Delta Farm and Nursery, Eugene, OR

Edgewood Flower Farm, Edgewood, WA
Flower World, Snohomish (Maltby), WA
Fuchsia Club Plant Sales
Johnson Brothers Greenhouses, Eugene, OR
Kildeer Farms, Ridgefield, WA
Mary's Country Garden, Kent, WA
Minter's Earlington Greenhouses, Seattle, WA
Molbak's, Woodinville, WA
Olympic Coast Garden, Sequim, WA
Squak Mountain Greenhouses, Issaquah, WA
Sundquist Nursery, Poulsbo, WA
Wildwood Nursery, Winston, OR
Windmill Gardens, Sumner, WA
Wileywood Nursery, Mill Creek, WA

GENERAL NURSERY STOCK

All Season Nursery, Kelso, WA
Alpine Nursery, Inc., Renton, WA
Al's Garden Center and Greenhouses, Woodburn, OR
Bainbridge Gardens, Bainbridge Is., WA
Bakerview Nursery, Bellingham, WA
Bay Hay and Feed, Bainbridge Is., WA
Bayview Farm & Garden, Langley, WA
Black Lake Organic Nursery, Olympia, WA
Boxhill Farm, Duvall, WA
Brim's Farm and Garden, Astoria, OR
Brown's Rose Lodge Nursery, Otis, OR
Cascade Nursery, Marysville, WA
Christianson's Stanwood Nursery, Stanwood, WA
City People's Garden Store, Seattle, WA
City People's Mercantiles, Seattle, WA
Cloud Mountain Farm, Everson, WA
Cornell Farm, Portland, OR
The Country Store & Gardens, Vashon Is., WA
DeLanceys' Garden Center, Ferndale, WA
DIG Floral and Garden, Vashon Is., WA
Edgewood Flower Farm, Edgewood, WA
Emery's Garden, Lynwood, WA
Flower World, Snohomish (Maltby), WA
Fremont Gardens Seattle, WA
Furney's Nursery, Des Moines, WA
Garden Spot, Bellingham, WA
Garden Spot, Seattle, WA
Garland Nursery, Corvallis, OR
Hayes Nursery, Issaquah, WA
Gray Barn Garden Center, Redmond, WA
Johnson Brothers Greenhouses, Eugene, OR
Julius Rosso Nursery, Seattle, WA
Kildeer Farms, Ridgefield, WA
Lazy-S-Nursery, Federal Way, WA
Magnolia Garden Center, Seattle, WA
Max and Hildy's Garden Store, Hillsboro, OR
Minter's Earlington Greenhouses, Seattle, WA
Molbak's Greenhouse and Nursery, Woodinville, WA
Olympic Coast Garden, Sequim, WA
Peninsula Gardens, Gig Harbor, WA
Portland Nursery, Portland, OR
Ravenna Gardens, Seattle, WA
Roadhouse Nursery, Poulsbo, WA
Savage Plants & Landscape, Kingston, WA
Saxe Floral & Greenhouse, Seattle, WA
(Molbak's) Seattle Garden Center, Seattle, WA
Skagit Valley Gardens, Mt. Vernon, WA
Sky Nursery, Shoreline, WA
Smokey Point Plant Farm, Arlington, WA
Southlands Nursery, Vancouver, B.C.
Spooner Creek Nursery, Birch Bay, WA
Squak Mountain Greenhouses, Issaquah, WA
Summersun Greenhouse Co., Mt. Vernon, WA
Sunnyside Nursery, Marysville, WA
Swanson's Nursery, Seattle, WA
Territorial Seed Company, Cottage Grove, OR
Thompson's Greenhouse, Sedro Wooley, WA

Thorsett Landscape Nursery, Kent, WA
Tillinghast Seed Co., La Conner, WA
Tsugawa Nursery, Woodland, WA
Tualatin River Nursery, West Linn, OR
Valley Nursery, Poulsbo, WA
West Seattle Nursery, Seattle, WA
Wight's Home and Garden, Seattle, WA
Wildwood Nursery, Winston, OR
Wileywood Nursery, Mill Creek, WA
Windmill Gardens, Sumner, WA

GRASSES — ORNAMENTAL

Amber Hill Nursery, Oregon City, OR
Bainbridge Gardens, Bainbridge Island, WA
Bayview Farm & Garden, Langley, WA
Bear Creek Nursery, Bellingham, WA
Bellweather Perennials, Lopez Is., WA
Boskey Dell Natives, West Linn, OR
Boxhill Farm, Duvall, WA
Burlingame Gardens, Hoquiam, WA
Carter's Greenhouse and Nursery, Dallas, OR
Clinton, Inc., Seattle, WA
Coastal Garden Center, Grayland, WA
Daryll's Nursery, Dallas, OR
Down to Earth, Eugene, OR
Fairie Perennial and Herb Gardens Nursery, Tumwater, WA
Farmington Gardens, Beaverton, OR
Fremont Gardens, Seattle, WA
Emery's Garden, Lynwood, WA
Hart's Nursery, Jefferson, OR
Heronswood Nursery, Kingston, WA
Joy Creek Nursery, Scappoose, OR
Julius Rosso Nursery, Seattle, WA
Magnolia Garden Center, Seattle, WA
Meadowsweet Nursery, So. Langley, B.C.
Minter's Earlington Greenhouses, Seattle, WA
Mitchell Bay Nursery, Friday Harbor, WA
Nora's Nursery, Port Townsend, WA
Oregon Trail Gardens, Boring, OR
Piriformis, Seattle, WA
Reflective Gardens, Poulsbo, WA
RoseHip Farm & Garden, Coupeville, WA
Savage Plants & Landscape, Kingston, WA
Secret Garden Growers, Canby, OR
Smokey Pt. Plant Farm, Arlington, WA
Squak Mountain Greenhouses, Issaquah, WA
Squaw Mt. Gardens, Estacada, OR
Sundquist Nursery, Poulsbo, WA
Swanson's Nursery, Saettle, WA
Thornton Creek Nursery, Seattle
Thorsett Landscape Nursery, Kent, WA
Tower Perennials, Spokane, WA
Trans-Pacific Nursery, McMinnville, OR
Trillium Gardens, Pleasant Hill, OR
Tualatin River Nursery, West Linn, OR
Valley Nursery, Poulsbo, WA
Valley View Nursery, Ashland, OR
Walker Mt. Meadows, Quilcene, WA
Wind Poppy Farm & Nursery, Ferndale, WA
Wine Country Nursery and Aquarium, Newberg, OR

GREENHOUSE / TROPICAL PLANTS

Christianson's Nurs., Mt. Vernon, Stanwood, WA
Flower World, Snohomish, WA
Johnson Brothers Greenhouses, Eugene, OR
Jungle Fever Exotics, Tacoma, WA
Logee's Greenhouses, Danielson, CT
Max and Hildy's Garden Store, Hillsboro, OR
Minter's Earlington Greenhouses, Seattle, WA
Molbaks, Woodinville, Seattle, WA
Oasis Water Gardens, Seattle, WA
Pat Calvert Greenhouse, Seattle, WA

Portland Nursery, Portland, OR
Raintree Garden and Gift Center, Seaside, OR
Saxe Floral & Greenhouse, Seattle, WA
Squak Mountain Greenhouses and Nursery,
   Issaquah, WA
Southlands Nursery, Vancouver, B.C.
Summersun Greenhouse Co., Mt. Vernon, WA
Swanson's, Seattle, WA
Thompson's Greenhouse, Sedro-Woolley, WA
Trans-Pacific Nursery, McMinnville, OR
Walker Mt. Meadows, Quilcene, WA
Watson's Greenhouse & Nursery, Puyallup, WA
Willamette Falls Nursery, West Linn, OR

GROUND COVERS

Alpine Nursery, Renton, WA
Al's Garden Center and Greenhouses, Woodburn, OR
Bainbridge Gardens, Bainbridge Island, WA
Bay Hay and Feed, Bainbridge Is., WA
Boskey Dell Natives, West Linn, OR
Collector's Nursery, Battle Ground, WA
Emery's Garden, Lynwood, WA
Furney's Nurseries, Des Moines, WA
Hayes Nursery, Issaquah, WA
Heronswood Nursery, Kingston, WA
Kinder Gardens Nursery & Landscaping, Othello, WA
Malone's Nursery, Maple Valley, WA
Molbak's, Woodinville, WA
Mountain Meadow Nursery, Kirkland, WA
MsK Rare Plant Nursery, Shoreline, WA
Reflective Gardens, Poulsbo, WA
Smokey Pt. Plant Farm, Arlington, WA
Sound Native Plants, Olympia, WA
Squak Mountain Greenhouses, Issaquah, WA
Squaw Mountain Gardens, Estacada, OR
Swanson's Nursery, Seattle, WA
Thorsett Landscape Nursery, Kent, WA
Trillium Gardens, Pleasant Hill, OR
Valley Nursery, Poulsbo, WA
Valley View Nursery, Ashland, OR
Wallace Hanson Native Plants, Salem, OR
Whispering Springs Nursery, Hillsboro, OR
Whitney Gardens & Nursery, Brinnon, WA
Woodbrook Nursery, Gig Harbor, WA

HEATHER (see ERICAS)

HELLEBORES

Avalon Nursery, Snohomish, WA
Boxhill Farm, Duvall, WA
Brim's Farm and Garden, Astoria, OR
Burlingame Gardens, Hoquiam, WA
Collector's Nursery, Battle Ground, WA
DIG Floral and Garden, Vashon Island, WA
Emery's Garden, Lynwood, WA
Enchanted Lily Garden, Redmond, WA
Dancing Oaks Nursery, Monmouth, OR
Gradens at Padden Creek, Bellingham, WA
Gossler Farm Nursery, Springfield, OR
Heronswood Nursery, Kingston, WA
Honeyhill Farms Nursery, Portland, OR
Madrona Nursery, Seattle, WA
Northwest Garden Nursery, Eugene, OR
Portland Nursery, Portland, OR
Reflective Gardens, Poulsbo, WA
Russell Graham Purveyor of Plants, Salem, OR

HERBS

A Lot of Flowers, Bellingham, WA
Alpine Herb Farm, Deming, WA
Barn Owl Nursery, Wilsonville, OR
Bayview Farm and Garden, Langley, WA
Bay Hay and Feed, Bainbridge Is., WA

Black Lake Organic Nursery, Olympia, WA
Blue Heron Herbary, Sauvie Island, OR
Bonnie's Greenhouse, Sedro-Woolley, WA
The Book Mine, Cottage Grove, OR
Bouquet Banque, Marysville, WA
Brothers Herbs & Peonies, Newburg, OR
Burlingame Gardens, Hoquiam, WA
Cedarbrook Herb Farm, Sequim, WA
Christianson's Nurs., Mt. Vernon, Stanwood, WA
Cultus Bay Nursery & Garden, Clinton, WA
Delta Farm and Nursery, Eugene, OR
Fairie Perennial and Herb Gardens Nursery,
   Tumwater, WA
Fairlight Gardens, Auburn, WA
The Flower Lady, Arlington, WA
Foxglove Farm, Anacortes, WA
Fremont Gardens Seattle, WA
Garden Spot, Bellingham, WA
Garden Spot, Seattle, WA
GardenScapes (The Herb and Perennial Farm), Port
   Orchard, WA
Goodwin Creek Gardens, Williams, OR
Gray Barn Garden Center, Redmond, WA
Hayes Nursery, Issaquah, WA
Horizon Herbs, OR
House of Whispering Firs, Newberg, OR
Hummingbird Farm, Oak Harbor, WA
Magnolia Garden Center, Seattle, WA
Malone's Nursery, Maple Valley, WA
Mary's Country Garden, Kent, WA
Millennium Farm, Ridgefield, WA
Molbak's, Woodinville, Seattle, WA
No Thyme Productions, Mercer Island, WA
Nora's Nursery, Port Townsend, WA
Nichols Garden Nursery, Albany, OR
Johnson's Brothers Greenhouses, Eugene, OR
Piriformis, Seattle, WA
Ponderings Plus, Medford, OR
Ravenna Gardens, Seattle, WA
Ravenhill Herb Farm, Saanitchiton, B.C.
Richters, Ontario, Canada
Seattle Garden Center, Seattle, WA
Smith Creek Nursery, Snohomish, WA
Smokey Pt. Plant Farm, Arlington, WA
Tower Perennial Gardens, Spokane, WA
Tualatin River Nursery, West Linn, OR
Valley Nursery, Poulsbo, WA
Wildwood Nursery, Winston, OR
Wisteria Herbs and Flowers, South Beach, OR
Wonderland Tea & Spice, Bellingham, WA

HOLLY (Ilex)

Colvos Creek Nursery, Vashon Is., WA
Pat Calvert Greenhouse, Seattle, WA
Heronswood Nursery, Kingston, WA

HOSTAS

A & D Nursery, Snohomish, WA
Avalon Nursery, Snohomish, WA
Bear Creek Nursery, Bellingham, WA
Caprice Farm Nursery, Sherwood, OR
Carter's Greenhouse and Nursery, Dallas, OR
Collector's Nursery, Battle Ground, WA
Cottage Creek Nursery, Woodinville, WA
Dancing Oaks Nursery, Monmouth, OR
Enchanted Lily Garden, Redmond, WA
Green Acres Gardens & Ponds, Yelm. WA
Meadowsweet Nursery, So. Langley, B.C.
Naylor Creek Nursery, Chimacum, WA
Oregon Trail Gardens, Boring, OR
Plantasia Specialty Nursery, Olympia, WA
Plant Delights Nursery, Raleigh, NC
Naylor Creek Nursery, Chimacum, WA

Rainforest Gardens, Maple Ridge, B.C.
Robyn's Nest Nursery, Vancouver, WA
Tower Perennial Gardens, Spokane, WA
Woodland Gardens Nursery, Eugene, OR

HOUSEPLANTS

Bakerview Nursery, Bellingham, WA
Bayview Farm and Garden, Langley, WA
Brown's Rose Lodge Nursery, Otis, OR
Delta Farm and Nursery, Eugene, OR
Emery's Garden, Lynwood, WA
Flower World, Snohomish (Maltby), WA
Garland Nursery, Corvallis, OR
Johnson Brothers Greenhouses, Eugene, OR
Magnolia Garden Center, Seattle, WA
Minter's Earlington Greenhouses, Seattle, WA
Molbak's, Woodinville, Seattle, WA
Portland Nursery, Portland, OR
Rainshadow Greenhouse, Sequim, WA
Seattle Garden Center, Seattle, WA
Sky Nursery, Seattle, WA
South Seattle Community College Garden Center,
   Seattle, WA
Summersun Greenhouse Co., Mt. Vernon, WA
Swanson's Nursery, Seattle, WA
Valley Nursery, Poulsbo, WA
Wight's Home and Garden, Seattle, WA

HYDRANGEAS

Country Gardens, Fall City, WA
Fremont Gardens, Seattle, WA
Gossler Farms Nursery, Springfield, OR
Greer Gardens, Eugene, OR
Heronswood Nursery, Kingston, WA
Reflective Gardens, Poulsbo, WA
Rosebriar Gardens & Design, Seattle, WA
Sundquist Nursery, Poulsbo, WA

IRISES

Aitkin's Salmon Creek Garden, Vancouver, WA
Avalon Nursery, Snohomish, WA
Caprice Farm Nursery, Aumsville, OR
Cooley's Gardens, Silverton, OR
Lorane Hills Farm and Nursery, Eugene, OR
Maxwelton Valley Gardens, Clinton, WA
Rainforest Gardens, Maple Ridge, B.C.
Olympic Coast Nursery, Sequim, WA
Oudean's Nursery, Snohomish, WA
Reflective Gardens, Poulsbo, WA
Rosebriar Gardens & Design, Seattle, WA
Schreiner's Iris Gardens, Salem, OR
Skagit Rose Farm, Mt. Vernon, WA
Trillium Gardens, Eugene, OR
Walker Mt. Meadows, Quilcene, WA
Wildwood Gardens, Molalla, OR
Walsterway Iris Gardens, Snohomish, WA

IVY

Molbak's, Woodinville, WA
Squaw Mt. Gardens, Estacada, OR

KALMIAS

Brim's Farm and Garden, Astoria, OR
Greer Gardens, Eugene, OR
Hazelwood Gardens, Newcastle, WA
Nelson Rhododendrons & Azaleas,
   Sedro-Woolley, WA
The Rhody Ranch Nursery, Port Angeles, WA
Spooner Creek Nursery, Blaine, WA
Whitney Gardens & Nursery, Brinnon, WA

KIWI

Cloud Mountain Farm, Everson, WA
One Green World Nursery, Canby, OR

Puget Sound Kiwi Co., Seattle, WA
Raintree Nursery, Morton, WA
Stanley and Sons Nursery, Boring, OR

LAVENDER

Barn Owl Nursery, Wilsonville, OR
Cedarbrook Herb Farm, Sequim, WA
Goodwin Creek Nursery, Williams, OR
Hummingbird Farm, Oak Harbor, WA
Plantasia Specialty Nursery, Olympia, WA
Purple Haze Lavender, Sequim, WA
Sundquist Nursery, Poulsbo, WA
Sweetwater Lavender, Ltd., Coupeville, WA
Wildwood Nursery, Winston, OR
Wisteria Herbs and Flowers, South Beach, OR

LILIES

B & D Lilies, Port Townsend, WA
Cascade Bulb and Seed, Scotts Mills, OR
Enchanted Lily Garden, Redmond, WA
The Lily Garden, Vancouver, WA
The Lily Pad, Olympia, WA
Paris Gardens, Coupeville, WA
Windy Meadows Nursery, Ferndale, WA

MAGNOLIAS

Avalon Nursery, Snohomish, WA
Baltzer's Specialized Nursery, Pleasant Hill, OR
Boxhill Farm, Duvall, WA
Brim's Farm and Garden, Astoria, OR
Fragrant Garden Nursery, Canby, OR
Gossler Farms Nursery, Springfield, OR
Heronswood Nursery, Kingston, WA
Sky Nursery, Seattle, WA
Southlands Nursery, Vancouver, B.C.
Stanley and Sons Nursery, Boring, OR
Thorsett Landscape Nursery, Kent, WA
Walker Mt. Meadows, Quilcene, WA
Whitman Farms, Salem, OR
Whitney Gardens & Nursery, Brinnon, WA
Wine Country Nursery and Aquarium, Newburg, OR

MAPLES / Japanese

Alpine Nursery, Renton, WA
Amber Hill Nursery, Oregon City, OR
Avalon Nursery, Snohomish, WA
Baltzar's Specialized Nursery, Pleasant Hill, OR
The Bovees Nursery, Portland, OR
Brim's Farm and Garden, Astoria, OR
F.W. Byles Co. Nursery, Olympia, WA
Courtyard Nursery, Tumwater, WA
Emery's Garden, Lynnwood, WA
Foliage Gardens, Bellevue, WA
Green Acres Gardens & Ponds, Yelm, WA
Greer Gardens, Eugene, OR
Hazelwood Gardens, Newcastle, WA
Heronswood Nursery, Kingston, WA
Julius Rosso Nursery, Seattle, WA
Lazy-S-Nursery, Federal Way, WA
Max and Hildy's Garden Store, Hillsboro, OR
Pollock and Son's, Battle Ground, WA
Portland Avenue Nursery, Tacoma, WA
RainShadow Gardens, Freeland, WA
Savage Plants & Landscape, Kingston, WA
Squak Mountain Greenhouses, Issaquah, WA
Stanley and Sons Nursery, Boring, OR
Thorsett Landscape Nursery, Kent, WA
Tsugawa Nursery, Woodland, WA
Tualatin River Nursery and Café, West Linn, OR
Valley Nursery, Poulsbo, WA
Walker Mt. Meadows, Quilcene, WA
Wells Medina Nursery, Medina, WA
Wells Nursery, Mt. Vernon, WA

Whitman Farms, Salem, OR
Whitney Gardens, Brinnon, WA
Wine Country Nursery and Aquarium, Newberg, OR
Yang's Nursery, Gig Harbor, WA

MUSHROOM SPAWN / KITS

Fungi Perfecti, Olympia, WA
Raintree Nursery, Morton, WA

NATIVE PLANTS

Barfod's Hardy Ferns, Bothell, WA
Bear Creek Nursery, Bellingham, WA
Berry Botanic Garden Plant Sales, Portland
Black Lake Organic Nursery, Olympia, WA
Bloomers, Eugene, OR
Blue Heron Farm, Rockport, WA
Boskey Dell Natives, West Linn, OR
Burnt Ridge Nursery & Orchards, Onalaska, WA
Cardinal Gardens Nursery, Mission, B.C.
Carter's Greenhouse and Nursery, Dallas, OR
Changing Seasons, Mt. Vernon, WA
Cloud Mt. Farm, Everson, WA
Colvos Creek Farm, Vashon Island, WA
DeWilde's Nursery, Bellingham, WA
Down to Earth, Eugene, OR
Emery's Garden, Lynnwood, WA
Forest Flor Recovery Nursery, Lummi Is. WA
Forestfarm, Williams, OR
Foxglove Farm, Anacortes, WA
Furney's Nursery, Des Moines, WA
Goodwin Creek Gardens, Williams, OR
The Greenery, Bellevue, WA
Hansen Nursery, North Bend, OR
Wallace W. Hansen Native Plants, Salem, OR
Heronswood Nursery, Kingston, WA
Lorane Hills Farm and Nursery, Eugene, OR
Madrona Nursery, Seattle, WA
Max and Hildy's Garden Store, Hillsboro, OR
Maxwelton Valley Gardens, Clinton, WA
Molbak's, Woodinville, WA
MsK Rare Plant Nursery, Seattle, WA
Mountain Meadow Nursery, Kirkland, WA
Mt. Tahoma Nursery, Graham, WA
Natives Northwest, Mossyrock, WA
Nothing But NW Natives, Battle Ground, WA
Oakhill Farms Native Plants, Oakland, OR
Olympic Nursery, Woodinville, WA
Piriformis, Seattle, WA
Plants of the Wild, Tekoa, WA
Reflective Gardens, Poulsbo, WA
Rocky Top Gardens, Olga, WA
Russell Graham, Salem, OR
Petersen's Perennials, Snohomish, WA
Shore Road Nursery, Port Angeles, WA
Sound Native Plants, Olympia, WA
Siskyou Rare Plant Nursery, Medford, OR
Skagit Rose Farm, Mt. Vernon, WA
Sky Nursery, Seattle, WA
Soos Creek Gardens, Renton, WA
Sound Native Plants, Olympia, WA
Spangle Creek Labs, MN
Steamboat Island Nursery, Olympia, WA
Trillium Gardens, Pleasant Hill, OR
Watershed Garden Works, Longview, WA
Wildside Growers, Lynden, WA
Woodbrook Nursery, Gig Harbor, WA

NUT TREES

Bear Creek Nursery, Northport, WA
Black Lake Organic Nursery, Olympia, WA
Burnt Ridge Nursery & Orchards, Onalaska, WA
Cloud Mountain Farm, Everson, WA
Lom Rombough, Aurora, OR

Raintree Nursery, Morton, WA
Whitman Farms, Salem, OR

ORCHIDS

Aitkin's Salmon Creek Garden, Vancouver, WA
Baker & Chantry Orchids, Woodinville, WA
Enchanted Garden, Seattle, WA
Indoor Sun Shoppe, Seattle, WA
Lazy-S-Nursery, Federal Way, WA
Red's Rhodies, Sherwood, OR
Southlands Nursery, Vancouver, B.C.
Spangle Creek Labs, MN

PEONIES

A & D Nursery, Snohomish, WA
Adelman Gardens, Brooks, OR
Brothers Herbs & Peonies, Newburg, OR
Burlingame Gardens, Hoquiam, WA
Caprice Farm Nursery, Aumsville, OR
Reflective Gardens, Poulsbo, WA
Rosebriar Gardens & Design, Seattle, WA
Tower Perennials, Spokane, WA
Twin Creeks Peonies, Enumclaw, WA

PERENNIALS

A & D Nursery, Snohomish, WA
All Season Nursery, Kelso, WA
A Lot of Flowers, Bellingham, WA
Al's Garden Center and Greenhouses, Woodburn, OR
Amber Hill Nursery, Oregon City, OR
Arbutus Garden Arts, Carlton, OR
Avalon Nursery, Snohomish, WA
Bainbridge Gardens, Bainbridge Is., WA
Bayview Farm & Garden, Langley, WA
Bear Creek Nursery, Bellingham, WA
Bellwether Perennials, Lopez Island, WA,
Bloomer's, Eugene, OR
The Book Mine, Cottage Grove, OR
Bouquet Banque, Marysville, WA
Boxhill Farm, Duvall, WA
Burlingame Gardens, Hoquiam, WA
Bush's, Arlington, WA
Canyon Creek Nursery, Oroville, CA
Carter's Greenhouse and Nursery, Dallas, OR
Changing Seasons, Mt. Vernon, WA
Christianson's Nurs., Mt. Vernon, WA
City People's Garden Store, Seattle, WA
City People's Mercantile, Seattle, WA
Coldsprings Garden Nursery, Duvall, WA
Collector's Nursery, Battle Ground, WA
Cora's Nursery & Greenhouse, Anacortes, WA
Cornell Farm, Portland, OR
Cottage Creek Nursery, Woodinville, WA
Cricklewood Nursery, Snohomish, WA
The Country Store & Gardens, Vashon Is., WA
Cultus Bay Nursery & Garden, Clinton, WA
Dancing Oaks Nursery, Monmouth, OR
Daryll's Nursery, Dallas, OR
DIG, Vashon Island, WA
Down to Earth, Eugene, OR
Duckworth's Nursery, Eugene, OR
Edgewood Flower Farm, Edgewood, WA
Emery's Garden, Lynwood, WA
Evans Farm Nursery, Oregon City, OR
Fairie Perennial and Herb Gardens Nursery,
   Tumwater, WA
Ferguson's Fragrant Nursery, St. Paul, OR
The Flower Lady, Arlington, WA
Forestfarm, Williams, OR
Foxglove Farm, Anacortes, WA
Fremont Gardens, Seattle, WA
Friends & Neighbors, Battle Ground, WA
The Gardens at Padden Creek, Bellingham, WA

Garden Spot Nursery, Bellingham, WA
Garden Spot (The Wallingford), Seattle, WA
GardenScapes (The Herb and Perennial Farm), Port Orchard, WA
Garland Nursery, Corvallis, OR
Goodwin Creek Gardens, Williams, OR
Gossler Farm Nursery, Springfield, OR
Gray Barn Garden Center, Redmond, WA
Gray's Garden Center, Eugene, OR
Green Acres Gardens & Ponds, Yelm, WA
The Greenhouse Nursery, Port Angeles, WA
Greer Gardens, Eugene, OR
Hart's Nursery, Jefferson, OR
Hayes Nursery, Issaquah, WA
Hedgerows Nursery, McMinnville, OR
Heronswood Nursery, Kingston, WA
Highfield Garden, Woodland, WA
Hoyt Arboretum, Portland, WA
Hummingbird Farm, Oak Harbor, WA
Hunter's Hardy Perennials, Renton, WA
Johnson Brothers Greenhouses, Eugene, OR
Joy Creek Nursery, Scappoose, OR
Julius Rosso Nursery, Seattle, WA
Kent's Payless Nursery, Bellingham, WA
Lakewold Garden Shop, Tacoma, WA
Little Red Farm Nursery, Springfield, OR
Lorane Hills Farm and Nursery, Eugene, OR
Madrona Nursery, Seattle, WA
Magnolia Garden Center, Seattle, WA
Mary's Country Garden, Kent, WA
Max and Hildy's Garden Store, Hillsboro, OR
Maxwelton Valley Gardens, Clinton, WA
McComb Road Nursery, Sequim, WA
Meadowsweet Nurs. So. Langley, B.C.
Medrona Nursery, Seattle, WA
Minter's Earlington Greenhouses, Seattle, WA
Mitchell Bay Nursery, Friday Harbor, WA
Molbak's, Woodinville, Seattle, WA
Moon Rose Perennials, LaConner, WA
Munro's Nursery, Kenmore, WA
Nora's Nursery, Port Townsend, WA
Northwest Garden Nursery, Eugene, OR
Olympic Coast Nursery, Sequim, WA
Oregon Trail Gardens, Boring, OR
Paul Sayers Landscaping & Nursery, Monroe, WA
Pepper's Nursery, Anacortes, WA
Perennial Gardens, Everson, WA
Petersen's Perennials, Snohomish, WA
Piriformis, Seattle, WA
Plantasia Specialty Nursery, Olympia, WA
Ponderings Plus, Medford, OR
Portland Nursery, Portland, OR
Rainforest Gardens, Maple Ridge, B.C.
RainShadow Gardens, Freeland, WA
Rainshadow Greenhouse, Sequim, WA
Raintree Garden and Gift Center, Seaside, OR
Ravenna Gardens, Seattle, WA
Red's Rhodies, Sherwood, OR
Reflective Gardens, Poulsbo, WA
Robyn's Nest Nursery, Vancouver, WA
Rocky Top Gardens, Olga, WA
RoseHip Farm & Garden, Coupeville, WA
Russell Graham Purveyor of Plants, Salem, OR
Savage Plants & Landscape, Kingston, WA
Saxe Floral & Greenhouse, Seattle, WA
Seattle Garden Center, Seattle, WA
Secret Garden Growers, Canby, OR
Siskiyou Rare Plant Nursery, Medford, OR
Sky Nursery, Seattle, WA
Smith Creek Nursery, Snohomish, WA
Southlands Nursery, Vancouver, B.C.
So. Seattle CC Garden Center, Seattle, WA
Stone Hollow Farm, Redmond, WA

Squak Mountain Greenhouses, Issaquah, WA
Summersun Greenhouse Co., Mt. Vernon, WA
Sundquist Nursery, Poulsbo, WA
Sunnyside Nursery, Marysville, WA
Territorial Seed Company, Cottage Grove, OR
Thompson's Greenhouse, Sedro-Woolley, WA
Thornton Creek Nursery, Seattle, WA
Thorsett Landscape Nursery, Kent, WA
Tower Perennial Gardens, Spokane, WA
Trans-Pacific Nursery, McMinnville, OR
Trillium Gardens, Pleasant Hill, OR
Tsugawa Nursery, Woodland, WA
Tualatin River Nursery, West Linn, OR
Valley Nursery, Poulsbo, WA
Valley View Nursery, Ashland, OR
Village Green Perennial Nursery, Seattle, WA
Walker Mt. Meadows, Quilcene, WA
Wildwood Nursery, Winston, OR
Wildside Growers, Lynden, WA
Willamette Falls Nursery, West Linn, OR
Wind Poppy Farm & Nursery, Ferndale, WA
Windy Meadow Nursery, Ferndale, WA
Wine Country Nursery and Aquarium, Newberg, OR
Wintergreen Tree Farm & Garden Shop, Snohomish, WA
Wisteria Herbs and Flowers, South Beach, OR
Woodland Gardens Nursery, Eugene, OR

PRIMULAS

A Plethora of Primula, Vader, WA
The Greenhouse Nursery, Port Angeles, WA
Heronswood Nursery, Kingston, WA
Mary's Country Garden, Kent, WA
Northwest Garden Nursery, Eugene, OR
Olympic Coast Garden, Sequim, WA
Rainforest Gardens, Maple Ridge, B.C.
Reflective Gardens, Poulsbo, WA
Russell Graham Purveyor of Plants, Salem, OR
Southlands Nursery, Vancouver, B.C.

RHODODENDRONS (see AZALEAS)

ROCK GARDEN PLANTS (see ALPINES)

ROSES / RUGOSAS

Antique Rose Farm, Snohomish, WA
Bainbridge Gardens, Bainbridge Island, WA
Cascade Nursery, Marysville, WA
Christianson's Nursery, Mt. Vernon, WA
City People's Garden Store, Seattle, WA
Cottage Creek Nursery, Woodinville, WA
Cricklewood Nursery, Snohomish, WA
Cultus Bay Nursery & Garden, Clinton, WA
Dancing Oaks Nursery, Monmouth, OR
Edmund's Roses, Wilsonville, OR
ForestFarm, Williams, OR
The Fragrant Garden Nursery, Canby, OR
Furney's, Des Moines, WA
Garden Spot, Bellingham, WA
Garden Spot, Seattle, WA
Garland Nursery, Corvallis, OR
Gray's Garden Center's, Inc., Eugene, OR
Hayes Nursery, Issaquah, WA
Heirloom Roses, St. Paul, OR
Heronswood Nursery, Kingston, WA
Hunter's Hardy Perennials, Renton, WA
Julius Rosso Nursery, Seattle, WA
Minter's Earlington Greenhouses, Seattle, WA
Molbak's, Woodinville, WA
Portland Nursery, Portland, OR
Raft Island Roses, Nursery & Garden, Gig Harbor, WA
Rainshadow Greenhouse, Sequim, WA
Rocky Top Gardens, Olga, WA
RoseHip Farm & Garden, Coupeville, WA

The Rose Guardians, St. Paul, OR
The Rose Petaller, Vashon Is., WA
Rosebriar Gardens & Design, Seattle, WA
Secret Garden Growers, Canby, OR
Skagit Rose Farm, Mt. Vernon, WA
Sky Nursery, Seattle, WA
Smokey Point Plant Farm, Marysville, WA
Southlands Nursery, Vancouver, B.C.
Sunnyside Nursery, Marysville, WA
Swanson's Nursery, Seattle, WA
Valley Nursery, Poulsbo, WA
Village Green Perennial Nursery, Seattle, WA
West Seattle Nursery, Seattle, WA
Wileywood Nusery, Mill Creek, WA
Wine Country Nursery and Aquarium, Newberg, OR

SEDUMS (see ALPINES)

SHADE PLANTS

A & D Peony Nursery, Snohomish, WA
Bainbridge Gardens, Bainbridge Island, WA
Bear Creek Nursery, Bellingham, WA
Boskey Dell Natives, West Linn, OR
Burlingame Gardens, Hoquiam, WA
Collector's Nursery, Battle Ground, WA
Cottage Creek Nursery, Woodinville, WA
Country Store and Gardens, Vashon Is., WA
Dancing Oaks Nursery, Monmouth, OR
Emery's Garden, Lynwood, WA
The Gardens at Padden Creek, Bellingham, WA
Heronswood Nursery, Kingston, WA
Highfield Garden, Woodland, WA
Lazy-S-Nursery, Federal Way, WA
Maxwelton Valley Gardens, Clinton, WA
Molbak's, Woodinville, WA
MsK Rare Plant Nursery, Seattle, WA
Naylor Creek Nursery, Chimacum, WA
Northwest Garden Nursery, Eugene, OR
Nothing But NW Natives, Battle Ground, WA
Reflective Gardens, Poulsbo, WA
Robyn's Nest Nursery, Vancouver, WA
Savage Plants & Landscape, Kingston, WA
Siskiyou Rare Plant Nursery, Medford, OR
Sunnyside Nursery, Marysville, WA
Wallace Hanson Native Plants, Salem, OR
Madrona Nursery, Seattle, WA
Maxwelton Valley Gardens, Clinton, WA
Naylor Creek Nursery, Chimacum, WA
Rainforest Gardens, Maple Ridge, B.C.
Reflective Nursery, Poulsbo, WA
Robyn's Nest Nursery, Vancouver, WA
Secret Garden Growers, Canby, OR
Smokey Pt. Plant Farm, Arlington, WA
Thorsett Landscape Nursery, Kent, WA
Tower Perennial Gardens, Spokane, WA
Trans-Pacific Nursery, McMinnville, OR
Trillium Gardens, Pleasant Hill, OR
Wisteria, Herbs and Flowers, South Beach, OR

TISSUE CULTURE

Cedar Valley Nursery, Centralia, WA

TOPIARIES

Alpine Nursery, Inc., Renton, WA
Furney's, Des Moines, Bellevue, WA
Rainshadow Greenhouse, Sequim, WA
Valley Nursery, Poulsbo, WA
Wells Medina, Medina, WA

TREES / SHRUBS

All Season Nursery, Kelso, WA
Alpine Nursery, Inc., Renton, WA
Al's Garden Center and Greenhouses, Woodburn, OR
Amber Hill Nursery, Oregon City, OR

Arbutus Garden Arts, Carlton, OR
Avalon Nursery, Snohomish, WA
Bainbridge Gardens, Bainbridge Is., WA
Bakerview Nursery, Bellingham, WA
Bay Hay and Feed, Bainbridge Island, WA
Bayview Farm & Garden, Langley, WA
Bear Creek Nursery, Northport, WA
Big Trees Today, Inc, Hillsboro, OR
Bloomer's, Eugene, OR
Boskey Dell Natives, West Linn, OR
The Bovees Nursery, Portland, OR
Boxhill Farm, Duvall, WA
Brim's Farm and Garden, Astoria, OR
Burlingame Gardens, Hoquiam, WA
Burnt Ridge Nursery and Orchards, Onalaska, WA
Changing Seasons, Mt. Vernon, WA
Christianson's, Mt. Vernon, WA
Cloud Mt. Farm, Everson, WA
Colvos Creek Farm, Vashon Island, WA
Cornell Farm, Portland, OR
Country Store & Gardens, Vashon Island, WA
Courtyard Nursery, Tumwater, WA
Dancing Oaks Nursery, Monmouth, OR
Daryll's Nursery, Dallas, OR
DeWilde's Nursery, Bellingham, WA
DIG Floral and Garden, Vashon Is., WA
Duckworth's Nursery, Eugene, OR
The Fragrant Garden Nursery, Canby, OR
ForestFarm, Williams, OR
Emery's Garden, Lynnwood, WA
Evans Farm Nursery, Oregon City, OR
Ferguson's Fragrant Nursery, St. Paul, OR
The Flower Lady, Arlington, WA
Forestfarm, Williams, OR
Furney's, Des Moines, WA
Garland Nursery, Corvallis, OR
Gossler Farms Nursery, Springfield, OR
Gray Barn Garden Center, Redmond, WA
Gray's Garden Center, Eugene, OR
Greer Gardens, Eugene, OR
Hayes Nursery, Issaquah, WA
Hazelwood Gardens, Newcastle, OR
Hedgerows Nursery, McMinnville, OR
Heronswood Nursery, Kingston, WA
Hoyt Arboretum, Portland, OR
Interstate Garden Center, Vancouver, WA
Julius Rosso Nursery, Seattle, WA
Jungle Fever Exotics, Tacoma, WA
Kent's Garden & Nursery, Bellingham, WA
Kinder Gardens Nursery & Landscaping, Othello, WA
Lazy-S-Nursery, Federal Way, WA
Little Red Farm Nursery, Springfield, OR
Malone's Nursery, Maple Valley, WA
Magnolia Garden Center, Seattle, WA
Mary's Country Garden, Kent, WA
Maxwelton Valley Gardens, Clinton, WA
McComb Road Nursery, Sequim, WA
Molbak's, Weoodinville, WA
Mountain Meadow Nursery, Kirkland, WA
MsK Rare Plant Nursery, Seattle, WA
Munro's Nursery, Kenmore, WA
Olympic Nursery, Woodinville, WA
One Green World Nursery, Canby, OR
Oregon Trail Gardens, Boring, OR
Pat Calvert Greenhouse, Seattle, WA
Pepper's, Anacortes, WA
Porterhowse Farms, Sandy, OR
Portland Nursery, Portland, OR
RainShadow Gardens, Freeland, WA
Rainshadow Greenhouse, Sequim, WA
Raintree Garden and Gift Center, Seaside, OR
Raintree Nursery, Morton, WA
Ravenna Gardens, Seattle

RoseHip Farm & Garden, Coupeville, WA
Savage Plants & Landscape, Kingston, WA
Saxe Floral & Greenhouse, Seattle, WA
Secret Garden Growers, Canby, OR
Shorty's Nursery, Vancouver, WA
Skagit Valley Gardens, Mt. Vernon, WA
Skipper and Jordan Nursery, Gresham, OR
Sky Nursery, Seattle, WA
Smokey Point Plant Farm, Marysville, WA
Soos Creek Gardens, Renton, WA
Squak Mountain Greenhouses, Issaquah, WA
Star Nursery & Landscaping, Seattle, WA
Steamboat Island Nursery, Olympia, WA
Summersun Greenhouse Co., Mt. Vernon, WA
Sunnyside Nursery, Marysville, WA
West Seattle Nursery, Seattle, WA
Summersun Greenhouse Co., Mt. Vernon, WA
Sundquist Nursery, Poulsbo, WA
Swans Trail Gardens, Snohomish, WA
Territorial Seed Company, Cottage Grove, OR
Thorsett Landscape Nursery, Kent, WA
Tillinghast Seed Co., La Conner, WA
Trans-Pacific Nursery, McMinnville, OR
Valley Nursery, Poulsbo, WA
Valley View Nursery, Ashland, OR
Walker Mt. Meadows, Quilcene, WA
Wells Medina Nursery, Medina, WA
Wells Nursery, Mt. Vernon
West Seattle Nursery, Seattle, WA
Whitney Gardens & Nursery, Brinnon, WA
Wild Bird Garden & Nursery, Grayland, WA
Wildside Growers, Lynden, WA
Willamette Falls Nursery, West Linn, OR
Windy Meadow Nursery, Ferndale, WA
Wintergreen Tree Farm & Garden Shop, Snohomish, WA

TULIPS (see BULBS)

VARIEGATED PLANTS

Heronswood Nursery, Kingston, WA
Oregon Trail Gardens, Boring, OR
Willamette Falls Nursery, West Linn, OR

VEGETABLE STARTS

Al's Garden Center and Greenhouses, Woodburn, OR
Bayview Farm and garden, Langley, WA
Black Lake Organic Nursery and Garden Store, Olympia, WA
The Book Mine, Cottage Grove, OR
Christianson's Nurs., Mt. Vernon, Stanwood, WA
Cindy's Plant Stand, Elma, WA
Delta Farm and Nursery, Eugene, OR
Down to Earth, Eugene, OR
Farmer's Markets
Food Co-ops, PCC in Seattle, WA
Fremont Gardens, Seattle, WA
Garden City Heirlooms, Snohomish, WA
The Garden Spot, Bellingham, WA
Hart's Nursery, Jefferson, OR
Master Gardener Plant Sales everywhere
Millennium Farm, Ridgefield, WA
Minter's Earlington Greenhouses, Seattle, WA
Molbak's, Woodinville, Seattle, WA
Nichols Garden Nursery, Albany, OR
Seattle Garden Center, Seattle, WA
Seattle Tilth Edibles Plant Sale, Seattle
Smokey Pt. Plant Farm, Arlington, WA
Territorial Seed Company, Cottage Grove, OR
Thompson's Greenhouse, Sedro-Woolley, WA
Tillinghast Seed Co., La Conner, WA
Valley Nursery, Poulsbo, WA

VINES

Bayview Farm & Garden, Langley, WA
Carter's Greenhouse and Nursery, Dallas, OR
Christianson's Nurs., Mt. Vernon, Stanwood, WA
Cloud Mt. Farm, Everson, WA
Cultus Bay Nursery & Garden, Clinton, WA
Cora's Nursery & Greenhouse, Anacortes, WA
Cottage Creek Nursery, Woodinville, WA
Daryll's Nursery, Dallas, OR
Dave's Taste of the Tropics, Shoreline, WA
Emery's Garden, Lynwood, WA
Forestfarm, Williams, OR
Fremont Gardens, Seattle, WA
Freshops, Philomath, OR
The Gardeners, Bainbridge Is., WA
Garden Spot, Bellingham, WA
Greer Gardens, Eugene, OR
Hedgerows Nursery, McMinnville, OR
Heronswood Nursery, Kingston, WA
Jungle Fever Exotics, Tacoma, WA
Kinder Gardens Nursery, Othello, WA
Mary's Country Garden, Kent, WA
Mitchell Bay Nursery, Friday Harbor, WA
Molbak's, Woodinville, WA
Northwest Garden Nursery, Eugene, OR
Oregon Trail Gardens, Boring, OR
Raintree Nursery, Morton, WA
Skagit Valley Gardens, Mt. Vernon, WA
Sky Nursery, Seattle, WA
Swans Trail Gardens, Snohomish, WA
Swanson's, Seattle, WA
Trans-Pacific Nursery, McMinnville, OR
Valley Nursery, Poulsbo, WA
Wells Medina, Bellevue, WA
Wells Nusery, Mt. Vernon, WA
Whispering Springs Nursery, Hillsboro, OR
Wine Country Nursery and Aquarium, Newberg, OR

WATER LILIES (see AQUATIC PLANTS)

WETLAND PLANTS / Mitigation (see also AQUATIC PLANTS)

Boskey Dell Natives, West Linn, OR
Wallace W. Hansen Nursery and Gardens, Salem, OR
Nothing But NW Natives, Battle Ground, WA
Olympic Nursery, Woodinville, WA
Sound Native Plants, Olympia, WA
Watershed Garden Works, Longview, WA

WILDFLOWERS

Boskey Dell Natives, West Linn, OR
Plants of the Wild, Tekoa, WA
We-Du Nuseries, Marion, N.C.
Whispering Springs Nursery, Hillsboro, OR

WOODLAND PLANTS (see also SHADE PLANTS)

Boskey Dell Natives, West Linn, OR
Dancing Oaks Nursery, Monmouth, OR
ForestFarm, Williams. WA
Forest Floor Recovery Nursery, Lummi Island, WA
Hansen Nursery, North Bend, OR
Wallace W. Hansen Nursery and Garden, Salem, OR
Heronswood, Kingston, WA
Honeyhill Farms Nursery, Portland, OR
Maxwelton Valley Gardens, Clinton, WA
Mt. Tahoma Nursery, Graham, WA
MsK Rare Plant Nursery, Seattle, WA
Naylor Creek Nursery, Chimacum, WA
Siskiyou Rare Plant Nursery, Medford, OR
Wild Bird Garden & Nursery, Grayland, WA
Wildside Growers, Lynden, WA

NURSERIES & GARDENS—

Indexed by Geographical Location

On the following pages, you will find lists of nurseries and gardens to visit in British Columbia, Oregon, and Washington, organized by city going from north to south. This symbol ❋ indicates a garden to visit; all other entries are nurseries, many of which have display gardens. We hope this gives you an at-a-glance idea of the geographic areas in which Northwest nurseries and gardens are located. Chapter 5, "Nurseries," and Chapter 13, "Gardens to Visit," provide addresses, driving directions, and contact information, but remember: there is no substitute for a good map to guide you to your destination. Many of the nurseries also offer maps and local directions on their websites under "How to find us." Or, better yet, call ahead for specific directions. Good luck!

BRITISH COLUMBIA

ROSEDALE
❋ Minter Gardens

HORNBY ISLAND
Old Rose Nursery

COQUITLAM
❋ Riverview Horticultural Centre,
Davidson Arboretum

NORTH VANCOUVER
❋ Park & Tilford Gardens

BURNABY
GardenWorks
Mandeville Garden Centre & Floral
Design

VANCOUVER
Art Knapp Plantland & Florist
Shop in the Garden & Plant Centre
Southlands Nursery
❋ Arthur Erickson Garden
❋ Bloedel Conservatory
❋ Dr. Sun Yat-Sen Classical Chinese
Garden
❋ Stanley Park
❋ Queen Elizabeth Park
❋ University of British Columbia
Botanical Garden & Centre for
Horticulture
❋ VanDusen Botanical Garden

MAPLE RIDGE
Hansi's Nursery
The Perennial Gardens

RICHMOND
Hawaiian Botanicals and Water
Gardens
Jones Nurseries Garden Centre

SURREY
❋ Wrenhaven Nursery
Darts Hill Garden Park
❋ The Glades, A Woodland
Rhododendron Garden

CHILLIWACK
Minter Country Gardens
Old Rose Nursery

LANGLEY
Brookside Orchid Gardens
Elizabeth's Cottage Perennials
Erickson's Daylily Gardens
Free Spirit Nursery
Rain Forest Nurseries

SOUTH LANGLEY
Kelly's Country Garden
Meadowsweet Farms Garden
Nursery

ABBOTSFORD
Tanglebank Farms Nursery

WHITE ROCK
The Potting Shed Antiques & Garden
Shop

SALTSPRING ISLAND
Foxglove Farm and Garden Supply
Fraser's Thimble Farms

SAANICHTON
Ravenhill Herb Farm

BRENTWOOD BAY
❋ Victoria Butterfly Gardens

VICTORIA
❋ Abkhazi Garden
❋ The Butchart Gardens
❋ Government House Gardens
❋ Hatley Park Gardens, at Royal
Roads University
❋ Horticulture Centre of the Pacific
❋ Royal British Columbia Museum,
Native Garden

WASHINGTON

U.S. Border to Everett

BLAINE
Spooner Creek Nursery

LYNDEN / EVERSON
Cloud Mountain Farm
Perennial Gardens
Wildside Growers

FERNDALE
DeLancey's Garden Center
Wind Poppy Farm & Nursery
Windy Meadow Nursery
❋ Fragrance Garden
❋ Hovander Homestead Park

DEMING
Alpine Herb Farm

BELLINGHAM
A Lot of Flowers
Bakerview Nursery and Garden
Center
Bear Creek Nursery
DeWilde's Nurseries Inc.
Forest Floor Recovery Nursery
(Lummi Island)
The Gardens at Padden Creek
Garden Spot Nursery
Kent's Garden & Nursery
❋ Big Rock Garden Park

BOW
Skagit Heights Dahlia Farm

SEDRO WOOLLEY
Bonnie's Greenhouse
Nelson Rhododendrons and Azaleas
Thompson's Greenhouse

ROCKPORT
Blue Heron Farm

BURLINGTON
Sakuma Brothers Farms

ANACORTES
Cora's Nursery & Greenhouse
Foxglove Farm
Pepper's Greenhouse & Nursery

SAN JUAN ISLANDS
Bellwether Perennials (Lopez Island)
Mitchell Bay Nursery (San Juan Island)
Rocky Top Gardens (Orcas Island)

WHIDBEY ISLAND
Bayview Farm and Garden (Langley)
Cultus Bay Nursery (Clinton)
Hummingbird Farm & Nursery (Oak Harbor)
Maxwelton Valley Gardens (Clinton)
RainShadow Gardens (Freeland)
RoseHip Farm & Garden (Coupeville)
Sweetwater Lavender (Coupeville)
❋ Crescent Moon Rose Garden (Oak Harbor)
❋ Meerkerk Rhododendron Gardens (Greenbank)

MT. VERNON
Changing Seasons
Christianson's Nursery
Roozengaarde
Skagit Valley Gardens
Summersun Greenhouse Co.
Wells Nursery
❋ Discovery Garden
❋ The Juntunen Gardens
❋ La Conner Flats

LA CONNER
Tillinghast Seed Co.
MoonRose Perennials

STANWOOD
Christianson's Stanwood Nursery

ARLINGTON
Barfod's Hardy Ferns
Bush's
Smokey Point Plant Farm

MARYSVILLE
Bouquet Banque
Cascade Nursery
Sunnyside Nursery

EVERETT
Moorehaven Water Gardens
❋ Evergreen Arboretum and Gardens

SNOHOMISH
A & D Nursery
Antique Rose Farm
Avalon Nursery
Cricklewood Nursery

Flower World, Inc.
Garden City Heirlooms
Garden Treasures Nursery
Oudean's Willow Creek Nursery
Petersen's Perennials
Smith Creek Nursery
Swans Trail Gardens
Walsterway Iris Gardens
Wintergreen Tree Farm & Garden Shop

MONROE
Paul Sayers Landscaping and Nursery

GOLD BAR
Fancy Fronds

MILL CREEK
Wileywood Nursery

Lynnwood to the Columbia River

LYNNWOOD
Emery's Garden
Wight's Home and Garden

BOTHELL
❋ Rhody Ridge Arboretum Park

KENMORE
Munro's Nursery
❋ Kenmore Rhododendron Park and Garden

WOODINVILLE
Baker & Chantry, Inc. Orchids
Bassetti's Crooked Arbor Garden
Cottage Creek Garden Nursery
Molbak's Greenhouse and Nursery
Olympic Nursery

SHORELINE
Dave's Taste of the Tropics
MSK Rare Plant Nursery
Sky Nursery
❋ The Kruckeberg Botanic Garden

SEATTLE
Beauty and the Bamboo
Bonsai Northwest
City People's Garden Store
Clinton, Inc.
Fremont Gardens
Garden Spot (The Wallingford)
Indoor Sun Shoppe
Julius Rosso Nursery
Madrona Nursery
Magnolia Garden Center
Minter's Earlington Greenhouses
Molbak's Seattle Garden Center
Oasis Water Gardens
Pat Calvert Greenhouse
Piriformis
Puget Sound Kiwi Company
Ravenna Gardens

Rosebriar Gardens & Design
Saxe Floral & Greenhouses
Sea-Tac Dahlia Gardens
South Seattle Community College Garden Center
Star Nursery & Landscaping
Swanson's Nursery
Thornton Creek Nursery
Village Green Perennial Nursery
West Seattle Nursery
❋ Bradner Demonstration Garden
❋ Carl S. English, Jr. Botanical Garden
❋ Center for Urban Horticulture
❋ E. B. Dunn Historic Garden Trust
❋ Elisabeth C. Miller Botanical Garden
❋ Erna Gunther Ethnobotanical Garden
❋ Good Shepherd Center
❋ Green Lake Park
❋ Kubota Garden
❋ Magnuson Community Garden
❋ Medicinal Herb Garden
❋ Pacific Science Center / Tropical Butterfly House
❋ Seattle Center Butterfly House
❋ The Seattle Chinese Garden
❋ Seattle's Japanese Garden
❋ Seattle Tilth Gardens
❋ Seattle University
❋ South King County Arboretum
❋ South Seattle Community College Arboretum
❋ Volunteer Park Conservatory
❋ Washington Park Arboretum
❋ Woodland Park Rose Garden
❋ Woodland Park Zoological Garden

REDMOND
Bamboo Gardens of Washington
Enchanted Lily Garden
Gray Barn Garden Center & Landscape Co
Russell Watergardens, Nursery, and Design Center
Stone Hollow Farm

KIRKLAND
Mountain Meadow Nursery
❋ Lake Washington Technical College Arboretum

MEDINA
Wells Medina Nursery

BELLEVUE
Foliage Gardens
Furney's Nursery
The Greenery
❋ Bellevue Botanical Garden
❋ King County / WSU Master Gardeners Urban Demonstration Garden

MERCER ISLAND
No Thyme Productions

FALL CITY
Country Gardens

ISSAQUAH
Hayes Nursery
Squak Mountain Greenhouses and
  Nursery

PRESTON
❋ Arboretum of the Cascades

NEWCASTLE
Hazelwood Gardens Rhododendron
  Nursery

RENTON
Alpine Nursery, Inc.
Hunter's Hardy Perennials
Soos Creek Gardens

KENT
Mary's Country Garden
Thorsett Landscape Nursery
❋ David F. Neely Homestead Garden

MAPLE VALLEY
B & J Nursery
Malone's Landscape & Nursery
Rhododendron Species Botanical
  Garden

AUBURN
Fairlight Gardens

FEDERAL WAY
Lazy-S-Nursery
❋ French Lake Conservation
  Demonstration Garden
❋ Pacific Rim Bonsai Collection
❋ Powellswood
❋ Rhododendron Species Botanical
  Garden

PUYALLUP / SUMNER
The Garden of Eden Nursery
Van Lierop Bulb Farm, Inc.
Watson's Greenhouse & Nursery
Windmill Gardens

ENUMCLAW
Twin Creeks Peonies
❋ Anderson Garden

GRAHAM
Mt. Tahoma Nursery
❋ The Chase Garden (Orting)

TACOMA
Lakewold Gardens
Jade Mountain Bamboo, Inc.
Jungle Fever Exotics
Portland Avenue Nursery
❋ Point Defiance Park
❋ Puget Gardens
❋ W. W. Seymour Conservatory

DUVALL
Boxhill Farm
Coldsprings Garden Nursery

OLYMPIA
Black Lake Organic Nursery
F.W. Byles Nursery
The Lily Pad
Plantasia Specialty Nursery &
  Display Gardens
Rockyridge Nursery
Sound Native Plants
Steamboat Island Nursery
❋ Delbert McBride Ethnobotanical
  Garden
❋ Yashiro Japanese Garden
❋ Zabel's Rhododendron Garden

TUMWATER
Courtyard Nursery
Fairie Perennial and Herb Gardens
  Nursery

YELM
Green Acres Gardens & Ponds

SHELTON
Heaths and Heathers

EATONVILLE
Coenosium Gardens

CENTRALIA
Cedar Valley Nursery

MORTON
Raintree Nursery

ONALASKA
Burnt Ridge Nursery & Orchards

VADER
Plethora of Primula

KELSO
All Season Nursery, Garden & Gifts

LONGVIEW
Watershed Garden Works

WOODLAND
Highfield Garden
Tsugawa Nursery
❋ Hulda Klager Lilac Gardens

RIDGEFIELD
Killdeer Farms
Millennium Farm

BATTLE GROUND
Collector's Nursery
Daybreak Gardens
Nothing But Northwest Natives
Pollock and Son's

VANCOUVER
Aitken's Salmon Creek Garden
The Lily Garden
Robyn's Nest Nursery

Shorty's Nursery Inc.
❋ Fort Vancouver Historical Gardens

Kitsap & Olympic Peninsulas

KINGSTON
Heronswood Nursery, Ltd.
Savage Plants and Landscape

POULSBO
Raven Nursery
Roadhouse Nursery
Sundquist Nursery
Valley Nursery

BAINBRIDGE ISLAND
Bainbridge Gardens
Bay Hay and Feed
Faylee Greenhouses
The Gardeners
❋ Bloedel Reserve
❋ Little and Lewis Water Gardens

BREMERTON
❋ Elandan Gardens

PORT ORCHARD
GardenScapes—The Herb and
  Perennial Farm

VASHON ISLAND
Colvos Creek Nursery
Country Store and Gardens
DIG Floral & Garden
The Rose Petaller

BURTON
Edgewood Flower Farm
❋ The Mukai Farm and Garden

GIG HARBOR
Peninsula Gardens
Raft Island Roses, Nursery and
  Garden
Woodbrook Nursery

PORT TOWNSEND
B & D Lilies
Nora's Nursery

CHIMACUM
Naylor Creek Nursery

QUILCENE
Walker Mountain Meadows

BRINNON
Whitney Gardens and Nursery

SEQUIM
Cedarbrook Herb Farm & Petals
  Garden Café
McComb Road Nursery
Olympic Coast Garden
Purple Haze Lavender
Rainshadow Greenhouse

PORT ANGELES
The Greenhouse Nursery

The Rhody Ranch Nursery
Shore Road Nursery

HOQUIAM
Burlingame Gardens

GRAYLAND
Coastal Garden Center

ELMA
Cindy's Plant Stand

OAKVILLE
Dan's Dahlias

Central & Eastern Washington

WENATCHEE
✺ Ohme Gardens

OTHELLO
Kinder Gardens Nursery &
Landscaping

SPOKANE
Tower Perennial Gardens

TEKOA
Plants of The Wild

OREGON

Oregon Coast

ASTORIA
Brim's Farm and Garden
✺ Butterflies Forever

SEASIDE
Raintree Garden and Gift Center

OTIS
Brown's Rose Lodge Nursery

LINCOLN CITY
✺ Connie Hansen Garden

SOUTH BEACH
Wisteria Herbs and Flowers

FLORENCE
✺ Darlingtonia Botanical Wayside

NORTH BEND
Hansen Nursery

COOS BAY
✺ Shore Acres State Park Garden

GOLD BEACH
Tradewinds Bamboo Nursery

BROOKINGS
Fragrant Garden Nursery

Greater Portland & South

SAUVIE ISLAND
Blue Heron Herbary

SCAPPOOSE
Joy Creek Nursery

PORTLAND
The Bovees Nursery
Cornell Farm
Honeyhill Farms Nursery
Hoyt Arboretum
Portland Nursery
✺ Berry Botanic Garden
✺ Crystal Springs Rhododendron
Garden
✺ Elk Rock, Bishop's Close
✺ Hoyt Arboretum
✺ International Rose Test Gardens
✺ Ladd's Addition Rose Blocks
✺ Leach Botanical Garden
✺ Peninsula Park Rose Garden
✺ Portland Classical Chinese Garden
✺ Portland's Japanese Garden
✺ Portland Rose Gardens

ALOHA
✺ Jenkins Estate

BEAVERTON
Farmington Gardens

TIGARD
✺ Home Orchard Society Arboretum

TUALATIN
Hughes Water Gardens

WEST LINN
Boskey Dell Natives
Tualatin River Nursery & Café
Willamette Falls Nursery and Ponds

OREGON CITY
Amber Hill Nursery
Evans Farm Nursery
✺ Clackamas Community College
✺ John Inskeep Environmental
Learning Center
✺ Horticultural Department Gardens

GRESHAM
Skipper & Jordan Nursery

BORING
Stanley and Sons Nursery

SANDY
Porterhowse Farms

ESTACADA
Squaw Mountain Gardens

CORBETT
Oregon Trails Daffodils

WILSONVILLE
Barn Owl Nursery
Edmund's Roses

CARLTON
Arbutus Garden Arts

HILLSBORO
Big Trees Today, Inc
Max & Hildy's Garden Store
Whispering Springs Nursery

NEWBERG
Brothers Herbs & Peonies
House of Whispering Firs
Wine Country Nursery & Aquarium

ST. PAUL
Ferguson's Fragrant Nursery
Heirloom Roses
The Rose Guardians
✺ Cecil & Molly Smith
Rhododendron Garden

SHERWOOD
Caprice Farm Nursery
Red's Rhodies

CANBY
Secret Garden Growers
Swan Island Dahlias

MOLALLA
One Green World
Wildwood Gardens
✺ Pauling Center Native Garden

HUBBARD
Mitsch Novelty Daffodils

WOODBURN
Al's Garden Center & Greenhouses
Oregon Native Plant Nursery
Wooden Shoe Bulb Company

MCMINNVILLE
Hedgerows Nursery
Trans-Pacific Nursery

SCOTTS MILLS
Cascade Bulb & Seed

DALLAS
Carter's Greenhouse and Nursery
Daryll's Nursery

MONMOUTH
Dancing Oaks Nursery

SILVERTON
Cooley's Gardens, Inc.
✺ Oregon Garden

SALEM
Russell Graham Purveyor of Plants
Schreiner's Iris Gardens
Wallace W. Hansen, Nursery &
Gardens
Whitman Farms
✺ Bush's Pasture Park
✺ Deepwood Gardens
✺ Martha Springer Botanical Garden

AURORA
Lon Rombough

BROOKS
Adelman Peony Gardens

JEFFERSON
Harts Nursery

ALBANY
Nichols Garden Nursery

CORVALLIS
Garland Nursery

PHILOMATH
Freshops
Northern Groves

MONROE
Earth's Rising Trees

EUGENE
Bloomer's Nursery, Inc.
Delta Farm and Nursery
Down to Earth
Duckworth's Nursery

Gray's Garden Centers, Inc.
Greer Gardens
Johnson Brothers Greenhouses
Lorane Hills Farm and Nursery
Northwest Garden Nursery
Woodland Gardens Nursery
❋ George Owen Memorial Rose
Garden
❋ Mount Pisgah Arboretum
❋ Sebring Rock Garden

SPRINGFIELD
Gossler Farms Nursery
Little Red Farm Nursery

COTTAGE GROVE
Territorial Seed Company

PLEASANT HILL
Baltzer's Specialized Nursery
Trillium Gardens

OAKLAND
Oakhill Farms Native Plant Nursery

WINSTON
Wildwood Nursery

MEDFORD
Ponderings Plus
Siskiyou Rare Plant Nursery
Valley View Nursery
❋ Jackson & Perkins Display & Test
Gardens

WILLIAMS
Forestfarm
Goodwin Creek Gardens
❋ Pacifica: Garden in the Siskiyous

ASHLAND
Valley View Nursery

GENERAL INDEX

Stephanie Feeney and Debra Prinzing

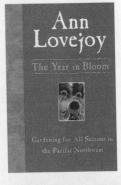